High Performance Computing

High Performance Computing
Modern Systems and Practices

Thomas Sterling

Matthew Anderson

Maciej Brodowicz

*School of Informatics, Computing, and Engineering,
Indiana University, Bloomington*

Foreword by C. Gordon Bell

ELSEVIER

MORGAN KAUFMANN PUBLISHERS

AN IMPRINT OF ELSEVIER

Notices

Knowledge and best practice in this field are constantly changing. As new research and experience broaden our understanding, changes in research methods, professional practices, or medical treatment may become necessary.

Practitioners and researchers must always rely on their own experience and knowledge in evaluating and using any information, methods, compounds, or experiments described herein. In using such information or methods they should be mindful of their own safety and the safety of others, including parties for whom they have a professional responsibility.

To the fullest extent of the law, neither the Publisher nor the authors, contributors, or editors, assume any liability for any injury and/or damage to persons or property as a matter of products liability, negligence or otherwise, or from any use or operation of any methods, products, instructions, or ideas contained in the material herein.

ISBN: 978-0-12-823035-0

For information on all Morgan Kaufmann publications visit our website at https://www.elsevier.com/books-and-journals

Publisher: Peter Linsley
Acquisition Editor: Stephen Merken
Editorial Project Manager: Helena Beauchamp
Project Manager: Haritha Dharmarajan
Cover Designer: Matthew Limbert

Printed in India

Typeset by TNQ Technologies

 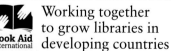

Working together to grow libraries in developing countries

www.elsevier.com • www.bookaid.org

Dedication to Paul Messina

The authors are pleased to dedicate this book to Dr. Paul C. Messina, in acknowledgment of and in gratitude for his exceptional contributions to and leadership in the field of high performance computing over a career of more than 4 decades. It is impossible to capture fully the importance of his impact, but many of the significant national programs have benefited from his guidance. Dr. Messina has been a visionary, a strategist, and a leader of programs, projects, initiatives, organizations, and, perhaps most importantly, the careers of individual scientists who would come to deliver technical accomplishments and leadership of their own. Among his many accomplishments, Dr. Messina was the founding director of the Mathematics and Computer Science Division at Argonne National Laboratory, a leading institution applying high performance computing to mission-critical problem domains of the US Department of Energy. He then founded and directed the Caltech Concurrent Supercomputing Consortium, which staged the Intel Touchstone Delta massively parallel processor that determined the future direction of high performance computing for the next 30 years. The Caltech Concurrent Supercomputing Consortium evolved into the Caltech Center for Advanced Computing Research, at which two of the authors spent some of their most formative years. Paul was particularly instrumental and served as co—principal investigator for the pioneering National Science Foundation Teragrid and the National Virtual Observatory. He directed the Department of Energy ASCI program for over 2 years, building up the nation's high performance computing capabilities toward the leadership-scale computing it currently demonstrates. Most recently Paul Messina led the Exascale Computing Project, America's biggest undertaking, achieving exascale computing performance by the beginning of the 2020s. For some, Paul has had a direct and meaningful effect on their individual careers. To author Thomas Sterling, Paul has been a colleague, leader, mentor, and friend for many years.

Contents

Foreword

High Performance Computing: Modern Systems and Practices is a much-needed follow-on to Becker and Sterling's 1994 creation of the Beowulf clusters recipe to build scalable high performance computers (also known as supercomputers) from commodity hardware. Beowulf enabled groups everywhere to build their own super-computers. Now, with thousands of Beowulf clusters operating worldwide, this comprehensive textbook addresses the critical missing link of an academic course for training domain scientists and engineers—and especially computer scientists. Competence involves knowing exactly how to create and run (e.g., controlling, debugging, monitoring, visualizing, evolving) parallel programs on the congeries of computational elements (cores) that constitute today's supercomputers.

Mastery of these ever-increasing, scalable, parallel computing machines gives entry into a comparatively small but growing elite and is the authors' goal for readers of this book. Lest the reader believes the name is unimportant: the first conference in 1988 was the ACM/IEEE Supercomputing Conference, also known as Supercomputing 88; in 2006 the name evolved to the International Conference on High Performance Computing, Networking, Storage, and Analysis, abbreviated SCXX. At the time of this writing, 11,830 attendees participated in the most recent annual meeting: SC22 in Dallas, Texas.

It is hard to describe a "supercomputer," but I know one when I see it. Personally, I never pass up a visit to a supercomputer, having seen the first one in 1961—the UNIVAC LARC (Livermore Advanced Research Computer) at the Department of Energy's Lawrence Livermore National Laboratory, specified by Edward Teller to run hydrodynamic simulations for nuclear weapons design. LARC consisted of a few dozen cabinets of densely packed circuit boards interconnected with a few thousand miles of wires and a few computational units operating at a 100 KHz clock rate. In 2022 the largest HPE Cray/AMD supercomputer, Frontier, at the Oak Ridge Leadership Computing Facility currently operates at 1.1 exaflops R_{max} (HPL benchmark), or more than a trillion times faster than LARC. Frontier incorporates almost 10,000 AMD Epyc "Trento" 64-core central processing units (CPUs) operating at a 2-GHz clock rate combined with almost 38,000 Radeon Instinct graphics processing units (GPUs) and consumes 21 MW. Its footprint (area) is approximately 7000 square feet. Today's challenge for computational program developers is designing the architecture and implementation of programs to utilize these mega-processor computers.

From a user perspective, the "ideal high performance computer" has an infinitely fast clock, executes a single-instruction stream program operating on data stored in an infinitely large and fast single memory, and comes in any size to fit any budget or problem. In 1957 Backus established the von Neumann programming model with Fortran. The first or "Cray" era of supercomputing from the 1960s (e.g., CDC-6600) through the early 1990s (e.g., CRI Cray-2) saw the evolution of hardware to support this simple, easy-to-use ideal by increasing processor speed, pipelining an instruction stream, processing vectors with a single instruction, and finally adding processors for a program held in the single-memory computer. By the early 1990s evolution of a single computer toward the ideal had stopped: clock speeds approached a few gigaHertz (GHz), and the number of processors accessing a single memory through interconnection was limited to a few dozen. However, the limited-scale, multiple-processor shared memory is likely to be the most straightforward to program and use!

Fortunately, in the mid-1980s the "killer microprocessor" arrived, demonstrating cost effectiveness and potentially extreme scaling just by interconnecting increasingly powerful computers. Unfortunately, this multicomputer era has required abandoning both the single memory and the single sequential program ideal of Fortran. Thus, "supercomputing" has evolved from a hardware engineering design challenge of the single (mono-memory) computer of the Seymour Cray era (1960–95) to a software engineering design challenge of creating a program to run effectively using multicomputers. Frontier comprises more than 600,000 CPUs and 8 million GPUs, forging the extended path at least to the end of this decade. So, in effect, today's high performance computing (HPC) nodes are like the supercomputers of a decade ago, as processing elements have grown 36% per year from 1000 computers in 1987 to 10 million processing elements (contained in 100,000 computer nodes).

High Performance Computing (second edition) is the essential guide and reference for mastering supercomputing, as the authors enumerate the complexity and subtleties of structuring for parallelism and creating and running these large parallel and distributed programs. For example, the largest climate models simulate ocean, ice, atmosphere, and land concurrently created by a team of a dozen or more domain scientists, computational mathematicians, and computer scientists in cooperation.

Program creation includes understanding the structure of the collection of processing resources and their interaction for different computers, from multiprocessors to multicomputers and the various overall strategies for parallelism. Other topics include synchronization and message-passing communication among the parts of parallel programs, additional libraries that form a program, file systems, long-term mass storage, and components for the visualization of results. Standard benchmarks for a system give an indication of how well your parallel program is likely to run. Techniques are described for controlling accelerators and special hardware cores, especially GPUs, attached to nodes to provide an extra two orders of magnitude more processing per node. These attachments are an alternative to the vector processing units of the Cray era and typified by the Compute United Device Architecture (CUDA) model and standard to encapsulate parallelism across different accelerators.

Unlike the creation, debugging, and execution of programs that run interactively on personal computers, on smartphones, or within browsers, supercomputer programs are submitted via batch processing control. Running a program requires specifying to the computer the resources and conditions for controlling your program with batch control languages and commands; getting the program into a reliable and dependable state through debugging; checkpointing, i.e., saving intermediate results on a timely basis as insurance for the computational investment; and evolving and enhancing a program's efficacy through performance monitoring.

This textbook concludes with a forward look at the problems and alternatives for moving supercomputers and the ability to use them to exascale and beyond. In fact, the only part of HPC not described in this book is the incredible teamwork and evolution of team sizes for writing and managing HPC codes. However, the most critical aspect of teamwork resides with the competence of the individual members. This book is your guide.

Gordon Bell
October 2023

Preface

Telescopes, microscopes, and other instruments enable scientists to see forms of reality from microns to megaparsecs beyond human senses, greatly expanding our knowledge of life, the universe, and everything. High performance computing (HPC) emerged in the latter half of the 20th century to open an entirely new vista of exploration through modeling, simulation, and data analytics. HPC enables approaching ever finer precision across myriad domains of knowledge up to the edge of intelligence itself. This introduces the 2nd edition of *High Performance Computing: Modern Systems and Practices*, based on the original textbook, first published in 2017.

While "HPC" also stands for "high performance computer," the machine platform that performs calculations at enormous speeds, it is much more than a particular system or a singular activity. HPC is an interdisciplinary field engaging many areas of distinct but interrelated expertise, knowledge, and skills. This field has experienced the single greatest gain of any technology of human history, with delivered performance growing exponentially over the last 7 decades by a factor of 10,000 million billion. Even more significant than its range of computing capability is its breadth of diversity of application domains to which it is employed. Science, engineering, medicine and drug design, national defense and cybersecurity, and data analytics and artificial intelligence (AI) are just some of the many and important areas in which HPC plays a critical role. The economic and societal impacts are and have been significant and are becoming more so with the advent of machine learning and AI. HPC is a driver of human advancement in the 21st century.

At the outset of this project, the creation of this textbook faced four significant but interrelated challenges. The first objective was to encompass an array of topics, ordinarily the subject of their own dedicated coverage, in a single textbook. The second objective was to present a narrative that integrates these topics in a unified flow that proceeds readily from one lesson to the next, each building on the others. The third objective of this textbook was to take a complex discipline and structure it to serve as an entry-level course with essentially no prerequisites. The final objective was to provide the material necessary for teaching faculty to formulate any one of a number of distinct courses depending on the chosen focus and duration. This includes the opportunity to conduct a two-semester course, introductory and advanced, if augmented with hands-on student projects.

These goals were achieved in the main through the first edition but at the expense of a tome of excess size, redundancy, and ancillary information not critical to the pedagogical purpose. These shortcomings have been rectified in this edition, although some repetitions will be noted to ensure that each chapter stands on its own. The publisher and authors have worked closely together to achieve a more compact work to better serve the students without losing the effectiveness of the presentation style. The instructor should be aware that one element of the first edition has been eliminated to save space. An attempt had been made to share with the reader the culture, contributors, and milestone achievements that have made up this field for 7 decades or more, its history, and its legacy. It was admitted that this thread of discussion is probably of more interest to the authors than the students in this fast-paced world.

A driving need for this follow-on edition is to update information that is time sensitive and easily grows stale in a few years. This is why some very good books on different topics within the domain of HPC have nonetheless become reduced in relevance and ultimately obsolete. The authors feel a commitment to the higher education community to continuously maintain the highest level of quality in reflecting the state of the art to keep the course material and the students current in the field. This was achieved in a number of ways. All tables and charts that give numeric data characterizing specific systems or performance achieved have been updated. Some chapters were dropped as they ultimately proved less useful, while new chapters were created, such as the one about machine learning, which has grown in interest substantially since the original edition.

The book has been reorganized into six parts to facilitate flexibility on the part of the instructor, as will be described in greater detail in Chapter 1, the introduction. The parts are structured such that they can be taught separately or in different combinations depending on the synopsis of the course. Part 1 provides a foundation for all of the other parts and should probably be used in any course.

Part 2 gives the means by which practicing computational scientists including those in other fields can employ HPC systems without writing their own programs but taking advantage of a vast expanse of infrastructure, libraries, and tools that can be used to construct workloads for end domain problems.

Part 3 presents the architecture of a major class of parallel computers and the methods of programming them through the widely used OpenMP shared-memory programming interface.

Part 4 does the same for scalable distributed-memory architecture using the message-passing interface.

Part 5 takes this one step further with heterogeneous computing combining graphics processing unit (GPU) accelerators with either symmetric multiprocessor or massively parallel processor class systems using OpenACC to construct basic application programs benefiting from GPUs.

Part 6 extends the utility of this work beyond the introductory level with elements of more sophisticated methods including machine learning. The full text can serve for a single comprehensive and fast-paced course.

With Part 1, separate course curricula in HPC can be based on Part 2, Part 3, or Part 4 without the others. These can provide the basis for shorter courses at universities on the quarter system. Part 5 can be added to any of these two-part courses to include GPU heterogeneous computing. For a more aggressive course, the ambitious educator may select topics from Part 6 to add to the body of topics presented. It is expected that a student successfully taking this course will be well positioned to assume entry-level positions in industry, national laboratories, and centers.

Acknowledgments

This second edition textbook is a product of many years of experience, commitment, and strong collaboration among the authors. Few writing projects are as challenging as that of crafting a textbook for a university-level technical discipline. Such was the case with this second edition and that of the original 2017 textbook as well. Far more than the substantial task of authorship, this unique textbook is the end result of many years of pedagogical practice having taught first-year graduate HPC first at Louisiana State University for half a dozen years and then at Indiana University for more than a decade. In addition to in-class teaching, substantial effort was dedicated to online education both in real-time and on-demand video lectures. More than 80 hours were "put in the can" to serve students within both the respective host institutions and many others around the nation and beyond. These years of hands-on experience with many students and cooperating faculty accrued to provide the foundations for the curriculum of the interdisciplinary course(s). Too many individuals were part of this journey to recognize explicitly, but they have the gratitude of the authors for the roles they played in the evolving process.

The authors wish to express their gratitude to Chirag Dekate and Dylan Stark, who both served as teaching assistants at Louisiana State University for multiple semesters of the original HPC course both in classroom setting and disseminated by high-bandwidth internet. Also, both expanded their formative contributions directly to the subject matter and their presentation material. Finally, the course was exported to tutorials in which Dekate and Stark directly participated.

The authors convey their appreciation to Bibrak Chandio and Prateek Srivastava, both of whom served as assistant instructors, each for multiple semesters, and were key to the success of the maturing course at Indiana University. In so doing, they contributed substantially to creative activities in producing test and problem set materials that have become permanent parts of the teaching material, strengthening the course, and sharing lessons from the experiences with students. Prateek also made direct contributions to the second edition of the textbook of significant value. He contributed two chapters to the work and reviewed and edited two others. In addition, he was responsible for innumerable diagrams and charts throughout the textbook, which made it much better.

Finally, the authors wish to thank Elsevier/Morgan Kaufmann for supporting this massive publishing project. Their guidance and patience throughout the process were critical to the ultimate success of this project.

An Introduction to High Performance Computing and This Textbook

1

Chapter outline

1.1 Preamble

Tools, their fabrication, their use, and ultimately their conceptualizations are among the distinguishing properties of humanity from essentially all other animals. For at least 2 million years, the *Homo sapiens* have manufactured implements, principally of stone, to modify the physical environment to better suit our desires, needs, and survivability. However, by the beginning of the third millennium BCE, an equally revolutionary domain of tool was derived—not to manipulate the physical world but rather that of the symbolic world of information. The invention was writing, and the ability to capture information, retain it for a long duration, and share it with others geographically and down through time would again transform the human condition and likely define civilization. The details of the process of this development are less important than the impact writing has had that, in addition to text, would result in numerical representations and the emergence of arithmetic and eventually the symbology of mathematics. The writing and recording of numeric values ultimately led to the descriptions of algorithms and the task of calculation.

Even before the common era, means and methods of facilitating the performing of calculations led to construction of simple but useful tools, including counting tables manipulating small stones, positions of which represented specific numbers.

High Performance Computing. https://doi.org/10.1016/B978-0-12-823035-0.00001-8

These eventually evolved into the more familiar form and methods of the abacus with beads replacing stones, but the essential idea largely stayed the same. The driving motivations for these millennial-old devices were speed and accuracy of calculating. The abacus was widely used throughout the world into the 20th century. The concept of mechanical calculating emerged as an important tool for commerce, navigation, civil engineering, and eventually science. Throughout the 19th century and well into the 20th, early concepts of calculating devices extending back to the 17th century (e.g., Pascaline) had transformed into an industry manufacturing mechanical calculators for a ready market into the 1960s.

The missing piece between calculation and computing was process—a recipe of instructions on how to make complicated computing tasks out of simple operations. How one got from one step to another was still all in the head of the purveyor and susceptible to error. For the relatively straight problem of enumeration for the US Census in the last decade of the 19th century, Hollerith devised a punched card—based solution that stored, counted, and added representative numeric data, cutting the time to complete the national task by many years. Descendants of this original mechanical data evaluator would lead to more than half a century of punched card business—related information processing.

It was not until the middle of the 20th century that the last piece fell into place. The von Neumann architecture model combined a stored program (in memory), with data storage and logical manipulation, and the inchoate digital electronic enabling technologies to create the first general-purpose high-speed computers (high speed for then but extremely slow for now). Initially, the challenges were great to progress beyond the crucible of ideas and engineering to the revolution that would come for practical (including affordable) programmable computers. There were many purposes to which the first two generations could be applied, and the commercial and scientific market opportunities proved enormous. But for the latter domain of computing, performance was a severe bottleneck. Computers far more powerful than the first vacuum tube—based platforms (<1 Kiloflops) needed. For this to be achieved, a new kind of digital electronic computer was required: the "supercomputer." The supercomputer was an entirely new class of digital computer with which a plethora of imperative uses would drive technology and design forward at an unprecedented rate, making sophisticated applications, once unthinkable, to become a reality. The first supercomputers emerged on the market and in the biggest data centers (machine rooms) by the 1960s. The fastest supercomputer today is a trillion times the performance of the early supercomputers and a quadrillion times as fast as the original machines of the early 1950s. It is without hyperbole to say that this rate of progress, literally within a single lifetime, is orders of magnitude greater than that of any other technology in human history.

Some basic terminology should be presented upfront to simplify discussions of the next sections. Supercomputers are very fast computers and historically have gotten faster at an exponential rate. Another synonym that will be used frequently is "high performance computer" or the acronym HPC, hence the title of this textbook. However, there are two variations of these terms: "supercomputing" and "high performance computing." These capture the notion of using a supercomputer to perform the act of using one, which by the way is an "application" or a "job" just like with regular computers. However, supercomputers are not like other computers, although there are many similarities. And supercomputing is not like computing, though again, there are similarities. To do regular computing, you run a "program" written in a "computer language" on a computer (once referred to as a "mainframe"). As long as you stay within the rules of the programming language, a result value or set of values will be produced and probably correctly. Supercomputing doesn't just call for the correct answer; it demands it quickly. The rules for the programming interface for supercomputing require a lot of knowledge about the supercomputer itself and what works and doesn't work well in computing very fast. Therefore, to successfully apply an HPC requires knowledge about the supercomputer and how it responds to different program sequences, data structures, hierarchies of system memory, forms of parallelism of actions, and even distances between different parts of the system.

This textbook *High Performance Computing Modern Systems and Practices* is carefully crafted to guide you through these various kinds of knowledge and others as well. To the student, upon completing a course based on this textbook, you will be able to perform all of the needed tasks to immediately serve at an industrial or government-grade environment at or above an entry-level position. More important, you may use your newly acquired knowledge to give you the necessary abilities to pursue your own studies and research using the power of supercomputers to solve problems of interest. For some, this may establish a foundation for future careers in HPC itself as a field in hardware design or software development. Yet others seeking the necessary background to manage such systems as "system administrators" will find this an excellent resource. However, whatever the goals, the topics of this text are interrelated, each mutually supporting the others.

One final word of this preamble: the field of HPC is dynamic and fast paced. Knowledge factors are likely to change over time. Such knowledge is provided throughout this volume and will serve you well but will ultimately get a bit stale. However, concepts are foundational and are a basis upon which supercomputing can be expected to rely from the distant past through to the next decades. This information is conveyed in a manner that highlights what serves as fundamental concepts such that you can have confidence in their relevance into the future. Finally, students are likely to want to learn how to do things—make it work and achieve results. For this purpose, this text delineates the chapters or sections that are crafted to convey "skills" almost in tutorial style but with explanations of why, not just how. The remainder of this introductory chapter provides an overview and quick but solid view of the field of HPC, the nature of such machines, and the means of making them work for you.

1.2 An Introduction to High Performance Computing

HPC is the discipline and practice of the development, operation, and application of the broad class of high-speed computers used to deliver superior rate of calculation or reduce time to solution. Also referred to more casually as "supercomputing," HPC is a cross-cutting field synthesizing interrelated domains of user application workloads and parallel algorithms, programming languages and compilers, runtime and operating system software, and enabling device technology and hardware architecture. Since the emergence of digital electronic computers in the mid-20th century, speed as a property of computation has driven HPC across a performance range of 15 orders of magnitude. In doing so, supercomputing has evolved from a specialized tool for a narrow range of applications (often government sponsored) to a broad span of diverse commercial, industrial, defense, and societal problem domains. Yet even as this second edition textbook is going to print, an almost explosive growth of new techniques in artificial intelligence (AI) for machine learning, natural language processing, medical diagnosis, and robotics (among many others) are ensuring that HPC will continue to drive the future of humankind well into this new century. Not just for lucky specialists, the expanding field and powerful tool of HPC is delivered to students and readers of this textbook.

HPC involves big machines with lots of capability, sometimes taking up thousands of square feet of machine room floor space and millions of watts of electrical power. But HPC is much more. As well as impressive and sometimes noisy hardware that may comprise rows of racks each containing dozens of "nodes" or "drawers," HPC involves software: millions of lines of code serving various essential purposes to ultimately deliver the results of an end user's application. Such software can be demarcated as 1) system software, and 2) libraries of complex functions constructed and optimized by experts and shared by many users for productivity, correctness including accuracy, and delivered performance. The third category, as anticipated, is the application code, developed either by the end user or for other users.

These three software domains are presented in the following chapters, although they have been carefully edited to select the specific useful parts for entry-level HPC computational scientists, hardware design engineers, HPC researchers, and heavily relied upon system administrators (thank you for your service, sincerely).

1.3 Impact of Supercomputing on Science, Society, and Security

The motivation for the invention and development of supercomputers and their means of use is not about hardware (as fascinating as that is) or even the software that makes it work but the problems that it solves both now and in the past. It would not be possible to provide an adequate let alone comprehensive listing of all the computational challenges that only supercomputing has solved. However, equally, it would be remiss to introduce the many facets of HPC without considering its many domains of application throughout its more than seven decades of evolution. Even then, this only touches on the digital electronic stored program generations of HPC class systems, omitting the previous half century of electromechanical tabulators (including the Harvard Mark 1), the many special purpose devices, and the decades of analog computers (e.g., Vannevar Bush machines). However, sampling some of these high-impact areas may impress future users and use of the state of the art in computing. Here is such a sample:

- **National Defense:** Beginning in the 1940s, vacuum tube–based electronic digital systems were used for what was then daunting computations in the areas of projectile ballistics, cryptography, nuclear physics, and intercontinental air defense. Over the following decades, most of these requirements and many others for defense continued to expand in scale and performance to the present while gaining in capability by a factor of a quadrillion (or more).
- **Human health:** Medical practices have been revolutionized by supercomputing such as personalized health, nonintrusive internal diagnostics (e.g., magnetic resonance imaging), genomics, and molecular dynamics for drug design.
- **Industrial engineering simulation:** Uses include computational fluid dynamics for aerospace design, automobile crash simulations, magnetohydrodynamics,
- **Meteorology and climate:** Uses include atmospheric, oceanic, ice flows, and topography with heat and mass transfer, mesoscale, and chemical speciation.
- **Nuclear reactors:** These are used for both fission of uranium and plutonium and fusion of hydrogen and helium isotopes in tokomak reactors.
- **Civil engineering:** Uses include concrete structures, bridges, tunnels, and steel building frames.
- **Material:** Uses include properties, fabrication, crack propagation, shockwave physics, alloying, and carbon nanotubes.
- **Cosmology:** Uses include special and general relativity, quantum mechanics, loop quantum fields, superstring theory, black holes and neutron stars (e.g., pulsars), dark matter, and dark energy.
- **AI:** Uses include supervised machine learning, unsupervised machine intelligence, and natural language processing.

Together, these areas are representative of modern extensive workflows but not presumed to be exhaustive. Indeed, it is expected that some of you (i.e., students) will contribute to the expansion of the list provided. Please feel free to share your thoughts on this with the authors.

1.4 **Supercomputer Performance**

In HPC, "performance" is its middle name. Upon first reflection, the idea of performance would appear intuitive with the principal feature being speed (of some kind). However, the realities of supercomputing are far more complex, subtle, and multidimensional. Issues of metrics, measurement, and means of comparative analysis, as well as how performance is achieved and the role of time all require sufficient explanation (Fig. 1.1).

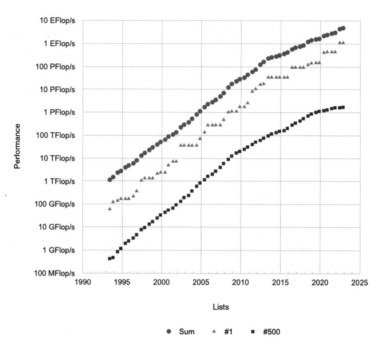

FIGURE 1.1 Performance of the Top 500 machines.

In its simplest form, performance can be measured in terms of work accomplished in unit time. Even then there is no single metric. Time is usually determined in seconds (or microseconds) but of what may vary. Work can take multiple forms. Even in the basic case of calculating integer operations, most computers can recognize different types and scales of integers. They may be of different bit lengths (e.g., 8, 16, or 32 bits) and signed or unsigned. Similarly, numeric data may be floating point (or approximate real numbers) usually of 32- or 64-bit length formats. For integers, the metric of operations per second or ops is a common unit. For floating-point numbers, performance is usually specified as floating-point operations per second or flops. Still, the numeric precision is assumed. Of course, no computer let alone a supercomputer is as slow as 1 ops or 1 flops. Therefore, actual units are presented in sets of three orders of magnitude. The earliest digital electronic computers operated at performances of 1 Kilo ops or Kops. Today a more common measure is Petaflops or Pflops. Even this notation is not universal with capitalizations changing and other distinctions such as Pflop/s as just one example. For the computation of a graph application, none of these is appropriate. A completely different unit of performance is therefore required: traversed edges per second or TEPS. Variations based again on orders of magnitude are widely used. As will be seen, there are different kinds of workflows and execution units such that there are a diversity of measures.

Another important measure depends on whether the data type is scalar or in a vector (or matrix). As a scalar, a value is fetched one at a time and cycled through the multiple layers of the execution unit, including potentially multiple stage of a pipelined floating-point unit, until producing a result value to be placed in a designated register. The time from original instruction fetch to final write-back determines the rate of floating-point operation. However, it is possible to be engaged in multiple (if independent) floating-point operations in which a succession of instructions read a sequence of floating-point operand values such that they are performed in execution and operational pipelines, albeit at different stages of their operation. This produces a higher measure of performance. A final approach is to use a floating-point vector instruction that informs the hardware instruction unit to rapidly stream the vectored sequence of values through the same units for maximal performance. Therefore, there are alternative methods of achieving the same class of work but by slightly different methods. One will still get a measure in flops, but which one is right? They all are, of course, but with different assumptions.

Over multiple decades, the supercomputing community has devised diverse sets of shared common tests called "benchmarks" that are bodies of code and sets of rules that together, when applied with veracity, assert meaningful measures of comparisons. Many such benchmarks are used among community vendors, and users to rank their respective supercomputing platforms. Not the least of these is high performance LINPACK (HPL), which has its legacy in more narrowly defined LINPACK for sequential computers many years before. HPL has been used since 1994 to rank all (submitted machines) supercomputers approximately every 6 months at ISC and SC, respectively. Others include the HPC Benchmarks, which is a set of workflow kernels. HPCG is a more stressful test of system resources. Graph-500 exercises traversal of graphs. Different supercomputers perform at different relative capabilities to these different benchmark measures. Therefore, no one benchmark serves as an all-encompassing and final means of evaluation with respect to other supercomputer systems. Different benchmarks stress machines to different degrees, and these distinctions are exposed by different tests.

One last and important aspect of HPC performance measure is the concept of "scalability." Although the term is somewhat arbitrary, It nonetheless conveys the notion of the effect of increase in size. Even at this introductory level, this is worth bringing to the student's attention. Two separate forms of scalability are commonly conceived and used in technical discourse. These are "weak scaling" and "strong scaling" that are also, respectively, associated with the terms of "capacity computing" and "capability computing." Weak scaling refers to simply the number of operations performed per unit time. With weak scaling, not only is the system to be measured increasing in size but the size of the computational problems, which may be independent, in the form of dataset sizes is increased proportionally as well.

Weak scaling reveals the total amount of work that a system has the capacity to conduct across multiple or many separate tasks or jobs at the same time. It could be an expansion of the number of jobs of the same application type being proportional to the number of system nodes. In a way, it is the easiest form of scalability and on a good day exhibits linear scaling, that is, the amount of throughput (the total operations per unit time increases proportionally to the size of the supercomputer or its increase in capacity). Strong scaling is more stringent. Although the supercomputer system increases in size, say by the number of nodes, the work to be performed or problem size remains constant. The actual measure of interest for this capability processing is how the time to solution decreases as the size of the supercomputer increases. Ideally, this would be linear. However, real-world practical systems may exhibit linear capability scaling with respect to system resources available over a limited range. Beyond some point of system resources available, the execution time will no longer continue to decrease. In the worst case, it will tend upward because of third-order effects.

The authors introduce a third degree of parallelism that may be perceived as a compromise between capacity and capability computing. Capacity computing increased the size of the workload proportionally with the size of the system in which the workload is presumed to be a set of independent tasks. The capability computing modality increases the system scale with a single task even as the system gets bigger. "Cooperative" computing is proposed to interleave the two boundary forms of scalability. Like both of the previous forms, cooperative scalability extends the size of the system. Like capability computing, cooperative computing and scaling involves a single task or job, even as the system is extended. Like capacity computing, cooperative computing does increase the workload size but within the scope of a single task, usually as it relates to the size of the input dataset. It is possible to increase a task size by other means as will be seen in future chapters. Cooperative computing, although not standard terminology in HPC, is in fact quite typical for methods of parallel programming described in this book including, for example, Message Passing Interface (MPI) and OpenMP. A single task is stretched somehow rather than feeding more concurrent jobs. Cooperative scaling and computing will prove important as we proceed forward.

1.5 Sources of High Performance Computing Performance

As will be shown, the property of performance is achieved through several factors, including enabling technologies, architecture structures, programming methods, and application algorithms. Although each is a separate area in its own right, there are substantial overlapping and mutual support. Future chapters explore these aspects in detail and show in what way the user, designer, and developer contribute to advance these characteristics separately and together. At a higher level of abstraction, there are really two factors that deliver performance and with which students will directly engage. The first is the raw or intrinsic speed of the enabling technologies from which the supercomputer is constructed. The second is the attribute of parallelism, or the degree and means by which a multiplicity of operations can be conducted at the same time.

The user, or in this case the student, is unlikely to come into contact with or have the means to make judgements regarding the underlying technologies incorporated within a high performance computer. The system to which students will most likely have access will determine the capabilities and capacities of that technology without direct engagement. However, a major contributor to the performance experienced is due to the extraordinary growth of enabling technologies. This was exponential for the better part of three quarters of a century and was unprecedented in the history of human technology. A conservative estimate of the gain factor of performance over that period is one quadrillion to present-day supercomputing capability. More than a factor of a million of this can be attributed directly to the enabling technologies themselves.

To be frank, it's been a wild ride across the evolution, or likely revolution, of the development of the generations of enabling technologies. To achieve speed of computing, a narrower set of parameters are responsible. Yet, other ancillary parameters are relevant to the overall value of a system's capabilities and services. At the risk of oversimplification, three functionalities have been essential since the 1940s: (1) the logic technology for switches and gates, (2) the memory technology for bit storage, and (3) data communication and transfer channels and networks. The speed and density of devices in each of these three cases have contributed to both the raw performance and to what capabilities and capacities can be incorporated within a single system at a particular design (cost) point.

Almost all of the remainder of this performance gain factor is due to parallelism: the operational ability to perform multiple (actually a lot) of operations at the same time. The user, student, or designer will be directly engaged with parallelism. This textbook shows how to do so. At the lowest level, parallelism is achieved through logic circuit design. Computer system architecture defines the levels and degree to which functional units are used to perform many streams of tasks simultaneously. The programming language or nested languages and the underlying compiler and potentially runtime software support parallel programming and execution. The user's job description asserts the actual work that can be undertaken at the same time. The ordering of such work segments provides associated and synchronized precedence. The parallel programming language provides the user or student with the expressiveness of how to order, coordinate, and organize the computational work to be performed and in so doing exploit computation parallelism to expedite the necessary processing.

Parallelism of computing is not created by the programming language but rather only represented by it as a medium of information exchange. The actual parallelism comes from the abstraction of the "algorithm," the formula or recipe by which the user or student describes how the computational work is to be performed. Although not a tangible element of the supercomputer, it is critical as an intermediary transformation between the problem to be solved and the method by which it is solved.

The algorithm includes the identification of the execution parallelism. The more computational work that can be done in parallel, the shorter the time required to conclude the program execution (strong scaling) or at least increase the amount of computational work that can be performed (throughput).

1.6 A Brief Description of a High Performance Computer

Without exaggeration, most likely any student reading this textbook is familiar, at least at an informal and casual level, with computer processors. More than one is buried, perhaps literally, under the hood of your automobile. It is at the core, again literally, of the cellphone and carried ubiquitously throughout the day. A modest number of such processor cores are managing the resources, operating system, input/output (I/O) drivers, and applications on every laptop, including the one on which this textbook is being compiled. Although in varying forms and packaging, their processor cores are not unlike those that compose supercomputers. The personal assistants that are mostly mobile are a significant element of the world's highest performing computers. So, what is the difference? Essentially everything, which is why inquiring students are engaged in the pursuit of necessary concepts, knowledge, and skills offered through this treaties. As a baseline, a laptop is likely to deliver a performance in excess of roughly 10 giga-ops. By some metrics, the fastest computer in the world, Frontier, at the Oak Ridge Computing Leadership Facility, is a factor of 100 million times faster. By the time the reader encounters these words, the numbers may be off by a factor of an order of magnitude or more. The numbers are astounding, and this is the power offered to students and future users in their pursuits and is the domain of this textbook.

1.6.1 Enabling Technologies

At the risk of an un-useful distraction or, worse, a disruption, the short history of supercomputing of approximately 7 decades did not take the form of systems described as earlier. It was only in the decade of the 1990s that this formula for essentially all future HPC systems emerged, replacing all of its varied predecessors. Before then, super-fast machines took on a number of differing forms because of existing enabling technologies and alternative architectures that were to a degree responsive to both those technologies and market niche requirements. The logic technologies of these previous 4 decades included vacuum tubes, transistors (germanium and then silicon), and small- and medium-scale integrated circuits of a few logic gates (RTL, DTL, TTL, ECL) that would grow in density and scale to large-scale integrated circuits and eventually very large-scale integrated digital electronic circuits. The number of transistors ranged from a few on a semiconductor die in the 1960s to billions after the turn of the century and more today as this exponential growth of decades ends with transistor feature size approaching a few nanometers. Memory technologies also spanned an array of physical devices, including, in some rough order: capacitors, paper tapes (with holes), punched cards (also with holes), mercury delay lines, Williams tubes (with phosphorous screens), magnetic drums (spinning), magnetic cores (a major advance), magnetic disks (also spinning), floppy disks, magnetic tapes, static random access memory (SRAM), and dynamic random access memory (DRAM). The last two are fabricated from semiconductor dies. Other logic and memory technologies are still being pursued.

1.6.2 Hardware Architecture

The past 3 decades, although still experiencing exponential growth in device density of both logic and memory, converged to a sequence of stages that at the macro level involved rows of racks lined up in parallel covering thousands of square feet of floor space at times, including today. Each rack mostly comprised equivalent drawers or modules referred to as "nodes," 32 per rack, more or less. Originally, each node comprised a single processor core, multiple memory chips, I/O ports, and a bunch of buses and wires connecting all of it together. Sometimes there were lights, usually red. Outside the racks of nodes were many wires or optical cables making up the system area network that integrates the whole of the supercomputer system.

The HPC node evolved with its underlying technology to include multiple processor sockets per node and further multiple cores per socket. This increasing multiplicity of computing devices proportionally increased the potential peak performance per node. In addition, the main memory within a node was shared among all of the processor cores of the node. Admittedly, the access time for any particular request by one core to a datum in any of the node's memory will vary in time because of the relative distances. In simpler days, these access times were all similar, and a system was characterized as a uniform memory access subsystem (UMA). But with the varying distances even within a single node, the behavior of a diversity of access times is instead referred to non-uniform memory access systems (NUMAs). The more salient aspect of the core to memory relationship is that all such interactions are coherent, even in the presence of their separate and sometimes partially shared caches; very fast memories transparent to the user that store copies of currently used data for high bandwidth and low access latency read and write operations. Consistency is a hardware-provided mechanism that keeps all copies of data among such caches up to date, a complicated trick that has evolved through the years. The result is that the multitude of cores making up the processing power of a system node is assured of acquiring access to the correct data values at any one time even if "owned" by some other core at the time.

The final evolutionary phase change of the modern HPC system is the move from homogeneity (the internals of a system node being the same) to heterogeneity (the internals of a system node being differentiated between the central processing unit (CPU) cores as described earlier and a second class of computing generally referred to as the graphical processing unit [GPU]) It is the addition of the GPU or GPUs in a multicore node that makes the node heterogeneous. Although the design of GPUs differs across generations and industrial providers, their role is to

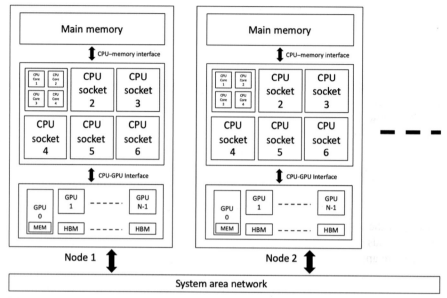

FIGURE 1.2 Node-level system architecture block diagram. *CPU*, Central processing unit; *GPU*, graphical processing unit; *HBM*, ***; *MEM*, memory.

dramatically accelerate the execution of specific computational idioms regular, highly parallel, and widely used for an important set of algorithms (Fig. 1.2).

As indicated earlier, the many nodes of a modern supercomputer are integrated into a single system by the system area network (SAN) that interconnects all of its racks and nodes. However, a significant distinction between the intranode computing paradigm and the internode computing exists, at least in a distributed scalable system. Although all of the processor cores within any one node have direct access to all of the main memory within that node, the separate nodes do not share their internal main memories with other nodes. Rather, the separation between nodes is a severe portioning of the system with good and bad consequences. The bad is, as discussed, the inability to directly share access to each other's memory. Between nodes, message passing is required. The *good* is the ability to scale such systems for very large, albeit it coarse-grained, parallelism. Both require that across the global system, an added protocol of messages is required to convey values, simple or compound, by send-receive message-passing protocols. Therefore, there are two modalities of parallel operation: (1) between nodes, data are explicitly exchanged by messages over the system area network while executing separate processes, and (2) within a node and its active process, there are multiple parallel threads being performed concurrently by its set of processor cores while exchanging information through the shared main memory of the node. Yet as mentioned earlier, there is yet a third modality within any single node (if so provisioned), that of offloading parts of the computation to GPUs. Often, but not always, partitions of a user application takes the form suitable for execution on the regular Single Instruction, Multiple Data (SIMD) pipelined hardware structures used by GPUs. A CPU may transfer control and data from a computation to a GPU, which can inherently perform that computing partition at an extreme throughput, in some cases greatly accelerating the performance for that piece and reducing its time to completion. There are overheads and effects of latency that degrade the ideal performance to some capability, but often these are offset by the significant advantage delivered by the GPU in such cases.

1.6.3 Supportive System Software

The complementary aspect of HPC beyond the architecture and its underlying hardware is software. Although understanding the hardware architecture is essential for mastery of the use of a supercomputer, the actual medium by which the expert conveys the needs and methods of the problem to be undertaken is established between one or more application programming interfaces (APIs). The workload management by other underlying software provides additional functionality and control of the target application. Next some major classes of software are briefly identified that are usually made available on a supercomputer and that in some form are discussed later within this textbook.

The initial user interface to a supercomputer is similar but not identical in form to the conventional operating system with which readers are familiar. The major challenge is the access to large dataset management through the users' file system, which may extend to the cloud. The other aspects of the operating system, at least as viewed by the user, are direct use of various system functions that may help with the details of directing the system in its allocation of physical and virtual resources and the mapping of the user's application onto them. Linux was originally introduced to HPC in the mid-1990s through the NASA Beowulf project and dominates this niche to this day as the operating system of choice for supercomputing.

The runtime system is an additional software environmental interface that delivers more refined control of the allocation of the parallel system resources to the parallel application modules. Although many forms of runtime systems have been developed and made available such as PBS, this textbook uses SLURM as the runtime utility of choice for this purpose. It is widely used, although other such system software systems may serve this purpose. Nonetheless, much of the functionality is shared even if with differences in syntax.

The question of the programming language for use with parallel computers is more complicated for several reasons. In most methods as used, a conventional programming language is used to express the basic computations. Most familiarly, these are Fortran, C, and C++. However, although some parallelism is implied by constructs within these otherwise sequential languages, additional binding frameworks are used to exploit the full effect of the parallel structures of modern system architectures as discussed earlier. To take advantage of the internal node architecture with its shared main memory and its multiple threads, the popular OpenMP is widely used. It provides the basic semantic constructs for demarcating threads, their points of barrier synchronization, the code segments that must only be performed one thread at a time although in any order, and the collective operations most widely required. OpenMP can be used if the target supercomputer consists only of a single node. Although this is not scalable (beyond the number of internal cores), it is the most common form of application platform used.

For multiple node systems, a different parallel API is required to establish the channels of message passing required and provide the broad set of send and receive semantic constructs to move data with such messages. A community-wide API for this is the MPI framework first developed in the mid-1990s by a joint committee from industry, government, and academia to create a shared standard. The version MPI 1.1 was heavily used, upgraded based on experience to MPI 2, and further enhanced with improvements by MPI 3 and MPI 4. MPI has more than 200 commands that supports the many syntactical mechanisms. They specify how messages are conveyed among nodes. They provide a wide array of alternative protocols for synchronization and collective operations among nodes. MPI is presented in two separate chapters for the basics and some advanced functions. One of the important advances in recent years has been the merger of the MPI and OpenMP programming interfaces to form a single framework for structuring an application code. Doing so takes advantage of the strengths of both while complementing their respective weaknesses. This method uses MPI as an outer layer expressing the patterns of communication between the potentially large number of system nodes. Within the MPI processes, OpenMP is used to convey how to use the multiple processor cores in each node to take advantage of local multiple threaded execution and the opportunity of efficient shared memory access by the threads within the same node. Together the combined usage of MPI with OpenMP gives HPC programmers the greatest control and flexibility in managing the parallelism of their application programs for best performance.

The best way to write a parallel application is to not do so. Rather, it is better to use a code already crafted by an expert in the field and provided through the availability of one of a large number of libraries that are easily accessible over the internet. If the problem to be addressed is not unique, then a library of function appropriate to that problem probably exists and can be used with the individual user's own input dataset. Many of these libraries are public and open source with minimum restrictions of their licensing agreement. More often, one may need to devise an application that is not exactly satisfied by any one open-source program. A style of problem formulation referred to as "workflow management" uses a "scripting" language to weave together multiple available library packages to customize to the particular needs of the end user's problem. Although scripting languages such as Perl have been available for decades, practitioners have gravitated to higher level languages such as Python to use for this purpose. This textbook does not directly discuss this methodology, not wishing to impose more than one language (i.e., C) on the readers. However, experience has shown the authors that some students do undertake this approach themselves for projects and even problem sets.

Finally, there are myriad tools, sometimes libraries, that provide greater functionality and power of HPC usage. These are described in many cases throughout the textbook. In addition to environments for parallel programming, software packages are available for scientific visualization; for mass storage of complex data structures; for debugging complex code and performance tuning; and, of course, for benchmarking as presented in following chapters.

1.7 **An Overview of This Textbook**

Students could spend a lifetime fully mastering all of the details of the many programming interfaces available in HPC. Fortunately, only a small portion of these are required to develop significant codes even by the inchoate programmer. Fortunately, this textbook has been developed by authors who have done exactly this so that students do not have to. If used judiciously both by students and faculty, this book can serve as the basis for a single semester course that is sufficient to embark on any of a number of areas of expertise, projects, and careers. Nonetheless, there is more than a minimalist presentation of content to provide flexibility in its adaptation to varying needs and preferences. Not every student will read every chapter or section. Rather, each student or lecturer will select a path through the offered material to optimize for impact of purpose. There are multiple ways described to craft parallel programs depending on the prescribed curriculum. Only one or two of these need to be mastered to become an effective contributor to areas of interests, relying on supercomputing as a tool. Similarly, distinct computer architectures are separately explained to refine the ability to combine any one of these with a chosen programming methodology for best performance. This may also be influenced by the nature of the application discipline and problem sets to which the supercomputers are to be used. Finally, ancillary areas of expertise that may prove interesting and useful are covered in their own chapters. These can serve well to expand one's abilities but are not necessarily demanded in the course of a single semester. Another way to cut and dice the course is to select a subset of sections in each of the many chapters to acquire the useful essentials without investing additional time on all the fine points.

The textbook is organized into six parts, each with multiple mutually supporting chapters.

Part 1, "Getting Started," presents a cross section of interrelated topics, all of which provide a foundation for understanding the domain of HPC and the basics for the succeeding components and lessons of the book.

Part 2, "Making High Performance Computing Work for You," may surprise you. It explains many techniques for using supercomputers, none of which require you to actually write an application code by yourself. In fact, the majority of *runs* of jobs on an HPC system is based on programs made available from other sources but still driven by the input data of a single user.

Part 3, "Writing Your Own Parallel Programs," describes in detail one widely used methodology that students can use to develop a new parallel application program. This partition of the textbook focuses on shared-memory multiple-threaded HPC architectures. Although this broad class of supercomputer is not scalable indefinitely, it yields between one and two orders of magnitude of performance advantage over conventional single-processor core laptop, desktop, or desk-side commercial-grade computers. The vast majority of HPC applications that are executed by users are performed on such machines. Furthermore, as will be seen, the techniques described and learned from Part 3 will be of use for the next family of supercomputer APIs that enables true scalability.

This brings us to Part 4 of the textbook, "Writing Your Own Scalable Distributed Programs." The lessons from this part of the textbook give you access to powerful techniques to use the biggest machines in the world such as the Frontiers Exaflops HPC system that came online in the summer of 2022 at Oak Ridge National Laboratory. Although this textbook is devised to enable even those with a minimum of prerequisites to succeed and elevate their knowledge and skillset to useful and usable levels of practical capability, it is not merely a beginners' guide and tutorial.

Part 5, "Writing Your Own Heterogeneous Programs," significantly expands discourse to a more advanced level, introducing important areas of modern methods and practices. Included, as alluded to in the title, is substantial material about heterogeneous computing, which goes even beyond multiple node scalable systems to those with nodes that incorporate not just CPUs but more specialized GPUs. For certain classes of computation, they can greatly accelerate the performance achieved. However, in addition to added hardware (the accelerator boards), heterogeneous computing requires yet another layer of programming interface, which is also explored and demonstrated here.

Part 6, "Intermediate High Performance Computing Means and Methods," expands the students exposure to the intermediate level. This final part of the textbook is required by the student of a one-semester course. But it contains much interesting material and provides future direction for the inquiring student. Chapter 19 introduces the student to Machine Learning which should expose the student to an entirely different class of application and programming discipline. Chapter 20 exposes the student to the important area of Mass Storage and Parallel File Systems; a must for any serious practitioner looking forward to a long career in which HPC will play a key part. Chapter 21, as previously advertised, expands the student's knowledge in MPI by taking them beyond the basics and expanding their facility with valuable details and expanded capabilities. Chapter 22 provides the means of checkpointing/restart; a requirement for conscientious users of HPC. Finally, Chapter 23 while not critical to the focused reader, nonetheless gives an overview of some of the future possibilities to a field at or near the end of Moore's Law and possible future directions.

1.8 **Summary and Outcomes**

- "High performance computing" and "supercomputing" are synonymous and refer to the fastest computers in the world, at least within certain classes of structure and use.
- Classical supercomputing is a single really big machine, first introduced in the 1960s at 1 Mflops and continuing to this day at 1+ Exaflops.
- As often as not, HPC systems are measured by the HPL benchmark or parallel LINPACK. The Top 500 list uses parallel LINPACK as the principal means for comparison among competing systems.
- This chapter is an introduction to the textbook (second edition) in which it resides.
- General-use cases for HPC include national defense, human health, industrial engineering simulation, meteorology and climate, nuclear reactors, civil engineering, materials, cosmology, and AI, although this is not an exhaustive list by any means.
- The HPC growth trends have been shown to be essentially exponential, although in recent years, the trend has slowed down (i.e., the slope of the curve has lessened).
- "Performance" is measured in multiple ways. Most simple are the time to perform a single operation and operation and the throughput or number of operations per unit time. Benchmarks and other means provide additional methods to capture performance evaluations such as LINPACK on the Top 500 list every 6 months.
- Weak scaling reveals the total amount of work that a system has the capacity to conduct across multiple or many separate tasks or jobs at the same time. It could be an expansion of the number of jobs of the same application type being proportional to the number of system nodes.
- Strong scaling is when the supercomputer system increases in size but the work to be performed remains constant. The actual measure of interest for this capability processing is how the time to solution decreases as the size of the supercomputer increases.
- Multiple generations of enabling technologies increase clock rates, densities, and types over 7 decades. These include vacuum tubes, transistors, small-scale integration and medium-scale integration, and very-large-scale integration for logic. Memory includes mercury delay lines, Williams tubes, core memories, SRAM, and DRAM.
- Machine architectures also evolved considerably over this period. These include uniprocessors, pipeline processors, vector processors, multiprocessors, distributed computers, and heterogeneous systems (GPUs).
- System software includes operating systems, runtime systems, workflow managers, and compilers, among many other elements.
- The organization of this textbook is Part 1, Getting Started; Part 2, Making High Performance Computing Work for You; Part 3, Writing Your Own Parallel

Programs; Part 4, Writing Your Own Scalable Distributed Programs; Part 5, Writing Your Own Heterogeneous Programs; and Part 6, Intermediate High Performance Computing Means and Methods.

1.9 Exercises

1. What is a high performance computer? Specify a way that it differs from a conventional computer of the same era.

2. Identify application programming interfaces used for programming supercomputers.

3. What are three kinds of HPC architecture functional elements that are usually found as part of supercomputers despite the generation of enabling technologies incorporated?

4. What are two of the major forms of parallelism exploited within a supercomputer?

5. What form of supercomputer architecture is programmed with MPI?

6. Identify domains of problem applications that benefit from the use of supercomputers.

Commodity Clusters

2

Chapter outline

2.1 Introduction

The class of "commodity clusters" has been the single most widely deployed form of supercomputing system for the last two decades; more if you include the sub-class of "constellations." Commodity clusters exploit mass produced and marketed

High Performance Computing. https://doi.org/10.1016/B978-0-12-823035-0.00002-X

technology advancements in the areas of very-large-scale integration microprocessors, dynamic random access memory (DRAM) memory, and high bandwidth networking (local area network [LAN]or system area network [SAN]) taking advantage of superior performance to cost through economy of scale of mass production for other broader markets. Commodity clusters achieve this by chiefly using multiple (sometimes many) integrated standalone computers (i.e., nodes). These are separately sold in a much larger market segment (than that of the narrower high performance computing [HPC] domain), delivering an economy of scale benefits from this much larger consumer base. Commodity clusters provide great flexibility of system configuration and tremendous accessibility for a broad range of users from the most arcane national lab scientists to high school students. In this, commodity clusters may constitute the fourth revolution in supercomputing since its inception in the late 1940s. For our purposes, the commodity cluster will serve as the archetype of the conventional scalable HPC system, and its description will delineate the many system component layers that compose a full supercomputer, both hardware and software.

2.1.1 Definition of "Commodity Cluster"

The commodity cluster is a system of multiple integrated computer systems. The component computers are standalone, capable of independent operation, and marketed to a much broader consumer base than the scaled clusters of which they are composed. The integration network used is separately developed and marketed to be used by a system's integrator. Mass storage devices are off-the-shelf devices and are either physically installed within the system nodes or connected externally. All interfaces adhere to industry standards for both attached devices (e.g., USB, PCIe) or system networking. Although not required, system software is usually open source, nonproprietary, and Linux based. Programming interface libraries are bound to C, C++, or Fortran and use Message Passing Interface (MPI), OpenMP, both, or additional libraries for attached graphical processing (GPU) accelerators. More recently, domain-specific software has become available for data analytics, machine learning, and general artificial intelligence.

2.1.2 Motivation and Justification for Clusters

Although the motivation for adopting commodity clusters may differ among individuals and institutions, there are clear attributes that have justified their adoption for the past 2 decades. Some of the most prevalent among these are briefly discussed as follows:

> **Accessibility:** More likely than not, access to a medium-scaled supercomputer is to a commodity cluster of a moderate number of nodes. This is in part because they are by far the most prevalent form of supercomputer available. But it is also true that because of their relatively low cost, commodity clusters make up a disproportionate number of systems deployed at institutions where entry-level experience is likely to be acquired.

Performance-to-cost ratio: The relative low cost of acquisition, and within some environments, the low cost of ownership, are often the dominant reasons for the procurement choice of commodity clusters over custom massively parallel processing (MPP). Simply put, one gets more peak performance for a given price range than more tightly coupled, admittedly more efficient, alternatives (per processor core). Upon their introduction, commodity clusters running Linux exhibited performance-to-cost benefits with respect to contemporary MPPs of between one and two orders of magnitude depending on workload.

Scalability: Unlike symmetric multiprocessing (SMP) systems, commodity clusters are scalable in that the number of nodes can vary widely dependent on need, space, power, and cost. As earlier, for a given scale, the cost is less than alternative custom systems. However, this claim may be primarily in the domain of throughput computing rather than capability computing for which the overheads, latencies, and bandwidths may be less substantial than competing custom systems.

Configurability: The flexibility of configuration for commodity clusters has been historically greater than vendor-configured custom systems. Not only is variability of scale more flexible, but topology of node interconnects, node memory and processor sockets, external input/output (I/O) components, and other properties can also be easily specified by the end-user institution; vendor offerings had been more limited. Because of exploitation of industry standards and multiple sources of system elements, a diversity of choices gives even greater flexibility and choice alternatives. Also, systems can be modified over time rather than remaining stagnant throughout their lifetimes. Software diversity, often through open-source options, has strengthened customer control of user environments.

Latest technology: Clusters are made up of subsystems that have large markets, hence the value of economy of scale through mass production. As a consequence, such subsystems are targets by vendors for incorporation of the latest technologies to remain competitive in these large markets such as enterprise servers or SMP platforms. The integration of these leading-edge subsystems guarantees that commodity clusters, even those provided by system integrators, will incorporate the state of the art in component technologies, possibly even earlier than their custom-designed counterparts using the same underlying technology base.

Programming compatibility: Although very different in appearance and cost, commodity clusters are compliant in form if not function to MPPs; therefore, the approach to programming both is quite similar although optimizations may differ. Both clusters and MPPs are made up of microprocessor cores, tightly coupled nodes of processors and memories, and integration networks of various topologies. This permits the use of MPI to be used in programming both classes of supercomputer and the use of OpenMP for programming the individual system nodes. Such compatibility permits application codes and libraries to be shared between clusters and MPPs and to permit similar skill sets to be used for both as well.

Empowerment: A sociological aspect of commodity clusters, unanticipated by their original developers, was that users in labs and academia principally found that they had control of their system and were not bound or constrained by commercial fixed product specifications or proprietary software. There emerged an excitement and enthusiasm about supercomputers, an ease of engagement doing it with off-the-shelf components, and it was fun. Due to this a whole new generation was attracted to at least this form of supercomputing and it continues to draw young people into the field to this day.

2.1.3 **Cluster Elements**

There are widely varying alternative structures for commodity clusters, this being one of their features of scalability and configurability. However, in one form or another, almost all clusters comprise the same four classes of component types. These include:

- **Node:** This is the principal element of the commodity cluster that contains the major processing and main memory components to perform the user computation. The node is a standalone computer capable of performing independent user workloads. Even as part of a larger cluster, a node may be used to perform a single computation with other nodes doing separate work in the mode of throughput computing. Additional components of nodes usually include communication channels for processor to memory access and processor to I/O controllers and the node "chip set" that manages the node transparently to the user while providing basic primitives for the operating system (OS) and boot-strapping the node from the powered-down state. The node may include a diversity of I/O controllers for various purposes, including (but not limited to) the SAN(s). A cluster can incorporate anywhere from a few nodes to a few thousand nodes, enabling a broad range of system scale.

- **System Integration Network** (or SAN)**:** This is the off-the-shelf communication channel(s) that interconnects all of the nodes together into a single distributed computing system. The network supports data message passing between nodes, interprocess synchronization such as global barriers, and other collective operations such as reduction operations. It also may support communication with external system I/O devices and the internet. The network consists of the physical data paths of either copper wires or fiber optics, network interface controllers (NICs) to move node data to the data paths, and routers for switching data between data paths to arrive at the intended destination node.

- **Host:** This is a special node to support user services, including login accounts, administration, resource allocation and scheduling, and user file directories. The host node may serve multiple users simultaneously even as it spatially partitions the compute nodes among user jobs. The host node may have its own secondary storage, use the clusterwide mass storage, or access an external file system. Users usually log in to the host node through an institution's LAN.

- **Filesystem:** Secondary storage associated with the commodity cluster provides persistent storage for user programs, input data, and result data associated with the jobs that run on the cluster. Logically, the storage is exported to the user through the OS filesystem. Physically, the storage is a set of disk drives (and possibly tape drives) combined with controller hardware and connections between the controllers and the hard drives. Each node may have its own disk(s) built into the node or have access to a set of disk drives composing the system-wide filesystem, sometimes referred to as the "storage area network." Alternatively, the filesystem may be external to a cluster in the form of a network file system.

The canonical commodity cluster block diagram is shown in Figure 2.1 with these principal components.

2.1.4 Impact on the Top 500 List

As previously discussed, the field of HPC tracks its progress by measuring the performance of systems executing a derivative of the LINPACK benchmark, high performance LINPACK (HPL), and listing the fastest 500 machines every 6 months. Over this period, observed performance has experienced a gain of more than 1 million. Figure 2.2 represents this history in terms of the class of HPC systems contributing to the list at any period of review. Commodity clusters did not even show up on the list until 1997 with the entry of the Network of Workstations (NOW) system. In 2005, commodity clusters constituted half of all systems of the Top 500 list. Today that proportion has grown to about 85%, and it has been above 80% for the past 12 years (see Fig. 2.2). The vast majority of these exhibit R_{Max} performance (according to the rules of the HPL benchmark) near two orders of magnitude lower than the #1 machine at the corresponding reporting date, indicating that the largest portion of users are of the smallest cluster machines.

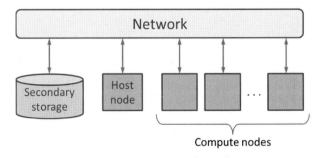

FIGURE 2.1

Commodity cluster components.

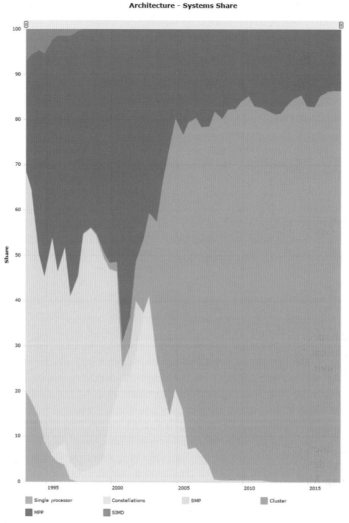

FIGURE 2.2

The dominant system architecture classes comprising the fastest 500 computers over the past 24 years. *MPP,* Massively parallel processing; *SIMD,* single instruction, multiple data; *SMP,* symmetric multiprocessing.

2.1.5 Brief History

The term "cluster" itself was first used in the late 1980s by Digital Equipment Corporation (DEC) for their Andromeda (M31) project. This early cluster combined 32 VAX 11/750 mini-computers and served as a testbed for experimental studies of hardware system interconnect and software support. This cluster system was never

FIGURE 2.3

The 1996 1-Gigaflops Beowulf cluster.

commercialized. In 1993, the NASA Beowulf project undertook an approach incorporating low-end consumer grade personal computers (PC) integrating them with the widely used Ethernet LAN. It also introduced Linux to the supercomputing community, providing at that time all of the Ethernet NIC driver software for Linux. For much of the succeeding 2 decades, this formula proved to dominate commodity clusters and ultimately supercomputing as a whole.

Throughout the late 1980s and the early 1990s, a series of message-passing programming interfaces had been developed by industry, national laboratories, and academia. These represented in one form or another the Communicating Sequential Processes execution model derived by Anthony Hoare in the late 1970s [6]. Ultimately, this body of work culminated in the community-wide application programming interface being developed and agreed upon, MPI. Shortly thereafter, MPICH was developed as a first reduction to practice by Argonne National Laboratory, making MPI widely accessible to a broad user community and establishing MPI as the premiere programming library for both MPPs and Beowulf-class commodity clusters (Fig. 2.3).

2.2 Hardware Architecture

The commodity cluster hardware is, by definition, all commodity off the shelf (COTS) to make maximum benefit of economy of scale to achieve the best performance to cost. The hardware architecture of the commodity cluster is therefore driven and constrained by this requirement. As briefly discussed in Section 2.1, the principal system components composing a commodity cluster are the (1) compute nodes, (2) SAN, (3) host node, and (4) mass storage. The architecture of a cluster exploits these resource classes but is also limited by these and additional support components (e.g., GPUs) that conform to industry interface standards. The hardware architecture of a cluster reflects the choices made of the specific component types, their number, and the structure in which they are organized and integrated via associated networks.

2.2.1 The "Node"

The principal system component of the commodity cluster is most commonly referred to as the "node," which includes most of the active components that make up the aggregate cluster computer. The replicated nodes, also referred to as "the compute node," in combination with the integrating interconnection network and the mass (secondary) storage, compose the complete scalable commodity cluster with associated mass storage. However, the node itself is a full and self-contained computer that alone and individually serves a much larger user market and therefore benefits from economy of scale to deliver exceptional performance to cost, at least for some important institutional workloads. The peak performance and capacity of a cluster is essentially the aggregate capability of all of the compute nodes in combination.

The responsibility of the node is to perform useful compute work for the end user. This is achieved through the collection of processor cores. A modern cluster node is made up of one or more multicore chips, also referred to as "processors," "sockets," "processor sockets," and so on. Depending on the type and number of cores on the chip, the term "many-core" may be used. A core is the workhorse of any modern computer. It issues a sequence of user instructions, each potentially designating multiple operations to be performed. A multistage execution pipeline carries out the micro operations required in succession to complete a given instruction and retire it when results are written back into the associated register, to the memory system, or to an I/O channel (other effects are possible as well). A processor socket contains multiple cores; one or more layers of memory cache for high memory bandwidth and low latency access; and one chip networks that integrate the cores, caches, and external I/O ports together. In many cases, a cluster node incorporates multiple multicore processor sockets. As will be discussed in more detail in following chapters, the micro-architecture of the node cores vary depending on manufacturer and system integrator. Popular processors have variants of two separate architectures by Intel, the IBM Power architecture family, x86 variants by AMD, and the ARM architecture, which is becoming increasingly interesting, although it has not as yet had a significant impact on the cluster market.

The node is also the container for the system main memory, which is primarily made of DRAM technology. Although there are many variants of technology and design, a typical DRAM bit cell consists of a switching transistor and associated capacitor for a high-density, low-cost, and moderate-speed data access, both read and write. Although core and main memory are both made from semiconductor devices, they are usually on separate chips because the respective fabrication processes of manufacturing are very different for optimal behavior of each. Multiple DRAM chips are mounted on single cards, and a number of cards are plugged into industry-standard interfaces. The sum of these cards determines the total main memory capacity of the node with the number of nodes then determining the total main memory of the commodity cluster.

The onboard network channels of the node support the intranode communication to move data between the processor sockets, the main memory boards, and the external I/O ports of the node. These networks are transparent to the user and are controlled either by the low-level "chip-set" also on the node motherboard or by the node OS. One of these communication channels is open to the user institution at the time of deployment or when reconfiguration is being conducted. The PCI "bus" is a standardized multi-port I/O fabric that permits additional subsystems to be added in a "plug-and-play" manner to the node without additional hardware changes. Several generations of PCI interconnects have been used in succession, the latest being PCI-Express (or PCIe). Even for this single specification, there are many distinct scales for each generation. Other interface ports, some of which go through the PCI bus on the node, are available such as the ubiquitous USB ports and more obscure accesses for maintenance and administration. Of particular importance is possible direct access to hard disk drives for secondary storage, network controllers for the LAN, and additional NICs for the SAN discussed next.

2.2.2 System Area Networks

The SAN is the central and differentiating attribute of a commodity cluster that varies in industry standards for communications. It is the principal distinction between a "commodity cluster" and a more generalized clustering of components in which the network is custom designed such as the Intel Omnipath. Many different networks have served this purpose. In 1994 to 1995, two approaches were explored. The first was the invention of the SAN by Chuck Seitz, former professor at Caltech, who created and manufactured the "Myrinet" that was very high performance and low latency for its day. It was also expensive. It was used by the University of California, Berkeley NOW project that used Sun Microsystems workstations (hence network of workstations), which were also relatively expensive.

The second was the adoption of the Ethernet LAN to this purpose by the NASA Beowulf project using low-cost but also lower performance personal computers based on the x86 Intel microprocessor architecture. Both approaches were used throughout the following decade in commodity clusters. Myricom, the vendor and distributor for Myrinet, is no more, but Ethernet continues to this day. Only recently has it been surpassed by the InfiniBand network architecture (IBA). Ethernet has dominated the low-cost SAN market and for clusters used primarily for throughput computing; IBA is widely used for more tightly coupled commodity clusters with higher bandwidth and significantly lower latency. Both branches of the SAN technology continue to evolve. Some commodity clusters will incorporate both types of network with the actual computing being conducted over the IBA network and the "out-of-band" activities for administration and system maintenance being performed over the Ethernet network.

SANs comprise physical channels for data transfer over distance of a few centimeters to hundreds of meters. These may be either conductors, usually copper, or optical fiber depending on issues of cost, energy, and bandwidth requirements. These are connected to nodes by NICs. These may be hardwired into the node motherboard such as is found with GigE (1 GB/sec Ethernet) in many cases or with separate NIC cards often plugged into the nodes' PCIe connectors. The NIC converts data provided by the processors or directly from main memory into message packets of varying length to be sent to destination nodes.

The third component is the router or switch used to create topologies of multi-layer network structures for higher degree of nodes. Switches are characterized by their degree (number of ports) and their time to transfer a packet from input port to output port, including the time to set up the internal switching configuration. For very large systems, switches can make up a large part of the system total cost as well as energy usage.

2.2.3 Secondary Storage

Persistent storage in one or more forms is essential for computing to indefinitely retain user programs, libraries, and input and result data. Commodity clusters may use hard disk drives or solid-state devices (SSD) built in to each node. Alternatively, a separate storage subsystem with its own controllers and possibly its own network may be included as a separate unit within the commodity cluster. Finally, the commodity cluster may access an external mass storage system via the LAN and share it with other user systems. A mix of these is possible and often used. One advantage of not having hard disks integrated within the node is a significant reduction in node power consumption and improved reliability. Disk drives are mechanical and therefore have a higher failure rate (like fans), so avoiding them in the node improves the node's down time. These are referred to appropriately as "diskless nodes." However, the recent rapid growth of use of nonvolatile memories, NVRAM, fabricated from semiconductors eliminates the use of mechanicals and can largely resolve this problem. Separate file systems are usually built from faster hard disks and incorporate redundancy (e.g., RAID) to circumvent downtime caused by single-disk failures. This is often a cost-effective and operational better approach to providing persistent storage to users.

2.3 Programming Interfaces

The principal programming modes for parallel programming involve using parallel library application programming interfaces that have bindings to sequential languages. This is the main modality that will be presented here.

2.3.1 **High Performance Computing Programming Languages**

Among programming languages frequently used in HPC, the most popular continue to be Fortran, C, and C++. Some other languages are growing in popularity for HPC applications, including the Python scripting language.

Fortran was developed by John Backus at IBM and first released in 1957. The name Fortran derives from the original description of the language as a formula translating system and is designed to be well suited for high-level programming of numerical calculations. In fact, many have described Fortran as a Domain Specific Language for mathematics. Subsequent standardizations followed, including Fortran 66, Fortran 77, Fortran 90, Fortran 95, Fortran 2003, and Fortran 2008.

The C language emerged in the late 1960s and early 1970s from Bell Labs from work by Dennis Ritchie. The C language was first standardized in 1988 and has gone through multiple updates, including C95, C99, and C11. In 1978, Brian Kernighan and Dennis Ritchie published one of the most influential books and tutorials on C programming titled *The C Programming Language*, which continues to influence C programmers today.

The C++ language emerged in the early 1980s developed by Bjarne Stroustrup. The name arises from the "++" increment operator and indicates the "evolutionary nature of the changes from C." Just as in the case for the C language, the C++ creator also wrote a highly influential book titled *The C++ Programming Language*, which has gone through multiple editions and continues to strongly influence C++ programmers. The C++ standard continues to evolve, from C++98, C++03, and C++11 to C++14.

2.3.2 **Parallel Programming Modalities**

There are three main parallel programming modalities present on most clusters today: throughput computing, message passing, and shared-memory multiple thread applications.

Throughput computing involves efficiently running a large number of jobs that may be either entirely independent of one another or otherwise require minimal communication or coordination between each other. An example is conducting an application parameter survey when a single application is run with thousands of different input parameters concurrently to explore its parameter space. Throughput computing is covered later in greater detail.

In contrast to throughput computing, a single message passing application requires a significant amount of communication and coordination within the application to speed up the time to solution. The principal programming model for achieving this speed up is the communicating sequential processes model as exemplified by the MPI.

Like message passing, shared-memory multiple thread applications also focus on speeding up the time to solution for a single application rather than efficiently executing a large number of mostly independent applications as in throughput computing. However, as the name implies, shared-memory multiple-thread applications are restricted to shared memory as opposed to distributed memory as in the case of message passing. The shared-memory multiple-thread parallel programming modality is exemplified by the OpenMP programming model.

2.4 Software Environment

The software environment is a critical element of every computer's operational infrastructure. It exposes and manages functionality supported by hardware, provides different access and usage modalities for different users, manages global and local resources, and offers tools to further expand the installed software base. The latter is accomplished through utilities focusing on development, testing, optimization, configuration, performance monitoring and tuning, and trackable incorporation of new software modules into the existing code base. The following is a necessarily brief discussion of common software components composing a cluster's operational environment. A number of usage examples are also provided to benefit readers who haven't been exposed to this class of systems before.

2.4.1 Operating Systems

The OS provides the software environment and services necessary to use the computer and execute custom applications. It consists of a *kernel* that manages hardware resources and arbitrates access to them from other software layers, *system libraries* that expose a common set of programming interfaces permitting the application writers to communicate with the kernel and underlying physical devices, additional system *services* performed by the background processes, and various administrator and user *utilities* that comprise programs invoked by users of the computer to accomplish specific minor tasks. Readers are likely to be familiar with OSs commonly found on desktop and laptop computers such as Microsoft Windows or Apple OS X. Traditionally, however, this space on "big iron" systems was reserved to several variants of the UNIX OS, a proprietary OS developed by Bell Laboratories in 1970. Thus, one could find AIX on IBM machines, HP-UX on Hewlett Packard Enterprise computers, UNICOS on Cray, IRIX on SGI or Solaris on Oracle products in addition to academic equivalents such as Minix and BSD, or Berkeley Software Distribution (and its subsequent forks OpenBSD, NetBSD, and FreeBSD). Note that the series of Apple Mac OSes mentioned is also a derivative of FreeBSD. Another important UNIX-like OS that has been steadily gaining in prominence over that past 2 decades is Linux. Linux is frequently used as the OS of choice on multitude of servers and clusters, although it is also used in a broad range of mobile computing devices, for example, providing the core implementation for Android OS. Although successful in mobile and enterprise markets, Linux desktop penetration oscillates around 1% to 2% depending on the statistics.

The development of Linux kernel was started by Linus Torvalds in 1991. Since then, many individual developers and companies contributed to its source, making it a truly multiplatform product, effectively supporting an impressive number of hardware devices through the available driver pool and execution environments and spanning from small embedded devices to large multiprocessor systems. The majority of systems on the Top 500 list are Linux derivatives. The Linux kernel is an open-source product licensed under GPLv2.

On most systems, the Linux kernel is accompanied by an open-source suite of libraries and utilities primarily contributed by the GNU Project. These tools were developed and refined over the course of several decades in a massive online collaboration that originated in 1983 and include, among many other entries:

- C library (*glibc*)
- C, C++, Fortran, and several other languages compiler (*gcc*)
- Debugger (*gdb*)
- Binary utilities comprising linker, assembler, symbol table tools, simple archive manager, and others (*binutils*)
- Application build system support (*make*, *autoconf*, *automake*, *libtool*)
- Command-line shell (*bash*)
- Core utilities that support low level operations on filesystems and contents of stored there files (*coreutils*, *less*, *findutils*, *gawk*, *sed*, *diffutils*)
- Text editors (*emacs*, *vi*, *nano*)
- E-mail utilities (*mailutils*)
- Terminal emulator (*screen*)
- Archivization and compression tools (*tar*, *gzip*)

Although these utilities provide a near-complete basic UNIX-like operating environment, most Linux distributions include additional open-source software packages, many of them released under a GPL license. They enable more flexible process management, bootstrap service configuration, network tools, improved e-mail client and server programs, graphical environments (X Window System, Wayland), and desktop environments (Gnome, KDE) in addition to a plethora of other special purpose programs. To ensure broad compatibility, most of the software conforms to the IEEE POSIX standards, effectively enabling drop-in replacement for proprietary implementations.

2.4.2 Resource Management

Large computers use resource management systems to coordinate accesses to multiple execution units, memory allocation, network selection, and persistent storage allocation. The number of users of even a single machine can easily reach several thousands, and each of them may potentially execute multiple applications with different properties, requirements, and runtimes. Manual management of every aspect of machine resource allocation by the operators is therefore prohibitive. Fortunately, numerous sophisticated resource management packages have been developed and are in extensive use today to automate the tasks related to distribution of user workloads across the compute nodes and monitoring the progress of their execution. One of such most widespread resource management systems is SLURM. The example commands described below may be directly used on any correctly configured system equipped with SLURM.

- The resource management programs encapsulate user workloads in self-contained units, or *jobs*, that specify at the very least a program to be run, its I/O datasets, the number of nodes (or cores) to be used for its execution, and the maximum duration of time the program is expected or required to execute. These parameters are encoded in *job scripts*, which are discussed in greater detail in a later chapter. The user informs the system of the intended workload and its resource requirements by submitting a job script to the execution queue. This is done using the *sbatch* command:

```
sbatch job_script
```

- If the script `job_script` is an existing file, the above command will create a new job, append it to the default job queue, and print a confirmation similar to the following:

```
Submitted batch job 12345
```

- In the output above, "12345" is a unique job number assigned by the system to the job that has just been queued. The user may subsequently refer to this number to examine the job status using the *squeue* command:

```
squeue -j 12345
```

The result output contains among other information the name of the queue job that was stored in (PARTITION field), name of the job (NAME), submitting user's ID (USER), and execution status (ST). The example output may look as follows:

```
    JOBID PARTITION     NAME     USER ST       TIME  NODES
NODELIST(REASON)
    12345     batch job_scri   user03  R       0:13      1
node01
```

In this particular case, the job was submitted to the "batch" queue by user "user03" and is already running (status "R") on one node of the cluster. Other noteworthy status flags include "CA" for canceled jobs, "CD" for completed,

"F" for failed, "TO" for timed out, and "PD" for pending. The latter marks jobs that await allocation of resources to avoid conflicts with other, already executing jobs.

- A pending or running job may be canceled at any time using the command:

```
scancel 12345
```

If successful, the command does not print any confirmation after removing job from the queue or killing the related executing application and releasing the affected nodes. Errors (e.g., invalid job number given as the argument) cause an explicit error message to be printed on the console.

2.4.2.1 Debugger

A debugger enables the programmer to step through code in execution, place breakpoints in the code, view memory, change variables, and track variables, among other capabilities. One of the most common serial debuggers available is the gnu debugger (gdb). The gdb debugger is a command line debugger with which the user can give a set of commands to set a breakpoint, continue execution, examine a variable, set a watchpoint, and so on. Table 2.1 gives a few of the basic gdb commands.

To debug a code, the code must be compiled with debugging information included. For most compilers, this is accomplished by adding the '-g' flag to the list of compiler flags when compiling. An example of this using the gnu debugger to alter the execution flow of a serial dot-product computation is provided in Figure 2.4.

TABLE 2.1 A Few Basic gnu Debugger Commands

gdb Command	Function
gdb <executable name>	Starts the gnu debugger on the specified executable
r	Starts executing the code
l	Lists the current source code in which execution is paused
bt	Provides a backtrace from the stack
p <variable name>	Prints the variable value
set var <var> = <value>	Sets the value of the specified variable
watch <var>	Sets watchpoint on specified variables
b <filename>:<line number>	Set breakpoint at specified source code line number
c	Continue execution after pausing after a breakpoint or some other pause.
quit	Quit

```
 1 #include <stdlib.h>
 2 #include <stdio.h>
 3
 4 int main(int argc,char **argv) {
 5    int i;
 6    // Make the local vector size constan
 7    int local_vector_size = 100;
 8
 9    // initialize the vectors
10    double *a, *b;
11    a = (double *) malloc(
12        local_vector_size*sizeof(double)
13    b = (double *) malloc(
14        local_vector_size*sizeof(double)
15    for (i=0;i<local_vector_size;i++) {
16      a[i] = 3.14;
17      b[i] = 6.67;
18    }
19    // compute dot product
20    double sum = 0.0;
21    for (i=0;i<local_vector_size;i++) {
22      sum += a[i]*b[i];
23    }
24    printf("The dot product is %g\n",sum)
25
26    free(a);
27    free(b);
28    return 0;
29 }
```

```
Launch gdb on the executable (a.out here):
andersmw@cutter:~/learn$ gdb ./a.out
Command line interaction with gdb:
Reading symbols from ./a.out...done.
(gdb) b dotprod_serial.c:17
Breakpoint 1 at 0x4005ef: file dotprod_serial.c, line 17.
(gdb) r
Starting program: /home/andersmw/learn/a.out

Breakpoint 1, main (argc=1, argv=0x7fffffffdfe8) at dotprod_serial.
17            b[i] = 6.67;
(gdb) p i
$1 = 0
(gdb) l
12            local_vector_size*sizeof(double));
13      b = (double *) malloc(
14            local_vector_size*sizeof(double));
15      for (i=0;i<local_vector_size;i++) {
16        a[i] = 3.14;
17        b[i] = 6.67;
18      }
19      // compute dot product
20      double sum = 0.0;
21      for (i=0;i<local_vector_size;i++) {
(gdb) set var i=100
(gdb) c
Continuing.
The dot product is 0
[Inferior 1 (process 24118) exited normally]
(gdb)
```

FIGURE 2.4

Example usage of the gnu debugger. The *left panel* illustrates a simple serial dot-product computation. The *right panel* illustrates command line interaction with the gnu debugger, including the setting of break points, printing variables, setting variables, and continuing execution. In the gnu debugger interaction, the loop variable in source code line 15 is reset to be 100, forcing the exit of the loop and the null dot product result.

Debugging a parallel application on a commodity cluster introduces several complications. These will be addressed in further detail. A simple and straightforward way to debug a parallel application on a commodity cluster is to launch a serial (nonparallel) debugger for each process. An example is provided in Figure 2.5.

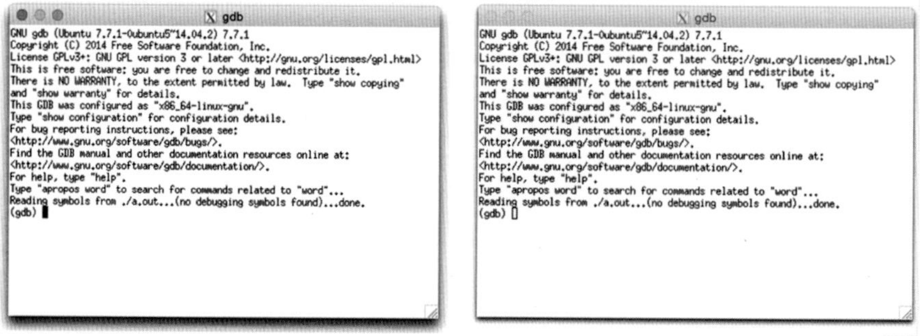

FIGURE 2.5

Using the "mpirun" command, the gnu debugger is launched for each process to enable parallel debugging. Two processes are launched here.

2.5.2.2 Performance Profiling

The profiling performance of an application on commodity cluster can be carried out in a very similar way to debugging by launching serial performance profilers on one or several processes. The Linux *perf* utility provides a simple interface for profiling a serial application and can be launched on a single process of a parallel application. An example of launching the serial performance profiler *perf* in conjunction with an MPI supercomputing code is given in Figures 2.6 and 2.7. Further discussion and details of performance profiling on supercomputers is given in *Performance Monitoring*.

2.5.2.3 Visualization

There are many open-source and proprietary solutions for visualization of data generated on a commodity cluster. One ubiquitous command line and script driven solution is *gnuplot*. One example of *gnuplot* visualization is provided in Figures 2.8 and 2.9. Visualization is covered later in greater detail: *Scientific Visualization*.

```
andersmw@cutter:~/learn$ mpirun -np 7 ./a.out : -np 1 perf record ./a.out
The sum of the ranks is 28
[ perf record: Woken up 1 times to write data ]
[ perf record: Captured and wrote 0.034 MB perf.data (~1474 samples) ]
```

FIGURE 2.6

In this example, a parallel application is run on eight cores where the serial Linux performance counter tool *perf* is run on the application (called a.out here) with just one of those cores. The *perf* utility is given the instruction to "record" the events in this example for postprocessing. Postprocessing is shown in Figure 2.7.

```
Samples: 125  of event 'cycles', Event count (approx.): 68985441
Overhead  Command  Shared Object         Symbol
   5.76%  a.out    ld-2.19.so            [.] do_lookup_x
   5.13%  a.out    ld-2.19.so            [.] _dl_lookup_symbol_x
   4.16%  a.out    libc-2.19.so          [.] memset
   4.07%  a.out    [kernel.kallsyms]     [k] perf_event_aux_ctx
   3.20%  a.out    libc-2.19.so          [.] __strncmp_sse2
   2.87%  a.out    [kernel.kallsyms]     [k] __d_lookup_rcu
   2.87%  a.out    [kernel.kallsyms]     [k] clear_page_c
   2.79%  a.out    [kernel.kallsyms]     [k] native_write_msr_safe
   2.63%  a.out    [kernel.kallsyms]     [k] format_decode
   2.58%  a.out    [kernel.kallsyms]     [k] shmem_getpage_gfp
   2.52%  a.out    [kernel.kallsyms]     [k] __rmqueue
   2.42%  a.out    libopen-pal.so.13     [.] opal_memory_ptmalloc2_malloc
   2.35%  a.out    libc-2.19.so          [.] vfprintf
   2.31%  a.out    libc-2.19.so          [.] malloc
```

FIGURE 2.7

In this example, the postprocessing of the results from the serial performance record in Figure 2.3 originating from a parallel execution is reported using the "*perf* report" command.

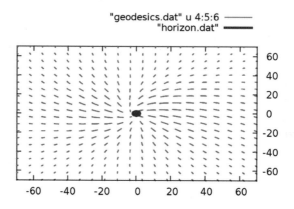

FIGURE 2.8

Visualization of the bending of light around a spinning black hole using gnuplot.

```
1 # To run this file, type: gnuplot -persist plot.gnu
2 sp[-70:70][-70:70][-50:50] "geodesics.dat" u 4:5:6 w lines
3 unset ztics
4 set style line 1 lt 1 lw 3 pt 3 linecolor rgb "blue"
5 replot "horizon.dat" with lines ls 1
6 # bottom
7 set view 0,0
8 replot
```

FIGURE 2.9

Script to generate Figure 2.8. The fourth to sixth columns of file "geodesics.dat" are used to plot the light rays; the spinning black hole horizon is added to the figure from the "horizon.dat" file. These data files are available for download on the textbook's website.

2.5 Basic Methods of Use

2.5.1 Logging On

Some readers may be already familiar with the login procedure on common desktop machines. It typically requires providing the user identifier (or clinking on a corresponding icon) and typing a correct password to verify that the person attempting to log on is the same as the one who set up the password before. Unfortunately, this method requires direct proximity to the target computer, which is not practical with systems hosting thousands of users or located far away. Hence, the login has to be performed over network using a computer local to the user to act as a connection client. Most supercomputers provide the Secure Shell (SSH) managed logins, which require that an SSH client is installed on the user's machine. Secure connections are preferred because they avert most eavesdropping attempts by using strong encryption of all communications, including login information and passwords. Most UNIX-like computers are typically configured to include the *ssh* program used for this purpose; on Windows, one can install a popular PuTTY package [] to achieve the same goal. Although PuTTY provides a dialog window that manages the login procedure, a login sequence using a command prompt in a terminal window or console is described later. For those unfamiliar with UNIX systems, launching the program called *xterm* is recommended to get the command prompt. Depending on the system, there may be other graphical terminal emulators available, such as *gnome-terminal*, *konsole*, or *urxvt*. If using a console directly (and after a successful login to the local computer), secure communication with a target computer is achieved after typing at the command prompt:

```
ssh -l user03 cluster.hostname.edu
```

In this example, the SSH client connects to the account of `user03` on the login node `cluster.hostname.edu`. Note that the user ID used here refers to the user's login name on the *target* machine, here identified as `cluster.hostname.edu` and not the one on which *ssh* was invoked. After the connection is established, the SSH client prints the password prompt on the client machine to which the user should supply the account password, again, for the target machine. Alternatively, the above command may be also invoked as:

```
ssh user03@cluster.hostname.edu
```

If the password is accepted, *ssh* will respond with the remote machine command prompt in the local terminal. Arbitrary commands may be entered at this prompt and executed in the same way as if they were invoked directly on the remote machine. To finish the interactive session on the remote computer and return to the local shell prompt, it is necessary to type `exit` or simultaneously press Control and D keys.

Another utility, *scp*, is a close companion to *ssh* and often installed together with it. It enables secure transfer of files between the local and remote computers. For example:

```
scp ./myfile user03@cluster.hostname.edu:
```

This copies the local file `myfile` from the current working directory on the local machine to the home directory on the `cluster.hostname.edu` host. Note that the colon following the remote host name is required to inform *scp* that the second argument is a host and not a file name. Transfer of directories is accomplished by specifying the `-r` option:

```
scp -r user03@cluster.hostname.edu:/tmp/user03/dir .
```

The command above copies the directory `/tmp/user03/dir` with all its contents to the current working directory on the local machine. An absolute path was specified for the source directory. However, only its last component, `dir`, will be created and populated on the local machine.

2.5.2 User Space and Directory System

Persistent information in a computer has to be stored in a secondary storage system (e.g., disk or SSD) because the contents of RAM are volatile. *Filesystems* organize this information into a hierarchical name space, where each chunk of data can be properly named and attributed for access. The individual datasets and program executables are stored in *files*. Which parts of data belong in each file and how to subdivide the computational datasets into files is at the discretion of the user. Each file in a filesystem has a unique name by which it can be accessed by executing programs. Files are stored in logical containers called *directories*; a directory may also include other directories, permitting building of tree-like structures with arbitrary depth. Like files, directories also have unique names. UNIX-like systems use a single-rooted name space for all filesystems in current use.

A *path* describes a file or directory identifier that is sufficient to locate it in the filesystem hierarchy. Path components, from left to right, name the subsequent containing directories in descending order (from root downward). The last component of a path identifies the target file or directory in its immediate containing unit. In UNIX (and therefore Linux), path components are separated by forward slashes ("/"), hence the individual directory or file names should not contain forward slashes to avoid confusion. By convention, "/" denotes the topmost directory in a filesystem, referred to as "root." "/tmp/myfile" identifies a file called "myfile" stored in a directory called "tmp," one level below the root. Typical location of files owned by a specific user on most machines is in directory "/home/*user*," in which "*user*" is substituted with login ID of that user. The users are free to create their own subtrees of directories and files in these locations. Although the exact details of name space taxonomy may vary from system to system, in Linux they are regulated by an informal specification Filesystem Hierarchy Standard (FHS) maintained by the Linux Foundation. It defines the typical layout as containing the following directories:

- "/bin" contains critical executables that may be used during system boot.
- "/sbin" contains critical system executables that may be used during system boot.
- "/lib" includes libraries for the essential executables in "/bin" and "/sbin."
- "/usr" is a root of secondary hierarchy containing mostly read-only data. Notable subdirectories of "/usr" include:
  - "/usr/bin" contains nonessential executables, typically system-wide application binaries.
  - "/usr/sbin" contains nonessential system executables such as auxiliary services and daemons.

- "/usr/lib" holds libraries used by executables in "/usr/bin" and "/usr/sbin"
- "/usr/include" contains include files (headers) used by compilers.
- "/usr/share" includes shared, architecture-independent data frequently associated with the installed system-wide applications.
- "/usr/local" stores local, host-dependent data. It has additional subdirectories similar to those of "/usr," such as "bin," "include," "lib," and others.
- "/home" hosts individual user subdirectories with their own settings, configuration files, and custom user datasets.
- "/tmp" is a system-wide storage for temporary data that is cleaned after every reboot. Although its capacity may be limited on desktop machines, on cluster compute nodes with dedicated storage, it is often configured to provide a sizable scratch space with its own data retention policy.
- "/dev" keeps entries representing physical and logical devices under control of the OS. These entries are not regular files and special care should be exercised when accessing them.
- "/etc" stores host-specific configuration files.
- "/var" contains logs, spools, e-mail, temporary files, and other variable datasets.
- "/root" provides the dedicated home directory for superuser (administrator).
- "/opt" is used to store optional packages, frequently third-party proprietary or licensed software.
- "/mnt" contains temporarily mounted filesystems.
- "/media" includes mount points for external, removable storage media such as USB drives (including flash), e-SATA drives, and CD- or DVD-ROMS.
- "/proc" and "/sys" are pseudo-filesystems (not backed up by physical storage devices) providing runtime process data, memory allocation, I/O statistics, performance information, and device configuration and status. These filesystems are frequently used by monitoring programs and scripts to obtain access from user space to certain types of information maintained by the OS kernel.

Unlike some other OSes, UNIX-compatible systems do not introduce distinct directory hierarchies for each storage device. Instead, the contents of a filesystem associated with a specific device are *mounted* under some predefined directory (called a *mount point*). Location of that directory in the hierarchy may be arbitrary and is typically preselected by the system administrator or suitable device access daemon. This offers a benefit of being potentially able to reach any of the files and directories available in the entire node by performing a recursive traversal of the hierarchy starting from its root. To examine the currently mounted filesystems, the user may issue the "disk free" command:

```
df -h
```

The example output may look as follows:

```
Filesystem            Size  Used Avail Use% Mounted on
udev                   16G   12K   16G   1% /dev
tmpfs                 3.2G  1.7M  3.2G   1% /run
/dev/sda2             235G  146G   78G  66% /
none                  4.0K     0  4.0K   0% /sys/fs/cgroup
none                  5.0M     0  5.0M   0% /run/lock
none                   16G  3.3G   13G  21% /run/shm
none                  100M     0  100M   0% /run/user
/dev/sda1             290M  175M   96M  65% /boot
/dev/mapper/vg0-home  6.8T  4.6T  1.9T  72% /home
```

The devices representing individual component filesystems are listed in the leftmost column, and the corresponding mount points in the rightmost column. The command also presents the actual size of storage devices suffixed with a proper unit ("K" for kilobytes, "M" for megabytes, "G" for gigabytes, and "T" for terabytes). For users generating a lot of data the "Avail" and "Use%" columns are of particular interest because they show how much free space is remaining on each device.

To list the contents of any directory, an *ls* command is used. If invoked without any options, it will simply print the names of all files in *current working directory* in several columns. It is far more useful to see also various attributes of files, such as their sizes, access permissions, modification timestamps, and so on. For example:

```
ls -halF /some/path
```

will output information about all files and directories contained in "/some/path" directory, or if "/some/path" is a file, only about that file. The output data produced with the "long" ("-l") option shows the file ownership (user and group), its size, the last modification date and time, and the file name. Other options add useful features: "-a" lists "hidden" entries (all items whose names start with a period "."), "-h" converts numbers to "human-readable" format with suffixes instead of printing size data in bytes, and "-F" appends a symbol after each name indicating the type of entry. Thus, directory entries end in "/" and executable files in "*." The *ls* command offers many more useful options; to see what they do, one can access the relevant manual page by typing:

```
man ls
```

Of course, the *man* command can display information also about other commands available in the system. Exploration is strongly encouraged!

To navigate the directory hierarchy, one of the most useful commands is "change directory." For example, typing at the prompt

```
cd ..
```

moves the shell context to the closest encompassing directory. The double dot notation is a special shortcut to denote the parent directory; similarly, single dot (".") has a special meaning indicating the current directory. This notation introduces another important concept, namely, that of *relative* paths. So far, all examples used paths that begin at root (the first character is "/"). To reach the final component of such a path called the *absolute* path, the system needs to start at root and traverse all component subdirectories. However, it is frequently more convenient (and on occasion faster) to indicate target location relative to the current working directory. Thus, specifying "../tmp/some_file" while located in "/usr" directory would effectively refer to a file described by an equivalent absolute path "/tmp/some_file." To verify that the directory change performed by the last command actually happened, a "print working directory" command may be called:

```
pwd
```

If the previous command was invoked in the user's home directory, the result of the last command will likely be "/home." Another useful path shortcut is a tilde ("~"), which expands to user's home directory. Hence, executing the following will change the working directory to the parent directory of user's home irrespective of where it is invoked:

```
cd ~/..
```

Both files and directories can be added to and removed from the hierarchy. To create a new directory, a "make directory" command is issued:

```
mkdir /tmp/user13
```

The above will create an empty "user13" subdirectory in the system-wide temporary data directory. Because it is owned by the creating user, it may be subsequently used to store arbitrary data attributed to that user. Very few system directories delineated by FHS have this property; typically creation of new entries in system directories by regular users will be denied (for good reasons!) because of insufficient access rights. Note that creating directories with paths containing multiple components that do not exist yet requires a "-p" option (for "parents"). Removal of files and directories is achieved with "remove" or *rm* command. Thus:

```
rm -r ~/my_jobs
```

Deletes "my_jobs" subdirectory from user's home. Although removing files does not require any special options, for directories, one needs to specify "-r" (meaning "recursive") to scan for and eliminate all the contents contained within the directory. Because the *rm* command is frequently configured with a fail-safe interactive mode that requires the user to confirm deletion of every entry, this is often impractical for subdirectories containing thousands of files. For this reason, an "-f" or "force" option may be specified to suppress any confirmation prompts.

Note: *rm −fr* **is one the most dangerous commands on UNIX systems.** Because there is no undelete functionality integrated with most filesystems, all deleted files and directories are usually irretrievably lost.

Another useful set of commands performs moving, renaming, and copying of filesystem entries. To relocate a file or directory to another location, a "move" command is used, with the first argument being the source path and the second being the destination path:

```
mv /tmp/user13/src ~/dst
```

Interestingly, the outcome of this command depends on whether "dst" exists and is a file or directory. If it is a directory, "src" will be removed from the "/tmp/user13" directory and stored in the "dst" directory (this works independently of the original "src" being a file or directory). If both "src" and "dest" are files, "src" will be removed from "/tmp/user13" and stored in the user's home under the new name, "dst." Because this operation also destroys the original contents of file "dst," *mv* typically will ask the user to confirm the operation. If "src" is a directory but "dst" is a file, the command unconditionally fails (one cannot move a directory into a file). Finally, if there is no object named "dst" in the home directory, the operation removes the original entry from "/tmp/user13" and stores it in user's home renamed to "dst." Because no preexisting files are overwritten, *mv* does not issue confirmation prompts in this case. As can be seen, the *mv* command is quite multifaceted in that it combines the semantics of relocating the objects in the filesystem hierarchy, object deletion, and object name modification.

Most of the remarks described for move can be applied for the copy command, or *cp*. There are two crucial differences between them: *cp* does not remove the original entry referenced by the source path, and the explicit "-r" option has to be specified for all operations in which the source path is a directory. Thus,

```
cp -r ~/data/set5
```

replicates the "set5" directory in the current working directory, leaving the source directory intact.

Although the presented guide introduces some of the most essential filesystem operations, the world of POSIX commands has much more to offer. Listed below are other commonly available commands suggested for further exploration that can be carried out by consulting the related manual pages (using *man* command) in a working system:

- *cat* concatenates the contents of multiple files but is also useful for printing their contents.
- *less* permits browsing of the contents of text files, scrolling it line by line or page by page or advancing directly to points requested by the user.
- *chmod* changes the access permission flags for a file or directory.
- *chown* changes the file ownership (user and group).
- *ln* creates a link (named reference) to a filesystem object.
- *du* computes total storage usage by a specific file or directory.
- *touch* updates the file timestamp or creates an empty file.
- *head* prints out the starting lines of a file.
- *tail* prints out the final lines in a file.
- *wc* computes the count of characters, words, and lines.
- *file* guesses the file format based on its contents (not extension).
- *find* searches for specific files and directories.
- *grep* searches for patterns and phrases in files.
- *uname* prints out a brief information about the system in use.
- *ps* lists processes in the system.
- *top* ranks the processes in order of resource usage.
- *kill* sends signals to processes, in particular allowing their termination.
- *bash* is the primary shell on most systems. The suggested topics to master include I/O redirection, pipelines, globing, command aliasing, user environment initialization, variable expansion, job control, and basics of scripting.

2.5.3 Package Configuration and Building

The source code of most software packages is distributed in the form of so-called *tar archives*. *tar* is a utility to create, examine, and unpack the contents of these archives. They retain the original directory layout and file contents of the package build directory and include the configuration data required to build the binaries on another platform. In addition, the archives may be compressed to save storage space. The following command lists the contents of archive "package.tgz":

```
tar tvf package.tgz
```

The archives may use different extensions depending on the used compression algorithm. Thus, ".tar" indicates an uncompressed archive, files ending in ".tgz" and ".tar.gz" were prepared using the *gzip* compression, and ".tbz2" and ".tar.bz2" are the result of applying the *bzip2* tool. Other compression formats are also possible. Recent versions of *tar* are capable of recognizing the compression algorithm automatically and do not require specific command line options for that purpose. The archive is unpacked by invoking:

```
tar xf package.tgz
```

Typically, the command creates a subdirectory tree in the current working directory containing the package source files and configuration scripts. There may also be README and INSTALL files providing additional configuration and installation instructions. Before initiating the build process, it is worthwhile to examine various configuration options to properly customize the features of created executables and libraries. After changing the working directory to the top directory of unpacked archive contents, it may be done with:

```
./configure --help
```

Most commonly, options such as "–prefix" that determines the final installation directory, "–with-mpi" that includes MPI support, and "–with-omp" that enables OpenMP based multi-threading are of interest. The final configuration may be then generated as:

```
./configure --prefix=/home/user13/some_package
```

The last command creates the necessary *makefiles*, which are files that contain various definitions, rules, and commands required to successfully execute the build process. Makefiles are used by the *make* utility, which optimizes the build process by only executing commands for which the dependencies are newer than the build target. Default makefile names include "makefile," "Makefile," and "GNUmakefile," although the latter should be used only for build scripts that contain GNU-specific extensions. To start the build process, one needs to issue:

```
make -j9
```

```
make install
```

Although the *make* command alone would suffice, the "-j" option initiates a much faster parallel build using multiple processors in the system. The commonly applied rule of thumb suggests passing it an argument that equals the number of available cores plus one. Therefore, the above command should work well on 8-core platforms. The final step when preparing new packages for use is installation of the generated programs, libraries, and data to the target directory.

2.5.4 **Compilers and Compiling**

Cluster supercomputers provide several suites of compilers and debugging tools to support the diverse user community using the cluster. The individual user environments are most frequently customized using the module system. Using modules, the compilers and relevant environment paths can be changed in a dynamic way transparent to the user. A list of the most common module commands is provided in Table 2.2. An example of module usage on a Cray XE6 is provided in Figure 2.10.

With the specific compiler flavor and version controlled by loading modules, compiling a source code usually translates into invoking a compiler wrapper and supplying compiler flags along with the source code in the same way as is done when compiling a serial (nonparallel) application. In cluster environments, the C compiler wrapper for applications using the MPI is most frequently called *mpicc*.

2.5.5 **Running Applications**

After accessing compute nodes from the resource management system as summarized in Section 2.5.2 and detailed elsewhere, the user can launch a parallel application on the compute nodes using a shell script to start the computation if using an application in a distributed memory context. In the case of using the MPI, this shell script is most often called *mpirun*. The most important argument it takes is the flag specifying the number of processes to launch, usually given by $-n$ <# of processes>. Other options and flags associated with the *mpirun* script can be found by passing to the script the help flag, *-h*. In the case of launching a shared memory application with OpenMP, no shell script is needed to start the application.

TABLE 2.2 A List of Commonly Used Module Commands for Dynamically Controlling the User's Software Environment[a]

Module Command	Description
module load [module name]	Loads the specified module
module unload [module name]	Unloads the specified module
module list	Lists the modules already loaded in the user environment
module avail <string>	Lists the available modules that can be loaded; if a string is provided, only modules starting with that string are listed
module swap [module 1] [module 2]	Swaps out module 1 for module 2

[a] An example of some of their usage is provided in Figure 2.6. Brackets indicate required arguments, and angle brackets indicate optional arguments.

```
hpstrn01@login1:/N/dc2/scratch/hpstrn01> module list
Currently Loaded Modulefiles:
  1) modules/3.2.10.3                      13) gni-headers/4.0-1.0502.10859.7.8.gem
  2) eswrap/1.1.0-1.020200.1231.0          14) xpmem/0.1-2.0502.64982.5.3.gem
  3) craype-network-gemini                 15) dvs/2.5_0.9.0-1.0502.2188.1.113.gem
  4) cce/8.4.6                             16) alps/5.2.4-2.0502.9774.31.12.gem
  5) craype/2.4.2                          17) rca/1.0.0-2.0502.60530.1.63.gem
  6) totalview-support/1.2.0.2             18) atp/1.8.3
  7) totalview/8.14.0                      19) PrgEnv-cray/5.2.82
  8) cray-libsci/13.2.0                    20) craype-interlagos
  9) udreg/2.3.2-1.0502.10518.2.17.gem     21) cray-mpich/7.2.6
 10) ugni/6.0-1.0502.10863.8.28.gem        22) moab/8.0.1
 11) pmi/5.0.10-1.0000.11050.179.3.gem     23) torque/5.0.1
 12) dmapp/7.0.1-1.0502.11080.8.74.gem
hpstrn01@login1:/N/dc2/scratch/hpstrn01> module avail PrgEnv

----------------------------------- /opt/cray/modulefiles ------------------------
PrgEnv-cray/5.2.82(default)   PrgEnv-intel/5.2.82(default)
PrgEnv-gnu/5.2.82(default)    PrgEnv-pgi/5.2.82(default)
hpstrn01@login1:/N/dc2/scratch/hpstrn01> module swap PrgEnv-cray PrgEnv-gnu
hpstrn01@login1:/N/dc2/scratch/hpstrn01> █
```

FIGURE 2.10

An example of using modules to dynamically control a user's software environment. The first command, module list, lists the modules already loaded. The second command lists the modules available for loading which begin with the string "PrgEnv." The last command swaps out the cray programming environment for the gnu programming environment.

2.6 Summary and Outcomes

- A commodity cluster is a system of integrated computer systems. The component computers are standalone, capable of independent operation, and marketed to a much broader consumer base than the scaled clusters of which they are composed. The integration network used is separately developed and marketed to be used by a systems integrator.
- A commodity cluster is constructed from a set of processing nodes, one or more interconnection network that integrates the nodes, and secondary storage.
- A node of a cluster contains all of the components required to serve as a standalone computer.
- Commodity clusters benefit from high performance to cost through the economy of scales achieved by mass production.
- A node incorporates one or more processor cores and sockets, main memory banks, a motherboard controller, onboard network connecting all of the components, and external I/O interfaces, including a NIC to the SAN, and possibly one or more disk drives for nonvolatile storage of data, user program code, and system libraries.
- The principal programming modes for parallel programming involve using parallel library application programming interfaces that have bindings to sequential languages.
- The OS provides software environment and services necessary to use the computer and execute custom applications. It consists of a *kernel* that manages hardware resources and arbitrates access to them from other software layers,

system libraries that expose a common set of programming interfaces permitting the application writers to communicate with the kernel and underlying physical devices, additional system *services* performed by the background processes, and various administrator and user *utilities* that comprise programs invoked by users of the computer to accomplish specific minor tasks.

- Large computers use resource management systems to coordinate accesses to multiple execution units, memory allocation, network selection, and persistent storage allocation.
- A debugger enables the programmer to step through code in execution, place breakpoints in the code, view memory, change variables, and track variables.
- A simple and straightforward way to debug a parallel application on a commodity cluster is to launch a serial (nonparallel) debugger for each process.
- Persistent information in a computer has to be stored in a secondary storage system (e.g., disk or SSD) because the contents of RAM are volatile. *Filesystems* organize this information into hierarchical name space, where each chunk of data can be properly named and attributed for access.
- Cluster supercomputers provide several suites of compilers and debugging tools to support the diverse user community using the cluster. The individual user environments are most frequently customized using the module system.

2.7 Questions and Exercises

1. What are the four principal components of a commodity cluster? Describe their functions.

2. Name the required and optional hardware components of a cluster node and describe their properties. Which of them would be more suitable for installation in a compute node and which in a host node? What would be their preferred traits and parameters in each of these environments?

3. Expand and explain the COTS acronym. What is the role of COTS components in a commodity cluster?

4. Contrast commodity cluster and NOW. What are the drawbacks and benefits of each?

5. List the elements of software environment critical to cluster operation. Which of these components directly involve interaction with the user?

6. What are the steps required to develop and execute a custom application on a cluster?

7. Describe two primary named entities supported by filesystems. Why is maintaining consistent organization of filesystem hierarchy such as the one suggested by FHS important to daily operation of a computing center?

Foundational Concepts of High Performance Computing Through a Brief History

3

3.1 Introduction: The Hammer of the Mind

Supercomputing (high performance computing [HPC]) is unique among human technologies in that its rate of progress has dramatically exceeded that of any other in the history of civilization. Within a single human lifetime, by the quantifiable metric of performance, HPC has gained by a factor of a quadrillion. This was not just doing it very wrong for decades and then suddenly finding out how to do it right. Rather, it was achieved through the continuous accrual of gains of more than two orders of magnitude every decade, accomplished through continued advances in

High Performance Computing. https://doi.org/10.1016/B978-0-12-823035-0.00003-1

device technologies and machine architecture. Understanding these compounding trends is not merely a history lesson in dates, names, and places. Rather, it is a continuum of fundamental concepts evolving over millennia from Neolithic counting sticks to digital electronic logic execution. These innovative concepts, each addressing a problem of their time, built the foundations of modern HPC. This chapter's narrative introduces the key concepts, some basic fundamentals, that have culminated in the fastest computing systems. For the purpose of this up-to-date textbook, these concepts frame the foundational ideas, knowledge, and skills for students to acquire essential capabilities and methods for using HPC platforms to solve real-world applications.

Although not necessary to the immediate practical outcomes of the textbook for the readers, there is a deeper issue associated with the human condition. Humanity is defined by the fabrication and use of tools as foundational to our genus, *Homo*. More than 2 million years ago in East Africa, a predecessor to our own species, *Homo habilis* ("handy man)," fabricated primitive stone artifacts for various purposes. Later, a more advanced species, *Homo erectus*, learned to craft finer elements through a delicate and precise process of chipping flakes of stone from larger cores, creating a sharp edge with a solid point. This "hand axe" or "Acheulian hammer" was used for more than 1 million years by these predecessors as they successfully migrated across much of the Earth's habitable terrain (excluding the Americas and Antarctica), creating many of humankind's first footprints. The Acheulian Hammer allowed *H. erectus* to manipulate and modify the form of the physical world to enhance human survivability. These "hammers" could be used to hunt and kill prey, cut through hides, slice meat from bones, shape tree limbs or animal bones, and chop edible plants. No doubt they found many other applications, even chopping wood for fires, which they harnessed at least half a million years ago or the assembly of simple but serviceable habitats. The Acheulian hammer made humankind the master of its physical domain. The ability to use a different kind of artifact as a tool to quickly and accurately represent, store, and manipulate quantities or numeric information, even primitively, was a revolutionary kind of tool. Values were not physical; rather, they were abstraction, occurring in the human brain. Instead of the Acheulian hammer affecting objects, such aids to calculating or eventually computing was invented to serve as the "hammer of the mind,"

3.2 The Foundations of Calculation

The rudiments of mechanically assisted calculation extend back to the third Millennium BCE and possibly further through the introduction of two major basics, albeit primitive, of "numeric storage" and "counting." A further step around 3000 BCE and the beginnings of the Bronze Age included the earliest forms of writing, proto-cuneiform, that made possible recording of complex data and their storage over the long term via baked clay tablets. Finally, techniques for robustly performing complicated calculations were achieved by various stone tables, and procedures for manipulating them ultimately led to the abacus. The abacus was used into the 20th century of the common era. Expanding on these tools and methods exposes most of the key conceptual elements of calculation through the first tools for storing quantities and counting extending to more sophisticated methods and devices and ultimately to modern digital electronic computers.

3.2.1 Counting Sticks: Primitive Number Storage and Counting

The first examples of assisted calculation are found throughout the Neolithic era at the end of the last glaciation with the use of counting sticks. These were usually wooden sticks or animal bone in which notches were created with sharp-edged stones or obsidian. Each such physical piece actually embodied the earliest instances of concepts ultimately found in supercomputers. These are a means of representing numeric values, storing them for future reference, and performing perhaps the first logical operation ever done mechanically, counting.

The creation and storing of a representation of a numeric value with a physical medium is a milestone of human advancement, both physically and conceptually. The counting stick "remembers" a value to be viewed many times. It predated general writing and may have led to it over time (e.g., proto-cuneiform at the beginning of the third millennium BCE). The means by which information is retained has changed dramatically over time but has remained central to machine calculation and ultimately computation.

The form of representation of numbers in a physical medium was the breakthrough idea. Although such schema would change enormously over the millennia to the current era, the very idea of doing so in any form was a paradigm shift. A notch represented "one" or "1." Adding a second notch to the first one on the same medium (e.g., a straight stick) conveyed the meaning of our number 2. Continuing this simple technique allowed small numbers to be captured in the base of 1, or unary, and stored indefinitely. The recorded number of notches conveyed the number wished to be recorded.

This process of recording a small-scale number in unary with notches also introduced the first arithmetic operation: incrementing, or the adding of 1 to the prior stored unary number; this was done by inserting yet another notch onto a specific stick. Furthermore, larger counts could be embodied by the accumulation of a number of such sticks. As trivial as this may appear, it made possible accounting of physical things such as units of volumes of grain by a farmer, the number of sheep in a shepherd's flock, or even precious items such as seashells or bear teeth. (It was a rough life.) Time was also tracked by counting days, full moons, or other durations clearly delineated for the purposes of planting and harvesting of wheat or barley, preparing for religious ceremonies, or traversing territory for hunting or meeting with other clans at a predetermined location (e.g., Gobekli Tepe). With a third operation, subtracting of 1 could also be performed by duplicating an old counting stick but with one fewer notch. Observe that incrementing or decrementing had a fixed repetitive procedure independent of the number incorporated.

To summarize, the important basic concepts, even if apparently trivial by today's experience, laid the foundations of all future methods of calculating even to this day. These are:

- The concept of physical manifestation of numeric values
- A representation schema for numbers, initially unary
- Operation on a stored value, specifically, incrementation (adding 1) or counting
- Multiple simple operations such as accumulation and subtraction
- Solution to problems of their times such as accounting, recording for future reference, and temporal tracking such as a primitive calendar

3.2.2 Writing

At the beginning of the third millennium BCE, associated with the start of the "Bronze Age" across the Mediterranean Sea and the Fertile Crescent, the most profound human invention (perhaps after fire) became a critical tool in support of expanding societies, towns and cities, and ultimately civilization as we know it. This is writing. Writing as a topic might seem a nonsequitur when related to computing technology. However, writing was fostered initially by simple accounting procedures and the ability to store information for future access, in some cases, for thousands of years.

Depending on location and century stone, baked clay tablets, and papyrus served as media for capturing numbers, symbols, names, and eventually complex statements. This greatly expanded the forms of information that could be recorded, starting with accounting and used for inchoate bureaucracies; religious texts; stories; and albeit by hand, more complicated calculations. Intermediate values could be captured and used to generate succeeding values through arithmetic procedures. This also permitted far more efficient bases for numeric calculation. Base 10, base 12, and base 60 were all common practice at different times and places in the second millennium BCE. Although writing was primarily a specialty practiced by scribes (like computer programming is today) and creating of copies was laborious, the means for government hierarchies, early trading enterprises, and long-distance communication became possible and by the end of the Bronze Age ubiquitous. Ordinarily, writing and calculation are distinguished. However, history shows as well as does the internet age that they are actually tightly related.

Again, to summarize the basic concepts to early means of human calculating, this time through writing, the following is offered:

- Storing complex information (beyond simple counts) for long-term access
- High-level bases for advanced number systems
- Complex arithmetic methods (e.g., multiplication)
- Association of data values with symbols that relate them
- Sets of symbols including character strings
- Long-distance communications of data via transfer of clay and papyrus written documents

3.2.3 **Abacus**

Major advances for performing arithmetic operations were the "abacus" and its predecessors, such as the "counting table." Among its many forms, some rudimentary, are those dating back at least to the second millennium BCE in Sumerian Mesopotamia. Many improvements over centuries and in many parts of the Eurasian continent culminated in the now familiar frame with columns of vertical rods, each with its own set of beads. In the abacus, every column is divided into two parts. Each bead of the lower part represents the count of 1, and the bead or beads of the upper part represent the quantity of 5. These beads can be moved up or down to create any digit, usually of base 10. To a limited extent, a column can be used to perform addition or subtraction. This abstraction of a physical element (a bead) and its position representing a quantity was a leap in humankind's ability to perform basic arithmetic. However, the second revolution was the association of each column of beads with a unique order of magnitude: 1, 10s, 100s, and so on. Therefore, the meaning of the set of beads is a number determined by the vertical position of the beads on the rod and the order of magnitude associated with the particular rod column. The relationship between an essentially mechanical condition or state and the quantitative meaning and ability to alter that value by changing the bead positions are foundational to the future of all means of computing systems.

The abacus is not a full calculating machine but rather just an aid to assist one in accomplishing such calculations. To do so introduces two more important properties ultimately required of all future computers. The first is the concept of procedure, an ordered set of steps or basic operation that if followed will produce the sought-after result. Such a procedure is made up of a sequence of basic actions, in this case moving the elemental beads, which when known will serve to always deliver a correct numeric answer. Simple operations when combined can be used to perform complicated calculations. With the abacus, even in its multiple possible forms throughout history, new complex operations became possible far beyond mere counting with tally sticks. The second property is the possibility of a number of more sophisticated numeric operations across a very wide range of values. These include the equivalent of unsigned integer addition, subtraction, multiplication, and even division.

The major weakness of the abacus is that it does not store values very long, although it does hold temporary values as one builds toward an answer through the proscribed sequence of basic steps. There is no place for the result values to be retained. For this, educated practitioners also involve the previously discussed invention, writing. For a tool to survive literally over millennia indicates its effectiveness in satisfying societal needs in government accounting, business and trade, and management of shared resources.

Again, this subsection concludes by summarizing the major contributions to high(er) speed computation made through the invention and application of early primitive assistants.

- Initial means representing full number system for positive integers
- A rich set of micro actions and procedures to perform basic integer operations with structured material assistance

- Methods of accomplishing more sophisticated arithmetic (integer) operations with sequencing of more simplistic actions and temporary storage of intermediate values
- The reliable and wide usage of mechanical arithmetic aids used over many centuries, albeit in varied forms

3.3 Mechanical Calculator: Automation of Arithmetic

The advent of mechanical technologies, such as shafts, levers, wheels, gears, cams, and sprockets, created a new and ultimately powerful medium for calculation in the past half millennium. Slowly and incrementally, first of wood but more recently of easily worked metals (e.g., brass), mechanical devices were developed primarily for clocks and precision astronomical instruments. Visionaries imagined means of harnessing them for automating arithmetic operations and even performing procedures (sequence of operations). These steps toward mechanical calculators emerged in the 17th century to eliminate the need for highly proficient users of the abacus. Their evolution and application continued into the first half of the 20th century with increasing sophistication. This nascent period of revolution in methods of calculation would invent and ultimately apply many of the functional mechanisms and capabilities required for basic automated arithmetic calculation found even in today's computers, albeit in greatly advanced form.

This epoch is characterized by the fundamental property of mechanical movement, physical connection, force transference, torque, and gear ratios, as well as components directly equated to numeric values. Such devices are physical, made up of moving parts. It was enabled but also limited by enabling technologies through the enlightenment and the industrial revolution. Before its conclusion, electricity and electrical devices in early form were incorporated to augment the ease and speed of machines. These could be found in regular use up through the 1960s. Thus, this is the beginning of technology as a prime mover (literally) of operational capability and the functions that could be produced and can interoperate.

3.3.1 The Dawning of the Age of Mechanical Calculating Machinery

Among the early and moderately successful of mechanical calculating devices was the "Pascaline" developed by Blaise Pascal in 1642. As simple as it appears today, at the time it was an amazing innovation. In its initial form, it performed addition and subtraction. But it did so using the actual number representation for both input and output. Access for the user was presented on the top of a metal box, which was about 2 feet long (left to right). Little windows in a line across the top of the unit displayed the digits (0—9) for about six places. Below these were corresponding dials, also each associated with one place of the integer value. These round wheels, rotated by the user, could represent the value of one digit of the number and were the means by which input values were fed to the mechanical calculator.

Internal to the device was a set of gears (details are not important here) that by clever interconnection allowed operations on the entire multidigit numeric value. The breakthrough of the Pascaline was its ability to handle carries. That is, when two digits were added such that their combined value exceeded 9, a carry action would be generated, and the value of 1 would be added to the next digit. Such carries could propagate along the sequence of digits as required.

The Pascaline exhibited features unequaled in previous centuries. The user interface presented both input and output to the calculator in user-friendly natural (integer) numbers. Also important, it automatically performed the carries (add 1 to the next place) without user intervention. One consequence was major reduction in errors. Another was accessibility to relatively nonexpert users, making it more widely available to common people. Admittedly, these units were hand-made and represented among the most sophisticated devices aside from contemporary clocks.

Half a century later, the German mathematician Gottfried Leibniz devised a far more advanced mechanical calculator. The Stepped-reckoner completed by the end of the 17th century was able to perform all four basic arithmetic operations on integer values, including addition, subtraction, multiplication, and division. The principal mechanism upon which this functionality relied was referred to as the "stepped cylinder" (also the "Leibniz wheel"). It was a sophisticated structure of gears and other mechanical devices. Although the original two prototypes were less than perfect because of limitations of the technology at that time, the stepped cylinder found wide use in future machines for more than 2 centuries, establishing the foundations for mechanical calculation systems. Both the Pascaline and the Leibniz calculator performed their operations in base 10; that is, the operations manipulated mechanical embodiments of single digits, each able to represent values from 0 to 9 in each place of the number. This counting system would continue into the 20th century, even when the underlying technologies would change dramatically. Ultimately, this would be replaced by base 2 numeric encoding (binary) in the second half of the 20th century.

The 17th century revolutionized methods of calculation and can justly be credited with a phase change in computing methods and devices, although this took some time. Underlying this major transition in computing are critical contributions that have been fundamental to all future advances, including:

- The vision of a full-capability device functionally able to perform basic operations without human intervention of micro-operations
- User interface for high-level representation of numeric data for input and output
- The recognition of the potential use of enabling technologies for calculating

3.3.2 Data Retention and Action Sequencing

By the latter half of the 19th century, a number of different mechanical calculators were produced and marketed to be used for a wide range of applications in business and formulating numerical tables. Still primarily used for simple arithmetic, they were used up into the middle of the 20th century. The British mathematician and enemy of London organ grinders designed but was unable to construct the "difference engine" to automate the creation of numerical tables. Even more ambitious was the differential analyzer that if it had been built would have been programmable using punched cards first invented for the Jacquard Loom. Punched cards were also used to store data. This was used and applied to the 1890 census by the enumerator developed by Herman Hollerith. Although a specialized machine, it proved to be the beginning of business data processing for the next half century and contributed to the founding of IBM. Throughout the period of almost a century, mechanical calculating machine designs were enhanced by the addition of electric motors to lead to electromechanical calculators.

By the late 1930s and into the next decade, the two critical ideas of automatic arithmetic calculation and punched card instruction sequencing were integrated into the Harvard architecture. Aiken, a Harvard professor, and IBM partnered to build the first fully functional electromechanical computer with the ability to perform sequences of operations. It was enormous in size and weight. But it was general purpose and programmable and delivered a performance of one instruction per second or 1 ops. At the same time in the first half of the 20th century, a number of advanced versions of the original Hollerith enumerators were developed and marketed by IBM and other manufacturers based principally on punched cards for business and some defense purposes.

This period of approximately a century and a half was a turning point for high-speed computing when high speed hovered around 1 second per In some cases, this could be ten times as much. The fundamental concepts contributed by this period are summarized here:

- Modern data retention was introduced with the punched card, first used by Jacquard to control the process of creating intricate patterns in textiles. Holes in a card represented information and were stored for future use or access. In the first half of the 20th century, the format and protocol for data representation in punched cards was known as Hollerith.
- Punched cards provided rapid manipulation of information with electromechanical business machines for usual operations performed in a "run."
- Simple instruction sequences can be represented. The concept of a "program" was devised and eventually became common practice—the transition from calculating to computing.
- Business data processing emerged.

3.3.3 The Synthesis of Concepts From Early Means of Calculation

It is ironic that what may be perceived as the culmination of thousands of years of mechanically assisted calculating from counting sticks and mechanical calculators through the idea of the programmable differential analyzer and punched card business machines would lead not to a golden age in numeric processing but rather the final obsolete example of a dead-end approach and end of a multi-millennial evolution. The Harvard Mark-1 would never be replicated. In some ways, it would be considered as archaic as the abacus, which actually outlived it. However, the foundational principles of automatic computation derived since the Bronze Age would be metamorphized through additional conceptual insights and a revolutionary technology to achieve astronomical capabilities by means of revolutionary HPC.

Although electromechanical calculating machines went into steep decline and were essentially extinct by the 1970s, the foundational concepts, both explicit and implied, through the centuries of methods driven by need while inhibited by available technologies remained valid and contributed to the unprecedented revolution that was yet to come. Here (pay attention) is a synopsis of all of these essential concepts:

1. **Information storage and retrieval:** The counting sticks allowed a particular kind of numeric data (unary) to be manifest in a physical medium and accessed when required.
2. **Mechanical-assisted arithmetic:** The abacus in its diverse forms throughout most of human civilization served to enable arithmetic operations with high reliability and relative speed, hinting that computation would leverage mechanism.
3. **Numeric representation:** This demonstrated that the state of a mechanical device could serve to represent the state of a calculation. Interestingly, this was repeatedly done through the angular orientation of gears, but it was the simpler two-positioned encoding of pebbles or beads that would prove the most efficient, fast, and reliable.
4. **Digital encoding:** The punched card was an array of two-state data. At any one point of rows and columns, there was either a hole or there wasn't. Today this is referred to as "digital", implying discretized rather than analog. So important is this distinction that the common computer including HPC is identified as "digital computing".
5. **Instructions can be data:** With the Jacquard loom and the differential analyzer (concept), it was recognized that in principle, not just numbers could be encoded, but so could commands in the same medium to cause arithmetic and other kinds of operations to be performed.
6. **Enabling technologies:** Automated calculation and computation at any one time are both made possible but are also limited by the available technologies and their capabilities. It is a challenge to find technologies good enough to conduct arithmetic operations as fast as possible. However, it is also essential to find ways to use existing or near-term technologies to perform the fastest calculations.
7. **Architecture is structure of simple elements:** The evolution of the mechanical calculator was enabled by the improving physical technologies (e.g., clock gears) but also the way these elements were organized and interconnected. This emphasis on organization of components and their interoperability has been the creative driver of more than 2 centuries but has continued and accelerated until the present as will be demonstrated.

8. **Computation is synthesis of data storage and data manipulation:** A computer is a programmable system that assimilates stored values and produces new values, which may be then stored. Aiken almost got that. So close.

3.4 Fundamental Principles of Digital Computation

Computers are embodiments of mathematics even when the data are not numerical. Mathematics devises schema of representation, relationships, transformations, responses, function, and proving truths. Perhaps it is the most pure (whatever that means) science evolved by humans. It is also still evolving. The history so far and the concepts developed and applied to facilitate the creation and application of aids to calculation were largely if not entirely a product of need served by invention, cleverness, and some trial and error. It is amazing what a few good ideas can do for a species. However, before a transformation to the next realization and application of computational machines, some further groundwork of a more formal nature was required upon which to erect the conceptual scaffoldings needed for the following advances to an ultimate high-performance computer of 1 Exaflops.

3.4.1 Bit: The Binary Digit

The binary digit, or "bit" is a medium that holds a value that can be in either of two states. The bit has served as the principal form or abstraction for the most basic representation of information. The bit is an element that alone distinguishes between two conditions or states often referred to as: "0" or "1," "T" or "F," "true" or "false," "high" or "low," "H" or "L," or other two-state designations. For the purposes of this textbook, the first two pairings will be used depending on context.

The bit is derived from the field of informatics, often credited to Claude Shannon in the early 1940s but also building on prior work such as that of Nyquist in the 1920s. It is based on the idea of communication capacity, noisy channels, entropy, and coding. This is really cool stuff, but although it is a foundational aspect of the advances in computing, it is outside the scope of this textbook. Familiarity of the two-state bit as the basic primitive of information representation, storage, and operations is sufficient for your purposes. You will see how, with the bit at its core, computing systems can rapidly encompass ever-increasing complexity of value, structure, and actions.

As fundamental and powerful as the bit is, it is clearly limited in the value that can be represented and sounds as far away as you can get from supercomputing. To expand beyond these limitations while building on the fundamentals, the modern age of computer design manipulates more than one bit at a time at least for most operations and instead uses groups of bits as single informational entities. The most universal of such bit-based format is the "byte," which is an ordered collection of 8 bits. The number of different values that can be encoded in a byte is 2^8 or 256. Assuming that the lowest such value is 00000000 or 0 (zero), the largest value that can be represented by a byte is 11111111 or 255. This could be considered an unsigned integer from 0 to 255. But it may also be used to reflect a signed integer from -128 to $+127$ with the most significant bit (left most) conveying the sign, $+$ or $-$. In this case, the value of zero, 0, is 00000000 as before. As will be seen, this numbering scheme is also referred to as "twos-complement." Less widely used now but mentioned for the sake of completeness is an alternative representation of signed integers with the byte. In this case, too, the most significant bit represents the sign of the integer as before. But the "ones complement" format has the remaining seven significant bits the same for the same absolute value. For example, whereas 00100110 is $+38$, 10100110 is -38. As a side comment, for one's complement 00000000 and 10000000 as the same value, 0. In many systems, individual bytes can be separably addressed. But a larger conglomeration of bits is also possible and widely used for reasons of greater numeric range and wider data access rate for higher bandwidth (how many bits can be accessed in a single memory cycle). Most common among these groupings are half-words (16 bits), words (32 bits), and double words (64 bits). These formats may be used both as signed or unsigned integers with the most significant bit still representing the sign bit.

3.4.2 Boolean Logic

In the 19th century, the British mathematician George Boole at University College at Cork developed a mathematical schema for performing logic based on values of "true" or "false" ("T" or "F" for simplicity). Here again, base-2 logic values could be represented by a single bit (although this is not always done). Boole showed that a full set of 16 functions with two inputs and one output represented a complete group; that is, all 16 logic functions individually or in combination could form all possible Boolean functions. This is an example of when mathematics played a major role in computer design of the 20th and 21st centuries, without prior intent.

Other than a side-bar curiosity, why is this important to the student of HPC? The answer is that essentially all (nonanalog) computing elements are based on digital electronic logic, the same logic as created by Boole (there are some, albeit few, notable exceptions). And this hints at the catalyst that ended the Harvard Mark 1's legacy almost before it started: "digital electronics."

3.4.3 Computability: The Turing Machine

What can or cannot be computed was a fundamental question that was included by the great mathematician Hilbert near the beginning of the 20th century when it was considered of theoretical interest. But in the latter half of the 1930s, both Alan Turing, a graduate student at Cambridge University in the United Kingdom, and Alonzo Church, a professor at Princeton University, took two different approaches to addressing this challenge by abstractly modeling computers. Both succeeded with Church developing the Lambda calculus and Turing conceiving of a less abstract model known as the "Turing machine." A computer to be general purpose is presumed to be "Turing equivalent." This laid the foundation of theoretical computer science, establishing the boundaries of what can and cannot be computed. By the way, this has nothing to do with the "Turing test," also devised by Alan Turing but related to artificial intelligence.

3.4.4 von Neumann Architecture: Stored Program

The model of modern digital electronic computing was conceived by the mathematician John von Neumann and collaborators, the same team that designed the ENIAC digital electronic calculator used for projectile trajectory determinations and other special-purpose applications. This new model was documented at the end of World War II and was referred to as "EDVAC." Today all such machines and their derivatives over 6 decades are universally called "von Neumann architecture." By today's standards, this is rudimentary. However, in the mid-20th century, it was revolutionary.

The von Neumann architecture in concept is user programmable as was Charles Babbage's "differential analyzer" (on paper only) and the Aiken "Harvard Mark 1," the electromechanical behemoth actually constructed and operated by IBM in the early 1940s. But the similarities end here.

The von Neumann architecture model is represented by five principal units integrated into a single computer. Commercial implementations of computers based on the von Neumann model would come to be called "central processing units," "CPUs," or more colloquially, "mainframes." Curiously, "CPU" is still often used even for vast massively parallel processing (MPP), inappropriately, as will be seen. These elements are:

1. Arithmetic and logic unit (ALU)
2. Main memory
3. Instruction pointer and control unit
4. Input and output units
5. Data communication buss

The ALU performed the actual calculation operations in combination with an "accumulator" (sort of a smart data buffer) and possibly one or two more buffers. The main memory was intended as a block of fast (relatively) read/write storage. A unique innovation of the von Neumann architecture was that not only did the main memory hold accessible data such as numbers, logical values, and characters, but the main memory also held the program instruction sequences, what quickly became known as the "code." At the risk of redundancy, the von Neumann innovative contribution is that execution data and instructions are stored in individual contiguously addressable and randomly accessible storage elements, more casually referred to as "memory locations." The ramifications are enormous, and no single conceptual advancement in computer design, including HPC, has ever been as important. Among other things, this allowed instructions to be modified based on the program itself and on the value of stored data, all in the same memory. To some, this marked the distinction between a stream of calculations and true computation. Others consider this a distinction without a difference, and this characterization has largely been lost to history.

The instruction pointer, or "program counter" (PC), is enabled by the von Neumann randomly accessible memory. If a sequence or list of entries is contiguously loaded into a partition of memory, then a reference pointer (itself possibly a word in memory) can be incremented to point to the next entry. This made it possible for the control unit to trace through the sequence of instructions by means of the program counter executing one operation at a time. The program could alter the order of instruction execution by "jump" or "branch" instructions, and these could be done conditionally based on the value of a stored value. Finally, the program could actually change one of its own instructions to form a different instruction in its place. Of particular value was the ability to store routines of code in different sets of locations using base plus offset addressing.

von Neumann, Turing, Shannon, and Boole laid down the theoretical concepts that have had practical and profound implications for the vast majority of digital electronic computing systems. Other important technologies, circuit designs, architecture innovations, and the entire realm of software would yet be developed before the current generation of supercomputers, some of which will be discussed at useful times within this textbook. But these four foundational theoretical concepts would stand the test of time and continue in importance to this day. In summary, the major take-home messages from this section are:

1. The binary digit or bit
2. Boolean logic
3. Computability and the Turing machine
4. von Neumann architecture and main memory

3.5 Performance

HPC's middle name is "performance." The narrative of the evolution of artifacts for assisting calculating suggests that performance can be increased, perhaps significantly, by devising structures and mechanisms that assume as much of the intricacies as possible. However, even as late as the World War II, the term "computer" was associated with a person who in large groups used electromechanical desktop calculators to perform very large (for the day) computations to create mathematical tables or undertake cryptanalysis, space flight, and atomic engineering, among others. By the end of the 1940s, digital electronic computers were beginning to replace humans in this task. Performance improved by orders of magnitude and continued to do so into the 21st century, as represented indirectly by Moore's law. The concept of computing performance was a product of this period. How it was achieved has proved complicated. However, three factors stand out: enabling technologies, parallelism of actions, and computer architecture.

As is discussed elsewhere, the apparently simple concept of performance is actually multifaceted and nuanced. Performance, how it is measured, and how it is compared between different applications or different machines running the same applications are nontrivial, with stated assumptions often required. Time is an essential dimension of performance characterization. However, under distinct circumstances, the duration of time involved can be as small as a fraction of a nanosecond to as long as many days. The rate at which a stream of instructions is sent into the execution pipeline (a central part of a modern processor) can be higher than one per nanosecond. However, the length of time it takes for a single instruction to be executed, which is its latency, is multiple nanoseconds, both a correct measure of performance but different in aspect. Similarly, performance may measure the rate at which instructions are performed in unit time, its throughput, or it can measure the amount of time a workload takes to execute, its time to solution. These appear to be the same, just in different wording. However, another facet of performance is the amount of work that is done under different conditions. Work can be defined as a fixed number of operations performed with the time varying or a fixed amount of time in which varying number of operations are done.

The distinguishing property is the scale (size) of the computer. For example, if a fixed size problem is performed on two different machines that are the same in every way except their sizes or clock rates, one would expect the time to solution to decrease proportionally with the change in resources or in speed of their logic. This is known as "strong scaling." But if a system twice the size runs for the same amount of time as the smaller system and more work is fed to the larger machine in that same time, then the total number of operations would be executed, suggesting greater performance. This is known as "weak scaling."

Finally, benchmarks are codes used with different computers to compare their relative capabilities. One of the most widely used benchmarks is the high performance Linpack (HPL). Its performance metric, R_{max}, includes a standard set of rules agreed upon by all users. However, one of these rules allows different workloads of different sizes for each competitor. This is not a cheat because it reflects not just the processor core speed but also its amount of main memory as well. HPL has been used for more than 2 decades to compare the 500 fastest computers in the world (every half year) and establish their rank in this hierarchy. Therefore, the measure of performance is complicated and depends on the factors that are measured and the conditions under which the measurements are done.

3.5.1 Enabling Technologies

Actual technologies for performing calculations changed and improved over thousands of years, at first slowly, then with increased rate of functionality over centuries, and ultimately with exponential growth over decades into the 21st century. Mechanical and electromechanical technologies served for calculating devices from the mid-19th to the mid-20th centuries, culminating with the programmable Harvard Mark 1. It was capable of an average speed of about 1 operation per second (ops).

As large as this machine was, it was almost immediately obsolete by the next revolution in enabling technology: digital electronics.

Logic circuits were developed by the mid-1940s using vacuum tubes. Up until that time, vacuum tubes had served well as analog devices for music amplifiers, radio transmission and receiving, and radar, creating the field of electronics. Vacuum tubes were also found to serve as electronic switches, turning on or off depending on their inputs. They could switch at potentially thousands of times that of mechanical devices. This two-state modality of operation fit nicely with the ideas of Shannon and Boole to create the first electronic logic functions and in combination to perform arithmetic. ENIAC was among the first vacuum tube electronic calculators. But guided by the von Neumann model, general-purpose computers were born. These included EDSAC, IBM 704, Whirlwind, and Univac 1. Their performance was roughly a thousand times faster than their electromechanical predecessors.

Digital logic rapidly evolved over succeeding decades. Vacuum tubes were replaced by germanium transistors invented at Bell Labs in 1947 and later silicon transistors with superior switching properties. By the mid-1960s, the CDC-6800 exceeded 1 Megaflops, or a thousand times faster than the early generation of vacuum tube−based computers. The integrated circuit (IC or chip) was developed by the end of that decade with multiple transistors connected in circuits that work like logic gates. Small-scale integration (SSI), medium-scale integration (MSI), and large-scale integration (LSI) evolved in rapid succession as the feature size of the transistors diminished and their speeds increased, both exponentially. By the late 1980s, performance had exceeded 1 Gigaflops or 1000 times the performance of the CDC-6800. Another factor of 1000 was first achieved in 1997 at a Teraflops, in 2008 at a Petaflops, and only in 2022 of an Exaflops.

An equivalent story can be told about the other major enabling technology: that of main memory. High-speed memories in the 1960s were actually made out of tiny ferromagnetic cores (toroids). But the semiconductor revolution impacted here as well with Kilobits integrated on a single die before 1980. Although exponential growth of bit densities was also achieved, the slope of the growth was significantly shallower than that of logic speeds per unit die area.

3.5.2 Parallelism

After enabling technology, the single most important performance factor was "parallelism", a term used to indicate the ability to accomplish more than one action at a time. The more actions that can be done at the same time, at least in principle, the greater the performance that may be achieved. Parallelism manifests in multiple ways that are mutually supporting. In hardware, parallelism is achieved through the use of more than one operational unit that can be driven by separate streams of operations with their own argument data. This can be done at many scales. Single Instruction, Multiple Data (SIMD) structures make it possible for many instances of the same operation to be performed on different data at the same time. Multiple Instructions, Multiple Data (MIMD) used at a higher scale lets separate threads of execution operate on their own data at the same time. All of the fastest machines use these and other forms of parallel hardware to achieve the highest throughput performance possible.

Parallelism also occurs in software. Threads of execution must be represented within application programs that both define the actions to be performed by every thread and specify which threads can be done concurrently and when. As will be seen in subsequent chapters, there are different formalisms represented by alternative application programming interfaces used to create such parallel programs. Although a plethora of forms of parallel semantics are available, they are distinguished by one key property related to their respective approaches to using data stored in main memory. The two primary classes of use are "shared memory" and "distributed memory." Both support parallel processing. Shared memory parallelism enables different processor cores to have access to the same memory and in so doing to exchange results of their respective computations by having access to all of the memory. Coordination requires synchronization among the independent threads of actions through the shared memory. Distributed memory parallelism partitions the total main memory of the system in to separate system "nodes," each with its own processor or processors. Within any given node, its resident processor core(s) can operate independently and execute its process as long as the data it needs to do so are local to the node. Parallelism is achieved by means of many nodes executing at the same time out of their own memory. However, there are points in the processor instruction sequence when intermediate result values by other nodes are needed to be acquired before the computation can continue. This is accomplished by a mechanism for passing messages between nodes carrying the values from one node (source of send action) to the other node (destination of the receive action). This method of communication of values allows the nodes to cooperate and engage in parallel processing.

3.5.3 Computer Architecture

The third major contributor to performance is the structure and semantics of the design of a specific computer. The von Neumann architecture was presented earlier as the archetype of super class of what would become generations of actual design implementations. Within the scope of this paradigm has been a trajectory of evolving architectures, each of which is optimized to balance the capabilities and limitations of the enabling technologies available at any point in time with the opportunities of ways that parallelism can be adopted. Over the past 3 decades, a level of parallelism has been many microprocessors working together. For more than a decade, additional computer architecture parallelism has been created by integrating multiple processor cores on a single semiconductor die. Within each core many subunits operate in parallel down to instruction-level parallelism. Finally, system-wide computer architecture comprises multiple nodes, which provides broad scalability. In essence, computer architecture brings the power of technology to the application descriptions (code).

3.6 **Summary and Outcomes**

- The earliest means of assisted calculation predates the rudiments of writing about 5000 years ago with "counting sticks".
- Counting sticks held numerical information and counted by adding a notch for each item being counted (base 1).
- The abacus extended the mechanics of counting to that of general integer addition (and subtraction) before the beginning of the common era.
- The abacus (in its many forms) represented a numeric placement system in which beads were used by sliding them along a rod (back and forth) while carries were propagated vertically.
- The mechanical calculator represented numeric digits (base 10) and an automated carry mechanism for addition. The Pascaline was among the first practical such machine in the 17th century and was superseded by more advanced devices in the following century by Leibniz and others.
- Charles Babbage designed but did not build the "differential analyzer" in the 19th century; it was a general-purpose programmable mechanical calculator.
- Alan Turing (Cambridge) and Alonzo Church (Princeton) theoretically addressed computability and the halting problem.
- Claude Shannon devised the "bit" as the foundation number from which all others could be derived.
- von Neumann derived the basic modern computer that served as the basis of the general-purpose calculation machine of the following decades.

3.7 **Exercises**

1. What was a very early form of assisted calculation predating human writing?

2. What base were counting sticks?

3. What are three operations that could be performed with counting sticks?

4. What was the abacus, and how did it perform calculations beyond counting sticks?

5. The Pascaline was a mechanical calculator that advanced mechanical calculation. What did it do beyond the abacus?

6. With what medium did the 1890 census get performed on?

7. Who conceptualized the "bit"?

8. Who is the father of the modern digital computer?

Models and Metrics for Machines

4

4.1 Introduction

Performance is a principal property of high performance computing (HPC) systems, almost by definition. Distinguishing between any two possible systems would in part be delineated by their differences in performance. Performance might at first seem intuitive: How fast does a computer run? However, the speed of a parallel computer system depends on the conditions under which it is executing and the workload upon which it is operating. One measure is peak performance, the number of operations that in principle could be performed in unit time given the total number of arithmetic units provided in hardware. Equation 4.1 gives a simplified means of estimating peak performance on a conventional multiprocessor. In practical terms, peak performance is unachievable in realistic computing scenarios, but it does provide an upper, not to be exceeded, bound.

High Performance Computing. https://doi.org/10.1016/B978-0-12-823035-0.00004-3

$$P_{peak} \sim N_{sockets} * N_{cores\ per\ socket} * R_{clock} * N_{operations\ per\ instruction} \qquad (4.1)$$

A real measure of performance is ascertained within the context of an actual workload; a specified driver test code. When such codes are formerly defined, often by committee, along with rules of their usage, they form benchmarks by which different systems may be measured and compared. Chief among these is HPL derived from LINPACK and widely used and documented twice yearly by the Top 500 list, which only recently exceeded 1 Exaflops R_{max}. Benchmarking is discussed in detail in a later chapter. There are a number of such widely used benchmarks, each stressing HPC systems in different ways and further reflecting the needs of distinct classes of algorithms.

For HPC, additional quantitative properties represent the importance of systems, even similar systems, of different sizes, reflecting the ability to deliver increased performance with increased system size. Two key properties are scalability and efficiency. Scalability relates to the effect that a system of increased size (e.g., number of processor cores) would deliver increased performance. But this may be offset by efficiency that measures the percentage of a system that can actually be used for the computation. Even as the size of a system increases in its number of processing cores, its performance improvement may be countered by a reduction in efficiency. The reason for this is that the degree of hardware parallelism may not be matched by the application parallelism. The next section delves more deeply into the subtleties of measuring performance with respect to scalability and efficiency.

4.2 Throughput Versus Time

Performance is not a simple metric but can represent multiple forms or attributes of scalability. These can include just streams of independent operations (or sequences of operations) or problems whose time to solution decreases (improves) with increased system scale. Introduced here is a combination of the two. This section elaborates on these varied scaling modalities.

4.2.1 Capacity Computing

"Throughput" is one measure of performance. Simply, it is the number of operations being performed in unit time. It is also referred to as "capacity computing." The workload assumed does not have to be tightly coupled or interrelated. It can be driven by many uncorrelated tasks being scheduled by the operating system simultaneously. Scalability for capacity computing is "weak scaling." The workload applied to a parallel system that is increased in size is also proportionally increased such that the allocated work to each computing unit (e.g., processor core) remains invariant, yielding constant efficiency. Ideally, weak scaling should deliver performance proportional to the scale of the system. Throughput computing for HPC is widely used because most large systems serve a large community of users. Many of the applications of a large user base are much smaller than an entire machine with many as small as a single node (symmetric multiprocessor) allowing potentially hundreds of independent jobs to proceed concurrently. Although this is a practical way to manage the balance between the amount of application demand and large-scale resources, it does not take full advantage of the full capability of a major HPC system for extreme problem size and speed.

4.2.2 Capability Computing

HPC performance can be more powerful than high-throughput computing of many jobs. Such a compute profile can be perceived as wasteful because much of the same workload could be handled by many smaller, less costly, and more efficient systems, even Linux commodity clusters. For leadership-class computers such as Frontier or the soon to be deployed Aurora, a different and perhaps more intuitive use profile is possible. As a generalized example, imagine a large system performing a single multiphysics multidimensional application intended to push the frontier boundaries of some leading-edge field (e.g., Tokomak controlled fusion) that takes a very long time to complete, say, more than a week like 8 days. That is within the time range of feasible computing but rapidly becomes the pacing item of the research work going forward, a non-ideal methodology. It would be very valuable to the end user's mission to reduce the time to solution of this time-critical application. Now, and this takes some imagination, the hosting data center is able to double the scale (size) of the leadership computer. For this experiment, the computation doesn't need to be larger; it just needs to be faster, much faster.

It is intuitive that if an application with the same dataset of the original computation is performed on an equivalent HPC system but of twice the scale, then the execution time should be reduced by half. Because the number of operations performed by both the $1\times$ and $2\times$ scale systems is the same, doing them on the larger system means that the resulting performance is doubled. Reducing the time to solution of a fixed workload is a very important alternative to merely increasing total workload on larger system for greater throughput.

The form of scaling that results in reduced execution time with increased system size is referred to as "strong scaling." Because it involves a single large application rather than an ensemble of many smaller jobs, this class of processing is also called "capability computing." It is much harder to achieve than throughput computing because the parallel algorithm and programming models as well as possible runtime system have to expose much more parallelism than that of mere job-stream coarse-grained parallelism. In addition, control of task scheduling of the application work and resource management of the computer system processors require far more sophisticated and often dynamic control strategies.

4.2.3 Cooperative Computing

In this textbook, an intermediate modality of parallel processing is identified that embodies aspects of both weak and strong scaling. This is not common terminology in the field and is offered instead as a pedagogical tool to clarify an important sub-domain of HPC processing. The term "cooperative computing" is adopted here to represent this form of scalability. The alternative term "coordinated computing" is also used interchangeably for this purpose.

Like capability computing, cooperative computing executes a single parallel application rather than an ensemble of disjoint jobs. Therefore, it is able to apply an entire parallel computer to one user problem. However, like capacity computing, cooperative computing exhibits weak scaling. As more computer resources are applied to a user problem, the bigger the problem—specifically, the proportionally bigger the application dataset is. Although this does not reduce the time to solution, it does enable another ability important to scientific computation and accomplishment: It makes possible larger and more precise problems of the same type. In fact, cooperative computing is widely used with the industry standard Message Passing Interface (MPI) library and programming model. MPI methods of programming are covered later in this textbook.

4.3 SLOWER: Performance Factors

The factors contributing to the effectiveness of a parallel computing system are many, diverse, and interrelated. They affect the properties of both the hardware design and programming methods. Architecture and algorithm choice directly impact their value toward overall operational behavior of efficiency, scalability, and performance. There is, no doubt, that a number of possible sets of fundamental metrics can be devised to serve as guiding indicators for optimal system design and use. Here is offered one such performance model that benefits from its simplicity and expanse even if weak in quantitative fidelity and predictive strength. The SLOWER performance model guides attention to specific elements of a system design or software structure exposing opportunities for operational improvement. Ideally, each of the constituent factors would be orthogonal with the others of the set. Unfortunately, there are mutual non-nil sensitivities of the second order that are not fully expanded on in this model. Nonetheless, SLOWER is a powerful first-order framework for considering design and programming decisions for improved operation and performance.

"SLOWER" is an acronym for six key parameters of parallel system operation. These are starvation, latency, overhead, waiting, energy, and resilience. Together they approximate the value measure of an overall HPC system delivered in the presence of an application workflow. Each of these factors represents a major state of the performance characterization that in turn serves as a sensitivity indicator for optimization. The following describes each of these factors.

4.3.1 Starvation

Parallel computing in its many forms achieves performance gain by executing many application operations at the same time using a multiplicity of hardware computing elements available from the computer architecture. Ideally, the peak performance that could be delivered is the product of the speed of any one computing element and the number of computing elements made available. If at any one time there are many more actions to be conducted than the computing units, then near-peak speed could be attained. However, this would depend on the parallelism of the application workload. If it is less, even significantly less, than the available hardware units, the delivered performance would be much lower than the peak capability. Starvation is this insufficiency of available parallel application work to keep all of the computing elements busy.

4.3.2 Latency

The movement of data from one place in a distributed computer to another can take significant time; in fact, in some cases, it can take much more than the time of a basic operation. The term "latency" is used to reflect this time of data transfer but has various precise interpretations. Here, for this purpose, latency is the measure of data transfer time from the output port of one element to the input port of another, not including the overhead work required to prepare the data for transfer at the source and that required to assimilate the transferred data at the destination. It is assumed for this purpose that the data transfer path (i.e., channel) is unloaded; there is no other pending data transfers at the same time potentially creating contention and therefore further delays in addition to the inherent latency.

4.3.3 Overhead

An application algorithm specifies a set of operations to be performed and their mutual dependencies. A special-purpose computer designed expressly in hardware to execute such an algorithm (e.g., systolic array) would require no additional work by the system. But conventionally, the management of the physical resources and the scheduling of concurrent tasks require additional computing that consumes time and resources. Even at the low level near or at the hardware, more work needs to be done. An example of this is the network interface card at the communication port of a communication channel. Other overheads might include cache management or address translation. These overheads add to the total time to solution of an application.

4.3.4 Waiting

Delays occur when more than one pending action seeks access to a shared physical or logical resource. Contention for common resources extends the time to completion of coarse-grained tasks (waiting for a processor core) or at the lowest level conflicting requests for communication channels or main memory banks. Waiting because of contention for access to resources can impose significant bottlenecks to further progress of parts of the parallel computation.

4.3.5 Energy Consumption

Energy is a key resource for HPC. At in excess of $1 million per megawatt-year, it can be an appreciable part of a large system's operational budget. However, the rate of energy consumption (i.e., power) may also have a direct effect on performance. Specifically, a key contributing factor for performance of a processor core is its clock rate. The faster the clock (usually measured in gigahertz), the higher the peak performance of the core and the shorter the time of execution for a given workload. Therefore, energy directly translates into time.

4.3.6 Resilience

The fraction of the lifetime of an HPC system that can be used for useful application work may be a measure of its resilience (or reliability). Planned or unplanned downtime degrades the overall resilience of the system, reducing its availability to conduct useful application work, increasing the time to produce results, and increasing the amortized cost of a user application run. Planned periods of downtime are used to perform hardware and software upgrades or to perform common repeatable maintenance tasks. Unplanned downtime is usually a consequence of hard or soft faults that preclude further computation until maintenance has been performed. Resilience can be translated into time and overall average peak performance.

4.4 Amdahl's Law

The effective operation of a parallel computer architecture, rather than its peak performance, can be characterized as the ratio of the delivered performance to the theoretical peak performance of the system. Amdahl's law is an important relation that captures a critical aspect of the SLOWER performance model, specifically, the effect of the program parallelism that provides the performance gain. If, with some simplification, a computation is divided between that part or fraction (f, in which $0 < f < 1$) that can benefit from acceleration and the remaining part of the computation ($1-f$) that is forced to perform at the rate of a single thread execution, then a bounded limit of potential performance gain can be formulated. The acceleration of the fraction of the program that can be parallelized may exploit a number of processor cores. The sequential part is limited to a single processor core. Then a total performance gain, S, with respect to the full computation being performed sequentially can be determined. This is illustrated in Figure 4.1.

In Figure 4.1, the upper line represents the computation being performed in a purely sequential manner from start to end over a period of T_0. The part of the total execution that is available for acceleration, shown as the green line segment, is T_F in which $T_F < T_0$ and the fraction of the computation that can benefit from performance gain is $f = T_F/T_0$. If with the acceleration applied to the fraction designated, the total speedup, $S = T_0/T_A$, in which T_A is the time to solution of the accelerated code. The derivation for S is shown in Equations 4.2 to 4.6 in which g is the gain of

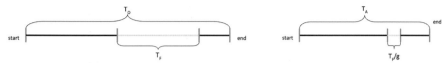

FIGURE 4.1 The time required to complete the serial execution (T_0) and accelerated (parallel) execution (T_A) of an application. A fraction of the application can be accelerated, indicated in *green*, requiring a nonaccelerated time of T_F and an accelerated time of T_F/g. The total performance gain of the acceleration, S, is T_0/T_F.

the accelerator with respect to the conventional execution rate. This is known as Amdahl's law:

T_0	Time for the nonaccelerated computation
T_A	Time for the accelerated computation
TF	Time of the portion of computation that can be accelerated
g	Peak performance gain for the accelerated portion of computation
f	Fraction of the non-accelerated computation to be accelerated
S	Speedup of the computation with acceleration applied

$$S = \frac{T_0}{T_A} \tag{4.2}$$

$$f = \frac{T_F}{T_0} \tag{4.3}$$

$$T_A = (1-f) * T_0 + \frac{f}{g} * T_0 \tag{4.4}$$

$$S = \frac{T_0}{(1-f) * T_0 + \frac{f}{g} * T_0} \tag{4.5}$$

$$S = \frac{1}{1 - f + \frac{f}{g}} \tag{4.6}$$

The fundamental consequence of Amdahl's law is that independent of the size of the accelerator's peak performance gain, g, the sustained performance is bounded by the fraction, f, of the original code that can be accelerated. As a trivial limit, imagine that you have an accelerator capable of instantaneous execution no matter what the code is and that half the problem can be executed this way; that is, consider the case of infinite gain of the accelerator. The speedup for infinite gain and f = 0.5 is only S = 2.0. Figure 4.2 shows the speedup with respect to fraction of code accelerated for several values of g.

Figure 4.3 shows that sustained speedup is highly sensitive to the fraction of the computation that can benefit from the acceleration. When the fraction, f, to which g can be applied is less than 0.5 or so, S remains relatively low even if g is greater than an order of magnitude. Only when f approaches 1.0 does dramatic reduction of time to solution result. For a parallel computer comprising p processor cores, g can be approximated by p_A which is the number of cores applied to the parallel segments of the code ($p_A \leq p$).

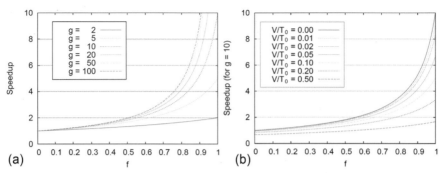

FIGURE 4.2 (A) The speedup with respect to the fraction of code accelerated for several values of g. (B) The speedup for various overhead ratios as a function of the fraction of code that can be accelerated for a fixed gain (g = 10).

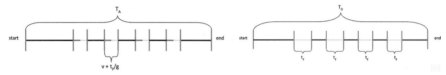

FIGURE 4.3 Timelines for nonaccelerated (T_0) and accelerated (T_A) executions similar to Figure 4.2 but including overhead.

Example

What is the minimum number of processor cores one must use in a computer to achieve a speedup of 3× in which 75% of the user application can be fully parallelized?

Here, S = 3, and f = 0.75 when we are seeking p_A as the minimum value of g required. Using the formulation for Amdahl's law derived earlier, the calculation follows:

$$3 = 1/(1 - 0.75 + (0.75 / g)) \text{ or } g = 9.$$

At least nine cores of the symmetric multi-processing (SMP) must be used to get a speed up of 3× with this code.

However, this is the good news. There are other sources of performance degradation that also come into play; in particular, overhead, v, of managing the parallel tasks that does not contribute to the problem's real work but does add to the critical time to solution. The timelines in Figure 4.1 suggests that all the work that can be accelerated occurs in one large chunk when in reality it is usually partitioned in a sequence of chunks, each controlled by some amount of overhead work as shown in Figure 4.3.

As seen in the sequential (nonaccelerated) timeline of Figure 4.2, the fraction of the computation that can be accelerated is broken into n = 4 partitions, which together make up the fraction f of the total work that can be accelerated. If this were the only difference, then with a bit of manipulation, the formulation of speedup would remain the same as that originally derived. However, for each partition of code to be accelerated, there is hopefully only a small amount of added overhead work to the critical path of execution time. Unfortunately, the size of the overhead is usually relatively constant independent of the granularity of the parallelized useful work parts. Furthermore, the more partitions, n, in which the work is divided, the more the additional overhead. By considering this overhead, a new extended version of Amdahl's law can be derived in Equations 4.7 to 4.9.

v	Overhead of accelerated work segment
V	Total overhead for accelerated work, $\sum_i^n v_i$

$$T_A = (1-f) * T_0 + \frac{f}{g} * T_0 + n * v \tag{4.7}$$

$$S = \frac{T_0}{T_A} = \frac{T_0}{(1-f) * T_0 + \frac{f}{g} * T_0 + n * v} \tag{4.8}$$

$$S = \frac{1}{(1-f) + \frac{f}{g} + \frac{n * v}{T_0}} \tag{4.9}$$

Using this new equation for speedup given in Equation 4.9, there is a new ratio added to the denominator that is proportional to the overhead v and the number of partitions n. If there is no overhead ($v = 0$), then the results are the same as the original formulation. If there is only a single large fraction of the code to be accelerated ($n = 1$), then it is almost the same. However, as the parallelism is increased in number of separate components, the overhead has an increasingly degrading effect. This is shown in Figure 4.2.

In Figure 4.2, the abscissa is the fraction of code that can be accelerated, f, but g here is constant for all curves. A new independent variable, overhead v, is added to the plot while T_0 is constant. As the overhead increases, performance gain, S, is reduced.

4.5 Memory Hierarchy

The "memory wall," or "von Neumann bottleneck," recognizes the mismatch between the peak demand rate of the processor core for data access and the possible delivered throughput and latency of the main memory technology, principally semiconductor dynamic random access memory (DRAM). Historically, whereas performance gains for processors increased on the average of 60%/year, that of main memory experienced only about a 9%/year improvement. Over time, this has led to a two-order-of-magnitude difference between processor speeds and memory speeds. To address this challenge and further into the domain of secondary storage, computer architecture in general and SMP architecture in particular have evolved a hierarchical structure of a sequence of layers of storage components with increasing density and capacity in one direction of the hierarchy and greater access speed, including higher bandwidth and lower latency, in the other direction. This is usually achieved through a cache hierarchy, intermediate layers of ever higher speed random access memory.

4.5.1 Data Reuse and Locality

Fundamental to success of parallel architecture is the strategy of data reuse through locality. If a value of a variable is used by a program repeatedly and frequently, storing it in a very high-speed memory device very close to the processor core will deliver near peak performance. This is "temporal locality," which reflects the property of data that associates the probability of usage with recent prior usage. High temporal locality suggests that a particular variable is accessed frequently in a moderate period of time. Low temporal locality indicates that a variable, if accessed at all, is probably only used once or a couple of times in the moderate contiguous period. A second form of locality often exploited is "spatial locality," which indicates an association of locality among adjacent or near neighbors in contiguous address space. High spatial locality suggests that the probability of a variable (virtually addressed value) being accessed is higher if one of its adjacent or neighboring variables has been recently accessed. These two forms of locality, concerning the reuse patterns of virtually addressed variables, provide the foundations for the structure and operation of the memory hierarchy to mitigate the effects of the discrepancies between bandwidths and latencies of processor and main memory technologies.

The second factor of practical concern is the tradeoff relationships between the characteristics of storage capacity per unit area, cycle time of access, and power consumption. Diverse data storage technologies vary in terms of these parameters. In general, faster memory technologies take up more room on a semiconductor die or other medium for the same amount of storage while consuming greater power. It is impractical to create a main memory layer that is big enough to hold all the software and data required for a given user application while running fast enough to keep the processor cores fully utilized at their peak instruction issue throughput.

4.5.2 Memory System Performance

The time to access a value from a specified variable in the memory system will vary dramatically depending on a number of factors, most specifically where the closest copy of the value is in the memory hierarchy. Although analyzing such a complex memory architecture can be very complicated because of the number of levels, the overheads involved, issues of contention, and so forth, a simplified version of the problem still exposes the principal tradeoffs and shows how dramatically the average memory access time can change depending on the hit rates to cache as a consequence of locality. For this purpose, cache is assumed as a single intermediate layer between processor core registers and main memory. Without doing a detailed queuing analysis or similar in-depth model, operational metrics are adopted to capture the specific properties of the architecture and application memory access profile as well as a quality metric of performance. An analytical model is derived to expose the sensitivity between delivered performance and the effectiveness of caching.

The quality metric of choice in this case is CPI or cycles per instruction. Time to solution, T, is proportional to cycle time, T_{cycle}, and the number of instructions to be executed for a user task, I_{count}. Because the purpose of this analysis is to expose the implications of memory behavior, instruction count will be partitioned between the instructions associated with the number of register-to-register arithmetic and logic unit (ALU) instructions, I_{ALU}, and the number of memory access instructions, I_{MEM}. For each of these two classes of instructions, there is a separate measure of cycles per instruction, one for the register-to-register ALU operation, CPI_{ALU}, and one for the memory instructions, CPI_{MEM}. The total value for time, I_{count}, and CPI can be derived from the breakdown between ALU and memory operations according to Equations 4.10 to 4.12.

$$T = I_{count} * CPI * T_{cycle} \tag{4.10}$$

$$I_{count} = I_{ALU} + I_{MEM} \tag{4.11}$$

$$CPI = \frac{I_{ALU}}{I_{count}} * CPI_{ALU} + \frac{I_{MEM}}{I_{count}} * CPI_{MEM} \tag{4.12}$$

The full set of parameters is defined as:

T	= total execution time
T_{cycle}	= time for a single processor cycle
I_{count}	= total number of instructions
I_{ALU}	= number of ALU instructions (e.g., register to register)
I_{MEM}	= number of memory access instructions (e.g., load, store)
CPI	= average cycles per instruction
CPI_{ALU}	= average cycles per ALU instruction
CPI_{MEM}	= average cycles per memory instruction
r_{miss}	= cache miss rate
r_{hit}	= cache hit rate
$CPI_{MEM-MISS}$	= cycles per cache miss
$CPI_{MEM-HIT}$	= cycles per cache hit
M_{ALU}	= instruction mix for ALU instructions
M_{MEM}	= instruction mix for memory access instructions

The idea of instruction mix simplifies representation of this distinction between ALU and memory operations providing ratios of each with respect to the total instruction count.

In addition, the parameter that expresses the effect of data reuse is defined as the hit rate or r_{hit} that establishes the percentage of time that a memory request is found in the cache. The opposite of this parameter can be useful and is $r_{miss} = (1 - r_{hit})$. One last distinction is made for CPI_{MEM} depending on whether a hit or a miss occurred. These represent the costs measured in number of cycles of the memory instructions' access times depending on whether there was a hit or a miss at the cache. $CPI_{MEM\text{-}hit}$ is a fixed value of the number of cycles required for an access that is served by the cache. $CPI_{MEM\text{-}miss}$ is the cost in cycles of going all the way to main memory to get a memory request serviced in the case of a cache miss. The relationships among these distinguishing parameters are demonstrated in Equations 4.13 to 4.17, associating them with the definition of full execution time.

Instruction mix:

$$M_{ALU} = \frac{I_{ALU}}{I_{count}} \tag{4.13}$$

$$M_{MEM} = \frac{I_{MEM}}{I_{count}} \tag{4.14}$$

$$M_{ALU} + M_{MEM} = 1 \tag{4.15}$$

$$CPI = (M_{ALU} * CPI_{ALU}) + (M_{MEM} * CPI_{MEM}) \tag{4.16}$$

$$T = I_{count} * [(M_{ALU} * CPI_{ALU}) + (M_{MEM} * CPI_{MEM})] * T_{cycle} \tag{4.17}$$

Finally, the values for CPI_{MEM} and T as functions of r_{miss} are presented in Equations 4.18 and 4.19. It may appear peculiar that the coefficient of $CPI_{MEM\text{-}HIT}$ is not r_{hit}. This is because the cost of getting data from or to the cache occurs whether or not a miss occurs.

$$CPI_{MEM} = CPI_{MEM-HIT} + r_{miss} * CPI_{MEM-MISS} \tag{4.18}$$

$$T = I_{count} * [(M_{ALU} * CPI_{ALU}) + M_{MEM} * (CPI_{MEM-HIT} + r_{miss} * CPI_{MEM-MISS})] * T_{cycle} \tag{4.19}$$

This shows the effect of the application-driven properties, including I_{count}, M_{MEM}, and r_{miss}. Architecture-driven properties are also reflected as T_{cycle}, $CPI_{MEM\text{-}miss}$, and $CPI_{MEM\text{-}HIT}$ in determining the final time to solution, T.

Example

As a case study, a system and computation are described in terms of the set of parameters presented earlier. Typical values are assigned to these to represent conventional practices, architectures, and applications. These are:

I_{count}	=1E11
I_{MEM}	=2E10
CPI_{ALU}	=1
T_{cycle}	=0.5 ns
$CPI_{MEM-MISS}$	=100
$CPI_{MEM-HIT}$	=1

The intermediate values for instruction mix are computed as follows:

$$
\begin{array}{l|l}
I_{ALU} & = I_{count} - I_{MEM} = 8E10 \\
M_{ALU} & = \frac{I_{ALU}}{I_{count}} = \frac{8E10}{1E11} = 0.8 \\
M_{MEM} & = \frac{I_{MEM}}{I_{count}} = \frac{2E10}{1E11} = 0.2
\end{array}
$$

It is the intent of this example to show the impact of the cache hit rate on the total execution time. This can prove to be one of the most important determining factors of application time to solution and one that the user has to be conscious of as data layout is considered. Two alternative computations are considered. The first is favorable to a cache hierarchy (this example simplifies with only one layer) with a hit rate of 90%. With this value established, the time to solution can be determined as shown in Equations 4.20 to 4.22.

$$r_{hit\ A} = 0.9 \tag{4.20}$$

$$CPI_{MEM\ A} = CPI_{MEM-HIT} + r_{MISS\ A} * CPI_{MEM-MISS} = 1 + (1 - 0.9) * 100 = 11 \tag{4.21}$$

$$T_A = 1E11 * [(0.8 * 1) + (0.2 * 11)] * 5E10 = 150\ sec \tag{4.22}$$

However, if the cache hit rate is lower, in this case at 50%, a recalculation with this new value shows a dramatic reduction of performance as shown in Equations 4.23 to 4.25.

$$r_{hit\ A} = 0.5 \tag{4.23}$$

$$CPI_{MEM\ B} = CPI_{MEM-HIT} + r_{MISS\ B} * CPI_{MEM-MISS} = 1 + (1 - 0.5) * 100 = 51 \tag{4.24}$$

$$T_B = 1E11 * [(0.8 * 1) + (0.2 * 51)] * 5E10 = 550\ sec \tag{4.25}$$

The difference is more than a factor of $3\times$ performance degradation, just because of the change in the cache hit rate.

4.6 Summary and Outcomes

- The speed of a parallel computer system depends on the conditions under which it is executing and the workload upon which it is operating.
- Peak performance is the maximum number of operations that in principle could be performed in unit time given the total number of arithmetic units provided in hardware.
- In practical terms, peak performance is unachievable in realistic computing scenarios but it does provide an upper, not to be exceeded, bound.
- Benchmarks are formerly defined codes along with rules of their usage by which different systems may be measured and compared.
- Scalability relates to the effect that a system of increased size (e.g., number of processor cores) would deliver increased performance.

- Efficiency measures the percentage of a system that can actually be used for useful computation.
- Throughput or capacity computing is a measure of performance based on the number of operations being performed in unit time without regard to the parallel flow of control.
- Strong scaling results in reduced execution time with increased system size. Because it involves a single large application rather than an ensemble of many smaller jobs, this class of processing is also called capability computing.
- Cooperative computing is weak scaling of a single parallel application that expands in terms of the size of its dataset proportionally with the increased size of the system resources.
- SLOWER is a powerful first-order performance model through which to consider design and programming decisions for improved operation and performance.
- Starvation is the insufficiency of available parallel application work to keep all of the system hardware computing elements busy.
- Latency is the measure of data transfer time from the output port of one element to the input port of another, not including the overhead work required to prepare the data for transfer at the source and that required to assimilate the transferred data at the destination.
- Overhead is the work beyond that of the user application required for management of the physical resources and the scheduling of concurrent tasks requiring additional computing that consumes time and resources.
- Contention is the delay of actions resulting from multiple simultaneous access requests to shared resources like memory banks and network ports.
- The energy consumption rate (i.e., power) determines, in part, the clock rate of the processor core with more power driving higher clock rates and greater performance.
- Resilience can be measured as the percentage of the lifetime of a computer system during which application work is able to be performed.
- Amdahl's law is a relation that captures the effect of the program parallelism that provides the delivered performance gain.
- A fundamental consequence of Amdahl's law is that independent of the size of the accelerator's peak performance gain, g, the sustained performance is bounded by the fraction, f, of the original code that can be accelerated.
- Locality of data access includes temporal locality and spatial locality
- The memory hierarchy or stack consists of layers of memory storage technology, each with different tradeoffs between memory capacity, costs, and cycle times that reflect bandwidths and latencies.

4.7 **Exercises**

1. What six factors make up the SLOWER performance model?

2. Capacity and capability computing are both valid models of conducting computation on parallel systems. What is their principal distinguishing characteristic?

3. Define "cooperative" computing and indicate its distinction from capacity and capability computing.

4. What is latency, and how is it differentiated from overhead in the SLOWER model?

5. Workload can be distinguished between purely serial (sequential) and that which may be performed concurrently. If the proportion of the workload that can be done in parallel is 75% and the gain of the parallel work is 10×, what degree of speedup is achieved by the accelerated system?

6. How much of a gain factor will be required of an accelerator to speed up the total computation by a factor of 4× when the proportion of the calculation can be speeded up by 80%.

7. If the overhead to launch parallel tasks is the fixed amount of additional work of for each task of 100 iterations (breaking the work in to 100 serial portions), the total amounting to 80% of the total workload, then what is the total speedup with respect to pure sequential execution?

8. Assume a single cache layer (for simplicity) and a cache hit rate of 85% with the cache cycle time of two cycles and the DRAM access upon a miss of 20 cycles. What is the speedup with the cache versus the operation without any cache?

Benchmarking

5

Chapter outline

5.1 Introduction

Benchmarking efforts for evaluating the performance of a computer have been ongoing since the beginning of the age of general-purpose computers. The nature of those benchmarks has reflected the intended purpose for which the computer was built while also providing an empirical performance measure that can be compared against the vendor's theoretical performance estimate. In the case of the first general-purpose electronic computer, the ENIAC (1946) [1], the de facto performance benchmark, was computing an artillery trajectory and comparing the time to solution against a human computing the same trajectory. Modern supercomputers employ a wide variety of benchmarks, ranging from linear algebra to machine learning, reflecting the diversity of users on modern systems. Just as in the case of the artillery trajectory calculation on the ENIAC, however, user applications have also been used on modern supercomputers as de facto benchmarks even though they were not initially designed for such operation.

One of the earliest general-purpose benchmarks for evaluating computer performance was the Whetstone benchmark [2], named after the Whetstone village in Leicestershire, England, where the Whetstone compiler was developed. This benchmark, first released in 1972, consisted of multiple programs that created

High Performance Computing. https://doi.org/10.1016/B978-0-12-823035-0.00005-5

synthetic workloads for evaluating kilo Whetstone instructions per second. In 1980 it was updated to report floating-point operations per second (flops). While this benchmark was a serial benchmark not specifically designed for supercomputing systems, it became an industry standard and is used to evaluate the performance of the microprocessors being used in some supercomputers.

In 1984 a benchmark with a standardized synthetic computing workload named Dhrystone was released. This benchmark, like Whetstone, would become an industry standard for measuring integer performance. Its name is a result of some word play on the Whetstone benchmark and is intended to complement the Whetstone benchmark by measuring integer performance rather than floating-point performance. Like Whetstone, Dhrystone was not created by itself as a supercomputing benchmark but has been used for evaluating microprocessor components of supercomputers. Dhrystone has since been superseded by the SPECint suite [3].

The genesis of one of the most widely used benchmarks in supercomputing is the Linpack benchmark, introduced by Jack Dongarra in 1979 and based on the Linpack linear algebra package developed by Dongarra, Jim Bunch, Cleve Moler, and Gilbert Stewart [4]. An interesting sidenote to this, one of the Linpack developers, Cleve Moler, later went on to invent MATLAB to make it easier for users to access the Linpack libraries. MATLAB has since become one of the most widely used scientific computing tools in both academia and industry. While the original Linpack linear algebra package has since been superseded by the LAPACK library [5] and other competitors, the Linpack benchmark continues to exert a strong influence in the field. It provides an estimate of the system's effective floating-point performance. Beginning in 1979, results from the Linpack benchmark on various systems have been collected by Dongarra. This list started with just 23 computer systems and grew to include hundreds of systems.

The Linpack benchmark employs a workload that solves a *dense* system of linear equations. That is, it solves for x in $Ax = b$, where b and x are vectors of length n and A is an $n \times n$ matrix with very few or no zero elements. The original Linpack benchmark solved matrices with $n = 100$ and was written for serial computation. No changes to the source code were allowed; only optimizations achieved through compiler flags were allowed. A second iteration of the benchmark used matrices with $n = 1000$ and allowed user modifications to the factorization and solver portions of the code. An accuracy bound on the final solution was also introduced. The third iteration of the benchmark, called the highly parallel computing Linpack (HPL), allows variations in the problem size and software and can run on a distributed memory supercomputer. This version of the benchmark is used to generate the Top 500 list that is frequently used to rank supercomputers throughout the world. Section 5.3.1 will discuss HPL in greater detail.

Today there are a wide variety of general-purpose benchmarks used for evaluating the performance of supercomputers and supercomputing elements. These benchmarks often originate from a specific application domain with a workload motivated by that application class rather than from a synthetic workload to achieve better relevance with respect to actual user applications. Table 5.1 provides a

Table 5.1 Brief Summary of Some Benchmarks Used in the HPC Community

Benchmark	Application Domain Workload	Aim	Parallelism	Characteristics
HPL	Dense linear algebra	Estimate system's effective flops	MPI	Part of HPC Challenge Benchmark; used for Top 500 list
STREAM	Synthetic	Estimate sustainable memory bandwidth (GB/s)	None	Part of the HPC Challenge Benchmark
RandomAccess	Synthetic	Estimate system's effective rate of integer random updates of memory—reported as giga updates per second (GUPS)	MPI, OpenMP	Part of the HPC Challenge Benchmark
HPCG	Sparse linear algebra	Estimate system's effective flops for those applications poorly represented by HPL	MPI + OpenMP	Used for HPCG list ranking
SPEC CPU 2006	Various	Estimate system's effective processor, memory, and compiler performance	None	Commercial
IS	Computational fluid dynamics	Estimate system's effective integer sort and random access performance	MPI, OpenMP	Part of the NAS Parallel Benchmarks
Graph500	Data-intensive applications	Estimate system's effective traversed edges per second (TEPS) for a graph traversal	MPI, OpenMP	Used for the Graph500 list ranking
MLPerf HPC	Machine learning applications	Measure wall clock time to train machine learning workload	Horovod (MPI), OpenMP	Part of the MLCommons consortium

summary of some of the benchmarks available for high performance computing (HPC) users along with their motivating application domain and characteristics. Some of the most universally used benchmarks come in suites containing multiple individual benchmarks. Two widely used suites of benchmarks are the HPC Challenge benchmark suite [6] consisting of seven individual benchmarks (including HPL) and the NAS parallel benchmarks (NPB) [7] consisting of more than eight benchmark specifications and reference implementations. These suites will be discussed further in Sections 5.5 and 5.7, respectively. With the rise of machine learning applications on supercomputing systems, it is no surprise that multiple machine learning benchmarks have also been developed covering distinct aspects of machine learning workflows including training and inference both at the edge for power-constrained technologies and in the datacenter where there are no power constraints. A discussion of these will be covered in Section 5.8.

5.2 Key Properties of an HPC Benchmark

HPC benchmarks fulfill several important roles in the HPC community. Benchmarks are frequently used to help decide the size and type of a supercomputer that an institution procures and can help to identify which technology is best to achieve the highest performance on a defined set of applications. In this role, many different benchmarks may be used to assess if a candidate supercomputer will adequately address the needs of its user community. In a similar role, benchmarks are often called upon to estimate the performance of certain user applications at processor scales and dataset sizes much larger than what is available to the user. Benchmarks also help identify and quantify performance upper bounds and limitations for specific application algorithms. For emerging technologies, benchmarks play a key role in comparing performance between conventional practice and the recent technology using the same workloads. On many supercomputing systems, benchmarks provide performance milestones against which users can compare their specific application performance and make assessments about the efficiency of their application. Benchmark results form an important historical record for exploring trends in HPC. Finally, benchmarks play a significant role in quantifying what percentage of the theoretical peak performance a supercomputer can achieve.

Good benchmarks share several key properties. First, they are relevant and meaningful to the target application domain. Second, they are applicable to a broad spectrum of hardware architectures. Third, they are adopted by both users and vendors and enable comparative evaluation.

Some other de facto properties of successful HPC benchmarks are also worth noting. One is that most HPC benchmarks are short. In Table 5.2 the line count for each of the nonproprietary benchmarks summarized in Table 5.1 is found. While many HPC user applications regularly exceed 100,000 lines of source code, the benchmarks used for evaluating supercomputing resources are much smaller.

Table 5.2 Approximate Line Count, Parallelism Application Programming Interface, and Language for Each of the Nonproprietary Benchmarks in Table 5.1

	Approximate Line Count	Parallelism	Language
HPL	26,700	MPI	C
STREAM	1500	None	C
RandomAccess	5800	MPI, OpenMP	C
HPCG	5700	MPI, OpenMP	C++
IS	1150	MPI, OpenMP	C
Graph500	1900	MPI, OpenMP	C
MLPerf HPC	25,000	Horovod, MPI	Python

HPC benchmarks in general specify guidelines about how the benchmark may be run and optimized. Similarly, the results from the benchmark can be archived and shared. Among the benchmarks in Table 5.2, there are four maintained supercomputer ranking lists associated with three benchmarks: HPL [8], high performance conjugate gradients (HPCG) [9], and Graph500 [10]. The top supercomputer for each of the lists in February 2023 is provided in Table 5.3.

Table 5.3 The Top-Performing Supercomputer in February 2023 for Each of the Four Benchmarks

Benchmark	Supercomputer	Location	Performance Result	Cores
HPL	Frontier	Oak Ridge, Tennessee, USA	1.1 exaflops	8,730,112
HPGC	Fugaku	Kobe, Japan	16.004 petaflops	7,630,848
Graph500-BFS	Fugaku	Kobe, Japan	102995 GTEPS	7,360,848

The rank of each supercomputer cross-listed on each list is in Table 5.4.

Table 5.4 The Ranking of the Top-Performing Supercomputers in February 2023 for Each of the Maintained Ranking Lists

Supercomputer	Top 500 List Ranking	Graph500 List Ranking	HPCG Ranking
Frontier	1		2
Fugaku	2	1	1

In addition to providing guidelines for execution, optimization, and result reporting, HPC benchmarks use standard parallel programming application programming interfaces (APIs) such as OpenMP, message-passing interface (MPI), or Horovod (discussed later in the chapters on MPI, OpenMP, and Deep Learning). They also provide some mechanism for flexibility in executing the benchmark to foster innovation, whether it be through changing the dataset size or tuning some portion of the implementation. For HPC benchmarks in general, while the type of workload may be the same within a list of benchmark results, the size of that workload may differ considerably.

One of the most important properties of an HPC benchmark is that its workload should represent some appropriate set of real supercomputer application workload. This is often one of the most difficult properties for a benchmark, and the performance impact from the type of workload can be significant. The HPCG benchmark mentioned in Tables 5.1−5.4 is intended to complement the HPL benchmark in exploring workloads with data access patterns not exhibited by HPL. The difference between the peak performance of these two types of workloads can be seen in Table 5.3. The fastest HPCG performance is typically less than 1% of the fastest HPL performance, illustrating a huge performance disparity between these two distinct types of workloads. HPC benchmarks with workloads that represent real applications enable better performance estimation and evaluation.

5.3 Standard HPC Community Benchmarks

Sections 5.4 through 5.9 explore several of the most widely used benchmarks in the HPC community. These sections give a brief description of the benchmark and how to compile and run it. The benchmarks themselves are run via command line and can be run on a laptop just as well as on a supercomputer if some basic prerequisite software is present. That software includes a C, C++, and Fortran compiler; the MPI libraries; BLAS; and cmake. For the machine learning benchmarks, the Tensorflow and Pytorch machine learning environments are needed in addition to Python. For ease of downloading benchmarks via command line, the wget software is also especially useful, as well as git for those benchmarks stored in github repositories. While most benchmarks can be easily compiled natively on a supercomputing system, machine learning benchmarks are most easily executed via a container platform for virtualization, such as docker or Singularity/Apptainer container.

The most widely cited benchmark in high performance computing is HPL and will be discussed in Section 5.4. The HPC Challenge benchmark suite contains seven different benchmarks including HPL as well as the STREAM memory bandwidth benchmark and will be discussed in Section 5.5. The HPCG benchmark, which is representative of memory-bandwidth-limited applications, will be explored in Section 5.6. Representing computational fluid dynamics applications, the NPB will be discussed in Section 5.7. Section 5.8 will cover the MLPerf benchmarks as well as the Graph500 benchmark. Finally, Section 5.9 will briefly cover a suite of microbenchmarks and miniapplications.

5.4 **Highly Parallel Computing Linpack**

HPL/Linpack is one of the most influential HPC benchmarks in the HPC community. It solves a dense system of linear equations and is well suited for floating-point intensive computations. As noted in Section 5.1, its genesis is the Linpack benchmark introduced by Jack Dongarra in 1979. HPL also serves as the benchmark for determining the supercomputer ranking on the Top 500 list. HPL is written in C and targets distributed memory computers.

The key workload algorithm in HPL is lower/upper (LU) factorization. Given a problem size n, HPL will perform $O(n^3)$ floating-point operations while only performing $O(n^2)$ memory accesses. Consequently, HPL is not strongly influenced by memory bandwidth and is well suited for empirically exploring the peak floating-point computation capability of a supercomputer.

HPL contains many variations in the way it can be executed so that the best-performing approach for a particular supercomputer can be found empirically. The user is also allowed to entirely replace the LU factorization and solver step reference implementation with an alternative implementation if so desired. Unlike the earlier versions of Linpack, there are no restrictions on problem size in HPL.

Here are the steps to install HPL on a laptop or supercomputer:

```
wget https://netlib.org/benchmark/hpl/hpl-2.3.tar.gz
tar -xf hpl-2.3.tar.gz
mkdir -p hpl-2.3/build
cd hpl-2.3/build
../configure; make;
```

The executable is called "xhpl" and is found in the build/testing subdirectory. Accompanying the *xhpl* executable is a parameter file to tune HPL for the supercomputer. An example of such a parameter file comes with HPL and is found in the source tree here: `hpl-2.3/testing/ptest/HPL.dat`. A quick test of the installation of xhpl can be run on four processes in the build/testing subdirectory using the provided default HPL.dat parameter file as follows:

```
mpirun -np 4 xhpl ../../testing/ptest/HPL.dat
```

It will report gigaflops for 864 parameter settings to the terminal in this format:

```
T/V       N  NB P  Q     Time     Gflops
WR00L2R4  35  3  4  1     0.00     3.0120e-01
```

```
||Ax-b||_oo/(eps*(||A||_oo*||x||_oo+||b||_oo)*N)= 2.09754958e-02  PASS==
```

The HPL.dat parameter file consists of 31 lines and the default HPL.dat file provided looks like this with the file line number shown on the left:

```
1 HPLinpack benchmark input file
2 Innovative Computing Laboratory, University of Tennessee
3 HPL.out   output file name (if any)
```

```
 4  6        device out (6=stdout,7=stderr,file)
 5  4        # of problems sizes (N)
 6  29 30 34 35 Ns
 7  4        # of NBs
 8  1 2 3 4   NBs
 9  0        PMAP process mapping (0=Row-,1=Column-major)
10  3        # of process grids (P x Q)
11  2 1 4    Ps
12  2 4 1    Qs
13  16.0     threshold
14  3        # of panel fact
15  0 1 2    PFACTs (0=left, 1=Crout, 2=Right)
16  2        # of recursive stopping criterium
17  2 4      NBMINs (>= 1)
18  1        # of panels in recursion
19  2        NDIVs
20  3        # of recursive panel fact.
21  0 1 2    RFACTs (0=left, 1=Crout, 2=Right)
22  1        # of broadcast
23  0        BCASTs (0=1rg,1=1rM,2=2rg,3=2rM,4=Lng,5=LnM)
24  1        # of lookahead depth
25  0        DEPTHs (>=0)
26  2        SWAP (0=bin-exch,1=long,2=mix)
27  64       swapping threshold
28  0        L1 in (0=transposed,1=no-transposed) form
29  0        U in (0=transposed,1=no-transposed) form
30  1        Equilibration (0=no,1=yes)
31  8        memory alignment in double (> 0)
```

The parameter space for tuning HPL is exceptionally large, so parameter inputs separated by a space on each line are run independently. For example, the default parameter file in the default HPL.dat will run HPL through 864 (= 4 × 4 × 3 × 3 × 2 × 3) distinct parameter combinations with a separate report of Gflops for each unique parameter combination since lines 6, 8, 11, 12, 17, and 21 of the default HPL.dat have space-separated parameter choices.

A brief explanation of the HPL.dat input file is as follows:

- Lines 1−2 are ignored.
- Line 3 specifies the name of the file where any output should be redirected if requested in line 4.
- Line 4 specifies whether to print the output to screen or to a file.
- Line 5 indicates the number of different problem sizes explored in this parameter file. It cannot be greater than 20.
- Line 6 gives a space-separated list of the matrix problem sizes. If the number of problem sizes given exceeds the number specified in line 5, those excess problem sizes will be ignored.

- Line 7 gives the number of block sizes explored in this parameter file.
- Line 8 gives a space-separated list of those block sizes.
- Line 9 indicates how MPI processes are mapped onto the nodes, whether row or column major.
- Line 10 indicates the number of process grid configurations specified in this parameter file.
- Lines 11−12 specify those process grid configurations.
- Line 13 specifies a threshold used for flagging residuals as failed. In general, residuals will be order 1. Specifying a negative threshold turns off checking and allows for faster parameter space sweeps.
- Lines 14−31 specify algorithmic variations in HPL. HPL has several different algorithm options, including six different virtual panel broadcast topologies (line 23), a bandwidth-reducing swap-broadcast algorithm (line 26), back substitution with look-ahead depth of one (line 24), and three different LU factorization algorithms (lines 21) among other options. Tuning these parameters on a specific supercomputer is a routine task with HPL.

For a certain problem size N_{max}, the cumulative performance in Gflops reaches its maximum value, called R_{max}. The R_{max} value is what is reported for the Top 500 list ranking supercomputers. Another interesting metric from the HPL benchmark is $N_{1/2}$. $N_{1/2}$ is the problem size where the maximum performance achieved is $R_{max}/2$.

5.5 HPC Challenge Benchmark Suite

The HPC Challenge benchmark suite consists of seven different tests that cover a range of application types and memory access patterns. The first, HPL/Linpack, has already been discussed in Section 5.4 because of its significant impact on the HPC community. The other six tests are:

- DGEMM—double-precision matrix−matrix multiplication.
- STREAM—synthetic workload to measure sustainable memory bandwidth.
- PTRANS—parallel matrix transpose.
- RandomAccess—reports the rate of integer random updates of memory in GUPS.
- FFT—double-precision complex one-dimensional discrete Fourier transform.
- B_eff—reports latency and bandwidth for several different communication patterns.

Here are the steps to install HPL on a laptop or supercomputer:

```
git clone https://github.com/icl-utk-edu/hpcc.git
cd hpcc/
```

In this directory you will need to manually adjust the setup.py script to indicate the location of the BLASS libraries and the MPI libraries on lines 47 and 53 by changing the MPDIR and LALIB variables for your specify host. Then run:

```
python setup.py
```

This script will create the Makefile for your architecture and give you the architecture name to use in building, e.g.,

```
make arch=darwin
```

When building is complete, the executable is called `hpcc` and it takes an input file called `hpccinf.txt` as input. A default version is provided in the directory but has an ampersand in front of it. This parameter file has the same format as the HPL input file but with five additional lines:

```
32 ##### This line (no. 32) is ignored (it serves as a separator). ######
33 0                        Number of additional problem sizes for PTRANS
34 1200 10000 30000            values of N
35 0                        number of additional blocking sizes for PTRANS
36 40 9 8 13 13 20 16 32 64   values of NB
```

These additional lines incorporate parameters specific to the matrix transpose benchmark, PTRANS.

To run a test of the installation, do the following:

```
cp _hpccinf.txt hpccinf.txt
mpirun -np 4 ./hpcc
```

All output will be written to a file called `hpccoutf.txt` containing the results for each of the seven benchmarks, e.g.,

```
Single DGEMM Gflop/s 220.882148
Single GUP/s 0.470213
```

5.6 High Performance Conjugate Gradients

The HPCG benchmark was created by Jack Dongarra (the HPL creator), Michael Heroux, and Piotr Luszczek (HPL developer), with the first release in 2000 and the most recent version released in 2015. It aims to complement the HPL benchmark in exploring memory and data access patterns in application workloads that are not well represented by HPL. The workload in HPCG centers on a sparse system of linear equations arising from the discretization of a three-dimensional (3D) Laplacian partial differential equation with a 27-point stencil. Like HPL, the workload in HPCG is geared for solving Equation (5.1), but the *A* matrix is dominated by zeros in the HPCG workload. Unlike HPL, the solution method in HPCG is driven by a

Krylov subspace solver known as conjugate gradient. Krylov subspace solvers are iterative solvers requiring multiple iterations to produce an approximate solution to Equation (5.1) to within a certain tolerance and are among the most common methods used for solving sparse linear systems of equations. Because the matrix in HPCG is dominated by zeros, the nonzero elements of the matrix are stored in contiguous memory locations for each row.

The sparse nature of the workload in this benchmark requires many more memory accesses than in HPL. For a problem size n, HPCG will perform $O(n)$ floating-point operations while also requiring $O(n)$ memory accesses. Given this, it is no great surprise that in Table 5.3 the peak flops measured for HPL and HPCG differ by over a factor of 68.

The HPCG benchmark incorporates five major kernels: sparse matrix vector multiplication, symmetric Gauss–Seidel smoothing, global dot product evaluation, vector update, and multigrid preconditioning. In addition, the benchmark provides seven different reference routines that can be replaced in their entirety by user code optimized for the intended supercomputer in accordance with some specific guidelines.

For Krylov subspace solvers, a sizable portion of the solve time is spent in sparse matrix vector multiplication, thereby making the HPCG sparse matrix vector multiplication kernel performance relevant to performance in many user applications. For a matrix of size $N \times N$ and a vector of size N, matrix vector multiplication is given by Equation (5.1):

$$x_i = \sum_{j=0}^{N-1} A_{ij} b_j \tag{5.1}$$

where A_{ij} is the (i,j)th element of the matrix, and b_j is the jth element of the vector. Because nonzero elements of sparse matrix are stored in contiguous memory locations for each row, Equation (5.1) can be modified to reflect that zero matrix entries in HPCG are neither stored nor manipulated:

$$x_i = \sum_{j=0}^{n_i} A_{ij} b_j \tag{5.2}$$

where n_i indicates the number of nonzeros in sparse matrix A for the ith row. The sparse matrix vector multiplication kernel in HPCG evaluates Equation (5.2) in distributed memory, requiring some exchange of needed b_j values between memory localities. This is an example of *halo exchange* and will be explored in detail in Chapter 9. Both the halo exchange routine and the entire sparse matrix vector multiplication kernel code in HPCG can be replaced or altered with certain restrictions by the user.

Gauss–Seidel smoothing is an iterative solution method for linear systems of equations. The Gauss–Seidel kernel in HPCG tests recursive execution and has memory access characteristics like that of the sparse matrix vector multiplication kernel. Like the sparse matrix vector kernel, the entire reference implementation of Gauss—Seidel smoothing can be modified or replaced in the benchmark by the user under specified guidelines.

One of the most important collective communication type operations in HPCG is computing a global dot product of two vectors in distributed memory to produce a single scalar value available to all processing elements. This type of operation is common in most user applications. HPCG reporting includes the min, max, and average MPI allreduce time when using MPI for the benchmark. A user-provided dot product routine can be substituted for the reference implementation. The same is true for the vector update and multigrid preconditioner, where all the key kernels of HPCG are tested using four different grid sizes.

Here are the basic instructions for installing and running the reference HPCG implementation on either a laptop or supercomputer:

```
wget https://hpcg-benchmark.org/downloads/hpcg-3.1.tar.gz
tar -xf hpcg-3.1.tar.gz
cd hpcg-3.1
mkdir build
../configure Linux_MPI
make
```

This will create an executable called `xhpcg` in the `hpcg-3.1/build/bin` directory. The default HPCG input file is also placed there. Unlike the HPL input file, the HPCG input file is noticeably short:

```
1 HPCG benchmark input file
2 Sandia National Laboratories; University of Tennessee, Knoxville
3 104 104 104
4 60
```

The first two lines are unused and can be replaced with user-motivated descriptions. The third line specifies the dimensions of the problem that are local to each MPI process. Consequently, the global problem size changes for HPCG depending on the number of processes launched, while the local problem size stays the same. In this sense, HPCG is already set up for weak scaling tests. The third line contains three space-separated numbers, which correspond to the number of collocation points in a cubic grid used for discretizing the 3D Laplacian partial differential equation that is at the heart of the HPCG workload. The fourth line specifies how long in seconds the benchmark should run (60 seconds in this example parameter file). To submit official HPCG results, the benchmark should run for at least 1800 seconds. The parameter file should reside in the same directory as the executable when running.

Like HPL, the HPCG executable is launched using mpirun:

```
mpirun -np 4 ./xhpcg
```

All output from the benchmark is written to two files named HPCG-Benchmark-3.1_<today's date and time>.yaml and hpcg<today's date and time>.txt. The hpcg file contains the log of output from the HPCG execution; the benchmark results are in the yaml file:

```
118 Final Summary=
119 Final Summary::HPCG result is VALID with a GFLOP/s rating of=3.31893
120 Final Summary::HPCG 2.4 rating for historical reasons is=3.37463
121 Final Summary::Reference version of ComputeDotProduct
used=Performance results are most likely suboptimal
122 Final Summary::Reference version of ComputeSPMV used=Performance
results are most likely suboptimal
123 Final Summary::Reference version of ComputeMG used=Performance
results are most likely suboptimal
124 Final Summary::Reference version of ComputeWAXPBY used=Performance
results are most likely suboptimal
125 Final Summary::Results are valid but execution time (sec) is=74.0185
126 Final Summary::Official results execution time (sec) must be at
least=1800
```

Current HPCG implementations achieve only a small fraction of peak flops on the fastest 10 supercomputers in the Top 500 list, while they achieve as much as 90% of the theoretical peak performance for HPL/Linpack. This highlights the different nature of the HPCG benchmark versus HPL even though they both report flops as the final overall rating.

5.7 **NAS Parallel Benchmarks**

NPB is a series of small self-contained programs that encapsulate the performance attributes of a large computational fluid dynamics application. NPB originated from the NASA Ames research center in 1991, and the first version of the benchmark consisted of eight problems that were specified entirely in a "pencil and paper" fashion. That is, there was no reference implementation, as in other benchmarks, and the benchmark programs were specified algorithmically. In 1995, the second version of NPB was announced, where reference versions based on MPI and Fortran77 would be distributed. Subsequently, a third version of NPB was released, which included several additions to the original eight problems as some additional parallel programming APIs beyond MPI, such as OpenMP, High Performance Fortran, and Java.

The original eight problems in NPB are a large integer sort for testing both integer computation speed and network performance, embarrassingly parallel random number generation for integral evaluation, a conjugate gradient approximation to compute the smallest eigenvalue of a sparse symmetric matrix, a multigrid solver for computing a 3D potential, a time integrator of a 3D partial differential equation using the fast Fourier transform, a block tridiagonal solver with a 5×5 block size, a pentadiagonal solver, and an LU solver for coupled parabolic/elliptic partial differential equations. These problems are referred to by the two-letter

Table 5.5 Some Characteristics of the NAS Parallel Benchmarks (NPB)

NPB	Approximate Line Count	Parallelism		Language	
		MPI	OpenMP	Fortran	C
IS—Integer Sort	1150	X	X		X
EP—Embarrassingly Parallel	400	X	X	X	
CG—Conjugate Gradient	1900	X	X	X	
MG—Multigrid	2600	X	X	X	
FT—Discrete 3D Fast Fourier Transform	2200	X	X	X	
BT—Block Tridiagonal solver	9200	X	X	X	
SP—Scalar Pentadiagonal Solver	5000	X	X	X	
LU—Lower Upper Gauss–Seidel Solver	6000	X	X	X	

abbreviations IS, EP, CG, MG, FT, BT, SP, and LU, respectively. A summary of these benchmarks is found in Table 5.5.

Here are the basic instructions on how to install and run the NPB on a laptop or supercomputer:

```
wget https://www.nas.nasa.gov/assets/npb/NPB3.4.2.tar.gz
tar -xf NPB3.4.2.tar.gz
cd NPB3.4.2/NPB3.4-MPI/config/
cp make.def.template make.def
```

The default compilers in the make.def file are mpif90 and mpicc (specified on lines 32 and 78, respectively). These can be adjusted for the system you are compiling in.

When compiling, three pieces of information must be given: the two letter (lowercase) reference to the benchmark problem, the number of processes on which to run, and the class of problem where the class is one of S, W, A, B, C, D, or E. S indicates a small problem size; W indicates a problem for a 1990s-era workstation; A, B, and C indicate standard problem sizes increasing by a factor of 4 with each letter; D and E indicate large test problems increasing by a factor of 16 by each letter. For example, to compile the integer sort benchmark for a small problem size to be run on four processes, in the NPB3.4-MPI directory we would issue this command:

```
make is NPROCS=4 CLASS=S
```

This will produce an executable called is.S.x in the NPB3.4-MPI/bin directory. Issue the following command:

```
mpirun -np 4 ./is.S.x
```

The output will be sent directly to the standard out of the terminal:

```
NAS Parallel Benchmarks 3.4 -- IS Benchmark
Size: 65536 (class S)
```

```
Iterations: 10
Total number of processes: 4
IS Benchmark Completed
Class           =              S
Size            =          65536
Iterations      =             10
Time in seconds =           0.00
Total processes =              4
Active processes   =           4
Mop/s total     =         703.93
Mop/s/process   =         175.98
Operation type  =    keys ranked
Verification =        SUCCESSFUL
Version         =          3.4.2
```

5.7 MLPerf

With machine learning workloads now taking up a significant fraction of HPC cycles, several efforts to create standard benchmarks to evaluate technology for this type of workload have emerged. Machine learning benchmarks are different in character from the other benchmarks discussed in this chapter because they require large datasets often exceeding 1 TB in size to adequately test the training phase of a machine learning workload. These benchmarks are invariably implemented in Python rather than Fortran, C, or C++ like the other benchmarks discussed in this chapter. Because they frequently involve vendor-specific drivers and multiple components from various machine learning software frameworks, it is easiest to deploy the benchmark using a container platform such as Docker or Singularity/Apptainer. While using a container to run a benchmark may add small performance cost, the convenience benefit achieved in setting up the software and driver prerequisites for the benchmark is worth the cost.

MLCommons (https://github.com/mlcommons) is a collaboration of over 50 members to create standard benchmarks for machine learning workflows, ranging from training to inference, while also establishing benchmarks to improve portability and reproducibility for machine learning workflows. The MLPerf HPC benchmark is one of the outcomes from this collaboration and consists of three machine learning benchmarks: cosmoflow, deepcam, and open_catalyst. Cosmoflow is a 3D convolutional network model implemented using Horovod and Tensorflow that uses dark matter simulations as the training data. Deepcam is a pattern detection model for climate data implemented using the PyTorch framework. Open catalyst is a machine learning model for investigating catalysts for renewable energy storage. Each of these benchmarks provides a docker recipe file for building a docker container to execute the benchmark. The datasets themselves for running the benchmarks can exceed 1 TB, so using a globus endpoint (https://docs.globus.org/faq/globus-connect-endpoints/) to access the data is important.

Installation instructions and execution of each of these benchmarks vary widely. As an example of a docker execution, here are the instructions for the object detection, which can be run on a single node of an HPC system with an NVIDIA graphics processing unit installed. The training data used is the Coco2017 annotated image dataset (cocodataset.org). The benchmark implementation uses the PyTorch machine learning framework.

```
git clone https://github.com/mlcommons/training.git
cd training/
source install_cuda_docker.sh
cd object_detection/
nvidia-docker build . -t object_detection
source download_dataset.sh
nvidia-docker run -v .:/workspace -t -i --rm --ipc=host object_detection
"cd training/object_detection && ./run_and_time.sh"
```

Performance results for the latest round of MLPerf benchmarks are published regularly; results from round 2.1 can be found here (https://mlcommons.org/en/training-normal-21/).

5.8 Graph500

The Graph500 benchmark was announced in 2010 and is intended to represent data-intensive workloads rather than floating-point-intensive computations, as in HPL. With support from an international steering committee of over 50 members and led by Richard Murphy, the Graph500 benchmark targets three key problems in the context of data-intensive applications: concurrent search, the single-source shortest path, and the maximal independent set. At present, only the concurrent search problem has been specified as Graph500 benchmark 1 and is sometimes also referred to as the Graph500 benchmark. In this section, the Graph500 benchmark 1 will be referred to as the Graph500 search benchmark to avoid confusion.

The Graph500 search benchmark implements the breadth-first search algorithm on a large graph. An illustration of the breadth-first search algorithm is given in Fig. 5.1.

The reference implementation comes with parallelism in several flavors, including MPI and OpenMP for distributed and shared memory settings, and was developed by David Bader, Jonathan Berry, Simon Kahan, Richard Murphy, Jason Riedy, and Jeremiah Willcock. It includes both a graph generator and a breadth-first search implementation. The benchmark starts with a root and finds all reachable vertices from that root; 64 unique roots are checked. There is only one kind of edge, and there are no weights between vertices. The output performance metric is traversed edges per second (TEPS). The resulting search tree is validated to ensure it is the correct tree given the root. The graph construction and the graph search are both timed in the Graph500 search benchmark.

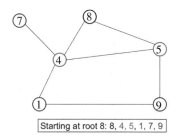

Starting at root 8: 8, 4, 5, 1, 7, 9

FIGURE 5.1 Example of the breadth-first search traversal of this graph data structure starting at vertex 8. The starting vertex is also called the root. The adjacent vertices to the root are 4 and 5, colored red. The adjacent vertices to those are 1, 7, and 9, colored blue. Lines connecting the vertices are called edges.

Installation and execution of the Graph500 benchmark are as follows:

```
wget https://github.com/graph500/graph500/archive/graph500-3.0.0.tar.gz
cd graph500-graph500-3.0.0/
cd src
make
```

This produces four executables: `graph500_reference_bfs_sssp`, `graph500_reference_bfs`, `graph500_custom_bfs`, and `graph500_custom_bfs_sssp`. Each executable requires at least one input to run and can take a second input. The first input supplies the code with the number of vertices:

$$N_{vertices} = 2^{scale} \tag{5.3}$$

The second input is the edgefactor. The number of edges is given by the product of the number of vertices and the edgefactor:

$$N_{edges} = \text{edgefactor} \times N_{vertices} \tag{5.4}$$

The default edgefactor is 16. Problem sizes in the Graph500 search benchmark are classified into six categories: toy, mini, small, medium, large, and huge. These are also referred to as levels 10–15, with level 10 being toy and level 15 being huge. The scale factor for each of these and the associated memory requirements for the graph are given in Table 5.6.

Table 5.6 The Problem Size Classes, Number of Vertices, and Memory Requirements for the Graph500 Search Benchmark

Level	Scale	Size	Vertices (Billions)	Terabytes
10	26	Toy	0.1	0.02
11	29	Mini	0.5	0.14
12	32	Small	4.3	1.1
13	36	Medium	68.7	17.6
14	39	Large	549.8	141
15	42	Huge	4398.0	1,126

The output from the Graph500 benchmark executables is TEPS. A list of the Graph500 benchmark results is maintained at https://graph500.org/ and updated every June and November.

5.9 Microbenchmarks and Miniapplications

Finding the optimal size for a benchmark is challenging. On the one hand, the benchmark should capture fundamental performance behavior without adding too many tangential details. On the other hand, the benchmark should give us some indication of how a real application will perform on a certain technology and help identify what the optimal technology is for that application. Sometimes to answer these questions, it is necessary to use a "microbenchmark" or a "miniapplication" rather than a traditional benchmark.

Microbenchmarks attempt to capture single performance characteristics of a specific operation. They are frequently used in characterizing various aspects of a network's performance. One of most widely used suites of microbenchmarks is the Ohio State University (OSU) Micro-Benchmarks (https://mvapich.cse.ohio-state.edu/benchmarks/). It contains communication benchmarks, including MPI benchmarks for point-to-point communication, collective operations, and one-sided communication. Installation and execution of the OSU microbenchmarks are as follows:

```
wget https://mvapich.cse.ohio-state.edu/download/mvapich/osu-micro-
benchmarks-7.0.1.tar.gz
tar -xf osu-micro-benchmarks-7.0.1.tar.gz
cd osu-micro-benchmarks-7.0.1
./configure CC=mpicc CFLAGS='-O3' CXX=mpicxx CXX_FLAGS='-O3'
make
```

The executables are then placed in the `libexec/osu-micr-benchmarks/mpi/` directory. For example, to run an All-to-All collective test, execute the following:

```
cd libexec/osu-micr-benchmarks/mpi/collective
mpirun -np 4 ./osu_all_to_all
```

The average latency as a function of message size is then reported.

At the other extreme from microbenchmarks are miniapplications, or "miniapps." As the name implies, miniapplications are smaller versions of real applications. They originate from many scientific disciplines and are generally much longer than HPC benchmarks. They do not output any standardized metric like flops or TEPS but do provide time to solution for various domain-specific scientific workloads, as well as strong and weak scaling information. Table 5.7 provides an overview of some common miniapplications from the Mantevo suite [12] organized by Michael Heroux (HPCG benchmark cocreator) and Richard Barrett.

Miniapplications fulfill several roles that are difficult for standard HPC benchmarks. Miniapplications enable large application developers to interact with a

Table 5.7 Some Characteristics of Miniapplications from the Mantevo Suite

Miniapplication	Approximate Line Count	Parallelism			Language		
		MPI	OpenMP	Other	Fortran	C	C++
MiniAMR	9400	X		CUDA, Cilk		X	
MiniFE	14,200	X	X				X
MiniGhost	12,770	X	X	OpenACC	X		
MiniMD	6500	X	X	OpenCL, OpenACC			X
CloverLeaf	9300	X	X	OpenACC, CUDA	X	X	
TeaLeaf	6500	X	X	OpenCL	X		

broader software engineering community by producing simplified, smaller, open-source versions of their application for outside scrutiny and optimization. Miniapplications also serve a key role in testing emerging programming models outside of the scope of conventional parallel programming APIs like MPI and OpenMP. Miniapplications are well suited for performing scaling studies, especially in the context of dynamic simulations running on emerging hardware architectures. Finally, miniapplications are sufficiently complex yet small enough to explore the parameter and interaction space of memory, network, accelerators, and processor elements.

The Mantevo suite contains a large number of open-source miniapplications from a wide array of application domains. Some of these are:

- MiniAMR—a miniapplication for exploring adaptive mesh refinement and dynamic execution with refinement and coarsening of meshes driven by objects passing through the mesh.
- MiniFE—a miniapplication for finite element codes.
- MiniGhost—a miniapplication for exploring halo exchange in the context of a finite differencing application on uniform 3D mesh.
- MiniMD—a miniapplication based on a molecular dynamics workload.
- Cloverleaf—a miniapplication for solving the compressible Euler equations.
- TeaLeaf—a miniapplication based on a workload for solving the linear heat conduction equation.

Some of these miniapplications will be revisited in the context of the software libraries discussion in the Libraries chapter.

In addition to the Mantevo suite, there are a large number of miniapplications maintained at the many supercomputing centers throughout the world. These miniapplications often complement standard HPC benchmarks by playing a significant role in procurement decisions. Consequently, these miniapplications have significant supercomputing vendor involvement as well.

5.10 Summary and Outcomes

- Benchmarking is a way to empirically measure the performance of a supercomputer. A benchmark provides some standardized type of workload that may vary in size or input dataset.
- Computational benchmark workloads come in two types: synthetic, where workloads are designed and created to impose a load on a specific component in the system, and application, where the workload is derived from a real-world application.
- Properties of a good benchmark: good benchmarks are relevant and meaningful to the target application domain, they are applicable to a broad spectrum of hardware architectures, and they are adopted by both users and vendors and enable comparative evaluation.

- Early benchmarks include the floating-point intensive Whetstone benchmark and the integer-oriented Dhrystone benchmark.
- The Linpack benchmark solves a dense, regular system of linear equations and provides an estimate of the system's effective floating-point performance.
- The HPL benchmark is used for ranking supercomputers in the Top 500 list.
- HPL is part of the HPC Challenge benchmark suite that contains seven widely used HPC benchmarks.
- The HPCG benchmark is meant to complement the HPL benchmark in exploring memory and data access patterns in application workloads that are not well represented by HPL. The workload in HPCG centers on a sparse system of linear equations arising from the discretization of a 3D Laplacian partial differential equation with a 27-point stencil.
- HPCG performance continues to be, at best, a small fraction of HPL performance on even the fastest supercomputers in the Top 500 list.
- NPB is a series of small self-contained programs that encapsulate the performance attributes of a large computational fluid dynamics application.
- NPB started as a pencil-and-paper benchmark, but later reference implementations became the benchmark itself in NPB iterations.
- Machine learning benchmarks are different from conventional HPC benchmarks in that they involve enormous dataset sizes.
- To complement HPC benchmarking efforts, both microbenchmarks and miniapplications can help provide a more targeted understanding of HPC technology and application behavior.
- Miniapplications fulfill several roles that are difficult for standard HPC benchmarks, including exploring the parameter and interaction space of memory, network, accelerators, and processor elements, especially in terms of emerging hardware and programming models.

5.11 Exercises

1. Run the HPL benchmark on an accessible supercomputer and on an available laptop. Tune the input parameters independently for each system to get the best possible performance. For what matrix size does the supercomputer give the best HPL performance? At what matrix size does the laptop give the best HPL performance? Explain your results in terms of the system architecture and memory characteristics of HPL.

2. Run the HPCG benchmark on an accessible supercomputer. Compare the peak HPCG performance versus the peak HPL performance. Which performs best and why?

3. Compile and run the HPC Challenge benchmark suite on an accessible supercomputer and on an available laptop. Provide a table with the results

(number and units) of each of the seven problems. Your table should have two columns: test name and a numeric value of a certain metric with its units. Pick only one metric for each problem. Compare the performance between the supercomputer and the laptop.

4. Run the OSU microbenchmarks for MPI on a supercomputer. Where is the sweet spot for message size at large node counts?

5. Explore the performance of the discrete 3D Fourier transform on an accessible supercomputer using the FT NPB. Plot the performance in gigaflops as a function of problem size. What are the peak gigaflops achieved for FT compared with the peak gigaflops achieved for the HPL benchmark on the same supercomputer?

References

1. Wikipedia. ENIAC. [Online] https://en.wikipedia.org/wiki/ENIAC.
2. Longbottom, Roy. History of Whetstone. [Online] http://www.roylongbottom.org.uk/whetstone.htm.
3. Standard Performance Evaluation Corporation. SPEC CPU 2006. [Online] https://www.spec.org/cpu2006/.
4. Netlib. Linpack FAQ. [Online] http://www.netlib.org/utk/people/JackDongarra/faq-linpack.htm.
5. LAPACK. [Online] http://www.netlib.org/lapack/.
6. Innovative Computing Laboratory, The University of Tennessee. HPC Challenge Benchmark Suite. [Online] http://icl.cs.utk.edu/hpcc/.
7. NASA. NAS Parallel Benchmarks. [Online] http://www.nas.nasa.gov/publications/npb.html.
8. Top500. Top500 List. [Online] https://www.top500.org/lists/.
9. HPCG. HPCG Benchmark. [Online] http://www.hpcg-benchmark.org/.
10. Graph500 Benchmark. [Online] https://graph500.org/.

Libraries

6

6.1 Introduction

Typical high performance computing (HPC) applications range from weather fore-casting applications like the Weather Researching and Forecasting (WRF) model to molecular dynamics simulation packages like GROMACS and density functional theory tools like the Vienna Ab Initio Simulation Package (VASP). While these ap-plications come from different computational science domains, their underlying al-gorithms share components that are similar to one another. Consequently, several software libraries have been developed for HPC resources to fill a specific computing need so that the application developers do not have to waste time rede-veloping supercomputing software components that have already been developed elsewhere. Subsequently, these libraries end up becoming required software depen-dencies across many user applications, and their performance and usage become critically important for an application's performance. Libraries targeting numerical linear algebra operations are the most common, given the ubiquity of linear algebra in scientific computing algorithms. Other libraries target operations like I/O, the fast Fourier transform, the finite element method, and solving ordinary differential equa-tions. These libraries have been highly tuned for performance, often for more than a decade, making it difficult for the casual application developer to easily match the library's performance using a homemade equivalent. Because of their ease of use and their highly tuned performance across a wide range of HPC platforms, the use of scientific computing libraries as software dependencies in computational sci-ence applications has become widespread.

Apart from serving as a repository for software reuse, libraries also serve the key role of providing a knowledge base for specific computational science domains.

High Performance Computing. https://doi.org/10.1016/B978-0-12-823035-0.00006-7

Table 6.1 A List of Some Widely Used Libraries on High Performance Computing Systems and Their Associated Application Domain

Application Domain	Widely Used Libraries on High Performance Computing Systems
Linear Algebra	BLAS (1), LAPACK (2), ScaLAPACK (3), GNU Scientific Library (4), SuperLU (5), PETSc (6), SLEPc, ELPA, Hypre (7)
Partial Differential Equations	PETSc (6), Trilinos
Graph Algorithms	Boost Graph Library (8), Parallel Boost Graph Library
I/O	HDF5, Netcdf, Silo
Mesh Decomposition	METIS, ParMETIS
Visualization	VTK
Parallelization	Pthreads, MPI, Boost MPI (8)
Signal Processing	FFTW
Performance Monitoring	PAPI, Vampir

These libraries in turn become community standards and serve as ways the community communicates with one another. Some examples of these are provided in Table 6.1. Among these libraries, BLAS and LAPACK stand out as the most widely used in scientific computing applications. This chapter will introduce these libraries and their usage.

6.2 The Basic Linear Algebra Subprograms

The Basic Linear Algebra Subprograms (BLAS) [1] provides a standard interface to vector, matrix—vector, and matrix—matrix routines that have been optimized for various computer architectures. In addition to the reference implementation [2], which provides both a Fortran 77 and C interface, and the Automatically Tuned Linear Algebra Software (ATLAS) project, which also provides a BLAS implementation, there are multiple vendor-provided BLAS libraries optimized for their respective hardware. Finally, the Boost libraries [8] provide a C++ template class with BLAS functionality called uBLAS.

The BLAS design and implementation was done by Charles Lawson, Richard Hanson, F. Krogh, D. R. Kincaid, and Jack Dongarra beginning in the 1970s, while the genesis of the idea for BLAS is credited to Charles Lawson and Richard Hanson while working at NASA's Jet Propulsion Laboratory. BLAS development coincided with the development of the LINPACK package introduced in Chapter 5. LINPACK was the first major package to incorporate the BLAS library.

The first BLAS routines developed were limited to vector operations, including inner products, norms, adding vectors, and scalar multiplication, and are typified by the operations

$$y = \alpha x + y$$

where x, y are vectors and α is a scalar value. These vector–vector operations are referred to as BLAS Level 1. At the time, the fastest supercomputer in the world was the Control Data Corporation (CDC) 7600 (shown in Fig. 6.1), which had such a small cache size that matrix operations were not possible, thereby limiting the first BLAS routines to vector operations. The CDC 7600 further motivated the BLAS creators to focus on developing a portable linear algebra interface so that others would not have to hand-compile assembly code to fully utilize the CDC 7600's capabilities.

In 1987, about 10 years after BLAS Level 1 was released, routines for matrix–vector operations became available, followed by matrix–matrix operations in 1989. These later additions are the Level 2 (matrix–vector) and Level 3 (matrix–matrix) BLAS operations, typified by

$$y = \alpha A x + \beta y$$

$$C = \alpha A B + \beta C$$

where x, y are vectors, α, β are scalars, and A, B, and C are matrices. Each routine in BLAS has a specific naming convention that specifies the precision of the operation, the type of matrix (if any) involved, and the operation to perform. BLAS is natively written in Fortran 77, but C bindings to BLAS are available via the CBLAS

FIGURE 6.1

A section of the CDC 7600. The CDC 7600 could achieve up to 36 Mflops and was the fastest computer available from 1969 to 1975.

and will be used in this chapter for illustration. For BLAS Level 1 operations, there is no matrix involved and so the naming convention for each routine begins with *cblas_*, after which a precision prefix is placed before the operation name. The core BLAS precision prefixes are summarized in Table 6.2. While these are the core precision prefixes, some BLAS operations support mixed precisions, resulting in combinations of the listed prefixes.

BLAS Level 1 operations can be subdivided into four different subgroups: vector rotations (Table 6.3), vector operations without a dot product (Table 6.4), vector operations with a dot product (Table 6.5), and vector norms (Table 6.6).

Table 6.2 List of Precision Prefixes Used by BLAS Routines

Prefix	Description
s	Single precision (float), 4 bytes
d	Double precision (double), 8 bytes
c	Complex, (two floats), 8 bytes
z	Complex * 16, (two doubles), 16 bytes

Some BLAS operations support mixed precision operations resulting in combinations of the prefixes used in the table as well.

Table 6.3 BLAS Level 1 Rotation Operations

Name	Description	Supported Precisions
rotg	Computes the parameters for a Givens rotation. That is, given scalars a and b, compute c and s so that $$ca + sb = r$$ $$-sa + cb = 0$$ where $$r = \sqrt{\|a\|^2 + \|b\|^2}$$	s,d
rot	Applies the Givens rotation. That is, provided two vectors as input, x and y, each vector element is replaced as follows: $$x_i = cx_i + sy_i$$ $$y_i = -sx_i + cy_i$$ where c and s are the parameters for the Givens rotation (see rotg).	s,d
rotmg	Computes the 2×2 modified Givens rotation matrix, $H = \{h_{ij}\}$. Given scaling factors $d1$ and $d2$ with Cartesian coordinates (x_1, y_1) of an input vector, compute the modified Givens rotation matrix H such that $$x_1 = \sqrt{d_1}h_{11}x_1 + \sqrt{d_2}h_{12}y_1$$ $$y_1 = \sqrt{d_1}h_{21}x_1 + \sqrt{d_2}h_{22}y_1$$	s,d
rotm	Applies the modified Givens rotation. That is, provided two vectors, x and y, compute: $$x_i = h_{11}x_i + h_{12}y_i$$ $$y_i = h_{21}x_i + h_{22}y_i$$ where h_{ij} are the elements of the modified Givens rotation matrix (see rotmg).	s,d

Table 6.4 BLAS Level 1 Vector Operations without a Dot Product

Name	Description	Supported Precisions
swap	Swaps vectors $x \leftrightarrow y$	s,d,c,z
scal	Scales a vector by a constant $y = \alpha y$	s,d,c,z,cs,zd
copy	Copies a vector $y = x$	s,d,c,z
axpy	Updates a vector $y = \alpha x + y$	s,d,c,z

Note that the scal operation supports mixed precisions, where the α is a single-precision or double-precision constant that can be multiplied by a complex vector.

Table 6.5 BLAS Level 1 Vector Operations Involving a Dot Product

Name	Description	Supported Precisions
dot	Dot product $x^T y$	s,d,ds
dotc	Complex conjugate dot product $x^h y$	c,z
dotu	Complex dot product $x^T y$	c,z
sdsdot	Dot product plus a scalar $\alpha + x^T y$	s,ds

Table 6.6 BLAS Level 1 Vector Operations Involving a Norm

Name	Description	Supported Precisions
nrm2	Compute the 2-norm $\sqrt{\sum |x_i|^2}$	s,d,sc,dz
asum	Compute the 1-norm $\sum |x_i|$	s,d,sc,dz
i_amax	Compute the ∞-norm $\max(|x_i|)$	s,d,c,z

BLAS Level 2 and Level 3 operations involve matrices and indicate the type of matrix they support in their name. Level 2 and Level 3 names are of the form *cblas_*pmmoo where the p indicates the precision, mm indicates the matrix type, and oo indicates the operation. Matrix types are listed in Table 6.7. Apart from general matrices, all other matrix types come in three storage scheme flavors: dense (default), banded (indicated by a "b" in the name), and packed (indicated by a

Table 6.7 Matrix Types Supported in BLAS Level 2 and 3

Matrix Type	Description
General: ge,gb	General, nonsymmetric, possibly rectangular matrix
Symmetric: sy,sb, sp	Symmetric matrix. This is a special class of square matrix that is equal to its own transpose. So, for matrix A with elements a_{ij}, a symmetric matrix would have elements that satisfy $a_{ij} = a_{ji}$.
Hermitian: he,hb,hp	Hermitian matrix. This is a special class of square matrix that is equal to its own Hermitian conjugate. So, for matrix A with elements a_{ml}, matrix A is Hermitian if all elements satisfy $a_{ml} = \overline{a_{lm}}$ where the overbar is the complex conjugate.
Triangular: tr,tb,tp	Triangular matrix. This is a special class of square matrices where all the entries above the diagonal are zero (lower triangular) or all the entries below the diagonal are zero (upper triangular).

"p" in the name). Dense storage schemes are either row-based or column-based storage in a continuous memory array. Packed storage schemes hold matrix values that are packed by rows or columns in a one-dimensional array, while band storage is applied to those sparse matrices where the nonzero entries lie in diagonal bands. An example of a banded matrix is a tridiagonal matrix that has nonzero column entries at the $i - 1$, i, and $i + 1$ columns for the ith row. In band storage for a banded matrix, the diagonal bands to the left of the main diagonal ("subdiagonals") and diagonal bands to the right of the diagonal ("superdiagonals") are placed in a two-dimensional array.

BLAS Level 2 and Level 3 operations are summarized in Table 6.8.

As an example, the name of the BLAS Level 3 routine *cblas_dgemm* indicates that this routine will perform a double-precision dense matrix—matrix multiplication. DGEMM is also the name for the matrix—matrix multiplication benchmark

Table 6.8 BLAS Level 2 and Level 3 Operations

Name	Description
mv	Matrix—vector product
sv	Solve matrix (only for triangular matrices)
mm	Matrix—matrix product, $C = \alpha AB + \beta C$ where A, B, C are matrices and α, β are scalars
rk	Rank-k update, $C = \alpha AA^{\mathsf{T}} + \beta C$ where A, C are matrices and α, β are scalars
r2k	Rank-2k update, $C = \alpha AB^{\mathsf{T}} + \overline{\alpha}BA^{\mathsf{T}} + \beta C$ where A, B, C are matrices and α, β are scalars

in the HPC Challenge Benchmark introduced in Chapter 5. Installation of *cblas* may be done as follows:

```
wget http://www.netlib.org/blas/blast-forum/cblas.tgz
tar -xf cblas.tgz
cd CBLAS/
make
```

The *cblas_dgemm* routine takes 14 arguments, shown here:

```
void cblas_dgemm(const enum CBLAS_ORDER Order, const enum
  CBLAS_TRANSPOSE TransA,
  const enum CBLAS_TRANSPOSE TransB, const int M, const int N,
  const int K, const double alpha, const double *A,
  const int lda, const double *B, const int ldb,
  const double beta, double *C, const int ldc)
```

- *Order* indicates the storage layout as either row-major or column-major. This input is either *CblasRowMajor* or *CblasColMajor*.
- *TransA* indicates whether to transpose matrix A. This input is either *CblasNo-Trans, CblasTrans,* or *CblasConjTrans*, indicating no transpose, transpose, or complex conjugate transpose, respectively.
- *TransB* indicates whether to transpose matrix B. Acceptable options are the same as those listed for A.
- *M* indicates the number of rows in matrices A and C.
- *N* indicates the number of columns in matrices B and C.
- *K* indicates the number of columns in matrix A and the number of rows in matrix B. This is the shared index between matrices A and B.
- *alpha* is the scaling factor for A * B.
- *A* is the pointer to matrix A data.
- *lda* is the size of the first dimension of matrix A.
- *B* is the pointer to matrix B data.
- *lbd* is the size of the first dimension of matrix B.
- *beta* is the scaling factor for matrix C.
- *C* is the pointer to matrix C data.
- *ldc* is the size of the first dimension of matrix C.

An example of matrix—matrix multiplication for 3×3 matrices is as follows:

```
1 #include <stdio.h>
2 #include <stdlib.h>
3 #include <cblas.h>
4
5 int main()
6 {
7 double *A, *B, *C;
8 int m = 3; // square matrix, number of rows and columns
9 int i,j;
10
11 A = (double *) malloc(m*m*sizeof(double));
12 B = (double *) malloc(m*m*sizeof(double));
```

```
13 C = (double *) malloc(m*m*sizeof(double));
14
15 // initialize the matrices
16 for (i=0;i<m;i++) {
17   for (j=0;j<m;j++) {
18     A[j + m*i] = j + m*i; // arbitrarily initialized
19     B[j + m*i] = 3.14*(j + m*i);
20     C[j + m*i] = 0.0;
21   }
22 }
23 double alpha = 1.0;
24 double beta = 0.0;
25
26 cblas_dgemm(CblasRowMajor, CblasNoTrans, CblasNoTrans,
27         m, m, m, alpha, A, m, B, m, beta, C, m);
28
29 for (i=0;i<m;i++) {
30   for (j=0;j<m;j++) {
31     printf(" A[%d][%d]=%g ",i,j,A[j+m*i]);
32   }
33   printf("\n");
34 }
35
36 for (i=0;i<m;i++) {
37   for (j=0;j<m;j++) {
38     printf(" B[%d][%d]=%g ",i,j,B[j+m*i]);
39   }
40   printf("\n");
41 }
42
43 for (i=0;i<m;i++) {
44   for (j=0;j<m;j++) {
45     printf(" C[%d][%d]=%g ",i,j,C[j+m*i]);
46   }
47   printf("\n");
48 }
49
50
51 free(A);
52 free(B);
53 free(C);
54 return 0;
55 }
```

The call to *cblas_dgemm* is on lines 26–27. Lines 29–48 are for printing the resulting matrices.

6.3 Linear Algebra PACKage

The Linear Algebra PACKage (LAPACK) [2] was developed by a collaboration between Jack Dongarra, James Demmel, and others and provides driver routines designed to solve complete problems such as solving a system of linear equations, solving eigenvalue problems, or solving singular value problems. It also provides computational routines that can perform specific tasks like lower/upper (LU) or Cholesky factorization. Certain auxiliary routines are provided for common subtasks. LAPACK requires BLAS Level 2 and Level 3 functionality, and it supersedes the LINPACK library. Unlike LINPACK, which also required BLAS but which targeted vector machines with shared memory, LAPACK is designed around the cache-based memory hierarchies found on modern supercomputers. It was initially written in Fortran 77 but switched to Fortran 90 in 2008. A C interface to LAPACK is provided by using LAPACKE.

The naming scheme for LAPACK routines is like BLAS. All routines are in the form of XYYZZZ where X is the data type (one of s, d, c, or z as in Table 6.2), YY is the type of matrix, and ZZZ is the computation performed. LAPACK matrix types share all the BLAS matrix types in Table 6.7 and use the same names. LAPACK also adds some additional matrix types, including unitary matrices and symmetric positive definite matrices, among others. Like BLAS, LAPACK provides support for dense, banded, and packed storage formats but not for general sparse matrices. Driver routines are summarized in Table 6.9. Expert versions of some of these

Table 6.9 LAPACK Driver Routines

Driver Name	Description
SV	Solver for system of linear equations: $Ax = b$
LS, LSY, LSS, LSD	Solver for linear least squares problems: minimize x in $||b - Ax||_2$ where A is not necessarily a square matrix, generally with more rows than columns, as would occur in an overdetermined system of linear equations
LSE	Linear equality-constrained least squares problems: minimize x in $||c - Ax||_2$ subject to the constraint that $Bx = d$ where A is an $m \times n$ matrix, c is a vector of size m, B is a $p \times n$ matrix, and d is a vector of size p, where $p \leq n \leq m + p$.
GLM	General linear model problems: minimize x in $||y||_2$ subject to the constraint that $d = Ax + By$ where A is an $m \times n$ matrix, B is an $n \times p$ matrix, d is a vector of size n, and $m \leq n \leq m + p$.
EV, EVD, EVR	Symmetric eigenvalue problems: find eigenvalues λ and eigenvectors k where $Ak = \lambda k$ for a symmetric matrix A.
ES	Nonsymmetric eigenvalue problems: find eigenvalues λ and eigenvectors k where $Ak = \lambda k$ for nonsymmetric matrix A.
SVD, SDD	Compute the singular value decomposition of an $m \times n$ matrix A: $A = UDV^T$ where matrices U and V are orthogonal and D is a diagonal real matrix of size $m \times n$ containing the singular values of matrix A.

Some of these drivers also come in an expert flavor accessible by appending an x to the name. The expert flavor provides additional functionality but also generally requires more memory. In some cases, multiple drivers are available to solve the same problem type using different algorithms.

drivers are available by appending an *x* to the name. The expert version provides more functionality but also generally requires more memory. In some cases, multiple driver routines are available to solve the same problem type reflecting different underlying algorithms.

While LAPACK is written in Fortran, C bindings to LAPACK are available through the LAPACKE library, which comes with LAPACK. Fortran routines in LAPACK can be called directly from C code, but the C bindings simplify code portability. The naming convention for LAPACKE remains the same as LAPACK but prefixes *LAPACKE_* to each routine. Installation of LAPACK may be done as follows:

```
wget https://github.com/Reference-LAPACK/lapack/archive/refs/tags/
v3.11.0.tar.gz
tar -xf v3.11.0.tar.gz
cd lapack-3.11.0/
mkdir build
cd build
cmake -DCMAKE_INSTALL_LIBDIR=$HOME/lapack_install ..
make
make install
```

An example solving a system of linear equations in double precision using LAPACK is given below. This example solves $Ax = b$ where A is a 3×3 matrix and b is a 3×1 vector.

```
1 #include <stdio.h>
2 #include <lapacke.h>
3
4 int main (int argc, const char * argv[])
5 {
6 double A[3][3]= {1,3,2,4,1,9,5,7,2};
7 double b[3]= {-1,-1,1};
8 lapack_int ipiv[3];
9 lapack_int info,m,lda,ldb,nrhs;
10 int i,j;
11
12 m = 3;
13 nrhs = 1;
14 lda = 3;
15 ldb = 1;
16
17 // Solve the linear system
18 info = LAPACKE_dgesv(LAPACK_ROW_MAJOR,m,nrhs,*A,lda,ipiv,b,ldb);
19
20 // check for singularity
21 if (info > 0 ) {
22 printf(" U(%d,%d) is zero! A is singular\n",info,info);
23 return 0;
```

```
24 }
25
26 // print the answer
27 for (i=0;i<m;i++) {
28 printf(" b[%i] = %g\n",i,b[i]);
29 }
30
31 printf( "\n" );
32 return 0;
33 }
```

In this example, the C interface to LAPACK is called in line 18; the matrix is defined on line 6; and the vector is defined on line 7. Lines 26–28 print the solution; notice that the solution is stored in the same memory as the input b vector to save space.

The LAPACK library is frequently a requirement for compiling and using many different supercomputing applications. LAPACK itself, however, does not use the message passing. There is a version of LAPACK that is built on message passing called ScaLAPACK [3] that, like LAPACK, supports dense and banded matrices but not general sparse matrices.

6.4 General Sparse Linear Algebra

The linear algebra operations supported in BLAS and LAPACK are designed for matrices that are dense (dominated by nonzero elements) or banded. However, when a matrix is dominated by zero entries outside of a banded structure, new techniques and libraries are needed to support this modality. Here is a brief overview of some widely used libraries for these types of operations:

- The GNU scientific library (GSL) [4] provides a wide array of linear algebra routines including an interface to BLAS for C and C++ and supports general sparse matrices as well as iterative solvers for sparse systems of linear equations.
- Supernodal LU (SuperLU) [5] is a library for direct solves of general sparse systems of equations through LU decomposition on HPC systems. It supports shared memory and distributed memory architectures and accelerator architectures such as graphical processing units (GPUs).
- The portable, extensible toolkit for scientific computation (PETSc) [6] was started in 1991 and led by William Gropp with the goal of providing a suite of data structures and routines to aid application scientists in solving partial differential equations on HPC resources. As the discretization of partial differential equations often results in a large system of sparse linear equations, PETSc provides a suite of parallel iterative linear equation solvers.
- The HYPRE library [7] provides a set of highly scalable preconditioners for systems of linear equations and scalable iterative solvers and algebraic multi-grid algorithms that have found broad usage in the HPC community.

6.5 Summary and Outcomes

- Several software libraries have been developed for HPC resources to fill a specific computing need so that the application developers do not have to waste time redeveloping supercomputing software that has already been developed elsewhere.
- Apart from serving as a repository for software reuse, libraries also serve the key role of providing a knowledge base for specific computational science domains.
- Libraries in turn become community standards and serve as ways the community communicates with one another.
- BLAS provides a standard interface to vector, matrix−vector, and matrix−matrix routines that have been optimized for various computer architectures.
- BLAS Level 1 operations involve vector operations. The naming scheme with C bindings is a *cblas_*, after which a precision prefix is placed before the operation name. Operations include dot products, norms, and rotations, among others.
- BLAS Level 2 and Level 3 operations involve matrices and incorporate the type of matrix they support in their name. Level 2 and Level 3 names are of the form *cblas_*pmmoo where the p indicates the precision, mm indicates the matrix type, and oo indicates the operation.
- LAPACK incorporates BLAS Level 2 and 3 to provide full problem drivers such as eigenvalue problems and linear solvers. A high performance version of LAPACK is available: ScaLAPACK.

6.6 Exercises

1. Explore the performance of matrix−matrix multiplication using the BLAS Level 3 dgemm routine for increasingly larger matrix sizes. Start with a randomly generated dense 3×3 matrix and incrementally increase the matrix size. For timing comparison, compute the matrix−matrix multiplication yourself just using for-loops without any BLAS calls for each matrix size explored. For each matrix size, which performs better, and by how much? Produce a plot comparing the time to solution for matrix−matrix multiplication with and without BLAS for each matrix size explored.

2. Using the DLATMR routine in LAPACK to generate random square test matrices, compute the vector $b = Au$ where u is a vector whose elements are all 1 and A is the random matrix. Then use LAPACK to solve the linear system $Ax = b$ for x. Check the solution to be sure that all elements of x are 1 after the solve. Produce a plot of the performance for solving $Ax = b$ for a wide variety of matrix sizes beginning with matrix sizes of 3×3 and exploring both symmetric and nonsymmetric test matrices.

3. The interfaces to BLAS and LAPACK can often be unwieldy. Domain-specific languages for numerical linear algebra can be much easier to read and use but often come with a performance penalty. Using the BLAZE domain-specific language (https://bitbucket.org/blaze-lib/blaze/src/master/), compare performance with BLAS. Which is faster, and by how much? Which is easier to use?

4. Use PETSc and the message-passing interface (MPI) to compute the sparse matrix vector product of a matrix and vector with randomly generated elements on a distributed memory architecture. Select several sparse matrices to explore from the Matrix Market repository (https://math.nist.gov/MatrixMarket/) and plot the time to solution as a function of the number of MPI processes used for the solve.

References

[1] BLAS (Basic Linear Algebra Subprograms). [Online] http://www.netlib.org/blas/.
[2] LAPACK—Linear Algebra PACKage. [Online] http://www.netlib.org/lapack/.
[3] ScaLAPACK—Scalable Linear Algebra PACKage. [Online] http://www.netlib.org/scalapack/.
[4] GSL—GNU Scientific Library. [Online] https://www.gnu.org/software/gsl/.
[5] SuperLU Developers. SuperLU. [Online] http://crd-legacy.lbl.gov/~xiaoye/SuperLU/.
[6] PETSc Team. Portable, Extensible Toolkit for Scientific Computation. [Online] https://www.mcs.anl.gov/petsc/.
[7] HYPRE. [Online] https://github.com/hypre-space/hypre.
[8] Boost C++ Libraries. [Online] https://www.boost.org/

The Essential SLURM: Resource Management

High Performance Computing. https://doi.org/10.1016/B978-0-12-823035-0.00007-9

7.1 **Managing Resources**

Supercomputer installation frequently represents a significant financial investment by the hosting institution. However, the expenses don't stop after the hardware acquisition and deployment is complete. The hosting data center needs to retain dedicated system administrators, pay for support contracts and/or a maintenance staff, and, finally, cover the cost of electricity used to power and cool the machine. Together these are referred to as "cost of ownership". The latter is frequently overwhelming for large installations. A commonly quoted average is over US$1 million for each megawatt of power consumed per year in the United States; in many other countries this figure may be much higher. It is not surprising that the institutions pay close attention to how the supercomputing resources are used efficiently and how to maximize their utilization.

Resource management software plays a critical role in how supercomputing system resources are allocated to user applications. It not only helps accommodate different workload sizes and durations but also exposes uniform interfaces across different machine types and their configurations, simplifying access to them and easing portability concerns. Resource management middleware provides mechanisms through which computing systems may be made available to various categories of users (even those external to the hosting institution) with accurate accounting and charging for the resource use. Resource management tools are the inherent part of the high performance computing (HPC) software stack. They perform three principal functions: resource allocation, workload scheduling, and support for distributed workload execution and monitoring. Resource managers commonly recognize the following resource types:

- *Compute nodes.* Increasing the number of nodes assigned to the parallel application is the simplest way to scale the size of the dataset (such as the number of grid points in a simulation domain) on which the work is to be performed or reduce the execution time for a fixed workload size by distributing the same dataset across the greater number of nodes. Node count is therefore one of the most important parameters requested when scheduling an application launched on a multicomputer. Even single physical computers may include various node types. They may differ in memory capacity, central processing unit (CPU) types, clock frequency, local storage characteristics, available interconnects, etc. Properly configured resource managers permit selection of the right kind of node for the job, precluding assigning of resources that will likely go unused.
- *Processing cores (processing units, processing elements).* Most modern supercomputer nodes feature one or more multicore processors, providing local parallelism to applications that support it through multithreading or by accommodating several concurrent single-threaded processes. For that reason, resource managers provide the option of specifying either *shared* or *exclusive* allocation of nodes to workloads. Shared nodes are useful in situations where already assigned workloads would leave some of the cores unoccupied. By

coscheduling different processes on the remaining cores, better utilization may be achieved. However, this comes at a cost: all programs executing on the shared node will also share access to other physical components, such as main memory, network interfaces, or input/output (I/O) buses. Users who perform careful benchmarking of their applications are frequently better off allocating the nodes in exclusive user mode to minimize the contention and resulting degradation caused by unrelated programs interfering with each other. Another reason to use exclusive allocation is for programs that rely on the affinity of the executing code to specific cores to achieve good performance. For example, programs that rely on the lowest communication latency may want to place the message sending and receiving threads on cores close to the PCI express bus connected to the related network card. This may not be possible when multiple applications enforce their own, possibly conflicting, affinity settings at the same time.

- *Interconnect.* While many systems are built with only one network type, there are installations that include multiple networks, in some instances involving different interconnect technologies such as Gigabit Ethernet (GigE) and Infiniband (IBA). Selection of the appropriate message fabric configuration depends on the application characteristics and needs. For example, is the program execution more sensitive to communication latency, or does it need as much communication bandwidth as possible? Can it take advantage of channel bonding using different network interfaces? Often, the answer may be imposed by the available version of the communication library with which the application has been linked. For example, it is common to see message-passing interface (MPI) installations with separate libraries supporting InfiniBand and Ethernet if both such network types are available. Selecting a wrong network type will likely result in less efficient execution.

- *Permanent storage and I/O options.* Many clusters rely on shared file systems that are exported to every node in the system. This is convenient since storing a program compiled on the head node and stored in such a file system will expose it to all of the compute nodes as well. Computations may also easily share a common dataset, with modifications visible to the relevant applications already during their runtime. However, not all installations provide efficient high-bandwidth file systems that are scalable to all machine resources and that can accommodate concurrent accesses by multiple users. For programs performing a substantial amount of file I/O, taking advantage of localized storage, such as local disks of individual nodes or burst buffers (fast solid-state device pools servicing I/O requests locally in predefined node groups), may be a better solution. Such local storage pools are typically mounted under a predefined directory path. The drawback to this is that the datasets generated this way will have to be explicitly moved to the front-end storage after job completion to permit general access for postprocessing (analysis, visualization, etc.). Unfortunately, there is no single solution available, requiring users to consult local machine guides to determine the best option for their application and how it can be conveyed to the resource management software.

- *Accelerators.* Heterogeneous architectures that employ accelerators (graphics processing units [GPUs], field programmable gate array modules, etc.) in addition to main CPUs are a common way to increase the aggregate computational performance while minimizing power consumption. However, it also complicates resource management, since the same machine may consist of some nodes that are populated with accelerators of one type, some nodes that are populated with accelerators of a different type, and some nodes that do not contain any accelerating hardware at all. Modern resource managers will permit the users to specify parameters of their jobs so that the appropriate node types are selected for a given application requirement. At the same time, programs that do not need accelerators may be confined to regular nodes as much as possible for the best resource utilization over multiple jobs.

Resource managers allocate the available computing resources to *jobs* specified by the users. A job is a self-contained work unit with associated input data that, during its execution, produces some output result data. The output may be as little as a line of text displayed on the console, a multiterabyte dataset stored in multiple files, or a stream of information transmitted over the local or wide area network to another machine. Jobs may be executed *interactively*, thus involving the user's presence at the console to provide additional input at runtime as required, or use *batch processing*, where all necessary parameters and inputs for job execution are specified before it is launched. Batch processing provides much greater flexibility to the resource manager since it can decide to launch the job when it is optimal from the standpoint of HPC system utilization, not being hindered by the availability of a human operator, for example, at night. For this reason, interactive jobs on many machines may be permitted to use only a limited set of resources.

Jobs may be monolithic or subdivided into a number of smaller *steps* or *tasks*. Typically, each such task is associated with the launch of a specific application program. Individual steps do not have to be identical in terms of used resources or duration of execution. Jobs may also mix parallel application invocations with instantiations of single-threaded processes, dramatically changing the required resource footprint. An example of that is a job that first preprocesses input data, copying them to storage local to its execution nodes, then launches the application that performs high-bandwidth access to the data, and finally copies the output files to shared storage using shell commands.

Pending computing jobs are stored in job *queues*. The job queue defines the order in which jobs are selected by the resource manager for execution. As the computer science definition of the word suggests, in most cases it is "first come, first serve" or "FIFO", although good job schedulers will relax this scheme to boost machine utilization, improve response time, or otherwise optimize some aspect of the system as indicated by the operator (user or system administrator). Most systems typically use multiple job queues, each with a specific purpose and set of scheduling constraints. Thus, one may find an interactive queue solely for interactive jobs. Similarly, a debug queue may be employed that permits jobs to run in a restricted parallel environment that is big enough to expose problems when running on multiple nodes using the same configuration as the production queue, yet small enough that the pool of nodes for production jobs may remain substantially larger. Frequently, there are multiple production queues available, each with a different maximum execution time imposed on jobs or on total job size (short versus long, large versus small, etc.). With hundreds to thousands of jobs with different properties pending in all queues of a typical large system, it is easy to see why scheduling algorithms are critical to achieving high job throughput as well as adequate user satisfaction. Common parameters that affect job scheduling include:

- *Availability of execution and auxiliary resources* is the primary factor that determines when a job can be launched.
- *Priority* permits more privileged jobs to execute sooner or even preempt currently running jobs of lower priority.
- *Resources allocated to the user* determine the long-term resource pool a specific user may consume while his or her account on the machine remains active.
- *Maximum number of jobs* that a user is permitted to execute simultaneously.
- *Requested execution time* estimated by the user for the job.
- *Elapsed execution time* may cause forced job termination or impact staging of pending jobs for the upcoming execution.
- *Job dependencies* determine launching order of multiple related jobs, especially in producer–consumer scenarios.
- *Event occurrence* when the job start is postponed until a specific predefined event occurs.
- *Operator availability* impacts the launch of interactive applications.
- *Software license availability* if a job is requesting the launch of proprietary code.

Resource managers use optimized mechanisms that enable efficient launching of thousands or more processes across a comparable number of nodes. Naïve approaches, such as repeated invocation of a remote shell, will not yield acceptable results at scale due to high contention when transferring multiple programs' executables to the target nodes. Job launchers employ hierarchical mechanisms to alleviate the bandwidth requirements and exploit network topology to minimize the amount of data transferred and overall launch time. Resource managers must be able to terminate any job that exceeds its execution time or other resource limits irrespective of its current processing status. Again, distributed termination should be efficient to release the allocated nodes to the pool of available nodes as quickly as possible. Finally, resource managers are responsible for monitoring the application execution and keeping track of related resource usage. The actual resource utilization data are recorded to enable accounting and accurate charging of the users for their cumulative system resource usage.

A number of resource management suites have been created that differ in their features, capabilities, and adoption level. The software commonly used today includes:

- *Simple Linux Utility for Resource Management (Slurm)* [1] is a widely used free open-source package and the example system discussed in this chapter.
- *Portable Batch System (PBS)* [2] was originally available as proprietary code developed by Altair Engineering and was open-sourced to the HPC community in 2016.
- *Moab Cluster Suite* [3], based on the open-source Maui Cluster Scheduler, is a highly scalable proprietary resource manager developed by Adaptive Computing Inc.
- *LoadLeveler* [4], currently known as the Tivoli Workload Scheduler LoadLeveler, is a proprietary IBM product originally targeting systems running the AIX operating system (OS) but later ported to POWER and x86-based Linux platforms.
- *Altair Grid Engine* [5] uses technology originally developed by Sun Microsystems, Oracle, and Univa that supports multiple platforms and OSs.
- *HTCondor* [6], formerly known just as Condor, is an open-source framework for coarse-grain high-throughput computing.
- *OAR* [7] provides database-centered resource and task management for both HPC clusters and some classes of distributed systems.
- *Apache Hadoop Yet Another Resource Negotiator (YARN)* [8] is a broadly deployed scheduler specifically tailored to MapReduce applications.

Unfortunately, there is no common standard specifying the command format, language, and configuration of resource management. Every system mentioned above uses its own interface and supports different sets of capabilities, although the basic functionality is essentially similar. Below is discussed possibly one of the most broadly adopted systems in the HPC community, Slurm.

7.2 The Essential Slurm

Slurm is an open-source, modular, extensible, scalable resource manager and workload scheduling software for clusters and supercomputers running Linux or other Unix-compatible OSs. Slurm origins date back to 2001, when a small team of developers led by Morris Jette at Lawrence Livermore National Laboratory originated the work on advanced scheduling systems for HPC. Since that time, Slurm development grew significantly, extending to nearly 200 contributors as well as multiple institutions, including SchedMD LLC (currently the core company responsible for its development, support, training, and consulting services), Linux NetworX, Hewlett-Packard Enterprise, Groupe Bull, Barcelona Supercomputing Center, Oak Ridge National Laboratory, Los Alamos National Laboratory, Intel, Nvidia, and many others. In April 2022 Slurm was among the most dominant resource management systems, being utilized in approximately 60% of machines in the Top 500 list [9].

The popularity of Slurm is in no small part due to its impressive list of operational features. As an open-source solution, it is available and affordable even to the smallest computing centers or schools. Its core functionality may be extended using plugins written in C or Lua, thus providing complex configuration options such as support for various interconnect types, scheduling algorithms, MPI implementations, accounting, and more. Slurm scales to the largest systems in use today, including the fastest supercomputer of 2023, Frontier at Oak Ridge National Laboratory, with over 9400 compute nodes. It can handle up to 1000 job submissions and 500 job executions per second. A number of strategies are available to optimize the power consumption, ranging from the ability to specify clock frequency for the CPUs to completely powering down the unused nodes—an important feature when power draw for the largest platforms may exceed 10 megawatts. Adjusted power levels can be entered in per job records to account more accurately for resource usage. Single points of failure are eliminated through the use of multiple backup daemons, permitting the affected applications to continue running and request resources to replace those that fail. Network topology factors into resource allocation to minimize the communication latency when it is critical to application execution. Slurm maintains detailed architectural information about each component node, including distribution of cores across NUMA domains and hyperthread affinities. The user may utilize these parameters to optimize binding of tasks to resources. Job sizes are not necessarily fixed over their execution time; they may grow or shrink in accordance with specified size and time limits. Sophisticated scheduling algorithms are available including gang scheduling and preemption. Control over scheduling policies is enabled through constraints specified by the user, a bank account, or quality-of-service metrics. Finally, Slurm integrates support for execution on heterogeneous components, such as GPUs and other accelerators. An optional database may be used to store each job's execution profile, detailing CPU, memory, network, and I/O usage, providing means for postmortem analysis and optimization of system allocation in the future.

7.2.1 **Architecture Overview**

To support its extensive functionality, Slurm employs a collection of daemons (programs continuously running in the background) to interpret user commands and distribute work to individual nodes in the system. Similar arrangements are commonly used also by other cluster resource management systems. Users, including programmers as well as system administrators, issue commands on one of the head nodes. These commands typically communicate with local control daemons *slurmctld*, which relay specific management tasks to the *slurmd* daemons running on the compute nodes. Some commands may directly interact with *slurmd* backends. Each *slurmd* daemon listens to a network connection to accept an incoming work item, execute it, return completion status, and wait for another work unit. These daemons are organized hierarchically to optimize communication and provide fault tolerance. This is illustrated in Fig. 7.1. Slurm may optionally

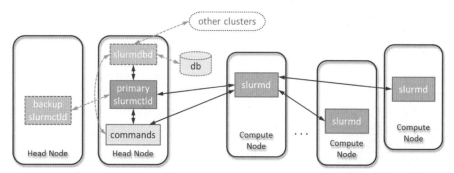

FIGURE 7.1 Simplified architecture of Slurm. Components framed by dashed lines are optional.

support a performance collection database, shown in the figure as an external storage component marked *db* managed by a dedicated daemon, *slurmdbd*. *Slurmdbd* may also connect to other machines to provide a central recording of accounting information for multiple clusters that run the Slurm software suite.

7.2.2 Workload Organization

One of the primary resource types managed by Slurm is the compute node. Nodes are divided into logical sets called *partitions*. Partitions in Slurm represent individual job queues and thus impose specific constraints on user jobs. Depending on the prevalent characteristics of computational workloads and user needs, the cluster administrator may decide to create completely disjoint or overlapping partitions. The latter may be useful to permit the allocation of all available execution resources to certain, usually severely constrained, job types.

The scheduler assigns the available nodes in the partition to the highest-priority eligible jobs until the pool of available nodes is exhausted. The individual tasks composing a job, called *job steps*, may utilize the entire set of nodes allocated to the parent job or only a fraction. The example in Fig. 7.2 shows a 20-node cluster that has been partitioned into two disjoint node sets, `Partition 1` and `Partition 2`. As illustrated in the figure, `Job 1` has been assigned all nodes in `Partition 1` and they are all currently utilized by `Job Step 1`. In `Partition 2`, the scheduler designated only 9 out of 12 available nodes for `Job 2`, and 8 of them are in use by two concurrent job steps, `Job Step 5` and `Job Step 6` (they could be a physics simulation application and connected visualization engine executing in parallel). The remaining three nodes in `Partition 2` could be allocated to another job concurrent with `Job 2` as long as its resource constraints can be satisfied. A typical system would use more meaningful partition names so they are indicative of their function in the system, such as `debug` or `main`. Similarly, good practice calls on the users to label their jobs in a way that permits easy identification of their purpose and configuration variant.

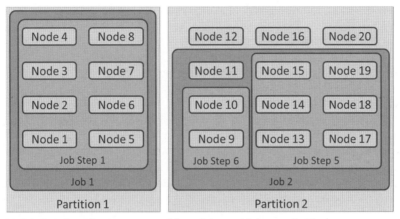

FIGURE 7.2 Relationships between partitions, jobs, and job steps in Slurm.

Slurm uses the concept of *job arrays* to provide highly efficient means for submission and management of collections of similar jobs. While their initial parameters, such as time limit or size, have to be identical, they may be changed later on a per-array or per-job basis. Job arrays may only be batch processed.

7.2.3 Slurm Scheduling

Slurm employs relatively simple default scheduling algorithms to comply with its design goals of efficiency and simplicity. Whenever a job is submitted or completed or system configuration changes, only a limited and predefined number of jobs at the front of the queue will be considered for scheduling. This is called "event-triggered scheduling". This algorithm is complemented by another that attempts to take into consideration all queued jobs before making scheduling decisions. Due to significantly increased overheads, the latter runs at much less frequent intervals. The scheduling algorithm marks the subset of highest-priority eligible jobs that in aggregate satisfy the available resource footprint as pending for execution. As long as there are any pending jobs in a partition, scheduling for that partition is disabled.

Slurm also provides a *backfill* scheduler plugin that can considerably improve the overall arrangement of job execution compared to the priority-based, first-come-first-serve scheduling. For example, low-priority jobs requesting a significant amount of resources could be delayed indefinitely in the queue if the influx of small, higher-priority jobs is high. Due to a larger number of jobs considered for execution, the system utilization may also improve. The backfill scheduler will attempt to start lower-priority jobs if that will not delay the expected start time of any of the higher-priority jobs. Making accurate scheduling decisions relies heavily on job-time-to-completion estimates, defined as the queue configuration parameters and submitted as wall-clock limit estimates with the individual jobs. Therefore, the administrators of many systems often recommend that their users specify these constraints as accurately as possible.

Job scheduling in Slurm is a complex topic, with many additional improvements and scheduler variants available through plugins. Below are briefly discussed some of the more prominent concepts.

7.2.3.1 Gang Scheduling

Gang scheduling supports a scheduling approach in which two or more jobs with similar characteristics are allocated the same set of resources. These jobs are then executed in an alternating fashion so that only one of them obtains the exclusive access to the resources at a time. The time for which a single job retains access to the resources, or a *timeslice*, is a configurable parameter. This scheduling mode permits shorter jobs to be started ahead of longer jobs as long as there are available resources instead of being forced to wait in the queue behind the longer job. As a result, they may be started (and finished) earlier, increasing the overall throughput of the system, measured as jobs completed at a given time.

Slurm spawns a dedicated timeslicer thread that prevents starvation of gang-scheduled jobs. The timeslicer wakes up periodically (at the start of each timeslice period) and checks for suspended jobs. If there are any, the currently running jobs are moved to the end of the queue. The timeslicer then calculates a new allocation for the partition by scanning the queue for suspended jobs that have been waiting the longest to run. If there are other active jobs that can be run concurrently with the newly computed allocation, they are added to it. All other currently running jobs that did not fit into the new allocation are suspended.

7.2.3.2 Preemption

Closely related to gang scheduling is preemption, or stopping of lower-priority jobs to permit the execution of higher-priority jobs. Preemption is implemented using a variant of gang scheduling. Whenever a high-priority job receives a resource allocation that overlaps that already assigned to one or more low-priority jobs, the affected low-priority jobs are preempted. They may resume once the high-priority job completes or, in newer versions of Slurm, be requeued and started by using a different set of resources.

7.2.3.3 Generic Resources

Generic resources (GRES) in Slurm terminology refer to other hardware devices associated with nodes, most frequently accelerators. Using the plugin mechanism, Slurm currently supports GPUs; CUDA Multi-Process Service (MPS), which allows allocation of a fixed percentage of Nvidia devices to different jobs; and a more generic sharing variant called *sharding*, but without isolating processes running on the same device. As there is no default configuration available, the system administrator has to specify the resource name, count, CPUs that may access the resource, device type, and file system pathname that can be used to access or exclusively allocate the device. Only the permitted CPUs may access the device, even though there may be no physical counter indications to disable the access for the remaining CPUs in the node. Unlike other execution resources, GRES allocated to a job will not become available to other jobs when that job gets suspended. The job steps may request fewer generic resources than the amount allocated to the parent job (by default they are allocated all the generic resources that the job holds). This permits easy partitioning of generic resources among concurrent job steps.

7.2.3.4 Trackable Resources

Slurm provides additional options to track the usage of or enforce custom constraints on various kinds of resources. Such trackable resources are identified by their types and names. Trackable resources (TRES) examples include burst buffers, CPUs, energy, GRES, licenses, memory, and nodes. This feature helps establish more accurate formulas to bill for computer usage in which predefined weights may be assigned to each TRES type.

7.2.3.5 Elastic Computing

Elastic computing refers to the computing scenario in which the overall resource footprint available in a system or consumed by a specific job can grow or shrink on demand. This usually relies on external cloud computing services, where the local cluster provides only a part of the resource pool available to all jobs. However, elastic computing may also be implemented on standalone clusters.

Elastic computing may improve power efficiency by explicitly turning off nodes that are not in use. These nodes will be restored to normal operation as soon as there are any jobs assigned to them. To prevent power surges, which are inevitable when powering up or down large groups of nodes, Slurm gradually may change the power consumption at a configurable rate. This typically requires CPU throttling support built into the OS kernel on the affected nodes. The power-saving algorithms drive the node provisioning logic in coordinating the reservation and relinquishing the external nodes to the cloud as needed.

7.2.3.6 High-Throughput Computing

Slurm provides rudimentary support for high-throughput computing, in which a large number of relatively small, loosely coupled jobs are launched over an extended period of time. A correctly tuned Slurm system may execute as many as 500 simple batch jobs per second (sustained), with bursts significantly exceeding this number. Slurm high-throughput job selection logic has been significantly optimized, roughly retaining half of the original scheduling code.

7.2.4 Summary of Commands

The purpose of this section is to familiarize the reader interested in using a system equipped with the Slurm resource manager with the basic commands to perform job submission, job status retrieval, system status query, and basic management of jobs. Commands targeting system administration are beyond the scope of this presentation. Along with each command description, listed are the most frequently used options (both short and long forms are provided if available) and usage examples. The option syntax used below shows literal parameter names and operators except for the following cases:

- Angle brackets, "<" and ">", signify a parameter name, which may expand to a number or a string depending on the context.
- Square brackets, "[" and "]" denote an optional entry.
- Braces, "{" and "}", encompass a list to describe selection of one of the items in that list.

Slurm commands start with lowercase "s" and include:

7.2.4.1 srun

```
srun [<options>] <executable> [<arguments>]
```

The srun command is used to start parallel jobs or job steps on a cluster. If the resources to run the job have not been allocated yet (for example, the command is executed on the head node's terminal), the resource allocation will be performed first. If invoked from an already started job, such as the job's batch script, srun starts a new job step. If the resources to start the job are available, the job is started immediately; otherwise, the command blocks until the resources become available.

The list of options presented below is comprehensive but in no way exhaustive. Many of these options also apply to resource allocation used by other Slurm commands. They are:

```
-N or --nodes=<min_nodes>[-<max_nodes>]
```

This allocates nodes for a job to be executed. The number of nodes has to be at least **min_nodes**, but not to exceed **max_nodes**. The numbers may be followed by the suffix "k" or "m" to signify the multiplier of 1,024 or 1,048,576. Slurm will allocate as many nodes in the range specified as possible without causing additional delays.

```
Example: srun -N1 /bin/bash
```

This starts an interactive shell on one of the compute nodes for the default period of time.

```
-n or --ntasks=<number_of_tasks>
-c or --cpus-per-task=<number_of_cpus>
```

The **ntasks** option specifies the number of tasks (processes) to run and requests allocation of a sufficient number of nodes for them. By default, one task per node is started, unless overridden by the **cpus-per-task** option, which defines the maximum number of cores assigned to each process. The latter may be used to launch multithreaded processes.

```
Example: srun -n4 -c8 my_app
```

This launches four processes using executable my_app, each limited to eight threads of execution. If the cluster has 16-core nodes, two nodes will be allocated for the job, unless the **exclusive** option is used (see below).

`--mincpus=<number_of_cpus>`

This allocates nodes for jobs that have at least number_of_cpus cores per node available.

`Example: srun -n4 -c8 --mincpus=32 my_app`

This will place all four instances of my_app on a single node.

`-B or --extra-node-info=<sockets_per_node>[:<cores_per_socket>[:<threads_`
`per_core>]]`
`--cores-per-socket=<number_of_cores>`
`--sockets-per-node=<number_of_sockets>`
`--threads-per-core=<number_of_threads>`

The first form allocates nodes with a specific number of sockets (physical processors), and optionally given count of cores per socket and threads per core. The last parameter applies to architectures that permit concurrent threads to effectively share execution units, such as Intel processors with hyperthreading. The remaining three options permit independent specification of each parameter.

`Example: srun -N1 -B2:4 my_app`
`        srun -N1 --cores_per_socket=4 -sockets_per_node=2 my_app`

Both examples are equivalent and will allocate one node for application my_app with at least two physical CPUs each containing at least four cores.

`-m or --distribution=<node_distr>[:<socket_distr>[:<core_distr>]]`
`[,{Pack,NoPack}]`

This specifies different distribution modes of the job's tasks across system resources. This may have dramatic implications for application performance, for example, due to grouping the related threads on topologically close resources and separating the unrelated tasks. The option argument contains up to three entries separated by colons, ":," that determine process assignment to nodes, sockets, and cores, respectively. Only the first entry (node distribution) is required. The argument may optionally contain the **Pack** or **NoPack** directive, which either directs the allocator to pack the tasks on the nodes as tightly as possible or forces as even a task distribution as possible. The node distribution parameters are as follows:

- * to accept the default distribution, typically **block.**
- **block** will try to assign consecutive tasks to the same node before moving to the next node.
- **cyclic** distributes consecutive tasks over consecutive nodes in a round-robin fashion.

- **plane = <size>** distributes the processes in blocks of specified **size.** After placing block of **size** processes on one node, it moves to the next node to assign the next block, and so on.
- **arbitrary** mode distributes the tasks in the order specified in the environment variable SLURM_HOSTFILE, defaulting to **block** if the variable is unspecified.

The supported socket and core distribution parameters are identical and include:

- * default mode: **cyclic** for sockets and derived from the socket distribution for cores.
- **block** assigns consecutive tasks to the same socket/core before moving to the next socket or core.
- **cyclic** will assign CPUs consecutively from the same socket/core to the same task and from the next socket/core for the next task in a round-robin fashion.
- **fcyclic,** or "full cyclic," assigns CPUs to tasks across consecutive sockets/cores in a round-robin fashion without trying to group them based on task boundary.

```
Example: srun -n6 -c2 -m'block:cyclic' my_app
         srun -n6 -c2 -mplane=2:fcyclic,NoPack my_app
```

If the first example is submitted on a machine equipped with dual quad-core processors (each core supporting a single thread of execution), two nodes are going to be allocated for the job. Assuming the first socket of node 0 includes cores numbered 0–3 and the second cores 4–7, task 0 will run on cores 0 and 1, task 1 on cores 4 and 5, task 2 on cores 2 and 3, and task 3 on cores 6 and 7. The remaining tasks are going to be instantiated on node 1, with task 4 using cores 0 and 1, and task 5 cores 4 and 5.

Launching the second example on the same platform results in allocation of three nodes. Tasks 0 and 1 are assigned node 0, tasks 2 and 3 node 1, and tasks 4 and 5 node 3. Individual tasks within the node use cores 0 and 4 (first task) and 1 and 5 (second task).

```
-w or --nodelist=<list_of_nodes>
```

This requests specific nodes for job execution. The list may contain individual node names separated by commas or node ranges. If **list_of_nodes** contains a "/" (forward slash character), it will be assumed to represent a path to a file containing the node list. Note that if the specified node list is not sufficient to support the job, the system will attempt to allocate additional nodes as required.

```
Example:srun —wnode0[4-6],node08 —N6 my_app
```

This will allocate nodes 4, 5, 6, and 8 plus two more not explicitly specified ones for the total of six required tasks.

```
--mem=<megabytes>
--mem-per-cpu=<megabytes>
```

These control the allocation of physical memory. The first form specifies the total memory per node required for job execution. The value of zero specified in the job step invocation restricts that job step to memory allocated to the parent job. The second option is used to limit the amount of memory allocated to individual processors.

Only one of these options may be specified at a time.

`Example: srun -N2 -c8 --mem-per-cpu=4096 my_app`

"my_app" will be allocated 32 GB of memory (or 4 GB per core) on each of the two assigned nodes.

`--hint=<type>`

This allocates resources based on a literal hint describing the job's properties:

- **compute_bound** causes allocation of all cores in each socket with one thread per core.
- **memory_bound** uses one core in each socket and one thread per core.
- **[no]multithread** instructs the system (not) to use multiple threads per core, which could improve the performance of communication-intensive applications.

`Example: srun -N48 --hint=compute_bound bh_mol`

This will start the compute-bound application "bh_mol" on all cores of 48 assigned nodes.

`--ntasks-per-core=<number>`
`--ntasks-per-socket=<number>`
`--ntasks-per-node=<number>`

These set the upper bound for the number of tasks per core, socket, and node, respectively. The last option is useful for starting mixed MPI/OpenMP jobs that require that only one MPI process is created per node that utilizes multiple threads for increased local parallelism.

`Example: srun -N16 --ntasks-per-node=16 mpirun my_sim`

This will launch an MPI application on 16 nodes utilizing a total of 256 threads.

`--multi-prog`

This runs a job consisting of different programs with different arguments. A configuration file listing the applications with related arguments for each task is required. A path to that file replaces the usual executable name at the end of the **srun** command line. The syntax of this file is explained in the section on job scripting.

`--exclusive[=user]`
`-s or --oversubscribe`

These affect resource undersubscription and oversubscription. The first option suppresses node sharing with other jobs. If the optional parameter **user** is specified, the node won't be shared with jobs submitted by other users but may be available to jobs owned by the same user. When used for job step launch, each of the concurrently executing job steps is assigned a separate processor. If such assignment is not possible at the time of invocation, launch of the job step may be deferred.

The **oversubscribe** option permits the resource oversubscription with other jobs that may apply to nodes, sockets, cores, and hyperthreads depending on system configuration. Jobs enabling oversubscription may obtain their resource allocation sooner and thus be started earlier than in exclusive mode.

Example: `srun -n4 -c2 --exclusive my_app`

This launches each of the four my_app instances on a separate node even if the nodes have four or more cores.

`--gres=<resource_list>`

The is used to specify generic resources. Each entry in the list has a format of **<name>[[:<type>]:count]**, where name is the name of the resource, count indicates the number of allocated units (one being the default), and type further restricts the resource to a specific class. When used with job steps, using **--gres=none** prevents specific the job step from using any of the resources allocated to the job (by default job steps are permitted to use all GRES allocated to the job). Simultaneous job steps may also partition the job resources by defining their own GRES allocations.

Example: `srun -N16 --gres=gpu:kepler:2 my_app`

The example allocates 16 nodes, each equipped with two Kepler GPUs, for the my_app job. To inquire for GRES descriptions available in the system, issue "`srun --gres=help`".

`-C or --constraint=<features>`

This specifies additional resource constraints to apply. The option parameter may be a feature name, a feature name with associated node count, or an expression formed by concatenating its clauses using the following operators:

- AND ("&"): only the nodes containing all specified features are selected.
- OR ("|"): only the nodes containing at least one of the listed features are chosen.
- Matching OR ("[<feature1>|<feature2>|...]"): variant of OR where precisely one of the alternatives is matched.

Currently, jobs steps may only use a single feature name as a constraint (no operators are supported). Features are defined by administrators and therefore meaningful only on a specific system.

Example: `srun -n4 -C 'big_mem*2|small_mem*4' my_app`
`        srun -N8 -C '[rack1|rack3|rack5]' my_app`

The first example reserves two large memory nodes or four nodes with small memory capacity and starts four user processes on the selection. The second command allocates eight nodes within a single rack selected from three possibilities.

`-t or --time=<time>`

One of the most frequently used options limits the total run time of job allocation. When the execution time limit is reached, all running tasks are sent a TERM signal followed soon thereafter by a KILL signal. Intercepting the first signal may be used to arrange for graceful termination of affected processes. Time resolution is 1 minute (seconds are rounded up to the next minute) with allowed specification formats of [<hours>:]<minutes>:<seconds>, <minutes>[:<seconds>], <days>-<hours> [:<minutes>[:<seconds>]]. Slurm is frequently configured to permit a reasonable grace period following the expiration of job allocation. A time value of zero imposes no temporal limit on the execution.

`Example: srun -N1 -t15 my_app`

`        srun -N8 -t1-3:30 my_app`

The first command executes the job for 15 minutes on one node. The second will allocate eight nodes for 1 day, 3 hours, and 30 minutes.

`-i or --immediate[=<seconds>]`
`--begin=<time>`
`--deadline=<time>`

These options additionally affect the temporal aspect of job scheduling. The first attempts to start the job within a specified period given in seconds (resources must be available right away if no argument is present). The job is not started if the resources cannot be allocated within the time indicated. The last two options may be used to either postpone the start of the job until a specific time (**begin**) or make sure that it finishes before a certain time (**deadline**). The latter removes the job if completion by the deadline is not possible. The time specification format for both is YYYY-MM-DD [THH:MM[:SS]] for each letter standing for year, month, day, hour (24-hour clock), minute, and second. The letter "T" separates date from time. If launching on the same day, just the time specification may be used without the letter "T" and with optionally appended "AM" or "PM". Both options offer additional time formats for convenience (see the examples).

`Example: srun -N4 --deadline=5/27-16:30 -t1-0 my_app`
`        srun -N8 --begin="now+300" my_app`
`        srun -N1 --begin=noon my_app`

The first example sets the completion deadline for an application estimated to run for a single day to May 27th at 4:30 p.m. in the current year. The second command will attempt to schedule the application within the next 5 minutes after submission (default units are seconds, but "minutes" and "hours" may be specified following the number). Finally, the third example will limit the job start to no later than noon (note that this may be current or the following day, depending on the time of submission). Other predefined times of day include **midnight**, **teatime** (4 p.m.), and **fika** (3 p.m.).

`-d or --dependency=<list_of_dependencies>`

This defers job execution until the listed dependencies are satisfied. This option applies only to full jobs and not job steps. List_of_dependencies may assume one of two forms, one using commas, ",", to separate the entries, while the other uses question marks, "?". With the first format, all specified dependencies must be satisfied in order for the job to be launched. The other form means that satisfying any of the dependencies is sufficient for the dependent job to be started. Each entry assumes one of the following expressions:

- **after:<id>[:<id>...]** delays the dependent job start until all listed jobs start the execution.
- **afterany:<id>[:<id>...]** defers the dependent job until the listed jobs terminate.
- **aftercorr:<id>[:<id>...]** is used to start tasks in the current job array after successful completion of the corresponding tasks in the listed job array.
- **afternotok:<id>[:<id>...]** specifies dependency on failed jobs (timed out, nonzero exit code, node failure, and others).
- **afterok:<id>[:<id>...]** starts the job after successful completion of listed jobs (completed with zero exit code).
- **expand:<id>** resources allocated to this job are used to expand the job <id>, which must execute in the same partition.
- **singleton** defers the execution of this job until all previously started jobs with the same name and by the same user terminate.

Example: srun -N4 --dependency=afterok:1234 my_app

This will not start the job involving "my_app" until job 1234 completes successfully.

-J or --job-name=<name>

This permits the user to specify the job name. The default is to use the submitted executable name. The job name is displayed alongside the job id when listing the queue contents.

Example: srun -N4 --job-name=gamma_ray_4n my_sim

This will change the default job name my_sim to gamma_ray_4n.

--jobid=<id>

This initiates a job step under an already allocated job with the specified id. For regular users, this command is limited to job step control only and should not be used for full job allocations.

--checkpoint=<time>
--checkpoint-dir=<path>
--restart-dir=<path>

This handles automatic checkpoint and restart. The first option will create checkpoints at regular intervals specified by the time argument. The time format is identical to that used by the **time** option. The default is not to generate checkpoints. The directory to store the checkpoint data is defined by the second option, defaulting to the current working directory. The third option specifies the directory from which the checkpoint data will be read when restarting a job or job step.

```
Example: srun -N4 -t40:00:00 --checkpoint=120 \
         --checkpoint-dir=/tmp/user036/chckpts my_app
```

This will run the job for 40 hours, checkpointing its state every 2 hours. The checkpoint files are going to be stored in a user's subdirectory on a temporary file system.

```
-D or --chdir=<path>
```

This changes the current working directory to the path specified before initiating job execution. The default is the working directory used for job submission. The path may be absolute or relative to the current working directory.

```
Example: srun -N64 -t10:00 -D /scratch/datasets/0015 dataminer.sh
```

This will switch the working directory to scratch storage before starting the application.

```
-p or --partition=<partition_name>
```

This specifies a partition (queue) to be used. A comma, ",", delimited list of partitions may be specified to accelerate the job allocation.

```
Example: srun -N4 -t30 -p small,medium,large my_app
```

This will start the application in the small, medium, or large job queue, whichever becomes available first.

```
--mpi=<mpi_type>
```

This identifies the MPI implementation to use. Supported types (which may not be supported on all systems) include:

- **openmpi** enables the use of OpenMPI library and implementation.
- **mvapich** supports MPI implementation on InfiniBand.
- **lam** with one *lamd* process per node and appropriate environment variables.
- **mpich1_shmem** launches one process per node and environment initialized for shared memory support in either MPICH1 or MVAPICH shared memory build.
- **mpichgm** to be used with Myrinet networks.
- **pmi2** if the underlying MPI implementation supports the PMI2 interface.
- **pmix** includes support for PMI1, PMI2, or PMIx and requires that Slurm is configured accordingly.
- **none** used for other MPI environments.

```
Example: srun -N64 -t300 --mpi=mvapich mpirun my_sim
```

This will run the MPI application `my_sim` on 64 nodes using InfiniBand interconnect.

```
-l or --label
```

This prepends a task number to every output line (for both stdout and stderr) generated while running the job. Since the output of all processes may be interleaved on the console, this option helps identify and sort the output lines printed by individual tasks. This has uses in debugging or postmortem analysis of applications.

```
Example: srun -N4 -1 hostname
```

A possible output is shown below:

```
1: node06
0: node05
3: node08
2: node07
-K or --kill-on-bad-exit[={0,1}]
```

This determines whether to terminate the job if one of its tasks fails (exists with nonzero status). The job will not be terminated if the argument of "1" is specified; in all other cases ("0" or no argument), task failure will imply the job's failure.

```
-W or ---wait=<seconds>
```

This specifies the waiting period in seconds for other task termination after completion of the first task. "0" signifies unlimited waiting time with a warning issued after the first 60 seconds. The **kill-on-bad-exit** option takes the precedence over **wait**, causing the immediate termination of other tasks after the first one exits with nonzero status.

7.2.4.2 salloc

```
salloc [<options>] [<command> [<command_arguments>]]
```

The **salloc** command obtains resource allocation and runs the command specified by the user. The allocation is relinquished after the user's command completes. **salloc** manipulates terminal settings and therefore should be executed in the foreground. The command may be an arbitrary program or possibly shell script containing **srun** commands. The job output is shown directly on the terminal from which the command was invoked. The resource allocation options are identical to those listed for **srun** above, with the addition of the following:

```
-F or ---nodefile=<path>
```

Similar to the nodelist option described above, this explicitly specifies the names of the nodes to be used for allocation. The names are stored in a file identified by the **path** argument. The node names may be listed in multiple lines. Duplicates and ordering do not matter, as the list will be sorted by Slurm.

7.2.4.3 sbatch

```
sbatch [<options>] [script [<arguments>]]
```

The **sbatch** command is used to submit batch scripts for execution to the Slurm system. This is the preferred way of running large or long jobs, as it allows the scheduler to pick the right moment for their launch to maintain high system utilization and job throughput. The job parameters are fully described by **sbatch** command line options and script contents, including input and output stream redirection. This frees the user from being continuously present at the terminal. The script may be a file or, if omitted on the command line, entered directly on the terminal. Batch script contents are described in more detail in the next section.

Normally, **sbatch** exits as soon as the script is successfully submitted to the Slurm controller daemon. This does not mean that the job has executed or even that it has been allocated resources, only that it has been queued. When the resources for execution are granted, Slurm starts a copy of the submitted script on the first of the assigned nodes. If commands executed by the script generate any output, it is stored in files with the name "slurm-%j.out", where "%j" is the job number. For job arrays, the output is captured in files named "slurm-%A_%a.out", with "%A" denoting the job identifier and "%a" the job index.

Like **sallocate**, **sbatch** recognizes many of the same resource allocation options but also supports a few of its own:

`-a or --array=<index_list>`

This submits a job array containing multiple jobs with the same parameters. The **index_list** specifies numerical ids of individual jobs and may use comma-delimited numbers, ranges (two numbers separated by a dash), and step functions (range followed by a colon and a number). Additionally, the user may put a restriction on a number of simultaneously executing tasks from the job array by suffixing the index_list with a "%" (percent sign) and a number.

```
Example: sbatch -N6 -a5-8,10,15%3 script.sh
         sbatch -N2 -a0-11:5 script.sh
```

This will create a six-job array with job indexes 5, 6, 7, 8, 10, and 15 while limiting the number of concurrent tasks to three. The second command creates a job array with three jobs indexed 0, 5, and 10.

`-o or --output=<pattern>`

This redefines the default file name to store the job script's output stream with **pattern**. The pattern may be an arbitrary literal that could be used as a file name by the underlying file system with special character sequences that are expanded by Slurm using current job parameters. They include:

- \\ to suppress the processing of expansion sequences.
- %% to insert the single "%" character.
- **%A** expands into the job array's master job allocation number.
- **%a** produces the job index within a job array.
- **%j** yields the job allocation number.
- **%N** is the node name of the first node used by the allocation.

- **%u** converts to the user's name.

```
Example: sbatch -N10 -o"ljs-%u-%j.out" ljs.sh
```

This will capture the job's output in file "ljs-joe013-1337.out" if submitted by user joe013 and the allocated job number was 1337.

```
-W or --wait
```

This postpones **sbatch** exit until the submitted job terminates. The exit code of **sbatch** will be the same as the exit code of the job and, for job arrays, the highest recorded exit code of all jobs in the array.

7.2.4.4 squeue

```
squeue [<options>]
```

The **squeue** command displays information about jobs and job steps in Slurm queues. It may be used to examine the status of queued, running, and suspended jobs, showing their resource allocations, time limits, associated partitions, and job owners. The frequently used options are:

```
--all
-l or --long
```

These force additional information to be shown. The **all** option displays the status of jobs in all partitions, including hidden partitions as well as partitions that are unavailable to the user invoking the command. The **long** option is specified to list the contents of additional fields, e.g., time limit for each job.

```
-M or --clusters=<cluster_list>
-p or --partition=<partition_list>
-u or --user=<user_list>
-t or --states=<state_list>
```

These restrict the reported information to specific clusters, partitions, users, or states. Each option accepts a single name or comma-separated list of applicable names (for the first three options they are system dependent). The **states** option accepts the following state IDs, listed here in full and shortened format: PENDING (PD), RUNNING (R), SUSPENDED (S), STOPPED (ST), COMPLETING (CG), COMPLETED (CD), CONFIGURING (CF), CANCELLED (CA), FAILED (F), TIMEOUT (TO), PREEMPTED (PR), BOOT_FAIL (BF), NODE_FAIL (NF), and SPECIAL_EXIT (SE). The state IDs are case insensitive.

```
Example: squeue -presearch -tPD,S -i60
```

This lists all pending and suspended jobs for the research partition of the currently used cluster and updates it every minute.

```
-i or --iterate=<seconds>
```

This repeatedly updates the displayed information every number of seconds. The timestamp of the last update is included in the header.

`--start`

This shows the expected start time and resource allocation for pending jobs if the Slurm scheduler is configured with the backfill plugin. The output is ordered by increasing start time.

`-r or --array`

This prints each job element per line when showing job arrays. If not specified, the output contains condensed information about job arrays combining all information about each job array into a single line.

7.2.4.5 scancel
`scancel [<options>] [<job_id>[_<array_id>][.<step_id>]]...`

The **scancel** command cancels or delivers signals to jobs, job arrays, and job steps. Besides the options, **scancel** accepts any number of arguments denoting the identifiers of specific jobs or job steps. An underscore ("_") is used to specify the individual elements of a job array. Both regular jobs and job array elements may append a step identifier after a period (".") to limit the scope of signal delivery to the specific job steps. The target job subset may also be identified through application of filters, in which case no explicit job identifiers need to be given.

The essential command options include:

`-s or --signal=<signal>`

This determines the type of Unix signal to be delivered. The **signal** argument may be either the signal's name or its number and is typically one of HUP, INT, QUIT, ABRT, KILL, ALRM, TERM, USR1, USR2, CONT, STOP, TSTP, TTIN, or TTOU. Absence of this option causes job termination.

`Example: scancel -sSTOP 12345`

This will send the STOP signal to job number 12345.

`-n or --name=<job_name>`
`-p or --partition=<partition_name>`
`-t or --state=<job_state>`
`-u or --user=<user_name>`

The above options restrict the set of jobs affected by **scancel**. The job filtering may be done by job name, partition name, state, or user ID of the job's owner, respectively. The job state must be of the following: PENDING, RUNNING, or SUSPENDED.

`Example: scancel -tPENDING -ujoe013`

This terminates all pending jobs owned by user "joe013".

`-i or --interactive`

This enables interactive mode, in which the user has to confirm the cancellation of each affected job.

7.2.4.6 sacct

```
sacct [<options>]
```

This retrieves job accounting data from Slurm logs or databases. The information is collected on jobs, job steps, their status, and exit codes. This command also may be used to access the status of no longer existing jobs to determine if they completed successfully. The options available to the regular user include the following:

```
-a or --allusers
-L or --allclusters
-l or --long
-D or --duplicates
```

The options listed above increase the amount of information reported by **sacct**. The first outputs data related to jobs owned by all users of the cluster (note that this may be restricted in some environments). Similarly, **allclusters** includes data collected for all clusters under Slurm control; otherwise, the output is limited to the machine from which the command is invoked. The **long** option provides practically all information that has been retained in logs pertaining to the finished job. Finally, the last option provides the information for all jobs that used the same ID. Normally, only the records with the most recent timestamp are reported for each job ID.

```
-b or --brief
-j or --job=<job>[.<step>]
--name=<jobname_list>
-s or --state_list=<state_list>
-i or --nnodes=<min_nodes>[-<max_nodes>]
-k or --timelimit-min=<time>
-K or --timelimit-max=<time>
-S or --starttime=<time>
-E or --endtime=<time>
```

Options in this group filter or otherwise restrict the output of the **sacct** command. The **brief** option shortens the listing to just job ID, status, and exit code. The **job** and **name** take arguments that identify the specific job (or job steps) and job names of interest. The **state_list** will list jobs that are pending, executing, or terminated in a specific state. The state mnemonics include (short form in parentheses) CANCELED (CA), COMPLETED (CD), COMPLETING (CG), CONFIGURING (CF), PENDING (PD), PREEMPTED (PR), RUNNING (R), SUSPENDED (S), RESIZING (RS), TIMEOUT (TO), DEADLINE (DL), FAILED (F), NODE_FAIL (NF), and BOOT_FAIL (BF). Option **nnodes** shows only entries that allocated a specific number of nodes (a range may be specified). The remaining options are used to limit the retrieved records by range of execution time limits (**timelimit-max** may only be specified if **timelimit-min** is set) and actual start and end times. The time format is the same as for the **srun time** option.

Example: sacct —sF,NF,BF —a -D

This will list all failed jobs (including errors due to node failures) on the current machine.

7.2.4.7 sinfo

sinfo [<options>]

This shows information about system partitions and nodes managed by Slurm. The options **all**, **long**, **clusters**, **partition**, and **iterate** are available and have the same semantics as described above for **squeue**. In addition to those, **sinfo** interprets the following options:

-n or --nodes=<node_list>

This displays information only about the specified nodes. Node names may be individually listed in a comma-separated list or use range syntax as described for the **nodelist** option of **srun**.

-r or --responding
-d or --dead

These limit the report to either alive (responding) or dead (nonresponding) nodes.

-e or --exact
-N or --Node

These change the way system information is presented. The first prevents grouping the data related to multiple nodes unless they have identical configurations. If not specified, the memory size, CPU count, and disk space are listed as a minimal value followed by a plus sign for all nodes in the same state and in the same partition. The **Node** option forces output of one line per node instead of using partition-oriented format.

Example: sinfo -N -pbatch

This produces the following output, showing the status of all nodes configured in the "batch" partition:

```
NODELIST                     NODES PARTITION STATE
node[01,04]                      2    batch* alloc
node[02-03,05-08,10-16]         13    batch* idle
node09                           1    batch* down*
```

7.2.5 Slurm Job Scripting

The majority of cluster execution resources are utilized by batch processing. Individual workloads (jobs) submitted to the batch queue must be correctly described through job submission scripts. While Slurm attempts to detect the errors as early as possible (which results in immediate job rejection), some errors are only manifest when the job is run. This section gives a brief introduction to the basics of batch script writing.

7.2.5.1 Script Components

Job submission script is a shell script, most commonly *sh* or *bash*. To indicate the type of shell to be used to execute the script contents, the very first line must be of the form

```
#!/bin/bash
```

Formally, the first character ("#") denotes a comment that spans to the end of line; therefore, the shell ignores its contents. By convention, if the comment marker is followed by the exclamation point ("!"), the remainder of the line is assumed to be the path to the executable that will interpret the script contents. It is good practice to use an absolute path to eliminate reliance on PATH environment variables, which may not always be set on compute nodes, and to ensure that a specific shell executable is started.

Additional job parameters and resource descriptions may be defined in the lines that follow. This part of the script is optional. Note that command line options for **sbatch** may override the settings specified in the script. Each line starts with a comment marker followed by "SBATCH" and relevant **sbatch** command option accompanied by an argument. For example:

```
#SBATCH --nodes=16
#SBATCH --time=100
#SBATCH --job-name=experiment4
```

The final portion of the batch script contains commands along with their options and arguments. The commands are executed in the order they are listed within the script. They may be regular Unix utilities or parallel programs, but in order to invoke them in parallel (create multiple processes), the **srun** command should be used. As mentioned before, when called from a batch script, the **srun** command initiates a new job step. This gives the script writer the means to modify the resource footprint assigned to individual applications through **srun** command-line options.

7.2.5.2 MPI Scripts

The simplest batch script to launch an MPI job looks as follows:

```
#!/bin/bash
mpirun hello_world
```

Since there are no job parameters set in the script, one should specify at least the required number of nodes or tasks and the estimated runtime on the **sbatch** command line. The execution may fail on some platforms due to the `mpirun` command not being found. As many platforms provide multiple MPI implementations, adding "`module load openmpi`" (or its equivalent on a local machine) before the last line will correctly initialize the MPI environment (library and executable search directories and possibly other critical environment variables). Finally, the command mpirun need not be preceded by `srun` since it has already been properly configured to interact with Slurm's parallel job launch facilities. The node count option to mpirun is no longer required, since it is derived from the environment set up by Slurm.

7.2.5.3 OpenMP Scripts

Since OpenMP applications do not cross the node boundary, they do not require any special treatment. The only requirement is to make the number of threads requested by the user known to the OpenMP environment. This is demonstrated by the script below:

```
#!/bin/bash
export OMP_NUM_THREADS=$SLURM_CPUS_PER_TASK
./omp_hello_world
```

7.2.5.4 Concurrent Applications

It is possible to use the batch system to launch different applications at the same time within the confines of the same job. The first way to do this involves the **multi-prog** option of **srun**. This option requires a configuration file that specifies in each line task numbers or their ranges followed by the command line (executable with options and arguments) for each application used. The program arguments in the configuration file may contain percent-sign ("%") expressions that will be replaced by relevant job parameters when actually run:

- **%t** is replaced by the task number under which the application executes.
- **%o** expands to task offset within the range specified at the start of the line for the application.

For example, let's create the file "multi.cf" with the following contents:

```
2,7      hostname
0-1,6    echo sample task A: task=%t offset=%o
3-5      echo sample task B: task=%t offset=%o
```

We use the script shown below to execute the job:

```
#!/bin/bash
#SBATCH --ntasks=8
#SBATCH --ntasks_per_node=4
srun -l --multi-prog multi.cf
```

Option **ntasks-per-node** forces the distribution of tasks across two nodes, while the **−l** option passed to **srun** causes it to prefix every output line with the number of the task that prints it out. Script execution produces the following output:

```
0: sample task A: task=0 offset=0
1: sample task A: task=1 offset=1
3: sample task B: task=3 offset=0
2: node02
5: sample task B: task=5 offset=2
6: sample task A: task=6 offset=2
7: node03
4: sample task B: task=4 offset=1
```

The second method to achieve concurrent execution of different applications is by spawning simultaneous job steps. The following script illustrates the concept:

```
#!/bin/bash
#SBATCH --ntasks=1536
#SBATCH --time=1:00:00
srun -n1 ./single_process &
srun -n16 mpirun ./small_mpi_app &
srun -n1024 mpirun ./big_mpi_app &
wait
```

The concurrent job steps are created by placing an ampersand ("&") at the end of the relevant lines, which causes the **srun** command to execute in the background. Note that unlike **multi-prog**, this method enables concurrent execution of parallel applications. The `wait` statement is required to prevent the script exit before all the background job steps complete. On systems with installed PMI, the `mpirun` commands may be dropped, since the MPI applications already include support for parallel launch. Also, the resource requests in the script header need not exactly match the aggregate resource allocations of all simultaneous job steps. However, if these resource requests are significantly overestimated, job execution may be delayed. As a general rule, creating multiple job steps is preferable to submitting multiple jobs, as the mechanisms used to launch the job steps introduce much lower overheads than full-scale job resource allocation and scheduling.

7.2.5.5 Environment Variables

The execution of scripts may be further modified by using environment variables that are provided by Slurm to reflect the details of resource assignment to the particular job and expose information that is not known prior to its execution. These environment variables (only a subset shown) may be categorized in the following groups:

- Propagated option values
  SLURM_NTASKS or **SLURM_NPROCS**
  SLURM_NTASKS_PER_CORE
  SLURM_NTASKS_PER_NODE

SLURM_NTASKS_PER_SOCKET
SLURM_CPUS_PER_TASK
SLURM_DISTRIBUTION
SLURM_JOB_DEPENDENCY
SLURM_CHECKPOINT_IMAGE_DIR
These variables reflect the values of **sbatch** options specified either on the **sbatch** command line or in the job script header. They correspond, respectively, to the **ntasks**, **ntasks-per-core**, **ntasks-per-node**, **ntasks-per-socket**, **cpus-per-task**, **distribution**, **dependency**, and **checkpoint-dir** options.

- Counts of resources allocated to the job:
  SLURM_JOB_NUM_NODES or **SLURM_NNODES** holds the total number of nodes allocated to the job.
  SLURM_JOB_CPUS_PER_NODE, depending on the scheduler, indicates the total number of CPUs (cores) available on the local node or the actual number of CPUs allocated to the job.
  SLURM_CPUS_ON_NODE indicates the number of CPUs on the current node.

- Runtime-assigned IDs and enumerations:
  SLURM_SUBMIT_HOST specifies the name of the host on which the job was submitted.
  SLURM_CLUSTER_NAME contains the name of the cluster on which the job is running.
  SLURM_JOB_PARTITION names the partition in which the job is running.
  SLURM_JOB_ID or **SLURM_JOBID** indicates the ID of the current job.
  SLURM_LOCALID indicates the ID of node-local task corresponding to the current process.
  SLURM_NODEID is the ID of the allocated node.
  SLURM_PROCID specifies the global relative ID of the current process (MPI rank if the process is a part of the MPI process group).
  SLURM_JOB_NODELIST or **SLURM_NODELIST** contains a list of node names that were allocated to the job. The list may contain node ranges or individual entries.
  SLURM_TASKS_PER_NODE shows the number of tasks executing on each node. The entries in the list correspond to host names in the
  SLURM_JOB_NODELIST variable, with some space-saving notation applied to identical consecutive entries (e.g., 4[×2] indicates two consecutive nodes with task count of 4).
  SLURM_ARRAY_TASK_ID stores the index of job array element.
  SLURM_ARRAY_TASK_MIN and **SLURM_ARRAY_TASK_MAX** provide the minimum and maximum indices used by the job array.
  SLURM_ARRAY_TASK_STEP indicates the step by which the index is increased in the job array.
  SLURM_ARRAY_JOB_ID specifies the ID of the master job in the job array.

- Other
  SLURM_SUBMIT_DIR contains the directory name from which the job was submitted.
  SLURM_RESTART_COUNT stores the current count if the job has been restarted due to failure or requeueing.

Import of the actual configuration parameters into the script and the application space through environment variables permits nearly arbitrary customization of job execution. It also enables creation of more flexible job scripts. For example, the following script calculates the total number of cores allocated to the job and selects the appropriate input configuration based on the outcome. It also provides a unique log file name to be generated by the master task, reflecting the job number and used resource geometry.

```
#!/bin/bash

job=$SLURM_JOB_ID
nodes=$SLURM_JOB_NUM_NODES
cores=$SLURM_JOB_CPUS_PER_NODE
total=$((nodes * cores))

config=small.conf
[ $total -ge 4096 ] && config=medium.conf
[ $total -ge 16384 ] && config=large.conf

mpirun ./my_sim -i $config -o sim_${job}_${nodes}x${cores}.log
```

Slurm environment variables may be helpful in staging files to a higher-performance file system than shared Network File System storage (frequently used to provide global access to home directories). The script listed below creates a unique temporary directory for each task in local temporary storage, copies the dataset data.in prepared in the submission directory, spawns tasks that modify it, and copies the results back. It assumes that the cluster supports a passwordless secure shell on login and compute nodes.

```
#!/bin/bash

host=$SLURM_SUBMIT_HOST
hostdir=$SLURM_SUBMIT_DIR
tmpdir=/tmp/${USER}/${SLURM_JOB_ID}

srun mkdir -p $tmpdir/$SLURM_PROCID
srun scp ${host}:${hostdir}/data.in $tmpdir/$SLURM_PROCID/data

srun ./update_file $tmpdir/$SLURM_PROCID/data
srun scp $tmpdir/$SLURM_PROCID/data

${host}:$hostdir/data.out.${SLURM_PROCID}
```

7.2.6 **Slurm Cheat Sheet**

This section contains a collection of commands that accomplish frequently performed tasks but may be sometimes difficult to locate in the manual. They are presented in the way they would be typed by a user at the login shell prompt, although
many of them can be converted to the equivalent job scripts. The examples below
serve primarily as a template, since in many cases the option arguments are strongly
platform dependent. For commands that require resource allocation, both time limit
and number of nodes or tasks are specified to enforce good practices.

Invoke interactive shell on the allocation:

```
srun -N4 -t30 --pty /bin/bash
```

Enable X windows forwarding for graphical applications (requires X11 plugin
installed):

```
srun -N1 -t30 --x11 xterm
```

(Here xterm is used as an example application.)

Submit job to the specific queue ("debug" in this case):

```
sbatch -N4 -t30 -pdebug job.sh
```

Submit multithreaded MPI job (MPI with OpenMP). The command below
spawns 16 MPI processes with 8 OpenMP threads each, placing two processes
per node:

```
env OMP_NUM_THREADS=8 sbatch -n16 -c8 -t30 --ntasks-per-node=2 job.sh
```

Specify memory requirements for the job (4 GB = 4096 MB per node shown):

```
sbatch --mem=4096 -n2 -t30 job.sh
```

Find out the estimated start of execution time (1234 is the queued job identifier):

```
squeue --start -j 1234
```

Ask to be notified by email when the job terminates or fails:

```
sbatch --mail-type=END,FAIL -N4 -t30 job.sh
```

Kill submitted or currently running job (1234 is the identifier of the queued job):

```
scancel 1234
```

7.3 **Summary and Outcomes**

• Resource management tools are the inherent part of the HPC software stack that
  perform three principal functions: resource allocation, workload scheduling,
  and support for distributed workload execution and monitoring.

- Resource allocation takes care of assigning physical hardware, which may span from a fraction of the machine to the entire system, to specific user tasks based on their requirements.
- Resource managers typically recognize the following resource types: compute nodes, processor cores, interconnects, permanent storage and I/O devices, and accelerators.
- Resource managers allocate the available computing resources to jobs specified by users.
- Jobs may be executed interactively or batch processed. Batch processing requires that all necessary parameters and inputs for job execution are specified before it is launched.
- Jobs may be monolithic or subdivided into a number of smaller steps or tasks. Each such task is associated with the launch of a specific application program.
- Pending computing jobs are stored in job queues, which define the order in which jobs are selected by the resource manager for execution.
- Most systems use multiple job queues, each with a specific purpose and set of scheduling constraints.
- Common parameters that affect job scheduling include availability of execution and auxiliary resources, priority, resources allocated to the user, maximum number of jobs, requested execution time, elapsed execution time, job dependencies, event occurrence, operator availability, and software license availability.
- Job launchers employ hierarchical mechanisms to alleviate the bandwidth requirements and exploit network topology to minimize the amount of data transferred and overall launch time.
- Resource managers must be able to terminate any job that exceeds its execution time or other resource limits irrespective of its current processing status.
- The software commonly used today includes Slurm, PBS, Moab Cluster Suite, LoadLeveler, Altair Grid Engine, HTCondor, OAR, and YARN. Some of these systems are tailored strictly to specific execution models (e.g., MapReduce in the case of YARN).
- There is no common standard specifying the command format, language, and configuration of resource management.
- Slurm is an open-source, modular, extensible, scalable resource manager and workload scheduling software for clusters and supercomputers running Linux or other Unix-compatible OSs.
- Slurm scales to the largest systems in use today, including the fastest supercomputer of 2023, Frontier, with its 9408 CPUs (over 8 million cores) and 37,632 GPUs. It is also used on 60% of the Top 500 machines. It can handle up to 1000 job submissions and 500 job executions per second.
- Single points of failure are eliminated through the use of multiple backup daemons, permitting the affected applications to continue running and request resources to replace those that fail.

- Job sizes are not necessarily fixed over their execution time; they may grow or shrink but should not exceed the maximum specified size and time limits. Sophisticated scheduling algorithms are available, including elastic scheduling, gang scheduling, and preemption.
- Slurm integrates support for execution on heterogeneous components, such as GPUs, field programmable gate arrays, and other accelerators with various resource-sharing schemes across jobs.
- Gang scheduling supports a scheduling approach in which two or more jobs with similar characteristics are allocated the same set of resources. These jobs are then executed in an alternating fashion so that only one of them obtains exclusive access to the resources at a time.

7.4 Exercises

1. Describe the role of resource management systems. Can they be implemented as a part of a conventional OS? Elaborate.

2. Based on Fig. 7.1, what are the primary software components of a resource management system in a cluster? Which physical system components do they rely on?

3. What are the two primary types of jobs? Why are they needed?

4. What are the differences between a job array and job step in Slurm?

5. Imagine you are a system administrator for a newly installed computer composed of 260 nodes total. Of those, 64 come equipped with GPUs and 36 have substantially larger memory capacity. Your users execute both regular and (infrequently) high-priority jobs. The latter require exclusive access to nonaccelerated hardware resources but never occupy more than 128 nodes.

    a. Propose a partitioning scheme (enumerate the types and sizes of Slurm partitions) that provides good utilization of the entire machine. Identify any partition overlaps.

    b. What kind of provisions would you implement to facilitate parallel job debugging?

    c. Which Slurm features would you take advantage of to minimize the impact of conflicts between jobs of different priorities?

6. What is backfill? How does it affect computer utilization?

7. Provide a couple of realistic use cases that would utilize job dependencies in batch processing. Why would emulating this functionality with blocking statements inside job scripts be ill advised?

8. Write a Slurm command line to schedule an MPI application "mpi_compute" that takes input file argument "my_file.dat" stored in the user's home directory. The application must run on 10,240 cores on a machine equipped with 16-core compute nodes that are available in the "production" partition. The anticipated execution time is 1.5 hours. Also provide an equivalent job script with a correctly formed header.

References

[1] SchedMD, Slurm Workload Manager Version 23.02, 2022 [Online]. Available: https://slurm.schedmd.com.

[2] PBS Works, a division of Altair Engineering, Inc., OpenPBS, Industry-Leading Workload Manager and Job Scheduler for High-Performance Computing, 2023 [Online]. Available: http://www.openpbs.org.

[3] Adaptive Computing, Inc., MOAB HPC Suite, 2023 [Online]. Available: http://www.adaptivecomputing.com/moab-hpc-suite/.

[4] IBM, Tivoli Workload Automation, Version 8.6.0, 2021 [Online]. Available: https://www.ibm.com/docs/en/workload-automation/8.6.0?topic=publications-libraries.

[5] Altair Engineering, Inc., Altair Grid Engine, 2023 [Online]. Available: https://www.altair.com/grid-engine/.

[6] University of Wisconsin-Madison Center for High Throughput Computing, HTCondor Software Suite, 2023 [Online]. Available: https://htcondor.org/.

[7] OAR Home Page, 2018 [Online]. Available: http://oar.imag.fr.

[8] Apache Software Foundation, Apache Hadoop YARN, 2023 [Online]. Available: https://hadoop.apache.org/docs/stable/hadoop-yarn/hadoop-yarn-site/YARN.html.

[9] Top 500. The List, 1993-2022 [Online]. Available: https://www.top500.org.

Visualization

Chapter outline

8.1 Introduction

Supercomputer applications frequently produce enormous amounts of output data that also must be analyzed and presented to understand the application outcome and draw conclusions on the results. This process, frequently referred to as "visualization", itself can require supercomputing resources and is a fundamental modality of supercomputer usage. Visualization may even incorporate machine learning models to extract and leverage metadata to aid communication of the results to the user.

Some of the principal reasons for visualizing data resulting from running an application on a supercomputer include debugging, exploring data, statistical hypothesis testing, and preparing presentation graphics. In some cases, the output from running an application on a supercomputer will be something as simple as a single file with comma-separated values. However, it is much more likely that the output from a supercomputing application will be in a special parallel input/output (I/O) library format, like one of those mentioned in Table 6.1 in Chapter 6, to manage and coordinate the simultaneous output from multiple compute nodes to a single file.

This chapter will discuss four key foundational visualization concepts frequently needed as part of high performance computing (HPC) visualization: streamlines, isosurfaces, volume rendering through ray tracing, and mesh tessellations. Visualization will then be practically explored using five different visualization tools that are frequently used in the context of HPC: (1) Gnuplot, (2) Matplotlib, the (3) VTK library, (4) ParaView, and (5) VisIt. Three of these tools (VTK, ParaView, and VisIt) already incorporate the ability to use distributed memory parallel processing to accelerate the visualization process itself. ParaView usage as a distributed memory parallel processing tool will be demonstrated. Finally, a discussion on tools supporting visual intelligence will be discussed.

8.2 Foundational Visualization Concepts

Among the most frequently used concepts for scientific visualization are streamlines, isosurfaces, volume rendering through ray tracing, and mesh tessellations. Streamlines like those illustrated in Fig. 8.1 take a vector field as input and show curves that are tangent to the vector field. Streamlines may be thought of as showing the trajectory that a massless particle would travel in the input vector field. While the starting point for each streamline can be specified explicitly, it is more common to use random starting points seeded inside a small geometric object like a sphere or cube.

An isosurface like that illustrated in Fig. 8.2 is a surface that connects points that have the same value. Isosurfaces are frequently used in medical visualization to extract surfaces that have the same density as those seen in a three-dimensional (3D) ultrasound. An isosurface is the 3D analog to a contour line in two-dimensional (2D) visualizations.

Volume rendering through ray tracing like that illustrated in Fig. 8.3 is where for each pixel a ray is used to sample the volume through which it passes. Based on a provided color transfer function, the ray is shaded while an opacity function alters

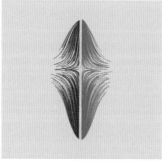

FIGURE 8.1

Streamline example using the gradient of the function f(x,y,z) = 2550sin(100x)sin(30y) cos(40z) as input. Two different three-dimensional views are provided.

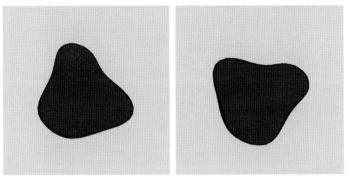

FIGURE 8.2

Isosurface example of the function f(x,y,z) = 2550sin(10x)sin(10y)cos(10z) as input with the isosurface value set at 200. Two different three-dimensional views are provided.

FIGURE 8.3

Example of low-resolution volume rendering of the function f(x,y,z) = 2550sin(50x) sin(50y)cos(50z). The color and opacity map were chosen arbitrarily. Two different three-dimensional views are provided.

the transparency of the data in the volume. This type of volume rendering can reveal internal structures in data, as well as produce blurry or sharp edges depending on the opacity function chosen.

A mesh tessellation like that seen in Fig. 8.4 is where a collection of data points and their connectivities to other data points are visualized through a set of polygons, frequently triangles, or quadrilaterals in 2D and tetrahedra or hexahedra in 3D. The meshes often provide important statistical information about a simulation, including error bounds and mesh adaptivity, while also visually conveying the scale at which simulation features are resolved.

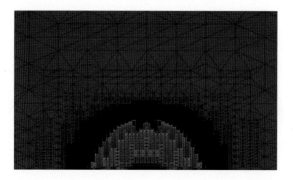

FIGURE 8.4

An example of a two-dimensional (2D) mesh tessellation for an adaptive mesh shock wave simulation. The mesh consisting of black lines is visualized on top of a 2D color plot of the shock wave density.

These foundational visualization concepts are usually not implemented directly by the application developer but rather accessed in the context of an existing visualization toolkit or library. Some of the most common visualization toolkits and libraries for HPC are discussed in the following sections.

8.3 Gnuplot

Gnuplot [1] is a freely available and open-source command-line-driven visualization tool that includes support for both 2D and 3D plots. Gnuplot has been around since 1986 and is frequently found in most Linux distributions and on supercomputer login nodes. Several other independent applications use Gnuplot for graphics output, including GNU Octave [6], which features a high-level programming language that is similar and often compatible with MATLAB [7].

Like most spreadsheet tools, Gnuplot is capable of a wide range of 2D plots. This is demonstrated here using the space separated text data, e.g.:

1. 1 -1
2. 2 -2
3. 3 -3
4. 4 -7

Gnuplot can be installed from the command line on a Linux-based operating system (e.g., *apt-get install gnuplot* on Ubuntu) and a Mac-based operating system (e.g., *brew install gnuplot*) or downloaded and installed for a Windows-based operating system from the Gnuplot website. To start Gnuplot, simply type "gnuplot" in a terminal.

The *plot* command is the main command for 2D plots in Gnuplot and takes the syntax as follows:

```
plot {<ranges>} <plot-element> {, <plot-element>, <plot-element>}
```

If no ranges are specified, a default is computed based on the specific plot member. A plot member may be a predefined function like *sin(x)* or data read from a file with space-separated text data. Each plot member may have its plotting style altered using a predefined plotting style such as *linespoints* or *circles*, for example. Referring to the example space-separated data shown earlier as the file called "*gnu_example.dat*", three separate ways of plotting with Gnuplot are illustrated in Figs. 8.5—8.7.

```
plot "gnu_example.dat" using 1:2 with linespoints
plot "gnut_example.dat" using 3:2 with linespoints
plot [0:4][-5:5] "gnu_example.dat" using 1:2 with linespoints title
"data", sin(x) title "sin(x)"
```

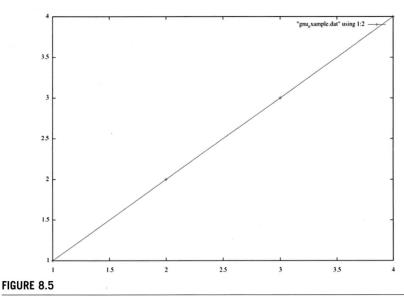

FIGURE 8.5

The first column of the example space-separated data is used as the x values and the second column as the y values. Default ranges are generated.

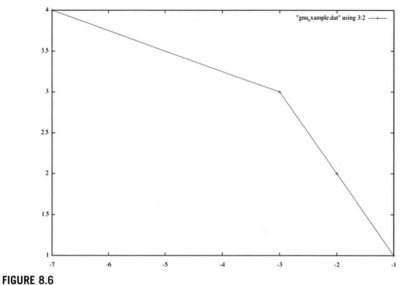

FIGURE 8.6

The third column of the example space-separated data is used as the x values and the second column as the y values. Default ranges are generated.

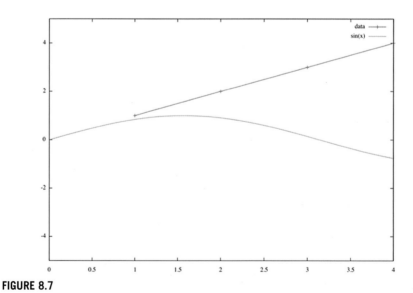

FIGURE 8.7

Plot containing the example space-separated text data as well as a plot of sin(x) with specified plot ranges.

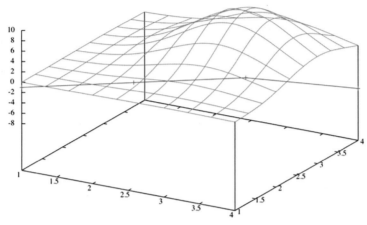

FIGURE 8.8

An example of a Gnuplot-generated three-dimensional plot showing both the data in
Fig. 8.5 and $f(x,y) = 10 \exp(-(x-3)^2 - (y-3)^2)$.

Gnuplot is also capable of 3D plots using the *splot* command and shares most of
the syntax with the 2D *plot* command. When plotting space-separated text data like
that of the example data, the first column gives the x values, the second the y values,
and the third column is the value of the function at that point. An example of this is
illustrated in Fig. 8.8.

```
splot "gnu_example.dat" with linespoints title "data", 10*exp(-(x-3)
**2-(y-3)**2) title "gaussian"
```

Among the many strengths of Gnuplot is the easy-to-use documentation accessed
via the *help* command in interactive mode.

8.4 Matplotlib

Matplotlib [2] is a freely available and open-source Python language-based visualization tool that has an interface with the look and feel of Matlab. It relies upon the
NumPy extension to Python as a required dependency for array and matrix support.
Like Gnuplot, Matplotlib is frequently found already installed on many supercomputer installations and is easily integrated into existing HPC application code bases
for application-specific visualizations. If Matplotlib is not already installed in your
Python distribution, you can create a conda environment with the Python version of
your choice and install Matplotlib via pip3, e.g.: (if on Mac) *brew install miniforge*

(if on Linux) wget "https://github.com/conda-forge/miniforge/releases/latest/download/Mambaforge-$(uname)-$(uname-m).sh"bash Mambaforge-$(uname)-$(uname -m).sh

```
conda create -n matplotlib_env python=3.11
conda activate matplotlib_env
pip3 install matplotlib
```

In this way there is no need to use or modify a system-installed Python to add Matplotlib, and this approach will not require system administrator intervention on a supercomputer. Most supercomputers will already have matplotlib installed in some environment.

Python is frequently used in scientific visualization, and in the case of Matplotlib, using Python is a requirement. While the Python syntax is simple and intuitive, a quick overview of Python syntax can be found in reference [8].

In interactive mode, Matplotlib is initialized by launching Python in the command line and loading NumPy and Matplotlib:

```
[$ python3
>>> import matplotlib.pyplot as plot
>>> import numpy
```

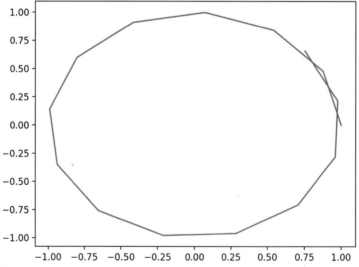

FIGURE 8.9

Matplotlib plotting the x and y coordinates of data written in HDF5 format. The code for this plot is given in Code 8.1.

Once Matplotlib has been started in interactive mode, data such as space-separated text data can be plotted interactively in a way analogous to that used with Gnuplot earlier:

```
data = numpy.loadtxt("gnu_example.dat",skiprows=0)
xvalues = data.T[0]
yvalues = data.T[1]
l1, = plot.plot(xvalues,yvalues)
plot.show()
```

Matplotlib easily integrates with the data storage libraries mention in Table 6.1 in Chapter 6, including HDF5 and netCDF, through their respective Python bindings. Data can then be easily manipulated using NumPy and plotted using Matplotlib. This is illustrated in Fig. 8.9.

In Fig. 8.9, *particles.h5*, is read into Python and the *x* and *y* values of the particles are plotted using Matplotlib. To do this, the Python bindings to HDF5 are loaded using the *import h5py* command in addition to loading Matplotlib and NumPy, as illustrated in the Python script in Code 8.1.

The HDF5 file can then be loaded using the *h5py.File* method. A specific dataset in the file can be accessed by passing the dataset name as a key to the file; in this case the dataset name is "particle data". A list of all datasets present in an HDF5 file can be found using the *h5ls* utility as well. The values in the dataset are copied to the

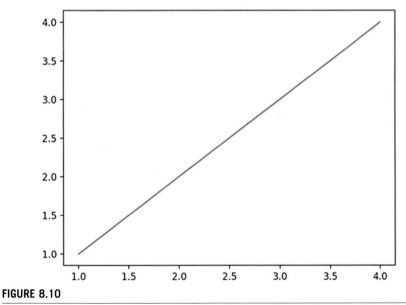

FIGURE 8.10

An interactive plot of the first and second columns of the example space-separated data using Matplotlib. This is analogous to the Gnuplot version shown in Fig. 8.5. The text file "gnu_example.dat" is read into the data variable using the loadtxt method from NumPy. The data is rotated upon read-in so the data variable is transposed using the "T" operation and the columns are loaded into variables xvalues and yvalues for plotting.

```
1 import h5py
2 import numpy as np
3 import matplotlib.pyplot as plot
4
5 f = h5py.File("particles.h5","r")
6 dataset = f["particle data"]
7 xvalues = np.zeros(dataset.shape) #initializing memory
8 yvalues = np.zeros(dataset.shape) #initializing memory
9 for idx,item in enumerate(dataset):
10   xvalues[idx] = item[0]
11   yvalues[idx] = item[1]
12
13 l1, = plot.plot(xvalues,yvalues)
14 plot.show()
```

CODE 8.1

Python code to plot the x and y values of the particle data stored in the "particles.h5" file.

```
1 import scipy.io as sio
2 from matplotlib.pyplot import figure, show
3 import numpy
4
5 A = sio.mmread("pgfem_big.mtx");
6
7 fig = figure()
8 ax1 = fig.add_subplot(111)
9
10 ax1.spy(A,markersize=1)
11 show()
```

CODE 8.2

Python script illustrating the ability to plot the sparsity pattern of a matrix. The matrix in this case, bcspwr06.mtx, comes from the Matrix Market collection [9]. The resulting sparsity pattern plot is shown in Fig. 8.11.

appropriate *xvalues* and *yvalues* NumPy arrays and plotted just like was done in Fig. 8.10.

Like Matlab, Matplotlib provides several tools for visualizing sparse matrices. One of the most common of these is the ability to plot the sparsity pattern of a matrix. This is illustrated in Code 8.2 and Fig. 8.11 for the matrix *"bcspwr06.mtx"* from the Matrix Market collection [9] and using the matrix market reader provided in the SciPy ecosystem [10].

Unlike Gnuplot, Matplotlib itself does not support 3D surface plots or other 3D-type visualizations. However, there are extension modules that can enable 3D plotting using Matplotlib, including mplot3d [11]. Matplotlib plots are also capable of integration with one of the most important and widely used libraries for 3D computer graphics, the Visualization Toolkit (VTK).

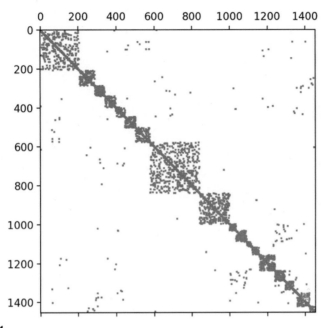

FIGURE 8.11

The sparsity pattern of a matrix plotted using Code 8.2.

8.5 **The Visualization Toolkit**

One of the most important open-source visualization libraries for HPC users is VTK
[3]. VTK provides many 3D visualization algorithms, parallel computing support,
and interfaces to interpreted languages like Python, which will be used for examples
in this section. VTK is also used in several full visualization tools, including Para-
View and VisIt, which are illustrated later in this chapter.

VTK can be installed in a conda environment just like Matplotlib:

```
conda create -n my_vtk_env python=3.11
conda activate my_vtk_env
pip3 install vtk
```

VTK can then be accessed from Python by importing VTK into your Python
script or interactive session, e.g.:

```
import vtk
```

The most recent VTK application programming interface is conceptually laid out
around the idea of a data pipeline incorporating maps with keys and values for passing information through the pipeline, objects for storing source data, algorithms and
filters, and a class for connecting and executing the pipeline. In VTK terminology,

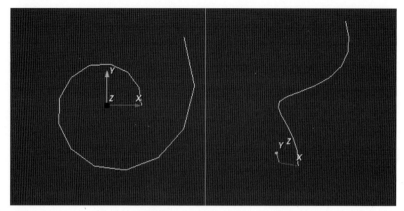

FIGURE 8.12

Two three-dimensional plots of the particle locations found in particles.h5 using VTK. The corresponding code for this visualization is found in Code 8.3.

"mappers" convert data into graphics primitives, while "actors" alter the visual properties of those graphics. The following example shown in Fig. 8.12 and Code 8.3 reads the HDF5 data "*particles.h5*" and plots a line in 3D through the points in the HDF5 dataset using VTK.

All other major scientific visualization components are available in VTK. Isosurfaces of 3D data can be produced using vtkContourFilter, as illustrated in Fig. 8.13. In VTK, filters like vtkContourFiler are optionally applied in the pipeline before applying mappers and actors, as illustrated in Code 8.4.

One way to execute volume rendering through ray tracing in VTK is using the SmartVolumeMapper class illustrated in Code 8.5 and Fig. 8.14. In this example, a color transfer function and opacity map are passed as properties to appropriately shade the rays as they pass through the volume.

Streamlines in VTK are accomplished using the StreamTracer class. Streamlines require vector data as input, but VTK also provides a means to take a gradient of scalar data and then assign output as a vector that can be visualized as a streamline. This entire pipeline is demonstrated in Code 8.6 and Fig. 8.15. The starting point for a single streamline can be specified as illustrated in the comment on line 31 of Code 8.6, or a streamline seed region can be created for starting multiple streamlines as illustrated in lines 23–27.

While the VTK library provides a complete visualization pipeline solution for HPC users, many users will prefer a turnkey visualization solution that is driven by a powerful graphical user interface and is ready for supercomputing usage without having to write any code. Two turnkey visualization tools that incorporate the powerful algorithms of VTK and are widely used include ParaView and VisIt.

```
1 import h5py     # the HDF5 Python interface
2 import vtk    # the VTK Python interface
3 f = h5py.File("particles.h5","r")  # read in the file "particles.h5"
4 dataset = f["particle data"]    # access the dataset "particle data" in "particles.h5"
5 points = vtk.vtkPoints()
6 points.SetNumberOfPoints(dataset.shape[0])  # create a list of points for particle locations
7 for idx,item in enumerate(dataset):
8  points.SetPoint(idx,dataset[idx][0],dataset[idx][1],dataset[idx][2]) # assign values
9
10 lines = vtk.vtkCellArray()
11 lines.InsertNextCell(dataset.shape[0])
12 for idx in range(0,dataset.shape[0]):    # assign the connectivity between the points
13 lines.InsertCellPoint(idx)
14
15 polygon = vtk.vtkPolyData()     # create a polygon geometric structure
16 polygon.SetPoints(points)
17 polygon.SetLines(lines)
18
19 polygonMapper = vtk.vtkPolyDataMapper()  # map the polygonal data to graphics
20 polygonMapper.SetInputData(polygon)
21 polygonMapper.Update()
22
23 axes = vtk.vtkAxesActor()             # create some axes
24 polygonActor = vtk.vtkActor()          # Manage the rendering of the mapper
25 polygonActor.SetMapper(polygonMapper)
26 renderer = vtk.vtkRenderer()          # The viewport on the screen
27 renderer.AddActor(polygonActor)
28 renderer.AddActor(axes)
29 renderer.SetBackground(0.1, 0.2, 0.3)
30
31 renderer.ResetCamera()
32
33 renderWindow = vtk.vtkRenderWindow()
34 renderWindow.AddRenderer(renderer)
35
36 interactive_ren = vtk.vtkRenderWindowInteractor()  # enable interactivity with visualization
37 interactive_ren.SetRenderWindow(renderWindow)
38 interactive_ren.Initialize()
39 interactive_ren.Start()
```

CODE 8.3

A Python script to read in and visualize the 3D trajectory of the particle data stored in particles.h5 using VTK. The resulting visualization is seen in Fig. 8.12.

8.6 ParaView

ParaView [4] is an open-source HPC-capable turnkey visualization solution based on VTK. Like other visualization tools examined in this chapter, significant support for the Python language is provided, enabling control of ParaView both from a graphical user interface (GUI) and from a script. Because ParaView is based on VTK, the naming of elements in the visualization pipeline follows that of the VTK application programming interface. ParaView has data readers for over 70 different data formats. An example dataset that comes with ParaView is demonstrated in Fig. 8.16.

The easiest installation route for ParaView is downloading one of the multiple binaries made available on http://paraview.org. These binaries are self-contained and can come bundled with MPI to enable running in a client-server mode with multiple servers running on distributed nodes.

FIGURE 8.13

An isosurface in VTK using Code 8.4.

```
1 import vtk       # the VTK Python interface
2
3 rt = vtk.vtkRTAnalyticSource() # data for testing
4
  27  contour_filter = vtk.vtkContourFilter() # isosurface filter
  27  contour_filter.SetInputConnection(rt.GetOutputPort())
7 contour_filter.SetValue(0, 190)
8
9 mapper = vtk.vtkPolyDataMapper()
10 mapper.SetInputConnection(contour_filter.GetOutputPort())
11
12 actor = vtk.vtkActor()
13 actor.SetMapper(mapper)
14
15 renderer = vtk.vtkRenderer()
16 renderer.AddActor(actor)
17
18 renderer.SetBackground(0.9, 0.9, 0.9)
19
20 renderWindow = vtk.vtkRenderWindow()
21 renderWindow.AddRenderer(renderer)
22 renderWindow.SetSize(600, 600)
23
24 interactive_ren = vtk.vtkRenderWindowInteractor() #enable interactivity with visualization
25 interactive_ren.SetRenderWindow(renderWindow)
26 interactive_ren.Initialize()
27 interactive_ren.Start()
```

CODE 8.4

Example isosurface using the ContourFilter filter; the value of the isosurface is set at line 7. Test data was provided using vtkRTAnalyticSource in line 3. The resulting visualization is shown in Fig. 8.13.

```
 1 import vtk
 2
 3 rt = vtk.vtkRTAnalyticSource()
 4 rt.Update()
 5
 6 image = rt.GetOutput()
 7 range = image.GetScalarRange()
 8
 9 mapper = vtk.vtkSmartVolumeMapper()                # volume rendering
10 mapper.SetInputConnection(rt.GetOutputPort())
11 mapper.SetRequestedRenderModeToRayCast()
12
13 color = vtk.vtkColorTransferFunction()
14 color.AddRGBPoint(range[0], 0.0, 0.0, 1.0)
15 color.AddRGBPoint((range[0] + range[1]) * 0.75, 0.0, 1.0, 0.0)
16 color.AddRGBPoint(range[1], 1.0, 0.0, 0.0)
17
18 opacity = vtk.vtkPiecewiseFunction()
19 opacity.AddPoint(range[0], 0.0)
20 opacity.AddPoint((range[0] + range[1]) * 0.5, 0.0)
21 opacity.AddPoint(range[1], 1.0)
22
23 properties = vtk.vtkVolumeProperty()
24 properties.SetColor(color)
25 properties.SetScalarOpacity(opacity)
26 properties.SetInterpolationTypeToLinear()
27 properties.ShadeOn()
28
29 actor = vtk.vtkVolume()
30 actor.SetMapper(mapper)
31 actor.SetProperty(properties)
32
33 renderer = vtk.vtkRenderer()
34 renderWindow = vtk.vtkRenderWindow()
35 renderWindow.AddRenderer(renderer)
36
37 renderer.AddViewProp(actor)
38 renderer.ResetCamera()
39 renderer.SetBackground(0.9, 0.9, 0.9)
40 renderWindow.SetSize(600, 600)
41
42 interactive_ren = vtk.vtkRenderWindowInteractor()
43 interactive_ren.SetRenderWindow(renderWindow)
44 interactive_ren.Initialize()
45 interactive_ren.Start()
```

CODE 8.5

Example volume rendering using VTK. Test data was provided using vtkRTAnalyticSource at line 3. Opacity and colormap settings were made based on the image scalar range. The resulting visualization is shown in Fig. 8.14.

FIGURE 8.14

An example volume rendering in VTK using Code 8.5.

Often in HPC a user will need to use more memory than is available on a single compute node to visualize a dataset. Sometimes the time needed to visualize a dataset can also be a limiting factor. To avoid this problem, ParaView comes bundled with MPI and can launch multiple servers. Here is a quick example. On a set of compute nodes, launch multiple ParaView servers, *pvserver*:

```
export   PATH=/usr/local/ParaView-5.11.0-MPI-Linux-Python3.9-x86_64/
bin:$PATH
mpiexec -np 16 pvserver
```

In this example, we assume that ParaView has been installed in the /usr/local/ directory, and we update the PATH variable to use the *mpiexec* and *pvserver* that come bundled with the installation. The *mpiexec* command will launch 16 ParaView servers on the compute nodes. Those servers will then wait for a client connection and output something like the following:

```
Waiting for client...
Connection URL: cs://compute-node-1:11111
Accepting connection(s): compute-node-1:11111
```

Now a ParaView client can be launched on a laptop or a different node:

```
paraview &
```

Select the "File" dropdown menu and then select "Connect". The option to add a server configuration will then appear as shown in Fig. 8.17.

```
 1 import vtk
 2
 3 rt = vtk.vtkRTAnalyticSource()  # data for testing
 4 rt.Update()
 5
 6 #calculate the gradient of the test data
 7 gradient = vtk.vtkImageGradient()
 8 gradient.SetDimensionality(3)
 9 gradient.SetInputConnection(rt.GetOutputPort())
10 gradient.Update()
11
12 # Make a vector
13 aa = vtk.vtkAssignAttribute()
14 aa.Assign("SCALARS","VECTORS","POINT_DATA")
15 aa.SetInputConnection(gradient.GetOutputPort())
16 aa.Update()
17
18 # Create Stream Lines
19 rk = vtk.vtkRungeKutta45()
20 streamer = vtk.vtkStreamTracer()
21 streamer.SetInputConnection(aa.GetOutputPort())
22
23 # seed the stream lines
24 seeds = vtk.vtkPointSource()
25 seeds.SetRadius(1)
26 seeds.SetCenter(1,1.1,0.5)
27 seeds.SetNumberOfPoints(50)
28
29 # options for streamer
30 streamer.SetSourceConnection(seeds.GetOutputPort())
31 #streamer.SetStartPosition(1.0,1.1,0.5)
32 streamer.SetMaximumPropagation(500)
33 streamer.SetMinimumIntegrationStep(0.01)
34 streamer.SetMaximumIntegrationStep(0.5)
35 streamer.SetIntegrator(rk)
36 streamer.SetMaximumError(1.0e-8)
37
38 mapStream = vtk.vtkPolyDataMapper()
39 mapStream.SetInputConnection(streamer.GetOutputPort())
40 streamActor = vtk.vtkActor()
41 streamActor.SetMapper(mapStream)
42
43 ren = vtk.vtkRenderer()
44 renWin = vtk.vtkRenderWindow()
45 renWin.AddRenderer(ren)
46 iren = vtk.vtkRenderWindowInteractor()
47 iren.SetRenderWindow(renWin)
48
49 ren.AddActor(streamActor)
50 ren.SetBackground(0.9,0.9,0.9)
51 renWin.SetSize(300,300)
52 iren.Initialize()
53 iren.Start()
```

CODE 8.6

Example code using vtkRTAnalyticSource to create streamlines with VTK. The gradient of the test data is computed in lines 7–10; the gradient is then assigned as vector data for use by the vtkStreamTracer filter for producing streamlines. The starting points for the streamlines are produced from point sources in a sphere computed in lines 24–27. A single starting point could also be assigned as illustrated in the comment in line 31. The result from this code is seen in Fig. 8.15.

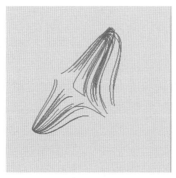 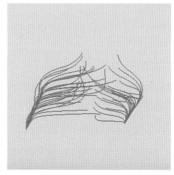

FIGURE 8.15

Streamlines in VTK using the gradient of the data shown in Figs. 8.13 and 8.14. The code that produced these streamlines in VTK is shown in Code 8.6.

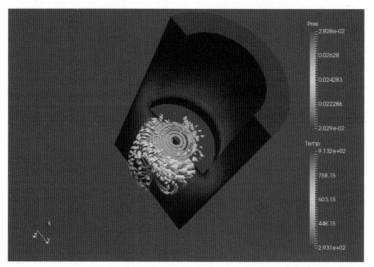

FIGURE 8.16

Example visualization that comes with ParaView illustrating streamlines with arrows and data slices.

The "Add Server" option is selected. The host (compute-node-1 in our example) and port specified (11111 in our example) when the *pvserver* was launched can be entered. Then click "Connect". The *pvserver* will report:

```
Client connected.
```

The user can then execute visualization across multiple nodes and visualize large datasets faster that would potentially not even fit in the memory of a single compute node.

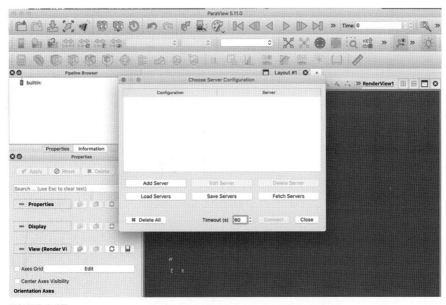

FIGURE 8.17

Option to add a server configuration in ParaView via the "File" dropdown menu and selecting the "Connect" option.

8.7 VisIt

VisIt [5] is another open-source HPC-capable turnkey visualization solution that uses VTK for several visualization algorithms. VisIt is particularly well suited for in situ visualization where visualization occurs while the supercomputing simulation that creates the data is ongoing. An example VisIt visualization is shown in Fig. 8.18 with a skewed color map to reveal features in the data that would not be otherwise apparent.

VTK accepts over 100 different data input formats and provides a simple scripting interface as an alternative to using the GUI for creating visualization.

8.8 Visual Intelligence

Visual intelligence workflows are more frequently complementing scientific data visualization on HPC systems. Image segmentation, illustrated in Fig. 8.19, where components of an image are partitioned into different objects identified via a machine learning algorithm, requires a separate set of tools than those visualization

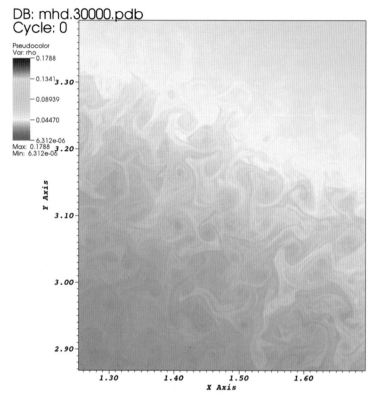

FIGURE 8.18

Example VisIt pseudocolor plot using a skewed color map to reveal a physical instability manifested as rolls in the data. The name of the visualized file appears in the upper left-hand corner, and the field variable name ("rho") is given above the color legend.

tools discussed earlier. Supervised machine learning models are used for image segmentation and require a large set of annotated visualizations for the model to perform image segmentation inference correctly.

Like conventional visualization tools, there are many tools for annotating visualizations to support image segmentation, ranging from commercial to open source. The annotation toolsets enable collaborative annotation efforts to support image segmentation and related machine learning efforts on HPC datasets. Some open-source examples include ScaLabel (https://github.com/scalabel/scalabel) and Label Studio (https://labelstud.io/). Many annotation tools already come as a docker container for easy installation and usage on an HPC system.

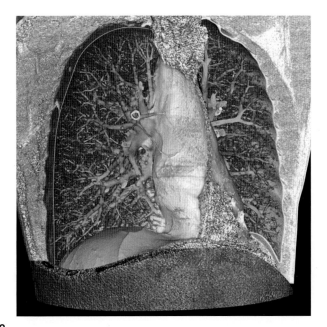

FIGURE 8.19

Three-dimensional image segmentation of a computed tomography (CT) scan of the thorax. Four colors are used to partition different elements of the CT scan distinguishing arteries and veins. Image segmentation driven by machine learning complements conventional visualization tools. (Image source: https://commons.wikimedia.org/wiki/File: 3D_CT_of_thorax.jpg)

8.9 Summary and Outcomes

- Motivations for visualizing data include debugging, exploring data, statistical hypothesis testing, and preparing presentation graphics.
- Many scientific visualizations incorporate at least one of some foundational visualization concepts: streamlines, isosurfaces, volume rendering by ray tracing, and mesh tessellations.
- Streamlines take a vector field as input and show curves that are tangent to the vector field.
- Isosurfaces are surfaces that connect data points that have the same value.
- Volume rendering by ray tracing casts rays through the data volume and sample the volume through which the ray passes.
- Mesh tessellations visualize data points and their connectivities to other data points using polygons.
- Gnuplot is a simple command-line visualization tool for 2D and 3D plots.
- Matplotlib is a Python-based visualization tool with easy integration to other libraries with Python bindings.

- VTK is an open-source collection of visualization algorithms for creating application-specific visualization solutions.
- ParaView and VisIt are turnkey visualization solutions incorporating VTK algorithms but providing a GUI and scripting interface for visualization.
- ParaView and VisIt already incorporate support for hundreds of widely used data formats on HPC systems.
- ParaView can come bundled with MPI to easily perform visualization across multiple compute nodes concurrently for visualizing large datasets that would not fit in the memory of a single node.
- Machine learning tools including image segmentation increasingly complement conventional visualization efforts.

8.10 Exercises

1. List all the factors that impact a decision to use a particular visualization approach for an HPC application. Create a table listing the trade-off space of the five visualization tools explored in this chapter.

2. Visualization tools provide many optional color legends. Why? In what circumstances is one color legend better than another?

3. Explore the parallel visualization capabilities of ParaView using HPC resources. Produce a strong scaling plot showing the time to solution for the visualization as a function of the number of computing resources employed.

4. Many HPC users interact with visualization tools like Matplotlib via a Jupyter Notebook or Lab. Test a visualization using Matplotlib and ParaView using a Jupyter Notebook instance. Are there any performance consequences?

5. Annotate a few frames of a visualization using ScaLabel and train an object detection and segmentation model to automatically segment the full visualization. How do any inaccuracies in the machine learning model impact the final segmented visualization?

References

[1] Gnuplot Homepage. [Online] http://www.gnuplot.info/.
[2] Matplotlib. [Online] http://matplotlib.org/.
[3] The Visualization Toolkit. [Online] http://www.vtk.org/.
[4] ParaView. [Online] http://www.paraview.org/.
[5] VisIt. [Online] https://wci.llnl.gov/simulation/computer-codes/visit.
[6] GNU Octave. [Online] https://www.gnu.org/software/octave/.

[7]   MathWorks. MATLAB. [Online] https://www.mathworks.com/products/matlab.html.

[8]   Python.org. Python Beginners Guide. [Online] https://wiki.python.org/moin/BeginnersGuide/Programmers.

[9]   National Institute of Standards and Technology. *Matrix Market Collection.* [Online] http://math.nist.gov/MatrixMarket/.

[10] SciPy Developers. *SciPy.* [Online] https://www.scipy.org/.

[11] Matplotlib. *mplot3d.* [Online] http://matplotlib.org/mpl_toolkits/mplot3d/.

Performance Monitoring and Measurement

9

Chapter outline

9.1 Introduction

Performance monitoring is both an inherent and a key step in application development. The code development process does not stop when the program appears to be doing what it was designed to do and the generated results are validated for correctness. Even when the application has been tested using a broad range of input parameters and datasets as well as multiple supported computational modes stressing individual program features, there still may be hidden problems preventing it from executing at the maximum performance permitted by the underlying platform. This is particularly important in parallel computing, where the impact of every inefficiency is effectively multiplied by the number of processor cores on which the application is running. Besides increasing the time necessary to arrive at a solution, this may also have financial implications, since often the user is charged for computer use in proportion to the consumed aggregate machine time. One of the most important reasons for performance monitoring is therefore to verify that the application is not impacted by any obvious or easily preventable degradation factors. One way to confirm this is a simple sanity check: is the actual computation time in line with the processor speed and the estimated total number of operations that need to be performed? Is the communication phase taking longer than estimated given the message sizes transmitted by the application and network bandwidth? Fortunately, these questions may be answered by performing simple instrumentation of application

High Performance Computing. https://doi.org/10.1016/B978-0-12-823035-0.00009-2

code to measure the time required to execute the segments of the program. This is discussed in Section 9.2.

Even a simple measurement, such as capture of a timestamp, impacts program execution due to greater than zero latency of the operation accessing the system timer and the nonzero resource footprint required to perform the operation. The more complex and frequent the measurements are, the more overhead is introduced into program execution, potentially skewing the measurement results and in the worst case completely changing the application execution flow. The latter may be particularly damaging, since the identification of sections of code that need to be revised for performance improvement may be incorrect and cause additional programmer effort with little or no benefit. One way to alleviate this problem is to apply statistical sampling. Instead of registering every occurrence of an event in a program, a snapshot of its state (sample) is taken at fixed intervals. The sampling period usually may be adjusted within a permitted range to increase the accuracy (again, at the cost of additional overhead) when there is a good possibility that some events were not accounted for, or lowered if the monitoring is discovered to be too intrusive or if a coarse execution profile is sufficient. Another, albeit limited, way to lower the instrumentation overheads is to use dedicated hardware to capture the events of interest. Modern central processing units (CPUs) implement dedicated registers that may be configured to count the occurrences of specific low-level events, such as branches, cache misses, instruction retirement, etc. Since the register updates are carried out entirely in hardware, executing software almost never sees the monitoring overhead. However, the consequence of a hardware implementation is that the classes of supported events are predefined and cannot be extended or customized.

9.2 Time Measurement

Execution time is one of the critical metrics of application performance and of primary importance to both application developers and end-users. Its measurement may be carried out at the whole program level as well as for selected sections of the monitored application. Each of these scenarios requires a different approach. The measurement of duration of application execution should typically be synchronized with the wall-clock time to establish a common reference permitting meaningful comparisons with results obtained on other platforms and environments. This is particularly important when application execution takes a significant amount of time, potentially counted in days. Most of computer system clocks are periodically synchronized over the network to a common high-accuracy standard typically derived from an atomic clock using protocols such as Network Time Protocol (NTP) [6]. This provides sufficiently good average accuracy in the long term, although it does not avoid the issue of local clock jitter.

Most Unix systems provide several utilities to access the wall-clock time from the command line. One of them is the *date* program that outputs the current date and time with accuracy down to single seconds. It may be used in batch job scripts to provide coarse timestamps for the start and end time of application execution (or any intermediate phases as long as they are represented by separate applications). Its output will be captured in a file storing the standard output stream of the job's execution shell for future inspection. An example output of the command as invoked from the shell prompt is shown below:

```
> date
Sun, Feb 05, 2017 6:17:33 PM
```

The date command also accepts custom date format specification as a command-line argument in case the default form shown above is not acceptable.

Since resolution at the full second level may not be sufficiently precise for short running applications, more accurate measurements may use the *time* utility that is available as a bash shell built-in command or a standalone system program. It has to be followed by a correctly formed command line fully describing the application with its options and command-line arguments. The specified application will be immediately spawned as specified, while the timing utility captures several key characteristics of its execution. For example:

```
> /usr/bin/time dd if=/dev/zero of=/dev/null bs=4096 count=1M
1048576+0 records in
1048576+0 records out
4294967296 bytes (4.3 GB, 4.0 GiB) copied, 0.482873 s, 8.9 GB/s
0.37user    0.10system    0:00.48elapsed    100%CPU    (0avgtext+0avgdata
415744maxresident)k
0inputs+0outputs (1643major+0minor)pagefaults 0swaps
```

The above times the execution of the *dd* program (available on any Linux distribution and used to copy and convert file data) that transfers 4 GB of zero-filled data to a null device. The first three lines contain output from the *dd* utility itself. In this case, the program execution took 0.48 s (as given by the elapsed time entry), of which 0.37 s were spent executing user code and 0.1 s for system (or kernel) code. The reported system and user times do not necessarily have to add to the elapsed time value. This is because program execution may be stalled, e.g., waiting for user input, completion of input/output (I/O) operations, or other external events. If the program could not fully utilize the allocated processor core(s), the reported utilization (as a percentage of the CPU) may be lower than 100%. The multithreaded programs may report values greater than 100%, since the displayed user and system times are the aggregate values over all compute threads spawned by the application.

The time utility also reports other details of program execution that may be helpful in analyzing the application's behavior. One of them, following the timings, provides the information about memory resources allocated by the application. The first number indicates the average size of memory used by program text (instruction pages), the second represents the average size of unshared program data, and the third shows the maximum size of physical memory (resident set) used by the application's process. These numbers are reported in kilobytes. The last line displayed by the time command lists the number of I/O operations performed by the program, the number of minor and major page faults, and how many times the process was swapped out from memory for disk. The difference between the major and minor page fault is that the first involves access to a storage device required to retrieve the contents of the memory page, while a minor fault only requires an update of page table entry. Therefore, the cost of a major fault is typically substantially higher than that of a minor fault. Similar to *date*, the output of the *time* command may be customized through the command-line option `-f` or `--format` to include additional parameters such as the number of involuntary and voluntary context switches, number of messages in socket-based communication, number of signals delivered to the process, and exit status of the process. The shell built-in *time* command reports only the user, system, and elapsed timings for the monitored program.

The timing utilities operating at the whole application level are not useful for measurement of the duration of execution of individual functions or code segments. For that purpose, a number of timing functions accessing the system's high-resolution clock are used. Individual implementations of high-resolution timers may differ from system to system depending on the actual processor type and system configuration. Since the native interfaces exposed by such timers are often not compatible with each other, typically the most portable way to access them is to use POSIX clock functions. The most frequently used call, `clock_gettime`, obtains the value of time that has elapsed from some fixed reference point in the past, typically machine boot time. It is as follows:

```
#include <time.h>
int clock_gettime(clockid_t id, struct timespec *tsp);
```

where `id` identifies one of the clocks available on the system and the structure to store the time data pointed to by `tsp` has two fields: `tv_sec` that contains the number of full seconds and `tv_nsec` that stores the number of nanoseconds expressing the remaining fraction of a second for the measured time interval. Both of these fields are integers of sufficient size to store the required data, frequently equal to the machine's native word size. The function returns zero on success. To verify the actual resolution of the accessed clock, POSIX provides the `clock_getres` function that takes the clock identifier argument and stores the measurement resolution value in a structure pointed to by `tsp`:

```
int clock_getres(clockid_t id, struct timespec *tsp);
```

For fine-granularity measurements, useful clock IDs include `CLOCK_MONOTONIC` and `CLOCK_MONOTONIC_RAW`. Unlike the system wall clock, which may be subjected to coarse changes of value due to the administrator manually adjusting the system time, the monotonic clock is only affected by incremental adjustments performed by the time synchronization protocol in effect (e.g., NTP). The raw monotonic clock has the same properties as the monotonic clock. However, it is not affected by external time adjustment. The POSIX interface also supports other clocks of interest: `CLOCK_BOOTTIME`, which is similar to the monotonic clock but includes the time that elapsed while the system was suspended; CLOCK_PROCESS_CPUTIME_ID, which measures the processor time consumed by all threads in the process that it was called in; and CLOCK_THREAD_CPUTIME_ID for the processor time clock that is limited to the specific thread. Selection of the suitable clock should be performed in the context of application and type of measurement; for most performance measurements on an "always on" platform, the monotonic clock is often sufficient as long as the overhead of several tens of nanoseconds per access is acceptable.

To take advantage of POSIX clocks, the user code needs to be explicitly instrumented with timing functions. To demonstrate this, a program performing matrix—vector multiplication with source code listed in Code 9.1 will be used. The same code will be subsequently subjected to analysis by other performance monitoring tools in the next sections of this chapter. The application allocates heap memory, initializes the matrix and multiplicand and product vectors (routine init, lines 6—15), performs the multiplication by invoking the CBLAS library function to compute dot products (mult function, lines 17—23), and verifies the result by performing an

```
001 #include <stdio.h>
002 #include <stdlib.h>
003 #include <cblas.h>
004 #include <time.h>
005
006 void init(int n, double **m, double **v, double **p, int trans) {
007    *m = calloc(n*n, sizeof(double));
008    *v = calloc(n, sizeof(double));
009    *p = calloc(n, sizeof(double));
010    for (int i = 0; i < n; i++) {
011       (*v)[i] = (i & 1)? -1.0: 1.0;
012       if (trans) for (int j = 0; j <= i; j++) (*m)[j*n+i] = 1.0;
013       else for (int j = 0; j <= i; j++) (*m)[i*n+j] = 1.0;
014    }
015 }
016
017 void mult(int size, double *m, double *v, double *p, int trans) {
018    int stride = trans? size: 1;
019    for (int i = 0; i < size; i++) {
020       int mi = trans? i: i*size;
021       p[i] = cblas_ddot(size, m+mi, stride, v, 1);
022    }
023 }
024
025 int main(int argc, char **argv) {
026    int n = 1000, trans = 0;
027    if (argc > 1) n = strtol(argv[1], NULL, 10);
028    if (argc > 2) trans = (argv[2][0] == 't');
029
030    double *m, *v, *p;
031    init(n, &m, &v, &p, trans);
032    mult(n, m, v, p, trans);
033    double s = cblas_dasum(n, p, 1);
034    printf("Size %d; abs. sum: %f (expected: %d)\n", n, s, (n+1)/2);
035    return 0;
036 }
```

CODE 9.1 Matrix—vector multiply code operating in row- and column-major modes.

```
     ...
025  double sec(struct timespec *ts) {
026     return ts->tv_sec+1e-9*ts->tv_nsec;
027  }
028
029  int main(int argc, char **argv) {
030     struct timespec t0, t1, t2, t3, t4;
031     clock_gettime(CLOCK_MONOTONIC, &t0);
032     int n = 1000, trans = 0;
033     if (argc > 1) n = strtol(argv[1], NULL, 10);
034     if (argc > 2) trans = (argv[2][0] == 't');
035
036     double *m, *v, *p;
037     clock_gettime(CLOCK_MONOTONIC, &t1);
038     init(n, &m, &v, &p, trans);
039     clock_gettime(CLOCK_MONOTONIC, &t2);
040     mult(n, m, v, p, trans);
041     clock_gettime(CLOCK_MONOTONIC, &t3);
042     double s = cblas_dasum(n, p, 1);
043     clock_gettime(CLOCK_MONOTONIC, &t4);
044     printf("Size %d; abs. sum: %f (expected: %d)\n", n, s, (n+1)/2);
045     printf("Timings:\n   program: %f s\n", sec(&t4)-sec(&t0));
046     printf("      init: %f s\n      mult: %f s\n       sum: %f s\n",
047           sec(&t2)-sec(&t1), sec(&t3)-sec(&t2), sec(&t4)-sec(&t3));
048     return 0;
049  }
```

CODE 9.2 Instrumented section of the matrix multiplication code.

absolute value sum on the elements of the product vector (cblas_dasum in line 33). Both initialization and multiplication can be performed in row- or column-major fashion, potentially impacting the duration of computations. This is controlled by the second command-line argument (transposition flag); the first one specifies the size of the matrix. To gather the timing information, clock_gettime functions were added to the main function of the source as shown in Code 9.2 (only the instrumented section is provided; the starting part of the program preceding line 25 is unchanged). Code 9.2 also defines the sec function that is used to convert the contents of the timespec structure to floating-point number of seconds, thus enabling a straightforward calculation of time intervals. The collection of timestamps is arranged with as little additional code as possible, and therefore the conversion of timing values to seconds and printout of final values are performed outside the timed regions.

Execution of the instrumented code in row-major mode with matrix size $10,000 \times 10,000$ yields:

```
> ./mvmult 20000
Size 20000; abs. sum: 10000.000000 (expected: 10000)
Timings:
  program: 1.148853 s
     init: 0.572537 s
     mult: 0.576276 s
      sum: 0.000037 s
```

Doing the same using less efficient, column-major operation results in:

```
> ./mvmult 20000 t
Size 20000; abs. sum: 10000.000000 (expected: 10000)
Timings:
  program: 12.126625 s
     init: 4.343727 s
     mult: 7.782852 s
      sum: 0.000043 s
```

As can be seen, program execution in transposed mode takes an order of magnitude longer. The change is attributed primarily to a substantial increase in execution time of initialization and multiplication subroutines that access the matrix data. The absolute sum performed in the verification phase takes roughly the same amount of time, since the layout of the input data (product vector) did not change.

9.3 Performance Profiling
9.3.1 Significance of Application Profiling

The goal of profiling is to provide an insight into application execution that may help identify potential performance problems. These may be related to the algorithmic code makeup, memory management, communication, or I/O. Profiling tools usually concentrate on *hotspot* analysis, that is, detection of parts of code the program spends most of the time executing. These may lead to identification of bottlenecks, or those hotspots that have unduly adverse effects on the application's performance. A bottleneck is usually apparent as a throughput-limiting component in processing flow. Typically, both the predecessor and successor components of a bottleneck are capable of providing higher-aggregate throughput than that of a bottleneck. Bottlenecks may sometimes be replaced by a less limiting implementation (optimized). This may cause a dominant program bottleneck to move to another location in the code. Not every hotspot is necessarily a bottleneck. Many tightly optimized numeric libraries, for example, will spend nearly all of their time performing floating-point unit computations. This doesn't mean they are inefficient (the evidence for this is provided when the machine reaches performance near its hardware peak or close to the theoretical throughput limit of the computational algorithm used). Profilers may record compute performance data at the system level (including all active processes, system daemons, and kernel code running on a node); the process level, where only data relevant to a specific process is collected; or individual threads of a process. Additionally, profiling may be restricted to a user space, kernel space, or both. Profiling requires that the analyzed application is *instrumented*, or modified in a way that permits the profiler to access the required runtime information. This process may be more (e.g., the programmer injecting the required function calls or macros in the relevant places of source code) or less (linking with a profiling library or attaching an external profiler to an already running process) invasive. The first often occurs when the tracking of user-defined events is necessary.

Besides analysis of computational performance, profiling tools may monitor other characteristics of the executed programs. One of them is memory usage over the course of program execution. This applies to the overall size of virtual memory allocated by the application, the amount of physical memory assigned to the program, the shared memory that may be accessible to other concurrently executing processes, and the sizes of a program's stack, data, and text segment. The other aspect is I/O, for which the profiler records the number of input and output operations, the amount of data transferred to or from the secondary storage or buffer cache, achieved data bandwidth, number of files opened, and so on. Finally, communication profiling registers the number and size of messages sent, their destinations, latencies, and bandwidths. This can be further categorized by network type (Ethernet, InfiniBand, etc.), communication endpoint type (sockets, RDMA), or protocol used. Information collected during profiling can be used to classify a program or its individual subroutines as *CPU* (or *compute*) *bound*, where execution time is dominated by processor speed; *memory bound*, for which execution time is primarily dictated by the amount of memory needed to store the program's data structures; or *I/O bound*, where a dominant fraction of execution time is spent performing I/O operations. The code characteristic may change as a result of optimization, e.g., from CPU bound to I/O bound.

9.3.2 Essential *gperftools*

The *time* utility discussed previously is an example of a simple profiler. Its usefulness is limited by reporting only the single average, cumulative, or maximum value of parameters of interest for the entire duration of program execution. This makes it impossible to pinpoint the moment in program execution when performance was degraded and cross-reference it to the responsible sections of source code.

Modern profiling tools attempt to address this issue. One of the commonly used profilers is available as a part of the *gperftools* [7] package. While originally named Google Performance Tools, the code is currently maintained by the community and is distributed under the BSD license. It provides a statistical CPU profiler *pprof* and several tools based around the *tcmalloc* (thread-caching malloc) library. Besides offering an improved memory allocation library for multithreaded environments, the *tcmalloc* library also supports memory leak detection and dynamic memory allocation profiling. To illustrate the use of these features, the program from Code 9.1 was compiled using the command shown below (note the addition of −lprofiler to the command line). To permit access to a program's symbol table, a -ggdb option was specified as well:

```
> gcc -O2 -ggdb mvmult.c —o mvmult -lcblas -lprofiler
```

The *gperftools* CPU profiler does not require any changes to the source code and after successfully linking the instrumented application may be executed. The location of the file containing the collected data must be specified using the CPU-PROFILE environment variable as demonstrated below:

```
> env CPUPROFILE=mvmult.prof ./mvmult 20000
Size 20000; abs. sum: 10000.000000 (expected: 10000)
PROFILE: interrupts/evictions/bytes = 115/0/376
```

The program execution proceeds as before with the expected output appearing on the console. The only change is the final line, which confirms that the profiling indeed took place and collected 115 data samples. To display the obtained information, pprof tool is used:

```
> pprof --text mvmult mvmult.prof
Using local file mvmult.
Using local file mvmult.prof.
Total: 115 samples
      58   50.4%   50.4%       58   50.4% ddot_
      57   49.6%  100.0%       57   49.6% init
       0    0.0%  100.0%       57   49.6% 0x00007f2c9485e00f
```

The produced output is organized in several columns. The first shows the sample count associated with each function. Whenever the profiler collects a sample, it records, among other things, the current address stored in the instruction pointer of the running program context. Subsequent analysis done by pprof assigns the collected addresses to individual program functions. This is shown in the second column. The result above indicates that practically the entire program time is spent in two functions: ddot_ and init. While init may be found in Code 9.1, ddot_ is a Fortran function indirectly called by CBLAS that computes the double-precision dot product. The third column lists the cumulative percentage of samples for all functions displayed so far. The fourth and fifth columns deal with the aggregate sample counts and percentages for the annotated function as well as all its callees. Hence, the unnamed function in the last line is the likely ancestor of the init function; it might be related to an early setup code that executes before the invocation of main. Finally, the last column lists the affected function names or, if not available, raw sampled addresses.

The default sampling frequency is 100 samples per second. This can be set to a custom value using the CPUPROFILE_FREQUENCY environment variable, although the maximum speed for most Linux platforms is limited to 1000 per second. Since the test application runs for only about a second, trying to increase the number of samples may offer additional insights:

```
> env CPUPROFILE=mvmult1K.prof CPUPROFILE_FREQUENCY=1000 ./mvmult 20000
Size 20000; abs. sum: 10000.000000 (expected: 10000)
PROFILE: interrupts/evictions/bytes = 1147/0/536
```

About 10 times as many samples were collected. Their analysis reveals the following:

```
> pprof --text mvmult mvmult1K.prof
Using local file mvmult.
Using local file mvmult1K.prof.
Total: 1147 samples
      576   50.2%   50.2%       576   50.2% ddot_
      571   49.8%  100.0%       571   49.8% init
        0    0.0%  100.0%       571   49.8% 0x00007f5fd0cda00f
```

Most of the test application execution is concentrated in the two functions identified before. However, pprof supports other analysis options that may be changed through command-line switches.

- --text displays the profile in a plain text form.
- --list=<regex> outputs only data related to functions whose names match the provided regular expression.
- --disasm=<regex>, like list, but performs disassembly of a relevant section of the program while annotating each line with a sample count.
- --dot, --pdf, --ps, --gif, and --gv generate annotated graphical representation of a call graph and output it to *stdout* in the requested format. Requires that the *dot* converter is installed in the system. The last option uses the *gv* viewer to open a window with call graph visualization.

The default output of pprof is performed at function granularity, but sometimes it is useful to change that to avoid lengthy output or zoom in more closely on to the source of the problem. Options to adjust this, in order of decreasing resolution, are:

- --addresses shows annotated code addresses.
- --lines annotates source code lines.
- --functions lists the statistics per function.
- --files switches to whole-file granularity.

To see how the samples are distributed within the init function, one may apply the following command to the set of profiling data collected before (to save space, the produced output was truncated and removed lines were replaced with "[...]"):

```
> pprof --list=init --lines mvmult mvmult1K.prof
Using local file mvmult.
Using local file mvmult1K.prof.
ROUTINE ====================== init in /home/maciek/perf/mvmult.c
   571       571 Total samples (flat / cumulative)
   [...]
     .         .    6: void init(int n, double **m, double **v, double **p, int
trans) {
     .         .    7:    *m = calloc(n*n, sizeof(double));
     .         .    8:    *v = calloc(n, sizeof(double));
     .         .    9:    *p = calloc(n, sizeof(double));
     .         .   10:    for (int i = 0; i < n; i++) {
     1         1   11:      (*v)[i] = (i & 1)? -1.0: 1.0;
```

```
     .          .     12:   if(trans)for(int j=0;j<=i;j++)(*m)[j*n+i]=1.0;
    570        570     13:   else for (int j = 0; j <= i; j++) (*m)[i*n+j] = 1.0;
     .          .     14:   }
     .          .     15: }
[...]
```

Not unexpectedly, this shows that most of the initialization time is spent within the main loop. Of that, the inner loop performing initialization of matrix rows dominates the execution time, while the multiplicand vector initialization is marginal by comparison. Since the sources of BLAS routines are not available, a disassembled code listing may be used to identify the fine-grain hotspots in that code (again, the output was shortened to the most interesting fragment):

```
> pprof --disasm=ddot_ mvmult mvmult.prof
Using local file mvmult.
Using local file mvmult.prof.
ROUTINE ====================== ddot_
    576      576 samples (flat, cumulative) 50.2% of total
[...]
     48       48      fcc0: movsd -0x8(%rax),%xmm0
      9        9      fcc5: add $0x28,%rax
      .        .      fcc9: add $0x28,%rcx
     60       60      fccd: movsd -0x20(%rax),%xmm2
     43       43      fcd2: mulsd -0x30(%rcx),%xmm0
      .        .      fcd7: mulsd -0x20(%rcx),%xmm2
      2        2      fcdc: addsd %xmm0,%xmm1
     26       26      fce0: movsd -0x28(%rax),%xmm0
      .        .      fce5: mulsd -0x28(%rcx),%xmm0
      .        .      fcea: addsd %xmm0,%xmm1
     81       81      fcee: addsd %xmm2,%xmm1
     93       93      fcf2: movsd -0x18(%rax),%xmm2
      9        9      fcf7: mulsd -0x18(%rcx),%xmm2
      .        .      fcfc: movapd %xmm1,%xmm0
     57       57      fd00: movsd -0x10(%rax),%xmm1
     13       13      fd05: mulsd -0x10(%rcx),%xmm1
      .        .      fd0a: cmp %rax,%rdx
      .        .      fd0d: addsd %xmm2,%xmm0
     70       70      fd11: addsd %xmm0,%xmm1
     65       65      fd15: jne fcc0 <ddot_+0x110>
[...]
```

It is not difficult to guess that the annotated instructions are performing the arithmetic operations (scalar double-precision multiplication and addition) and managing the data movement between memory and floating-point registers (denoted as % xmm with a numeric suffix). The listed code segment captures the innermost loop, as evidenced by the backward conditional branch in the last line. The overhead of memory access is comparable to the cost of computation. The fact that only scalar arithmetic operations were used indicates an optimization opportunity, since the dense algebra algorithms frequently benefit from single-instruction multiple data (SIMD) support available on modern CPUs. Further investigation reveals that CBLAS was linked to the reference BLAS library instead of any of the optimized versions.

For completeness, profile data of the transposed case sampled at 100 samples/ second are available below. While the program's execution is still confined to the same functions as before, the ratio of their timing has changed: initialization is less affected by column-major layout. At this point it is difficult to ascertain the reason for the difference in performance based solely on CPU profile data.

```
> pprof --text mvmult mvmult_trans.prof
Using local file mvmult.
Using local file mvmult_trans.prof.
Total: 13577 samples
    9240  68.1%  68.1%     9240  68.1% ddot_
    4335  31.9% 100.0%     4335  31.9% init
       2   0.0% 100.0%        2   0.0% ddotsub_
       0   0.0% 100.0%     4335  31.9% 0x00007f6440b6900f
```

One of the features of *gperftools* is the ability to detect memory leaks. To enable this functionality, it is necessary to link the application with the *tcmalloc* library or set environment variable LD_PRELOAD to libtcmalloc.so. Before launching the application, the leak detector needs to be informed about the flavor of checking that should be performed. This is accomplished by storing one of the keywords minimal, normal, strict, or draconian in the HEAPCHECK environment variable. They differ in scope and level of detail performed by the heap allocation checker; for most purposes normal mode is sufficient. The compilation command line and results of the instrumented program execution are shown below.

```
> gcc -O2 mvmult.c -o mvmult -lcblas -ltcmalloc
> env HEAPCHECK=normal ./mvmult 20000
WARNING: Perftools heap leak checker is active -- Performance may suffer
tcmalloc: large alloc 3200000000 bytes == 0xe9e000 @ 0x7f887688eae7
0x4009b1 0x400b95
Size 20000; abs. sum: 10000.000000 (expected: 10000)
Have memory regions w/o callers: might report false leaks
Leak check _main_ detected leaks of 3200160000 bytes in 2 objects
```

Since the program in Code 9.1 performs explicit memory allocation in init but that memory is never freed, the heap checker reports a leak at the end of main. *tcmalloc* also prints statements whenever large amounts of memory are allocated.

The tool may also profile memory management similarly to CPU profiling. In this case the source code needs to be explicitly instrumented: a HeapProfilerStart function has to be inserted before the profiled section of code, and a HeapProfilerStop function must be added at the end. The first function takes one argument describing the file name prefix used to store the profiling data. Multiple files may be generated. Each of them has a unique number and ".prof" extension added automatically. The prototypes of these functions are defined in header file "gperftools/heap-profiler.h." The profiler's behavior may be adjusted through dedicated environment variables:

- HEAP_PROFILE_ALLOCATION_INTERVAL—each time the specified number of bytes is allocated, the profile data is stored in file; defaults to 1 GB.
- HEAP_PROFILE_INUSE_INTERVAL—as above but the profile is written every time the total memory use by the program increases by the specified value; defaults to 100 MB.
- HEAP_PROFILE_TIME_INTERVAL—stores data every time period in seconds (default: 0).
- HEAP_PROFILE_MMAP—in addition to the usual C and C++ memory allocation calls such as `malloc`, `calloc`, `realloc`, and `new`, also profiles `mmap`, `mremap`, and `sbrk` calls. By default it is disabled (false).
- HEAP_PROFILE_ONLY_MMAP—constrains the profiling to only `mmap`, `mremap`, and `sbrk` functions; the default value is false.
- HEAP_PROFILE_MMAP_LOG—enables logging of `mmap` and `munmap` calls; default is false.

To illustrate the use of the memory profiler, the following sequence of commands compiles the instrumented application (the file prefix was set to "mvmult") and launches it with profiling enabled. The threshold is set to a low value to capture all allocation calls.

```
> env HEAP_PROFILE_ALLOCATION_INTERVAL=1 ./mvmult_heap 20000
Starting tracking the heap
tcmalloc: large alloc 3200000000 bytes == 0x2258000 @ 0x7fd915a2eae7
0x400a71 0x400c55
Dumping  heap  profile  to  mvmult.0001.heap  (3051  MB  allocated
cumulatively, 3051 MB currently in use)
Dumping  heap  profile  to  mvmult.0002.heap  (3051  MB  allocated
cumulatively, 3051 MB currently in use)
Dumping  heap  profile  to  mvmult.0003.heap  (3052  MB  allocated
cumulatively, 3052 MB currently in use)
Dumping  heap  profile  to  mvmult.0004.heap  (3052  MB  allocated
cumulatively, 3052 MB currently in use)
Size 20000; abs. sum: 10000.000000 (expected: 10000)
```

After the program execution completes, four data dump files may be found in working directories named from "mvmult.0001.heap" to "mvmult.0004.heap." The pprof may display the information in one of four modes determined by an additional command-line switch:

- `--inuse-space`—shows the number of megabytes currently in use (the default).
- `--inuse-objects`—shows the number of objects in use.
- `--alloc_space`—shows the number of allocated megabytes.
- `--alloc-objects`—shows the number of allocated objects.

Thus, to display the allocated data captured by the last sample, the following command is used:

```
> pprof --text --alloc_space mvmult_heap mvmult.0004.heap
Using local file mvmult_heap.
Using local file mvmult.0004.heap.
Total: 3052.1 MB
  3052.1 100.0% 100.0%    3052.1 100.0% init
     0.0   0.0% 100.0%       0.0   0.0% __GI__IO_file_doallocate
     0.0   0.0% 100.0%       0.2   0.0% 0x00000000c0e19fff
     0.0   0.0% 100.0%    3051.9 100.0% __libc_csu_init
```

While *gperftool* suite directly supports profiling of individual applications, it is also possible to use it for inspection of message-passing interface (MPI) programs. Since an application's performance data must be written to a specific file, one way to avoid collisions is to make sure that each monitored MPI process is assigned a different file. This is accomplished by adding the following statement to the application's source at a point following `MPI_Init` invocation:

```
ProfilerStart(filename);
```

The prototype of this function is available in `gperftools/profiler.h` along with other calls that may be helpful to control the profiler's operation. The *filename* parameter must be a different string for each MPI process. This is typically arranged by deriving it from the rank of the process within `MPI_COMM_WORLD`. For example:

```
int rank;
MPI_Comm_rank(MPICOMM_WORLD, &rank);
char filename[256];
snprintf(filename, 256, "my_app%04d.prof", rank);
ProfileStart(filename);
```

9.4 Monitoring Hardware Events
9.4.1 Perf

The *perf* framework [8], also referred to as *perf_events*, is a performance monitoring tool and event tracer closely integrated with the Linux OS kernel. Its primary functionality is based on the *sys_perf_event_open* [9] system call introduced in the 2.6 series of Linux. The system call enables access to special-purpose registers of the CPU that may be configured to collect the counts of specific hardware-level events. These events may vary from processor to processor, but their main categories include:

- Cache related: misses and references issued. They may be further grouped by cache level (L1 through L3), cache type (instruction and data), and access type (loads and stores).

- Translation lookaside buffer (TLB) related. These may also be subdivided into instruction and data categories and by access type (load/store).
- Branch statistics. This includes counts of overall branch occurrences and missed branch target loads.
- Instructions and cycles. *Perf* can also provide the number of executed instructions or count of CPU cycles that occurred during program execution.
- Stalled or idle cycles. They further subdivide into front-end and back-end stalls. The first indicate an inability to completely fill the available capacity of the first stages of the execution pipeline and may be caused by instruction cache or TLB misses, mispredicted branches, or unavailability of translation into micro-operations for specific instruction(s). The back-end issues may be caused by interinstruction dependencies (e.g., long latency instruction delaying the execution of other dependent instructions, such as division) or availability of memory units.
- Node-level statistics: prefetches, loads and stores, and misses. Prefetch misses are counted separately to avoid false inflation of statistics describing actual data accesses generated by the monitored code.
- Collected by processor's performance management unit. These counters provide the aggregate values for the whole CPU, including primarily *uncore*-related events. Uncore is a term coined by Intel to describe segments of CPU logic that are not part of the core execution pipeline and thus are shared by the cores. They include memory controllers and their interfaces, a node-level interconnect bus that provides NUMA functionality, last-level cache, coherency traffic monitor, and power management.

The *perf* tool also provides access to many software-level kernel events that may be of great use for performance analysis. They comprise counts of context switches; context migrations; data alignment faults; major, minor, and aggregate page faults; accurate time measurements; and even custom events defined using the Berkeley Packet Filter framework. The complete list of events supported on the local system is obtained with:

```
> perf list
```

Perf may be invoked in several modes of operation selected by the first argument on the command line. The frequently used commands are:

- `stat`, which executes the provided application with arguments while collecting the counts of specified events or a default event set.
- `record`, which enables per-thread, per-process, or per-CPU profiling.
- `report`, which performs analysis of data collected by `perf record`.
- `annotate`, which correlates the gathered profiling data to assembly code.
- `top`, which displays the statistics in real time using a format resembling that of Unix *top* utility for visualization of process activity.
- `bench`, which invokes a number of predefined kernel benchmarks.

To test this functionality in practice, profile the test application shown in Code 9.1. The result for row-major (nontransposed) mode is presented below:

```
> perf stat ./mvmult 20000
Size 20000; abs. sum: 10000.000000 (expected: 10000)

Performance counter stats for './mvmult 20000':

         1219.404556      task-clock (msec)         #    1.000 CPUs utilized
                   1      context-switches          #    0.001 K/sec
                   0      cpu-migrations            #    0.000 K/sec
             781,490      page-faults               #    0.641 M/sec
       3,898,266,727      cycles                    #    3.197 GHz
       2,283,166,328      stalled-cycles-frontend   #   58.57% frontend
cycles idle
       1,372,252,385      stalled-cycles-backend    #   35.20% backend
cycles idle
       3,764,331,355      instructions              #    0.97 insns per
cycle
                                                    #    0.61 stalled
cycles per insn
         495,220,268      branches                  #  406.116 M/sec
             815,338      branch-misses             #    0.16% of all
branches
         1.219967824 seconds time elapsed
```

Invoking the same for column-major layout produces:

```
Performance counter stats for './mvmult 20000 t':

        12212.530334      task-clock (msec)         #    1.000 CPUs utilized
                  11      context-switches          #    0.001 K/sec
                   0      cpu-migrations            #    0.000 K/sec
           1,213,417      page-faults               #    0.099 M/sec
      42,933,883,759      cycles                    #    3.516 GHz
      39,567,001,587      stalled-cycles-frontend   # 92.16% frontend
cycles idle
      37,181,761,140      stalled-cycles-backend    # 86.60% backend
cycles idle
       6,077,067,370      instructions              #    0.14 insns per
cycle
                                                    #    6.51 stalled
cycles per insn
         918,790,187      branches                  # 75.233 M/sec
           1,276,503      branch-misses             #    0.14% of all
branches
        12.213751102 seconds time elapsed
```

Besides the duration of program execution, there are several other noticeable differences between the two modes of operation. First, the number of front-end and back-end stalls is significantly increased. The effective number of stalls per instruction is an order of magnitude higher. The instruction throughput per cycle is also much lower. Serious inefficiencies are introduced in the processing pipeline. Curiously, despite using a nearly identical algorithm, the number of executed instructions is 60% greater for the column-major case. The code also encounters a much higher number of page faults in that mode.

Since the types of executed instructions are likely similar for both cases, the increased number of stalls may indicate caching issues. A higher count of page faults might also suggest TLB problems. To confirm this, the codes are reexecuted with custom selection of events. *perf* may accommodate a greater number of events in a single invocation than available hardware slots in the processor using a technique called *multiplexing*. It means that at any given moment only a subset of requested events is configured on the processor; this subset is periodically replaced with one that contains other requested events. This is repeated cyclically to permit all specified events to be active for an approximately equal share of time during application execution. The additional options that may be passed to *perf* invocation are:

- -e *event* [:*modifier*][,*event*[:*modifier*]]...
  Explicitly specifies the kinds of monitored events. Each event name may be followed by one or more modifiers, such as u for measuring only the events when the application executes in user mode or k when it is in kernel mode (and others that are not relevant here).

- -B
  Separates groups of every three digits in numbers by commas for easier readability.

- -p *pid*
  Instead of directly launching an application, the profiler attaches to an existing process with the specified *pid.*

- -r *integer*
  Repeatedly runs the command, collecting the aggregate statistics. The result shows the mean values for each event and deviation from the mean.

- -a
  Forces *perf* to collect data for all CPUs, including profiles of other applications running at the same time. The default is to monitor only the specified application's threads.

To put this into practice, the code was run again with the monitoring of cache misses and TLB load misses enabled:

```
> perf stat -B -e cache-misses,dTLB-load-misses,iTLB-load-misses
./mvmult 20000
Size 20000; abs. sum: 10000.000000 (expected: 10000)

Performance counter stats for './mvmult 20000':
```

```
29,307,244        cache-misses
 3,121,156        dTLB-load-misses
     4,224        iTLB-load-misses
```

In transposed version:

```
Performance counter stats for './mvmult 20000 t':

   79,004,606        cache-misses
  405,044,765        dTLB-load-misses
       33,124        iTLB-load-misses

   12.185000849 seconds time elapsed
```

The collected data show a significant increase for all three figures. Particularly damaging is the two orders of magnitude jump in data-TLB misses. This is caused by strided access to matrix elements; the consecutive references not only touch different cache lines but also involve different memory pages (8-byte entries with 20,000-element stride are effectively separated by 160 KB, which is far greater than the default page size of 4 KB). This emphasizes the importance of selecting algorithms that exhibit good spatial locality of access.

To verify that the change is caused by different data layouts used by the main compute functions, the performance data were recorded in sampling mode using the command shown below. The -F option controls the sampling frequency; in this case 1000 samples per second are requested.

```
> perf record -F 1000 -e cache-misses,dTLB-load-misses,iTLB-load-mis-
ses ./mvmult 20000 t
Size 20000; abs. sum: 10000.000000 (expected: 10000)
[ perf record: Woken up 4 times to write data ]
[ perf record: Captured and wrote 0.834 MB perf.data (17967 samples) ]
```

The collected information may be analyzed using the "perf report" command. The most significant excerpts of the result are listed below.

```
# Samples: 6K of event 'cache-misses'
# Event count (approx.): 78141963
#
# Overhead  Command  Shared Object      Symbol
#
#
    33.64%  mvmult   libblas.so.3.6.0   [.] ddot_
    27.12%  mvmult   [kernel.vmlinux]   [k] clear_page
    24.04%  mvmult   mvmult             [.] init
     6.73%  mvmult   [kernel.vmlinux]   [k] _raw_spin_lock
     3.93%  mvmult   [kernel.vmlinux]   [k] page_fault
[...]
# Samples: 10K of event 'dTLB-load-misses'
# Event count (approx.): 405199968
#
```

```
# Overhead Command Shared Object Symbol
#
#
    99.03%  mvmult    libblas.so.3.6.0   [.] ddot_
     0.63%  mvmult    [kernel.vmlinux]   [k] page_fault
     0.14%  mvmult    [kernel.vmlinux]   [k] handle_mm_fault
[...]
# Samples: 1K of event 'iTLB-load-misses'
# Event count (approx.): 33857
#
# Overhead Command Shared Object Symbol
#
#
    15.57%  mvmult    libblas.so.3.6.0   [.] ddot_
     8.86%  mvmult    libcblas.so        [.] cblas_ddot
     6.16%  mvmult    mvmult             [.] init
     5.97%  mvmult    [kernel.vmlinux]   [k] cpumask_any_but
     5.74%  mvmult    [kernel.vmlinux]   [k] page_fault
     5.54%  mvmult    [kernel.vmlinux]   [k] notifier_call_chain
     4.62%  mvmult    [kernel.vmlinux]   [k] flush_tlb_mm_range
     4.57%  mvmult    libcblas.so        [.] ddotsub_
     3.27%  mvmult    [kernel.vmlinux]   [k] smp_apic_timer_interrupt
     2.90%  mvmult    [kernel.vmlinux]   [k] apic_timer_interrupt
     2.33%  mvmult    [kernel.vmlinux]   [k] update_vsyscall
     2.10%  mvmult    mvmult             [.] mult
[...]
```

As can be seen, the ddot_ function is the primary contributor of cache and TLB misses. A large percentage of cache misses are also caused by the kernel's page-clearing function, most likely called as a consequence of using the calloc function to allocate the memory for matrix and vectors. The init function is the source of a significant fraction of cache misses.

Unlike *gperftools*, *perf* can only record the performance data in a file with a fixed name. This makes it harder to analyze the performance of all component processes composing an MPI application. The workaround on a machine with dedicated local storage partitions (e.g., in /tmp) could be by starting the application in node-exclusive mode (one process per node) after changing the working directory to one on the local file system. After the application terminates, the generated data files may be copied (and renamed) for analysis to a shared file system using *scp*. If all component processes of the application execute a similar workload, it may suffice to set up monitoring only for one of them as delineated in Section 3.5.2.2. The approximate counts for the whole application are then derived by multiplying single process counts by the number of executed MPI processes. Note that monitoring of arbitrary rank can also be arranged by subdividing the processes into correctly sized groups using the −np *n* option to *mpirun*, while remembering that they have to add up to the total count of processes required by the application and only one instance may invoke *perf*.

9.4.2 Performance Application Programming Interface

The Performance Application Programming Interface (PAPI) [10] is a performance monitoring toolkit developed at the Innovative Computing Laboratory at the University of Tennessee. It provides C and Fortran library and header files containing prototypes of functions that may be used to instrument user applications. The application programming interface (API) categories comprise library initialization and shutdown; event description and translation between symbolic event names and their codes; creation and manipulation of event sets; starting and stopping of event counters; retrieval, accumulation, resetting, and initialization of counter values; system parameter queries; and various timing functions. The package also provides a number of practical utilities:

- `papi_avail` prints the symbolic names of *preset* events annotated with availability flags on the local systems and whether they are counted directly or derived by using more than one counter. Using option `-a` limits the display only to events locally available.
- `papi_native_avail` similarly displays so-called *native* events, which typically comprise uncore and node-level events.
- `papi_decode` outputs more detailed event descriptions in csv format.
- `papi_clockres` determines the practical resolution of various time and cycle measurement interfaces.
- `papi_cost` checks the latency of invocation of various API functions in different configurations.
- `papi_event_chooser` prints out events that may be added without conflict to a set containing events specified by the user.
- `papi_mem_info` shows the local machine cache and TLB hierarchy information.

PAPI events are less portable across processor architectures than those exposed by the *perf* tool. The user always needs to confirm whether a specific event is available on the target platform by using `papi_avail` or `papi_native_avail`. Due to the growing complexity of microprocessor designs, the interpretation of seemingly the same events may change even between different iterations of the same architecture. On the other hand, PAPI may be used to instrument the application in precise locations of the code and enables use of events that are normally not supported by *perf*.

To showcase the use of the interface, Code 9.1 was instrumented with two counters that tally the occurrences of double-precision operations; however, one counts instances of all floating-point operations converted to scalar operations (`PAPI_DP_OPS`) and the other vector operations (`PAPI_VEC_DP`). The counters are activated just before the initialization (line 45), and their values are retrieved after return from the `init`, `mult`, and `cblas_dasum` functions (lines 48, 50, and 52). To guard against silent failures, a PAPI_CALL macro was defined in lines 25–30 to verify that called PAPI routines completed successfully. As before, only the modified portion of the source code is provided (not counting the inclusion of the PAPI header, papi.h, in the top section of the source file) in Code 9.3.

For correct compilation, the program must be linked with the PAPI library as shown below:

```
> gcc -O2 mvmult_papi.c -o mvmult_papi -lcblas -lpapi
```

Running the instrumented program produces the following output:

```
> ./mvmult_papi 20000
Size 20000; abs. sum: 10000.000000 (expected: 10000)
PAPI counts:
   init: event1:              0 event2:              0
   mult: event1:      804193640 event2:              0
    sum: event1:          20276 event2:              0
```

```
  ...
025 #define PAPI_CALL(fn, ok_code) do { \
026   if (ok_code != fn) { \
027     fprintf(stderr, "Error: " #fn " failed, aborting\n"); \
028     exit(1); \
029   } \
030 } while (0)
031
032 #define NEV 2
033
034 int main(int argc, char **argv) {
035   int n = 1000, trans = 0;
036   if (argc > 1) n = strtol(argv[1], NULL, 10);
037   if (argc > 2) trans = (argv[2][0] == 't');
038
039   int evset = PAPI_NULL;
040   PAPI_CALL(PAPI_library_init(PAPI_VER_CURRENT), PAPI_VER_CURRENT);
041   PAPI_CALL(PAPI_create_eventset(&evset), PAPI_OK);
042   PAPI_CALL(PAPI_add_event(evset, PAPI_DP_OPS), PAPI_OK);
043   PAPI_CALL(PAPI_add_event(evset, PAPI_VEC_DP), PAPI_OK);
044   double *m, *v, *p;
045   PAPI_CALL(PAPI_start(evset), PAPI_OK);
046   init(n, &m, &v, &p, trans);
047   long long v1[NEV], v2[NEV], v3[NEV];
048   PAPI_CALL(PAPI_read(evset, v1), PAPI_OK);
049   mult(n, m, v, p, trans);
050   PAPI_CALL(PAPI_read(evset, v2), PAPI_OK);
051   double s = cblas_dasum(n, p, 1);
052   PAPI_CALL(PAPI_stop(evset, v3), PAPI_OK);
053   printf("Size %d; abs. sum: %f (expected: %d)\n", n, s, (n+1)/2);
054   printf("PAPI counts:\n");
055   printf("  init: event1: %15lld event2: %15lld\n", v1[0], v1[1]);
056   printf("  mult: event1: %15lld event2: %15lld\n", v2[0]-v1[0], v2[1]-
v1[1]);
057   printf("   sum: event1: %15lld event2: %15lld\n", v3[0]-v2[0], v3[1]-
v2[1]);
058   return 0;
059 }
```

CODE 9.3 Instrumented section of Code 9.1 for collection of floating-point operation counts using PAPI.

Since the reference BLAS implementation does not use vector floating point, the count of vector operations stays at zero. The theoretical count of scalar operations should be $20,000^2$ for multiplication and $20,000*19,999$ for addition, for a grand total of 799,980,000 in the `mult` function and 19,999 operations (since the absolute value computation requires only clearing the sign bit) in `cblas_dasum`. The counters consistently register higher values most likely due to speculative execution.

After replacing the reference BLAS library by a highly optimized Intel Math Kernel Library [11] that takes advantage of the vector instructions supported by the target machine, the application was reexecuted to produce the following values:

```
PAPI counts:
   init: event1:                 0 event2:                 0
   mult: event1:        1055372246 event2:         527686123
    sum: event1:             24674 event2:             12337
```

The count of vector operations was roughly half of the scalar figure. This indicates that the library selected the use of vector instructions with two floating-point numbers per instruction. Indeed, the machine on which the test was performed supports the Streaming SIMD Extensions (SSE) instruction set with up to two operands per vector. As a result of this change, the execution time dropped from 1.22 s to 1.08 s.

9.5 Summary and Outcomes

- Performance monitoring is closely associated with application development and optimization. It detects the most frequently executed sections of code and measures an application's resource footprint.
- The act of performing the measurement disturbs the measured system. Performance monitors employ minimally intrusive solutions to collect the performance metrics, possibly leveraging dedicated low-overhead implementations such as hardware event counters whenever available.
- Monitored programs need to be instrumented, i.e., modified through insertion of suitable measurement and result collection functions. This may be accomplished at the source level, using compiler techniques, library-level instrumentation, or executable level. Each of these mechanisms differs in the degree of user involvement, measurement scope and precision, supported features, and intrusiveness.
- One of the fundamental metrics is time. Its measurement may be invoked from the command line using the *time* system utility or by instrumenting an application with timestamp collection functions such as *clock_gettime*.
- Profiling is one of the elementary techniques of performance monitoring. It is used to identify a program's execution hotspots and potentially capture other runtime metrics, such as memory size, communication parameters, and I/O activity. They may be used to classify the program as compute bound, memory bound, or I/O bound.

- Hotspots are parts of code the program spends most of the time executing. Bottlenecks are hotspots that have unduly adverse effects on the application's performance. Program optimization may relocate the bottleneck to another part of the code.
- One of the commonly used general-purpose profilers is provided by the *gperf-tools* suite. It can detect hotspots and memory management issues without modifications to the source code.
- The *perf_events* and *PAPI* packages are commonly used interfaces accessing hardware event counters. The first may be used from the command line, while the other enables instrumentation of arbitrary application sections.

9.6 Questions and Exercises

1. Discuss the differences between hotspots and bottlenecks. Provide examples to illustrate your answer.

2. Why do hardware event counters often provide better insight into the runtime behavior of an application? What are their limitations?

3. Write a program that estimates the overhead of time measurement using POSIX clocks. Make sure you collect numbers for both "hot" (i.e., initialized) and "cold" (uninitialized) cache scenarios.

4. Consider the following program:

```
001 #include <stdio.h>
002
003 int main() {
004     long sum = 0;
005     for (int i = 0; i < 1000000; i++)
006         if (i&1 != 0) sum += 3*i;
007     printf("sum=%ld\n", sum);
008     return 0;
009 }
```

Instrument the `for` loop using PAPI to count all conditional branches and taken conditional branches. Estimate the counts and verify your numbers by executing the instrumented code. How do the values change when the program is compiled with optimizations enabled compared to the unoptimized version? Why?

Note: to explain the discrepancies, it may be helpful to look at the generated assembly code. For gcc it can be done using the following command:

```
gcc -S -fverbose-asm program.c
```

The resultant assembly listing annotated with variable names will be placed in the file `program.s`.

5. Profiling a program with the *perf* tool produces the following output:

```
Performance counter stats for './a.out':

      14207.022284      task-clock:u (msec)        #    1.000 CPUs
utilized
                 0      context-switches:u         #    0.000 K/sec
                 0      cpu-migrations:u           #    0.000 K/sec
            10,301      page-faults:u              #    0.725 K/sec
    50,036,833,663      cycles:u                   #    3.522 GHz
    49,799,684,446      stalled-cycles-frontend:u  #   99.53% frontend
cycles idle
    46,725,530,082      stalled-cycles-backend:u   #   93.38% backend
cycles idle
     1,059,912,928      instructions:u             #    0.02 insn per
cycle
                                                   #   46.98 stalled
cycles per insn
       115,260,873      branches:u                 #    8.113 M/sec
            55,407      branch-misses:u            #    0.05% of all
branches

      14.208427535      seconds time elapsed
```

What may be inferred about the code based on the above statistics?

Symmetric Multiprocessor Architecture

10

Chapter outline

10.1 Introduction

A widely used form of a high performance computer is the symmetric multiprocessing (SMP) architecture. It represents a class of parallel architectures that exploits multiple processor cores to increase performance through parallelism (multiple threads) while maintaining a single-system image of shared memory across the entire parallel computer. A global virtual address space shared by all of

High Performance Computing. https://doi.org/10.1016/B978-0-12-823035-0.00010-9

the incorporated processors minimizes the changes from that of a single processor machine, thus simplifying the transformation from sequential applications to parallel programs. SMPs are also referred to as *shared-memory* (SM) machines or *cache coherent* computers. The "S" in SMP stands for symmetric, which refers to the property of equal access times by any processor core to any of the main memory banks. As will be seen, this is at best an approximation because secondary effects cause some variability in the time experienced for load/store operations. But overall, SMPs provide balanced operation in which data placement need not be a major consideration. SMPs maintain cache coherence such that access by any core of any virtual addressed memory locations is consistent with its most recent value without user intervention. This differs from distributed memory systems that are discussed in detail elsewhere in the text.

The principal strength of the SMP architecture family is that it is tightly coupled (i.e., all the components are close together in terms of time—distance of operations, data manipulation, and communication). Some examples of SMPs and their characteristics are provided in Table 10.1.

10.2 Architecture Overview

An SMP is a full-standing self-sufficient computer system with all subsystems and components needed to serve the requirements and support actions necessary for conducting the computation of an application. It can be used independently for user applications cast as shared memory multiple threaded programs or as one of many equivalent subsystems integrated to form a scalable distributed memory massively parallel processing (MPP) or commodity cluster. An SMP can also operate as a throughput computer supporting multiprogramming of concurrent independent jobs or as a platform for multiprocess message passing jobs even though the interprocess data exchange is achieved through shared memory transparent to the parallel programming interface. In the following sections of this chapter, the key subsystems are described in greater detail to convey how they contribute to achieving performance, principally through parallelism and diverse functionality through distinct technologies. Here is a brief overview of the full organization of an SMP architecture and the basic purposes of its major components to provide a context in which to establish the later discussions.

Like any general-purpose computer, an SMP serves a key set of functions on behalf of the user application either directly or indirectly through the supporting operating system. These are typically:

1. Instruction issuance and execution (control logic)
2. Memory management
3. Communication management
4. Input/output (I/O) interfaces
5. Mass store

TABLE 10.1 Some Examples of Symmetric Multiprocessing and Their Characteristics

Vendor	Name	Processor	Number of Cores	Cores per CPU	Memory Capacity	PCIe Slots	Storage Slots
IBM	Power S1024	IBM Power 10 4 GHz	48	24	8 TB	4 PCIe G4 x16 or G5 x8 slots 4 PCIe G5 x8 slots 2 PCIe G4 x8 slots	16 NVMe U.2
HPE	Proliant DL385 Gen11	AMD EPYC 4.4 GHz	192	96	6 TB	8 PCIe G5 x16	8 LFF 8 SFF 12 EDSFF
Dell EMC	PowerEdge R940xa	Intel Xeon Gen 2 2.7 GHz	112	28	15.36 TB	12 PCIe G3 x16	4 NVMe 32 SAS/SATA
Oracle	Sparc M8-8	SPARC M8-8 5.0 GHz	256	32	32 TB	32 PCIe G3 x16	24 NVMe 30 SAS/SATA/SSD
Lenovo	ThinkSystem SR860 V2	Intel Xeon 2.9 GHz	256	32	24 TB	11 PCIe G3 x16	24 SAS/SATA/SSD 12 NVMe
Supermicro	SuperServer 7089P-TR4T	Intel Xeon	112	28	6 TB	8 PCIe G3 x16	8 SAS/SATA 2 NVMe

10.2.1 Flow Control

The SMP cores perform the primary execution functions for the applications. Their principal operation is to identify the next instruction in memory to execute, read that instruction into a special instruction register, and decode its binary format to determine the sequence of hardware control signals. The instruction then is issued to the execution pipeline with its data. Proceeding through a sequence of micro-operations, the final result is determined. Usually, the initial and resulting data are acquired and deposited by special storage elements, "registers", that are high-speed (high-bandwidth, low-latency) latches holding temporary values. Five classes of operation make up the functionality of the processor:

1. The basic register to register integer, logic, and character operations
2. Floating-point operations on real values
3. Conditional branch operations to control the instruction sequence
4. Memory access operations to move data between the registers and the main memory
5. Actions that initiate control of and data through external I/O

Until the turn of the century, essentially all processors were single microprocessor integrated circuits. Semiconductor technology advances, limitations of instruction-level parallelism (ILP), and clock rates caused by power constraints drove the development multicore sockets. Contemporary processors may comprise a few cores, 6 to 16. New architectures permit sockets of greater than 60 smaller cores on a chip. An SMP may incorporate one or more such sockets to deliver its processing capability. Peak performance (theoretical performance that can be achieved in ideal conditions) of an SMP is approximated by the product of the number of sockets, the number of cores per socket, the number of operations per instruction, and the clock rate summarized in Equation 10.1.

$$P_{peak} \sim N_{sockets} * N_{cores \ per \ socket} * R_{clock} * N_{operations \ per \ instruction} \qquad (10.1)$$

10.2.2 Memory Hierarchy

SMP memory consists of layers of storage to balance the need for large capacity with high speed of the core's data and instruction streams. Complex control logic manages data access, vertical migration through the cache hierarchy, and cache consistency across the many cache stacks supporting the processor cores. SMP memory is three separate kinds of hardware technology. Already mentioned are the processor core registers, very fast latches that have their own name space and that provide the fastest access time (less than one cycle) and lowest latency. Each core has its own sets of registers that are unique to it and separated from all others. The main memory of the SMP is a large set of processor modules divided into memory banks that are accessible by all the processors and their cores. Main memory is implemented on separate dynamic random access memory (DRAM) chips and plugged into the SMP motherboard's industry standard memory interfaces (physical, logical, and electrical). Data in main memory are accessed through a virtual address that the processor translates to a physical address location in the main memory.

Between the processor core register set and the SMP main memory banks are the caches. Cache attempts to bridge the gap of speeds between the rate at which the processor core wants to access data and the rate at which the DRAM can provide it. The difference between these two is easily 2 orders of magnitude with a core fetch rate on the order of two accesses per nanosecond and the memory cycle time on the order of 100 nanoseconds. The cache layers exploit temporal and spatial locality, relying on data reuse. Ideally, data access requests are satisfied with data present in the level 1, L1, cache that operates at a throughput equivalent to the demand rate of a processor core and a latency of one to four cycles. This assumes that the sought-after data had already been acquired before (temporal locality) or that the data required are very near the data already accessed (spatial locality). Under these conditions, a processor core could operate very near its peak performance capability. But because of size and power requirements, L1 caches (both data and instruction) are relatively small and susceptible to overflow; there is a need for more data than can be held in the L1 cache alone. To address this, a level two, L2, cache is almost always incorporated, again on the processor socket for each core or sometimes shared by a pair of cores. The L2 cache holds both data and instructions and is much larger than the L1 caches but much slower. L1 and L2 caches are implemented with SRAM. As the separation between core clock rates and main memory cycle times grew, a third level of cache, L3, was included, although these were usually implemented as a DRAM chip integrated within the same MCM packaging of the processor socket. The L3 cache is often shared among all cores of the processor package.

The symmetric multiprocessing attribute of coherency requires that copies of main memory data values held in caches for fast access be mutually consistent (hold the same value). Specifically, when two or more copies of a value with a virtual address are in distinct physical caches, a change to the value of one of those copies must be reflected by the values of all others. Sometimes the actual value may be changed to the updated value, although more frequently, the other copies are merely invalidated so that an obsolete value is not used. Many hardware protocols ensure the correctness of data copies started as early as the 1980s with the MESI protocols. The necessity to maintain such data coherence across caches within an SMP adds design complexity, time to access data, and increased energy.

10.2.3 Mass Store

Many SMP systems incorporate their own secondary storage for high information capacity. They do so in a persistent manner so as to not lose stored information after the associated applications finish, other users use the system, or the system is powered down. Mass storage has usually been achieved through hard magnetic disk technology with one or more spinning disk drives. More recently, though with somewhat lower density, solid-state drives (SSDs) have served this purpose. Although more expensive, SSDs exhibit superior access and cycle times and better reliability because they have no moving parts. Mass storage presents two logic interfaces to the user. Explicitly, it supports the file system consisting of a graph structure of directories, each holding other directories and end-user files of data and programs. A complete set of specific file and directory access service calls are made available to users as part of the operating system to use the secondary storage. A second abstraction promoted by the mass storage is the virtual memory system in which "pages" of block data with virtual addresses may be kept on disk swapped in and out of main memory as needed. When a page request is made for data that are not found in memory, a page fault is indicated. The operating system performs the necessary tasks to make room for the requested page in main memory. A less used page in memory is migrated to the disk, and the desired page is moved to the memory. Address translation tables are updated transparently to the user. But it can take a orders of magnitude times longer than a similar data access request to L1 cache. Some SMP nodes, especially those used as subsystems of commodity clusters or MPPs, may not include their own secondary storage. Referred to as "diskless nodes", these instead share secondary storage, which is itself a subsystem of the supercomputer or even external file systems shared by multiple computers and workstations. Diskless nodes are smaller, cheaper, lower energy, and more reliable. But, of course, they do not contain full system storage capacity.

10.2.4 Input/Output Interface

Every SMP has multiple I/O channels that communicate with external devices (outside the SMP), user interfaces, data storage, system area networks, local area networks, and wide area networks, among others. Every user is familiar with many of these because they are also found on desk-side and laptop systems. For local area and system area networks, interfaces most frequently to Ethernet and Infini-Band are provided to connect to other SMPs of a larger cluster or to institutional infrastructure. Universal Serial Bus (USB) has become so widely used for a diversity of purposes, including portable flash drives, that it is ubiquitous and available on essentially everything larger than a screen pad or laptop and certainly on every desk-side or rack-mounted SMP. The Joint Test Action Group (JTAG) is widely used for system administration and maintenance. SATA is widely used for external disk drives. There is usually a connection specifically provided for a directly connected user keyboard. Depending on the system, there may be a number of other I/O interfaces (Fig. 10.1).

10.3 Processor Core Architecture

The modern multicore processor consists of a number of cores per socket for computation, a complex cache hierarchy per core, one or more interfaces to an external shared main memory, I/O buses, and ancillary logic. Although differing in design

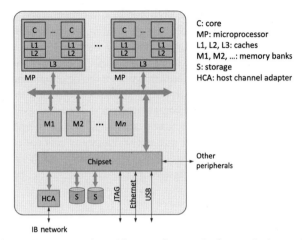

C: core
MP: microprocessor
L1, L2, L3: caches
M1, M2, ...: memory banks
S: storage
HCA: host channel adapter

FIGURE 10.1 Internal to symmetric multiprocessing are the intranode data paths, standard interfaces, and motherboard control elements.

TABLE 10.2 Characterization of Several Symmetric Multiprocessing Processors

Processors	Clock Rate	Caches (per Core)	ILP (Each Core)	Cores per Chip	Processor and Die Size	Power (W)
AMD EPYC 9004	3.7 GHz	L3: 256 MB (Total) L2: 16 MB	32 intops/cycle 32 fpops/cycle	96	5 nm	400
IBM Power 10	4 GHz	L3: 120 MB (Total) L2: 7.5 MB	32 intops/cycle 16 fpops/cycle	15	7 nm	230
Intel Xeon 8368Y	3.6 GHz	L3: 47.5 MB (Total) L2: 0.5 MB	2 intops/cycle 2 fpops/cycle	40	10 nm	300

detail, most common processors can be characterized by a shared set of parameters as shown in Table 10.2. Among these are the number of cores per socket, the size and interconnectivity of the cache levels (usually two or three levels), the clock rate of the core, the number and type of arithmetic logic units per core, ILP, the semiconductor die size (between one and four square centimeters), the fabrication feature size (line width) which spans a range mostly between 15 nanometers and 5 nms, and the delivered performance for one or more standardized application benchmarks. For application programmers, many of the details may not appear of direct importance because they are not actionable in the development of application programs. But the rate at which instructions are issued, the number of operations performed per instruction fetch, the average time per memory access, and the delays due to I/O requests are principal factors determining the delivered performance. Section 10.5 examines the memory and cache hierarchy in depth to explain the role of data locality and reuse in reducing average memory access time. In this section, the major structures of the processor core related to forms of operational parallelism are described.

10.3.1 Execution Pipeline

The earliest generation of sequential computers issued and completed one instruction at a time using the oft quoted "fetch-execute-writeback" cycle. This was sufficient with relatively low clock rates (1−100 kilohertz) delivered by early vacuum tube and transistor technologies. As clock rates improved with advanced semiconductor technologies (e.g., small-scale integration and medium-scale integration), this micro-stepwise sequential control method proved inadequate. The complexity of the full issue to completion times of instructions required too many successive phases of micro-operations through a sequence of logical stages. The latency of each stage was significantly lower than the full instruction operation if performed in one logic structure. However, the total accumulated latency of any one instruction propagating through multiple stages of simpler logic is greater than that of the single logic structure. An early form of architectural parallelism serves as a mitigating strategy (Fig. 10.2).

A pipelined structure of multiple micro-operation stages has been adopted to partition the full compute operation into a sequence of micro-operations that together achieved the same functionality. The time from instruction issue to completion would actually take longer than would a single logical function of the same purpose. But each stage of the pipeline takes much less time. Because the clock rate was limited by the instruction issue cycle time, which was itself determined by the

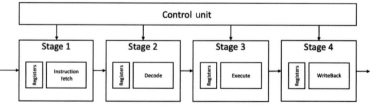

FIGURE 10.2 An example of a four-stage pipeline.

propagation delay through the longest stage of the pipeline, an execution pipeline with as many stages as possible, each of the same delay, permitted the clock rate to increase appreciably. Early execution pipelines of four and five stages were eventually superseded with much longer ones. The consequence of exploiting execution pipeline parallelism is that although instructions could be fetched much more quickly than before, multiple operations are being processed (in flight) in the pipeline at the same time, each at a different stage for greater throughput but at a cost of longer time to complete any single fetched instruction. Many benefits accrue, but challenges to this strategy invoked additional innovations to execution pipelines, including:

1. The size of the total function limits the maximum number of pipeline stages.
2. Imbalance of stage logic length reduces throughput to that of the slowest.
3. The interface overhead between pipeline stages added propagation delay.
4. Functions requiring more stages than other waste some hardware.
5. Intermediate values of one operation could force a stall when a following has to wait.
6. Conditional operations complicate the efficient use of an execution pipeline.

To speed up execution despite these inhibiting factors, core architecture has evolved in a number of forms and functions to be briefly described in the following subsections.

10.3.2 Instruction-Level Parallelism

ILP is a form of parallelism that executes multiple operations within an instruction in parallel. For instance, "superscalar" architectures enable multiple operations to be launched by a single instruction issue. This is achieved through the incorporation of multiple arithmetic and logic units, including both floating point and integer/logical functional units, among others. Additional Single Instruction, Multiple Data units may also be included to perform the same operations on multiple data values from the same instruction. ILP provides fine-grained parallelism within a core. For special cases, this can have a dramatic impact on total throughput. Unfortunately, the average benefits of ILP prove marginal.

10.3.3 Branch Prediction

Branch prediction is a statistical technique that predicts the next instruction to a conditional operation (or a branch instruction) to prepare the system and potentially increase performance. When a branch instruction is issued, the hardware guesses which of two alternative instructions to follow. The key idea is that depending on the role of the particular branch, one of two paths is more likely. If a branch is used at the bottom of a loop, it is more likely that the predicate will redirect the execution flow to the top of the loop rather than immediately continue on. If a branch is associated with error handling, it is highly unlikely that that path will be pursued and rather that the next instruction to be issued should be part of the regular computation stream. There will always be cases in which the wrong choice is made. In these cases, the hardware architecture has to be capable of rolling back the computation to take the other path. System software is branch intensive, and branch prediction architecture support can go a long way in improving efficiency.

10.3.4 Forwarding

Key to the concept of the execution pipeline is that the time to issue successive instructions is potentially far shorter than the time of completion through the many stages of the pipeline. It is possible that two succeeding instructions may impose one or more precedence constraints such that the second instruction requires the result value of the preceding (first) instruction issued. Usually, an instruction will acquire its operands from the core's register set. But in the condition described, there will not have been enough time for the resulting value of the first instruction to be calculated and written back into the register bank before the second instruction would ordinarily read the same value from that register. Forwarding is added data transfer channels that move data from downstream execution pipeline segments to the appropriate upstream segment, making the argument value available in time for the instructions to follow closer in succession. Combined with compiler reordering where necessary gaps can be filled with one or more unrelated instructions, pipeline stages can be filled eliminating bubbles.

10.3.5 Reservation Stations

Different operations take different amounts of time to complete, and the execution pipeline becomes multipath with shorter links through a simple Boolean logic operation than for a floating point multiply, for example. If strict ordering were preserved, then the rate of instruction processing would be constrained by the slowest operations, forcing repeated stalls of backstream instructions. This problem is addressed by reservation stations. A reservation station is a special purpose buffer register, invisible to the user, that temporarily holds a previous result value. Its special feature is that it "knows" what follow-on instructions require the captured value and those instructions know the corresponding reservation station(s) from which to acquire their argument values. If the instruction tries to get the operand value before its availability in the designated reservation station, then the instruction will be delayed at the reservation station but not impede the progress of the execution pipeline. There are many alternative architecture methods by which this complex out-of-order scheduling mechanism can be achieved (often referred to as the "Tomasulo algorithm" shown in Fig. 10.3). But in every case, the use of a reservation station permits substantial flexibility in operation of the execution pipeline and greater efficiency.

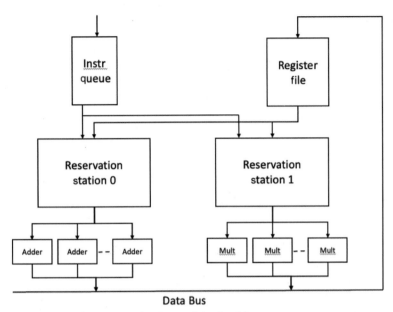

FIGURE 10.3 Block diagram showing Tomasulo's algorithm

10.3.6 Multithreading

So far, the discussion of the processor core's execution pipeline assumes a single stream of instructions, each with one or more associated operations. Although these can prove complex in detail, they still are based on the original von Neumann concept of a single program counter (or instruction pointer) that is incremented for each instruction issue except for branch instructions. This is a clean and elegant approach but suffers from a number of edge conditions. Many of these problems are due to the interrelationships among adjacent or neighboring instructions of a single instruction stream. One way to address this challenge in a single processor core was introduced by Burton Smith, the concept of "multithreading". In its simplest version, multithreading incorporates multiple instruction streams or threads through sets of multiple instruction pointers and their associated register sets. The rest of the execution pipeline is shared, and a round robin instruction issue scheduler selects each of the successive instruction fetches from different threads if pending. This hides the latency of the execution pipeline, and if sufficient threads are used, the latencies to main memory as well.

10.4 Memory Hierarchy

The "memory wall", or "von Neumann bottleneck", recognizes the mismatch between the peak demand rate of the processor core for data access and the possible delivered throughput and latency of the main memory technology, principally semi-conductor DRAM. Historically, performance gains for processors increased on the average of 60%/year, but that of main memory experienced only about a 9%/year improvement. Over time, this has led to a 2-order-of-magnitude difference between processor speeds and memory speeds. To address this challenge and further into the domain of secondary storage, computer architecture in general and SMP architecture in particular have evolved a hierarchical structure of a sequence of layers of storage components with increasing density and capacity in one direction of the hierarchy and greater access speed including higher bandwidth and lower latency in the other direction.

10.4.1 Data Reuse and Locality

Fundamental to success of SMP architecture is the strategy of data reuse through locality. If a value of a variable is used by a program repeatedly and frequently, storing it in a very high-speed memory device very close to the processor core will deliver near peak performance. This is "temporal locality", which reflects the property of data that associates the probability of usage with recent prior usage. High temporal locality suggests that a particular variable is accessed frequently in a moderate period of time. Low temporal locality indicates that a variable, if accessed at all, is probably only used once or a couple of times in the moderate contiguous period. A second form of locality often exploited is "spatial locality", which indicates an association of locality among adjacent or near neighbors in contiguous address space. High spatial locality suggests that the probability of a variable (virtually addressed value) being accessed is higher if one of its adjacent or neighboring variables has been recently accessed. These two forms of locality, concerning the reuse patterns of virtually addressed variables, provide the foundations for the structure and operation of the memory hierarchy to mitigate the effects of the discrepancies between bandwidths and latencies of processor and memory technologies.

The second factor of practical concern is the tradeoff relationships between the characteristics of storage capacity per unit area, cycle time of access, and power consumption. The diverse data storage technologies vary in terms of these parameters. In general, faster memory technologies take up more room on a semiconductor die or other medium for the same amount of storage while consuming greater power. It is impractical to create a main memory layer that is big enough to hold all the software and data required for a given user application while running fast enough to keep the processor cores fully utilized at their peak instruction issue throughput.

10.4.2 Memory Hierarchy

The conventional solution for modern computing architectures and including SMP systems to address these tradeoffs through the exploitation of the data locality is the structure of the memory hierarchy, also known as the "memory stack".

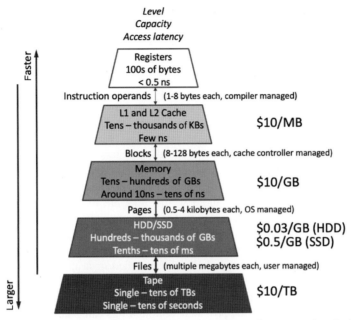

FIGURE 10.4 The memory hierarchy delineated by memory capacity, cost, and cycle times. *GB*, Gigabytes; *HDD*, ***; *MB*, megabytes; *SSD*, solid-state drive; *TB*, terabytes.

As shown in Figure 10.4, the memory hierarchy or 'stack' consists of layers of memory storage technology, each with different tradeoffs between memory capacity, costs, and cycle times reflecting their specific bandwidths and latencies. By far the slowest but also the highest capacity is the use of tape archival storage, often consisting of possibly thousands of tape modules physically stored in a robotic library with total capacities approaching Exabytes. Tapes are admittedly an old technology and format. But in an unloaded system, access to stored data could take upwards of 1 minute even though the cost of a megabyte is a fraction of a cent. Tape robots provide part of mass storage called "tertiary storage", although they may not be found at some current data processing facilities. Also, part of mass storage is secondary storage made of hard disk drives. Disks such as tapes use magnetic storage medium. Both are nonvolatile in that they retain the data stored on them indefinitely, even when removed from the immediate system. But unlike tapes, which present one long serial stream of storage that can take a long time to go from one end to the other, data on disks are laid out in concentric rings (called "cylinders") that spin on an axis. A radial arm moving in and out across the spinning disk selects the appropriate cylinder and waits for the required data to come around to be detected by the arm's head. A typical disk drive may hold several terabytes, deliver data at a peak streaming rate of 300 MB per second, and impose an overall access time of around 10 ms. Although this is 100,000 times longer than access to main memory, it may hold 1000 times as much stored data and exhibit a latency 10,000 times shorter than tape drives. A third technology, NVRAM, recently introduced commercially, is increasingly being used as a partial replacement for disk drives for response much faster than disks but slower than main memory. It, too, is nonvolatile (hence the "NV"). Mass storage is presented to the user usually in the form of logical data modules called files and directories that hold files as well as other directories.

At the other (top) end of the memory hierarchy are the processor core registers that operate at the speed of the clock rate and support multiple access ports, allowing multiple reads and writes into or out of the register bank's each instruction cycle. Although operating at native processor speeds, registers take up a lot of room and consume significant energy per cycle. Registers also have their own independent address space not associated with the memory address name space. The instruction set architecture is logically structured so that data are explicitly moved between identified registers and the variables in the main memory (or cache). These are also referred to as "load store" architectures.

The main memory is provided by DRAM semiconductor devices. DRAM is volatile, requiring data cells to be periodically refreshed or at the time of an access. Many such components are mounted on PC cards, which are plugged into sockets compliant with industry-standard interfaces. As much as 16 GB of memory per processor core for an SMP is often provided, although this can drop to as low as 1 GB per core depending on the number of cores per socket. But access times from register to DRAM can be between 100 and 200 clock cycles, far too much for effective computing.

Between processor core registers and SMP main memory modules is the cache system to bridge between these two extremes in timing and bandwidth. Logically, the cache system is transparent to the user in that it is not separately addressable. Instead, the cache accepts memory access requests. If the variable address requested by a core has a copy of the variable value somewhere within its cache, then the cache provides that value in the case of a load operation to the designated core register. If such a copy does not exist, then the cache system automatically passes the request to the main memory itself to perform the access request. Where data locality applies, a cache "hit" is likely, and the access time will be that of high-speed cache rather than the much slower main memory.

In a modern SMP, the cache is usually not a single layer of higher speed memory but rather multiple layers to find an optimal balance of speed, size, and power. Typically, there are three layers: L1, L2, and L3. L1 is the fastest and smallest, although it usually consists of two separate caches, one for data and the other for instructions to provide enough peak bandwidth. L2 is slower but much larger and like L1 is made from SRAM circuits. The L3 cache is much larger than the lower layer caches but is slower. Unlike the first two, the L3 is usually a separate chip of DRAM rather than SRAM circuits to achieve the greater density.

A simple hierarchical structure provides each core with its own separate L1, L2, and L3 caches. However, often multiple cores are working on the same set of data, and the amount of data in a layer that would be possible could be increased by allowing more than one core to share at least some of the cache. Typically, the L1 cache is not shared because of the need for maximum individual bandwidth. Also, typically, the L3 cache is shared among the processor cores or some subset of them. With regard to the L2 cache, it may be either dedicated to a single core or shared among two or more cores. Part of the tradeoff is also about bandwidth and possible contention for cache access among sharing cores.

10.5 External I/O Interfaces

An SMP node, although internally self-sufficient for computation, requires external interfaces to the many other facilities of a data processing infrastructure. SMP nodes are interconnected to a diversity of physically separate but logically integrated classes of functional support. Examples include user-terminal access, external secondary mass storage (e.g., SSD, spinning disk drives) for file management, system administrator network ports, high-bandwidth system area network (when connected to other nodes), I/O devices (e.g., shared laser printers), and connection to the internet, among others. The SMP node incorporates a number of I/O interfaces for this purpose. In most cases (but not all), the ports for these interfaces are accessible from the back of the node's physical package. The motherboard incorporates the interface controller logic for each of the I/O interfaces. Although there are custom interfaces for special situations, the majority of the interfaces are industry standard for interoperability between system components from the widest range of hardware vendors. Also, driver system software is provided by both those hardware vendors and the sources of the operating system, runtime system, and programming-language compilers. A couple of I/O interfaces are physically internal to the node for adapter cards that export diversity of functionality such as network interface controllers (NICs). The key I/O interfaces of an SMP are the network interface controllers including PCI-e, Ethernet and InfiniBand, SATA for mass storage devices, JTAG for low-level hardware interface, and USB for connecting peripheral devices such as keyboards. The following briefly describes the prevalent external I/O interfaces incorporated as part of most SMP systems.

10.5.1 PCI-e Bus

The PCI-e external interface is a widely adopted industry standard for SMP I/O connectivity to a broad range of supporting devices and is used by hundreds of computer systems and peripheral devices. The Peripheral Component Interconnect Express (hence, PCI-e) is found in essentially all current or recent generation SMP systems. It enables system extensibility, providing high bandwidth serial data transfer paths to diverse peripheral devices such as disk controllers, graphics cards, Ethernet network, medical instrumentation, and other attached capabilities. PCI-e has had five versions delivered to the market with backwards compatibility. Version 6 is in production, and version 7 is going through the specification process. Scaling to the desired bandwidth is accomplished by adding more links, called "lanes", in PCI-Express vernacular. Specifications permit up to 32 lanes per card slot, although practical implementations rarely exceed 16 lanes. PCI-Express is a dominant standard for attaching high-performance communication with expansion boards on different machines that may use different processor architecture than the original Intel x86 variant. The PCI-Express specifications are continuously updated and refined to reflect modern technological trends.

10.5.2 Ethernet

Ethernet is a standardized computer networking technology that has become ubiquitous. The official Ethernet standard is IEEE 802.3, and the technology continues to develop. The state of the art for Ethernet is currently at 100 GB/s. Ethernet was originally used as a local area network, connecting single processor nodes to shared (among other nodes) resources such as printers and file servers. It was adopted as a low-cost system area network for Beowulf-class commodity clusters delivering superior performance to cost and configuration flexibility (using Linux operating system). Much of the original Ethernet driver software for the Linux operating system was developed and distributed open source by the NASA Beowulf Project. Most motherboards manufactured currently incorporate Gig-E (1 GB/s Ethernet) interfaces as standard, thus eliminating the need for additional Ethernet NIC cards.

10.5.3 InfiniBand

InfiniBand, frequently denoted as IB, is an alternative to Ethernet for computer networking technology. Unlike Ethernet, IB does not need to run networking protocols on the CPU. These are handled directly on the IB adapters. IB also supports remote direct memory access (RDMA) between nodes of a supercomputer without requiring a system call thereby reducing overhead. IB hardware is produced by Mellanox and Intel with IB software developed through the Open-Fabrics Open-Source Alliance. The state of the art for IB transfer rates is the same as the fastest transfer rate supported by the PCI Express bus (25 GB/s for enhanced data rate). In the Top 500 list of supercomputers, InfiniBand technology is the second most used internal system interconnect technology. Many multi-SMP node systems, some used for high performance computing, use a combination of separate InfiniBand and Ethernet networks with the former for application execution and the latter for many system-housekeeping and administrative chores.

10.5.4 SATA

Serial ATA, or Serial Advanced Technology Attachment, is a computer interface and communication protocol. SATA specifications are currently developed by the independent, nonprofit Serial ATA International Organization (SATA-IO) led by multiple industry partners that include dominant computing systems and storage manufacturers. It is used primarily to provide connectivity to mass storage devices including secondary hard disks and SSD. SATA replaces the older PATA technology that was characterized by lower data transfer bandwidths, bulky ribbon cables frequently obstructing air flow in the node's case, and lack of proper support for hot-swapping of I/O devices. SATA interfaces may be found on most modern internal (i.e., housed inside computer enclosure and therefore nonportable) hard disk drives, solid-state drives, and optical drives (CD-ROM, DVD-ROM, BD-ROM, and their data-writer equivalents). SATA supports only point-to-point topology between storage devices and controllers or port multipliers. Data transmission is performed over high-speed serial links that use similar technology to PCI-Express and share many of the same quality characteristics with it. Serial links also take advantage of matched impedance cables, guaranteeing signal integrity over distance of at least 1 m. Most of the computer motherboards manufactured today support multiple SATA data ports (typically 2−8), and common power supplies provide multiple SATA-compatible power hookups. Signaling speeds for current generation SATA is 16 Gbps with the corresponding peak data rate of nearly 2 GB/s.

10.5.5 JTAG

JTAG is a low-level hardware interface specified by IEEE Standard 1149 to facilitate verification and test methods for electronic circuits. Although most of casual computer users are likely never going to have an opportunity to use JTAG directly, it is broadly adopted by the industry for postproduction printed circuit board testing (detection of shorts, mismatched and detached pins, "stuck" bits, in-silicon logic defects, and so on). Additionally, JTAG permits in-circuit debugging of embedded applications by being able to access most (if not all(of the device register state, including the status of I/O pins. Coupled with Built-In Self-Test (BIST) functionality commonly implemented by the manufacturers in most of the LSI and very-large-scale integration logic circuits, JTAG identifies many chip failure modes before allowing them to enter the supply chain. Because it can directly manipulate the device hardware state, JTAG is also occasionally used to perform firmware updates in cases when more user-friendly options may not be available or desirable. JTAG functionality relies on the presence of four signals: TCK (test clock), TDI (test data in), TDO (test data out), and TMS (test mode select). Multiple JTAG-equipped devices may be daisy-chained as illustrated in Figure 10.5. Neither JTAG connector nor its clock frequency is standardized; the latter may range from single to multiple tens of MHz. The host may enable bypass operation in any device on a chain, thus avoiding full communication with it if not required.

10.5.6 USB

Computers usually need to communicate with relatively low-speed attached peripheral devices, such as keyboards or printers. The need for a low-profile broadly

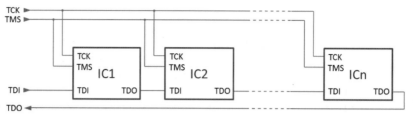

FIGURE 10.5 Joint Test Action Group chain with n devices. Integrated circuit blocks represent individual integrated circuits that may be located on single or multiple printed circuit boards. *TCK,* Test clock; *TDI,* test data in; *TDO,* test data out; *TMS,* test mode select.

applicable industry-standard interface has been driven, in part, by the introduction and high adoption of "laptop" mobile personal computers. The USB standard successfully resolve these issues and become the lingua franca of consumer-grade interconnectivity, perhaps the most familiar to users. It is currently guided by the USB Implementers Forum, Inc. (USB-IF), a nonprofit corporation involving representatives of 894 hardware and software companies including, among others, Intel, HP, NEC, Renesas, Samsung, ST Microelectronics, Infineon, Philips, Sony, Apple, and Microsoft. The standard has been designed with low cost and simplicity as the primary features. USB standard defines architecture, data flow model, mechanical and electrical properties of connectors and cables, signaling and physical layer, and power supply and management, as well as transaction protocols. It is currently implemented in many categories of peripheral devices, including keyboards, mice, printers, scanners, cameras, mobile phones, media players, mass storage, modems, network adapters, game controllers, and more. In USB 3.1, the maximal signal rate to 10 Gbps required introduction of the type-C connector. The specification limits the cable length of low-speed devices to 5 m, full-speed devices to 3 m, and 5 m for high-speed devices. USB 3.0 currently does not impose cable length constraints.

10.6 **Summary and Outcomes**

- The most widely used form of a high performance computer is SMP.
- SMPs are also referred to as SM machines or *cache coherent* computers.
- SMP architecture integrates a number of processor cores with a single shared main memory system by means of a common interconnection network.
- The symmetric multiprocessing attribute requires that copies of main memory data values that are held in caches for fast access be consistent (cache coherency).
- Every SMP has multiple I/O channels that communicate with external devices (outside the SMP), user interfaces, data storage, system area networks, local area networks, and wide area networks, among others.
- Defining characteristics of processors include the number of cores per socket, the size and interconnectivity of the cache levels (usually two or three levels), the

clock rate of the core, the number and type of arithmetic logic units per core (ILP), the die size (between one and four square centimeters), the feature size, and the delivered performance for one or more standardized benchmarks.

- The pipeline logic structure is a general way of exploiting a form of very fine-grained parallelism as each of the pipeline stages is operating simultaneously.
- Multithreading incorporates multiple instruction streams or threads through sets of multiple instruction pointers and their associated register sets.
- The "memory wall" recognizes the mismatch between the peak demand rate of the processor socket for data access and the possible delivered throughput and latency of the main memory technology, principally semiconductor DRAM.
- The memory hierarchy or stack consists of layers of memory storage technology, each with different tradeoffs between memory capacity, costs, and cycle times that reflect bandwidths and latencies.
- In a modern SMP, the cache is usually not a single layer of higher speed memory but rather multiple layers to find an optimal balance of speed and size.
- PCI-Express is a dominant standard for attaching and high-performance communication with expansion boards on different machines that may use different processor architecture than the original Intel x86 variant.
- The two most ubiquitous network interface controllers are Gigabit Ethernet and InfiniBand.
- SATA is used primarily to provide connectivity to mass storage devices.
- JTAG is broadly adopted by the industry for postproduction printed circuit board testing.
- The USB standard provides a relatively low-speed method for communication with attached peripheral devices.

10.7 Questions and Exercises

1. List and describe components of an SMP node. When applicable, name their most significant operational parameters along with units they are measured in. Approximate values these parameters may assume in common server hardware.

2. Expand and define each of the following acronyms. What are their application domains?

   a. SMP

   b. ILP

   c. CPI

   d. PCIe

   e. SATA

   f. USB

3. Why is standardization of I/O and expansion buses important? Provide examples.

4. You are an IT specialist at a small computational research institution. The scientists require a peak 100TFLOPS machine to conduct their studies. The approved vendor offers 2U rackmount nodes with 2 CPU sockets that may accommodate either 12-core processors clocked at 3.4-GHz frequency or 20-core processors operating at 2.5G-Hz frequency. Each core can perform four floating-point operations per clock cycle. Given that there is 32U space for nodes available in each rack, answer:

   a. Which type of processor would you recommend to minimize the floor space occupied by racks?

   b. How many racks are needed to reach the required peak throughput?

   c. With all racks filled, what is the final peak computational throughput of the machine?

5. A sequential version of a simulation takes 90 minutes to compute 10,000 iterations. Each iteration can be accelerated using multiple threads of execution, but the overhead of assigning work to the threads is 100 ms. If the sequential setup of the application takes 10 minutes regardless of the number of iterations subsequently executed, how many cores are needed to bring the execution of a program performing 1000 iterations down to 12 minutes? What maximum speedup is possible assuming unlimited execution resources?

6. Execution of a 1,000,000-instruction program takes 2.5 ms on a 2.5-GHz core. Hardware monitor reports cache miss ratio of 6% for the application. Main memory access takes on average 80 ns, and cache access has a latency of 800 ps. Given that all ALU instructions are executed effectively in a single clock cycle, calculate:

   a. The fraction of application instructions that performed ALU operations

   b. If the core has a 16KB cache and doubling the cache size decreases miss rate by 1% for that particular application, what would be the required cache size (in powers of 2) to cut the execution time in half?

   c. What would be the program run time and resulting speedup if all accessed data fit in the cache?

The *Essential* OpenMP

Chapter outline

11.1 Introduction

OpenMP is an application programming interface (API) to support the shared-memory multiple-thread model of parallel application development. "OpenMP" stands for "**Open M**ulti-**P**rocessing". It greatly simplifies the development of multiple-threaded parallel programming compared to, for example, low level OS support services for threads and shared memory. OpenMP incorporates separate sets of bindings for the sequential programming languages Fortran, C, and C++. It gives easy access to the resources of this general class of SMP computers for parallel applications.

High Performance Computing. https://doi.org/10.1016/B978-0-12-823035-0.00011-0

This chapter describes the syntax of constructs related to the C programming language. OpenMP provides extensions to C in the form of compiler directives, environment variables, and runtime library routines to expose and execute parallel threads in the context of shared memory systems. A principle of the design philosophy is to permit incremental changes to sequential C code for ease of use and natural migration from initial C-based applications to parallel programs. In so doing it provides a practical and powerful means of parallel computing, admittedly within the limits of the SMP class of parallel computers.

OpenMP is among the most widely used parallel programming APIs. However, it is limited in scalability to those hardware system architectures providing near uniform memory access (UMA) shared-memory. This chapter provides a first introductory treatment of the essentials of OpenMP and how to program in parallel with it. Although an initial coverage assuming no prior experience with parallel programming, this chapter provides all necessary concepts and semantic constructs to enable the development of useful real-world applications. This presentation is primarily focused on release 2.5 of OpenMP, which is core to later releases and is probably the most widely used version as well as more broadly supported.

Shared memory parallel architectures were first developed in the 1980s and a number of APIs were devised to assist in programming these. The OpenMP specification standard process began in 1997 based on this prior work. An earlier draft of this interface, ANSI X3H5, was released in 1994. The oversight of OpenMP evolution is provided by the OpenMP Architecture Review Board consisting of industry and government partners. The first C-based specification, C/C++ 1.0, was released in 1998 followed by C/C++ 2.0 in 2002. C and Fortran specifications have been released together since 2005 with OpenMP 2.5, 3.0, 4.0, and 5.0 released in 2005, 2008, 2013, and 2020, respectively. The most recent version, 5.2, was released in 2021.

11.2 Overview of OpenMP Programming Model

OpenMP provides a shared memory multiple threads programming model. It assumes underlying hardware support for efficient management of shared memory including virtual addresses and cache coherency among processor cores and across multiple sockets. This is the principal defining facet of the class of SMP (Symmetric Multi-Processor) class of parallel computers. All processor cores have direct access to all memory shared within the system. A simple but illustrative representation of this class of parallel computers suitable for OpenMP programming is shown in Figure 11.1. The key elements are the processor cores, P, that perform the concurrent threaded computing, the memory banks, M, that are assumed equally accessible by the threads, and the connectivity among both the P and M elements that convey the shared memory architecture and execution models.

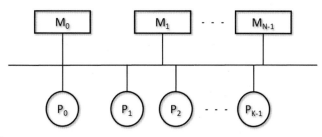

FIGURE 11.1

Shared Memory Multiprocessor. The key elements are the processor cores, P, that perform the concurrent threaded computing, the memory banks, M, that are equally accessible by the threads, and the connectivity among both the P and M elements that convey the shared memory architecture and execution models.

11.2.1 Thread Parallelism

Threads are the principal means of providing parallelism of computation. A thread is an independently schedulable sequence of instructions combined with its private variables and internal control. Usually, there are as many threads allocated to the user computation as there are processor cores assigned to the computation. However, this is not required. Threads are divided among the Master thread and the Worker threads. The single Master thread exists for the lifetime of the computation from its initiation to its termination. Sometimes, the Master thread is the only thread being performed at one time. The Worker threads provide additional paths of concurrency of execution for performance gain. Worker threads are controlled by the Master thread and are delineated by OpenMP directives. Like the number of threads, how the threads are scheduled is determined by environment variables and can be static or dynamic.

OpenMP supports the fork-join model of parallel computing. At particular points in the execution the Master thread spawns a number of Worker threads and with them performs a part of the program in parallel. The point in time of multiple Worker thread initiation is referred to as the *fork*. Usually, all these threads perform their calculations separately and when they come to their respective completion wait for the other threads to finish as well. This succeeding point is the *join* of the parallel threads. The default at the join is an implicit barrier synchronization. All the threads must complete before computation is continued beyond this point of control. An OpenMP parallel program mostly consists of a sequence of such fork-join Worker and Master thread parallel segments separated by lone sequential Master thread segments as shown in Figure 11.2. Segments of concurrent Master/Worker threads often have all the threads the same differentiated only by the values of their private variables. This is the SPMD or *Single Process Multiple Data* model. Alternatively, the concurrent threads may each execute different code blocks, separately delineated by

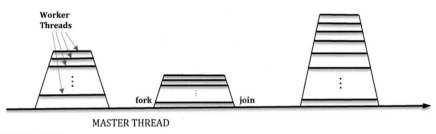

Worker
Threads

fork

join

MASTER THREAD

FIGURE 11.2

Fork-join model of Master/Worker Treads. The horizontal axis represents time from left to right while the vertical access shows work in terms of one or more concurrent threads. The single lowest line is the Master thread that continues from the beginning to the end of the OpenMP program. At key fork points, multiple threads are launched of works that can be performed concurrently. These threads may be somewhat irregular in that they do not execute exactly the same work even if their code is the same. When all the concurrent threads have completed at the join synchronization point, only then the computation can proceed.

appropriate directives. In either case, join synchronization at the end of the concurrent threads is enforced unless explicitly avoided through added directives for this purpose. The figure illustrates this parallel control flow. The horizontal axis represents time from left to right while the vertical access shows work in terms of one or more concurrent threads. The single lowest line is the Master thread that continues from the beginning to the end of the OpenMP program. At key fork points, multiple threads are launched of works that can be performed concurrently. These threads may be somewhat irregular in that they do not execute exactly the same work even if their code is the same. When all the concurrent threads have completed at the join synchronization point, only then the computation can proceed; in each case below by the Master thread alone until the next thread fork is encountered.

OpenMP permits the representation of nested parallelism such that inner fork-join segments of parallel threads can themselves be embedded into threads of outer parallel thread segments. However, while the syntax is supported and will execute correctly, not all implementations will take advantage of this additional parallelism and may treat it as sequential code, one inner thread after another. An example of nested parallelism is illustrated in Figure 11.3. Again, the lower horizontal line represents the Master thread with time increasing from left to right. First a set of worker threads are created when the Master thread encounters a forking point of parallelism; this is at the *outer fork*. Each of these outer threads then separately encounter its own *inner fork* to create a second level of parallel threads, exposing more concurrency for scalability. The inner threads of each outer thread then synchronize with their respective matching inner join, after which the outer thread proceeds until it encounters the outer join synchronization point with the outer threads. The OpenMP scheduler uses this added parallelism to improve performance when possible.

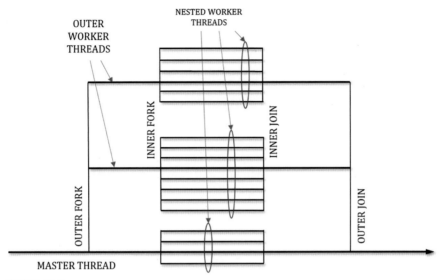

OUTER WORKER THREADS

NESTED WORKER THREADS

INNER FORK

INNER JOIN

OUTER FORK

OUTER JOIN

MASTER THREAD

FIGURE 11.3

Nested Parallel Threads. The lower horizontal line represents the Master thread with time increasing from left to right. First a set of worker threads are created when the Master thread encounters a forking point of parallelism; this is at the *outer fork*. Each of these outer threads then separately encounter its own *inner fork* to create a second level of parallel threads, exposing more concurrency for scalability. The inner threads of each outer thread then synchronize with their respective matching inner join, after which the outer thread proceeds until it encounters the outer join synchronization point with the outer threads. The OpenMP scheduler uses this added parallelism to improve performance when possible.

11.2.2 Thread Variables

OpenMP is a shared memory model allowing direct access to global variables by all threads of a user process. In order to support the SPMD modality of control where all concurrent threads run the same code block simultaneously, OpenMP also provides private variables. These have the same syntactical names but their scoping is limited to the thread in which they are used. Private variables of the same name have different values in each thread in which they occur. A frequently occurring example is the use of index variables accessing elements of a vector or array. While all threads will use the same index variable name, typically 'i', when accessing an element of the shared vector, perhaps '$x[i]$', the range of values of the index variable will differ for the separate concurrent threads. For this to be possible, the index variable has to be private, rather than shared. In fact, this particular idiom is so common that the default for such variable usage is private although for most common variables the default is shared. Directive clauses are available for explicit setting of these properties of variables by users. Another variant on how variables may be used relates to reduction operators such as sum or product. In this specialized case, the reduction variable is a mix of private and global as will be discussed in detail in section 11.5.

11.2.3 Runtime Library and Environment Variables

An OpenMP parallel application program consists of the syntax of the core language (i.e., Fortran, C, C++) with additional constructs to guide parallel threaded execution and set specific operational properties. These include environment variables, compiler directives, and runtime libraries. Environment variables define operational conditions and policies under which the executing OpenMP program will run. Their values can be set at the system shell through OS user interface commands. From within the program, they can be accessed through runtime library routines. Compiler Directives appear as comments but through the OpenMP extensions and pragmas are treated as commands to guide parallel execution. Additional functionality is provided through Runtime Library routines that help manage parallel programs. Many runtime library routines have corresponding environment variables that can be controlled by users. Examples include determining the number of threads and processors, scheduling policies to be used, and portable wall-clock timing.

11.2.4 Environment Variables

OpenMP provides environment variables for controlling execution of parallel codes. These can be set from the OS command line or equivalent. Prior to execution of the application program use *export* or *setenv* commands depending on the user shell. However, these variables have default settings so that they only have to be set explicitly if an optional value is required. There are four main environment variables:

OMP_NUM_THREADS — controls the parallelism of the OpenMP application by specifying the number of threads to be used by the user program. This will usually determine the number of cores allocated to the user program but not always. When more threads are requested than available, they may be associated with OS Pthreads requiring the operating system to context switch adding additional overheads to the computing. The default option is system dependent. To set the value of this environment variable to 8 use the following bash command:

```
export OMP_NUM_THREADS=8
```

OMP_DYNAMIC — enables dynamic adjustment of number of threads for execution of parallel regions. Under certain conditions, this provides a level of adaptability that makes optimal use of task granularity to minimize the effects of overhead and irregularity. However, it also incurs additional overhead within the runtime system and may not always improve performance. The default value for this environment variable is FALSE which implies that the number of threads employed remains fixed at the value set in the environment variable

OMP_NUM_THREADS. To change this to enable dynamic thread allocation, use the following bash command:

```
export OMP_DYNAMIC=TRUE
```

OMP_SCHEDULE — manages the load distribution in loops such as the parallel for pragmas (discussed in the next section). This environment variable sets the schedule type and chunk size for all such loops. The chunk size can be provided as an integer number. The default value for the OMP_SCHEDULE is 1. To set this tuple variable use the following form:

```
export OMP_SCHEDULE=<schedule>,<chunk>
```

OMP_NESTED — permits nested parallelism in OpenMP applications. This may open up the opportunity for more parallelism, which may increase scalability but at the risk of finer granularity in the presence of fixed overheads, possibly reducing efficiency. The default value for this Boolean environment value is FALSE, permitting only the top level of fork-join parallelism to be used. To set this environment variable to support multi-level parallelism, use the following form:

```
export OMP_NESTED=TRUE
```

11.2.5 Runtime Library Routines

Runtime library routines help manage parallel application execution including accessing and using environment variables such as those above. Prior to using these routines in the code, the following *include* statement must be added:

```
#include <omp.h>
```

Two important routines allow the program to know how many threads are operating concurrently and to identify a unique rank for each thread among their total set. The first function,

```
omp_get_num_threads()
```

returns the total number of threads currently in the group executing the parallel block from where it is called. Usually, this is a direct reflection of the environment variable OMP_NUM_THREADS.

The second important runtime routine,

```
omp_get_thread_num()
```

returns a value to each thread executing the parallel code block that is unique to that thread and can be used as a kind of identifier in its calculations. When the Master thread calls this function, the value of 0 is always returned identifying its special role in the computation. A call to this routine by a worker thread will return a value between 1 and the environment variable value OMP_NUM_THREADS -1 (inclusive).

11.2.6 **Directives**

OpenMP directives are a principal class of constructs used to convert initially sequential codes incrementally to parallel programs. They serve a multitude of purposes primarily about controlling parallelism through delineation and synchronization. The following sections describe in detail the directives for parallelism, mutual exclusion of shared variables through synchronization, and reduction calculations. All directives take the following form:

```
#pragma omp <directive> <clauses> <statement/code block>
```

As will be seen in the examples, such directives may be treated one at a time in a nested organization or in many cases combined to simplify textual presentation. The clauses permit optional conditions to be satisfied like declaring the scope of a variable (e.g., private).

11.3 **Parallel Threads and Loops**

11.3.1 **Parallel Threads**

In the tradition of C programming and the teaching thereof, the first program to present is "Hello World". Using OpenMP, a very simple parallel program can be constructed to print this statement by multiple threads. It requires only one OpenMP command:

```
#pragma omp parallel
```

to turn the classic sequential C code to a parallel code. This simplicity of transformation from serial to parallel is one of the hallmark strengths of OpenMP. Parallel hello-world is written as follows:

```
01 #include <stdio.h>
02 #include <omp.h>
03
04 int main() {
05 #pragma omp parallel
06 {
07    printf("Hello World \n");
08 }
09
10    return 0;
11 }
```

Code 1. Parallel Hello World example.

```
Hello World
Hello World
Hello World
Hello World
```

Output 1. The result from Code 1 with the environment variable OMP_NUM_THREADS set to 4.

When compiled and run, the result will be a succession of printed lines of text: Hello World. The number of such lines is determined by the environment variable OMP_THREAD_NUM. The only difference between this and the conventional C version of this code is the parallel version: the single OpenMP directive *#pragma omp parallel*. The effect of the parallel pragma is to fork the number of allocated threads and for each such thread to execute the designated block of code. As a result, every thread executes the *printf* statement once, each printing "Hello World". This demonstrates the use and power of the parallel pragma, perhaps the most important directive in OpenMP. It creates the fork and subsequent join of parallel threads throughout the program.

11.3.2 **Private**

In the simple version of hello-world, above, there is nothing to differentiate among the separate executed threads. For threads to become useful they need to support distinct work even if the code block is the same. Some local state for each thread is usually required although there are some special cases (like reduction variables). The *private* clause within directives is the principal means of achieving this. It declares a variable within the code block to be local to each thread. By this means, each thread has its own copy of the named variable permitting each instance to have its own value, independent of the other threads executing the same code block.

```
01 #include <stdio.h>
02 #include <omp.h>
03 int main() {
04    int num_threads, thread_id;
05 #pragma omp parallel private(num_threads, thread_id)
06 {
07       thread_id = omp_get_thread_num();
08       printf("Hello World. This thread is: %d\n", thread_id);
09       if (thread_id == 0) {
10          num_threads = omp_get_num_threads();
11          printf("Total # of threads is: %d\n", num_threads);
12       }
13 }
14    return 0;
15 }
```

Code 2. An example hello world code where each OMP thread prints out its thread id.

```
Hello World. This thread is: 0
Total # of threads is: 4
Hello World. This thread is: 3
Hello World. This thread is: 1
Hello World. This thread is: 2
```

Output 2. The output from Code 2 with the environment OMP_NUM_THREADS set to be 4.

There are two variables, *num_threads* and *thread_id*, that are declared as private and therefore separate copies of both are provided for each and every thread with the values potentially different. In this case *num_threads* is only used by the Master thread, thread 0. The *omp_get_num_threads* runtime function is called only by the Master thread. Each thread has its own copy of *thread_id*. The runtime function *omp_get_thread_num()* will return a different and unique value to each thread for the respective version of thread-id.

11.3.3 Parallel for

Among the most useful sources of parallelism is the distribution of loops among threads. In C, loops are defined by the for construct specifying the number of iterations of a code block through a designated range of an index variable local to that loop code. Here is a sequential code block to add two arrays together.

```
01 #include <stdio.h>
02 #include <stdlib.h>
03
04 int main (int argc, char *argv[])
05 {
06    const int N = 20;
07    int nthreads, threadid, i;
08    double a[N], b[N], result[N];
09
10    // Initialize
11    for (i=0; i < N; i++) {
12       a[i] = 1.0*i;
13       b[i] = 2.0*i;
14    }
15
16    for (i=0; i<N; i++) {
17       result[i] = a[i] + b[i];
18    }
19
20    printf(" TEST result[19] = %g\n",result[19]);
21
22    return 0;
23 }
```

Code 3. Serial example of adding two arrays together.

```
TEST result[19] = 57
```

Output 3. The output from Code 3.

This program has three parts like many real-world programs. These are initialization, calculation, and output. In this simple program most of the lines of text are dedicated to the declaration and initialization of program variables. Here, these include integers i, k, and N as well as the double vectors a, b, and *result*. A for-loop is included to initialize the vector elements to (admittedly gratuitous) double values. The output of the computation is given by the single *printf* statement that sends the last element of the result vector to standard I/O (usually the screen or a file).

This program can be readily converted to be executed in parallel to increase the computational performance and reduce the time to solution. Three additions are required to transform the above program to parallel.

1. Include the OpenMP header,
2. Delineate the code block to be made parallel, and
3. Specify the loop to be distributed among the concurrent threads.

The first two of these semantic constructs have already been discussed. The OpenMP libraries are incorporated through the command:

```
#include <omp.h>
```

The parallel code block is established through the directive:

```
#pragma omp parallel
{
    ...
}
```

The new construct is the parallel 'for' instruction. This directive enables work sharing where the total work of a loop is divided among the assigned threads. The effect is to divide the range of the private index variable of the for loop into sub ranges, preferably of equal span, one each assigned to one of the parallel threads. Thus, each thread is responsible for part of the total work of the loop and by all of the threads working on their respective parts separately but at the same time, parallel computing is performed. Optimally, the speedup would be equal to the number of threads being used. For a number of reasons to be discussed later, it is infrequent that this level of scaling is fully realized. The parallel for directive is given as the following:

```
#pragma omp for
```

The parallel version of the vector addition example is presented in Code 4 with OpenMP header in line 1, and the additional OpenMP directives in lines 17 and 20:

```
01 #include <omp.h>
02 #include <stdio.h>
03 #include <stdlib.h>
04
05 int main (int argc, char *argv[])
06 {
07   const int N = 20;
08   int i;
09   double a[N], b[N], result[N];
10
11   // Initialize
12   for (i=0; i < N; i++) {
13     a[i] = 1.0*i;
14     b[i] = 2.0*i;
15   }
16
17 #pragma omp parallel
18   { // fork
19
20   #pragma omp for
21   for (i=0; i<N; i++) {
22     result[i]= a[i] + b[i];
23   }
24
25   } // join
26
27   printf(" TEST result[19] = %g\n", result[19]);
28
29   return 0;
30 }
```

Code 4. OpenMP parallel for version of Code 3. OpenMP additions are seen in lines 1, 17, and 20. The output of Code 4 is the same as Code 3, shown in Output 3.

While correct, the code above is a bit verbose. OpenMP allows some compression of code text by merging different directives where it makes sense. For example, the parallel and for directives can be combined into a single statement as shown in Code 5:

```
01 #include<omp.h>
02 #include<stdio.h>
03 #include<stdlib.h>
04
05 int main (int argc, char *argv[])
06 {
07   const int N = 20;
08   int i;
```

```
09   double a[N], b[N], result[N];
10
11   // Initialize
12   for (i=0; i < N; i++) {
13       a[i] = 1.0*i;
14       b[i] = 2.0*i;
15   }
16
17   #pragma omp parallelfor
18   for (i=0; i<N; i++) {
19       result[i] = a[i] + b[i];
20   }
21
22   printf(" TEST result[19] = %g\n", result[19]);
23
24   return 0;
25 }
```

Code 5. Combining the parallel and for directives from Code 4 into a single statement.

Notice that the braces are not required because a single statement makes up the code block now.

In order to find out which thread executes which index of the vector addition, some additional statements are needed as shown in Code 6.

```
01 #include<omp.h>
02 #include<stdio.h>
03 #include<stdlib.h>
04
05 int main (int argc, char *argv[])
06 {
07   const int N = 20;
08   int nthreads, threadid, i;
09   double a[N], b[N], result[N];
10
11   // Initialize
12   for (i=0; i < N; i++) {
13       a[i] = 1.0*i;
14       b[i] = 2.0*i;
15   }
16
17 #pragma omp parallel private(threadid)
18   { // fork
19   threadid = omp_get_thread_num();
20
21   #pragma omp for
22   for (i=0; i<N; i++) {
23       result[i] = a[i] + b[i];
24       printf(" Thread id: %d working on index %d\n",threadid,i);
25   }
```

```
26
27  } // join
28
29  printf(" TEST result[19] = %g\n",result[19]);
30
31  return 0;
32 }
```

Code 6. In this example of vector addition, the identity of the thread performing the operation for each index is printed to screen.

In Code 6, a new variable is introduced called *threadid*. It contains the OpenMP thread index and is initialized inside the OpenMP parallel region. Because it is declared outside the scope of the parallel region, it would by default be considered a global variable by OpenMP. Therefore, it is necessary to declare it as private in the clause following the OpenMP parallel pragma in line 17.

```
Thread id: 0 working on index 0
Thread id: 0 working on index 1
Thread id: 0 working on index 2
Thread id: 0 working on index 3
Thread id: 0 working on index 4
Thread id: 0 working on index 5
Thread id: 0 working on index 6
Thread id: 1 working on index 7
Thread id: 1 working on index 8
Thread id: 1 working on index 9
Thread id: 1 working on index 10
Thread id: 1 working on index 11
Thread id: 1 working on index 12
Thread id: 1 working on index 13
Thread id: 2 working on index 14
Thread id: 2 working on index 15
Thread id: 2 working on index 16
Thread id: 2 working on index 17
Thread id: 2 working on index 18
Thread id: 2 working on index 19
TEST result[19] = 57
```

Output 4. The output from Code 6 when using OMP_NUM_THREADS=3. The default thread scheduler in OpenMP will break the for-loop into 3 roughly equal pieces where thread 0 works on array indices 0 through 6, thread 1 works on array indices 7 through 13, and thread 2 works on array indices 14 through 19.

The behavior controlling which thread works on which index can be altered by using the schedule clause as noted in section 11.2.3.1. This is illustrated in Code 7.

```
01 #include <omp.h>
02 #include <stdio.h>
03 #include <stdlib.h>
04
05 int main (int argc, char *argv[])
06 {
07   const int N = 20;
08   int nthreads, threadid, i;
09   double a[N], b[N], result[N];
10
11   // Initialize
12   for (i=0; i < N; i++) {
13     a[i] = 1.0*i;
14     b[i] = 2.0*i;
15   }
16
17   int chunk = 5;
18
19 #pragma omp parallel private(threadid)
20   { // fork
21   threadid = omp_get_thread_num();
22
23   #pragma omp for schedule(static,chunk)
24   for (i=0; i<N; i++) {
25     result[i] = a[i] + b[i];
26     printf(" Thread id: %d working on index %d\n", threadid,i);
27   }
28
29   } // join
30
31   printf(" TEST result[19] = %g\n", result[19]);
32
33   return 0;
34 }
```

Code 7. An example of the schedule clause. Work in the for-loop will be statically divided into chunks of size 5.

```
Thread id: 0 working on index 0
Thread id: 0 working on index 1
Thread id: 0 working on index 2
Thread id: 0 working on index 3
Thread id: 0 working on index 4
Thread id: 0 working on index 15
Thread id: 0 working on index 16
Thread id: 0 working on index 17
Thread id: 0 working on index 18
Thread id: 0 working on index 19
Thread id: 1 working on index 5
Thread id: 1 working on index 6
Thread id: 1 working on index 7
Thread id: 1 working on index 8
Thread id: 1 working on index 9
```

```
Thread id: 2 working on index 10
Thread id: 2 working on index 11
Thread id: 2 working on index 12
Thread id: 2 working on index 13
Thread id: 2 working on index 14
TEST result[19] = 57
```

Output 5. Output from Code 7 when run using OMP_NUM_THREADS=3. The for-loop is statically divided into chunks of size 5 among 3 threads. Hence thread 0 operates on array indices 0 through 4 and 15 through 19 while thread 1 operates on array indices 5 through 9 and thread 2 operates on array indices 10 through 14.

11.3.4 Sections

OpenMP provides a second powerful method for specifying work sharing among parallel code blocks. The 'sections' directive describes separate code blocks, each of a different sequence of instructions, which may be performed concurrently. There is one thread allocated to each code block. The full set of parallel blocks is initiated with the following directive:

```
#pragma omp sections
{
    ...
}
```

Within this structure are the set of nested code blocks, each begun by the directive:

```
#pragma omp section
{ <code block> }
```

with the exception of the first code block that does not require its own section pragma (the sections pragma serves this second duty) heading. A simple example of a sections code block structure could look like this:

```
#pragma omp parallel
{
    #pragma omp sections
    {
        {
          <1st parallel code block>
        }
        #pragma omp section
        {
          <2nd parallel code block>
        }
        #pragma omp section
        {
          <3rd parallel code block>
        }
    }
}
```

This nested structure of code blocks can be extended as necessary to represent as many distinct and concurrent blocks as necessary. But depending on the number of threads specified by the environment variable, not all of these may be executed simultaneously.

The following example in Code 8 demonstrates the use of the sections and nested section directives to specify three separate code blocks to be executed concurrently. The three calculations determine statistics about a set of integer values, x. The first determines the minimum and maximum values of the set. The second computes the mean. The third computes the mean of the square of the values, which is used later to provide the variance.

```
01 #include <stdio.h>
02 #include <stdlib.h>
03 #include <omp.h>
04
05 int main()
06 {
07    const int N = 100;
08    int x[N], i, sum,sum2;
09    int upper, lower;
10     int divide = 20;
11      sum = 0;
12     sum2 = 0;
13
14 #pragma omp parallelfor
15    for(i = 0; i < N; i++) {
16       x[i] = i;
17    }
18
19
20 #pragma omp parallel private(i) shared(x)
21 {
22
```

```
23 // Fork several different threads
24 #pragma omp sections
25   {
26       {
27         for(i = 0; i < N; i++) {
28           if (x[i] > divide) upper++;
29           if (x[i] <= divide) lower++;
30         }
31         printf("The number of points at or below %d in x is %d\n", divide, lower);
32         printf("The number of points above %d in x is %d\n", divide, upper);
33       }
34 #pragma omp section
35       { // Calculate the sum of x
36         for(i = 0; i < N; i++)
37           sum = sum + x[i];
38         printf("Sum of x = %d\n", sum);
39       }
40 #pragma omp section
41       {
42         // Calculate the sum of the squares of x
43         for(i = 0; i < N; i++)
44           sum2 = sum2 + x[i]*x[i];
45
46         printf("Sum2 of x = %d\n", sum2);
47       }
48   }
49 }
50   return 0;
51 }
```

Code 8. Example of sections in OpenMP.

11.4 Synchronization

A strength of OpenMP is the sharing of global data among multiple concurrent threads. This "shared memory" model presents a view of program data similar to that experienced with the use of conventional sequential programming interfaces like the C programming language. This is distinguished from "distributed memory" models where special send-receive message-passing semantics are required to exchange values among concurrent processes such as found with the MPI programming libraries. But with this ease of use comes a serious challenge: control of the order of access to shared variables. This problem in a different form was encountered when the distinction between private and shared variables was made. By designating a variable as private, it was possible to avoid the out-of-order problem among multiple threads; here, copies of a named variable disassociated the accesses of separate threads. However, communications between or among threads through shared memory is a frequent and efficient means of computation cooperation, if appropriately coordinated. OpenMP incorporates semantic constructs to enable coordination in the shared use of global memory for the class of SMP parallel architectures.

On a shared memory system communication between threads is mainly through read and write operations to shared variables. Where two threads are both reading the value of a shared variable, previously set, the order of accessing the variable by the threads is irrelevant; either thread can perform the read first, followed by the second one. But if one thread is responsible for setting the value through a global write for the other thread to read and use, then clearly the order of access is important and failing to ensure proper order will likely result in an error. This can become more complex when many threads are involved beyond just two.

Synchronization defines the mechanisms that help in coordinating execution of multiple parallel threads that use a shared context (shared memory) in a parallel program. Without synchronization, multiple threads accessing a shared memory location may cause conflicts. This can occur by two or more threads attempting to modify the same location concurrently. It can also happen if one thread is attempting to read a memory location while another thread is updating (writing) the same location. Without strict control of ordering, a race condition may result making the result of these actions non-determinant; the result cannot be guaranteed to always produce the same answer. Synchronization helps to prevent such race conditions. Access conflicts are resolved by providing explicit coordination among multiple threads. These include implicit event synchronization and explicit protection by synchronization directives.

Implicit synchronization determines the occurrence of an event across multiple threads. Barriers are a simple form of event synchronization in OpenMP that coordinate multiple threads such that they are aligned in time. A barrier establishes a point in a parallel program where each thread waits for all of the other like threads to reach the same point in their respective execution. This ensures that all of the computing threads have completed their computation prior to that specific instruction. Only after all threads have reached the barrier can any of them proceed.

Explicit synchronization directly controls access to a specific shared variable. This guarantees that access to the identified data location is limited to at least one thread at a time. This is particularly important when the thread needs to perform a compound atomic sequence of operations such as a read-modify-write on a data element without intrusion of another thread. While this does not fix the order of access, it does protect a variable until any one thread's activity associated with the variable has been completed without conflict. This class of synchronization constructs provides mutual exclusion.

11.4.1 *Critical* Synchronization Directive

The OpenMP pragma "critical" provides mutual exclusion for access to shared variables by multiple threads. This provides protection against race conditions with the minimum of performance degradation for the case when all likely accesses to a given shared variable are from multiple concurrent threads of the same code sequence. The critical directive delineates a block of code that only one thread is permitted to execute at a time. Any global variable that is accessed within that sequence of instructions is protected from attempts by multiple concurrent executing threads of the same code block. Once one thread enters the critical region, the other threads have to wait until it has exited the region. The order in which the different threads perform the critical code block is undetermined. Only the limit of one such thread at a time entering and completing the specified code is guaranteed. The critical pragma permits atomic read-modify-write operation sequences to be safely conducted on a shared variable.

The critical pragma has the form:

```
#pragma omp critical
{
   ...
}
```

An example of its use to safely perform compound atomic operations is the following:

```
int n;
n = 0;
...
#pragma omp parallel shared(n)
{
   #pragma omp critical /* delineate critical region */
     n = n + 1; /* increment n atomically */
} /* parallel end */
```

This simple code allows many threads to increment the shared variable n without the possibility of a race condition among them corrupting the resulting value. Independent of the order in which the critical regions of the separate threads are performed, the resulting value of n will be the same.

11.4.2 The *Master* Directive

The master directive provides another, and perhaps simpler, way of protecting a shared variable among threads to avoid race conditions and possible corruption of result values. As the name implies, master gives total control to the master thread for a specified code block. Such a code block delineated by the master pragma is executed only by one thread, the master thread. When the master thread encounters the master directive, it proceeds to perform it like any other code. But when any thread other than the master thread, all of the worker threads, reaches a master block, it does not execute it and skips over this part of the code. Thus, this particular code block is only performed once, and that by the master thread. Therefore, there is no possibility of a race condition because only one thread is allowed to access the global shared variables referred to within the master code block. There is no barrier implied by the master region. The worker threads that do not perform this code go right past it and continue without any delay due to the master region. The master directive takes the following syntactical form:

```
#pragma omp master
{
   ... /* protected code block */
}
```

11.4.3 The *Barrier* Directive

The barrier pragma puts the computation in a known control state. It synchronizes all the shared variables. When encountering a given barrier directive, all threads halt at that location in the code until all other threads have reached the same point of execution. Only when all the threads have gotten to the barrier can any of them proceed beyond it. Once all the threads have performed the barrier operation, they all continue with the computation after it.

The barrier operation is used to ensure that all the threads have completed the preceding computations no matter what order they are scheduled in or at what rate they are executing. An important purpose of this idiom is to implement the bulk synchronous parallel or BSP protocol, a very common form of parallel computation. With this approach, a set of threads read from shared memory and performs the necessary arithmetic on their values. Then a barrier is performed. Only when all the threads have completed their computation and have reached the barrier, can they go ahead and write the resulting values back to the shared variables. In one form (there are several), after writing to shared memory every thread encounters a second barrier and again waits for all the other threads to complete their shared memory write-back operation as well. Having safely performed all of the writes, the threads can repeat the next step of the parallel calculation safely by reading the newly updated shared variables guaranteed to be correct by the barriers.

```
#pragma omp barrier
```

11.4.4 The *Single* Directive

The 'single' directive combines a form of dynamic scheduling with synchronization. It expands the master pragma to permit any thread to perform the action and combines this with an implicit barrier at the end. The delineated code block is executed by only one thread like the master directive. Unlike master, the executing thread can be any of the running threads, but only one of them. The first thread to reach the single pragma construct in its sequence of instructions will perform the designated code block. The remaining threads will not perform that code. But, all of the threads will encounter a barrier that blocks them from proceeding passed the end of the single pragma code block until all of them have reached that point in their execution.

Only after the thread executing the code designated by the single pragma has completed and exited that code can all of the other threads continue.

```
#pragma omp single
{
  … /* protected code executed by only one thread */
}
```

11.5 Reduction

Reduction operators are a means of bringing together a large number of values to produce a single result value. Familiar examples are numeric (integer or real) summation and logical OR over a range of variables. While this can be achieved through functions of more primitive operations, OpenMP (like other programming interfaces) provides a convenient way to accomplish reductions and in some cases do so in parallel for performance speedup (over sequential implementations). The reduction pragma may take the following form:

```
#pragma omp reduction(op : result_variable)
{
result_variable=result_variable op expression
}
```

The reduction operator, *op*, is one of the following:
+, *, -, /, &, ^, |

The *result_variable* is of a scalar value with one such element as a private variable for every thread.

```
01 #include <stdio.h>
02 #include <omp.h>
03
04 int main ()
05 {
06     int    i, n = 16, chunk = 4;
07     float a[16], b[16], result = 0.0;
08
09     for (i = 0; i<n; i++) {
10            a[i] = i * 1.0;
11            b[i] = i * 2.0;
12     }
13
```

```
14 #pragma omp parallel for      \
15      default (shared )private(i) \
16      schedule(static,chunk)      \
17      reduction(+:result)
18
19    for (i=0; i<n; i++)
20           result += (a[i] * b[i]);
21
22    printf("Result = %f\n", result);
23    return 0;
24 }
```

Code 9. Example of reduction.

```
Result = 2480.000000
```

Output 6. Output from Code 9.

11.6 **Summary and Outcomes**

- "OpenMP" stands for "Open Multi-Processing".
- OpenMP is an application programming interface for parallel computing that has bindings to programming languages such as Fortran and C.
- OpenMP supports programming of shared memory multiprocessors including SMP (Symmetric Memory Processors) and DSM (Distributed Shared Memory processors) class of parallel computer systems.
- OpenMP supports the fork-join model of parallel computing. At particular points in the execution the Master thread spawns a number of threads and with them performs a part of the program in parallel. The point of multiple Worker thread initiation is referred to as the *fork*. Usually, all these threads perform their calculations separately and when they come to their respective completion wait for the other threads to finish as well at the join of the parallel threads.
- OpenMP provides environment variables for controlling execution of parallel codes. These can be set from the OS command line or equivalent prior to execution of the application program.
- Runtime library routines help manage parallel application execution including accessing and using environment variables such as those above. The library routines are provided in the omp.h file and must be included (#include <omp.h>) prior to using any of these routines.
- Threads are the principal means of providing parallelism of computation. A thread is an independently schedulable sequence of instructions combined with its private variables and internal control. Usually, there are as many threads

allocated to the user computation as there are processor cores assigned to the computation. However, this is not required.

- `omp_get_num_threads()` returns the total number of threads currently in the group executing the parallel block from where it is called.
- `omp_get_thread_num()` returns a value to each thread executing the parallel code block that is unique to that thread and can be used as a kind of identifier in its calculations. When the Master thread calls this function, the value of 0 is always returned identifying its special role in the computation.
- OpenMP directives are a principal class of constructs used to convert initially sequential codes incrementally to parallel programs. They serve a multitude of purposes primarily about controlling parallelism through delineation and synchronization.
- The parallel directive delineates a block of code that will be executed separately by each of the computing threads.
- The parallel for directive permits work sharing of an iterative loop among the executing threads with one or more iterations performed by each thread.
- The private clause in a directive establishes that each thread has its own copy of a variable and when accessing that designated variable will read or write its own private copy rather than a shared variable.
- The sections directive describes separate code blocks, each of a different sequence of instructions, which may be performed concurrently. There is one thread allocated to each code block.
- Synchronization directives define the mechanisms that help in coordinating execution of multiple parallel threads that use a shared context (shared memory) in a parallel program to preclude race conditions.
- The *critical* directive provides mutual exclusion of access to shared variables by permitting only on thread at a time to perform a given code block at a time. When a thread enters the critical code section, all other threads that attempt to do so are deferred until the thread doing it has completed. Other threads are then free to execute the critical section of code themselves but only one at a time.
- The *master* directive delineates a block of code that is only executed by the master thread with all other threads skipping over it.
- The *single* directive delineates a block of code that is performed by only a single thread but it can be any of the executing threads, whichever one gets to that code block first. All threads wait until whatever thread executing that code completes it.
- The *barrier* directive is a form of synchronization. When encountering a given barrier directive, all threads halt at that location in the code until all other threads have reached the same point of execution. Only when all the threads have gotten to the barrier can any of them proceed beyond it. Once all the threads have performed the barrier operation, they all continue with the computation after it.

- Reduction operators combine a large number of values to produce a single result value. A number of operations can be used for this purpose such as $+$ or $|$ among others.

11.7 **Exercises**

1. Can you spot any mistakes in the following code? Please correct them.

```
01 #include <stdio.h>
02 #include <omp.h>
03
04 // compute the dot product of two vectors
05
06 int main() {
07    int const N=100;
08    int i, k;
09    double a[N], b[N];
10    double dot_prod= 0.0;
11
12    // Arbitrarily initialize vectors a and b
13    for(i = 0; i < N; i++) {
14       a[i] = 3.14;
15       b[i] = 6.67;
16    }
17
18 #pragma omp parallel
19    {
20    #pragma omp for
21       for(i = 0; i < N; i++)
22          dot_prod= dot_prod+ a[i] * b[i]; // sum up the element-wise product of the
two arrays
23    }
24
25    printf("Dot product of the two vectors is %g\n",dot_prod);
26
27    return 0;
28 }
```

2. In line 23 of Code 7 in section 11.3.3 the static scheduler was demonstrated. How would the output of this code change if the dynamic scheduler were used instead?

3. In Code 8 of section 11.3.4, the sections pragma was introduced. What would happen to Code 8 if the number of OpenMP threads were fewer than the number of sections?

4. Write a matrix-vector multiply and parallelize with OpenMP directives.

CHAPTER

Examples for Multiple-Thread Shared-Memory Programs

12

Chapter outline

When altering a serial application for a high performance computer, leveraging multiple threads inside a shared-memory modality is frequently one of the quickest approaches to take advantage of the computing resources of the supercomputer. In this chapter, two full stand-alone examples of multiple-thread shared-memory programs are presented using OpenMP. To get started, here is a quick test to ensure that OpenMP has been installed properly on your system.

```
 1 #include <stdio.h>
 2 #include <omp.h>
 3 int main(void){
 4     #pragma omp parallel
 5     {
 6         printf("Hello World from thread %d out of %d\n",
omp_get_thread_num(), omp_get_num_threads());
 7     }
 8
 9     return 0;
10 }
```

Assuming the compiler with OpenMP support is gcc, compile this code as follows, assuming the code has been named *test.c*:

```
gcc -fopenmp test.c -o test
```

Assuming the bash shell syntax, set the number of OpenMP threads desired for testing using the OMP_NUM_THREADS environment variable:

```
export OMP_NUM_THREADS=4
```

Then execute the test case:

```
$ ./test
```

High Performance Computing. https://doi.org/10.1016/B978-0-12-823035-0.00012-2

If OpenMP has been installed properly, something like the following will appear as output:

```
Hello World from thread 1 out of 4
Hello World from thread 2 out of 4
Hello World from thread 0 out of 4
Hello World from thread 3 out of 4
```

The order in which the threads print to screen can vary.

12.1 Solving the Black–Scholes Equation

The Black–Scholes partial differential equation is a backward parabolic partial differential equation used for pricing financial instruments that derive their value from some other underlying asset at a future time. It was named after economists Fischer Black and Myron Scholes and requires only a very small number of input parameters, making it a very simple model to use. While there is an analytic solution to the Black–Scholes equation, financial practitioners often modify the basic formulation by creating different flavors of Black–Scholes, such as pricing baskets of instruments or adding stochastic components; in these cases, there is generally no analytic solution, and numerical computation is needed to solve the system. Financial practitioners then use the solution to assess and adjust the risk of a portfolio based on differentiated values of the solution known as the Greeks (delta, gamma, theta, vega, rho). The Black–Scholes equation is:

$$\frac{\partial f}{\partial t} + \frac{1}{2}\sigma^2 S^2 \frac{\partial^2 f}{\partial S^2} + \mu S \frac{\partial f}{\partial S} - \mu f = 0$$

where f is the price of the derivative, S is the price of the underlying asset, σ is the future volatility of the underlying asset, and μ is the interest rate. This equation is usually solved via Monte Carlo by reexpressing the equation as a random walk in the equivalent Black–Scholes stochastic differential equation:

$$dS = \mu S\,dt + \sigma S\,dz$$

where dz is a Wiener process. Here is a stand-alone OpenMP example solving the Black–Scholes equation using the stochastic differential equation approach for a call option at strike price K, expiry t, volatility σ, and expected interest rate μ, with the current underlying price (or spot price) at f_0:

```
1 #include <stdio.h>
2 #include <stdlib.h>
3 #include <math.h>
4 #include <omp.h>
5 #include <time.h>
6
7 double NoD(double x);
8
9 int main(int argc, char *argv[]) {
```

```
10
11    if ( argc != 7 ) {
12       printf(" Usage: bs <f0><K><T to expiry><sigma><mu><Monte Carlo
cycles>\n");
13       exit(0);
14 }
15 double f0 = atof(argv[1]);
16 double K = atof(argv[2]);
17 double T = atof(argv[3]);
18 double sigma = atof(argv[4]);
19 double mu = atof(argv[5]);
20 int mc_cycles = atoi(argv[6]);
21
22 printf("-----------------------------\n");
23 printf(" Parameter choices:\n");
24 printf("-----------------------------\n");
25 printf("            Spot: %g\n",f0);
26 printf("          Strike: %g\n",K);
27 printf("   Time to expiry: %g\n",T);
28 printf("           sigma: %g\n",sigma);
29 printf("              mu: %g\n",mu);
30 printf("Monte Carlo cycles: %d\n",mc_cycles);
31
32 double pi = 4.*atan(1.0);
33 double a,b,result,eps;
34 double S;
35 int i;
36 double *payoff;
37
38 payoff = (double *) malloc(mc_cycles*sizeof(double));
39
40 // Timing
41 clock_t begin = clock();
42
43 double variance, mean;
44
45 #pragma omp parallel private ( i )
46 {
47
48 #pragma omp for
49    for (i=0;i<mc_cycles;i++) {
50       result = rand();
51       a = (1.0*result)/RAND_MAX;
52       result = rand();
```

```
53      b = (1.0*result)/RAND_MAX;
54      if ( a <= 0.0 || a > 1.0 ||
55          b <= 0.0 || b > 1.0 ) {
56        printf(" Random number generator problem : %g %g\n",a,b);
57        exit(0);
58      }
59      /* Standardized normal distribution */
60      eps = sqrt(-2.*log(a))*cos(2.*pi*b);
61
62      S = f0*exp( (mu-0.5*sigma*sigma)*T + sigma*eps*sqrt(T) );
63
64      payoff[i] = exp(-mu*T)*(S - K);
65      if ( payoff[i] < 0.0 ) payoff[i] = 0.0;
66      }
67  }
68      /* find the mean and variance of the payoff */
69      mean = 0.0;
70       variance = 0.0;
71
72  #pragma omp parallel private ( i )
73  {
74  #pragma omp for reduction ( + : mean)
75    for (i=0;i<mc_cycles;i++) {
76       mean += payoff[i];
77    }
78  }
79
80  #pragma omp parallel private ( i )
81  {
82  #pragma omp for reduction ( + : variance)
83    for (i=0;i<mc_cycles;i++) {
84       variance+=(mean/mc_cycles-payoff[i])*(mean/mc_cycles-payoff[i]);
85  }
86  }
87    variance /= mc_cycles;
88    mean /= mc_cycles;
89    double std = sqrt(variance);
90    double error = std/sqrt(mc_cycles);
91
92    clock_t end = clock();
93    double time_to_solution = (double) (end-begin)/CLOCKS_PER_SEC;
94
```

```
95    printf(" Mean: %g Estimated Error: %g std dev: %g\n",mean,error,std);
96    printf(" True price should be in range: %g to %g with 0.95 confidence.\n",
97        mean-1.96*error,mean+1.96*error);
98    printf(" Time to solution: %g\n",time_to_solution);
99
100   /* Analytic result */
101   double d1 = ( log(f0/K)+(mu+0.5*sigma*sigma)*T )/( sigma*sqrt(T) );
102   double d2 = d1 - sigma*sqrt(T);
103
104   double price = f0*NoD(d1) - K*exp(-mu*T)*NoD(d2);
105   printf(" Analytic BS result: %g\n",price);
106
107   free(payoff);
108
109   return 0;
110 }
111
112 // Cumululative Normal Distribution Function
113 double NoD(double x) {
114   double gamma = 0.2316419;
115   double a1 = 0.319381530;
116   double a2 = -0.356563782;
116   double a2 = -0.356563782;
117   double a3 = 1.781477937;
118   double a4 = -1.821255978;
119   double a5 = 1.330274429;
120   double pi = 4.0*atan(1.0);
121   double k;
122
123   double N;
124   double Nprime;
125 if ( x >= 0.0 ) {
126    k = 1./(1.+gamma*x);
127    Nprime = 1./sqrt(2.*pi)*exp(-0.5*x*x);
128    N = 1. - Nprime*(a1*k
129                    +a2*k*k
130                    +a3*k*k*k
131                    +a4*k*k*k*k
132                    +a5*k*k*k*k*k);
133     return N;
134 } else {
135    x *= -1.0;
136    k = 1./(1.+gamma*x);
137    Nprime = 1./sqrt(2.*pi)*exp(-0.5*x*x);
```

```
138    N = 1. - Nprime*(a1*k
139                    +a2*k*k
140                    +a3*k*k*k
141                    +a4*k*k*k*k
142                    +a5*k*k*k*k*k);
143    return 1.-N;
144    }
145  }
```

The function for the cumulative normal distribution function (lines 112−145) is a polynomial approximation accurate to six decimal places and is only added to compute the analytical solution for comparison with the numerical result. The key OpenMP components of this example are lines in just three locations, all beginning with *#pragma omp parallel*. In the first of these locations in lines 45−67, each OpenMP thread computes a payoff trajectory concurrently, and the total amount of concurrency that can be extracted is limited by the number of Monte Carlo iterations specified. Concurrency is extracted by means of *#pragma omp for*, which distributes the work in the for-loop over the available OpenMP threads.

The example code contains two reduction sections: 72−78 and 80−86. In these sections, the sum of the shared variables *mean* and *variance* across the different threads is computed and broadcast. This is accomplished using *reduction* in the *#pragma omp for* directive. The syntax of the directive requires the specification of the type of reduction (addition, subtraction, multiplication, etc.) and the name of the shared variable. For example:

```
#pragma omp for reduction ( + : variance)
```

This directive specifies that the shared variable *variance* needs to be summed across all threads and then broadcast to all threads at the end of the for-loop.

The example code can be compiled with a standard compiler like gcc. For example, if the source code is stored in a file called bsm.c, it can be compiled for OpenMP as follows:

```
gcc -fopenmp bsm.c -o bsm
```

This command will create an executable called *bsm*. To run the example, six input arguments are needed: the spot price, call option strike price, time to expiry, volatility, interest rate, and number of Monte Carlo iterations. The larger the number of Monte Carlo iterations, the more accurate the solution will be. Suppose we are pricing a call option with a strike price of $50 and expiration in 3 months, where the underlying asset is currently trading at $45 and the historical volatility of the asset is 0.2 with interest rate 0.05. We set the number of OpenMP threads first according to the number of cores available on the node:

```
export OMP_NUM_THREADS=96
```

We then run the code in the command line and specify to compute 100,000 Monte Carlo iterations:

```
./bsm 45 50 0.25 0.2 0.05 100000
-----------------------------
      Parameter choices:
-----------------------------
              Spot: 45
            Strike: 50
    Time to expiry: 0.25
             sigma: 0.2
                mu: 0.05
Monte Carlo cycles: 100000
   Mean: 0.435049 Estimated Error: 0.00436639 std dev: 1.38077
   True price should be in range: 0.42649 to 0.443607 with 0.95 confidence.
   Time to solution: 0.00012077
   Analytic BS result: 0.448759
```

The system computes the price of the option to be $0.435; the analytic Black−Scholes result is $0.449. The numerical solution converges to the analytic solution as the number of Monte Carlo iterations increases. Setting the number of OpenMP threads to be one will still give a correct answer, but the time to solution will be slower.

12.2 Solving the Wave Equation

The wave equation is a second-order hyperbolic partial differential solved numerically as an initial value problem. The wave equation in one spatial dimension is

$$\frac{\partial^2 \varphi}{\partial t^2} = \frac{\partial^2 \varphi}{\partial x^2}$$

where $\varphi(x, t)$ is subject to boundary conditions at some initial time and the edges of the x domain. It is often reduced to two first-order partial differential equations by introducing two new variables:

$$u = \frac{\partial \varphi}{\partial t}, v = \frac{\partial \varphi}{\partial x}$$

The wave equation then becomes

$$\frac{\partial u}{\partial t} = \frac{\partial v}{\partial x}, \frac{\partial v}{\partial t} = \frac{\partial u}{\partial x}$$

Here is a stand-alone OpenMP example solving the wave equation in one spatial dimension using finite differencing to solve these two first-order partial differential equations. It takes the number of points used to discretize the spatial dimension as the only input.

```
 1 #include <stdio.h>
 2 #include <stdlib.h>
 3 #include <math.h>
 4 #include <omp.h>
 5
 6 void compute_dx(double *du,double *u,int nx, double hx)
 7 {
 8   int i,j;
 9   double ohx = 1.0/(2.0*hx);
10 #pragma omp parallel private (i)
11 {
12 #pragma omp for
13   for (i=1;i<nx-1;i++) {
14     du[i] = ohx*( u[i+1] - u[i-1] );
15   }
16 }
17
18 }
19
20 int main(int argc,char *argv[]) {
21   if ( argc < 2 ) {
22     printf(" Usage: wave <nx>\n");
23     exit(0);
24   }
25   int nx = atoi(argv[1]);
26   if ( nx%2 == 0 ) {
27     printf(" Only use odd grid sizes\n");
28     exit(0);
29   }
30   int i,j,it;
31   FILE *fp;
32
33   // Domain size
34   double maxx = 10.0;
35   double minx = -10.0;
36   double tmax = 3.0;
37
38   // Discretization
39   double hx = ( maxx - minx )/(nx - 1.0);
40
41   double cfl = 0.1;
42   double dt = cfl*hx;
43
44   int tsteps = (int) (tmax/dt);
```

```
45
46    // Allocate memory for the grid
47    double *u,*up1,*v,*vp1;
48    double *dx_u, *dx_v;
49    u = (double *) malloc(nx*sizeof(double));
50    up1 = (double *) malloc(nx*sizeof(double));
51    v = (double *) malloc(nx*sizeof(double));
52    vp1 = (double *) malloc(nx*sizeof(double));
53    dx_u = (double *) malloc(nx*sizeof(double));
54    dx_v = (double *) malloc(nx*sizeof(double));
55
56 #pragma omp parallel private (i)
57 {
58    // Specify initial data
59 #pragma omp for
60    for (i=0;i<nx;i++) {
61       double x = minx + i*hx;
62       u[i] = 2*x*exp(-x*x);
63       v[i] = -2*x*exp(-x*x);
64    }
65 }
66
67    // Output the initial data
68    fp = fopen("u_start.txt","w");
69    for (i=0;i<nx;i++) {
70       double x = minx + i*hx;
71       fprintf(fp,"%g %g\n",x,u[i]);
72    }
73    fclose(fp);
74
75    for (it=0;it<tsteps;it++) {
76       printf(" Computing step %d of %d\n",it,tsteps);
77       // compute derivatives
78       compute_dx(dx_u,u,nx,hx);
79       compute_dx(dx_v,v,nx,hx);
80
81 #pragma omp parallel private (i)
82 {
83       // Compute the next time step
84 #pragma omp for
85       for (i=1;i<nx-1;i++) {
86       up1[i] = u[i] + dt*dx_v[i];
87       vp1[i] = v[i] + dt*dx_u[i];
88       }
```

```
89  }
90
91      // Boundary conditions
92      up1[0] = 0; up1[nx-1] = 0;
93      vp1[0] = 0; vp1[nx-1] = 0;
94
95      // Swap pointers
96      double *swap;
97      swap = u;
98      u = up1;
99      up1 = swap;
100
101      swap = v;
102      v = vp1;
103      vp1 = swap;
104
105    }
106    // Simulation is complete
107    // Output the result after the last step
108    fp = fopen("u_finish.txt","w");
109    for (i=0;i<nx;i++) {
110      double x = minx + i*hx;
111      fprintf(fp,"%g %g\n",x,u[i]);
112    }
113    fclose(fp);
114
115    free(u);
116    free(up1);
117    free(v);
118    free(vp1);
119    free(dx_u);
120    free(dx_v);
121    return 0;
122  }
```

The code is compiled with a standard C compiler like gcc:

```
gcc -fopenmp wave.c -o wave
```

The number of OpenMP threads used is set via the environment variable OMP_NUM_THREADS:

```
export OMP_NUM_THREADS=96
```

The executable takes an integer as an argument to indicate the number of points used to discretize the spatial domain:

```
./wave 1001
```

Output is written in two text files, u_start.txt and u_finish.txt, that can be plotted in gnuplot and show the wave moving to the right as shown in Fig. 12.1. The gnuplot commands used to plot the data and reproduce the plot in Fig. 12.1 are as follows:

```
gnuplot> plot "u_start.txt" with linespoints
gnuplot> replot "u_finish.txt" with linespoints
```

The OpenMP pragmas located in the time integration are where the parallel concurrency is extracted. Because of the hyperbolic nature of the wave equation, it is difficult to extract concurrency in the time direction and so the OpenMP pragmas are limited to the computing derivatives in the spatial domain or to updating the right-hand side of the time difference equation to achieve a speedup. However, because of the diffusive nature of the finite difference approximation, high spatial resolution is needed to solve the system accurately, thereby giving plenty of concurrency to extract via OpenMP for larger grid sizes.

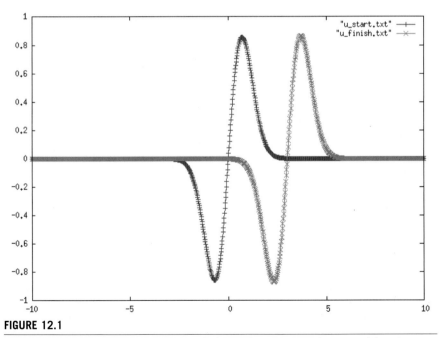

FIGURE 12.1

The initial condition and the computed solution to the wave equation several timesteps later are plotted here using gnuplot. The initial waveform is initially centered on the zero x coordinate and then moves to the right later.

12.3 **Summary and Outcomes**

- Two full OpenMP examples have been presented using different numerical methods for solving very common partial differential equations: the Black-Scholes equation and the Wave equation.
- For the Black-Scholes equation, each OpenMP thread computes a payoff trajectory concurrently.
- For the wave equation, each OpenMP thread computes the numerical derivatives or time difference equation across a portion of the spatial domain.

12.4 **Exercises**

1. For smaller grid sizes, the wave equation example will run slower on multiple OpenMP threads than just on a single thread. Why? At what grid size does it begin to make sense to use multiple OpenMP threads?

2. What would happen to the Black–Scholes example if the omp parallel sections in lines 72 and 80 were combined into the omp parallel section of line 45?

3. Why are shared variables not declared explicitly in the omp parallel sections?

4. Modify the wave equation example to solve the wave equation in two spatial dimensions. How does the OpenMP implementation change?

5. What happens if OpenMP is used as part of the output for the wave equation example? When does it make sense to use OpenMP to accelerate the input/output portion of the simulation?

Distributed Memory Architecture

13

Chapter outline

13.1 Introduction

The distributed memory architecture is the single most widely used system structure for scalable high performance computing (HPC). It incorporates a hierarchical (multilevel) organization, each layer of which embodies an explicit form of parallelism integrated into a single composite system. The primary system scaling parameters that distinguish among various distributed configurations include:

- Number of nodes per system, each node comprising one or more processor sockets, main memory banks, and ancillary logic, circuits, and interfaces
- Type and number of processor sockets and number of cores per socket in each node
- Main memory capacity per node and total system main memory
- Intranode structure is shared-memory communicating via local main memory
- Internode structure is fragmented for distributed memory using message passing to communicate between system nodes
- System area network (SAN) protocol, bandwidth, and diameter integrating the system nodes
- Power consumption, footprint (floor space area), and cost
- Software infrastructure including user interface, operating system (OS), and scheduler

Even within these boundaries, there is and has been a broad range of design choices for potential distributed memory system architectures. By 1990, supercomputers had entered the 3-decades-long era but struggled to be capable of more than a

High Performance Computing. https://doi.org/10.1016/B978-0-12-823035-0.00013-4

few Gigaflops sustained performance even by the largest such machines. In every case, nodes were single-processor core entities. The Intel Touchstone Paragon, CRI T3E, TMC CM-5, Tera MTA, Convex C3, and many others were the initial massively parallel processing (MPP) constituents of this class of HPC system. These were fully custom with the nodes designed from scratch but based on generational microprocessors. Others were a mix of commodity-off-the-shelf (COTS) components such as microprocessors and custom node designs, including their system area networks (SANs). In 1991, a consortium of agencies with Intel deployed the Touchstone Delta at Caltech with more than 500 microprocessors and a custom mesh network. The Delta was capable of 10 Gigaflops of sustained performance and served as the prototype of the Touchstone Paragon family of supercomputers. This class of systems in its many variations became the general architecture model for the following decades: custom-designed nodes and SANs with off-the-shelf state-of-the-art microprocessors. These are referred to as "massively parallel processors" and were a mix of shared memory and distributed memory architectures.

The Top 500 list of fastest supercomputers was begun in 1993 to 1994 based on the high performance LINPACK (HPL)benchmark derived from the earlier LIN-PACK benchmark by Jack Dongarra and colleagues. The Top 500 list recognized a number of distinct classes of supercomputers even including uniprocessors at its beginning. But only the class of MPP has survived from the list's beginning to the present day even as it has spanned the performance range of approximately from 100 Gigaflops to 1 Exaflops R_{max} or a factor of about 10 million in 3 decades.

The critical distinction between symmetric multiprocessing (SMP) and scalable MPP is the logical and physical separation of the "nodes" from each other for the MPP. Although the processor cores of the SMP share the same communication fabric and main memory, the individual nodes of the MPP incorporate their own local main memory independent of that of other nodes. SMP processor cores communicate through their shared memory. MPP processor cores communicate not through shared memory but by means of messages passed between nodes through the external SAN. This is very different both for hardware and programming. As will be seen in this chapter, MPPs reflect the communicating sequential processes model, more commonly referred to as "message passing". Using this semantic strategy yields dramatic expansion of scalability to tens, hundreds, even thousands of nodes at the sacrifice of a simpler programming model.

Finally, a variation of the MPP strategy was adopted for the special case where both microprocessor nodes and SANs are off-the-shelf. Both Network of Workstations (NOW) and Beowulf Linux Commodity Clusters pursued this approach in the mid-1990s, exploiting the economy of scale derived from the nodes being widely marketed standalone computers and the SAN using networks used for general local area networks (LANs) such as Ethernet, Myrianet, and InfiniBand. Although they experienced different performance and performance to cost, together they ultimately represented the single mostly widely deployed class of computing system on the Top 500 List. Because Chapter 2 discusses commodity clusters in detail, they won't be further amplified on here. What is important is that the programming model used for scalable MPPs can also be used on commodity clusters. With expanded nodes that leverage the improved SMP nodes of a growing number of multicore chips, this hierarchy has been, if anything, strengthened over the years until current generation nanoscale technology.

13.2 **Massively Parallel Processor**

MPPs are a genus of distributed memory computer systems. Like SMPs, they use microprocessors, even multiple microprocessors in any single node. Unlike SMPs, computing nodes do not logically or physically share the system's total main memory in a single unified shared memory structure. Instead, the system main memory is partitioned or fragmented (separated) among its multiplicity of nodes. The principal disadvantage is that the single-system image to the application program is discarded. Its shared memory model among multiple processor cores is sacrificed for an important alternative advantage: MPPs are scalable at least to a very large degree. Bigger application codes and datasets, in some cases by order of magnitudes, than those of SMPs are achievable. The largest HPC systems are MPPs with Frontier at ORNL being the highest performing HPL rated system of 1.1 Exaflops R_{max} and Aurora coming online at the time of this writing.

The two major elements of the MPP (in its basic form) are the processing nodes and the SAN (Fig. 13.1). Nodes incorporate the computing components, the main memory, external interfaces, and ancillary integration logic. Frontier incorporates

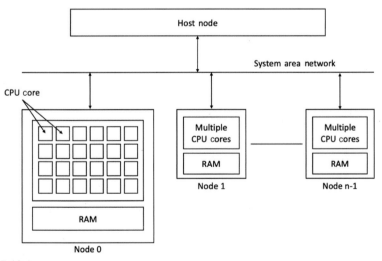

FIGURE 13.1

An example of massively parallel processor architecture. *CPU*, Central processing unit; *RAM*, random access memory.

FIGURE 13.2

Frontier supercomputer (massively parallel processor) at Oak Ridge National Laboratory.

9472 nodes with 74 racks taking up 7300 square feet of floor space. The SAN interconnects all of the nodes via their interfaces and incorporates data transfer channels, data routing switches, and network interface controllers. Both copper and optical cabling are used for the interconnect of Frontier. Although this description is overly simplistic, even in its limitations, it captures the essential functional elements and their operations that perform scalable computing. Many other physical pieces such as power distribution, liquid or air cooling, and secondary mass storage combine to form a modern practical and highly capable computing system that in its largest form factors can have a footprint at or in excess to 10,000 square feet of very large data center floor space. MPPs can be super big as well as super-fast (Fig. 13.2).

13.3 Node Microprocessor

The node of any HPC system serves a similar purpose; that is, it performs part of the computations of extended application programs stored across multiple or many nodes' main memory. These nodes exchange intermediate result data values with other nodes of the same system communicating among the nodes via message passing. Yet nodes of differing HPC system designs may vary widely in physical form and logical function.

Initially, in the 1990s and even slightly before, a node of a multinode MPP would have one microprocessor per node to provide the computing power for each node. However, even in this early era, the idea of incorporating a small number of processors was considered because a shared memory system had already been marketed in the previous decade. The Intel Touchstone Delta and succeeding Touchstone Paragons integrated three Intel i860 RISC microprocessors within a single node with a two-processor variant also available in some cases. In 1994, a Paragon was rated as the fastest computer in the world at 170 Gigaflops R_{max}.

The generic MPP compute node incorporates multiple distinct functional elements that are tightly coupled to perform general-purpose data processing. The processor core is responsible for all calculations done for the user application as well as the system software. Over the past 3 decades, many different microprocessors served in this role. Because of a dominant technology trend referred to as Moore's law, transistor density doubled approximately every 2 years (until recently), and clock rates also increased exponentially (again until recently). Over almost 3 decades, HPC performance gains increased by a factor of greater than 10 million.

The node microprocessor over that period also grew in complexity and sophistication, incorporating many innovations over time. These included many specific advances of which the most significant are as follows:

- Complex internal flow control execution pipeline
- Pipelined and instruction-level parallelism
- Reservation stations
- Single Instruction, Multiple Data parallel computation
- Branch prediction
- Speculative execution
- Cache memory hierarchy
- Virtual address translation
- Multiple register sets
- Other sometimes very clever mechanisms for optimal operation under specific but important conditions

It is outside the scope of this text to present details on each of these, and for this readers are directed to excellent books by Patterson and Hennesy on computer architecture. Many of these add to the exploitation of fine-grained parallelism to increase instruction level throughput. Others take advantage of temporal and spatial locality to minimize latency effects, including registers and caches.

13.4 **Node Main Memory**

The code and data for a user application are stored in main memory of any single node. The size of the application that can be computed is largely determined by the memory capacity of the computer and therefore of the node of an HPC system. Like the technology trends for microprocessors, that of dynamic random access memory (DRAM), which is the principal large memory device, experienced exponential growth in density and capacity over previous decades. Unlike logic DRAM, speeds grew much more slowly, and the speed gap between logic and storage cells widened appreciably.

In the late 1970s, the first DRAM chips were available on the market with a total capacity of 1 K bits. Today, DDR5 chips have a capacity of as much as 16 Gigabits per die. And there are many semiconductor dies in each node. This technology trajectory has been a major contributor to the transformative evolution and impact of

HPC. Nonetheless, another metric tracked through this epoch, the ratio of the memory capacity to the peak system performance, has diminished by orders of magnitude. At the beginning of this period, a common rule of thumb was a bytes/flops ratio of approximately 1.0. Today, typically, this has shrunk by 2 orders of magnitude or more or about 0.01. It turns out that studies have shown that a wide array of applications can be effectively performed without such an extreme storage capacity. However, such requirements vary widely with some problems being limited by available main memory.

Perhaps ironically, an important part of the memory hierarchy is not in the main memory at all. Rather it is the cache or caches that reside instead in or with the processor cores in the same socket. The purpose of cache is to bridge the speed and capacity gap between the main memory and the processor core. A cache is an intermediate level of memory, usually static random access memory (SRAM), with much smaller storage capacity than a DRAM but much faster access speed. Modern systems may incorporate three levels of cache. The second driver for caches is to dramatically reduce stored data access latency from that of the DRAM main memory banks only. Caches are hidden from the programmer in an attempt to minimize the burden of explicitly managing this complex subsystem. To do this, the caches use two operational properties: associative addressing and data locality. Associative addressing enables dynamic placement of temporarily stored data and processor core access. But which data is held in cache? This is determined by the property of "locality".

In many cases, data access patterns exhibit temporal or spatial locality (or both). Temporal locality relies on the greater likelihood that a variable to be accessed has already been acquired shortly before. Thus, a strategy of favoring storing data in the cache that is most recently used exploits temporal locality and may greatly increase the probability of finding requested values in the cache rather than resorting to the relatively long access time to main memory banks of DRAM. Spatial locality recognizes and exploits bias toward data near values already accessed such that they are favored to be accessed. Spatial locality is exploited by caches by storing multiple adjacent words in a single cache line. Spatially co-located data in a single cache line under many conditions is more likely to be accessed than randomly accessed data. Together, both forms of locality under favorable access patterns can greatly increase the rate at which requested data are found in cache, dramatically reducing the effective memory access time for higher performance.

13.5 Multicore Nodes

Throughout the first decade (1990s) of the MPP revolution, in most architecture designs, each node incorporated a single processor core. There were exceptions as previously noted. This led to a logical as well as a practical organization. Among other factors, it avoided the complication of enabling multiple processors to work together in a coordinated fashion, especially when sharing main memory, in particular, the challenge of maintaining consistency of copies of data across the caches of different processors. And with space on the PC boards and backplanes at a premium, there were many other aspects of the node architecture design that took precedent.

Distributed Memory MPP architectures achieved performance gain through scalability, the number of processor cores making up the system. The other performance factor of an MPP is the capability of each core, in part, proportional to the core's clock rate. A simple relation for MPP scalability is

$$N_{cores} = N_{nodes} \times N_{p/node} \times N_{cores/p}$$

in which N_{cores} is the number of cores in a given MPP, N_{nodes} is the number of nodes in a given MPP, $N_{p/node}$ is the number of processor sockets per node, and $N_{cores/p}$ is the number of cores per processor socket.

Distributed Memory MPP systems have gained much, if not most, of their parallelism based on the number of nodes of which they are constructed. There is a minor exception, which is a class of MPPs called "constellations". Constellations are MPPs for which the number of cores per node is greater than the total number of nodes. These play at most a small role within the field of contemporary HPC but did so a decade ago or more for a few years. Depending on the evolution of computer architecture in the post—Moore's law era through to the end of this decade, it is possible that constellations may reemerge as an architecture of choice. But now they need not be considered. Currently, nodes dominate MPP parallelism.

Within a node, additional opportunity for expanded parallelism is offered through a combination of two possible features. One of these is multiple processor sockets (and therefore cores) incorporated in each node. As previously noted, a formidable problem for this is cache coherency in which the veracity of all copies of memory data within the caches of the multiple processors is assured or at least invalidated. For the sake of performance, the protocols to guarantee this are implemented in hardware, potentially complicating the architecture design.

It would be possible to circumvent this problem by designing a node such that each of multiple processors has its own main memory and so do not share data across processors in the node. But this makes little sense because it merely repackages multiple nodes into a single unit. Nonetheless, it is a feasible organization.

The first attempts at addressing the problem of cache coherency were undertaken not for MPPs but rather for early SMPs in the 1980s. The logical protocol that integrated the memory hierarchy and that was implemented in hardware included MESI. This was a snooping model made possible by a shared bus. Several processor boards were interconnected by a single shared bus such that all access requests to main memory could be simultaneously observed by all of the processors. In one of many implementations, each processor would determine if its cache contained a copy of the requested memory address. If not, no action need be taken by that processor. But if a processor's cache does contain the requested address, one of several alternative actions is possible. The details are interesting to students of hardware architecture but are beyond the scope of this introductory text. The lesson to be drawn from this is that multiple processors can be integrated to form a single shared memory SMP permitting multithreaded shared memory execution and programming.

The second modality for MPP parallelism is the integration of multiple cores within a single socket. This configuration was not pursued into almost 2010 because as the enabling technology improved, there were many opportunities to design advanced cores with improved performance than would be delivered by more than one lesser cores on the same chip. By this period, the first large-scale systems did emerge, including the Roadrunner machine by IBM that in 2008 was recognized as the first MPP rated at 1 Petaflops R_{max}. Other systems such as the Blue Gene system also followed this path. Most MPPs on the Top 500 List fall into this category, although interestingly, Frontier specifies a node as a single AMD processor core with attached accelerators.

13.6 System Area Network and Message Passing

MPP nodes do not share main memory beyond relatively small number of cores in any given node. SMPs do. Their application threads and processes coordinate and cooperate through variables in main memory. If MPPs do not communicate through main memory, how do the potentially thousands of processors in the system work together on a single computation? The answer is message passing, and the medium of information exchange is the SAN.

The structure and operation of SANs is an entire discipline. They may differ by number of node ports, bisection bandwidth, topology, intermediate switching elements, and communication latency as well as message-packet transport protocol. The system-level parallelism through the SAN is the principal means of achieving scalability for potential performance gain. But it also imposes greater, even severe, latency and contention disparities dependent on relative connectivity of source and destination of message transfer. Topologies can vary in form and contention, emphasizing different properties considered important. Mesh or toroidal structures may exhibit very high nearest neighbor bandwidths but impose significant latencies and variability thereof highly sensitive to relative positioning. Star topologies (almost never used anymore) may yield order constant latencies but limit bandwidth.

MPP architecture may be delineated by source of its SAN technology. Custom networks are optimized for a specific architecture. Historically, this was frequently the case. The Touchstone Delta and Touchstone Paragon used a custom global two-dimensional mesh network. The TMC CM-5 used a custom modified fat-tree network. Frontier, currently the leading MPP on the Top 500 list, is based on the HPE Cray EX system architecture. The network is based on the HPE Slingshot switch with 64 ports in the Dragonfly topology. Both optical and copper are used in the Frontier SAN.

13.7 **Clusters and Other Massively Parallel Processing Variants**

The other category of MPP based on source of SAN is the commodity cluster. This was introduced by the NASA Beowulf project in 1994 along with the Linux operating system that now dominates essentially all systems on the Top 500 list. The commodity cluster uses off-the-shelf networks that benefit from the economy of scale based on its many market niches. One such network is the many generations of Ethernet, which is widely in use. Ethernet initially served in the 1980s as a LAN to connect mini-computers and workstations to peripheral devices (e.g., laser printers) and to shared file servers. Its technology was mature in 1995 with 100 Megabits/s bandwidth and nonblocking 16-way routing switches. The second widely used SAN is the InfiniBand Architecture that was designed expressly for this purpose and delivers improved performance and lower latency. Most HPC systems on the Top 500 list are commodity clusters, which are discussed in detail in Chapter 2 at some length.

This chapter has provided a concise presentation of the most widely used class of scalable HPC, the distributed computing MPP. The next chapter teaches students how to construct application programs with MPI for MPPs, including commodity clusters. But there have been other variants of systems. Some have attempted to bridge the gap between SMP and MPP to provide scalable shared memory HPC. Among these were the CRI T3E, the SGI Altix, the KSR, and the Convex SPP. Each embodied some unique features and operational characteristics. In principle, some of these and others exported a cc-NUMA programming interface, which was intended to simplify user programming.

Perhaps the biggest innovation to MPPs is that of heterogeneous system architecture and the introduction of graphical processing unit (GPU) accelerators, many from Nvidia but also AMD, which is the basis for the HPE Frontier 1 Exaflops HPC. GPUs, their architecture, and how to program them will be presented in detail later in this text.

13.8 **Summary and Outcomes**

- Most HPC systems are distributed memory MPP architecture.
- MPPs are scalable unlike shared memory SMPs.
- Message passing is used to communicate data between MPP nodes.
- The Top 500 list tracks the fastest HPCs based on the HPL benchmark.
- The purpose of cache is to bridge the speed gap between the main memory and the processor core.
- Distributed Memory MPP systems have gained much, if not most, of their parallelism based on the number of nodes of which they are constructed.
- MPP parallelism is also provided by the number of processor sockets in a node and the number of cores in a socket in a node.

- Nodes of MPPs are integrated by a SAN interconnection.
- Ethernet and InfiniBand are the most widely deployed COTS SAN.
- Caches exploit temporal and spatial locality to achieve high hit rates.

13.9 Exercises

1. What is the principal differentiating property of a scalable distributed architecture (MPP) from that of an SMP?

2. The node of a scalable distributed MPP incorporates four processor sockets. Each socket of a node has a two-dimensional array of four processors on a side. How many processor cores can be available in this MPP of 1024 nodes?

3. Describe the Dragonfly network and specify its principal advantage.

4. From the recent Top 500 list, of the top 5 machines, which has the largest number of cores per node and how many?

5. If Frontier is the fastest (or near fastest) HPL system, what is the top machine for performing the Graph-500 computation?

The Essential MPI

14

Chapter outline

High Performance Computing. https://doi.org/10.1016/B978-0-12-823035-0.00014-6

14.1 Introduction

A major form of high performance computing (HPC) systems that enables scalability is the distributed-memory multiprocessor. Both massively parallel processors (MPPs) and commodity clusters are examples of system-level architectures of this form. The distinguishing property of this important class of supercomputer is that the main memory of the system is partitioned into fragmented components, each associated with one or more processor cores and ancillary components that together compose what has become casually referred to as a "node". Multiple nodes integrated by means of one or more interconnect networks constitute the full high performance computer. A distributed-memory system is such that a processor core is able to directly access the memory intrinsic to its resident node, but not the memory or the external nodes. Exchange of data, cooperation and coordination of the tasks running on the separate nodes, and overall operation of the system as a single entity is achieved through the transfer of messages between nodes by means of the system area network.

The major advantage of the distributed-memory multiprocessor is its scalability. Within the constraints of power and cost, essentially any number of nodes can be incorporated within a single supercomputer. A downside to that is the programmer being forced to manage the program locality explicitly, making pieces of work fit within the confines of an individual node. This has resulted in a generation of scalable application software and libraries that has achieved a million times greater throughput performance than previous-generation computing models and architecture classes.

Over as many as 3 decades there have been many software application programming interfaces (APIs) and implementation libraries that supported the communicating sequential processes model of computation, casually referred to as the "message-passing model". These were developed by industry, within academia, and from national labs and centers, among others. However, by far the most impactful has been MPI [1]. MPI was, and in its most recent versions still is, a community-driven specification. Starting in late 1992, representatives of industry, government, and academia began a community-led process to develop a standard programming interface based on these principles, first laid out by Anthony Hoare in the mid-1970s [2]. The strength of this approach to community building was the ready acceptance of the result and the rapid development of useful applications. The weakness was that to achieve an agreed-upon initial standard, many more controversial semantics, constructs, and mechanisms were initially discarded for the sake of unity, resulting in a more simplistic and admittedly limited interface. However, despite such sacrifices of sophistication, this proved to be the right path for evolutionary progress that was much needed at the time. At the risk of hyperbole, there was probably no greater achievement of practical utility for the advancement of HPC than the development of MPI. Even in its most basic form MPI has proven a powerful, flexible, and usable programming interface. With its hundreds of commands, it deals with a rich and diverse set of circumstances. Yet, a very small subset of them described in this chapter is sufficient to write a wide array of parallel applications. In doing so it gives the student a powerful tool set for harnessing distributed-memory supercomputers and empowering the opportunity in computational end-user problems that are enabled by it.

14.2 Message-Passing Interface Standards

From 1992 to 1994, a community representing both vendors and users decided to create a common interface to message-passing calls in the context of distributed-memory parallel computers to address the lack of standardization of existing message-passing environments. MPI-1 was the result. From the very beginning, MPI was "just" an API, not a language. This was achieved by adding constructs for parallelism, data exchange communication, synchronization, and collectives through bindings to existing conventional sequential programming languages. These were initially Fortran 77 and ANSI C, later updated to Fortran 2008 and ISO C. Language bindings permit the semantics and syntax of existing languages to be exploited from the frameworks of libraries for concurrency management. These bindings permitted the widest possible use of existing application kernels, compilers, and user skill sets while augmenting them with the needed concepts of communication frameworks for coordination, cooperation, and concurrency. The MPI standard can be found online, including its most recent version 4.0 [3].

Probably equally as important as the community-derived API was for MPI was the first reduction to practice, that is, the first reference implementation called "MPI over Chameleon" (MPICH), developed at Argonne National Laboratory [4]. This was delivered in 1995 and served as the template for the many other implementations of MPI to come afterward. Led by William Gropp, the MPICH project provided both important experience in the implementation of MPI and a platform upon which the earliest practical applications were developed and run on the MPP systems of the time, such as the CM-5 (Fig. 14.1). Since then, the number of available MPI implementations grew to include OpenMPI [5], a joint effort merging several earlier message-passing libraries, and MVAPICH [6], focusing primarily on the InfiniBand interconnect, as well as multiple commercial packages.

14.3 Message-Passing Interface Basics

While the latest versions of MPI include literally hundreds of commands, a simple parallel program can be created using only three basic commands. This subsection presents how to do that. The bindings presented all assume the use of the C programming language, with which examples and descriptions are presented.

FIGURE 14.1

A connection machine 5 (CM-5) with 512 nodes and theoretical maximum capability of 65.5 Gflops, operational between 1991 and 1997.
Photo: https://en.wikipedia.org/wiki/FROSTBURG.

14.3.1 **Message-Passing Interface Header File**

Every MPI program in C must contain the preprocessor directive:

```
#include <mpi.h>
```

The `mpi.h` file contains the definitions and declarations necessary for compiling an MPI program. This file is usually found in the "include" directory of most MPI installations. This directive can be positioned in any order with other directives but must precede the beginning of the program with the `main` call.

14.3.2 **Message-Passing Interface Initialization**

The part of the user application code that will contain function calls for MPI program constructs must begin with the single call to `MPI_Init` and expects arguments of the following form, returning an integer error value:

```
int MPI_Init(int *argc, char ***argv)
```

MPI_Init initializes the execution environment for MPI. This command has to be called before any other MPI call is made, and it is an error to call it more than a single time within the program. The number of arguments passed internally to all of the parallel processes is pointed to by `argc`. The vector of the arguments' list is pointed to by `argv`, as is consistent with the C language and command-line argument variables passing. Every process launched by `MPI_Init` inherits copies of these two program argument variables and is achieved by the call:

```
MPI_Init(&argc, &argv);
```

prior to any of the other MPI calls within the application.

14.3.3 Message-Passing Interface Finalization

In a sense, the other bookend to `MPI_Init` is the `MPI_Finalize` command. `MPI_Finalize` cleans up all the extraneous mess that was first put into place by `MPI_Init`. It brings to an end the computing environment for MPI. There are no arguments to this MPI service call, which has the simple syntax as follows:

```
MPI_Finalize();
```

This does not have to be the end of the entire program. Many other C statements can follow it. Also, its exact position in the code sequence is not particularly important as long as it comes after any other MPI commands in the program.

14.3.4 Message-Passing Interface Example—Hello World

Somewhat sadly, there is a rite of passage that every neophyte programmer in just about any programming language has to go through: it is writing "Hello World", a most trivial program first sketched out by Kernighan and Richie in their original book on C [7]. This is the most minimalist program one can imagine that actually works. Getting this far is a major milestone for a student, crossing the line from never having successfully written an actual computer program in the language of choice to being a programmer (sort of). So, for the sake of tradition and with a justified nod to those giants who preceded us, here is "Hello World" in MPI with C bindings.

```
01 #include <stdio.h>
02 #include <mpi.h>
03
04 int main(int argc,char **argv)
05 {
06   MPI_Init(&argc,&argv);
07   printf(" Hello, World!\n");
08   MPI_Finalize();
09   return 0;
10 }
```

CODE 14.1

A trivial example of "Hello World" using message-passing interface.

The example in Code 14.1 is compiled and run using the MPICH implementation of MPI on a Beowulf class cluster as follows:

```
> mpicc code1.c -o code1
> mpirun -np 4 ./code1
  Hello, World!
  Hello, World!
  Hello, World!
  Hello, World!
```

The `mpicc` compiler wrapper links in the appropriate MPI libraries and gives the path to the file location of the mpi.h header. `mpirun-np 4` launches four instances of the code executable in the runtime environment. While using `mpicc` and `mpirun` to compile and launch MPI applications is very common, they are not part of the MPI standard, and the specific compile and launching approach may differ for different machines. For example, on a Cray XE6 MPP, Code 14.1 is compiled and launched as follows:

```
> cc code1.c -o code1
> aprun -n 4 ./code1
  Hello, World!
  Hello, World!
  Hello, World!
  Hello, World!
```

In this MPP case, the `cc` compiler wrapper links in the appropriate MPI libraries and finds the appropriate headers, while the launch script `aprun` launches the four instances of the executable in the runtime environment.

The only work performed by Code 14.1, of course, is to print the character stream "Hello World!" on the standard input/output (I/O) device, which is the user's terminal screen. However, unlike the equivalent sequential version of this simple program, this string will be printed multiple times; in fact, it will print out as many times as there are processes running under MPI at the same time. Although all output lines look the same (note that the \n character in line 7 of Code 14.1 causes a new line), the actual order in which they are output is unspecified. A later example will be more revealing of this nondeterminacy. The resulting parallelism is a consequence of the pairing of the `MPI_Init` and the `MPI_Finalize` calls. There is no interaction among the separate processes in this example, however. To get the different processes to interact, the concept of communicators is needed.

14.4 Communicators

The "Hello World" example in Code 14.1 in the previous section was very simple. However, it represents a broad range of parallel computing known as "throughput" computing, where every hardware node is running the same program but on different local data. This can be scaled to a very large degree, and additional examples of this will be demonstrated in succeeding chapters. However, the principal weakness of this limited form of processing is that the processes on different nodes run entirely independent of each other. It is a "share nothing" modality, in which the outcome of any one of the concurrent processes can in no way be influenced by the intermediate results of any of the other processes. Without interprocess interaction, this type of computing only supports the pure weak scaling or capacity computing as distinguished earlier. It cannot enable capability or coordinated computing, both of which are far richer in parallel computational forms and functions. Key to this advance is the means by which the concurrent processes can interact. This is achieved through the concept and implementation of "communicators" (Fig. 14.2).

MPI programs are made up of concurrent processes executing at the same time that in almost all cases are also communicating with each other. To do this, an object called the "communicator" is provided by the MPI. A communicator has its own address space and various properties. In particular, it encompasses a set of MPI processes and specific attributes. It is through the communicator that the processes of which it consists can communicate with other processes. Not only does a communicator consist of multiple coexisting MPI processes but also a process may be associated with more than one communicator at the same time. Thus, the user may specify any number of communicators within an MPI program, each with its own set of processes. However, all versions of MPI provide one common communicator, `MPI_COMM_WORLD`. This communicator contains all of the concurrent processes making up an MPI program and does not have to be explicitly created by the programmer. For simplicity and ease of understanding, the examples presented in this chapter will take advantage of `MPI_COMM_WORLD` as it manages the communications between concurrent processes. Advanced operations on communicators will be introduced in Chapter 21.

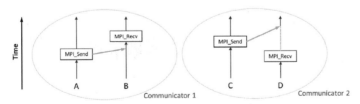

FIGURE 14.2

Idealized view of point-to-point communication in message-passing interface. To exchange data, communicating processes must belong to the same communicator (communicator 1 for processes A and B or communicator 2 for processes C and D). A process may be associated with multiple communicators. As a general rule, each message send must be paired with a corresponding receive. The act of sending or receiving a message doesn't need to be explicitly synchronized; if a message is not ready to be received, it will cause the calling process to idle (as is the case for process D).

14.4.1 **Size**

A communicator embodies a number of attributes, many of which may be referenced by the user program. Among those most widely used is "size". This property, as its name implies, indicates some aspect of a communicator's scale, specifically related to processes. The size of a communicator is the number of processes that makes up the particular communicator. The following function call provides the value of the number of processes of the specified communicator:

```
int MPI_Comm_size(MPI_Comm comm, int *sizep)
```

The function name is `MPI_Comm_size`, required to return the number of processes; `comm` is the argument provided to designate the communicator, recognizing that any process may be part of more than one communicator. The resulting value is returned to a variable pointed to by `sizep` within the process context. A typical statement for this purpose could be:

```
int size;
MPI_Comm_size(MPI_COMM_WORLD, &size);
```

This will put the total number of processes in the `MPI_COMM_WORLD` communicator in the variable size of the process data context. As this is the same for all processes of the communicator, their respective copies of the variable size will receive the same value.

14.4.2 **Rank**

A second widely used attribute of a communicator is the identification of each of the processes within the communicator. Every process within the communicator has a unique ID, referred to as its "rank". The MPI system automatically and arbitrarily assigns a unique positive integer value starting with 0 to all of the processes within the communicator. The MPI command to determine what is the process's rank is:

```
int MPI_Comm_rank(MPI_Comm comm, int *rankp)
```

The function call `MPI_Comm_rank` indicates that the rank value of the calling process is to be returned to the process. The first argument, `comm`, indicates the communicator to which the process belongs within which it requires its rank. The second argument, `rankp`, is a pointer to the variable that will assume the value returned by the command. A typical statement for this purpose could be:

```
int rank;
MPI_Comm_size(MPI_COMM_WORLD, &rank);
```

In the case of the `MPI_COMM_WORLD` communicator, all the processes of the application will have a unique value of rank returned. Each process within this communicator when calling this function will receive a different value in its copy of the variable rank.

14.4.3 **Example**

As a trivial example that nonetheless demonstrates the functionality of communicators and these simple but powerful commands, the following example is offered. This is a minor elaboration of the earlier and iconic "Hello World" problem.

The purpose of this application program is for every process that exists within the MPI_COMM_WORLD communicator to identify itself by printing a statement to the standard output. The structure of this parallel program is the same as the previous, with the potentially interprocess communicating part of the code delimited by the pair of MPI_Init and MPI_Finalize commands. Between these two statements are the working parts of the program, such as the printf construct shown before. However, added here are also the two service calls associated with the communicator: MPI_Comm_rank and MPI_Comm_size. The complete MPI code is given in Code 14.2.

```
01 #include <stdio.h>
02 #include <mpi.h>
03
04 int main(int argc,char **argv)
05 {
06   int rank, size;
07   MPI_Init(&argc,&argv);
08   MPI_Comm_rank(MPI_COMM_WORLD,&rank);
09   MPI_Comm_size(MPI_COMM_WORLD,&size);
10   printf(" Hello from rank %d out of %d processes in
MPI_COMM_WORLD\n",rank,size);
11   MPI_Finalize();
12   return 0;
13 }
```

CODE 14.2

Example where each process prints its rank and the MPI_COMM_WORLD communicator size.

This code is compiled and executed on a Beowulf class cluster as follows:

```
> mpicc code2.c —o code2
> mpirun —np 4 ./code2
  Hello from rank 0 out of 4 processes in MPI_COMM_WORLD
  Hello from rank 1 out of 4 processes in MPI_COMM_WORLD
  Hello from rank 3 out of 4 processes in MPI_COMM_WORLD
  Hello from rank 2 out of 4 processes in MPI_COMM_WORLD
```

Code 14.2 illustrates the use of the two most common calls related to communicators. The two commands bracketed by MPI_Init and MPI_Finalize are MPI_Comm_rank (line 8), which determines the id of the process, and MPI_Comm_size (line 9), which finds the number of processes. In both cases they refer to the MPI_COMM_WORLD communicator as specified as the first operand in each of the two calling sequences. The second argument in each case indicates the process variable in which the related integer value is put. The printf I/O service call not only outputs the string "Hello" but also prints out two integers, one for the process's rank, which is unique for each process, and the other giving the size of the MPI_COMM_WORLD communicator in terms of the number of processes it contains. The size for all processes within the same communicator is the same. The order of printing the output is undetermined, as mentioned before. With each process now uniquely identified within the communicator, it is now possible to begin sending messages between processes.

14.5 Point-to-Point Messages

Among its most important functionalities, MPI manages the exchange of data between processes within a selected communicator. The medium of this exchange is referred to as messages. Messages provide point-to-point communication from a source process and a corresponding destination process, each with its own unique rank by which it is identified. In its simplest form, two commands are required to achieve the passing of a message. The sending of the message from the source process is accomplished by a send command. The receiving of the message by the corresponding destination process is accomplished by a receive command. Messages are matched between the two commands. While there are a number of variants of both the send family and receive family of commands, the most basic of these are MPI_Send and MPI_Recv.

The message specification can be considered as a combination of the connection and the data of the message. The connection describes the points forming the communication. These include:

1) The source process rank.
2) The destination process rank.
3) The communicator of which both processes are a part.
4) The tag, which is a user-controlled value that can be used to discriminate among a set of possible messages between the same two processes.

14.5.1 Message Send

The send function is used by the source process to define the data and establish the connection of the message. The send construct has the following syntax:

```
int MPI_Send(void *message, int count, MPI_Datatype datatype, int dest,
             int tag, MPI_Comm comm)
```

There are six arguments to the MPI_Send call to provide this information. The first three operands establish the data to be transferred between the source and destination processes. The first argument points to the message content itself, which may be a simple scalar or a group of data elements. The message data content is described by the next two arguments. The second operand specifies the number of data elements of which the message is composed. These are all the same in form. The third operand indicates the data type of the elements that make up the message (see the next subsection for details). These three values give the data to be moved by the message. The connection of the message is established by the second three operands. These are the rank of the destination process, the user-defined tag field, and the communicator in which the source and destination processes reside and for which their respective ranks are defined.

14.5.2 Data Types

MPI defines its own data types. This might appear redundant as programming languages like C explicitly define data types as well. However, for the sake of robustness where different processes may be written in different languages or run on different kinds of processor architectures, MPI makes explicit what is intended. Like other interfaces, MPI provides a set of primitive data types. More complex structured data types can be user defined, as will be shown in the intermediate MPI chapter (Chapter 21). The set of the most common primitive data types is presented in Table 14.1 along with the C data type equivalent.

Table 14.1 Some of the Basic MPI Data Types and Their C Data Type Equivalent

MPI Data Type	C Data Type Equivalent
MPI_CHAR	signed char
MPI_SHORT	signed short int
MPI_INT	signed int
MPI_LONG	signed long int
MPI_UNSIGNED_CHAR	unsigned char
MPI_UNSIGNED_SHORT	unsigned short int
MPI_UNSIGNED	unsigned int
MPI_UNSIGNED_LONG	unsigned long int
MPI_FLOAT	float
MPI_DOUBLE	double
MPI_LONG_DOUBLE	long double
MPI_BYTE	No direct equivalent but like unsigned char; just one byte

14.5.3 **Message Receive**

The MPI_Recv command mirrors the MPI_Send command to establish a connection between the source and destination processes within the specified communicator. Like the send command, the receive command describes both the data to be transferred and the connection to be established. It is structured as follows:

```
int MPI_Recv(void *messagep, int count, MPI_Datatype datatype, int source,
             int tag, MPI_Comm comm, MPI_Status *statusp)
```

The information provided to describe the data to be exchanged is represented in a form similar to those operands of the MPI_Send command. The message itself will be placed in a buffer variable designated here as "message". The number of data elements making up the full message is given by the integer count. The data type of the element of the message is one of the MPI data types defined in the previous subsection or a user-defined data type to be described later.

The connection information of the MPI_Recv command is similar but not identical to that of the MPI_Send command. The source field designates the rank of the process sending the message. As before, a tag variable is provided for a user-defined integer that is provided in the send command and can be extracted for user code manipulation by the receiving process. As in all cases, the communicator in which both processes reside is specified. A final argument variable, "status", is included as the final operand of the receive. This is a record of two fields about the actual message received. The first field indicates the process rank from which the message was actually received. The second provides the tag.

14.5.4 **Example**

A third example is presented in Code 14.3 based on "Hello World" to illustrate MPI commands; in this case the send and receive commands. This example expands our experience in a couple of important ways:

1) It shows the syntactical details for setting up the information, including declarations for the MPI commands to be used.
2) It illustrates an important idiom related to how to control the concurrent execution and the idea of the manager—worker form of computing using MPI.
3) It solves the problem of the previous examples that we've witnessed with the out-of-order printf commands.

```
01 #include <stdio.h>
02 #include <stdlib.h>
03 #include <mpi.h>
04 #include <string.h>
05
06 int main(int argc,char **argv)
07 {
08    int rank, size;
09    MPI_Init(&argc,&argv);
10    MPI_Comm_rank(MPI_COMM_WORLD,&rank);
11    MPI_Comm_size(MPI_COMM_WORLD,&size);
12
13    int message[2];     // Buffer for sending and receiving messages
14    int dest, src;      // Destination and source process variables
15    int tag = 0;
16    MPI_Status status;
17
18    // This example has to be run on more than one process
19    if (size == 1) {
20      printf(" This example requires more than one process to execute\n");
21      MPI_Finalize();
22      exit(1);
23    }
24
25    if (rank != 0) {
26      // If not rank 0, send message to rank 0
27      message[0] = rank;
28      message[1] = size;
29      dest = 0;    // Send all messages to rank 0
30      MPI_Send(message,2,MPI_INT,dest,tag,MPI_COMM_WORLD);
31    } else {
32      // If rank 0, receive messages from everybody else
33      for (src=1;src<size;src++) {
34        MPI_Recv(message,2,MPI_INT,src,MPI_ANY_TAG,MPI_COMM_WORLD,&status);
35        // This prints the message just received. Notice it will print in rank
36        // order since the loop is in rank order.
37        printf("Hello from process %d of %d\n",message[0],message[1]);
38      }
39    }
40
41    MPI_Finalize();
42    return 0;
43 }
```

CODE 14.3

"Hello World" example where all processes with ranks greater than 0 send their rank and size to the process with rank 0 for printing.

```
> mpicc code3.c -o code3
> mpirun -np 4 ./code3
  Hello from process 1 of 4
  Hello from process 2 of 4
  Hello from process 3 of 4
```

Much of this example is similar to the previous ones shown in this chapter. Commands such as MPI_Init, MPI_Finalize, MPI_Comm_rank, and MPI_Comm_size are all the same in their usage. And as in the other examples, the communicator used is MPI_COMM_WORLD. However, at this point the similarities end.

The biggest difference is the important idiom of the manager–worker organization, in which one process, the manager, coordinates the execution of the other processes, the workers. Sometimes the manager is also referred to as the "root" process. All processes, whether root or worker, receive and execute the same process code (procedure). Therefore, it is within the user code itself that the distinction between manager and worker has to be prescribed. In this example, the manager is assumed to be of rank 0 and the workers are identified as $1 <$ rank $<$ size $-\ 1$. Therefore, the code is separated between manager and workers by the conditional on line 25. If true, a message array of size 2 is populated with the rank and size variables. The message is then sent using the MPI_Send command to the destination process (line 30), which is always rank 0 in this case.

The magic occurs in the body of code executed by the root process within the otherwise bounded sequence in line 31. The ordered iterative loop embodied by the for block (line 33) accepts the messages using the MPI_Send command in rank-ordered fashion and prints them out in that order, guaranteeing the sequence of outputs. The control by the root process makes certain that the output information from the worker processes is presented in a deterministic form, i.e., a rank-ordered list. This is an important idiom of control in MPI using the manager–worker paradigm. Because only one message is sent from each nonroot process, the MPI_Recv command is told to ignore the tag with the useful MPI_ANY_TAG field (line 34).

14.6 Synchronization Collectives

While point-to-point communication is the backbone of MPI management of data exchange, additional communication constructs that involve more processes at one time are a powerful addition to simplifying MPI programming and improving performance efficiency. These are referred to as "collective operations" or simply "collectives".

14.6.1 Overview of Collective Calls

A communication pattern that encompasses all processes within a communicator is known as "collective communication". One of the important aspects of a communicator is the set of processes within an MPI program to which the programmer wants to apply collective operators, and this may not be all of the processes used by the program as a whole. MPI has several collective communication calls. The most frequently used are synchronization collectives, communication collectives, and reduction collective operators. Synchronization collective operations bring all the processes of a communicator up to a known place in the control flow even though their separate processes are executing asynchronously, some further ahead than others. Communication collectives exchange data in different patterns among two or more processes within a communicator. Reduction collective operators perform a common communicative operator across versions of the same variable of all the processes.

14.6.2 Barrier Synchronization

The MPI_Barrier() command creates, as the name implies, a point of barrier synchronization among all of the processes of the specified communicator. This command has a simple syntax of a single operand:

```
int MPI_Barrier(MPI_Comm communicator)
```

where communicator is the communicator of the processes engaged in the synchronization. The barrier requires that all the processes reach that point in their respective code and then wait for all the other processes of the communicator to do the same before proceeding with their separate computations. Thus, all processes block at the point of the barrier until they determine that all other processes have arrived there as well.

Fig. 14.3 illustrates the barrier operation. Processes P0 through P3 enter the point of barrier synchronization at different times and potentially in unpredictable order. None of the processes proceed beyond this point in the computation until all of the

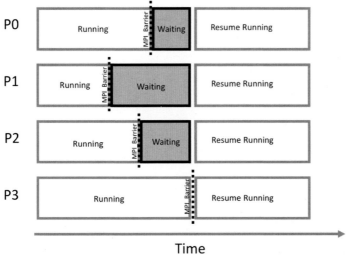

FIGURE 14.3

An illustration of the MPI_Barrier operation. Processes P0 through P3 enter the point of barrier synchronization at different times and potentially in unpredictable order. None of the processes proceed beyond this point in the computation until all of the processes reach this point. Only then do the four processes continue on to their next operations.

processes reach this point. Only then do the four processes continue on to their next operations. In this way, all processes can be assured of the completion of the necessary work by the others. This can be an important condition to avoiding a number of different failure modes resulting from the uncertainty imposed by asynchronous operation.

14.6.3 Example

A somewhat artificial example of the use of the MPI_Barrier collective command is presented in Code 14.4 to demonstrate its syntax. It is also an opportunity to introduce another occasionally useful MPI function, MPI_Get_processor_name, that gives access to the actual hardware for purposes of identification. Depending on the MPI implementation, this might simply be the output from gethostname or something more detailed.

```
01 #include <stdio.h>
02 #include <mpi.h>
03
04 int main(int argc, char **argv)
05 {
06   int rank, size, len;
07   MPI_Init(&argc,&argv);
08   char name[MPI_MAX_PROCESSOR_NAME];
09
10   MPI_Barrier(MPI_COMM_WORLD);
11
12   MPI_Comm_rank(MPI_COMM_WORLD,&rank);
13   MPI_Comm_size(MPI_COMM_WORLD,&size);
14   MPI_Get_processor_name(name,&len);
15
16   MPI_Barrier(MPI_COMM_WORLD);
17
18   printf(" Hello, world! Process %d of %d on %s\n",rank,size,name);
19
20   MPI_Finalize();
21   return 0;
22 }
```

CODE 14.4

Example of MPI_Barrier and MPI_Get_processor_name.

```
> mpicc code4.c —o code4
> mpirun —np 4 ./code4
  Hello, world! Process 2 of 4 on cutter01
  Hello, world! Process 3 of 4 on cutter01
  Hello, world! Process 0 of 4 on cutter01
  Hello, world! Process 1 of 4 on cutter01
```

The example code above inserts two synchronization points with the two highlighted instances of the `MPI_Barrier` command. The first is just before the conventional MPI commands getting the size of the `MPI_COMM_WORLD` communicator and the unique rank identifiers of the individual process within that communicator. The second barrier is just after the newly introduced MPI_Get_processor_name command. Every process is blocked at both points until all processes have arrived at the respective barrier.

The MPI_Get_processor_name reminds the student that there is a difference between the abstraction of the executing process and the physical processor core resource upon which the process is computing. This command, as the name implies, acquires the character string that MPI uses to uniquely represent each processor core. In the example above, this character string is simply the output from gethostname, which was cutter01, the name of the compute node on which the example was run. MPI has a lot of special constants that describe key values of its operation. Here one is used to specify the greatest possible length of the character string representing the processor name. This constant is MPI_MAX_PROCESSOR_NAME and is referred to near the beginning of the code where the variable "name" is declared as a character buffer.

14.7 **Communication Collectives**

Communication collective operations can dramatically expand interprocess communication from point-to-point to n-way or all-way data exchanges. These commands can greatly simplify user programming and provide the opportunity for greater execution efficiency by telling MPI what one actually wants to happen. Communication collective operations are among the most powerful contributing capabilities of MPI for weaving many individual processes into a single scalable computation. While there are many variants of communication collectives, a few are very widely employed in support of parallel algorithms.

Collective data movement relates to different patterns by which compound data may be exchanged among concurrent processes within a specific communicator. The requirements for these data distributions are a function of the parallel algorithms being employed and the degree to which intermediate results of any process need to be shared with one or more other processes to continue the evolving distributed computation. Such patterns can be diverse, but five basic patterns satisfy most algorithmic requirements of data exchange: broadcast, scatter, gather, allgather, and alltoall. They are described in detail throughout the remainder of this section.

14.7.1 **Broadcast**

The broadcast communication collective operation is perhaps the simplest of the collectives and among the most important as well. As illustrated in Fig. 14.4, it shares a value or structure that exists within the context of one process with all the other

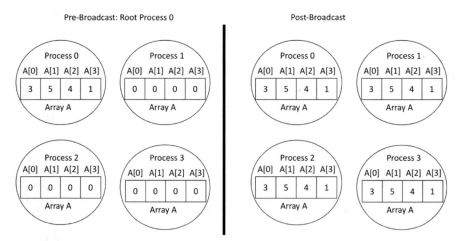

FIGURE 14.4

The broadcast operation. Broadcast shares a value or structure that exists within the context of one process with all the other processes of a communicator. In this example the root process 0 shares the integer array A of length 4 with all the other processes.

processes of a communicator. The values in the A integer array in process 0 are copied to the equivalent arrays in all of the other processes so they all have the same information. Broadcast, like other collective communications, provides the means by which the intermediate results of any one process are efficiently shared with all the other processes.

The syntax of the broadcast operation takes the following form:

```
int MPI_Bcast(void *shared_data, int number, MPI_Datatype datatype,
                int source_process, MPI_Comm communicator)
```

The operands define the form and source of the data to be sent to all of the processes. The broadcast is performed within the scope of a communicator specified by the last argument of type MPI_Comm, and the broadcasted data is sent to all of the processes within it. The data comes from a single process identified by its rank within the communicator by source_process (or root process), which is the penultimate argument of MPI_Bcast. Like many other message-passing commands, the data to be sent is determined by the first three arguments: the name of the data, here shared_data in the first argument; the type of the data elements of which it is composed, here datatype of type MPI_Datatype in the third argument; and the number of elements of the data type making up the data to be broadcast.

The equivalent MPI code to the broadcast illustrated in Fig. 14.4 is given in Code 14.5.

```
01 #include <stdio.h>
02 #include <mpi.h>
03
04 int main(int argc,char **argv)
05 {
06   int rank, size, i;
07   MPI_Init(&argc,&argv);
08   MPI_Comm_rank(MPI_COMM_WORLD,&rank);
09   MPI_Comm_size(MPI_COMM_WORLD,&size);
10
11   int A[4];
12
13   // Initialize array
14   for (i=0;i<4;i++) {
15     A[i] = 0;
16   }
17
18   int root = 0;  // Define a root process
19
20   if (rank == root) { // Initialize array A
21     A[0] = 3;
22     A[1] = 5;
23     A[2] = 4;
24     A[3] = 1;
25   }
26
27   MPI_Bcast(A,4,MPI_INT,root,MPI_COMM_WORLD);
28
29   printf("Rank %d A[0] = %d A[1] = %d A[2] = %d A[3] = %d\n",
30          rank,A[0],A[1],A[2],A[3]);
31
32   MPI_Finalize();
33   return 0;
34 }
```

CODE 14.5

An example of MPI_Bcast that corresponds to the illustration in Fig. 14.4.

Due to the nondeterministic execution order of print statements, the example may produce different outputs, one of which is shown below:

```
> mpirun —np 4 ./code5
Rank 0 A[0] = 3 A[1]= 5 A[2]= 4 A[3]= 1
Rank 2 A[0] = 3 A[1]= 5 A[2]= 4 A[3]= 1
Rank 1 A[0] = 3 A[1]= 5 A[2]= 4 A[3]= 1
Rank 3 A[0] = 3 A[1]= 5 A[2]= 4 A[3]= 1
```

14.7.2 Scatter

The scatter communication collective operation distributes data of one process in separate parts to all the processes (including itself) within the scope of a communicator. The communicator of size processes disseminates the data of the source process in size-equal partitions. The distribution will be in rank order across the set of processes and the linear dimension of the dataset. This is a particularly important construct for scalable matrices across a distributed-memory system.

The scatter communication pattern is illustrated in Fig. 14.5. Like broadcast, it shares data of one process with all the other processes of a communicator. But in this case, it partitions a set of data elements of one process into subsets and sends one subset to each of the processes. To be clear, each receiving process gets a different subset, and there are as many subsets as there are processes. In Fig. 14.5, the process 0 has a set of data that is partitioned, in this case, into four distinct partitions: A[0], A[1], A[2], and A[3], which is equal to the number of processes, i.e., processes 0 through 3 of the communicator. The first partition is returned to the source (root) process, process 0. Data partition A[1] is sent to the second process, process 1. Partition A[2] is sent to process 2, and so on. In this way the original data in process 0 is distributed equally among all the processes of the communicator.

The scatter operation is performed by means of the MPI_Scatter command:

```
int MPI_Scatter(void *send_data, int send_number, MPI_Datatype datatype,
                void *put_data, int put_number, int source_rank,
                MPI_Comm communicator)
```

The operands define the form and source of the data to be sent to all of the processes. The scatter is performed within the scope of a communicator specified by the last argument, here communicator of type MPI_Comm, and the data is sent to all of the processes within it. The data comes from a single process identified by its rank

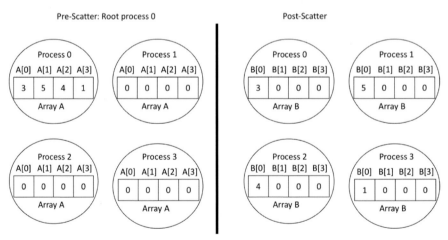

FIGURE 14.5

The scatter operation. The scatter pattern shares data of one (root) process with all the other processes of a communicator. It partitions a set of data elements of the root process into subsets and sends one subset to each of the processes. Each receiving process gets a different subset, and there are as many subsets as there are processes. In this example, the send array is A and the receive array is B (B is initialized to zero). The root process (process 0 here) partitions the data into subsets of the same length and sends each subset to a separate process.

within the communicator by `source_rank`, which is the next to last argument of MPI_Scatter. Like many other message-passing commands, the data to be sent is determined by the first three arguments: the name of the data, here `shared_data` in the first argument; the type of the data elements of which it is composed, here datatype of type `MPI_Datatype` in the third argument; and the `send_number` of elements of the data type making up the data to be distributed. Where the data is to be put in the receive process is specified by `put_data`, and the size of the data of data type is given by the integer put_number. The equivalent MPI code to the scatter operation illustrated in Fig. 14.5 is given in Code 14.6.

```
01 #include <stdio.h>
02 #include <stdlib.h>
03 #include <mpi.h>
04
05 int main(int argc,char **argv)
06 {
07   int rank, size, i;
08   MPI_Init(&argc,&argv);
09   MPI_Comm_rank(MPI_COMM_WORLD,&rank);
10   MPI_Comm_size(MPI_COMM_WORLD,&size);
11
12   if (size != 4) {
13     printf("Example is designed for 4 processes\n");
14     MPI_Finalize();
15     exit(0);
16   }
17
18   // A is the send buffer and B is the receive buffer
19   int A[4], B[4];
20
21   // Initialize array
22   for (i=0;i<4;i++) {
23     A[i] = 0;
24     B[i] = 0;
25   }
26
27   int root = 0;   // Define a root process
28
29   if (rank == root) { // Initialize array A
30     A[0] = 3;
31     A[1] = 5;
32     A[2] = 4;
33     A[3] = 1;
34   }
35
36   MPI_Scatter(A,1,MPI_INT,B,1,MPI_INT,root,MPI_COMM_WORLD);
37
38   printf("Rank %d B[0] = %d B[1] = %d B[2] = %d B[3] = %d\n",
39          rank,B[0],B[1],B[2],B[3]);
40
41   MPI_Finalize();
42   return 0;
43 }
```

CODE 14.6

An example of MPI_Scatter that corresponds to the illustration in Fig. 14.5.

A possible result of execution of the scatter example is given below:

```
> mpirun −np 4 ./code6
Rank 0 B[0] = 3 B[1]= 0 B[2]= 0 B[3]= 0
Rank 2 B[0] = 4 B[1]= 0 B[2]= 0 B[3]= 0
Rank 1 B[0] = 5 B[1]= 0 B[2]= 0 B[3]= 0
Rank 3 B[0] = 1 B[1]= 0 B[2]= 0 B[3]= 0
```

14.7.3 Gather

The gather collective communication pattern, as illustrated in Fig. 14.6, is, in a sense, the opposite of the scatter collective. In the case of the gather, as the name might suggest, data from all of the processes is sent to a particular process, which therefore is gathering up the data from the other processes. Of course, it is actually each process sending its respective designated data to the consumer process that organizes all of the separate data partitions into one cumulative structure.

The syntax of the gather operation takes the following form:

```
int MPI_Gather (void *send_data, int send_number, MPI_Datatype send_datatype,
                void *put_data, int put_number, MPI_Datatype put_datatype,
                int destination_rank, MPI_Comm communicator)
```

The operands of the MPI_Gather define the form and source of the data to be sent to the single receiving process and the form and destination of the data being received. The gather is performed within the scope of a communicator specified by the last

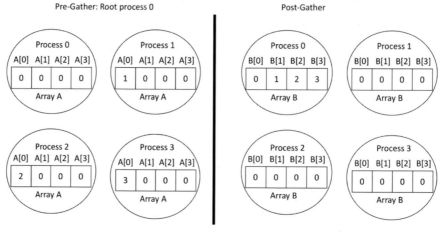

FIGURE 14.6

The gather operation. The gather collective communication pattern is the opposite of the scatter collective. Data from all of the processes is sent to the root process, which is gathering them up at unique offsets in the destination buffer. In this example A is the send array and B is the receive array. B is initialized to 0 prior to the gather.

argument, here communicator of type MPI_Comm, and the data is sent from all of the processes within it to the single receiving process. The data to be sent is determined by the first three arguments: the name of the data, here send_data in the first argument; the type of the data elements of which it is composed, here send_datatype of type MPI_Datatype in the third argument; and the send_number of elements of the data type making up the data to be distributed. Where the data is to be put in the receive process is specified by put_data, of type put_datatype, and the size of the data of the data type is given by the integer put_number. The process to which all the data across the processes is accumulated in the communicator is specified by the integer argument destination_rank, which is the seventh operand. The equivalent MPI code to the gather operation illustrated in Fig. 14.6 is shown in Code 14.7.

```
01 #include <stdio.h>
02 #include <stdlib.h>
03 #include <mpi.h>
04
05 int main(int argc,char **argv)
06 {
07   int rank, size, i;
08   MPI_Init(&argc,&argv);
09   MPI_Comm_rank(MPI_COMM_WORLD,&rank);
10   MPI_Comm_size(MPI_COMM_WORLD,&size);
11
12   if (size != 4) {
13     printf("Example is designed for 4 processes\n");
14     MPI_Finalize();
15     exit(0);
16   }
17
18   // A is the sendbuffer and B is the receive buffer
19   int A[4], B[4];
20
21   // Initialize array
22   for (i=0;i<4;i++) {
23     A[i] = 0;
24     B[i] = 0;
25   }
26   A[0] = rank;
27
28   int root = 0;   // Define a root process
29
30   MPI_Gather(A,1,MPI_INT,B,1,MPI_INT,root,MPI_COMM_WORLD);
31
32   printf("Rank %d B[0] = %d B[1] = %d B[2] = %d B[3] = %d\n",
33           rank,B[0],B[1],B[2],B[3]);
34
35   MPI_Finalize();
36   return 0;
37 }
```

CODE 14.7

An example of MPI_Gather that corresponds to the illustration in Fig. 14.6.

Example output is presented below:

```
> mpirun —np 4 ./code7
Rank 1 B[0] = 0 B[1]= 0 B[2]= 0 B[3]= 0
Rank 2 B[0] = 0 B[1]= 0 B[2]= 0 B[3]= 0
Rank 3 B[0] = 0 B[1]= 0 B[2]= 0 B[3]= 0
Rank 0 B[0] = 0 B[1]= 1 B[2]= 2 B[3]= 3
```

14.7.4 Allgather

The extension of gather that makes it possible for all processes to use the results across the entire communicator is allgather, illustrated in Fig. 14.7. This is equivalent to first performing a gather of data from all of the processes to a single receiving process and then broadcasting the accumulated data back to all of the processes so that all processes have all of the resulting data.

The syntax of the MPI_Allgather operation is nearly identical to that of the MPI_gather operation except that there is no longer any need to provide a destination rank because of the broadcast implicit in the operation.

```
int MPI_Allgather(void*send_data, int send_number, MPI_Datatype send_datatype,
                  void*put_data, int put_number, MPI_Datatype put_datatype,
                  MPI_Comm communicator)
```

The equivalent MPI code to the allgather operation illustrated in Fig. 14.7 is shown in Code 14.8.

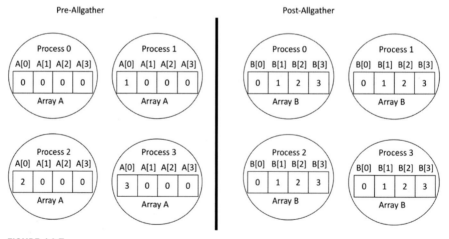

FIGURE 14.7

The allgather operation. This operation is equivalent to a gather operation followed by a broadcast of the array so that each process contains an identical receive array. In this example, the A array is the send array and the B array is the receive array. B is initialized to zero.

```
01 #include <stdio.h>
02 #include <stdlib.h>
03 #include <mpi.h>
04
05 int main(int argc,char **argv)
06 {
07   int rank, size, i;
08   MPI_Init(&argc,&argv);
09   MPI_Comm_rank(MPI_COMM_WORLD,&rank);
10   MPI_Comm_size(MPI_COMM_WORLD,&size);
11
12   if (size != 4) {
13     printf("Example is designed for 4 processes\n");
14     MPI_Finalize();
15     exit(0);
16   }
17
18   // A is the send buffer and B is the receive buffer
19   int A[4], B[4];
20
21   // Initialize array
22   for (i=0;i<4;i++) {
23     A[i] = 0;
24     B[i] = 0;
25   }
26   A[0] = rank;
27
28   int root = 0;  // Define a root process
29
30   MPI_Allgather(A,1,MPI_INT,B,1,MPI_INT,MPI_COMM_WORLD);
31
32   printf("Rank %d B[0] = %d B[1] = %d B[2] = %d B[3] = %d\n",
33          rank,B[0],B[1],B[2],B[3]);
34
35   MPI_Finalize();
36   return 0;
37 }
```

CODE 14.8

An example of MPI_Allgather that corresponds to the illustration in Fig. 14.7.

Running the example may produce the following result:

```
> mpirun −np 4 ./code8
Rank 0 B[0] = 0 B[1]= 1 B[2]= 2 B[3]= 3
Rank 1 B[0] = 0 B[1]= 1 B[2]= 2 B[3]= 3
Rank 2 B[0] = 0 B[1]= 1 B[2]= 2 B[3]= 3
Rank 3 B[0] = 0 B[1]= 1 B[2]= 2 B[3]= 3
```

FIGURE 14.8

The alltoall communication pattern extends allgather, where distinct data is sent to each receiver and each sender is also a receiver. The ith data partition is sent to the jth process. The communication pattern looks like a matrix transpose when listing the data in each process in rows and the data partitions in each process as the columns. In this example, each data partition in each process only contains a single integer, and the number of processes has been limited to four to better see the alltoall communication pattern.

14.7.5 Alltoall

There is an important extension to the MPI_Allgather pattern that frequently appears in scientific computations: the alltoall communication pattern. In this pattern, distinct data is sent to each of the receivers and each sender is also a receiver. When displayed as a matrix with rows representing processes and columns representing data partitions, the alltoall communication pattern looks exactly like a matrix transpose (that is, placing the contents of input matrix rows in the corresponding output matrix columns), illustrated in Fig. 14.8.

The MPI_Alltoall operation uses the following syntax:

```
int MPI_Alltoall(void *send_data, int send_number, MPI_Datatype send_
datatype,
                void *put_data, int put_number, MPI_Datatype put_datatype,
                MPI_Comm communicator)
```

As an extension to MPI_Allgather, MPI_Alltoall takes the exact same arguments as MPI_Allgather even while the communication pattern is different, as illustrated in Fig. 14.8. The MPI version of the operation illustrated in Fig. 14.8 is shown in Code 14.9.

```
01 #include <stdio.h>
02 #include <stdlib.h>
03 #include <mpi.h>
04
05 int main(int argc,char **argv) {
06
07   MPI_Init(&argc,&argv);
08   int rank, size, i;
09   MPI_Comm_rank(MPI_COMM_WORLD,&rank);
10   MPI_Comm_size(MPI_COMM_WORLD, &size);
11
12   if (size != 4) {
13     printf("This example is designed for 4 proceses\n");
14     MPI_Finalize();
15     exit(0);
16   }
17
18   int A[4], B[4];
19
20   for (i=0;i<4;i++) {
21     A[i] = i+1+4*rank;
22   }
23
24   // Note that the send number and receive number are both one.
25   // This reflects that fact that the send size and receive size
26   // refer to the distinct data size sent to each process.
27   MPI_Alltoall(A,1,MPI_INT,B,1,MPI_INT,MPI_COMM_WORLD);
28
29   printf("Rank: %d   B: %d %d %d %d\n",rank,B[0],B[1],B[2],B[3]);
30
31   MPI_Finalize();
32
33   return 0;
34 }
```

CODE 14.9

The MPI example that corresponds to the illustration in Fig. 14.8.

Possible output produced by this example is:

```
> mpirun —np 4 ./code11
Rank: 0 B: 1 5 9 13
Rank: 1 B: 2 6 10 14
Rank: 2 B: 3 7 11 15
Rank: 3 B: 4 8 12 16
```

14.7.6 Reduction Operations

Reduction operations are collectives similar to gather but perform simple computation on the gathered data, such as calculating a sum, finding a maximum value, or performing some user-defined operation. Predefined reduction operations in MPI are given in Table 14.2.

Table 14.2 Predefined Reduction Operations in MPI and Supported Predefined MPI Data Types

Reduction Operation	MPI Name	Supported Type
Maximum	MPI_MAX	MPI_INT, MPI_LONG, MPI_SHORT, MPI_FLOAT, MPI_DOUBLE
Minimum	MPI_MIN	MPI_INT, MPI_LONG, MPI_SHORT, MPI_FLOAT, MPI_DOUBLE
Summation	MPI_SUM	MPI_INT, MPI_LONG, MPI_SHORT, MPI_FLOAT, MPI_DOUBLE
Product	MPI_PROD	MPI_INT, MPI_LONG, MPI_SHORT, MPI_FLOAT, MPI_DOUBLE
Logical AND	MPI_LAND	MPI_INT, MPI_LONG, MPI_SHORT
Bit-wise AND	MPI_BAND	MPI_INT, MPI_LONG, MPI_SHORT, MPI_BYTE
Logical OR	MPI_LOR	MPI_INT, MPI_LONG, MPI_SHORT
Bit-wise OR	MPI_BOR	MPI_INT, MPI_LONG, MPI_SHORT, MPI_BYTE
Logical XOR	MPI_LXOR	MPI_INT, MPI_LONG, MPI_SHORT
Bit-wise XOR	MPI_BXOR	MPI_INT, MPI_LONG, MPI_SHORT, MPI_BYTE
Maximum value and location	MPI_MAXLOC	Pair datatypes: MPI_DOUBLE_INT (a double and an int), MPI_2INT (two ints)
Minimum value and location	MPI_MINLOC	Pair datatypes: MPI_DOUBLE_INT (a double and an int), MPI_2INT (two ints)

The syntax for the reduction operation in MPI is as follows:

```
int MPI_Reduce(const void *send_data, void *put_data, int send_number,
          MPI_Datatype datatype, MPI_OP operation, int destination_rank,
          MPI_Comm communicator)
```

where the first two arguments are the data sent to the reduction operation by each process and the location at the destination rank is specified by put_data, both of type datatype. The size of the data sent is given by the send_number. The reduction operation is either one of those listed in Table 14.2 or user defined. An example of MPI_Reduce in a vector dot product calculation is presented in Code 14.10.

```
01 #include <stdlib.h>
02 #include <stdio.h>
03 #include <mpi.h>
04
05 int main(int argc,char **argv) {
06     MPI_Init(&argc,&argv);
07     int rank, p, i, root = 0;
08     MPI_Comm_rank(MPI_COMM_WORLD,&rank);
09     MPI_Comm_size(MPI_COMM_WORLD,&p);
10
11     // Make the local vector size constant
12     int vector_size = 100;
13
14     // Compute the global vector size
15     int n = p*vector_size;
16
17     // Initialize the vectors
18     double *a, *b;
19     a = malloc(vector_size*sizeof(double));
20     b = malloc(vector_size*sizeof(double));
21     for (i=0;i<vector_size;i++) {
22         a[i] = 3.14*rank;
23         b[i] = 6.67*rank;
24     }
25
26     // Compute the local dot product
27     double partial_sum = 0.0;
28     for (i=0;i<vector_size;i++) {
29         partial_sum += a[i]*b[i];
30     }
31
32     double sum = 0;
33     MPI_Reduce(&partial_sum,&sum,1,MPI_DOUBLE,MPI_SUM,root,MPI_COMM_WORLD);
34
35     if (rank == root) {
36         printf("The dot product is %g\n",sum);
37     }
38
39     free(a);
40     free(b);
41     MPI_Finalize();
42     return 0;
43 }
```

CODE 14.10

Example of MPI_Reduce, which computes the dot product of two vectors. The two vectors here, a and b, are initialized arbitrarily (lines 21–24). The local dot product is computed in lines 27–30 and then the partial sum of the dot product from each process is summed using MPI_Reduce in line 33. Note that the global vector sizes change as a function of the number of processes used, while the size of the vector segments local to the process remains constant, consistent with weak scaling.

The companion to `MPI_Reduce` is `MPI_Allreduce`, which behaves the same as `MPI_Reduce` except that the result of the reduction is broadcast to all processes in the communicator. As such, the syntax for usage is nearly identical except that no "destination rank" input is needed since all ranks will receive the result, as shown in Code 14.11.

```
01 #include <stdio.h>
02 #include <mpi.h>
03
04 int main(int argc,char **argv) {
05
06    MPI_Init(&argc,&argv);
07    int rank;
08    MPI_Comm_rank(MPI_COMM_WORLD,&rank); // identify the rank
09
10    int input = 0;
11    if (rank == 0) {
12       input = 2;
13    } else if (rank == 1) {
14       input = 7;
15    } else if (rank == 2) {
16       input = 1;
17    }
18    int output;
19
20    MPI_Allreduce(&input,&output,1,MPI_INT,MPI_SUM,MPI_COMM_WORLD);
21
22    printf("The result is %d rank %d\n",output,rank);
23
24    MPI_Finalize();
25
26    return 0;
27 }
```

CODE 14.11

An example of MPI_Allreduce. The sum of the input variable is computed and broadcast to all processes. If run on three processes or more, each process should have as output the value 10.

```
int MPI_Allreduce(const void *send_data, void *put_data, int send_number,
          MPI_Datatype datatype, MPI_OP operation, MPI_Comm communicator)

> mpirun −np 4 ./code10
The result is 10 rank 0
The result is 10 rank 1
The result is 10 rank 2
The result is 10 rank 3
```

14.8 **Summary and Outcomes**

- There was probably no greater achievement of practical utility for the advancement of HPC than the development of MPI.
- MPI is a community-driven specification that continues to evolve.
- MPI is a library with an API, not a language.
- MPICH was the first reduction to practice of the MPI standard.
- Key elements of MPI are point-to-point communication and collective communication.
- MPI has a set of predefined data types for use in library calls.
- Point-to-point communication calls are typified by the `MPI_Send` and `MPI_Recv` calls.
- Collective communication is typified by the broadcast, gather, and scatter operations.
- Important extensions of these collective operations are allgather, alltoall, and reduce.
- Nonblocking point-to-point communications are frequently used to simplify code development and avoid deadlocks.
- User-defined data types can be built up starting from existing MPI datatypes and used in MPI function calls.

14.9 **Exercises**

1. Find errors in the following MPI program and fix them. Explain the reasons for malfunction.

```
01 #include <stdio.h>
02 #include <stdlib.h>
03 #include <mpi.h>
04
05 int main(int argc,char **argv)
06 {
07   int rank, size, neigh = 0;
08   MPI_Status stat;
09   MPI_Init(&argc,&argv);
10   MPI_Comm_rank(MPI_COMM_WORLD,&rank);
11   MPI_Comm_size(MPI_COMM_WORLD,&size);
12
13   switch (rank) {
14     case 0:
15       MPI_Send(&rank,1,MPI_INT,1,0,MPI_COMM_WORLD);
16       MPI_Recv(&neigh,1,MPI_INT,3,3,MPI_COMM_WORLD,&stat);
17     break;
```

```
18    case 1:
19        MPI_Recv(&neigh,1,MPI_INT,0,1,MPI_COMM_WORLD,&stat);
20        MPI_Send(&rank,1,MPI_INT,2,1,MPI_COMM_WORLD);
21    break;
22    case 2:
23        MPI_Send(&rank,1,MPI_INT,3,2,MPI_COMM_WORLD);
24        MPI_Recv(&neigh,1,MPI_INT,1,1,MPI_COMM_WORLD,&stat);
25        break;
26    default:
27        MPI_Send(&rank,1,MPI_INT,0,3,MPI_COMM_WORLD);
28        MPI_Recv(&neigh,1,MPI_INT,2,2,MPI_COMM_WORLD,&stat);
29        break;
30    }
31
32    printf("Rank %d: neighbor %d says hello!\n",rank,neigh);
33
34    MPI_Finalize();
35    return 0;
36 }
```

2. Write a matrix–vector multiplication code using MPI. Use a dense matrix and a dense vector. Call CBLAS in each process for the local matrix–vector multiplication.

3. Rewrite Code 14.9 using point-to-point communication. Generalize your program to use an arbitrary number of processes. Compare the performance of MPI_Alltoall with your point-to-point communication implementation.

4. Rewrite Code 14.10 so that the global vector sizes stay the same as the number of processes varies. This will require changing the local vector size depending on the number of processes on which MPI is launched. Plot the time to solution for your program as a function of the number of processes for various global vector sizes.

References

[1] MPI Forum, "MPI Standardization Forum," [Online]. Available: https://mpi-forum.org/.
[2] C.A.R. Hoare, Communicating Sequential Processes, Prentice Hall International Series in Computer Science, 1985.
[3] M.P.I. Forum, MPI: A Message Passing Interface Standard Version 4.0, 9 June 2021 [Online]. Available: https://www.mpi-forum.org/docs/mpi-4.0/mpi40-report.pdf.
[4] Argonne National Laboratory, "MPICH," [Online]. Available: https://www.mpich.org.

[5] The Open MPI Project, Open MPI: Open Source High Performance Computing, 2023 [Online]. Available: https://www.open-mpi.org.

[6] Network-Based Computing Laboratory, MVAPICH: MPI over InfiniBand, Omni-Path, Ethernet/iWARP, RoCE, and Slingshot, The Ohio State University, 2023 [Online]. Available: https://mvapich.cse.ohio-state.edu.

[7] B. Kernighan, D. Ritchie, The C Programming Language, Prentice Hall, 1988.

Examples for Message-Passing Programs

15

Chapter outline

The message-passing interface (MPI) libraries are the main channel by which high performance computing applications leverage message-passing capabilities to extract concurrency. MPI applications fall under the single-program multiple data category in Flynn's taxonomy of computer architectures. In this chapter, two full stand-alone examples of message-passing applications are presented using MPI. To get started, here is a quick test to ensure that MPI has been installed properly on your system.

```c
1 #include <stdio.h>
2 #include <mpi.h>
3
4 int main(int argc,char** argv) {
5   MPI_Init(NULL,NULL);
6   int size,rank,len;
7   char name[MPI_MAX_PROCESSOR_NAME];
8   MPI_Comm_size(MPI_COMM_WORLD,&size);
9   MPI_Comm_rank(MPI_COMM_WORLD,&rank);
10  MPI_Get_processor_name(name,&len);
11  printf("Hello world! From %s, rank %d out of %d\n",name,rank,size);
12  MPI_Finalize();
13  return 0;
14 }
```

After saving the code in a file called hello.c, it can be compiled using the mpicc wrapper for the compiler:

```
mpicc hello.c -o hello
```

The executable is run using either the mpirun or mpiexec script:

```
mpirun -n 4 ./hello
```

High Performance Computing. https://doi.org/10.1016/B978-0-12-823035-0.00015-8

Something like this will appear as output:

```
Hello world! From compute-1.local, rank 0 out of 4
Hello world! From compute-1.local, rank 1 out of 4
Hello world! From compute-1.local, rank 2 out of 4
Hello world! From compute-1.local, rank 3 out of 4
```

The order in which the processes print to screen may not be the same as shown.

15.1 Solving a Stochastic Differential Equation With Runge–Kutta

Stochastic differential equations permeate scientific and industrial high performance computing applications. They are typically solved using a stochastic Euler or stochastic Runge–Kutta integration method requiring Monte Carlo iterations. Concurrency is extracted by performing the Monte Carlo integrations concurrently on different processes and combining the results with a gather operation to determine the final solution. These types of applications are well suited for message passing and tend to scale extremely well. In this example, we solve the following coupled set of stochastic differential equations using stochastic Runge–Kutta as the numerical method:

$$dF = \mu F + aF^{\beta}dW_1 \quad da = vadW_2$$

where F is the price of an asset, a is the volatility of that asset, v is the volatility of the volatility, β is an adjustable parameter, and dW_1, dW_2 are separate Wiener processes. The system is known as the SABR model [1] and was introduced in 2002 to help account for volatility smile risk in pricing derivative instruments. In this standalone MPI example solving these two equations, the price of a call option at a given strike price, interest rate, volatility, and volatility of volatility is computed. The parameters for the pricing are given in lines 41–47.

```
1 #include <stdio.h>
2 #include <stdlib.h>
3 #include <math.h>
4 #include <time.h>
5 #include <mpi.h>
6
7 int main(int argc, char *argv[]) {
8
9 double K,T,beta;
10 double f,a,f_0,a_0,nu,mu;
11 int mc_cycles,timesteps;
12 double pi = 4.*atan(1.0);
13 double a1,b1,result;
```

```
14 double **eps;
15 int i,j,m;
16 double *payoff;
17 double k[4],k_h[4],k_t[4],k_c[4];
18
19 double ma[4][4];
20 double ma_h[4][4];
21 double ma_t[4][4];
22 double ma_c[4][4];
23
24 int id,ntasks,err;
25
26 err = MPI_Init(&argc, &argv); /* Initialize MPI */
27 if (err != MPI_SUCCESS) {
28   printf("MPI initialization failed!\n");
29   exit(1);
30 }
31 err = MPI_Comm_size(MPI_COMM_WORLD, &ntasks);
32 err = MPI_Comm_rank(MPI_COMM_WORLD, &id);
33
34 // Number of Monte Carlo cycles
35 mc_cycles = 10000;
36
37 // Number of timesteps for the integration
38 timesteps = 1000;
39
40 // Parameters for the stochastic differential equation
41 K = 50;
42 beta = 1.0;
43 T = 0.3;
44 f_0 = 45;
45 a_0 = 0.4;
46 nu = 2.8;
47 mu = 0.05;
48
49 clock_t start;
50 if ( id == 0 ) {
51   printf("----------------------------\n");
52   printf("      Parameter choices:\n");
53   printf("----------------------------\n");
54   printf("          Strike: %g\n",K);
55   printf("            Spot: %g\n",f_0);
56   printf("      volatility: %g\n",a_0);
57   printf("         vol-vol: %g\n",nu);
```

```
58   printf("  interest rate: %g\n",mu);
59   printf("     log(K/f): %g\n",log(K/f_0));
60   printf("  Time to expiry: %g\n",T);
61   printf("          beta: %g\n",beta);
62   printf("Monte Carlo cycles: %d\n",mc_cycles);
63   printf("    timesteps: %d\n",timesteps);
64   start = clock();
65 }
66
67 int seed = id;
68 srand(seed);
69
70 /* parameters for stochastic runge-kutta */
71 ma[0][0] = 0.0; ma[0][1] = 0.0; ma[0][2] = 0.0; ma[0][3] = 0.0;
72 ma[1][0] = 1./2; ma[1][1] = 0.0; ma[1][2] = 0.0; ma[1][3] = 0.0;
73 ma[2][0] = 1./4; ma[2][1] = 1./4; ma[2][2] = 0.0; ma[2][3] = 0.0;
74 ma[3][0] = 1./3; ma[3][1] = -2.0; ma[3][2] = 8./3; ma[3][3] = 0.0;
75
76 ma_h[0][0]=0.0; ma_h[0][1]=0.0; ma_h[0][2]=0.0; ma_h[0][3]=0.0;
77 ma_h[1][0]=1./2; ma_h[1][1]=0.0; ma_h[1][2]=0.0; ma_h[1][3]=0.0;
78 ma_h[2][0]=1./4; ma_h[2][1]=1./4; ma_h[2][2]=0.0; ma_h[2][3]=0.0;
79 ma_h[3][0]=1./3; ma_h[3][1]=-2.0; ma_h[3][2]=8./3; ma_h[3][3]=0.0;
80
81 ma_t[0][0]=0.0; ma_t[0][1]=0.0; ma_t[0][2]=0.0; ma_t[0][3]=0.0;
82 ma_t[1][0]=1./2; ma_t[1][1]=0.0; ma_t[1][2]=0.0; ma_t[1][3]=0.0;
83 ma_t[2][0]=0.0; ma_t[2][1]=1./2; ma_t[2][2]=0.0; ma_t[2][3]=0.0;
84 ma_t[3][0]=0.0; ma_t[3][1]=0.0; ma_t[3][2]=1.0; ma_t[3][3]=0.0;
85
86 ma_c[0][0]=0.0; ma_c[0][1]=0.0; ma_c[0][2]=0.0; ma_c[0][3]=0.0;
87 ma_c[1][0]=-1.0; ma_c[1][1]=0.0; ma_c[1][2]=0.0; ma_c[1][3]=0.0;
88 ma_c[2][0]=-13./32; ma_c[2][1]=5./32; ma_c[2][2]=0.0; ma_c[2][3]=0.0;
89 ma_c[3][0]=-7./24; ma_c[3][1]=1./8; ma_c[3][2]=1./6; ma_c[3][3]=0.0;
90
91 payoff = (double *) malloc(mc_cycles*sizeof(double));
92 eps = (double **) malloc(2*sizeof(double**));
93 for (i=0;i<2;i++) {
94   eps[i] = (double *) malloc(2*sizeof(double));
95 }
96
97 if ( timesteps == 1 ) {
98   printf(" Problem: choose timesteps to be greater than 1.\n");
99   exit(0);
100 }
```

```
101 double dT = T/(timesteps-1);
102 double nnu = 1.0;
103
104 if ( mc_cycles%ntasks != 0 ) {
105   fprintf(stderr,"Problem: number of tasks %d needs to be a divisor
of mc_cycles %d\n",ntasks,mc_cycles);
106   exit(1);
107 }
108 int mstart = (mc_cycles/ntasks)*id;
109 int mend = (mc_cycles/ntasks)*(id+1);
110 int localsize = mend - mstart;
111 double *localpayoff;
112 localpayoff = (double *) malloc(localsize*sizeof(double));
113
114 for (i=mstart;i<mend;i++) {
115   f = f_0;
116   a = a_0;
117   /* Stochastic integration */
118   for (m=0;m<timesteps;m++) {
119    /* dW terms */
120    result = rand();
121    a1 = (1.0*result)/RAND_MAX;
122    result = rand();
123    b1 = (1.0*result)/RAND_MAX;
124    if ( a1 <= 0.0 || a1 > 1.0 ||
125        b1 <= 0.0 || b1 > 1.0 ) {
126     printf(" Random number generator problem : %g %g\n",a1,b1);
127    }
128    /* Standardized normal distribution */
129    eps[0][0] = sqrt(-2.*log(a1))*cos(2.*pi*b1);
130
131    result = rand();
132    a1 = (1.0*result)/RAND_MAX;
133    result = rand();
134    b1 = (1.0*result)/RAND_MAX;
135    if ( a1 <= 0.0 || a1 > 1.0 ||
136        b1 <= 0.0 || b1 > 1.0 ) {
137     printf(" Random number generator problem : %g %g\n",a1,b1);
138    }
139    /* Standardized normal distribution */
140    eps[0][1] = sqrt(-2.*log(a1))*cos(2.*pi*b1);
141
142    result = rand();
143    a1 = (1.0*result)/RAND_MAX;
```

```
144    result = rand();
145    b1 = (1.0*result)/RAND_MAX;
146    if ( a1 <= 0.0 || a1 > 1.0 ||
147        b1 <= 0.0 || b1 > 1.0 ) {
148     printf(" Random number generator problem : %g %g\n",a1,b1);
149    }
150    /* Standardized normal distribution */
151    eps[1][0] = sqrt(-2.*log(a1))*cos(2.*pi*b1);
152
153    result = rand();
154    a1 = (1.0*result)/RAND_MAX;
155    result = rand();
156    b1 = (1.0*result)/RAND_MAX;
157    if ( a1 <= 0.0 || a1 > 1.0 ||
158        b1 <= 0.0 || b1 > 1.0 ) {
159     printf(" Random number generator problem : %g %g\n",a1,b1);
160    }
161    /* Standardized normal distribution */
162    eps[1][1] = sqrt(-2.*log(a1))*cos(2.*pi*b1);
163
164    // Stochastic Runge-Kutta
165    // First SDE
166    k[0] = mu*(f);
167    k_h[0] = a*pow(f,beta);
168    k_t[0] = a*pow(f,beta);
169    k_c[0] = a*pow(f,beta);
170
171    k[1] = mu*(f + dT*ma[0][1]*k[0]
172           + eps[0][0]*sqrt(dT)*ma_h[0][1]*k_h[0]
173           + eps[0][1]*sqrt(dT)/sqrt(3.0)*ma_t[0][1]*k_t[0]);
174    k_h[1] = a*pow(f + dT*ma[0][1]*k[0]
175             + eps[0][0]*sqrt(dT)*ma_h[0][1]*k_h[0]
176             + sqrt(nnu*dT)*ma_c[0][1]*k_c[0],beta);
177    k_t[1] = a*pow(f + dT*ma[0][1]*k[0]
178             + sqrt(nnu*dT)*ma_c[0][1]*k_c[0],beta);
179    k_c[1] = a*pow(f + sqrt(nnu*dT)*ma_c[0][1]*k_c[0],beta);
180
181    k[2] = mu*(f + dT*(ma[0][2]*k[0] + ma[1][2]*k[1])
182           +eps[0][0]*sqrt(dT)*(ma_h[0][2]*k_h[0]+ma_h[1][2]*k_h[1])
183           +eps[0][1]*sqrt(dT)/sqrt(3.0)*(ma_t[0][2]*k_t[0]+ma_t[1][2]
           *k_t[1]) );
184    k_h[2] = a*pow(f + dT*(ma[0][2]*k[0]+ma[1][2]*k[1])
185             +eps[0][0]*sqrt(dT)*(ma_h[0][2]*k_h[0]+ma_h[1][2]*k_h[1])
186             + sqrt(nnu*dT)*(ma_c[0][2]*k_c[0]+ma_c[1][2]*k_c[1])
187             ,beta);
```

```
188    k_t[2] = a*pow(f + dT*(ma[0][2]*k[0]+ma[1][2]*k[1])
189              + sqrt(nnu*dT)*(ma_c[0][2]*k_c[0]+ma_c[1][2]*k_c[1])
190            ,beta);
191    k_c[2] = a*pow(f + sqrt(nnu*dT)*(ma_c[0][2]*k_c[0]+ma_c[1][2]*k_c
[1]),beta);
192
193    k[3] = mu*(f + dT*(ma[0][3]*k[0] + ma[1][3]*k[1] + ma[2][3]*k[2])
194            + eps[0][0]*sqrt(dT)*(ma_h[0][3]*k_h[0]+ma_h[1][3]*k_h[1]
            +ma_h[2][3]*k_h[2])
195            +eps[0][1]*sqrt(dT)/sqrt(3.0)*(ma_t[0][3]*k_t[0]+ma_t[1][3]
            *k_t[1]+ma_t[2][3]*k_t[2]) );
196    k_h[3] = a*pow(f + dT*(ma[0][3]*k[0]+ma[1][3]*k[1]+ma[2][3]*k[2])
197              + eps[0][0]*sqrt(dT)*(ma_h[0][3]*k_h[0]+ma_h[1][3]
            *k_h[1]+ma_h[2][3]*k_h[2])
198              + sqrt(nnu*dT)*(ma_c[0][3]*k_c[0]+ma_c[1][3]*k_c[1]
            +ma_c[2][3]*k_c[2])
199            ,beta);
200    k_t[3] = a*pow(f + dT*(ma[0][3]*k[0]+ma[1][3]*k[1]+ma[2][3]*k[2])
201              + sqrt(nnu*dT)*(ma_c[0][3]*k_c[0]+ma_c[1][3]*k_c[1]
            +ma_c[2][3]*k_c[2])
202            ,beta);
203    k_c[3] = a*pow(f + sqrt(nnu*dT)*(ma_c[0][3]*k_c[0]+ma_c[1][3]
*k_c[1]+ma_c[2][3]*k_c[2]),beta);
204
205    f += (1./6*k[0]-2./9*k[1]+8./9*k[2]+1./6*k[3])*dT
206       +(1./6*k_h[0]-2./9*k_h[1]+8./9*k_h[2]+1./6*k_h[3])*eps[0][0]
       *sqrt(dT)
207       +1./sqrt(3.0)*(1./6*k_t[0]-2./9*k_t[1]+8./9*k_t[2]-5./6*k_t[3])
       *eps[0][1]*sqrt(dT)
208       +(-1./18*k_c[1]+8./9*k_c[2]-5./6*k_c[3])*sqrt(3.*dT);
209
210    // Second SDE
211    k[0] = 0.0;
212    k_h[0] = nu*(a);
213    k_t[0] = nu*(a);
214    k_c[0] = nu*(a);
215
216    k[1] = 0.0;
217    k_h[1] = nu*( a + dT*ma[0][1]*k[0]
218             + eps[1][0]*sqrt(dT)*ma_h[0][1]*k_h[0]
219             + sqrt(nnu*dT)*ma_c[0][1]*k_c[0] );
220    k_t[1] = nu*( a + dT*ma[0][1]*k[0]
221             + sqrt(nnu*dT)*ma_c[0][1]*k_c[0] );
222    k_c[1] = nu*( a + sqrt(nnu*dT)*ma_c[0][1]*k_c[0] );
```

```
223
224    k[2] = 0.0;
225    k_h[2] = nu*( a + dT*(ma[0][2]*k[0]+ma[1][2]*k[1])
226                +eps[1][0]*sqrt(dT)*(ma_h[0][2]*k_h[0]+ma_h[1][2]*k_h[1])
227                + sqrt(nnu*dT)*(ma_c[0][2]*k_c[0]+ma_c[1][2]*k_c[1])
228                );
229    k_t[2] = nu*( a + dT*(ma[0][2]*k[0]+ma[1][2]*k[1])
230                + sqrt(nnu*dT)*(ma_c[0][2]*k_c[0]+ma_c[1][2]*k_c[1])
231                );
232    k_c[2] = nu*( a + sqrt(nnu*dT)*(ma_c[0][2]*k_c[0]+ma_c[1][2]*k_c
       [1]) );
233
234    k[3] = 0.0;
235    k_h[3] = nu*( a + dT*(ma[0][3]*k[0]+ma[1][3]*k[1]+ma[2][3]*k[2])
236                + eps[1][0]*sqrt(dT)*(ma_h[0][3]*k_h[0]+ma_h[1][3]
                   *k_h[1]+ma_h[2][3]*k_h[2])
237                + sqrt(nnu*dT)*(ma_c[0][3]*k_c[0]+ma_c[1][3]*k_c[1]
                   +ma_c[2][3]*k_c[2])
238                );
239    k_t[3] = nu*( a + dT*(ma[0][3]*k[0]+ma[1][3]*k[1]+ma[2][3]*k[2])
240                + sqrt(nnu*dT)*(ma_c[0][3]*k_c[0]+ma_c[1][3]*k_c[1]
                   +ma_c[2][3]*k_c[2])
241                );
242    k_c[3]=nu*( a + sqrt(nnu*dT)*(ma_c[0][3]*k_c[0]+ma_c[1][3]
       *k_c[1]+ma_c[2][3]*k_c[2]) );
243
244    a += (1./6*k[0]-2./9*k[1]+8./9*k[2]+1./6*k[3])*dT
245        +(1./6*k_h[0]-2./9*k_h[1]+8./9*k_h[2]+1./6*k_h[3])*eps[1][0]
            *sqrt(dT)
246        +1./sqrt(3.0)*(1./6*k_t[0]-2./9*k_t[1]+8./9*k_t[2]-5./6*k_t[3])
            *eps[1][1]*sqrt(dT)
247        +(-1./18*k_c[1]+8./9*k_c[2]-5./6*k_c[3])*sqrt(3.*dT);
248    }
249
250    localpayoff[i-mstart] = (f - K);
251    if ( localpayoff[i-mstart] < 0.0 ) localpayoff[i-mstart] = 0.0;
252 }
253
254 /* Communicate payoff vector to processor 0 */
255 err = MPI_Gather(localpayoff,localsize,MPI_DOUBLE,payoff,localsize,
MPI_DOUBLE,0,MPI_COMM_WORLD);
256
257 if ( id == 0 ) {
258  /* find the mean and variance of the payoff */
259  double mean = 0.0;
```

```
260   double variance = 0.0;
261   for (i=0;i<mc_cycles;i++) {
262    mean += payoff[i];
263   }
264   mean /= mc_cycles;
265
266   for (i=0;i<mc_cycles;i++) {
267     variance += (mean-payoff[i])*(mean-payoff[i]);
268   }
269   variance /= mc_cycles;
270
271   double std = sqrt(variance);
272   double error = std/sqrt(1.0*mc_cycles);
273
274   printf("Mean: %g Estimated Error: %g std dev: %g\n",mean,error,std);
275   printf("True price should be in range: %g to %g with 0.95 confidence.\n",
276      mean-1.96*error,mean+1.96*error);
277
278   clock_t end = clock();
279   double time_to_solution = (double) (end-start)/CLOCKS_PER_SEC;
280   printf("Time to solution: %g\n",time_to_solution);
281 }
282
283 free(payoff);
284 free(localpayoff);
285 free(eps);
286
287 err = MPI_Finalize(); /* Terminate MPI */
288 return 0;
289 }
```

The key MPI call is in line 255, where the local integrations of each MPI process are gathered to the process with rank 0 and the price is calculated. A different random seed is used for each process as seen in line 68 to ensure different random numbers are computed on each process. The MPI initialize and finalize calls are at lines 26 and 287. The partitioning of the Monte Carlo iterations among processes is done in lines 108–109. Each MPI process only computes a fraction of the total number of requested iterations.

The code, called sabr.c here, can be compiled using the mpicc wrapper:

```
mpicc sabr.c -o sabr
```

The executable takes no arguments and can be run using either the mpirun or mpiexec scripts:

```
mpirun -np 4 ./sabr
-----------------------------
   Parameter choices:
-----------------------------
        Strike: 50
         Spot: 45
     volatility: 0.4
        vol-vol: 2.8
   interest rate: 0.05
        log(K/f): 0.105361
   Time to expiry: 0.3
          beta: 1
Monte Carlo cycles: 10000
      timesteps: 1000
   Mean: 2.78577 Estimated Error: 0.130003 std dev: 13.0003
   True price should be in range: 2.53097 to 3.04058 with 0.95 confidence.
   Time to solution: 0.355749
```

The predicted price for the call option is $2.79. The executable scales nearly perfectly with the number of processes and enables real-time pricing of instruments for which there is no analytic solution.

15.2 Differentiating Field Variables by Finite Difference

Message-passing operations are frequently used to support differentiating a field variable discretized on a regularly spaced grid. For example, an approximation of the first derivative of a variable on a regularly spaced grid with discretization dx is as follows:

$$\frac{df}{dx} \approx \frac{1}{12dx}\left(f(x-2dx) - 8f(x-dx) + 8f(x+dx) - f(x+2dx)\right)$$

In this formula, an accurate estimate of the first derivative of a variable can be found if the value of that variable is known at four locations: $x - 2dx$, $x - dx$, $x + dx$, and $x + 2dx$. When a grid is partitioned across multiple processes to extract concurrency, artificial boundaries due to the partition are introduced such that the values needed to estimate a derivative near one of those boundaries are not available for performing the differentiation. This is where message-passing operations come in. The needed field values can be communicated by message. This type of message-passing operation, known as halo exchange, is present in many scientific computing applications and is critical for solving partial differential equations via discretization on high performance computers. In this stand-alone MPI example, the first partial derivatives of $\sin x + \sin y + \sin z$ are computed and distributed on a three-dimensional domain using message passing. Each MPI process computes the derivative on a portion of the domain. The core of the computation is encompassed in this finite difference routine:

```
1 Int_t deriv_x(Real_t *dxsol,Real_t *sol,Int_t nx,Int_t ny,Int_t nz,Real_t dx)
2 {
3  Int_t i,j,k;
4
5  Real_t idx = 1.0/dx;
6  Real_t idx_by_2 = 0.5*idx;
7  Real_t idx_by_12 = idx/12.0;
8
9  for (k=0;k<nz;k++) {
10    for (j=0;j<ny;j++) {
11     i = 0;
12     dxsol[i+nx*(j+ny*k)] = ( - 3.0*sol[i +nx*(j+ny*k)]
13                     + 4.0*sol[i+1 +nx*(j+ny*k)]
14                     - sol[i+2 +nx*(j+ny*k)]
15                   ) *idx_by_2;
16
17     i = 1;
18     dxsol[i+nx*(j+ny*k)] = ( - sol[i-1 +nx*(j+ny*k)]
19                     + sol[i+1 +nx*(j+ny*k)]
20                   ) *idx_by_2;
21
22     for (i=2;i<nx-2;i++) {
23     dxsol[i+nx*(j+ny*k)] = ( sol[i-2 +nx*(j+ny*k)]
24                     -8.0 *sol[i-1 +nx*(j+ny*k)]
25                     +8.0 *sol[i+1 +nx*(j+ny*k)]
26                     - sol[i+2 +nx*(j+ny*k)]
27                   ) *idx_by_12;
28     }
29     i = nx-2;
30     dxsol[i+nx*(j+ny*k)] = ( - sol[i-1 +nx*(j+ny*k)]
31                     + sol[i+1 +nx*(j+ny*k)]
32                   ) *idx_by_2;
33
34     i = nx-1;
35     dxsol[i+nx*(j+ny*k)] = ( sol[i-2 +nx*(j+ny*k)]
36                     - 4.0*sol[i-1 +nx*(j+ny*k)]
37                     + 3.0*sol[i +nx*(j+ny*k)]
38                   ) *idx_by_2;
39
```

```
40   }
41 }
42 return 0;
43 }
```

This routine and its analogous versions in the *y* and *z* dimensions compose the core work accomplished on each MPI process.

The global three-dimensional grid must be partitioned among the processes so that each process only works on a small subportion of the global grid. The subportions of the global grid must overlap each other to create a halo so that derivatives can be computed on the artificial boundaries created by partitioning. We use the MPI_Dims_create function (line 58) to assist with this. The initial data is specified on line 313, while derivatives are computed in lines 322–324, which can be done inside an iterative loop as would be done when solving a partial differential equation like the wave equation.

```
 1 #include <stdio.h>
 2 #include <stdlib.h>
 3 #include <assert.h>
 4 #include <math.h>
 5 #include <mpi.h>
 6
 7 typedef int Int_t ;
 8 typedef double Real_t ;
 9
10 Int_t TAG_SYNC_DATA = 4;
11
12 Int_t main(Int_t argc,char *argv[])
13 {
14  Int_t numRanks, myRank;
15  MPI_Init(&argc, &argv) ;
16  MPI_Comm_size(MPI_COMM_WORLD, &numRanks) ;
17  MPI_Comm_rank(MPI_COMM_WORLD, &myRank) ;
18
19  if ( argc < 2 ) {
20    printf(" Usage: fd <nx,y,z>\n");
21    MPI_Abort(MPI_COMM_WORLD,0);
22  }
23  Int_t n = atoi(argv[1]);
24  if ( n%2 == 0 ) {
25    printf(" Only use odd grid sizes!\n");
26    MPI_Abort(MPI_COMM_WORLD,0);
27  }
28  Int_t i,j,k;
```

```
29
30 // relevant parameters for domain decomposition
31 Int_t ghostwidth = 9;
32 Int_t bound_width = 7;
33 Int_t mindim = 16;
34 Int_t refine_factor = 2;
35 Int_t minsize = ghostwidth/refine_factor + mindim;
36 Int_t gwc = ghostwidth/refine_factor + 1;
37
38 Real_t maxx0 = 10.0;
39 Real_t maxy0 = 10.0;
40 Real_t maxz0 = 10.0;
41 Real_t minx0 = -10.0;
42 Real_t miny0 = -10.0;
43 Real_t minz0 = -10.0;
44
45 Int_t nx0,ny0,nz0;
46 nx0 = n;
47 ny0 = n;
48 nz0 = n;
49 // give a domain
50 Real_t hx = ( maxx0 - minx0 )/(nx0 - 1.0);
51 Real_t hy = ( maxy0 - miny0 )/(ny0 - 1.0);
52 Real_t hz = ( maxz0 - minz0 )/(nz0 - 1.0);
53 // create the placement of the distributed meshes
54 Int_t dims[3];
55 dims[0] = 0;
56 dims[1] = 0;
57 dims[2] = 0;
58 MPI_Dims_create(numRanks,3,dims);
59
60 // Domain decomposition
61 Int_t boxcount = 0;
62 Int_t fixcount;
63 Int_t fixminx,fixminy,fixminz;
64 Int_t fixmaxx,fixmaxy,fixmaxz;
65 Int_t minus,plus;
66 Int_t lengthi,lengthj,lengthk;
67
68 fixminx = 0;
69 fixminy = 0;
70 fixminz = 0;
71 fixmaxx = 0;
72 fixmaxy = 0;
```

```
73 fixmaxz = 0;
74
75 Int_t maxx[1];
76 Int_t maxy[1];
77 Int_t maxz[1];
78 Int_t minx[1];
79 Int_t miny[1];
80 Int_t minz[1];
81
82 Int_t ii = 0;
83 maxx[ii] = n;
84 minx[ii] = 1;
85 maxy[ii] = n;
86 miny[ii] = 1;
87 maxz[ii] = n;
88 minz[ii] = 1;
89
90 const Int_t maxnum = 400;
91 Int_t bmaxx[maxnum];
92 Int_t bmaxy[maxnum];
93 Int_t bmaxz[maxnum];
94 Int_t bminx[maxnum];
95 Int_t bminy[maxnum];
96 Int_t bminz[maxnum];
97
98 fixcount = boxcount;
99 lengthi = nint( (maxx[ii] - minx[ii])/dims[0] );
100 lengthj = nint( (maxy[ii] - miny[ii])/dims[1] );
101 lengthk = nint( (maxz[ii] - minz[ii])/dims[2] );
102
103 // Decide how we partition:
104 //      (1) partition as per MPI_DIMS_Create() says
105 //
106 //      (2) Else partition into "minsize" pieces
107 Int_t numx,numy,numz;
108 if (lengthi < minsize && dims[0] > 1 ) {
109   numx = (maxx[ii] - minx[ii])/minsize;
110   if ( numx <= 0 ) numx = 1;
111   lengthi = nint( (maxx[ii] - minx[ii])/numx );
112 } else {
113   numx = dims[0];
114 }
115 if (lengthj < minsize && dims[1] > 1 ) {
116   numy = (maxy[ii] - miny[ii])/minsize;
```

```
117  if ( numy <= 0 ) numy = 1;
118  lengthj = nint( (maxy[ii] - miny[ii])/numy );
119  } else {
120   numy = dims[1];
121  }
122 if (lengthk < minsize && dims[2] > 1 ) {
123   numz = (maxz[ii] - minz[ii])/minsize;
124   if ( numz <= 0 ) numz = 1;
125   lengthk = nint( (maxz[ii] - minz[ii])/numz );
126  } else {
127   numz = dims[2];
128  }
129 if ( (numx > 1 || numy > 1 || numz > 1) &&
130      (maxnum >= (boxcount + numx*numy*numz)) ) {
131   for (k=1;k<=numz;k++) {
132    for (j=1;j<=numy;j++) {
133    for (i=1;i<=numx;i++) {
134     boxcount = boxcount+1;
135     bminx[boxcount] = minx[ii] + (i-1)*lengthi;
136     bmaxx[boxcount] = minx[ii] + i *lengthi;
137     bminy[boxcount] = miny[ii] + (j-1)*lengthj;
138     bmaxy[boxcount] = miny[ii] + j *lengthj;
139     bminz[boxcount] = minz[ii] + (k-1)*lengthk;
140     bmaxz[boxcount] = minz[ii] + k *lengthk;
141     //Force overlap:
142     plus = bound_width/2;
143     if ( (bound_width%2) == 0 ) {
144      minus = plus;
145     } else {
146      minus = plus + 1;
147     }
148     bminx[boxcount] -= minus;
149     bmaxx[boxcount] += plus;
150     bminy[boxcount] -= minus;
151     bmaxy[boxcount] += plus;
152     bminz[boxcount] -= minus;
153     bmaxz[boxcount] += plus;
154
155     // In case dimensions don't divide evenly
156     // and overrule the overlap at the bounds,
157     // make sure we cover the whole box:
158     if (i == 1 ) bminx[boxcount] = minx[ii];
159     if (j == 1 ) bminy[boxcount] = miny[ii];
160     if (k == 1 ) bminz[boxcount] = minz[ii];
```

```
161    if (i == numx ) bmaxx[boxcount] = maxx[ii];
162    if (j == numy ) bmaxy[boxcount] = maxy[ii];
163    if (k == numz ) bmaxz[boxcount] = maxz[ii];
164    if ( bminx[boxcount] != minx[ii] &&
165        bminx[boxcount] <= minx[ii] + gwc-1 ) {
166     if ( (minx[ii]+gwc-bminx[boxcount]) > fixminx ) {
167        fixminx = minx[ii]+gwc-bminx[boxcount];
168     }
169     bminx[boxcount] = minx[ii] + gwc;
170    }
171    if ( bmaxx[boxcount] != maxx[ii] &&
172        bmaxx[boxcount] >= maxx[ii] - gwc+1 ) {
173     if ( (bmaxx[boxcount]-(maxx[ii]-gwc)) > fixmaxx ) {
174        fixmaxx = (bmaxx[boxcount]-(maxx[ii]-gwc));
175     }
176     bmaxx[boxcount] = maxx[ii] - gwc;
177    }
178    if ( bminy[boxcount] != miny[ii] &&
179        bminy[boxcount] <= miny[ii] + gwc-1 ) {
180     if ( (miny[ii]+gwc-bminy[boxcount]) > fixminy ) {
181        fixminy = miny[ii]+gwc-bminy[boxcount];
182     }
183     bminy[boxcount] = miny[ii] + gwc;
184    }
185    if ( bmaxy[boxcount] != maxy[ii] &&
186        bmaxy[boxcount] >= maxy[ii] - gwc+1 ) {
187     if ( (bmaxy[boxcount]-(maxy[ii]-gwc)) > fixmaxy ) {
188        fixmaxy = (bmaxy[boxcount]-(maxy[ii]-gwc));
189     }
190     bmaxy[boxcount] = maxy[ii] - gwc;
191    }
192    if ( bminz[boxcount] != minz[ii] &&
193        bminz[boxcount] <= minz[ii] + gwc-1 ) {
194     if ( (minz[ii]+gwc-bminz[boxcount]) > fixminz ) {
195        fixminz = minz[ii]+gwc-bminz[boxcount];
196     }
197     bminz[boxcount] = minz[ii] + gwc;
198    }
199    if ( bmaxz[boxcount] != maxz[ii] &&
200        bmaxz[boxcount] >= maxz[ii] - gwc+1 ) {
201     if ( (bmaxz[boxcount]-(maxz[ii]-gwc)) > fixmaxz ) {
202        fixmaxz = (bmaxz[boxcount]-(maxz[ii]-gwc));
203     }
204     bmaxz[boxcount] = maxz[ii] - gwc;
```

```
205     }
206
207     } } }
208
209     // Fix the boxes on the border
210     for (k=fixcount;k<boxcount;k++) {
211      if ( fixminx > 0 && bminx[k] == minx[0] ) {
212       bmaxx[k] += fixminx;
213        if ( bmaxx[k] > maxx[ii] ) bmaxx[k] = maxx[ii];
214      }
215      if ( fixmaxx > 0 && bmaxx[k] == maxx[ii] ) {
216       bminx[k] -= fixmaxx;
217        if ( bminx[k] < minx[ii] ) bminx[k] = minx[ii];
218      }
219      if ( fixminy > 0 && bminy[k] == miny[ii] ) {
220       bmaxy[k] += fixminy;
221        if ( bmaxy[k] > maxy[ii] ) bmaxy[k] = maxy[ii];
222      }
223      if ( fixmaxy > 0 && bmaxy[k] == maxy[ii] ) {
224       bminy[k] -= fixmaxy;
225        if ( bminy[k] < miny[ii] ) bminy[k] = miny[ii];
226      }
227      if ( fixminz > 0 && bminz[k] == minz[ii] ) {
228       bmaxz[k] += fixminz;
229        if ( bmaxz[k] > maxz[ii] ) bmaxz[k] = maxz[ii];
230      }
231      if ( fixmaxz > 0 && bmaxz[k] == maxz[ii] ) {
232       bminz[k] -= fixmaxz;
233        if ( bminz[k] < minz[ii] ) bminz[k] = minz[ii];
234      }
235     }
236 } else {
237   boxcount -= 1;
238   bminx[boxcount] = minx[ii];
239   bmaxx[boxcount] = maxx[ii];
240   bminy[boxcount] = miny[ii];
241   bmaxy[boxcount] = maxy[ii];
242   bminz[boxcount] = minz[ii];
243   bmaxz[boxcount] = maxz[ii];
244 }
245
246 if (boxcount == -1 ) {
247   boxcount = 1;
248   bminx[0] = 1;
```

```
249  bminy[0] = 1;
250  bminz[0] = 1;
251  bmaxx[0] = n;
252  bmaxy[0] = n;
253  bmaxz[0] = n;
254  } else {
255  for (i=1;i<=boxcount;i++) {
256   bminx[i-1] = bminx[i];
257   bmaxx[i-1] = bmaxx[i];
258   bminy[i-1] = bminy[i];
259   bmaxy[i-1] = bmaxy[i];
260   bminz[i-1] = bminz[i];
261   bmaxz[i-1] = bmaxz[i];
262  }
263  }
264
265 Real_t *dminx,*dminy,*dminz,*dmaxx,*dmaxy,*dmaxz;
266 dminx = (double *) malloc(boxcount*sizeof(double));
267 dminy = (double *) malloc(boxcount*sizeof(double));
268 dminz = (double *) malloc(boxcount*sizeof(double));
269 dmaxx = (double *) malloc(boxcount*sizeof(double));
270 dmaxy = (double *) malloc(boxcount*sizeof(double));
271 dmaxz = (double *) malloc(boxcount*sizeof(double));
272 for (i=0;i<boxcount;i++) {
273  dminx[i] = minx0 + hx*(bminx[i]-1);
274  dminy[i] = miny0 + hy*(bminy[i]-1);
275  dminz[i] = minz0 + hz*(bminz[i]-1);
276
277  dmaxx[i] = minx0 + hx*(bmaxx[i]-1);
278  dmaxy[i] = miny0 + hy*(bmaxy[i]-1);
279  dmaxz[i] = minz0 + hz*(bmaxz[i]-1);
280  }
281
282 if ( myRank == 0 ) {
283  printf(" boxcount %d\n",boxcount);
284  for (i=0;i<boxcount;i++) {
285   printf(" min %d %d %d max %d %d %d nx %d ny %d nz %d\n",bminx[i],
bminy[i],bminz[i],bmaxx[i],bmaxy[i],bmaxz[i ],
286            bmaxx[i] - bminx[i]+1,
287            bmaxy[i] - bminy[i]+1,
288            bmaxz[i] - bminz[i]+1);
289  }
290  }
291
```

```
292 if ( numRanks < boxcount ) {
293   printf(" Problem : numRanks %d boxcount %d\n",numRanks,boxcount);
294   MPI_Abort(MPI_COMM_WORLD,0);
295 }
296 Real_t *sol,*dxsol,*dysol,*dzsol,*dcoord;
297 Int_t nx = bmaxx[myRank] - bminx[myRank]+1;
298 Int_t ny = bmaxy[myRank] - bminy[myRank]+1;
299 Int_t nz = bmaxz[myRank] - bminz[myRank]+1;
300 sol = (Real_t *) malloc(nx*ny*nz*sizeof(Real_t));
301 dcoord = (Real_t *) malloc((nx+ny+nz)*sizeof(Real_t));
302 dxsol = (Real_t *) malloc(nx*ny*nz*sizeof(Real_t));
303 dysol = (Real_t *) malloc(nx*ny*nz*sizeof(Real_t));
304 dzsol = (Real_t *) malloc(nx*ny*nz*sizeof(Real_t));
305
306 // Specify initial data
307 for (k=0;k<nz;k++) {
308   for (j=0;j<ny;j++) {
309     for (i=0;i<nx;i++) {
310       Real_t x = dminx[myRank] + i*hx;
311       Real_t y = dminy[myRank] + j*hy;
312       Real_t z = dminz[myRank] + k*hz;
313       sol[i+nx*(j+ny*k)] = sin(x) + sin(y) + sin(z);
314     }
315   }
316 }
317
318 Int_t it,nits;
319 nits=1; // just one iteration is sufficient to illustrate differentiation
320 for (it=0;it<nits;it++) {
321   // Take derivative
322   deriv_x(dxsol,sol,nx,ny,nz,hx);
323   deriv_y(dysol,sol,nx,ny,nz,hy);
324   deriv_z(dzsol,sol,nx,ny,nz,hz);
325
326 // Sync
327 level_syncbnd_local(numRanks,myRank,boxcount,
328         bminx,bminy,bminz,
329         bmaxx,bmaxy,bmaxz,
330         dminx,dminy,dminz,
331         dmaxx,dmaxy,dmaxz,hx,bound_width,sol);
332
333 Real_t error = dsol_check(dxsol,dysol,dzsol,nx,ny,nz,
334         dminx,dminy,dminz,hx,myRank);
335
```

```
336  Real_t l2error;
337  MPI_Reduce(&error,&l2error,1,MPI_DOUBLE,MPI_SUM,0,MPI_COMM_WORLD);
338  if ( myRank == 0 ) {
339    printf(" Measure difference from analytical differentiation
%g\n",l2error/numRanks);
340    }
341  }
342  // end for loop
343  // ----------
344  free(sol);
345  free(dcoord);
346  free(dxsol);
347  free(dysol);
348  free(dzsol);
349  free(dminx);
350  free(dminy);
351  free(dminz);
352  free(dmaxx);
353  free(dmaxy);
354  free(dmaxz);
355
356  MPI_Finalize();
357  return 0;
358 }
```

The halo exchange between the partitioned subdomains occurs in line 327, consisting of a nonblocking send and receive and cycling through the grids in a round-robin fashion. Finally, a reduction operation in line 327 enables the evaluation of the l2 norm of the difference between the computed finite difference approximation and the analytic result. The full code is provided in the supplementary material and can be compiled with the mpicc wrapper:

```
mpicc finite_difference.c -o fd
```

The executable takes one argument that is the grid size in each of the three dimensions:

```
mpirun -np 4 ./fd 101
boxcount 4
  min 1 1 1 max 54 54 101 nx 54 ny 54 nz 101
  min 47 1 1 max 101 54 101 nx 55 ny 54 nz 101
  min 1 47 1 max 54 101 101 nx 54 ny 55 nz 101
  min 47 47 1 max 101 101 101 nx 55 ny 55 nz 101
  Measure difference from analytical differentiation 1.63944e-05
```

15.3 **Exercises**

1. Adjust the differentiation example to use a wider finite difference stencil that requires eight neighboring points rather than four and adjust the halo exchange to accommodate this. How does a wider halo exchange impact scalability?

2. Adjust the stochastic differential equation solve to solve a coupled system of 500 assets to model the S&P 500. How many Monte Carlo iterations does it take to converge to price an option on the S&P 500? How many processes would you have to use to get an answer for this problem in less than 5 seconds?

3. Adjust the differentiation example to solve the wave equation as an initial value problem. Produce a strong scaling plot for the time to solution as a function of the number of MPI processes used.

4. Adjust the differentiation example to solve the heat equation. Produce a strong scaling plot for the time to solution as a function of the number of MPI processes used.

5. Adjust the stochastic differential equation example to solve the vanilla Black–Scholes equation from the multiple-thread shared-memory examples Chapter 12 using stochastic Runge–Kutta integration.

Reference

[1] P.S. Hagan, D. Kumar, A.S. Lesniewski, & D.E. Woodward. Managing Smile Risk, Wilmott, 2002, pp. 84–108.

Heterogeneous and Graphical Processor Unit Computer Architecture

16

Contributed by Prateek Srivastava

Chapter outline

16.1 Heterogeneous System Organization

Heterogeneity at a system scale can be identified by the existence of multiple instruction set architectures (ISAs). In a central processing unit (CPU)–graphical processing unit (GPU) system, both the CPU and the GPU have their own distinct ISAs. Heterogeneous systems often involve a CPU with connected coprocessors or accelerators as shown in Figure 16.1.

The physical separation of CPU and GPU logic in the same system has both advantages and disadvantages. The implementation of each can be independently optimized (GPUs for scale, CPUs for thread performance), potentially using different manufacturing processes. They can be independently upgraded as long as the connectivity options (industry standard buses, e.g., PCI-Express shown in Figure 16.2) remain compatible across silicon generations. The resulting system topology is more flexible because more GPUs can be added to the system to populate the available interconnect slots. The memory interfaces can be tailored to provide data feed bandwidths and access latencies matching the dominant processing characteristics of either component. Many heterogeneous supercomputing installations, including those used to run applications that were recently awarded the Gordon Bell prize, use discrete GPUs. However, because the computations in both domains proceed

High Performance Computing. https://doi.org/10.1016/B978-0-12-823035-0.00016-X

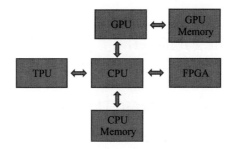

FIGURE 16.1

An example heterogeneous system block design. *CPU,* central processing unit; *GPU,* graphical processing unit; *TPU, ****.

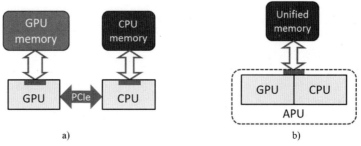

a)　　　　　　　　　　　　b)

FIGURE 16.2

(A) System structure with a discrete central processing unit (CPU) and graphical processing unit (GPU). (B) Heterogeneous system architecture—enabled architecture. *APU,* accelerated processing unit.

independently, there is always an associated overhead when the involved datasets must cross the domain boundary. Because the available system interconnects operate at substantially slower rates than those of memory banks, data copying detracts from overall performance. Moreover, application programmers frequently need to anticipate and manage data movement so that it overlaps with the ongoing computations as much as possible. Note that the additions to Pascal GPUs discussed in the previous section cannot prevent data copies, and naïvely arranged on-demand page migration is still going to produce substantial delays between the first access, causing a page fault and actual data availability in local memory. To alleviate these problems, AMD proposed the Heterogeneous System Architecture (HSA) that places cooperating hardware devices on the same bus and uses shared memory to physically co-locate the processed datasets. This concept is illustrated in Figure 16.2.

a)	b)

The HSA specifications are developed by the nonprofit HSA Foundation, including a host of industrial and academic members, among others, AMD, ARM, Texas Instruments, Samsung, Qualcomm, MediaTek, Imagination Technologies, and several US national laboratories. HSA's goal is to reduce the programming complexity of systems incorporating heterogeneous components by providing ISA-independent runtime and system architecture application programming interfaces (APIs). The specification identifies two types of compute units: a latency compute unit (LCU, e.g., a CPU) and a throughput compute unit (TCU, e.g., a GPU). These components share cache-coherent virtual memory hardware implementing a unified virtual address space. As a result, cooperating devices use the same page tables, enabling data sharing simply by exchanging pointers and thus incurring no memory copy penalties. This is accomplished by custom memory management units that coordinate access to both coherent and noncoherent system memory. Support for page faulting eliminates the need for high-overhead driver-managed pinned memory pools. HSA also obviates the need for the high-overhead system calls by promoting user-level dispatch of work units to TCU queues. Furthermore, it defines a mechanism by which TCU hardware may directly switch between individual application queues without operating system involvement, accomplishing faster scheduling and requiring less power. The HSA specifications do not define any custom or specific language for application programming. Instead they attempt to leverage a number of existing high-level languages and programming models such as C++, Java, Python, C#, OpenMP, and OpenCL.

HSA is of primary interest to Systems on Chip components in which efficiency and low power consumption are paramount. It is less likely to see it applied to flagship GPUs because co-location of different device types on the same die might take away the resources and thus reduce the effective throughput of the TCU. A good example of mainstream HSA hardware is the AMD accelerated processing unit (APU) starting with the Kaveri architecture. It combines a few x86_64 compatible processor cores with GPUs. An overview of their main parameters is presented in Table 16.1.

16.2 Graphical Processing Unit Structure Overview

At the core of a GPU are its lightweight cores that can execute instructions in parallel as part of a Single Instruction, Multiple Data (SIMD)pipeline. These GPUs have thousands of cores unlike CPUs, which have typically between 4 and 64 cores. The term "cores" is misleading because the definition becomes ambiguous based on the architecture being considered. A CPU core is different from a GPU core. A GPU core could be different for manufacturer 1, say NVIDIA, and from a manufacturer 2, say AMD. Generically speaking, if a CPU has 64 cores, it could theoretically imply 64 concurrent "different" executing threads, ignoring hyperthreading. A CPU could potentially have 64 different instructions executing concurrently on different data. However, this is not be true for GPUs. An NVIDIA Hopper

Table 16.1 Properties of Select HSA-compliant AMD APUs

Architecture Codename	Fabrication Process (nm)	Die Size (mm²)	CPU			GPU		Memory Support	Max. TDP (W)
			Architecture	Clock (GHz)	Max. Cores	Clock (MHz)	Shaders		
Kaveri	28	245	Steamroller	4.1/4.3	4	866	512	DDR3-2133	95
Carrizo	28	245	Excavator	2.1/3.4	4	800	512	DDR3-2133	35
Bristol Ridge	28	250	Excavator	3.7/4.2	4		512	DDR4-2400	65

GPU(GH100) has about 18,432 cuda cores. This does not mean that this GPU can work on 18,432 different instructions. It still means that there could be 18,432 instruction streams, which may be not different but executing concurrently.

The GPU is a SIMD machine. A SIMD machine is capable of executing a single instruction on separate data simultaneously. To multiply (Hadamard product) two vectors A and B of n dimension, a single instruction produces the pairwise product of vectors operand1 by operand2. A SIMD machine is very efficient at performing such operations, in which each corresponding element is subjected to the same instruction. Every operation works on different data because each element is different (not the value but from memory). The GPU works in a similar way. At the fundamental level, a GPU accepts a SIMD instruction and lets its lightweight cores execute that instruction by all the ALUs and floating-point units (FPUs) in it on their respective argument data. In our Hadamard product example, each tiny ALU/FPU works on a single corresponding index of the vectors A and B, executing the operation of multiplication in parallel.

This example is an oversimplification of workings of a GPU but captures its essence. GPUs are more complicated, and every manufacturer has its own optimizations and ways of executing this underlying SIMD architecture. The following section describes GPUs from two different manufacturers to give examples of modern real-world GPUs.

16.2.1 NVIDIA GPU

The state-of-art GPU is NVIDIA's H100 Hopper Architecture, at least at time of writing. Figure 16.3 shows the majority of the die area is occupied by the green elements, which are "cuda cores", the lightweight cores that are the functional units in a SIMD pipeline.

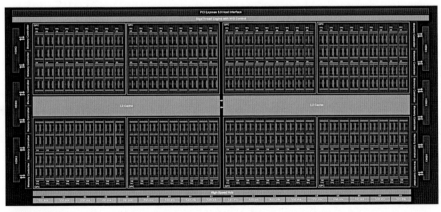

FIGURE 16.3

Block diagram of GH100 Hopper graphical processing unit architecture.

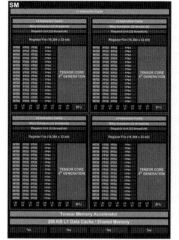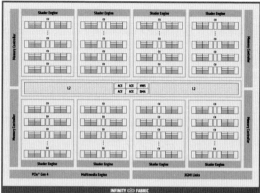

FIGURE 16.4

(A). Streaming multiprocessor in NVIDIA GH100. (B) AMD Instinct MI100 accelerator graphical processing unit architecture.

The GH100 shows the existence of 8 graphics processing clusters (GPCs), which contain 9 tensor processing clusters (TPCs) per GPC, totaling 72 TPCs. Each TPC contains 2 streaming multiprocessors (SMs) per TPC totaling 144 SMs. Each SM contains 128 32-bit single-precision floating-point cuda cores (FP32), 64 32-bit integer cores(INT32), and 64 64-bit double-precision floating-point cuda cores. Each SM also contains a tensor core that specializes in a matrix multiplication and an aggregation operation. This is extensively used for machine learning applications. Simplifying all of these specifications of this GPU, it is illustrated in Figure 16.4 that each SM (equivalent to a generic core) has four SIMD pipelines (blocks) and is capable of taking different instructions. Each block can only execute a single instruction on all the cuda cores within it at a certain time albeit with different data (memory location).

16.2.2 AMD Graphical Processing Unit

In Figure 16.4, for the AMD GPU, the command processor reads commands from user visible dynamic random access memory (DRAM) command queues and submits them to the shader engine's workload manager. Each shader engine is a SIMD pipeline in which the workload manager has a single instruction executing on multiple data among its computing units, which are essentially SIMD functional units.

16.3 **Graphical Processing Unit Memory Components**

The memory hierarchy in a GPU is constructed to minimize off-chip communication. Typically, it consists of a large DRAM-based global memory shared among its cores or "SIMD pipeline" that contain SIMD functional units within them. The GPU also consists of different levels of caches depending on the size of the GPU and the hierarchical organization of its computing elements within the SIMD pipeline. In Figure 16.3, the GPU has HBM3 (high-bandwidth stacked DRAM chips) components as its main memory. This memory is globally addressed followed by an L2 cache, which is shared by four GPCs. Inside the GPCs, we have the streaming processors (the "core" that has SIMD functional units, cuda cores). An SM is shown in Figure 16.4, which consists of 4 blocks that share an L1 Cache. Each of the blocks within the SM contains separate L0 instruction and data caches.

When using external memories, error detection and correction consumes part of memory capacity (storage for parity data) and requires an additional logic stage to rebuild the original data word. These respectively decrease the effective data bandwidth and increase access latency. The important benefit of HBM3 is that error correction is active at all times without imposing a bandwidth penalty.

16.3.1 **Optimizations of the Graphical Processing Unit Memory Hierarchy**

1. *Minimizing CPU—GPU transfers*

   One of the main problems plaguing GPU programming is effective arrangement of data transfers between the CPU and GPU memories. As the local interconnect (typically multilane PCI-Express bus) is an order of magnitude slower than the aggregate bandwidth of Graphics Double Data Rate RAM attached to GPU controllers. Also, the size of GPU memory is often a small fraction of system memory, allocation of GPU memory, and orchestrating data movement at the right time. All of this has substantial impact on performance.

2. *Unification of CPU—GPU virtual address space*

   GPUs often support unified virtual address space through which the GPU can access all GPU and CPU memory present in the system. Unified memory, originally introduced in the CUDA6 programming model, can create a shared memory allocation that is accessible to both CPU and GPU via a single pointer. The use of this feature in the past was limited because of the need for synchronization of any portion of memory modified by the CPU before it could be used by kernels running on the GPU.

3. *Page fault mechanism*

   Some GPUs support page faulting mechanisms. These bring in the necessary data pages into the accelerator's memory on demand. Explicit offload of the entire datasets is no longer necessary. Moreover, the pages to be accessed may stay at their current location and be mapped into GPU address space for access over PCI-Express or NVlink. Page migration is system-wide and symmetric: Both CPU and GPU may request migration of pages from CPU's or other GPU's address space. The page faulting mechanism also guarantees global memory data consistency. To reduce the translation lookaside buffer (TLB) impact of GPU paging, large pages up to 2-MB size are supported. These techniques allow oversubscription of physical memory on a GPU and permit finetuning of data movement performance through API hints ("cudaMemAdvise").

16.4 Parallel Flow Control

A GPU's execution model is also called Single Instruction Multiple Threads (SIMT), and its programming model is referred to as Single Program Multiple Data (SPMD). The idea behind SIMT is that multiple threads work on different data using the same instruction, in which each thread maps on to each functional unit in a SIMD pipeline. SPMD makes this execution easy because it allows a single program to run in parallel by splitting the work in tiny chunks and distributing it in a system or the functional units of a SIMD pipeline or threads in the case of SIMT.

Having examined the hardware architecture of a GPU, it is observed that a streaming multiprocessor or SMs in the Hopper architecture are SIMD pipelines (each SM has four SIMD pipelines). Each SM consists of cuda cores, which are the functional units in the pipeline. From an application layer perspective, we can look at each functional unit or cuda core running a thread and each SM capable of running blocks of such threads. A block of threads in GPU terminology is called a "Warp". In Figure 16.4, a warp scheduler manages these threads among the cuda cores within an SM.

The warp methodology executes parallel applications using Leslie Valiant's "bulk synchronous parallel" paradigm shown in Figure 16.5. With this model, threads synchronize within an SM using global barriers. Figure 16.6 shows a toy example of a matrix-vector dot product in which data is partitioned between two blocks and two threads per block. Here there is a GPU with 1 SM and two blocks within an SM and two cuda cores per block. Each thread is running on a single cuda core.

Thread-level computation

Communication

Synchronization using barriers

FIGURE 16.5

Bulk synchronous parallel model of parallel computation.

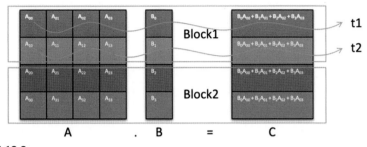

FIGURE 16.6

An example showing data and computation partitioning among blocks and threads assuming two threads per block

16.5 Central Processing Unit–Graphical Processing Unit Interoperability

GPUs are most efficiently used if certain types of work can be offloaded to them. CPUs do a good job in offloading such tasks. This is why the most common way of setting up a GPU is with a CPU. Computations in a GPU are offloaded in a three-step process, as shown in Figure 16.7: (1) communication (input/output [I/O]) from the CPU to the GPU, (2) GPU executes instructions of the GPU kernel, and (3) GPU sends the results back to the CPU (I/O).

16.5.1 Performance Considerations

- **SLOWER:** SLOWER is a performance model that examines an architecture in a six-dimensional tradeoff space, namely, starvation, latency, overheads, waiting for contention, energy, and reliability. In the context of this chapter, GPUs may be analyzed in terms of SLOW.
- **Starvation:** Starvation is defined by insufficiency of computational work to fully use available computing units. Figure 16.8 shows an example of starvation where a GPU with two warps; the warp 0 starves after executing instruction 0 because of the lack of availability of instruction 3. GPUs have an inherent bottleneck implicit because of their SIMD style of execution model. The workload manager cannot execute another instruction until all the functional units in the SIMD pipeline have finished their previous instruction. Thus, the entire pipeline is stalled until the slowest cuda core finishes, creating a starvation condition for the faster cores. For computations such as dense linear algebra, it doesn't matter because all the cuda cores are executing similar instructions with almost similar time per operation. However, starvation could be a significant performance bottleneck in the case of sparse linear algebraic operations.

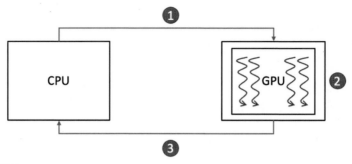

FIGURE 16.7

Central processing unit (CPU)—graphical processing unit (GPU) interoperability.

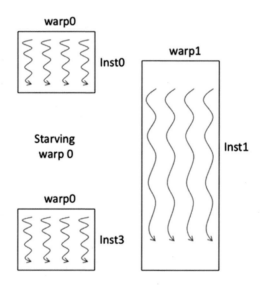

FIGURE 16.8

Starvation in graphical processing units.

- **Latency:** Latency is defined as the time taken to move data from source to destination in an otherwise unloaded system (no contention). GPUs have very low on-chip latencies. However, the off-chip communication latencies between CPU and GPU can impose a bottleneck. As an example: the bandwidth of a PCIe bus (sixth generation) is about 128 GB/s. However, an intel core i9 CPU has a peak performance of approximately 1.1 TFLOPs, and a hopper GPU has a single precision peak performance of approximately 51 TFLOPS. Here each operation manipulates 32-bit numbers so 51 TFLOPS could correspond to manipulation of 200 TB ($51 * 10^{12} * 4$) of data per second. The bus is slowing the computation down because it can only transfer 128 GB of data per second.

With these numbers, processing speed of CPUs or GPUs is much faster than the communication speed between them. This is even getting worse since the advances in speeds of GPUs or CPUs are faster than the speed at which the buses are getting faster.

- **Overhead:** Overhead is defined by the work done to manage parallelism, both physical resources and concurrent calculations. Overheads are permeated throughout a parallel machine. These are in multilevels of cache that permit data copying, which is an overhead. The warp scheduler partitions the data into its cuda cores. Partitioning is an overhead. The warp scheduler deals with reducing time to solution by increasing the parallelism, which is true. But, it also adds an overhead. These overheads when aggregated can sometimes overwhelm a system and are important measures to be considered when dealing with optimizations.
- **Waiting for contention:** This is time lost because of waiting for a shared resource. Contention creeps into a system whenever there are shared resources. Primarily, contention is of two types, memory contention and network contention, both directly related to their respective bandwidths. GPUs have a global address space, which means that different execution threads could contend for reading and updating a global data structure. Similarly, caches and register files within SMs are shared and are also contended. For network contention, the finite number of I/O channels cause contention for off-chip communication. Every interface within a GPU also faces some sort of network contention whenever communicating outside the boundaries of its computation.

16.5.2 Optimization Techniques

All the discussed performance degradation factors are limiting. But they have some scope of hiding or eliminating them. Some optimizations focus on improving the enabling technology itself. Faster processors reduce computation latencies. Faster buses reduce network latencies. Wider buses increase the bandwidth. There are some architectural optimizations such as overlapping computation with communication. While a cuda core performs a computation, the network is smart enough to use the time to fetch off-chip data. There are other techniques such as memory coalescing, divergence, and exploiting spatial and temporal locality that are used to improve some of these performance degradation factors.

16.6 Summary and Outcomes

- A typical heterogeneous system is one or more shared memory processor cores affiliated with the system main memory connected through industrial standard I/O interface such as PCIe to the socket GPU or any other accelerator.
- The physical separation of CPU and GPU logic in the same system has both advantages and disadvantages. It makes upgrading the system flexible while adding bottlenecks on off-chip communication.

- Structure of a GPU at its core is a collection of SIMD pipelines exploiting fine-grained data-level parallelism compared with a CPU.
- GPUs have high bandwidth on-chip memory to reduce off-chip communication as much as possible because they have high latency.
- GPUs are hardware devices that speed up certain types of computation. While controlled and coordinated by the main processor in the system, they are capable of performing these computations independently.
- GPUs implementations leverage different set of tradeoffs and design constraints driven by the available technology in each time period. The technology determined the level of integration with the main CPU, work offload mechanisms, and effective performance.
- The first floating-point accelerators were coprocessors. They operated in lock-step with the primary CPU and required custom hardware interfaces to operate.
- GPUs evolved to become the modern era floating-point accelerators through continued unification of previously hardwired functions specialized to support the individual stages of graphics rendering pipeline and explicit addition of other features required by HPC such as double-precision floating point.
- Large scale of integration affording high transistors counts per chip enables additional performance and programmability optimizations by combining multiple traditionally disjoint devices on a single die.

16.7 Exercises

1. What motivated the introduction of accelerators in computing systems?

2. Briefly characterize the coprocessor enhanced architecture. Which properties made the coprocessors cumbersome to use? Given that modern CPU transistor budgets frequently go into billions, would it be worthwhile to revisit the concept and include specialized coprocessor logic on processor die?

3. Which components of modern GPUs make them suitable for generic computing applications? Which architectural solutions may prevent them from reaching the peak processing throughput with arbitrary computing problems?

4. What are the benefits of using a unified memory system in HSA versus discrete GPU-CPU approach? What are the drawbacks?

5. What are the parameters that can decide the maximum number of threads in a warp?

6. A floating-point accelerator with 256 FPUs clocked at 512 MHz and equipped with 512 MB of local memory is used to speed up the multiplication of two

16K × 16K matrices containing double precision floating-point numbers. The multiplication nominally takes 200 seconds on host CPU. The accelerator is attached through PCI-Express bus with sustained data transfer rate of 1 GB/s in each direction. Each of its FPUs performs a fused multiply-add operation within a cycle. Assuming that the overheads of local data movement and space required to store the executable code in the accelerator may be ignored, and the setup of data transfer between CPU and accelerator takes a negligible amount of time, calculate:

7. Matrix multiplication speedup if executed only by the accelerator. Remember that the input matrices are originally stored in host memory; the result matrix should be placed there as well.

8. With optimal workload distribution, how would the speedup change if both accelerator and host CPU worked in tandem?

9. The chapter talks about two GPUs from two different vendors or manufacturers. Analyze the different tradeoff space those GPUs have exploited for optimizations.

10. What are the advantages and disadvantages of a SIMD execution model?

11. What is the difference between a GPU in a consumer-grade graphics card versus a GPU used for scientific applications?

12. Categorize increase in time to solution in the following scenarios as starvation, latency, overhead, or a contention problem. Explain the reason for the categorization.

13. Note: More than one answer is possible.

14. Due to increased CPU–GPU communication

15. Due to a narrow GPU interface

16. Due to a smaller cache

17. Due to suboptimal data partitioning

18. Analyze the tradeoff between having a smaller number of SIMD pipelines that are deeper versus a larger number of SIMD pipelines that are shallow.

19. Discuss the properties of a GPU that makes it suitable for dense linear algebra.

The Essential OpenAC

17

By Maciej Brodowicz

Chapter outline

17.1 Overview of GPU Programming

As discussed in Chapter 15, graphics processing units (GPUs) are currently one of the most dominant accelerator types employed in high performance computing (HPC). In contrast to conventional multicore processors, their programming is a much more complex task. The main reason for that stems from the relatively young age of GPU technology, resulting in a dearth of mature programming tools and environments. Various aspects of the technology are constantly improved and modified, which further complicates the development of general-purpose programming approaches and compilers. Compared to conventional hardware, the accelerators also use a completely different execution model. For many practical purposes each core on a multicore central processing unit (CPU) could be considered a separate context of execution, but the same is not true for a thread ensemble running on a GPU core. A core on a GPU is one of many functional units that is a part of a single-instruction multiple data (SIMD) pipeline that can be considered as a separate context with multiple execution streams. Conventional processor architecture in combination with an optimizing compiler hides many implicit components of program execution (register allocation, cache management, data consistency enforcement, optimization of branches, instruction reordering, speculative execution, and many others) from the user, enabling them to focus on the essential program algorithms and data structures in a high-level programming language. In GPUs, many details of the architecture still need to be explicitly addressed by the programmer who is interested in extracting the highest level of performance. Due to the much larger number of execution resources but also stronger emphasis on parallelism, resource allocation and management become far more critical to achieving a good level of performance. This often has to be done by taking into account the physical structure, count, and resource limits on GPUs, especially if many computational kernels with different memory footprints and performance characteristics need to be scheduled concurrently. GPU memory capacity is traditionally smaller compared to the host machine. The data locality plays a critical role in maximizing performance, which requires efficient scheduling of data offloads, adding another dimension to the complexity. Note that offload speeds are usually constrained by the available bandwidth of the peripheral component interconnect express (PCIe) bus, potentially resulting in significant latencies when transferring large amounts of data. To offer any advantage over the nonaccelerated model of computation, these costs would have to be amortized by performance gains over the entire course of an application execution. Moreover, the question of what is the right placement for a specific kernel in a heterogeneous architecture is not always easy to answer. It has to be weighed against the individual programmer's experience in GPU code development, familiarity with the architectural features of the target GPU, programming tools available, and ported algorithm characteristics. Even then it may turn out that due to unforeseen overheads or latencies the speedup gained through execution on an accelerator does not present any practical advantage compared to conventional hardware. This directly impacts a programmer's productivity; their time would have likely been spent better developing and optimizing a multicore implementation of the algorithm, or even better, linking with an optimized external library providing the required functionality. Finally, to take advantage of both worlds, one might attempt to balance the computation across all available execution resources in the system. While potentially yielding the best performance, this approach is also the most difficult to manage. Strong disparities between the execution environments involved make the predictable scheduling of computations very difficult to attain, save for the most trivial and well-characterized problems.

Initially, GPU programs leveraged three-dimensional graphics application programming interfaces (APIs) such as OpenGL nullN and DirectX nullN to perform operations on vectors and dense matrices since they were natively supported by the graphics pipeline. One of the first algorithms accelerated on a GPU was matrix multiplication using 8-bit (with 16-bit internal precision) fixed-point arithmetic published in 2001 nullN. To trick the graphics hardware into performing the desired operations, the authors used two textures corresponding to the input matrices and mapped multiple copies of them onto the interior of a cube, keeping one parallel and the other perpendicular to the projection plane. The partial products obtained through multitexturing in modulate mode were summed onto the front face of the cube using blending in orthographic view (to avoid perspective distortions). The final result (image) was then retrieved using GPU-to-CPU memory copy. The reader will immediately notice that this method of performing computations is not very practical. To provide a more convenient programming environment, a number of custom interfaces specialized for GPU and in some cases targeting general heterogeneous platforms were developed throughout the 2000s. As the feature set of newer GPUs grew richer and after introduction of new architectural capabilities (programmable shaders, double-precision floating point, support for dynamic parallelism, etc.), many of these interfaces were also revised to include the appropriate support for added extensions. It is not uncommon for many of these APIs to undergo several specification revisions over the relatively short span of their existence, the newest of which frequently require the recent versions of graphics hardware to provide the full set of operational features. A brief overview of several popular toolkits that expose different programming models, supported features, portability, and scope is presented below.

CUDA. This widespread proprietary GPU programming toolkit, originally known as the Compute Unified Device Architecture (CUDA) nullN, only works with devices manufactured by Nvidia, including the GeForce, Quadro, and Tesla family. Frequently used HPC languages such as C, C++, and Fortran are supported through compiler extensions and a runtime library. Different vendors provide different compilers, debuggers, and profilers for C, C++, and Fortran.

For the C family of languages, Nvidia provides `nvcc`, a low-level virtual machine-based compiler, whereas Fortran support is available from the Portland Group's (PGI) CUDA Fortran compiler. The programming environment is supplemented by libraries optimized for specific tasks, such as fast Fourier transform computation, basic linear algebra subprograms, random number generation, dense and sparse solvers, graphs analytics, and game physics simulation. CUDA exposes several performance-oriented features that are typically not available through standard graphics-based interfaces, such as scattered memory reads, unified memory access, fast on-GPU shared-memory access, improved speeds of offload and state retrieval, additional data types, mixed-precision computing, supplementary integer and bit-wise operations, and profiling support. As of November 2023, the most recent revision of the toolkit is 12.3.

OpenCL. Open Computing Language nullN, initially released in 2009 by the nonprofit Khronos consortium, is an open standard attempting to define a unified heterogeneous programing framework. It provides an API on top of the C language (ISO/IEC 9899:1999) and C++14 (starting with revision 2.2) that supports using the target device's memory and processing elements (PEs) for program execution. Execution in a heterogeneous environment places substantial constraints on language features that are permitted; for example, recursion, type identification, goto statements, virtual functions, exceptions, and function pointers may not be used at all or with severe limitations. Device vendors determine how and which PEs are actually exposed to the user. OpenCL permits up to four levels of memory hierarchy to be implemented by the device. It includes global memory (large, but with substantial latency), read-only memory (small and fast, but writable by host only), local memory shared by a subset of PEs, and per-PE private memory (e.g., registers). Corresponding qualifiers (`global`, `local`, `constant`, `private`) are integrated with the language and understood by the compiler when used in variable declarations. Functions executing on accelerators are marked with the `kernel` attribute and accept argument declarations tagged with the address space qualifiers listed above. Kernels defined as source code may be compiled in runtime by the appropriate online compiler if the platform is *full profile* compliant; otherwise, an offline, platform-specific compilation is used (*embedded profile*). Besides explicitly defined kernels, devices may provide built-in functions that are enumerated and exposed by OpenCL. The framework supports execution synchronization at three levels: workgroup, subgroup, and command. Revision 3.0 of the OpenCL specification was released in September 2020.

C++ AMP. Developed by Microsoft, C++ Accelerated Massive Parallelism nullN is a compiler and set of extensions to C++ that enable the acceleration of C++ applications on platforms that support various forms of data-parallel execution. The accelerator does not necessarily have to be an external device such as a GPU; it could be integrated on the same die as the main CPU, or even be an extension of the main processor's industry-standard architecture, such as streaming SIMD extensions or advanced vector extensions provided by some members of the x86 processor family. Its device model assumes that the accelerator may be equipped with a private memory that is not accessible to the host or that both host and device share the same memory. The C++ AMP runtime performs or avoids memory copies as required by a particular implementation. The framework defines two types of function restriction specifiers, `cpu` and `amp`, the latter of which marks the relevant code for execution on the accelerator. Functions tagged this way must conform to the C++ subset that is permitted by the underlying hardware type. Accelerators are represented by `accelerator` objects with an associated logical *view* (more than one view per accelerator is possible) that implement command buffers for computational tasks to be processed by the accelerator. Commands may be submitted for execution immediately or deferred; completion of the accelerator workload may be synchronous (blocking) or asynchronous, using future-based markers for a single task or task group. Data types are based on n-dimensional arrays with related n-dimensional *extent* (determining array bounds) and *index* objects (referring to specific elements). To exercise control over data copying and caching with minimum overhead, *array views* are provided that permit access to a segment of a relevant array. Array views may be accessed locally or in a different coherence domain, implying the necessary data copies for the latter. C++ AMP also supports a range of atomic operations and a `parallel_for_each` construct to launch parallel operations. The current revision of the specification is v1.2, released in 2013.

OpenACC. The Open Accelerator framework nullN, also known as "directives for accelerators", differs from the approaches described above in that it attempts to significantly simplify the accelerator programming interface, making the code development for GPUs and other attached devices more approachable to a casual developer. It also focuses on better code and performance portability across different platforms. The initial OpenACC specification was created by PGI, CAPS enterprise, Cray, and Nvidia in 2011. Since then it has been joined by multiple industries, national labs, and academic members, including AMD, Pathscale, and Sandia and Oak Ridge National Laboratories. Since the directive-based approach requires compiler support, commercial tools from PGI—now a part of Nvidia HPC Software Development Kit (support for multiple target platforms with OpenACC compatibility version 2.7) and Cray (for Cray systems only) are available. Several open-source compilers have also been developed, including OpenUH from the University of Houston nullN, OpenARC provided by Oak Ridge National Laboratory nullN, and GCC. The latter included experimental OpenACC v2.0a support starting with version 5.1, to be further refined in the GCC 6 release series. Since OpenACC resembles another directive-based parallel programming framework, OpenMP, it is expected that the two environments will be eventually combined and will share a single programming specification. The most recent (November 2023) revision of the OpenACC API is 3.3. Its essential features are discussed in more detail in the remainder of this chapter.

17.2 Programming Concepts

OpenACC supports offloading of designated parts of the program onto accelerator devices connected to the local host computer. Segments of code that may benefit from parallel execution must be explicitly identified by the programmer through relevant directives, or *pragmas* in C and C++, and by specially formatted comments in Fortran. Automatic detection of the offloadable sections of program is not supported. The applied method is portable between different CPU types, supported accelerator devices, and underlying operating systems. The details of initialization of accelerator hardware and suitable functions responsible for parallel code execution, management of workload offload, and result retrieval from the accelerator are hidden from the programmer and are performed implicitly by the compiler and runtime system. OpenACC currently doesn't support automatic workload distribution across multiple accelerator devices, even if such are available on the same host machine. Similarly to OpenMP, the directives are simply ignored if the relevant functionality is not supported or not enabled in the compiler.

The execution of the user application is controlled by the host, which nominally follows most of the control flow within the program and initiates transfer of work and data constituting the identified parallel regions to the accelerator. For these code segments, the host may be involved in the allocation of sufficient memory on the device to accommodate the computational kernel's dataset, performing the relevant data transfer between the host and accelerator memory (frequently over the direct memory access [DMA] channel), sending the executable code, marshalling and forwarding the input arguments for the parallel region, queuing the code for execution, waiting for completion, and finally fetching the computation results and releasing the memory allocated on the device. Accelerators typically support several levels of parallelism: coarse grain, referring to parallel execution on multiple execution resources; fine grain, involving one of multiple threads within a processing element; and function unit level, which exposes SIMD or vector operations within each fine-grain execution unit. In OpenACC, these levels are matched respectively by *gang*, *worker*, and *vector* parallelism as illustrated in Fig. 17.1. The accelerator device executes a number of gangs, each of which contains one or more workers. In turn, a worker may take advantage of available vector parallelism by executing SIMD or vector instructions.

Execution of a compute region on accelerator starts in so-called *gang-redundant* (GR) mode, in which each gang has a single worker executing the same code. Once the control flow in the program reaches the region marked for parallel execution, the execution switches to *gang-partitioned* (GP) mode. In this mode, the work

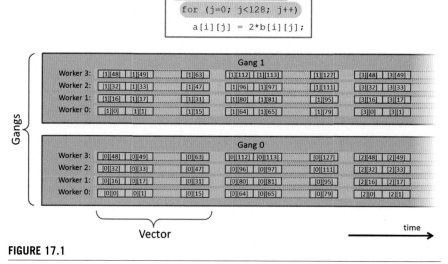

FIGURE 17.1

Example mapping of nested loop iterations onto OpenACC parallelism levels with 2 gangs (each gang typically maps onto a streaming multiprocessor), 4 workers (each worker typically maps to a block consisting of threads, also known as a warp within a gang), and 16 vector lanes (each vector lane is a thread). The numeric indices of the accessed matrix element in a specific iteration are shown in square brackets. In this case, the outer loop is partitioned across gangs, while the inner loop iterations are divided among workers and vector lanes.

performed by different iterations of one loop or multiple loops is distributed across the gangs, but still with only one worker active in each gang. In both of these scenarios program execution proceeds in *worker-single* (WS) mode; similarly, if only one lane of vector processing is used by the worker, the program operates in *vector-single* (VS) mode. If the parallel region or its section has been marked for worker-level work sharing, all workers in a gang are activated and the execution continues in *worker-partitioned* (WP) mode. Note that parallel regions may enable GP and WP modes at the same time, which causes distribution of available work among all workers in all gangs. A similar distinction applies to vector parallelism: it may be enabled on a per loop or loop nest basis to partition the parallel operations across available SIMD or vector units, thus executing in *vector-partitioned* (VP) mode. VP mode for the specific portion of workload may be activated concurrently with any combination of gang and worker modes.

Explicit synchronization involving barriers or locks across gangs, workers, and vector operations is discouraged. Due to differences between OpenACC implementations and accelerator architectures, some of the gangs may not even begin to execute before others complete. A similar observation applies to workers and vector lanes; since scheduling of worker or vector operations is not always defined deterministically, a specific workload synchronization method that works on one accelerator architecture may lead to a deadlock on another.

Both hosts and accelerators use the concept of a thread, albeit with some differences. Host threads are closely tied to processor execution units, such as cores or hyperthread slots, depending on the actual architecture. What constitutes an accelerator core strongly depends on the accelerator type or even the particular implementation of the same device type. For example, AMD demarcates core boundaries on their GPUs differently from Nvidia. OpenACC defines the accelerator thread as a single lane of a single worker in a gang; this unambiguously corresponds to a single parallel execution context. Most accelerator threads can operate asynchronously from host threads. The framework permits submitting the work units to one or more *activity queues* on the device. Operations entered in a single queue will execute in submission order; however, operations stored in different activity queues may execute in arbitrary order. The usage of other multithreading environments on the host, such as OpenMP, concurrently with OpenACC is generally unrestricted, although the users should take care to avoid oversubscription of execution resources if OpenACC code regions are also scheduled to run on the host processors.

The conscientious OpenACC programmer must be aware of the consequences of the memory model exposed by the framework. Many accelerators, especially PCIe-attached GPUs, are equipped with separate memories from that of the host computer. It means that the host is incapable of directly accessing the device memory, and conversely, the device cannot efficiently access the host memory. Data movement between the two memory pools has to be orchestrated through other means, such as DMA. The programmer must take this into account when writing portable Open-ACC code, since the overhead of scheduling and performing a data transfer between host and accelerator memory usually impacts the overall execution performance and may vary from instance to instance. When computing on a large amount of data, the programmer must also be aware of memory size limitations, which are typically much more restrictive on the accelerator side. The datasets accessed by the application must be appropriately partitioned into pieces that may individually fit in device memory, in some cases imposing changes on the computational algorithm. Data structures containing raw pointers to data in the host memory may also have to be redesigned. Many GPUs utilize a weak memory model in which operations between accelerator threads are performed in arbitrary order unless synchronized by a memory fence, thus potentially producing different results for multiple runs of the same code. Similar considerations apply to unified memory architectures or those exposing shared-memory space between the host and accelerator or multiple accelerators. Explicit synchronization to make sure that updates to shared data are fully carried out before they are accessed by the consumer entity is strongly recommended.

17.3 Compilation and Installation

To get started with openacc, the first step is installation of the toolchain that can be found at https://www.openacc.org/tools. For the rest of the chapter, nvc, the Nvidia GNU-compatible C compiler, will be used for the demonstrations. Once the compiler toolchain is in place, the type of accelerator should also be checked. Fig. 17.2 shows an example of having an Nvidia GPU in the system using the Nvidia System Management Interface (nvidia-smi) tool and AMD GPU using the lsmod tool.

The following program is to test if the installation has been done correctly. At this point the nuances of the program can be ignored. Let's say the following program shown in Code 17.1 was stored in a file "test.c".

```
001 #include <stdio.h>
002
003 #define N 1000
004 int array[N];
005
006 int main () {
007
008 #pragma acc parallel loop
009    for (int i = 0; i < N; i++) {
010       array[i] = 3.0;
011    }
012    printf("Success!\n");
013
014    return 0;
015 }
```

CODE 17.1

Example code illustrating a basic parallel loop.

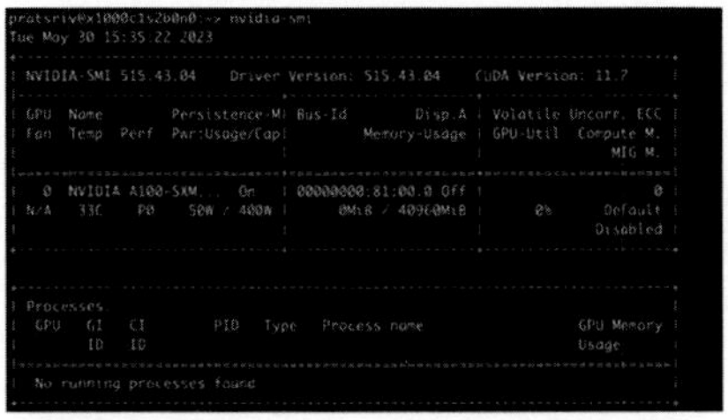

```
$ lsmod | grep amd
amdgpu              4575232  11
amd_iommu_v2          20480  1 amdgpu
gpu_sched             32768  1 amdgpu
ttm                  106496  1 amdgpu
drm_kms_helper       184320  1 amdgpu
drm                  487424  7 gpu_sched,drm_kms_helper,amdgpu,ttm
i2c_algo_bit          16384  1 amdgpu
```

FIGURE 17.2

Example screenshots confirming Nvidia GPU and AMD GPU.

To compile the program, use:

```
>nvc test.c
```

OpenACC allows compiling programs for different targets, such as host, multicore, or GPU:

- Host: Compiles OpenACC directives for serial execution on host CPU.
- Multicore: Compiles OpenACC directives for parallel execution on host CPU.
- GPU: Compiles OpenACC directives for parallel execution on GPU.

To compile the program, use:

```
> nvc -Minfo=all -acc=host test.c
main:
      9, Memory set idiom, loop replaced by call to __c_mset4

> nvc -Minfo=all -acc=multicore test.c
main:
      6, Generating Multicore code
          9, #pragma acc loop gang
      9, Memory set idiom, loop replaced by call to __c_mset4

>nvc -Minfo=all -acc=gpu test.c
main:
      6, Generating Tesla code
          9, #pragma acc loop gang, vector(128) /* blockIdx.x
threadIdx.x */
      6, Generating implicit copyout(array[:]) [if not already
present]
```

17.4 Environment Variables

Currently, OpenACC defines only three environment variables that may be used to modify the runtime behavior of applications. They include:

- `ACC_DEVICE_TYPE` determines the default device type that will be used to accelerate the marked parallel regions of the code. This value is implementation dependent. For example, the PGI compiler permits the following values: `NVIDIA`, `RADEON`, and `HOST` to signify respectively the selection of an Nvidia- or MD-branded GPU as the target accelerator device or to permit the execution on the host processor. The program has to be compiled in a way that enables the use of multiple accelerator devices.

Example:

```
export ACC_DEVICE_TYPE=NVIDIA
./openacc_app
```

Or:

```
env ACC_DEVICE_TYPE=NVIDIA ./openacc_app
```

These will accelerate the "openacc_app" application using the available Nvidia GPU. Note that the actual command line used to invoke the application may be subjected to additional requirements imposed by the runtime environment on the target platform, in particular the job management subsystem.

- `ACC_DEVICE_NUM` is a nonnegative integer that identifies the physical accelerator device to be used. The number should not be greater than or equal to the number of the attached accelerator devices on the host node; otherwise the behavior is implementation dependent.

Example:

```
export ACC_DEVICE_NUM=0
./openacc_app
```

This will execute parallel regions of code on the first physical accelerator in the system. The second invocation form as shown for ACC_DEVICE_TYPE may also be used.

- `ACC_PROFLIB` selects the appropriate profiling library, if such is available on the target system.

Example:

```
export ACC_PROFLIB=/usr/lib/libaccprof.so
./openacc_app
```

This will profile the execution of parallel regions in the application "openacc_app."

17.5 **Library Calls**

OpenACC provides a number of predefined values and library functions that may be invoked from user applications. Note that in general none of these functions are required to create fully functional OpenACC programs. They are used in situations when additional information has to be retrieved from the system or explicit management of runtime functions may yield better execution performance. Specifications subdivide the library interfaces into five major sections: definitions, device-oriented functions, asynchronous queue management, device functionality tests, and memory management. Since application of many of them requires an in-depth understanding of host—accelerator interactions, only a small subset of the available interfaces is discussed below.

Since the actual OpenACC implementations may conform to different revisions of the specification, one of the macros provided by the OpenACC library may be used to test for the provided functionality. It is called _OPENACC and expands to a six-digit decimal string in which the first four digits denote the year and the remaining two the month of the specification release date the library is based on. The _OPENACC macro may be used to enable conditional compilation of code segments that rely on more recently introduced features.

The OpenACC library definitions comprise prototypes of runtime functions and internal data types used by the library that specifically describe runtime function arguments and enumerations that identify accelerator types or variants of asynchronous request queue management. The commonly used runtime calls include:

```
int acc_get_num_devices(acc_device_t devtype);
```

This returns the number of attached accelerator devices of the type specified by devtype. It must not be used inside parallel regions offloaded to an accelerator. Even though symbolic identifiers describing permitted devtype values may depend on the actual implementation, the standard recommends the following:

- acc_device_nvidia for Nvidia GPUs.
- acc_device_radeon for AMD GPUs.
- acc_device_xeonphi for Intel Xeon Phi processors.

```
acc_device_t acc_get_device_type();
```

This indicates the device type currently set as the target accelerator. It may return acc_device_none if the accelerator device has not been selected. Similar to acc_get_num_devices, it may not be called inside the accelerator region.

```
void acc_set_device_type(acc_device_t devtype);\
```

This sets the type of device to be used as an accelerator for parallel regions of code. The device type is indicated by the input argument. Calling this function may result in undefined behavior (including program abort) if the devices of the requested type are not available or if the program was not compiled to support execution on the specified accelerator type. This function may not be called inside the accelerated region of code.

```
int acc_get_device_num(acc_device_t devtype);
```

This function returns the number (index) of the accelerator device of the specified type that will be used by the current thread to offload the parallel computations. As before, it may not be called inside the code region to be executed on the accelerator.

```
void acc_set_device_num(int n, acc_device_t devtype);
```

This defines which accelerator device of a specified type may be used to execute parallel regions by the current thread. If the value of n is negative, the implementation will select a default accelerator device. If devtype is zero, the specified number will be assumed for all attached accelerator types. Function execution may result in undefined behavior if n is greater than or equal to the number of devices available of the indicated type. acc_set_device_num may not be called from within the accelerated code region.

Example:

```
001 #include <stdio.h>
002 #include <openacc.h>
003
004 int main() {
005   printf("Supported OpenACC revision: %d.\n", _OPENACC);
006
007   int count = acc_get_num_devices(acc_device_nvidia);
008   printf("Found %d Nvidia GPUs.\n", count);
009   int n = acc_get_device_num(acc_device_nvidia);
010   printf("Default accelerator number is %d.\n", n);
011
012   return 0;
013 }
```

CODE 17.2

Example code illustrating the use of the OpenACC library functions.

The example program shown in Code 17.2 invokes several library functions and has been compiled to run on an HPE Cray EX supercomputer containing AMD EPYC 7742 CPUs and Nvidia Ada GPUs. Launching it on a node equipped with a single GPU prints the following:

```
Supported OpenACC revision: 201711.
Found 1 Nvidia GPU(s).
Default accelerator number is 0.
```

The retrieved release date is November 2017, which corresponds to OpenACC specification revision 2.6. All of the following code examples presented in this chapter were executed in the same environment.

17.6 Directives

The primary method of controlling the parallel execution of OpenACC programs is achieved through *directives* interspersed within the source code of the program. In C and C++, the directives have the following format:

```
#pragma acc directive-name [clause-list]
```

Each directive line must be terminated with a newline character. The initial # may be optionally preceded and followed by a white space. Note that the remainder of the directive (shown above in italics) is subjected to standard conventions governing C and C++ programs, such as macro substitution. It also means that it is case sensitive.

The following sections will use the same syntax format as presented above. The required literals are entered in boldface, while symbolic names referring to various components of a directive are italicized. Optional syntax components are placed inside square brackets.

17.6.1 Parallel Construct

The `parallel` directive is used to identify parallel execution regions. When the flow control in the program reaches the parallel directive, it creates one or more gangs to execute the following code region. The number of gangs, workers per gang, and vector lanes per worker remain constant throughout the execution of the parallel region. Initially, all gangs begin the execution of the specified code in a gang-redundant mode, unless changed by the appropriate clause (see below). By default, the parallel execution is terminated by an implicit barrier at the end of the region, thus blocking the execution of the next segment of the program until all work in the parallel region is finished. Note that code inside the parallel region may not branch out or be entered as a result of an external branch. The syntax of the `parallel` construct is as follows:

```
#pragma acc parallel [clause-list]
structured-block
```

The structured-block is typically a curly brace-delimited section of the code that effectively determines the scope of the parallel region, but it could also be a single statement, such as a loop as shown in Code 17.3. The clause-list includes async, wait, num_gangs, num_workers, vector_length, device_type, if, self, reduction, copy, copyin, copyout, create, no_create, present, deviceptr, attach, private, firstprivate, and default.

```
001 #include <stdio.h>
002 #include <time.h>
003
004 const int N = 1000;
005
006 int main() {
007    int vec[N];
008    int cpu_sum = 0, gpu_sum = 0;
009
010    // initialization
011    for (int i = 0; i < N; i++) vec[i] = i+1;
012
013    printf("gpu begins computation at : %lu", clock());
014    #pragma acc parallel
015    for (int i = 100; i < N; i++) gpu_sum += vec[i];
016
017    printf("cpu begins computation at : %lu", clock());
018    // the following code executes after waiting for GPU result
019    for (int i = 0; i < 100; i++) cpu_sum += vec[i];
020
021    printf("Result: %d (expected: %d)\n", gpu_sum+cpu_sum, (N+1)*N/2);
022
023    return 0;
024 }
```

CODE 17.3

An example of a parallel construct.

The example application listed in Code 17.3 sums all components of a 1000-element vector, where the latter 900 are offloaded to a GPU. The offloading occurs at line 14, where the directive executes the loop in parallel on the device. The parallel directive allows the user to precisely define the way in which the affected workload is parallelized, but by default it is not going to parallelize anything (the execution is started in GR mode). As there are no additional parallelization clauses (discussed below) specified in line 14, the compute region in line 15 is not going to be vectorized. Since the code doesn't use any OpenACC library calls or macros, it is not necessary to include the OpenACC header file. The program produces the following output:

```
gpu begins computation at : 8070
cpu begins computation at : 351362
Result: 500500 (expected: 500500)
```

However, the CPU waits for the GPU to sum the last 900 elements before it can start summing up the first 100.

Some of the most often used clauses in the parallel construct include:

- async[(*integer-expression*)]
  This removes the synchronization barrier at the end of the parallel region, permitting the host processor to execute the nonaccelerated code concurrently

with the offloaded parallel computations. Optionally, it may be paired with a nonnegative integer-valued argument that is later used in a corresponding `wait` clause (or directive) to make sure the host control thread blocks until the specific asynchronous computation is completed. The number can be thought of as the number of activity queues to which the workload is submitted. Therefore, two regions with async clauses having the same argument will be executed in order on the accelerator.

- `wait[(integer-expression-list)]`
  This blocks the current host thread until the asynchronous workload units indicated by the argument values have been completed. The specified numbers should match the arguments passed to `async` clauses. If no arguments are listed, the control thread blocks until all submitted asynchronous work has been executed.

- `num_gangs(integer-expression)`
  The `num_gangs` clause is used to explicitly specify the number of gangs the workload is distributed across. If absent, an implementation-specific default is used. Note that restrictions imposed by the target architecture may cause the implementation to choose a lower number of gangs than requested.

Note:

OpenACC exposes three levels of parallelism:
1. Gang: Gang parallelism is coarse grained. A number of gangs are launched on the accelerator. Gangs are organized in one-, two-, and three-dimensional grids.
2. Workers: Worker parallelism is fine grained. Each gang has one or more workers.
3. Vector: Vector parallelism is for SIMD operations within a worker.

When an execution starts on a device, one or more gangs are launched with one or more workers with one or more vector lanes. The computation starts in GR mode, where one worker in each gang is executing the same code redundantly. Each gang has a dimension and is denoted GR1, GR2, or GR3. When the control reaches a loop marked with gang-level work sharing, the program starts executing in GP mode for that particular dimension and is denoted GP1, GP2, or GP3. Here, the iterations of the loop or loops are partitioned across gangs in the respective dimension for truly parallel execution but still with one worker per gang and one vector lane per worker active. The program may be in different gang modes for different dimensions.

Similarly, when only one worker is active in any gang-level execution mode, the program is in WS mode. If a program reaches a loop marked with worker-level work sharing, the gang transitions to WP mode, activating all workers of the gang. If any worker reaches a loop marked with vector-level work sharing, the worker transitions to VP mode, activating all the vector lanes.

- num_workers(*integer-expression*)
  Analogously to num_gangs, this clause requests a specific number of workers per gang, which is used for execution of a parallel workload in WP mode. The default number of workers is chosen if not specified, in which case it is not guaranteed to be consistent between different parallel regions (marked by the parallel or kernel directives) invoked by the program. As mentioned above, the particular implementation may modify the number of workers due to architectural constraints.
- vector_length(*integer-expression*)
  This requests a specific number of vector lanes to be assigned for each worker for code segments annotated by the vector clause with loop directive (discussed later). Due to the arrangement of execution resources, the implementation is free to choose a value that better matches hardware specifications.

In addition to these, data management clauses may be present and will be discussed in Section 17.6.3.

Example:

```
001 #include <stdio.h>
002
003 const int N = 1000;
004
005 int main() {
006    int vec[N];
007    int cpu_sum = 0, gpu_sum = 0;
008
009    // initialization
010    for (int i = 0; i < N; i++) vec[i] = i+1;
011
012    #pragma acc parallel async
013    for (int i = 100; i < N; i++) gpu_sum += vec[i];
014
015    // the following code executes without waiting for GPU result
016    for (int i = 0; i < 100; i++) cpu_sum += vec[i];
017
018    // synchronize and verify results
019    #pragma acc wait
020    printf("Result: %d (expected: %d)\n", gpu_sum+cpu_sum, (N+1)*N/2);
021
022    return 0;
023 }
```

CODE 17.4

Example of concurrent GPU and CPU execution triggered by the async clause.

The example application listed in Code 17.4 sums all components of a 1000-element vector. The first 100 elements are added on a CPU, while the GPU asynchronously sums the remaining 900 numbers at the same time. The synchronization with GPU is achieved in line 19 preceding the result output. It uses directly a `wait` directive and not a `wait` clause on the `parallel` directive, since the latter would require executable workload to be specified. That way, the `printf` statement immediately following in line 20 is executed by the host. The `parallel` directive allows the user to precisely define the way in which the affected workload is parallelized, but by default it is not going to parallelize. As there are no additional parallelization clauses specified in line 12, the compute region in line 13 is not going to be vectorized. Since the code doesn't use any OpenACC library calls or macros, it is not necessary to include the OpenACC header file. The program produces the following output:

```
Result: 500500 (expected: 500500)
```

More details and examples on different clauses on the parallel construct can be found in OpenACC specification: https://www.openacc.org/specification.

17.6.2 Kernels Construct

The compiler encountering the `kernels` directive performs the analysis of a marked section of the code and converts it into a sequence of parallel kernels that will be executed in order on the accelerator device. The number of gangs and workers and vector size may be different for each such kernel. The workload subdivision is typically performed in a way that creates one kernel for each loop nest present in the code. The primary difference between the `kernels` construct and the `parallel` directive is that the latter relies on the programmer to configure various parameters that divide the workload across accelerated execution resources. Therefore, the use of the `kernels` directive is recommended for beginners to OpenACC programming; however, it may not always yield the best-performing code. Its syntax is shown below:

```
#pragma acc kernels [clause-list]
    structured-block
```

The `kernels` construct accepts `async` and `wait` clauses that behave as described for the `parallel` clause, as well as data management clauses discussed further in Section 17.7. Similar restrictions to those of the parallel directive apply: the code may not branch out or into the accelerated region.

Example:

```
001 #include <stdio.h>
002 #include <stdlib.h>
003
004 const int N = 500;
005
006 int main() {
007    // initialize triangular matrix
008    double m[N][N];
009    for (int i = 0; i < N; i++)
010      for (int j = 0; j < N; j++)
011        m[i][j] = (i > j)? 0: 1.0;
012
013    // initialize input vector to all ones
014    double v[N];
015    for (int i = 0; i < N; i++) v[i] = 1.0;
016
017    // initialize result vector
018    double b[N];
019    for (int i = 0; i < N; i++) b[i] = 0;
020
021    // multiply in parallel
022    #pragma acc kernels
023    for (int i = 0; i < N; i++)
024      for (int j = 0; j < N; j++)
025        b[i] += m[i][j]*v[j];
026
027    // verify result
028    double r = 0;
029    for (int i = 0; i < N; i++) r += b[i];
030    printf("Result: %f (expected %f)\n", r, (N+1)*N/2.0);
031
032    return 0;
033 }
```

CODE 17.5

Accelerated matrix—vector multiply using `kernels` directive.

The program listed in Code 17.5 performs multiplication of a matrix and a vector, the dimensions of which are known at compile time and fixed. The accelerated region of the code follows the kernels directive in line 22 and contains a loop nest: the outer loop iterates over matrix rows (index i) and the inner loop over the columns (index j). Unlike Code 17.4, the execution of the parallel region is synchronous (there is no `async` clause), meaning the program won't proceed to the result verification until the accelerated kernel computation is finished. The result of program execution is shown below:

```
Result: 125250.000000 (expected 125250.000000)
```

For more directives, look at Chapter 2 of the OpenACC specification version 3.3 (https://www.openacc.org/sites/default/files/inline-images/Specification/OpenACC-3.3-final.pdf).

17.7 Data Movement Commands

The resultant speedup of an accelerated program strongly depends on the efficiency of data transfers between the host and accelerator memories. In some cases, such as for AMD accelerated processing units, the accelerator shares the address space with the host processor. The overheads of communicating the data structures between the two components are minimal, as they are simply accomplished through pointer passing without any explicit data copies. If an accelerator needs to perform computation on certain elements of a data array, it only has to compute the resulting address of the data element based on the supplied pointer value, element index, and data type and dereference it (fetch the desired element from memory), just like the host processor would. Unfortunately, many accelerator devices utilized in current supercomputing installations feature separate memory modules that necessitate explicit data transfers. Ideally, such transfers would be orchestrated without involving any unnecessary data or even entirely avoiding communication when not required. The first case is apparent when performing computation only on a subset of array or vector elements; copying the entire structure would only increase the latency data offload. The second scenario may arise when a dataset produced as a result of GPU computation overwrites the contents of an array originally created on the host. Copying the initial state of such an array to GPU before performing the accelerated computation is obviously unnecessary.

Unfortunately, due to the complexity of C and C++ code, static analysis of data access patterns by the compiler cannot always determine with certainty which portions of the affected data structures should be offloaded to the accelerator. OpenACC by default chooses correctness over efficiency and performs full bidirectional copies, i.e., transfer of the initial state of all involved data structures to the device before initiating accelerated computations and copying back the possibly updated state of involved datasets after the accelerated region's execution completes. Note that this is supported implicitly only when the dimensions of the involved arrays are known at compile time; for dynamically allocated arrays or arrays that are passed by the pointer, it is a good idea to explicitly specify the ranges of data that should be offloaded to avoid potential out-of-bound access errors during runtime. OpenACC implementations may further optimize (or even avoid) the data transfers if the accelerator is capable of accessing the host memory directly.

OpenACC provides the following data clauses that can appear in different constructs (parallel, serial, kernel, or data) and directives (enter, exit, or declare) to control data copying between the host and accelerator memories:

- copy(*variable-list*)
  This performs data copies upon entry to and exit from the parallel region. First, for each variable specified in the variable list, the runtime system checks if the required data exist in the accelerator memory. If so, its reference count is incremented. Otherwise, a sufficient accelerator memory is allocated and a data copy from the host memory to the allocated memory is arranged. The

corresponding reference count for the data structure is set to one. On exit from the parallel region, the reference count is decremented. If it reaches zero, the corresponding data are copied back to the host memory and the allocated memory segment on the accelerator is deallocated.

- copyin(*variable-list*)
  This performs data copies upon entry to the parallel region. It behaves as a one-directional version of the copy clause. All operations specified for region entry in the copy clause are executed without modification. However, on exit from the parallel region, the reference counts for all data structures specified in the variable list are decremented. If the count for a specific variable reaches zero, the corresponding device memory is deallocated, but no data transfer to the host memory takes place.

- copyout(*variable-list*)
  This performs data copies upon exit from the parallel region. The copyout clause may be viewed as a complement of the copyin clause. Upon entry to the parallel region, if the data are already present in the accelerator memory, their reference counter is incremented. If not, the sufficient memory segment is allocated in the device memory and the reference count for it is set to one. The allocated memory is not initialized (and no data transfer takes place).
  Upon exit, the reference count for the involved data structures is decremented. If it reaches zero, the data are copied back to the host memory and the corresponding memory segment on the device is deallocated.

- create(*variable-list*)
  This creates a data structure on the accelerator to be used by local computation. The create clause never transfers any data between the host and accelerator memory. When the affected parallel region is entered and the data structure already exists in the device memory, the runtime increments the reference counter. Otherwise, a suitable amount of device memory will be allocated with the reference count set to one. On exit, the reference count is decremented, and if it reaches zero, the corresponding memory is deallocated.

The *variable-list* specifier accompanying the clauses listed above contains identifiers of program variables that are subjected to data copy operations. The identifiers are separated by a comma (","). They may be optionally followed by range specification consisting of a pair of square brackets per dimension, each enclosing the index range specification. The index range consists of two integer expressions separated by a colon (":"), with the first integer value denoting the starting index and the second value indicating the length (number of contiguous elements per dimension). If the first number is omitted, zero is assumed. The second number may be omitted if the size of the array is known at compile time and implies that the full dimension is used. Thus, a[5:t] describes the range of elements of vector a starting at index 5 and containing t elements, i.e., the sequence a[5], a[6], ..., a[5+t-1]. Analogously, mat[:N][16:32] refers to a rectangular segment of the array mat that comprises 32-element-long fragments of its first N rows. Each such fragment starts at index 16. The entire dataset thus includes N × 32 array elements.

Thanks to compiler support, OpenACC supports several different ways in which arrays may be defined in C and C++ programs. They include:

1. Statically allocated arrays with fixed bounds, such as:

```
int cnt[4][500];
```

One important restriction related to specifying the data transfer range for statically allocated arrays is that it must identify a contiguous chunk of memory. Only the range specifier for the first dimension may describe a subset of elements, while the specifiers for the remaining dimensions must identify full bounds. Therefore, for the declaration above, `cnt[2:2][:500]` (the last two rows of the matrix cnt) is legal, whereas `cnt[:4][0:100]` (the first 100 columns of the matrix cnt) is not.

2. Pointers to fixed-bound arrays:

```
typedef double vec[1000];
vec *v1;
```

3. Statically allocated array of pointers:

```
float *farray[500];
```

4. Pointer to array of pointers:

```
double **dmat;
```

Multidimensional array definitions may include mixed declarations involving static bounds and pointers. To correctly follow the range specification constraints in a general case, it may be helpful to realize that the runtime system will mirror the organization of the source data structures from the host on the accelerator, allocating pointers where necessary and filling in their values. Once the data structures are defined, modification of the embedded pointers on the host or device is discouraged.

Example:

```
001 #include <stdio.h>
002 #include <stdlib.h>
003
004 int main(int argc, char **argv) {
005   unsigned N = 1024;
006   if (argc > 1) N = strtoul(argv[1], 0, 10);
007
008   // create triangular matrix
009   double **restrict m = malloc(N*sizeof(double *));
010   for (int i = 0; i < N; i++)
011   {
012     m[i] = malloc(N*sizeof(double));
013     for (int j = 0; j < N; j++)
014       m[i][j] = (i > j)? 0: 1.0;
015   }
016
017   // create vector filled with ones
018   double *restrict v = malloc(N*sizeof(double));
019   for (int i = 0; i < N; i++) v[i] = 1.0;
020
021   // create result vector
022   double *restrict b = malloc(N*sizeof(double));
023
024   // multiply in parallel
025   #pragma acc kernels copyin(m[:N][:N], v[:N]) copyout(b[:N])
026   for (int i = 0; i < N; i++)
027   {
028     b[i] = 0;
029     for (int j = 0; j < N; j++)
030       b[i] += m[i][j]*v[j];
031   }
032
033   // verify result
034   double r = 0;
035   for (int i = 0; i < N; i++) r += b[i];
036   printf("Result: %f (expected %f)\n", r, (N+1)*N/2.0);
037
038   return 0;
039 }
```

CODE 17.6

OpenACC matrix–vector multiply with improved data transfers.

To demonstrate the application of improved data management techniques to Code 17.5, it has been rewritten to support dynamically allocated arrays storing the main matrix data and input and output vectors. The result is listed in Code 17.6. The size of the involved arrays may be defined (within reason) on the command line. To preserve the double-index notation when accessing the elements of matrix m, rather than flattening it to a vector, it has been declared as a pointer to a vector of pointers to dynamically allocated rows (this corresponds to scenario 4 described above). The pointers are declared with the restrict attribute telling the compiler that it should not expect pointer aliasing and potentially leading to a better optimized code. Since both the input matrix m and vector v are not modified by the computation, they are declared in the copyin clause. Vector b does not need to be initialized from host memory, since its entire content is overwritten by computation. It is therefore declared as a copyout variable. Since the accelerator can easily zero out individual elements of b before accumulating partial dot product values into it, this part of the computation has been explicitly moved to the accelerated region. We can see this behavior at compile time using the compilation flags as follows:

```
> nvc -Minfo=accel -acc=gpu code6.c
main:
      22. Generating copyout(b[:N]) [if not already present]
          Generating copyin(v[:N],m[:N][:N]) [if not already
present]
      26. Loop is parallelizable
          Generating Tesla code
          26. #pragma acc loop gang, vector(128) /* blockIdx.x
threadIdx.x */
          29. #pragma acc loop seq
      29. Complex loop carried dependence of b-> prevents
parallelization
          Loop carried dependence of b-> prevents parallelization
          Loop carried backward dependence of b-> prevents
vectorization
          Inner sequential loop scheduled on accelerator
```

Running the program with argument 2000 yields:

```
Result: 2001000.000000 (expected 2001000.000000)
```

17.8 Variable Scope

It should be apparent at this point that the OpenACC treatment of variables participating in the computation varies depending on whether they are loop indices or data structures and where they are declared in the code. Loop variables are considered private to each thread that executes loop iterations. Variables declared in a block of code that is marked for execution in vector-partitioned mode are private to the thread that is associated with each vector lane. For code executed in worker-partitioned, vector-single mode, the variables are private to each worker but shared across vector lanes associated with that worker. Similarly, variables declared in a block marked for worker-single mode are private to the containing gang but shared across the threads operating at the worker and vector levels in that gang.

OpenACC defines a `private` clause that may be used to further restrict the sharing of variables. It may be declared alongside the `parallel` or `loop` directive and accepts a list of variable names as argument. In the first case, a copy of each variable in the list is generated for each parallel gang. In the loop context, a copy of each variable is created for each thread associated with each vector lane (vector-partitioned mode). In vector-single, worker-partitioned mode, a copy of every item in the list will be created and shared for each set of threads associated with vector lanes in each worker. Otherwise, a variable copy is created and shared across all vector lanes of every worker in each gang. A `firstprivate` variant of the `private` clause is also available for the `parallel` directive with the same access semantics, except the variable copies are additionally initialized to the value of these variables inherent to the first thread encountering the `parallel` construct during the code execution.

17.9 Synchronization Commands

Parallelization of code across multiple execution resources on occasion calls for synchronization of accesses to some data structures that should be carried out in a predefined order. This is enforced by the `atomic` construct with syntax described below:

```
#pragma acc atomic [atomic-clause]
        statement;
```

Supported atomic clauses include `read`, `write`, `update`, and `capture` depending on the type of access synchronization. If absent, an `update` clause is assumed. The `read` clause is used to force atomic access to variables on the right-hand side of the equals sign in the assignment statement. Analogously, the `write` clause protects writes to variables on the left-hand side of the equals sign in assignments. The `update` clause enforces correct updates of values of variables that have to be performed using the read—modify—write sequence of operations. Their examples include prefix and postfix increment and decrement operators as well as updates in the form of *op=*, where *op* is a binary operator such as +, -, *, etc. The `capture` clause refers to assignment statements in which the right-hand side is an atomic update expression, such as the one described for the `update` clause, while the left-hand side is a variable that is supposed to capture the original or final value of the atomically modified variable (depending on the operation type).

Example:

```
001 #include <stdio.h>
002
003 int main(int argc, char **argv) {
004   if (argc == 1) {
005     fprintf(stderr, "Error: file argument neede!\n");
006     exit(1);
007   }
008   FILE *f = fopen(argv[1], "r");
009   if (!f) {
010     fprintf(stderr, "Error: could not open file \"%s\"\n", argv[1]);
011     exit(1);
012   }
013
014   const int BUFSIZE = 65536;
015   char buf[BUFSIZE], ch;
016   // initialize histogram array
017   int hist[256], most = -1;
018   for (int i = 0; i < 256; i++) hist[i] = 0;
019
020   // compute histogram
021   while (1) {
022     size_t size = fread(buf, 1, BUFSIZE, f);
023     if (size <= 0) break;
024     #pragma acc parallel loop copyin(buf[:size])
025       for (int i = 0; i < size; i++) {
026         int v = buf[i];
027         #pragma acc atomic
028         hist[v]++;
029     }
030   }
031   // print the first highest peak
032   for (int i = 0; i < 256; i++)
033     if (hist[i] > most) {
034       most = hist[i]; ch = i;
035   }
036   printf("Highest count of %d for character code %d\n", most, ch);
037
038   return 0;
039 }
```

CODE 17.7

Program showing the application of the `atomic` clause.

The program presented in Code 17.7 calculates a histogram of ASCII character occurrences in a file given as the command-line argument. The `atomic` directive in line 27 (implied `update` clause) ensures the correct increment of the histogram bin for a specific character. Running the code for the file containing the first paragraph of the "lorem ipsum" text nullN produces:

```
Highest count of 68 for character code 32
```

17.10 **Parallel Loops**

The `loop` directive is one of the fundamental OpenACC constructs responsible for identifying and fine-tuning the parallelization of accelerated workloads. It may be specified either as a separate directive:

```
#pragma acc loop [clause-list]
        for (...)
```

or as a clause combined with a parent `parallel` or `kernels` directive. In any case, it applies to the for-loop immediately following the clause or directive. The available loop control clauses include:

- `collapse(integer-expr)`
  This specifies how many nested loop levels indicated by the argument value are affected by the scheduling clauses present in the directive. Normally, only the nearest loop following the directive is considered. The argument must evaluate to a positive integer.
- `gang`
- `gang([num:] integer-expr [, integer-expr...] )`
- `gang(static:integer-expr)`
- `gang(static:*)`
  This distributes iterations of the affected loop(s) across gangs created by the parent `parallel` or `kernels` directive.
  When used with the `parallel` construct, the number of gangs is determined by the parent directive; hence, only the static argument is permitted in one of two forms listed above. It indicates the *chunk* size, that is, a count of loop iterations that is used as a unit of workload assignment. Chunks are assigned to gangs in a round-robin fashion. If the last form of gang specification is used, chunk size is determined by implementation. It should be stressed that for correct results, loop iterations must be data independent (except for the reduction clause described below), since the compiler is not going to perform the full code analysis, as when using the `kernels` directive.
  If the `loop` clause is associated with the `kernels` construct, all forms are permitted with some restrictions. The first two variants may be specified only if `num_gangs` does not appear in the parent `kernels` construct. If used with a numeric argument, it specifies the number of gangs to be used for parallel execution of the loop. The meaning of the static argument is as described above for the `parallel` construct.
- `worker`
- `worker([num:]integer-expr)`
  This causes the loop iterations to be distributed across the workers in a gang. When used with the `parallel` construct, only the first form is allowed. It causes the gang to switch to the worker-partitioned execution. The loop iterations must be data independent.
  When the parent directive is `kernels`, the form with an argument may be used only if `num_workers` was not specified in the parent construct. The expression must evaluate to a positive integer that indicates the number of workers per gang to be used.

- vector
- vector([length:]*integer-expr*)

  This enables execution of loop iterations in vector or SIMD mode. The conditions of use are analogous to those of the worker clause, except they apply to vector-level parallelism.

- auto

  This forces analysis of data dependencies in the loop to determine whether it can be parallelized. It is implied in every kernel directive that does not contain the independent clause.

- independent

  This instructs the compiler to treat the loop iterations as data independent, thus enabling more possibilities for parallelization. It is implied for all parallel directives that do not specify auto clauses.

- reduction(*operator* : *variable*[,*variable*...])

  The reduction clause marks one or more of the specified variables as a participant in the reduction operation performed at the end of the loop. The variable may not be an array element or a structure member. The supported operators include +, *, max, min, &, |, &&, and || for sum, product, maximum, minimum, bitwise-and, bitwise-or, logical-and, and logical-or, respectively.

Example:

```
001 #include <stdio.h>
002 #include <stdlib.h>
003
004 const int N = 10000;
005
006 int main() {
007   double x[N], y[N];
008   double a = 2.0, r = 0.0;
009
010   #pragma acc kernels
011   {
012     // initialize the vectors
013     #pragma acc loop gang worker
014     for (int i = 0; i < N; i++) {
015       x[i] = 1.0;
016       y[i] = -1.0;
017     }
018
019     // perform computation
020     #pragma acc loop independent reduction(+:r)
021     for (int i = 0; i < N; i++) {
022       y[i] = a*x[i]+y[i];
023       r += y[i];
024     }
025   }
026
027   // print result
028   printf("Result: %f (expected %f)\n", r, (float)N);
029
030   return 0;
031 }
```

CODE 17.8

Program using the loop directive with parallelism and reduction clauses.

The program listed in Code 17.8 showcases the use of the `loop` directive to perform accelerated vector scaling and accumulation reminiscent of the LAPACK *daxpy* routine. For demonstration purposes, the initialization code has also been moved to the accelerator. It requests parallelization in WP mode with the default number of gangs and workers. The parallelization parameters of the computational loop are left to the discretion of the implementation. The loop is explicitly marked as data independent to promote this and avoid the compiler analysis that would be performed by default for the `kernels` construct (less sophisticated compilers may interpret the update of `y[i]` as data dependence). To verify the correctness of the result, a reduction clause is used that sums all elements of the result vector `y` into variable `r`. The generated output is printed below:

```
Result: 10000.000000 (expected 10000.000000)
```

17.11 Summary and Outcomes

- There are several programming environments for accelerators that differ in approach, scope, supported features, and availability. The most commonly used include CUDA, OpenCL, OpenACC, and C++ AMP.
- OpenACC is a GPU and accelerator programming framework that attempts to simplify parallel programming and achieve better programmability by using a directive-based approach similar to OpenMP. It requires a specialized compiler capable of generating executable accelerator code following the static analysis of appropriately marked source code. Compilers with OpenACC support are available from Nvidia, Cray, and several open-source communities (OpenUH, OpenARC, GCC).
- The main method of identifying potential parallel execution regions is through addition of suitable "`#pragma acc`" directives in the relevant places in the source code. In addition to directives, the execution of programs is affected by predefined library calls and environment variables.
- OpenACC programs rely on the host machine to initiate the program computations and offload the data and executable code to the accelerator at appropriate times. Accelerated code execution is by default synchronized with the execution of the nonaccelerated sections of the program on the host machine. Additional speedup may be obtained by asynchronously coscheduling computations on the GPU with computations on the host processor.
- Performance gains in regions executed on the accelerator are realized through parallelization at three levels: gang, worker, and vector (from the coarsest to the finest grain). The programmer retains control of parameters influencing each level, although he/she may also select implementation defaults.

- There are two main compute directives: "`parallel`" and "`kernels`". The first foregoes much of the correctness analysis of the source code, relying on the programmer to verify data independence between concurrently executing accelerator threads. The second performs thorough static analysis of the code and enables vectorization and parallel execution only if it is safe to do so.
- Distribution of regular and nested loop iterations across the accelerated execution resources is one of the primary methods of increasing application performance gains. It is controlled by the `loop` clause. The loop clause also supports an accelerated set of reduction operations.
- Overall application performance depends on the efficiency of data transfers between the accelerator and host memory. OpenACC supports additional control clauses to optimize this aspect of execution (`copy`, `copyin`, `copyout`, `create`).

OpenACC provides simple mechanisms for synchronization of accesses to critical variables from multiple accelerator threads to ensure the correctness of program execution. Four modes of atomic access are supported: `read`, `write`, `update`, and `capture`.

17.12 **Questions and Problems**

1. Characterize directive-based programming. How does it differ from using functionality provided by software libraries?

2. Write an OpenACC program to compute the approximation of the natural logarithm of 2 using the first 10,000,000 terms of Maclaurin expansion:

$$\ln(1 + x) = x - \frac{1}{2}x^2 + \frac{1}{3}x^3 - \frac{1}{4}x^4 + \dots$$

Make sure the generated accelerator code is parallelized.

3. Modify Code 17.7 to compute the frequency of alphabetic digraph (two-letter sequence) occurrence in a block of text. Ignore case sensitivity.

4. Write a simple OpenACC program that computes the average value of elements occupying the lower triangular part (i.e., all elements on and below the main diagonal) of a large square matrix. Is it possible to optimize the program so that:

a) efficiency of data transfers is improved (by avoiding copying data not used by computation)?

b) the work performed in each iteration is balanced across GPU threads?

Implement optimizations that are possible. How do they affect performance? Test several different matrix sizes.

5. To debug an OpenACC program, the irrelevant portions of the code were removed, yielding the following:

```
001 #include <stdio.h>
002
003 const int N = 100, M = 200;
004
005 int main() {
006    int m[N][M];
007    for (int i = 0; i < N; i++)
008      for (int j = 0; j < M; j++)
009        m[i][j] = 1;
010
011    #pragma acc kernels
012    for (int i = 0; i < N; i++)
013      for (int j = M-i; j < M; j++)
014        m[i][j] = i+j+1;
015
016    // verify result
017    int errcnt = 0;
018    for (int i = 0; i < N; i++)
019      for (int j = 0; j < M; j++) {
020        int expect = (j >= M-i)? i+j+1: 1;
021        if (m[i][j] != expect) errcnt++;
022      }
023    printf("Encountered %d errors\n", errcnt);
024    return errcnt != 0;
025 }
```

The code fails (produces nonzero error count) when compiled with certain OpenACC compilers. What may be the reason for that? How may the errors be prevented?

References

[NaN] Khronos Group, OpenGL: The Industry's Foundation for High Performance Graphics. Version 4.6, 2023. https://www.khronos.org/api/opengl. (Accessed 28 November 2023).

[NaN] Khronos Group, Khronos OpenCL Registry: OpenCL 3.0 Unified Specifications. Version 3.0, 2023. https://registry.khronos.org/OpenCL/. (Accessed 28 November 2023).

[NaN] E.S. Larsen, D. McAllister, Fast matrix multiplies using graphics hardware, SC '01: Proceedings of the 2001 ACM/IEEE Conference on Supercomputing (2001), https://doi.org/10.1145/582034.582089.

[NaN] S. Lee, J.S. Vetter, OpenARC: Extensible OpenACC compiler framework for directive-based accelerator programming study, WACCPD: Workshop on Accelerator Programming Using Directives in Conjunction with SC'14 (2014), https://doi.org/10.1109/WACCPD.2014.7.

[NaN] Lorem Ipsum Generator. https://loremipsum.io/generator/. (Accessed 28 November 2023).

[NaN]   Microsoft Corporation, C++ AMP: Language and Programming Model, 2012. https://download.microsoft.com/download/4/0/e/40ea02d8-23a7-4bd2-ad3a-0bfffb640f28/cppamplanguageandprogrammingmodel.pdf. (Accessed 28 November 2023).

[NaN]   Microsoft Corporation, Getting Started with DirectX Graphics, 2012. https://learn.microsoft.com/en-us/windows/win32/getting-started-with-directx-graphics. (Accessed 28 November 2023).

[NaN]   Nvidia Corporation, CUDA Toolkit Documentation 12.3 Update 1, 2023. https://docs.nvidia.com/cuda/index.html. (Accessed 28 November 2023).

[NaN]   OpenUH - Open Source UH Compiler (Source Repository), 2017. https://github.com/uhhpctools/openuh. (Accessed 28 November 2023).

[NaN]   OpenACC-Standard.org, The OpenACC Application Programming Interface. Version 3.3, 2022. https://www.openacc.org/sites/default/files/inline-images/Specification/OpenACC-3.3-final.pdf. (Accessed 28 November 2023).

Examples of GPU Programs

18

Chapter outline

Applications leveraging graphics processing unit (GPU) devices in a high performance computing system may utilize a vendor programming model like NVIDIA's CUDA or a programming standard like OpenACC to take advantage of the GPU resource. For users running machine learning training on a GPU, the explicit GPU programming is mostly hidden from the user by the machine learning framework being used. For users running linear algebra computations on GPUs, vendor-provided BLAS libraries like cuBLAS simplify utilizing a GPU workflow. This chapter will provide two examples of GPU programs: one where the GPU programming is hidden from the user and one where the GPU programming is explicit. The CUDA programming model will be used in the explicit example. To get started, here is a quick test to ensure that CUDA has been installed properly on your system:

```
1 #include <stdio.h>
2 #include <assert.h>
3
4 int main(void)
5 {
6 // Print device and precision
7 cudaDeviceProp prop;
8 cudaGetDeviceProperties(&prop, 0);
9 printf("\nDevice Name: %s\n", prop.name);
10 printf("Compute Capability: %d.%d\n\n", prop.major, prop.minor);
11
12 return 0;
13 }
```

This example, test.cu, can be compiled using the nvcc compiler as follows:

```
nvcc test.cu -o test
```

High Performance Computing. https://doi.org/10.1016/B978-0-12-823035-0.00018-3

Running the executable will produce output indicating the type of GPU and compute capability for the device, e.g.:

```
./test
Device Name: NVIDIA A10
Compute Capability: 8.6
```

To test if a machine learning framework has been built with GPU support, the following commands can be executed in Python. For Tensorflow:

```
>>import tensorflow as tf
>> tf.test.is_gpu_available()
```

At some point is_gpu_available() is scheduled to be removed from Tensorflow; the replacement is tf.config.list_physical_devices('GPU').

For PyTorch:

```
>> import torch
>>torch.cuda.is_available()
```

A machine learning framework user can also monitor the nvidia-smi output to ensure the GPU is being used as follows:

```
$nvidia-smi
+-------------------------------------------------------------+
| NVIDIA-SMI 515.65.01   Driver Version: 515.65.01   CUDA Version: 11.7   |
|-----------------------------+----------------------+---------------+
| GPU  Name      Persistence-M| Bus-Id      Disp.A | Volatile Uncorr. ECC |
| Fan Temp Perf Pwr:Usage/Cap|      Memory-Usage | GPU-Util Compute M. |
|                 |           |       MIG M. |
|=============================+======================+===================|
| 0 NVIDIA A10       On | 00000000:06:00.0 Off |          0 |
| 0%  31C  P8  19W / 150W|    0MiB / 23028MiB |   0%       Default |
|                 |           |        N/A |
+-----------------------------+----------------------+---------------+

+-------------------------------------------------------------+
| Processes:                          |
| GPU  GI  CI   PID  Type   Process name            GPU Memory |
|   ID  ID                         Usage     |
|=============================================================|
| No running processes found                    |
+-------------------------------------------------------------+
```

18.1 cuBLAS Example

The BLAS library discussed in Chapter 6 has been implemented on top of NVIDIA's CUDA programming model for use on GPU devices. It retains the look and feel of working with the original BLAS library but is optimized for GPU execution. The original cuBLAS application programming interface requires the matrix to be stored in the GPU memory, although later versions will take care of the transfer for the user. Here is an example of a cuBLAS application multiplying the first column of a 5×5 matrix by 10.

```
1 #include <stdio.h>
2 #include <stdlib.h>
3 #include <math.h>
4 #include <cuda_runtime.h>
5 #include "cublas_v2.h"
6 #define M 5
7 #define N 5
8
9 int main (void){
10     cudaError_t cudaStat;
11     cublasStatus_t stat;
12     cublasHandle_t handle;
13     int i, j;
14     float* gpuA;
15     float* matrix_A = 0;
16     float pi = 4.0*atan(1.0);
17     matrix_A = (float *)malloc (M * N * sizeof (*matrix_A));
18     if (!matrix_A) {
19         printf ("CPU memory allocation failed");
20         return EXIT_FAILURE;
21     }
22
23     // Initialize the matrix
24     for (j = 0; j < N; j++) {
25       for (i = 0; i < M; i++) {
26          matrix_A[i + j*M] = (float) sin(0.5*pi*(i+j*M)/(M*N));
27       }
28     }
29
30     // Allocate memory on the GPU
31     cudaStat = cudaMalloc ((void**)&gpuA, M*N*sizeof(*matrix_A));
32     if (cudaStat != cudaSuccess) {
33         printf ("GPU memory allocation failed");
34         return EXIT_FAILURE;
35     }
36     stat = cublasCreate(&handle);
37     if (stat != CUBLAS_STATUS_SUCCESS) {
38         printf ("CUBLAS initialization failed\n");
39         return EXIT_FAILURE;
40     }
```

```
41
42      // Copy the matrix to the GPU memory
43      stat = cublasSetMatrix (M, N, sizeof(*matrix_A), matrix_A, M, gpuA, M);
44      if (stat != CUBLAS_STATUS_SUCCESS) {
45         printf ("problem sending matrix to GPU memory");
46         cudaFree (gpuA);
47         cublasDestroy(handle);
48         return EXIT_FAILURE;
49      }
50
51      // multiple matrix by a scalar value alpha
52      float alpha = 10.0;
53      cublasSscal (handle, N, &alpha, &gpuA[0], N);
54
55      // Copy the matrix back to the CPU memory
56      stat = cublasGetMatrix (M, N, sizeof(*matrix_A), gpuA, M, matrix_A, M);
57      if (stat != CUBLAS_STATUS_SUCCESS) {
58         printf ("problem sending matrix to CPU memory");
59         cudaFree (gpuA);
60         cublasDestroy(handle);
61         return EXIT_FAILURE;
62      }
63      cudaFree (gpuA);
64      cublasDestroy(handle);
65
66      // Print the matrix to screen
67      for (j = 0; j < N; j++) {
68        for (i = 0; i < M; i++) {
69           printf ("%f ", matrix_A[i+j*M]);
70        }
71        printf ("\n");
72      }
73      free(matrix_A);
74      return EXIT_SUCCESS;
75 }
```

The call to cublasSscal in line 53 is the GPU equivalent of calling sscal in BLAS. The matrix is initialized in line 26 and copied to the GPU memory in line 43. Once the GPU BLAS operation has completed, the matrix is copied back to central processing unit (CPU) memory in line 56 and the result is printed to screen in line 67.

The code, blas_example.c, can be compiled using the nvcc compiler as follows:

```
nvcc blas_example.cu -lcublas -o blas_example
```

The executable takes no arguments and produces this output:

```
./blas_example
0.000000 0.062791 0.125333 0.187381 0.248690
3.090170 0.368125 0.425779 0.481754 0.535827
5.877852 0.637424 0.684547 0.728969 0.770513
8.090170 0.844328 0.876307 0.904827 0.929776
9.510566 0.968583 0.982287 0.992115 0.998027
```

The first column of the matrix has been scaled by a factor of 10; the initial matrix was as follows:

```
0.000000 0.062791 0.125333 0.187381 0.248690
0.309017 0.368125 0.425779 0.481754 0.535827
0.587785 0.637424 0.684547 0.728969 0.770513
0.809017 0.844328 0.876307 0.904827 0.929776
0.951057 0.968583 0.982287 0.992115 0.998027
```

This GPU-enabled BLAS provides a straightforward way for many high performance computing applications to leverage GPU devices without having to write low-level CUDA code.

18.2 Differentiating Field Variables by Finite Difference

GPU operations are well suited for computing partial derivatives on a field variable discretized on a regularly spaced grid. In this example, the partial derivative of the function $\sin x + \sin y + \sin z$ is computed using the CUDA programming model on the GPU. The stencils used for the finite difference are as follows:

$$\frac{df}{dx} \approx \frac{1}{12dx}(f(x-2dx) - 8f(x-dx) + 8f(x+dx) - f(x+2dx))$$

$$\frac{df}{dx} \approx \frac{1}{2dx}(-f(x-dx) + f(x+dx))$$

$$\frac{df}{dx} \approx \frac{1}{2dx}(-3f(x) + 4f(x+dx) - f(x+2dx))$$

$$\frac{df}{dx} \approx \frac{1}{2dx}(f(x-2dx) - 4f(x-dx) + 3f(x))$$

The stencil chosen depends on the proximity of the grid boundary. The default stencil used is the 4-point stencil whenever possible. The example for finite difference computation on the GPU is as follows:

```
1 #include <stdio.h>
2 #include <stdlib.h>
3 #include <assert.h>
4 #include <math.h>
5
```

```
 6 typedef int Int_t ;
 7 typedef double Real_t ;
 8
 9 dim3 grid[3], block[3];
10
11 // stencil coefficients
12 __constant__ Real_t c_a1, c_b1, c_c1;
13 __constant__ Real_t c_a2, c_b2;
14 __constant__ Real_t c_a3, c_b3, c_c3, c_d3;
15 __constant__ Real_t c_a4, c_b4, c_c4;
16
17 #define cudaSafeCall(x) x;cudaCheckError()
18
19 #ifndef NDEBUG
20
21 #define cudaCheckError() {                                    \
22  cudaDeviceSynchronize();                                     \
23  cudaError_t err=cudaGetLastError();                          \
24  if(err!=cudaSuccess) {                               \
25   fprintf(stderr, "Cuda error in file '%s' in line %i : %s.\n",   \
26        __FILE__, __LINE__, cudaGetErrorString( err) );            \
27   exit(EXIT_FAILURE);                              \
28  }                                           \
29 }
30
31 #else
32
33 #define cudaCheckError() {                             \
34  cudaError_t err=cudaGetLastError();                   \
35  if(err!=cudaSuccess) {                          \
36   fprintf(stderr, "Cuda error in file '%s' in line %i : %s.\n",   \
37        __FILE__, __LINE__, cudaGetErrorString( err) );        \
38   exit(EXIT_FAILURE);                          \
39  }                                    \
40 }
41 #endif
42
43 inline
44 cudaError_t checkCuda(cudaError_t result)
45 {
46 #if defined(DEBUG) || defined(_DEBUG)
47  if (result != cudaSuccess) {
48   fprintf(stderr, "CUDA Runtime Error: %s\n", cudaGetErrorString(result));
49   assert(result == cudaSuccess);
50  }
```

```
51 #endif
52   return result;
53 }
54
55 __global__ void dd_deriv_x_(Real_t *f, Real_t *df,Int_t nx,Int_t
ny,Int_t nz) {
56
57   extern __shared__ Real_t s_f[];
58
59   Int_t i = threadIdx.x;
60   Int_t j = blockIdx.x*blockDim.y + threadIdx.y;
61   Int_t k = blockIdx.y;
62   Int_t si = i + 4;
63   Int_t sj = threadIdx.y;
64   Int_t globalIdx = k * nx * ny + j * nx + i;
65
66   Int_t lnx = nx + 8;
67
68   s_f[si + lnx*sj] = f[globalIdx];
69
70   __syncthreads();
71   if ( i == 0 ) {
72     df[globalIdx] =
73       ( c_a1 * s_f[sj*lnx+si]
74       + c_b1 * s_f[sj*lnx+si+1]
75       + c_c1 * s_f[sj*lnx+si+2] );
76   } else if ( i == 1 || i == nx-2 ) {
77     df[globalIdx] =
78       ( c_a2 * s_f[sj*lnx+si-1]
79       + c_b2 * s_f[sj*lnx+si+1] );
80   } else if ( i == nx-1 ) {
81     df[globalIdx] =
82       ( c_a4 * s_f[sj*lnx+si-2]
83       + c_b4 * s_f[sj*lnx+si-1]
84       + c_c4 * s_f[sj*lnx+si] );
85   } else {
86     df[globalIdx] =
87       ( c_a3 * s_f[sj*lnx+si-2]
88       + c_b3 * s_f[sj*lnx+si-1]
89       + c_c3 * s_f[sj*lnx+si+1]
90       + c_d3 * s_f[sj*lnx+si+2] );
91   }
92 }
93
```

```
94 Int_t main(Int_t argc,char *argv[])
95 {
96  Int_t deviceCount, dev;
97  cudaDeviceProp prop;
98
99  Int_t n = 200;
100 cudaSafeCall( cudaGetDeviceCount(&deviceCount) );
101 if (deviceCount == 0) {
102   fprintf(stderr, "no devices supporting CUDA.\n");
103   exit(1);
104 }
105 dev = 0;
106 printf("setting CUDA device %d\n",dev);
107 cudaSafeCall( cudaSetDevice(dev) );
108 cudaSafeCall( cudaGetDeviceProperties(&prop, dev) );
109 printf("\nDevice Name: %s\n", prop.name);
110 printf("Compute Capability: %d.%d\n\n", prop.major, prop.minor);
111
112 Real_t maxx = 10.0;
113 Real_t maxy = 10.0;
114 Real_t maxz = 10.0;
115 Real_t minx = -10.0;
116 Real_t miny = -10.0;
117 Real_t minz = -10.0;
118
119 Int_t nx,ny,nz,i,j,k;
120 nx = n;
121 ny = n;
122 nz = n;
123 // give a domain
124 Real_t hx = ( maxx - minx )/(nx - 1.0);
125 Real_t hy = ( maxy - miny )/(ny - 1.0);
126 Real_t hz = ( maxz - minz )/(nz - 1.0);
127 Int_t bytes = nx*ny*nz*sizeof(Real_t);
128 Real_t *sol,*dxsol;
129 sol = (Real_t *) malloc(nx*ny*nz*sizeof(Real_t));
130 dxsol = (Real_t *) malloc(nx*ny*nz*sizeof(Real_t));
131 Real_t *d_sol,*d_dxsol;
132 checkCuda( cudaMalloc((void**)&d_sol, bytes) );
133 checkCuda( cudaMalloc((void**)&d_dxsol, bytes) );
134
135 // Initial data
136 for (k=0;k<nz;k++) {
137   for (j=0;j<ny;j++) {
```

```
138    for (i=0;i<nx;i++) {
139      Real_t x = minx + i*hx;
140      Real_t y = miny + j*hy;
141      Real_t z = minz + k*hz;
142      sol[i+nx*(j+ny*k)] = sin(x) + sin(y) + sin(z);
143    }
144   }
145 }
146
147 // copy sol to device memory
148 checkCuda( cudaMemcpy(d_sol, sol, bytes, cudaMemcpyHostToDevice) );
149
150 // parameters for finite differencing
151 Real_t idx = 1.0/hx;
152 Real_t idx_by_2 = 0.5*idx;
153 Real_t idx_by_12 = idx/12.0;
154
155 Real_t a1 = Real_t(-3.0) * idx_by_2;
156 Real_t b1 = Real_t( 4.0) * idx_by_2;
157 Real_t c1 = Real_t(-1.0) * idx_by_2;
158 checkCuda( cudaMemcpyToSymbol(c_a1, &a1, sizeof(Real_t), 0,
    cudaMemcpyHostToDevice) );
159 checkCuda( cudaMemcpyToSymbol(c_b1, &b1, sizeof(Real_t), 0,
    cudaMemcpyHostToDevice) );
160 checkCuda( cudaMemcpyToSymbol(c_c1, &c1, sizeof(Real_t), 0,
    cudaMemcpyHostToDevice) );
161
162 Real_t a2 = Real_t(-1.0) * idx_by_2;
163 Real_t b2 = Real_t( 1.0) * idx_by_2;
164 checkCuda( cudaMemcpyToSymbol(c_a2, &a2, sizeof(Real_t), 0,
    cudaMemcpyHostToDevice) );
165 checkCuda( cudaMemcpyToSymbol(c_b2, &b2, sizeof(Real_t), 0,
    cudaMemcpyHostToDevice) );
166
167 Real_t a3 = Real_t( 1.0) * idx_by_12;
168 Real_t b3 = Real_t(-8.0)* idx_by_12;
169 Real_t c3 = Real_t( 8.0)* idx_by_12;
170 Real_t d3 = Real_t(-1.0)* idx_by_12;
171 checkCuda( cudaMemcpyToSymbol(c_a3, &a3, sizeof(Real_t), 0,
    cudaMemcpyHostToDevice) );
172 checkCuda( cudaMemcpyToSymbol(c_b3, &b3, sizeof(Real_t), 0,
    cudaMemcpyHostToDevice) );
173 checkCuda( cudaMemcpyToSymbol(c_c3, &c3, sizeof(Real_t), 0,
    cudaMemcpyHostToDevice) );
```

```
174 checkCuda( cudaMemcpyToSymbol(c_d3, &d3, sizeof(Real_t), 0,
    cudaMemcpyHostToDevice) );
175
176 Real_t a4 = Real_t( 1.0) * idx_by_2;
177 Real_t b4 = Real_t(-4.0) * idx_by_2;
178 Real_t c4 = Real_t( 3.0) * idx_by_2;
179 checkCuda( cudaMemcpyToSymbol(c_a4, &a4, sizeof(Real_t), 0,
    cudaMemcpyHostToDevice) );
180 checkCuda( cudaMemcpyToSymbol(c_b4, &b4, sizeof(Real_t), 0,
    cudaMemcpyHostToDevice) );
181 checkCuda( cudaMemcpyToSymbol(c_c4, &c4, sizeof(Real_t), 0,
    cudaMemcpyHostToDevice) );
182
183 // Compute the partial derivative in the x direction
184 grid[0] = dim3(ny / 5, nz, 1);
185 block[0] = dim3(nx, 5, 1);
186 int sharedmem = 5*(nx+8)*sizeof(Real_t);
187 dd_deriv_x_<<<grid[0],block[0],sharedmem>>>(d_sol,d_dxsol,nx,ny,nz);
188
189 // copy the derivative to CPU
190 checkCuda( cudaMemcpy(dxsol, d_dxsol, bytes, cudaMemcpyDeviceToHost) );
191
192 // Check the accuracy of the derivative
193 double maxerror = 0.0;
194 for (k=0;k<nz;k++) {
195   for (j=0;j<ny;j++) {
196     for (i=0;i<nx;i++) {
197       Real_t x = minx + i*hx;
198       Real_t y = miny + j*hy;
199       Real_t z = minz + k*hz;
200       if ( abs(cos(x) - dxsol[i+nx*(j+ny*k)]) > maxerror ) {
201         maxerror = abs(cos(x) - dxsol[i+nx*(j+ny*k)]);
202       }
203     }
204   }
205 }
206 printf(" Max error of x derivative: %g\n",maxerror);
207
208 free(sol);
209 free(dxsol);
210 checkCuda( cudaFree(d_sol) );
211 checkCuda( cudaFree(d_dxsol) );
212 return 0;
213 }
```

The field variable is initialized on the three-dimensional grid in lines 136–145. The finite difference kernel is defined in lines 55–92; this is where the finite difference stencils shown earlier are implemented. The stencil coefficients are copied to constants in GPU memory for performance considerations. The field variable that is finite differenced is copied to GPU memory in line 148, while the finite-differenced result is copied back to CPU memory in line 190. A comparison between the analytic partial derivative and the numerical partial derivative is computed in lines 193–205.

The code, fd.cu, is compiled with the nvcc compiler as follows:

```
nvcc fd.cu -o fd
```

The executable takes no arguments when executed:

```
./fd
setting CUDA device 0
Device Name: NVIDIA A10
Compute Capability: 8.6
Max error of x derivative: 0.00295294
```

The size of the grid is hard coded in line 99 to be $200 \times 200 \times 200$, but this can be changed to explore convergence of the numerical solution to the analytic solution. The finite difference computation in this example is done in double precision (fp64), so performance will be best on GPU hardware with native double-precision support, as is typical for supercomputer and data center GPUs.

18.3 **Questions**

1. The finite difference example computed the partial derivative of the field variable only in the x direction. Adjust the code to compute the partial derivative in the y and z directions. What must change about the derivative kernel?
2. Adjust the CUDA BLAS example to compute general matrix multiplication. What is the speedup compared with an equivalent CPU implementation?
3. While the GPU backend for machine learning frameworks is mostly hidden from the user, training on a GPU via these frameworks is a common example of a GPU program on high performance computing systems. What is the speedup when training the MNIST dataset on a GPU versus a CPU? What is the speedup when training Yolov4 on a GPU versus a CPU?
4. Linear algebra packages like PETSc are increasingly providing GPU support. What is the speedup when running a linear solve via PETSc on a GPU versus a CPU?

Machine Learning

19

Chapter outline

19.1 Introduction

Machine learning algorithms are distinct from most other types of number-crunching algorithms typically found on high performance computing systems because of the computational demand for data. Additionally, machine learning models have not just one but two different computationally demanding phases: training and inference. In the training phase, prolific amounts of data are read in batches and the model's weights and biases are adjusted to represent the statistical mean of the data. The inference phase is where a prediction is made by the trained model on an input dataset. The training phase typically takes orders of magnitude more time to execute than the inference phase. While high performance computing may be used to accelerate both phases, it is typically used only in the training phase of a model.

Machine learning is based on the concept of the artificial neuron originally proposed in 1943, which led to the first neural network machine, the Stochastic Neural Analog Reinforcement Calculator (SNARC), in 1951. The backpropagation algorithm started appearing for use in training the weights and biases of the neural network in the 1980s. The concept of deep learning was formally proposed in 2006 by Geoffrey Hinton and Ruslan Salakhutdinov at the University of Toronto [1], which subsequently led to an explosion in deep learning research. While deep learning is a relatively recent arrival for applications on high performance computing systems, the applications are so vast that a large percentage of compute cycles are now dedicated entirely to deep learning networks. These networks include convolutional neural networks, recurrent neural networks, and generative adversarial networks.

The computational demand for data inherent to machine learning training drives most model training efforts away from devices like central processing units (CPUs)

High Performance Computing. https://doi.org/10.1016/B978-0-12-823035-0.00019-5

due to their traditionally lower cumulative memory bandwidth and toward devices like graphics processing units (GPUs) with higher cumulative memory bandwidth and where the single-instruction multiple data operations are well suited for the matrix—matrix multiplications that are fundamental to training a machine learning model. As a result, GPU support is ubiquitous among machine learning frameworks and critical for training production models. Machine learning models are almost always implemented using Python so that the explicit GPU programming is mostly hidden from the user by the machine learning framework.

19.2 Handwritten Digits

The Modified National Institute of Standards and Technology (MNIST) database [2] is frequently used to illustrate an example of machine learning where images of handwritten digits of the numbers 0 through 9 are used to train a neural network to learn to recognize handwritten numbers. The dataset consists of a training set with 60,000 images and a test set with 10,000 images; the images are 28×28 pixels and are 8-bit grayscale. Examples of the handwritten numbers are shown in Fig. 19.1.

Here is a brief example using the MNIST database within the TensorFlow machine learning framework using the Keras application programming interface (API). TensorFlow can be easily installed through the conda package manager in a conda environment. To set up a conda environment, you can download and run miniforge as follows:

```
wget "https://github.com/conda-forge/miniforge/releases/latest/down-
load/Mambaforge-$(uname)-$(uname -m).sh"
```

FIGURE 19.1

Example of handwritten numbers from the MNSIT database. Each image is labeled to indicate which digit class (0 through 9) it belongs to. There are 10 classes. Image from https://commons.wikimedia.org/wiki/File:MnistExamples.png

Alternatively, miniforge installers can be downloaded here: https://github.com/conda-forge/miniforge. This will put conda in your path for creating a conda environment. Here are quick installation instructions for TensorFlow using the conda package manager:

```
conda create -n tensorflow python=3.11
conda activate tensorflow
conda install -c conda-forge tensorflow
```

When the command line for Python is launched, the Keras API can be loaded:

```
>>> from tensorflow import keras
```

Some additional libraries will also be beneficial for this example:

```
>>> import numpy as np
>>> from tensorflow.keras import layers
```

The MNIST database can be downloaded and loaded into memory directly using Keras:

```
>>> (X_train, Y_train), (X_test, Y_test) = keras.datasets.mnist.load_
data()
```

The variable X_train holds 60,000 handwritten images, while X_test holds an additional 10,000 handwritten images. These are broken into two sets so that the machine learning model can be trained on images that are different from those used to test the model's accuracy once trained. The labels (0 through 9) for each image are loaded into Y_train and Y_test. The first time this command is run, Keras will download the MNIST database and place it in the .keras directory of your home directory. Subsequent calls to load the data will then just use this downloaded dataset. Since many compute nodes of high performance computing systems are configured to not have internet access, it is usually easiest to download the MNIST dataset on a login node with internet access first if planning to train on a compute node without internet access.

For a classification example like this, the goal of the network is to classify what label (0 through 9) belongs to each image. The output layer of the neural network must therefore be of size 10—one for each class. The labels for each image need to be placed in a matrix format where each row has only one nonzero "1" in the column representing the handwritten image class. This is done using the to_categorical method with "10" as the number of classes of handwritten images:

```
>>> Y_train = keras.utils.to_categorical(Y_train, 10)
>>> Y_test = keras.utils.to_categorical(Y_test, 10)
```

The images stored in variables X_train and X_test are 8-bit grayscale with pixel values ranging up to 255. The neural network will train better by rescaling these values to be between 0 and 1:

```
>>> X_train = X_train.astype("float32") /255
>>> X_test = X_test.astype("float32") /255
```

The shape of the X_train and X_test arrays will be (60000,28,28) and (10000,28,28) at this point. We add one more dimension to the arrays using numpy so the input shape of each image will be (28,28,1):

```
>>> X_train = np.expand_dims(X_train, -1)
>>> X_test = np.expand_dims(X_test, -1)
```

The size of the arrays will now be (60000,28,28,1) and (10000,28,28,1).

A simple model can be defined to classify the images. Convolutional neural networks are often used for image classification because of their ability to capture spatial dependencies and edges in an image. Convolutional layers have fewer trainable parameters compared to their fully connected layer counterparts with more reusable weights. A convolutional layer has a kernel or filter that traverses the image and captures high-level features. For image problems, the kernel is a two-dimensional square matrix with an odd number of rows/columns, usually 3×3 or 5×5. The pooling layer then performs a dimensionality reduction on the kernel to capture only the most important information. Pooling options include max pooling and average pooling. In max pooling, only the maximum value of the kernel convolution over a particular region of the image is kept. In average pooling, the average value of the kernel convolution of the traversed region of the image is kept. In either case, the pooling layer reduces the computational expense for training the network while capturing the spatial dependencies in the network. In this example, we create a model using two convolutional layers with the Rectified Linear Unit (ReLu) activation function and a final dense layer consisting of 10 neurons— one for each class in the classification problem. The final activate function is the softmax activation function to normalize the output to a value between 0 and 1 that can be interpreted as a probability or likelihood for a particular classification. The dropout layer will randomly set a specified percentage of neurons in the network to zero to prevent overfitting the network.

```
>>> model = keras.Sequential(
... [
...     keras.Input(shape=(28,28,1)),
...     layers.Conv2D(32, kernel_size=(3, 3), activation="relu"),
...     layers.MaxPooling2D(pool_size=(2, 2)),
...     layers.Conv2D(64, kernel_size=(3, 3), activation="relu"),
...     layers.MaxPooling2D(pool_size=(2, 2)),
...     layers.Flatten(),
...     layers.Dropout(0.5),
...     layers.Dense(10, activation="softmax"),
... ]
...)
```

With the model defined and the data prepared for training, the model can be compiled and trained for a given number of epochs.

```
>>> model.compile(loss="categorical_crossentropy", optimizer="adam",
metrics=["accuracy"])
```

There are two required choices when compiling the model: the loss function and the optimizer. The optimizer is the algorithm used to solve the stochastic optimization problem to reduce the loss function. A typical choice for this is the Adam optimizer. The loss function measures how well the neural network represents the training data. Cross entropy and mean-squared error are common choices. When compiling the model, an additional function can be used to evaluate how the model performs on the data. Accuracy is a common metric for classification problems.

A batch size determines the number of samples read in during each model update cycle within the epoch. For training on a GPU, the best batch size is a power of two.

```
>>> batch_size = 256
>>> epochs = 10
```

The model is trained using the fit method; the training data and labels are the first arguments:

```
>>> model.fit(X_train, Y_train, batch_size=batch_size, epochs=epochs,
validation_split=0.1)
```

A validation_split separates out a percentage of the training data for use in metrics evaluation. Metrics and loss function are reported each epoch during training, c.g.:

```
Epoch 1/10
211/211 [==============================] - 14s 65ms/step - loss: 0.5012 -
accuracy: 0.8495 - val_loss: 0.0994 - val_accuracy: 0.9727
Epoch 2/10
211/211 [==============================] - 14s 64ms/step - loss: 0.1326 -
accuracy: 0.9590 - val_loss: 0.0656 - val_accuracy: 0.9825
Epoch 3/10
211/211 [==============================] - 14s 66ms/step - loss: 0.0962 -
accuracy: 0.9708 - val_loss: 0.0539 - val_accuracy: 0.9857
```

Once trained, the model can be used for predictions:

```
>>> predictions = model.predict(X_test)
```

The prediction output for each input image is an array of length 10 containing the likelihood for each class, e.g.:

```
>>> predictions[901]
array([0., 0., 0., 0., 1., 0., 0., 0., 0., 0.], dtype=float32)
```

For the 901st test image, the model predicts that the most likely classification is "4" with a likelihood of 1. The true label for the image can be explicitly verified:

```
>>> print(Y_test[901])
4
```

For a large computer vision model like the darknet implementation of Yolo (https://github.com/AlexeyAB/darknet), training may require more than 500,000 epochs and require days of training on multiple data center GPUs. Large machine learning models with enormous training datasets now commonly require high performance computing resources to adequately train the model.

19.3 Distributed Machine Learning Training

Machine learning training is the most expensive computational phase, often taking orders of magnitude more time and resources than the inference phase. While high performance computing resources can be applied in both phases to accelerate the time to completion, most methods focus on accelerating the training phase. There are two modalities by which concurrency is extracted to accelerate machine learning training: model parallelism and data parallelism. Model parallelism is where the model itself is split into segments that can be executed concurrently. Data parallelism is where the training data is split and used for training in the same model replicated across multiple devices; a communication collective like allreduce ensures the different model instances are updated with the gradient updates from each other. The concurrency is extracted by using training concurrently on different segments of data. An illustration of these two modalities is given in Fig. 19.2.

In the case of either model parallelism or data parallelism, some changes to the machine learning code are required. For many frameworks, model parallelism implementations require explicitly assigning certain components of the model to a resource and that the different components of the model can indeed be evaluated concurrently. The data parallelism modality has the look and feel of a single-program multiple data approach already familiar to high performance computing users who write message-passing codes using the message-passing interface

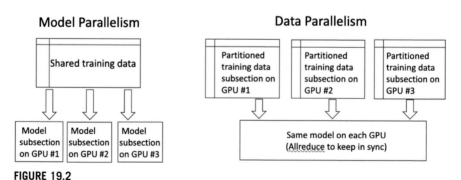

FIGURE 19.2

Two modalities for extracting concurrency when training a deep learning model. In model parallelism, the portions of the model itself that can be executed concurrently are assigned to different devices while the training data is shared. In data parallelism, the training data is partitioned among the different devices while the model is the same. The gradient updates from each device are communicated via an allreduce-type collective to keep the shared model consistent among the devices.

(MPI) libraries. Many machine learning frameworks support data parallelism, and there are even libraries built on MPI to simplify deploying model parallelism training at scale.

Horovod [3] is a simple-to-use library that can leverage the MPI libraries for implementing distributed model training using the data parallelism modality. It has been used to train models on over 27,000 GPUs [4] and is easily installed with the pip package installer on a laptop or supercomputer. Horovod has the look and feel of an MPI-based application, with Horovod.init() instead of MPI_Init and a distributed optimizer rather than a serial optimizer. Horovod-based machine learning codes can be launched via *mpirun* much like other MPI-based applications.

Horovod can be easily installed using the pip package installer as follows:

```
HOROVOD_WITH_TENSORFLOW=1  HOROVOD_WITH_MPI=1  pip  install  horovod
[tensorflow,keras]
```

Supported frameworks apart from TensorFlow and Keras include PyTorch, MXNet, and Spark. The Horovod installation can be tested with a very simple Python script as follows:

```
1 import tensorflow
2 import horovod.tensorflow as hvd
3 hvd.init()
4 print(hvd.rank())
```

This script can be saved in a file called *print_rank.py*. This example can be run using the *horovodrun* script, which comes with Horovod and is analogous to *mpirun* or *mpiexec*. The example *print_rank.py* is then run as follows:

```
$ hovorodrun -np 4 python print_rank.py
```

It will print out the rank (0−3 in this case) for each node it ran on. Alternatively, a user can use *mpirun* rather than *horovodrun* to launch a Horovod-driven machine learning training. Here is an example command to run a Horovod case with Open-MPI directly, which avoids the *horovodrun* script:

```
mpirun -bind-to none -map-by slot -x NCCL_DEBUG=INFO -x LD_LIBRARY_-
PATH -x PATH -mca pml ob1 -mca btl ˆopenib python print_rank.py
```

The *horovodrun* script encapsulates this information already to simplify running Horovod-based training. Notice that Horovod can leverage the Nvidia Collective Communications Library (NCCL) to speed up multi-GPU communications.

Adding distributed training support under the data parallelism model to an existing serial machine learning code requires a few additions and modifications. The MNIST handwritten digits code from the previous section provides a good example for this. We import TensorFlow and Keras layers just like before:

```
import tensorflow
from tensorflow.keras import layers
```

However, we must load Horovod and the Horovod Keras:

```
import hovorod
import horovod.tensorflow.keras as hvd
```

Horovod is initialized as follows:

```
hvd.init()
```

Each MPI process will be pinned to a single GPU device if GPU hardware is available:

```
gpus = tf.config.experimental.list_physical_devices('GPU')
for gpu in gpus:
    tensorflow.config.experimental.set_memory_growth(gpu, True)
if gpus:
    tensorflow.config.experimental.set_visible_devices(gpus
    [hvd.local_rank()], 'GPU')
```

The handwritten images can now be loaded in for training. This command will download the MNIST data if it hasn't already been downloaded and placed in the .keras directory.

```
(mnist_images, mnist_labels), _=tf.keras.datasets.mnist.load_data(path=
'mnist-%d.npz' % hvd.rank())
```

For example, if running on four processes, in the ~/.keras/datasets directory there will be four files named mnist-0.npz, mnist-1.npz, mnist-2.npz, and mnist-3.npz. If running on a compute node without internet access, this step would fail if the dataset hasn't already been downloaded. The entire dataset is loaded separately for each rank for simplicity rather than explicitly partitioning the training dataset for each Horovod rank.

Just as in the original MNIST example, we rescale the image pixel values to be between 0 and 1:

```
dataset = tensorflow.data.Dataset.from_tensor_slices(
    (tensorflow.cast(mnist_images[..., tensorflow.newaxis] / 255.0,
    tensorflow.float32),
    tensorflow.cast(mnist_labels, tensorflow.int64)))
```

The image order is also shuffled so that the model doesn't see the same order of training data for each epoch and on each Horovod rank:

```
dataset = dataset.repeat().shuffle(10000).batch(128)
```

The model is the same as was used previously:

```
mnist_model = tensorflow.keras.Sequential([
    layers.Conv2D(32, [3, 3], activation='relu'),
    layers.MaxPooling2D(pool_size=(2, 2)),
    layers.Conv2D(64, [3, 3], activation='relu'),
```

```
    layers.MaxPooling2D(pool_size=(2, 2)),
    layers.Flatten(),
    layers.Dropout(0.5),
    layers.Dense(10, activation='softmax')
])
```

The original learning rate used in the previous section was the default: 0.001. When running training across multiple Horovod ranks, the learning range needs to be increased according to the number of ranks because the effective batch size has already been increased by using more ranks:

```
scaled_learning_rate = 0.001 * hvd.size()
adjusted_optimizer = tensorflow.keras.optimizers.Adam(scaled_learning_
rate)
```

The loss function is kept the same as before:

```
loss = tensorflow.losses.SparseCategoricalCrossEntropy()
```

When training a large model, it is a good idea to write checkpoints in the event of an unexpected failure:

```
checkpoint_dir = './mnist_checkpoints'
checkpoint = tensorflow.train.Checkpoint(model=mnist_model,optimizer=
adjusted_optimizer)
```

Unlike the example of the previous section, when using Horovod for distributed training, the initial state of the variables needs to be broadcast to all the Horovod ranks:

```
@tensorflow.function
def training_step(images, labels, first_batch):
  with tensorflow.GradientTape() as tape:
    probs = mnist_model(images, training=True)
    loss_value = loss(labels, probs)

  tape = hvd.DistributedGradientTape(tape)
  grads = tape.gradient(loss_value, mnist_model.trainable_variables)
  adjusted_optimizer.apply_gradients(zip(grads,
mnist_model.trainable_variables))

  # Initial variable state is broadcast to all ranks
  if first_batch:
    hvd.broadcast_variables(mnist_model.variables, root_rank=0)
    hvd.broadcast_variables(adjusted_optimizer.variables(),
root_rank=0)

  return loss_value
```

The number of training steps is adjusted based on the number of Horovod ranks; the loss is printed out each 10th step here during training:

```
for batch, (images, labels) in enumerate(dataset.take(1000 // hvd.size())):
    loss_value = training_step(images, labels, batch == 0)
    if batch % 10 == 0 and hvd.local_rank() == 0:
        print('Step #%d\tLoss: %.6f' % (batch, loss_value))
```

Finally, when running with Horovod in distributed mode, checkpointing is only done on one rank so that other ranks don't try to concurrently overwrite the checkpoints and corrupt them:

```
if hvd.rank() == 0:
    checkpoint.save(checkpoint_dir)
```

Output to the terminal for this example appears as follows:

```
Step #0 Loss: 2.302912
Step #10 Loss: 1.372778
Step #20 Loss: 0.544705
```

The usage on the GPUs can be explicitly verified by using *nvidia-smi* or *gpustat* for NVIDIA GPUs.

19.4 Summary and Outcomes

- Machine learning workloads come in two phases: training and inference. The training phase is the most typical phase seen on high performance computing systems.
- Machine learning training workloads are fundamentally different from most other high performance computing workloads because of their enormous computational demand for data.
- The computational demand for data in machine learning workloads tends to drive applications toward devices like GPUs rather than CPUs for the training phase.
- Machine learning frameworks are typically programmed in Python with backend support for GPUs. They can be installed in conda environments using either the pip or conda package managers.
- The two principal modalities for training a machine learning model in distributed mode are model parallelism and data parallelism.
- Model parallelism requires executing separate components of the machine learning model concurrently.
- Data parallelism is where multiple devices train on different portions of the data concurrently and then rely on an all reduce-type collective for synchronization. This approach has many analogies with MPI-style programming.
- Horovod is a highly scalable tool for training machine learning models in distributed mode using the data parallelism approach.

19.5 Exercises

1. Try adjusting the MNIST handwritten image code provided as an example in this chapter. How much impact is there in removing the first MaxPooling layer and adding a fully connected layer? How sensitive is the model to changes in terms of accuracy?

2. Perform a strong scaling study on the MNIST handwritten image example using Horovod.

3. The PyTorch machine learning framework provides features in torch.distributed for running in distributed mode using data parallelism without requiring an external library like Horovod. Compare and contrast the PyTorch mechanisms for training in distributed mode versus Horovod.

4. Machine learning inference can also be accelerated on high performance computing systems. Tools like frugally deep (https://github.com/Dobiasd/frugally-deep) are thread-safe and can concurrently infer from multiple threads. What options exist to reduce inference latency for deep learning models?

5. Using the darknet implementation of Yolo (https://github.com/AlexeyAB/darknet), how long does it take to train Yolov4 for 50,000 epochs when using four GPUs? How long when using eight GPUs?

References

[1] G.E. Hinton, R.R. Salakhutdinov, Reducing the dimensionality of data with neural networks, Science 313 (2006) 504–507.
[2] MNIST Database. http://yann.lecun.com/exdb/mnist/. Accessed March 2023.
[3] Horovod. https://horovod.ai/. Accessed March 2023.
[4] N. Laanait, J. Romero, J. Yin, M. Young, S. Treichler, V. Starchenko, A. Borisevich, A. Sergeev, M. Matheson, Exascale Deep Learning For Scientific Inverse Problems. https://arxiv.org/pdf/1909.11150.pdf.

Mass Storage and File Systems

20

20.1 Introduction

The storage subsystem is one of the key components of every computing platform. Although the organization, speed, capacity, and supported functions of storage vary depending on platform class, its presence is always required for the computations to be carried out. In high performance computing (HPC), one can observe quite possibly the broadest variety of storage options and involved storage technologies, as well as range of implementation scales. This chapter discusses the segment of storage technology and low-level techniques utilized to reliably support the

High Performance Computing. https://doi.org/10.1016/B978-0-12-823035-0.00020-1

requirements of HPC systems to preserve the high volume of computational state in the form of both scientific data and elements of the operating environment. The state retention must be persistent between the power cycles of the machine for it to be able to execute bootstrap procedures on restart, attain the correct operational status, and resume interrupted computational tasks. This part of the storage hierarchy is referred to as "mass storage" to reflect its capability to retain large amounts of data. Mass storage is not concerned with volatile devices, such as main memory or processor registers. Besides input and output datasets used by and produced as a result of computation, mass storage also preserves the code (executables and libraries) necessary to run the operating system (OS), its associated background management processes, configuration and update scripts, and the user's and the system administrator's tools and utilities. Finally, mass storage plays an integral role in checkpoint and restart of compute applications, alleviating the impact of temporal and system resource limits imposed on application execution.

Traditionally, storage hierarchy is subdivided into four levels that differ in access latency and supported data bandwidth, with latencies increasing and effective transfer bandwidth dropping when moving away from the top level of the hierarchy. At the same time, storage capacity rapidly grows. The commonly recognized hierarchy levels include:

- *Primary storage* that comprises system memories, caches, and central processing unit (CPU) register sets. This type of storage is predominantly volatile (loses data contents when powered off), with the exception of read-only memories (ROMs) that store firmware or CPU boot code. The data access latencies range from a single CPU clock cycle (fraction of a nanosecond) for registers to several hundred cycles for dynamic memories in remote nonuniform memory access domains; the respective bandwidths span from over 100 GB/s (single-instruction multiple data registers in a single core) down to a few tens of GB/s per bank of double data rate memory still in use. Aggregate memory size in HPC ranges from a few tens of gigabytes for small nodes to several terabytes for multisocket nodes dedicated to memory-intensive tasks.
- *Secondary storage* is the first level of storage that leverages mass storage devices. Normally, CPUs cannot directly access the secondary (or higher-level) storage, and therefore transfers of data between the primary and secondary storage have to be mediated by the OS and computer chipset. The granularity of data access is typically limited to fixed-size blocks, while most of the primary storage components operate at byte or word resolution. The most commonly used technology in this tier is the solid-state drive (SSD), which offers the industry's best data bandwidths with reasonable cost per unit of storage. For the past decade, SSDs have been successively replacing the stalwart of storage technology, the hard disk drives (HDDs), which still hold the capacity crown in terms of total storage provided by a single device (over 20 TB). The random access latency of secondary storage media may be less than 100 μs for the fastest SSDs to as much

as tens of milliseconds for HDDs. The bandwidths may range from just below 100 MB/s for slower HDDs to more than 10 GB per second for the fastest SSDs.

- *Tertiary storage* is distinguished from secondary storage in that it usually involves large collections of storage media or storage devices that are nominally in an inaccessible or powered-off state but that may be reasonably quickly enabled for online use. This is typically accomplished by automated mechanisms, such as robots that physically move the requested mass storage medium from its assigned long-term retention slot to the specified online access device (drive). To lower the contention between multiple users, tertiary storage equipment typically hosts several independent media drives that may be accessed concurrently. Examples of tertiary storage equipment include tape libraries and optical jukeboxes. The access latency to tertiary storage may be substantially greater than that of secondary storage. It typically takes single tens of seconds for the robot to grab and mount the medium; the achieved single-device bandwidths are comparable to those of secondary storage. The storage capacity of robotic jukeboxes may reach as much as multiple hundreds of petabytes.

- *Offline storage* requires human intervention to enable access to the storage medium. It is primarily employed to archive, frequently in a secure location off-site, precious information. Since the storage unit is not under direct control of any computer, this provides a much-needed "air gap" to protect the security, confidentiality, and integrity of the archives. Offline storage is in principle similar to tertiary storage, although lack of predictability related to medium load requests results in highly random latency figures and may not be considered a practical high performance solution other than for some niche applications.

20.2 Brief History of Storage

Technological progress brought dramatic improvements in both capacity and performance of mass storage devices over the course of several decades. As illustrated in Fig. 20.1, starting with punched cards as the first external information store in the mid-1940s, through tape drives in the early 1950s, and continuing with HDDs from the mid-1950s to the present day, the storage capacity grew an amazing 11 orders of magnitude. The increases in device storage capacity were reflected by the corresponding improvements in device input/output (I/O) bandwidth (Fig. 20.2), which advanced six orders of magnitude over the same period. However, the access latency improvements were far more modest, since they decreased from single and tens of seconds for punched cards and tape to a few milliseconds in modern HDDs. Latency still remains one of the biggest performance bottlenecks plaguing most of the I/O devices in use today.

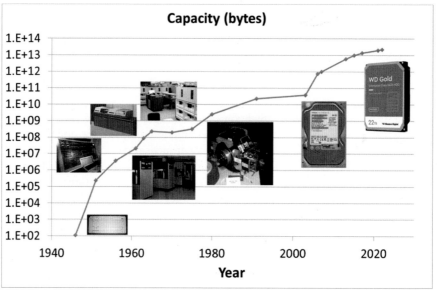

Capacity (bytes)

FIGURE 20.1

Increases in mass storage capacity. Represented systems include a punch card on the ENIAC (1946), a UNISERVO tape drive (1951), IBM 350 (1956), IBM 1301 (1961), IBM 1302 (1963), IBM 2314 (1965), IBM 3330 (1970), IBM 3350 (1975), IBM 3380 (1980), IBM 3390 (1991), Western Digital Raptor (2003), Seagate Barracuda 7200.10 (2006), HGST Deskstar 7K1000 (2007), HGST Ultrastar He6 (2013), HGST Ultrastar He10 (2015), Western Digital DC HC620 (2017), Seagate Exos X20 (2021), and Western Digital Gold Enterprise (2022).

20.3 Storage Device Technology

The technology of hardware storage devices continuously evolved to support the ever-increasing demands in storage capacity and data access bandwidth. Currently, the majority of storage systems utilize four main types of mass storage devices: HDDs, SSDs, magnetic tapes, and optical storage. Although they serve largely the same purpose, they substantially differ in the underlying physical phenomena used to implement data retention and their operational characteristics and cost. The fundamental properties and working principles of modern storage devices are discussed below.

20.3.1 Hard Disk Drives

HDDs have a long history as a data storage device in computing. Introduced in 1956, the first hard drive used in the IBM 350 RAMAC system [1] was approximately 68 inches high, 60 inches deep, and 29 inches wide and weighed approximately 1 ton. It

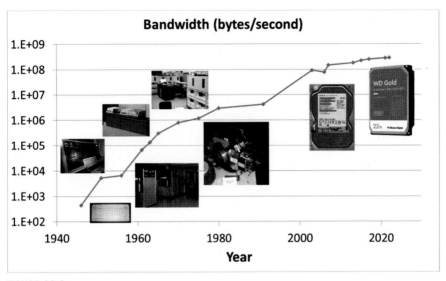

FIGURE 20.2

Improvements in I/O data access bandwidth. Represented systems include a punch card on the ENIAC (1946), a UNISERVO tape drive (1951), IBM 350 (1956), IBM 1301 (1961), IBM 1302 (1963), IBM 2314 (1965), IBM 3330 (1970), IBM 3350 (1975), IBM 3380 (1980), IBM 3390 (1991), Western Digital Raptor (2003), Seagate Barracuda 7200.10 (2006), HGST Deskstar 7K1000 (2007), HGST Ultrastar He6 (2013), HGST Ultrastar He10 (2015), Western Digital DC HC620 (2017), Seagate Exos X20 (2021), and Western Digital Gold Enterprise (2022).

contained 50 platters (disks serving as the recording medium for data) with a diameter of 24 inches rotating at 1200 revolutions per minute (RPM). It stored 5 million 6-bit characters that were transferred at a rate of 8800 per second. The progressive miniaturization, development of better materials, and signal processing techniques resulted in creation of drives vastly exceeding the performance of these first attempts, measured in total data capacity, transfer bandwidth, access time, and overall size.

The principal internal components of an HDD are annotated in Fig. 20.3. The information is recorded on one or both surfaces of a disc-shaped *platter*. While the base material for platters is typically glass due to several well-mastered technological processes that guarantee the maximum surface flatness, the platters may also be made of aluminum or ceramics. The platters are polished to a roughness of less than $1 \text{ Å } (10^{-10} \text{ m})$ and are covered with several thin (single-nanometer) layers of various materials that exhibit high coercivity, i.e., the ability to retain the acquired magnetization in the presence of an external magnetic field. The platter also receives a protective carbon-based coating through ion-beam or plasma-enhanced vapor deposition. Finally, a lubricant coat is added to the active surfaces and bonded. Storage densities of media manufactured may exceed 1 Tbit per square inch. A typical

platter

recirculation filter

actuator housing with
permanent magnets

spindle

actuator arm

read-write heads

SATA data connector

SATA power connector

FIGURE 20.3

A hard disk drive with removed top part of the enclosure (2-TB Seagate HDD shown).

HDD stacks several platters on the same axle (spindle) to achieve the desired total storage capacity. The spindle is a part of a direct drive brushless motor that rotates at several thousand RPM (commonly used speeds are 5400, 7200, and occasionally 10,000 and 15,000 RPM in high-end devices). Data is retrieved from and written to the platters using multiple read–write heads mounted at the end of the actuator arm. The arm can move in an arc over the platters to be able to locate a specific data track; the information is stored on platters in the form of concentric circles, referred to as *cylinders* to emphasize the three-dimensional aspect of the data layout. The actuator motion is controlled by the so-called *voice coil,* named in analogy to a dynamic loudspeaker construction that has coils surrounded by permanent magnets that push the sound-generating membrane.

Read–write heads are not attached directly to the actuator arms, but to *sliders*— tiny (that is, a fraction of a millimeter in the longest dimension and weighing a fraction of a gram), aerodynamically shaped carriers that are responsible for maintaining the correct, nearly constant distance between the head and spinning medium. Due to the precision involved, it is not difficult to see that foreign contaminants present a serious damage risk to HDDs. Most drives have ventilation outlets protected by additional filters to stop the foreign matter. Some HDD versions are hermetically sealed and use inert gases such as nitrogen or helium to support the operation.

The peak media transfer speeds of current HDDs are on the order of 100–300 MB/s. In addition to user data, the recorded information also contains error-correcting codes (ECCs) to detect and, if possible, correct the malformed data. The information in each track is subdivided into a number of sectors of constant size, each requiring an identifier, synchronization information, and explicit gap separating it from its nearest neighbors. The standard for sectors was 512 bytes for several decades; modern, large-capacity drives forced manufacturers to migrate to 4096-byte sectors (called Advanced Format) to lower the spatial overheads of metadata, primarily ECCs, associated with each sector (see Fig. 20.4(a)). Older disks maintained a fixed number of sectors in each cylinder, hence producing a nonuniform recording density between the innermost and outermost tracks. Since the platters spin mostly at a constant rate, the solution was to introduce zone bit recording, illustrated in Fig. 20.4(b). The platter surface is subdivided into concentric zones with different radii. Each zone features a specific number of sectors per track, thus allowing an increased number of sectors to be stored in outer cylinders.

HDDs are described using a number of parameters that help determine their usefulness for a specific application (Table 20.1):

- **Storage capacity** is typically expressed in gigabytes or terabytes. Unlike memory capacities, it is measured in powers of 10; hence, 1 TB is 10^{12} bytes.
- **Seek time** (in milliseconds) expresses the duration taken by the read–write head to move to a specific cylinder. Average seek time is determined statistically involving travel distances over one-third of all tracks on a disk. Of specific interest are also track-to-track latency (moving the head between the adjacent tracks) and full-stroke latency that involves travel between the innermost and the outermost cylinders.
- **RPM** is the number of rotations the platters perform in 1 minute.
- **Rotational latency** (in milliseconds) describes the time required to position a specific sector under the read–write head. Average latency is typically given as

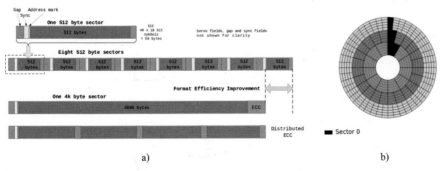

a)   b)

FIGURE 20.4

Physical information layout on HDDs: (a) advantage of larger sectors, (b) zone bit recording. Image source: Wikipedia

Table 20.1 Comparison of Hard Disk Drive Properties Characteristic of Different Market Segments

Manufacturer and Drive	Capacity (TB)	Media Transfer Rate (MB/s)	Seek Time (ms)		RPM	DRAM Cache (MB)	MTBF (million hours)	Avg. Power (W)		UER	Acoustic Noise (dB(A))		Form Factor (inches)	Market Segment
			Track to Track	Full Stroke				Seek	Idle		Seek	Idle		
WDC WUH722222AL5204	22	291			7200	512	2.5	9.6	6.0	<1 in 10^{15}	32	20	3.5	Enterprise
WDC WD60EZRZ	6	175			5400	64		5.3	3.4	<1 in 10^{14}	28	25	3.5	Economy desktop
HGST HTS721010A9E631	1	161	1	20	7200	32		2.1	0.8		27	25	2.5	Mobile
Seagate ST20000VE002	20	248/260 max.			7200	256	2.5	7.5	3.5	<1 in 10^{15}	32	28	3.5	A/V streaming

the time it takes the drive to perform half rotation of the platter and is directly dependent on its RPM rating.

- **Access time** (in milliseconds) is a delay between the time the request for data is submitted by the host and the time the data are returned by the drive. It is a compound metric involving a combination of rotational latency and seek time typically determined through a synthetic benchmark that exercises various access scenarios.
- **Media transfer rate** (in megabytes per second) measures how fast the signal processing chain and controller can read the data from the platter.
- **Burst rate** (in megabytes per second) describes how fast the data may be transmitted between the host and disk cache using transfers that do not exceed the cache capacity.
- **Areal density** (in gigabits per square inch) provides the achievable upper limit of information density per surface area on a recordable medium. Related metrics involving linear densities are tracks per inch (TPI) and bits per inch.
- **Mean time between failures (MTBF)** (in millions of hours) estimates the drive's resilience to nonrecoverable faults.
- **Uncorrectable error rate (UER)** (no unit) estimates the probability of receiving data containing a hard error, i.e., an error that either could not be detected or fixed by the built-in ECC mechanisms or could not be corrected through operation retries.
- **Power consumption** (in watts) describes the average energy requirements of a drive in several possible scenarios: during regular operation, during power-up (spin-up), while idle, and during standby.
- **Acoustic noise** (in dB(A)) provides an upper bound on noise level produced by the device during active operation.
- **Shock resistance** (in g) describes the device's resilience to external mechanical impact.
- **Size** (in inches) provides the mechanical dimensions of the drive so that a proper enclosure may be adopted for its use.

20.3.2 Solid-State Drive Storage

Advances in semiconductor technology enabled practical realization of high-capacity persistent storage in solid state. The most broadly utilized SSDs today are the descendants of electrically erasable programmable read-only memory (EEPROM) technology, introduced by Toshiba in 1984. EEPROMs can store small amounts of data using floating-gate metal oxide semiconductor transistor arrays similar to regular field-effect transistors with oxide isolators, but they sandwich an additional electrode between the oxide layers above the transistor's channel.

Increasing the device capacity necessitated reduction of control structure and the number of internal connections, resulting in two dominant flash memory types: NOR and NAND (introduced in 1987). The names of flash memory configurations are derived from an internal structure resembling that of NOR gate, with parallel

Table 20.2 Comparison of Principal Properties of NOR and NAND Flash Memory

Property	NOR Flash	NAND Flash
Capacity	Low	High
Cost per bit	High	Low
Read speed	High	Medium
Write speed	Very slow	Slow
Erase speed	Very slow (10s to 100s of ms)	Medium (single ms)
Erase cycles (endurance)	100,000–1,000,000	1,000–10,000
Active power	High	Low
Standby power	Low	Medium
Random access	Easy	Hard
Block storage	Medium	Easy

arrangement of output n-type transistors and series connection of n-type transistors in the NAND gate. The comparison of their characteristics is shown in Table 20.2.

Charge leakage is one of the main factors that limits the miniaturization of storage cells. Moreover, the amount of charge per cell cannot be decreased indefinitely. Originally, NAND storage used single-level cell (SLC) implementation. Commercial devices available today resort to multilevel cells (MLCs) with 2 bits per cell; triple-level cells (TLCs) with 3 bits stored in a cell, thus representing eight data states; and even quadruple-level cells (QLCs) with 4 bits per cell. Sizes of the cells used in MLC devices are somewhat larger than those of SLCs to provide a reasonable margin of error, but even then, their endurance drops effectively to about 3000 erase cycles.

Table 20.3 presents examples of commercially available SSD with their parameters. Since solid-state storage performs multiple short accesses with much better performance than HDDs, the number of I/O operations per second (IOPS) is given. The limited rewrite count of flash is reflected through the terabytes written (TBW) statistic that estimates the total volume of data a drive is guaranteed to accommodate over its lifetime, taking into account wear leveling. An alternative metric is data writes per day, indicating how many times a drive's entire size may be overwritten each day over the warranty period before that drive becomes unreliable.

20.3.3 Magnetic Tape

Magnetic tape has a long history as a computer data medium. Having been used as secondary storage (manufactured by UNISERVO) in UNIVAC in 1951, it predates HDDs by approximately 5 years. It consisted of 0.5-inch-wide and 0.0015-inch-thick nickel-plated phosphor bronze metal tape wound on open reels, was up to 1500 feet long, and recorded information at a density of 128 bits per inch. The

Table 20.3 Examples of Currently Manufactured SSD Devices and Their Operational Properties

Manufacturer and Device	Capacity (TB)	Sequential Read (MB/s)	Sequential Write (MB/s)	Max. 4-KB Random Reads [kIOPS]	Max. 4-KB Random Writes [kIOPS]	Endurance	Memory Type	Form Factor and Interface
Crucial CT4000T700SSD5	4	12,400	11,800	1500	1500	2400 TBW	232-layer TLC NAND[3]	M.2 2280, PCIe5 x4, NVMe 2.0
Samsung MZ7L37T6HBLA-00B7C	7.68	550	520	98	30	1 DWPD (5 yr)	TLC V-NAND	2.5", SATA 6Gbps

Table 20.4 Operational Parameters of Example Recent-Generation Tape Drives

Manufacturer and Drive Model	Capacity (TB)	Sustained Data Rate (MB/s)	Burst Rate (MB/s)	Max. Continuous Power (W)	Cartridge Types Supported	Interface
IBM 3588-S9C (SAS) IBM 3588-F9C (FC)	Up to 18 TB uncompressed Up to 45 TB compressed	400 (SAS) 700 (FC)	1200 (SAS) 800 (FC)	37	LTO Ultrium 9, LTO Ultrium 8	12 Gbps (SAS) 8 Gbps (FC)

sustained data bandwidth was 7200 characters per second. A single reel with tape weighed about 3 pounds.

Along with increases in data density and length of tape stored on a reel, improvements in tape and deck technology brought more practical implementations of replaceable storage media. Instead of using independent reels, they were packaged into a *tape cartridge* that combined reels, tape, and some elements of a guiding mechanism into a single enclosure. Lack of widely accepted standards for tape storage resulted in proliferation of mutually incompatible cartridge families, including DDS (digital data storage, from 1989), DAT (digital audio tape, originated in 2003), DLT (digital linear tape, 1984–2007), and finally LTO (linear tape-open, 2000–current). The latter is an example of the longest-surviving tape technology. It was established in response to proprietary tape formats and developed by a consortium founded by HP, IBM, and Quantum. Its current generation, LTO-9, supports up to 18 TB of data per cartridge packed on a tape that is 1035 m long, 12.65 mm wide, and 5.2 μm thick.

Table 20.4 lists the operational parameters of currently available LTO-9-compatible internal tape decks.

20.3.4 Optical Storage

While there were many attempts to apply optical means for storage and retrieval of digital information, none of them attained widespread popularity before the commercial release of the compact disc (CD) in 1982. The CD is the result of collaboration between Philips and Sony, which jointly developed the Red Book CD-DA (digital audio) specifications and agreed to manufacture compatible hardware. Even though originally intended as a medium of music distribution, the CD was soon used to store photographs, graphics, artwork, sound samples, video, and, of course, data.

Physically, the CD is a 1.2-mm-thick plastic disc with a diameter of 120 mm. The base material is polycarbonate with an impressed spiral pattern of elongated pits to encode the data. The data track is covered with a reflective metal layer (usually aluminum) before sealing it with a protective layer of lacquer and artwork (Fig. 20.5(b)). The information is retrieved from the spinning disc using an infrared

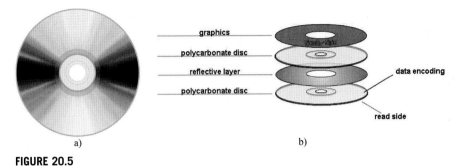

FIGURE 20.5

Compact disc: (a) physical medium and (b) component layers.

laser beam equipped with appropriate collimating optics and tracking mechanism. Most discs have just one active surface that is used to read the data and store 74–80 minutes of audio or up to 700 MB of data packed into 2352-byte sectors. For data storage, the CD-ROM variant retains the basic organization of information on the disc; however, the effective number of data bytes per sector is reduced to 2048 due to the stronger ECC schemes employed. As CD-ROM's content is fixed at the factory, compact disc-recordable (CD-R) and later compact disc-rewritable (CD-RW) formats detailed by the Orange Book specification were developed. While CD-R discs may be "burned" (written) only once due to the laser beam effectively destroying the underlying organic dye, CD-RW, deploying a phase-change medium, may be rewritten up to about 1000 times.

When advances in semiconductor laser technology enabled cheap visible light lasers, larger-capacity formats became possible. In 1995, Philips, Sony, Toshiba, and Panasonic introduced DVD (digital versatile disc), accessed with a red laser with a wavelength of 650 nm. While DVDs have the same external dimensions as CDs, they store up to 4.7 GB of data in a single layer or 8.5 GB in two layers per disc. Their recordable versions are known as DVD-R and DVD+R and their rewritable versions as DVD-RW, DVD+RW. Blue lasers operating at a 405 nm wavelength gave birth to the Blu-ray Disc (BD) format in 2008, capable of storing 25 GB in a single layer up to as much as 128 GB in quad-layer configuration (BDXL). Table 20.5 lists some of the performance parameters of the consumer-grade optical disc reader/recorder.

20.3.5 Aggregated Storage: Redundant Array of Independent Disks

Redundant array of independent disks (RAID; formerly redundant array of inexpensive disks, attributed to David Patterson, Garth Gibson, and Randy Katz of the University of California at Berkeley) attempts to address reliability issues of conventional mass storage devices. All storage devices, including HDDs and SSDs, have a limited lifespan and undergo random mechanical or electrical failures. RAID works by extending the pool of drives containing actual data with additional

Table 20.5 Parameters of a Typical Consumer-Grade BXDL-Capable Optical Drive

Manufacturer and Drive	BD Access Time (ms)	DVD Access Time (ms)	CD Access Time (ms)	Max. Data Rate			Buffer Size (MB)	Interface
				BD-ROM Read	CD-ROM Read	DVD-ROM Read		
LG BH16NS40	180	160 (ROM) 180 (RAM)	150	53.94 MB/s 12×	7.2 MS/s 48×	22.16 MB/s 16×	4	SATA (internal)

devices to provide *redundancy*. By treating such an array of drives as a single, virtualized I/O device, the impact of individual component failures may be alleviated. Below, a number of commonly used RAID configurations (called *levels*) are presented along with their operational parameters.

20.3.5.1 RAID 0: Striping

RAID 0 is not a proper RAID level in that it does not provide any data redundancy should drive failures occur. It describes a configuration in which the data blocks are simply distributed (stripped) across available disks in a round-robin fashion, as shown in Fig. 20.6. A *stripe* is a sequence of blocks spanning all disks in the array; for example, block 4—block 5—block 6 in the figure constitutes a stripe. An arbitrary number of disks may be arranged this way; however, assuming that failure occurrences are independent and have exponential probability distribution, the reliability for the whole array including d data disks will be a fraction of that for a single drive:

$$MTBF_0 = \frac{MTBF_D}{d}$$

Thus, building an array of four enterprise drives, each with a good MTBF rating of 1,200,000 hours, will result in an MTBF for the array of 300,000 hours—equivalent to an average consumer drive. With independent controllers, data on the drive may be accessed concurrently, providing increased read and write bandwidths in proportion to the number of drives:

$$B_{R_0} = d \cdot B_{R_D}$$

$$B_{W_0} = d \cdot B_{W_D}$$

where B_{R_D} and B_{W_D} are respectively read and write bandwidths of a single drive.

Finally, the storage capacity of the whole array is a sum of component drive capacities:

$$C_0 = d \cdot C_D$$

where C_D is the capacity of a single drive.

20.3.5.2 RAID 1: Mirroring

RAID 1 is the lowest RAID level supporting data protection (Fig. 20.7). This is accomplished by storing replicas of used data blocks that reside on the primary

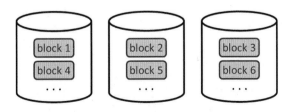

FIGURE 20.6

RAID 0 data layout.

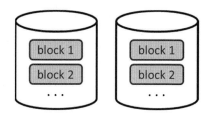

FIGURE 20.7

RAID 1 data layout.

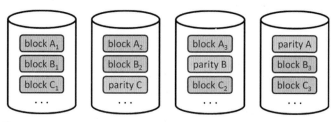

FIGURE 20.8

RAID 5 data layout.

data drive on all other drives in the array (data mirroring). Most typical installations use just one redundant drive (mirror) in addition to the primary drive. Hence, the number of data disks is fixed at $d = 1$; assuming a general case with p mirror drives, the RAID 1 array can tolerate up to p concurrent drive failures without data loss. While read accesses can take advantage of all I/O devices to issue concurrent requests for a better throughput, write operations need to store data replicas on all mirror drives, achieving the write throughput of a single drive. The resulting formulae are:

$$d = 1, p \geq 1$$

$$B_{R_1} = (p + 1) \cdot B_{R_D}$$

$$B_{W_1} = B_{W_D}$$

$$C_1 = C_D$$

20.3.5.3 RAID 5: Block-Level Striping with Single Distributed Parity

RAID 5 is one of the most commonly used data protection schemes. The additional (marked green in Fig. 20.8) parity blocks computed for each stripe are distributed in round-robin fashion across all participating devices. This enables the system to achieve high read bandwidth, effectively matching that of RAID 0 with an equal number of disks. The main issue of RAID 5 storage is its high vulnerability in a degraded state, i.e., after it has suffered a drive failure. Even if the replacement drive is quickly furnished, the rebuild process for the whole array may take several hours. During that time the component drives are accessed at close to full bandwidth, exposing the remaining devices to increased stress levels. A second device malfunction during that time may effectively destroy the nonrebuilt fraction of data stored in the array.

$$d \geq 2, p = 1$$
$$B_{R_5} = (d + 1) \cdot B_{R_D}$$
$$B_{W_5} = d \cdot B_{W_D}$$
$$C_5 = d \cdot C_D$$

20.3.5.4 RAID 6: Block-Level Striping with Dual Distributed Parity

To maintain the array operation in a degraded state with no more than two failed drives, RAID 6 associates two parity drives with each group of data drives. Much like RAID 5, the parity blocks are distributed over all drives in the array. Parity information, denoted in Fig. 20.9 by indexes p and q, must be computed using different methods, e.g., conventional bitwise XOR on the original contents of the stripe and XOR on the stripe contents transformed by an irreducible binary polynomial selected using Galois field [2] theory. Following a single drive failure, the array may be reconstructed using the conventional parity, which is fast to compute.

$$d \geq 2, \quad p = 2$$
$$B_{R_6} = (d + 2) \cdot B_{R_D}$$
$$B_{W_6} = d \cdot B_{W_D}$$
$$C_6 = d \cdot C_D$$

20.3.5.5 Hybrid RAID Variants

The most common hybrid RAID configurations are illustrated in Fig. 20.10. RAID 10, also denoted RAID 1+0, combines data mirroring at a lower level and striping at a higher level. This provides the benefits of a simple-to-implement redundancy scheme (mirroring) with improved data access performance due to striping. The main drawback is the low storage utilization of 50%. The configuration shown in Fig. 20.10 can tolerate two drive failures (one per mirror group). A variant of RAID 10 that improves storage utilization replaces the mirroring with RAID 5 at the lowest level and is known as RAID 50. As the smallest number of devices supported by RAID 5 is three, the minimum layout of RAID 50 consists of six devices.

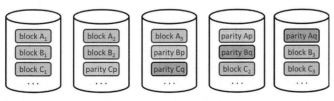

FIGURE 20.9

RAID 6 data layout.

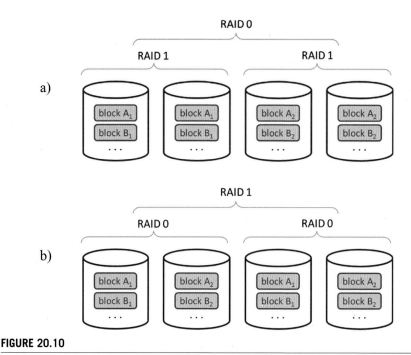

FIGURE 20.10

Diagram of data distribution in (a) RAID 10 (stripe of mirrors) and (b) RAID 01 (mirror of stripes).

RAID 01 (or 0+1) has the same storage utilization, capacity, and access performance as RAID 10 with an equivalent number of mirrors and stripe units. However, while RAID 10 still is able to operate with one failed drive per mirror group, in RAID 01 the loss of a single drive equals the loss of the entire stripe. This has dramatic consequences for rebuild performance: RAID 10 can accomplish this by simply copying the contents of the remaining drive in its mirror group without disturbing other components of the array, while RAID 01 must pull the data from another functional mirror, potentially interfering with its regular operation. RAID 01 has, however, practical application when portions of the array are distributed over the network. Having a fully functional local RAID 0 setup is more important in the event of a network outage than having a mirror containing partial data.

20.4 **Role and Function of File Systems**

The mass storage devices discussed before expose only limited types of data access interfaces. They are closely related to the low-level protocols used for data transfers between the device and the system's memory, and to the physical data layout and storage partitioning permitted by the device. The stored data may only be accessed at predefined granularities depending on the particular device, namely at the level of physical *blocks* (occasionally also referred to as *records* or *sectors*) that typically vary in size from 512 bytes to as much as 16 Kbytes. Carrying out small modifications of stored data or appending to it information in smaller-than-block-sized amounts may require a sequence of multiple read and write operations. Such direct data accesses necessitate correct calculation of physical addresses of relevant blocks. Even though direct access to the physical medium is on occasion necessary to extract a predictable level of performance from a storage device or to ensure strict control of data state replication in some applications, it is far too inconvenient for general use in multitasking and multiuser environments.

File systems provide many usability and convenience features, including storage space management and organization, a consistent programming interface that is portable and mostly independent from the underlying mass storage device types, and extensions that expose functions of other system components through the same application programming interface (API). The most notable features commonly supported by file systems are as follows:

- **Organization.** The file system imposes a hierarchical layout using *directories* and *files* as its primary components. Directories serve as containers for other directories and files, while the files contain the actual datasets written to or read from the mass storage. File systems rarely impose limitations on what kinds of information may be stored inside files; this is usually decided by the applications creating and accessing files. In many cases additional conventions (such as file name extensions) and even software are required to decipher the actual contents of files, which otherwise may be viewed only as anonymous byte streams. Depending on a file system, file size is usually limited to some large value that rarely interferes with the practical aspects of file access.
- **Namespace.** One of the most important aspects of a file system is the support of a persistent and system-architecture-independent naming scheme for stored information. All logical names of files and directories are expressed in the form of *paths*, or multicomponent strings in which each element names the containing directory ordered from the topmost in the hierarchy to the lowest level at the path's leaf. Thus, each file system component is uniquely identified by its symbolic name. While some details of path construction and how many roots (i.e., top-level hierarchy entry points) are supported differ between the individual file systems, the overall naming scheme often conforms to the same common model across many implementations.
- **Metadata.** Due to the shared nature of file systems, access to certain datasets must be constrained to only preapproved users in the system. In Unix, this is commonly arranged at the level of the file or directory owner, specific multiuser group, and "others" (all users). In each of these categories, the access rights may be individually enabled for reading, writing, and executing a specific file system entry. Some implementations also support more fine-grained access schemes, such as access control lists (ACLs), through which arbitrary permissions can be

assigned to arbitrary user sets. Metadata are also used to describe other properties of files, most notably their size in bytes.

- **Programming interface (API).** From the user's perspective, one of the fundamental operational properties of a file system is to permit creation of, writing to, and reading back the contents of files. This is accomplished through library calls that internally invoke the lower-level system functions. The files are identified by their symbolic names (paths) before the actual data access functions are enabled. The API then relies on shorter and fixed-type handles associated with files open for access. Besides file data access, it also supports the manipulation of storage hierarchy, such as directory traversal, file and subdirectory deletion, and creation of new subdirectories.

- **Storage space management.** As all physical devices have explicit capacity limits, the file system must carefully monitor the usage of space on the storage medium, which may be shared potentially between millions of files and directories. Additionally, the space allocation for the newly created files should be performed in a way that ensures good access performance for the specific device type. Thus, for standard HDDs, the file system typically strives to reserve the space for a file in continuous segments that reside on the same platter and cylinder since the sequential access offers the highest effective data bandwidth and latency.

- **File system mounting.** Computers frequently utilize multiple storage devices at the same time. Some of them are made available for use at an arbitrary time, such as removable media. This is performed in a process called *mounting*, in which the hierarchy defined by the imported file system is exposed to the OS. In single-namespace file systems (e.g., Unix), this requires support to expand the existing name hierarchy. In such OSs the *mount points* at which the external file systems are imported can conceivably be any existing directories. After the mount operation is completed, the imported file system hierarchy replaces the original layout below the mount point.

- **Special files.** The Unix environment is commonly known for employing the "everything is a file" model. This means that the file system namespace may be used to provide access to other system entities and software constructs such as raw devices, named pipes, and sockets to, e.g., obtain additional performance benefits or implement interprocess communication. Unfortunately, the elegance of the abstraction breaks when access to advanced features or adjustment of control parameters is necessary.

- **Fault handling.** A properly designed file system can minimize the impact of device failures on stored data integrity. These faults can span from individual bad blocks to whole devices. Due to often-used data caching in memory, a commonly occurring problem is caused by power fluctuations or system crashes that may affect the result of a write operation in progress or destroy unwritten data in memory. Many file systems deal with this by scanning the contents of data structures on the storage device during bootstrap and fixing incompatible entries using a dedicated utility program, such as *fsck* in Unix.

The landscape of currently available file systems covers many instances with different features and characteristics, deployment environments, target storage devices and media, and applications. There are file systems specifically optimized for use with HDDs, SSDs, flash memories, tapes, and optical media. File systems may transparently support compression to save space and encryption to protect the confidentiality of the stored information. Pseudo file systems are used to expose details related to arbitrary installed devices and system data structures using familiar semantics (such as *procfs*, *sysfs*, and *devfs* in Linux). Particularly important to HPC are distributed and parallel file systems, which support multiple clients communicating with storage devices over network or computer interconnects. However, they do not share file contents at the physical block level but implement a service layer translating and executing received requests. Not all distributed file systems can necessarily provide a high performance concurrent access to the same file from multiple clients, instead focusing on supporting the shared namespace and metadata and achieving significantly better throughputs when each client operates on its own, disjoint set of files. This issue is better addressed by parallel file systems, making them more suitable for supercomputing applications that may read or write various sections of the same file or file set from multiple compute nodes. Note that this mode of operation is associated with several nontrivial challenges. First, a file parallel system needs to employ appropriate mechanisms to accommodate multiple storage devices by distributing the contents of files over multiple disks or SSDs (striping). This is necessary to extract the required aggregate data throughput. The stripe unit has to be carefully chosen so as to not impose too high an overhead (small blocks) or to not destroy striping benefits for smaller files (large blocks). Second, the file system is expected to provide the abstraction of a single server to the accessors: the details of the underlying architecture, physical arrangement of supporting hosts and storage devices, fault tolerance measures, file striping parameters, and many other aspects should be hidden from users who are not interested in optimizing the I/O performance for specific applications. A familiar file access interface (such as the Portable Operating System Interface [POSIX]) should be provided to reduce the learning curve for new users and facilitate application porting. Third, both metadata and data have to utilize appropriate consistency protocols, since there must be no discrepancies between the file contents, sizes, and their other attributes when simultaneously viewed by different nodes. While multiple readers of a file can be easily accommodated, the addition of even a single writer may complicate the way information is propagated to and possibly replicated on the participating nodes. Parallel file systems may also resort to relaxing access atomicity (i.e., guarantee that no portion of data read or written in a single call is ever modified by overlapping preceding or subsequent accesses) to be able to attain reasonable data throughput rates. Finally, the governing algorithms must scale to support not only a large number of concurrent accessors, possibly extending to the total number of compute nodes in the system, but also growing storage pools.

20.4.1 The Essential POSIX File Interface

The POSIX standard [3] describes the elements of runtime API, shells, and utilities, specifying compatibility requirements for variants of the Unix OS. The file I/O interface is part of the specification. The necessarily limited overview presented here focuses only on a subset of data transfer functions, with a few auxiliary calls that are frequently used in parallel programs. Directory access and manipulation, link creation, file deletion, and other namespace and metadata functions are not discussed as they are rarely invoked directly from applications, instead being typically handled by job scripts using appropriate system utilities. File access functions come in two flavors: system calls and buffered I/O. Both are described below along with usage examples and enumeration of their semantic differences.

20.4.1.1 System Calls for File Access

System calls are used to directly invoke OS kernel functions. While all system calls typically share the same generic invocation format, a thin wrapper layer is additionally provided by the runtime library for user convenience and to facilitate first-level argument checking. Since system calls incur greater overheads than regular user-space function invocation, this interface should be used to transfer larger amounts of data (several memory pages or more) per call. The interfaces described below show function arguments and the necessary "include" files defining their prototypes and optional argument macros. Since system calls are often used to access other entities in the system, such as terminals, pipes, or sockets, only semantics related to regular file access are discussed below.

File open and close

```
#include <sys/stat.h>
#include <fcntl.h>
#include <unistd.h>

int open(const char *path, int flags, ...);
int close(int fd);
```

The open call allocates an integer *file descriptor* that shall be used in all subsequent accesses to the file whose name is specified in *path*. The descriptor returned is the lowest integer not currently used for file access by the calling process and identifies the kernel data structure associated with the opened file. The *flags* argument consists of exactly one of *O_RDONLY, O_WRONLY,* and *O_RDWR,* respectively, for read-only, write-only, and mixed read-and-write access. The access mode flag can be bitwise or-ed with other flags, some of which are listed below:

- *O_APPEND* causes the initial file offset to be set to the end of a file instead of its beginning.
- *O_CREAT* creates the file if it doesn't exist and is otherwise ignored as long as *O_EXCL* is not set. The file is created with access rights specified in the third argument that conform to conventional owner/group/other permissions.

- *O_EXCL* when used together with *O_CREAT* will cause the call to fail if the file exists. If the flag is specified without *O_CREAT*, the result is undefined.
- *O_TRUNC* truncates the existing file to zero length if the access mode is *O_WRONLY* or *O_RDWR*. Using this flag in read-only mode produces an undefined result.

The successful `open` call returns a nonnegative integer that is a valid file descriptor. A negative one is returned on failure and a corresponding code is set in the global *errno* variable. Error causes may include insufficient access or file creation rights, invalid path, exceeded maximum number of simultaneously opened files in the system, and requested file creation with exclusive flag but the target file already exists. A failed `open` cannot modify an existing file status or create a new file.

The opened files may be closed by passing their descriptor to the close call. This causes deallocation of the file data structure and releases the file descriptor for reuse within the calling process.

Sequential data access

```
#include <unistd.h>

ssize_t read(int fd, void *buf, size_t n);
ssize_t write(int fd, void *buf, size_t n);
```

The *read* function attempts to read at most *n* bytes at the current offset from a file identified by *fd* into a user buffer pointed to by *buf*. Successful invocation returns the actual number of bytes stored in the user buffer. The call may return a value less than *n* if the number of bytes between the current offset associated with *fd* and the end of the file is smaller than the requested value. A successful call will increase the file offset by the number of bytes transferred to the user buffer and update the file access time to the system time at which the access was carried out.

The *write* call attempts to transfer *n* bytes provided in the user buffer pointed to by *buf* to a file identified by the descriptor *fd*. The position at which the data are stored in the file is determined by the current value of the file offset associated with the descriptor. If the offset of the last written byte is greater than the file length, the file length will be updated to the position of the last written byte increased by one. A successful call returns the actual number of bytes written; the internal file offset is incremented by this value and its modification and status change timestamps.

Either function returns −1 on error and sets the global variable *errno* to indicate the error cause. These include the use of an invalid file descriptor, exceeding the maximum offset, a read operation that has been interrupted by a signal without having started yet, and a write that would exceed the maximum size of the file without the possibility to perform a partial data transfer.

Data access with explicit offset

```
#include <unistd.h>

ssize_t pread(int fd, void *buf, size_t n, off_t offs);
ssize_t pwrite(int fd, void *buf, size_t n, off_t offs);
```

The *pread* and *pwrite* calls provide explicit offset variants of read and write functions and therefore may be used to perform data access in any location in the file. The value of the implicit file offset associated with the descriptor *fd* is not modified by the calls.

Synchronization with storage device

```
#include <unistd.h>

int fsync(int fd);
```

The *fsync* function transfers all data and metadata associated with the file identified by *fd* to the underlying storage device. The call blocks until all data are transferred or an error occurs. On success, zero is returned; otherwise it is −1.

File status query

```
#include <fcntl.h>
#include <sys/stat.h>

int lstat(const char *restrict path, struct stat *restrict buf);
int fstat(const char *restrict path, struct stat *restrict buf);
```

Both calls retrieve metadata of the file system entity identified either by path (for *lstat*) or the opened file descriptor *fd* (for *fstat*) into a status structure pointed to by *buf*. They return the value of zero on success and −1 otherwise. Individual metadata entries are stored in different fields of *struct stat* and include, among others:

- **st_size**—size of file in bytes.
- **st_blksize**—size of block used by file system in I/O operations.
- **st_mode**—file type and mode. If set, bit flags S_IRUSR, S_IWUSR, S_IRGRP, S_IWGRP, S_IROTH, and S_IWOTH identify enabled read and write access rights for user, group, and other users in the system.
- **st_uid**—user ID of file owner.
- **st_gid**—group ID of file owner.
- **st_atim**—time of last file access.
- **st_mtim**—time of the last modification of file.
- **st_ctim**—last status change time.

Code 20.1 shows an example code using the system call file interface to write a number of integers to a created (or truncated) file, flush it to persistent storage, and read back a smaller section of written file.

```
001 #include <stdio.h>
002 #include <stdlib.h>
003 #include <unistd.h>
004 #include <sys/stat.h>
005 #include <fcntl.h>
006
007 #define BUFFER_SIZE 4096
008 #define HALF (BUFFER_SIZE/2)
009
010 int main(int argc, char **argv)
011 {
012    // initialize buffer
013    int wbuf[BUFFER_SIZE], i;
014    for (i = 0; i < BUFFER_SIZE; i++) wbuf[i] = 2*i+1;
015
016    // open file, write buffer contents, and flush it to the storage
017    // the file is accessible (read/write) only to the creator
018    int fd = open("test_file.dat", O_WRONLY | O_CREAT | O_TRUNC, 0600);
019    int bytes = BUFFER_SIZE*sizeof(int);
020    if (write(fd, wbuf, bytes) != bytes) {
021       fprintf(stderr, "Error: truncated write, exiting!\n");
022       exit(1);
023    }
024    fsync(fd);
025    close(fd);
026
027    // retrieve the second half of the file and verify its correctness
028    int rbuf[HALF];
029    fd = open("test_file.dat", O_RDONLY);
030    bytes /= 2;
031    if (pread(fd, rbuf, bytes, bytes) != bytes) {
032       fprintf(stderr, "Error: truncated read, exiting!\n");
033       exit(1);
034    }
035    close(fd);
036
037    for (i = 0; i < HALF; i++)
038       if (wbuf[i+HALF] != rbuf[i]) {
039          fprintf(stderr, "Error: retrieved data is invalid!\n");
040          exit(2);
041       }
042    printf("Data verified.\n");
043
044    return 0;
045 }
```

CODE 20.1

Example demonstrating the use of I/O system calls to create, write, and read data from a file.

20.4.1.2 Buffered File Input/Output

Buffered file access is implemented by the Unix runtime system library, *libc*. It introduces additional data buffers in the application's address space that may improve performance if frequent operations involving small amounts of data are performed.

The buffers and their control parameters are not exposed directly to the application. Whenever possible, I/O calls issued by the user are satisfied by copying the data between the user buffer in the application and the internal library buffer, thus avoiding the overhead of system calls. This interface is also known as the *streaming* interface (and related file description structures are known as *streams*) since the best performance is achieved for sequential data access. This interface is also a part of the *stdio.h* chapter of the ISO/IEC C language standard [4] and therefore far more portable than functions based on system calls.

File open and close

```
#include <stdio.h>

FILE *fopen(const char *restrict path, const char *restrict mode);
int fclose(FILE *stream);
```

The *fopen* call opens or creates a file identified by *path* and associates it with a stream. The first character of the mode argument determines the file access mode and may be one of the following:

- "r"—opens the file for reading.
- "w"—creates a file or truncates the file to zero length if it already exists and opens it for writing.
- "a"—creates or opens a file for write access at the end of the file (append mode).

The mode string may also contain a "+" character, which enables access in *update* mode, or both reading and writing performed in any order. The other characteristics defined by the first character of the mode string are preserved. If the file is used in update mode, the application must ensure that I/O operations are separated by a seek call or, in case of reads following writes, *fflush*.

A successful call to *fopen* returns a valid stream pointer, or NULL otherwise. The opened streams may be closed using the *fclose* function. The side effect of the close operation is propagation of the contents of data buffers to the file.

Sequential data access

```
#include <stdio.h>

size_t fread(void *restrict buf, size_t size, size_t n, FILE
*restrict stream);
size_t fwrite(const void *restrict buf, size_t size, size_t n,
            FILE *restrict stream);
```

The *fread* and *fwrite* functions are stream equivalents of *read* and *write* calls. They attempt to respectively read or write an integral number of elements *n*, each of size *size*, from an opened stream *stream* by transferring them from or to the user buffer pointed to by *buf*. Both functions return the number of elements successfully transferred. The return value may be less than *n* only if the end of the file has been encountered while reading or an error has occurred during writing. The file offset associated with the stream is increased by the number of bytes successfully transferred. If an error occurs, the value of the offset for the file associated with the stream is unspecified.

Offset update and query

```
#include <stdio.h>

int fseek(FILE *stream, long offs, int whence);
long ftell(FILE *stream);
```

The `fseek` function sets the value of the file offset for a specified *stream* in accordance with the values of *offs* and *whence* arguments. The latter can be one of *SEEK_-SET*, *SEEK_CUR*, or *SEEK_END*. The first variant sets the file offset to *offs*, the second to the sum of the current file offset and value of *offs*, and the last to the length of file increments by *offs*. If the file offset is advanced beyond the current end of the file, the file size is updated accordingly and the yet-unwritten regions of the file will read as zeroes. Upon success, *fseek* returns 0, or −1 on error.

The *ftell* call returns the current value of the internal file offset associated with stream *stream* measured in bytes from the start of the file. The error is indicated by −1 as the return value.

Buffer flush

```
#include <stdio.h>

int fflush(FILE *stream);
```

The *fflush* function forces the unwritten data stored in a buffer associated with the *stream* that has been opened in write or update mode to be written to the underlying file. If the stream has been opened for reading, the call will set the offset of the underlying file to the current offset position of the stream. If *stream* is a null pointer, the function will perform the described action for all opened streams. The call returns zero on success and EOF on error.

Conversion between streams and file descriptors

```
#include <stdio.h>
#include <unistd.h>

FILE *fdopen(int fd, const char *mode);
int fileno(FILE *stream);
```

On occasion it may be useful to convert between streams and file descriptors to be able to invoke alternative interface functions. Thus, *fdopen* accepts an open file descriptor and mode string, whose meaning is the same as for the *fopen* call, and creates and returns a corresponding stream descriptor. The supplied *mode* argument has to be compatible with the access mode of the file referred to by the descriptor *fd*. The offset of the returned stream will be set to the same value as that of the opened file indicated by `fd`. A failed call returns a null pointer. The converse operation, *fileno*, extracts the descriptor of the underlying file from the specified stream structure or returns −1 to indicate the error.

Code 20.2 presents a converted version of a program originally listed in Code 20.1 that uses a buffered I/O interface instead of system calls. While the transformation is obvious for most of the I/O functions used, one detail is particularly noteworthy. Since the *fflush* call native to the *stdio* library can only push the contents

```
001 #include <stdio.h>
002 #include <stdlib.h>
003 #include <unistd.h>
004
005 #define BUFFER_SIZE 4096
006 #define HALF (BUFFER_SIZE/2)
007
008 int main(int argc, char **argv)
009 {
010   // initialize buffer
011   int wbuf[BUFFER_SIZE], i;
012   for (i = 0; i < BUFFER_SIZE; i++) wbuf[i] = 2*i+1;
013
014   // open file, write buffer contents, and flush it to the storage
015   FILE *f = fopen("test_file.dat", "w");
016   size_t count = BUFFER_SIZE;
017   if (fwrite(wbuf, sizeof(int), count, f) != count) {
018     fprintf(stderr, "Error: truncated write, exiting!\n");
019     exit(1);
020   }
021   fflush(f); fsync(fileno(f));
022   fclose(f);
023
024   // retrieve the second half of the file and verify its correctness
025   int rbuf[HALF];
026   f = fopen("test_file.dat", "r");
027   count /= 2;
028   fseek(f, count*sizeof(int), SEEK_SET);
029   if (fread(rbuf, sizeof(int), count, f) != count) {
030     fprintf(stderr, "Error: truncated read, exiting!\n");
031     exit(1);
032   }
033   fclose(f);
034
035   for (i = 0; i < HALF; i++)
036     if (wbuf[i+HALF] != rbuf[i]) {
037       fprintf(stderr, "Error: retrieved data invalid!\n");
038       exit(2);
039     }
040   printf("Data verified.\n");
041
042   return 0;
043 }
```

CODE 20.2

Equivalent program to Code 20.1 that uses the streaming I/O interface.

of stream buffers to the kernel, the actual propagation of dirty data to storage has to be performed by a system call (*fsync*). To provide the file descriptor expected as an input argument to that call, *fileno* is used to retrieve it from the stream descriptor.

20.4.2 Network File System

The Network File System (NFS) is one of the oldest and at the same time one of the most broadly deployed distributed file systems in computing installations. Originally conceived at Sun Microsystems in 1984, it is currently an open standard that has spurred many implementations, including several open-source versions. Its main appeal is that a regular file system, the access to which would otherwise be confined to a single host, can be "exported" to permit remote access to its contents (files, directories, links, etc.) from multiple client machines. There are no significant restrictions regarding the properties of the underlying file system; any POSIX-compliant file system can be accessed via NFS, and in some cases (e.g., new technology file system through Microsoft Subsystem for UNIX-based Applications) even file systems with non−POSIX-compliant interfaces are available. The remote file system can be transparently mounted at any place in the directory hierarchy and accessed as if it was local.

NFS services can utilize both transmission control protocol (TCP) (connection-oriented) and user datagram protocol (UDP) (datagram) messages. At the heart of the protocol stack is the support for Remote Procedure Call (RPC), which permits sending requests from clients to a remote host, invocation of a function local to the host, and propagation of returned data and operation status in reply packets. Originally based on Sun RPC implementation, it is now defined by the Open Network Computing RPC specification [5]. Due to the requirement to support hosts with different data type properties and byte order, an external data representation [6] layer is used to serialize and retrieve the call arguments and other data that are conveyed as packet payload. To support RPC, *port mapper* services on a dedicated port 111 must be configured on the participating machines.

The basic architecture of NFS is illustrated in Fig. 20.11. Before the users are permitted to issue any data access requests, the remote file system has to be mounted on the client host. This is accomplished by the mount program parsing the name of the NFS server and asking it to provide the handle for the remote directory. If the requested directory exists and is permitted to be exported, the server returns its handle. This causes the local kernel to access the VFS layer and create a virtual node (vnode), or translation from a symbolic path to an arbitrary accessed file system object, for the remote directory. Among other things, vnodes store information whether the target object is local or remote. Thus, the subsequent open request for the remote file issued by the user finds that the parent portion of the file's path translates to a vnode marked as remote, retrieves the stored server address, sends the *lookup* request to the server utilizing the RPC code stubs on the client and server, and creates an opened file entry using the retrieved file attributes provided by the server. The corresponding descriptor index is then returned to the user program.

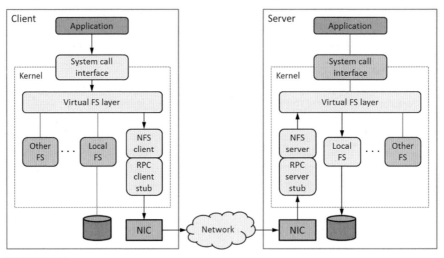

FIGURE 20.11

Architecture of Network File System (NFS) and its integration with other kernel components in Linux. The arrows show the propagation of the client request to the server and remote file system. The virtual file system (VFS) layer provides an implementation-independent interface to access the underlying file system(s). The NFS client relies on the Remote Procedure Call (RPC) service to enable transparent invocation of file system functions on a remote node as requested by the client.

The lookup procedure is used since the server does not execute a regular *open* call to avoid creation of state; as a result of lookup, a specially formed *handle* is returned that uniquely identifies the file to the server. Data access, such as read operations, proceed similarly, except that since the client may be permitted to cache the file data locally in newer NFS revisions, a local cache lookup is performed to check if the data are available locally. NFS servers also use a simple strategy to deal with request duplication, such as that caused by packet retransmits due to network errors. This applies only to *nonidempotent* requests, i.e., those that would fail if retransmitted, such as directory or file removal. The servers maintain *request replay cache* in which all nonidempotent requests are kept for a predetermined period; finding that a newly received request's transaction ID, source address, and port match one already in the cache will suppress its execution and cause the cached reply to be reemitted.

The first publicly released version of NFS was version 2 (NFSv2). Since it was developed in the late 1980s, it is considered dated by today's standards. It was replaced by NFSv3, a much-improved revision of the protocol that still preserved the "stateless" design. It may still be found in use today, although many data centers and institutions switched to the next version that introduces some minimal state at the server to handle features that otherwise would have to be supported externally. The current revision of NFS was heavily influenced by design of the Andrew File

System [7] and Microsoft's Common Internet File System [8]. NFSv4 [9] supports operations that inherently require server-side state, such as file locking. The new protocol is capable of byte-range locking that is lease based. Since clients may crash before releasing active locks, it forces them to stay in touch with the server for the duration of locked operations. Otherwise, the locks are revoked after a preset time-out. A new approach to caching of file contents called *delegation* has been introduced. It permits the clients to modify the files locally in its own cache without communication with the server. Read delegation can be granted to multiple clients simultaneously, while write delegation may be permitted to only one client at a time. When a conflict is detected for the currently held delegation(s), they may be revoked using a callback mechanism. Version 4 improves the overall response time by permitting compound RPCs, i.e., calls that combine several commonly executed request sequences (such as lookup, open, and read) into one. The security of operation and authentication has been substantially augmented through introduction of Kerberos 5 [10] and SPKM/LIPKEY [11]. The administrative overhead required to coordinate numeric user and group IDs across multiple hosts and to enforce conventional Unix permission flags is reduced thanks to the new ACL mechanism that interoperates with both POSIX and Windows ACLs. Finally, the NFSv4 protocol implements file migration and replication. Despite these improvements, NFS best supports *session semantics*, in which clients have exclusive access to files and the updates to them are propagated on file close (i.e., session finish).

20.4.3 Lustre File System

Lustre is a parallel distributed file system originally released in 2003. Its name has been derived from "Linux" and "clusters", indicating the intended target platforms for its deployment. Its development was initially carried out under the Department of Energy Accelerated Strategic Computing Initiative (ASCI) Path Forward [12]. Corporate ownership of the project and its code base changed hands several times and included Sun Microsystems, Oracle, Whamcloud, and, since 2012, Intel. Lustre provides a POSIX-compliant file system interface with atomic semantic support for most operations, thus avoiding data and metadata inconsistencies. Its design is highly scalable, making it a preferred file system for HPC by supporting multiple tens of thousands clients, petabytes of storage, and I/O bandwidths reaching multiple hundreds of GB/s. Deployment of multiple clusters is simplified with Lustre, as it permits aggregation of both the capacity and performance of multiple storage subsystems. The storage space and I/O throughput can also be dynamically increased by providing additional storage servers as needed. Lustre takes advantage of high performance networking infrastructure, such as low-latency communication and remote direct memory access (RDMA) over InfiniBand with OpenFabrics Enterprise Distribution (OFED) [13]. Lustre software enables bridging of multiple RDMA networks and provides integrated network diagnostics. The file system supports high availability with multiple failover modes using shared storage partitions and interfacing with different high-availability managers. This implements automatic failovers with no single point of failure as well as transparent application recovery. The chances of file system corruption are minimized through the multiple-mount protection feature. Particularly noteworthy is the online distributed file system check (LFSCK) that is capable of operating while the file system is in use to restore the data consistency after a major file system error is detected. The security of operation is enforced by permitting TCP connections only on privileged ports and application of ACLs and extended attributes based on POSIX ACLs with custom additions, such as *root squash* (reduction of effective access rights for the remote superuser). Lustre uses a distributed lock manager (LDLM) to permit file locking with byte granularity as well as fine-grain metadata locks to permit concurrent operation of multiple clients on shared files and directories. Lustre software is open sourced under the GPL 2.0 license; its current major revision is v2.15 (2022). Many of these features account for the popularity of Lustre deployment in HPC systems: as of June 2023, the majority of the 10 fastest supercomputers (Frontier, LUMI, Leonardo, TaihuLight, Perlmutter, Selene, Tianhe-2A) on the Top 500 list integrated Lustre or a Lustre-based file system as their storage management layer.

The schematic view of Lustre architecture is shown in Fig. 20.12. The primary functional components of a Lustre system include:

- **Management server** (MGS) is responsible for storing, managing, and supplying the configuration information to other Lustre components. It interacts with all targets (configuration providers) and clients (configuration accessors) in the

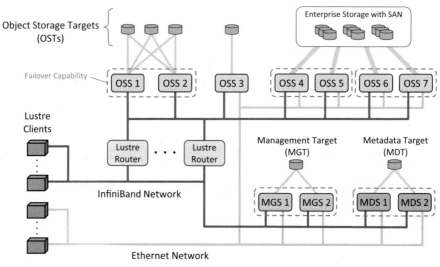

FIGURE 20.12

Layout of typical Lustre deployment at scale.

system. While MGS typically works using a dedicated set of storage devices for independent operation, the storage could also share the physical devices present in the metadata server pool.

- **Management target** (MGT) provides storage space for the MGS. Its space requirements rarely exceed 100 MB even on large-scale Lustre installations. While the performance of the underlying storage is not critical for the operation of the system (seeks and writes of small amounts of data), its reliability is paramount. MGT may leverage redundant storage structures such as RAID1 to provide it. Multiple MDTs per system are supported.

- **Metadata server** (MDS) is responsible for management of the names and directory contents. The namespace in Lustre may be distributed across multiple MDSs. Each MDS also handles network requests for one or more MDTs. MDS failovers are supported, in which a standby MDS assumes functions of a failed active MDS.

- **Metadata target** (MDT) stores various metadata, including directories, file names, permissions, and file layout information, on physical storage associated with an MDS. There is nominally one MDT per file system, although recent revisions support multiple MDTs under the distributed namespace environment (DNE). The primary MDT makes up the root of the file system, while the additional MDSs with their own attached MDTs may hold various sub-directories. It is also possible to distribute the contents of a single directory across multiple MDT nodes, thus creating a *striped directory*. MDT storage usually accounts for 1%–2% of the total file system capacity.

- **Object storage server** (OSS) services file data I/O requests and other network requests for up to 32 object storage targets (OSTs). A common Lustre configuration involves MDT on a dedicated hardware node, two or more OSTs on every OSS node, and an I/O client on every compute node of a system. The ratio of OSTs to OSSs typically varies between two and eight.

- **Object storage target** (OST) manages physical storage for user file contents. The file data is contained in one or more objects, each of which is under control of a specific, separate OST. The number of objects a file is divided into is configurable by the user. Single OST capacity is limited to 128 TB (256 TB on ZFS, an advanced file system originally developed at Sun Microsystems); the total file system capacity is the sum of the capacities of all OSTs.

- **Clients** execute the applications generating the I/O data. They may include conventional compute nodes, but also loosely associated desktops, workstations, or visualization servers that are permitted to mount the file system.

- **Lustre Networking** (LNET) provides the communication infrastructure for the whole system. Its main features include concurrent access to and support of many common network types (Ethernet, InfiniBand, Omni-Path, Gemini) and protocols emphasizing RDMA if available, routing between individual network segments, and high availability and recovery from network errors. Bonding of multiple network interfaces for increased bandwidth is also supported.

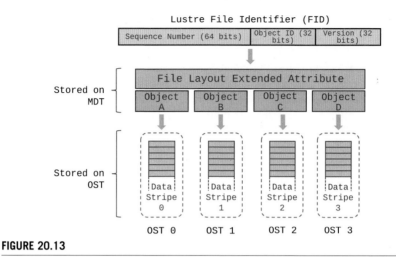

FIGURE 20.13

Lustre file layout.

The high-level organization of a file in Lustre is depicted in Fig. 20.13. The files are referred to by 128-bit file identifiers (FIDs) that consist of a unique 64-bit sequence number, a 32-bit object ID (OID), and a 32-bit version number. The FID identifies an object in MDT whose extended attributes encode the layout information: one or more pointers to OST objects that contain the file data. Since the objects must be stored on different OSTs, the data is striped in a round-robin fashion across all OSTs (obviously, no striping is applied if only one OST is associated with the file). The number of stripes, stripe size, and target OSTs are user configurable. The default stripe count is one and the default stripe size is 1 MB. There may be up to 2000 objects per file. Since the client performing data I/O operations on a file must first fetch the layout data from the MDT object identified by the FID, further data transfers can be arranged directly between the client node and the related OSS nodes storing the file data.

Efficient synchronization of file operations in parallel file systems is a key factor in achieving a good level of performance. Lustre resources are associated with locks that may be local or global. The distributed lock manager is based on a locking algorithm utilized by VAX DLM [14].

One of Lustre's strengths is fault management, which can be applied to most of its functional components. Two basic failover modes are available: active/passive and active/active. In the first configuration the active server processes client requests and provides resources while the passive server stays idle. In case of active node failure, the passive server becomes active and takes over. The second scenario involves multiple active servers, each providing a subset of resources. If one of them fails, the remaining ones take over the failed node's resources.

Table 20.6 Select Operational Parameters of Lustre

Parameter	Design Target	Production Tested
Maximum file size	32 PB (ldiskfs) 8 EB (ZFS)	Multiple TB
Maximum file count	1 trillion	25 billion
Maximum storage space	512 PB (ldiskfs) 1 EB (ZFS)	700 PB
Number of clients	≤131,072	50,000+
Single-client I/O performance	90% network bandwidth	15 GB/s data I/O
Aggregate-client I/O performance	50 TB/s	10 TB/s
OSS count	1000 OSSs, up to 4000 OSTs	450 OSSs with 900 750TB OSTs 1024 OSSs with 1024 72TB OSTs
Single OSS performance	15 GB/s	10 GB/s
Aggregate OSS performance	50 TB/s	20 TB/s
MDS count	≤256 MDTs, ≤256 MDSs	40 MDTs, 40 MDSs
MDS performance	1M create ops/s 2M stat ops/s	100K create ops/s 200K stat ops/s

Excerpted from Intel Corp., Lustre Software Release 2.x Operations Manual [Online]. Available: http://doc.lustre.org/lustre_manual.pdf

An overview of various operational parameters of the Lustre file system is presented in Table 20.6. Since the underlying file system can be selected by the system administrator as either *ldiskfs* (a modified and patched revision of the Linux *ext4* journaling file system) or ZFS, some of the absolute limits listed depend on the file system type used. As Lustre continues to be deployed in installations of increasing scales and capacities, some of the listed configurations tested in production may be out of date by the time of publication.

20.5 **Summary and Outcomes**

- Mass storage enables computational state retention to be persistent between power cycles of the machine.
- The majority of storage systems utilize four main types of mass storage devices: HDDs, SSDs, magnetic tapes, and optical storage. Although they serve largely the same purpose, they substantially differ in the underlying physical phenomena used to implement data retention as well as their operational characteristics and cost.

- The storage hierarchy is subdivided into four levels that differ in access latency and supported data bandwidth, with latencies increasing and effective transfer bandwidth dropping when moving away from the top level of the hierarchy.
- Primary storage comprises system memories, caches, and CPU register sets.
- Secondary storage is the first level of storage that leverages mass storage devices. Normally, CPUs cannot directly access the secondary (or higher-level) storage and therefore transfers of data between the primary and secondary storage have to be mediated by the OS and computer chipset.
- Secondary storage capacity grew 12 orders of magnitude between the 1940s and 2022. Device I/O bandwidth advanced six orders of magnitude over the same period.
- The most commonly used technologies in the secondary storage tier are HDDs and SSDs, which offer the industry's best cost per unit of storage coupled with satisfactory reliability.
- RAID attempts to address the reliability issues of conventional mass storage devices.
- Latency remains one of the biggest performance bottlenecks plaguing most of the I/O devices in use today.
- File systems provide an abstraction necessary to manage the information kept on mass storage devices. They organize the information in a hierarchical layout, provide the human-accessible namespace to uniquely identify individual stored entities, maintain attributes describing access permissions and various properties of individual entries, verify the consistency of stored information, provide fault recovery mechanisms, and expose the user interface for access.
- Distributed file systems are file systems that are capable of handling I/O requests issued by multiple clients over the network. To keep up with the demands of scaling, they frequently span multiple server nodes while providing a "single view" access to the stored data and related namespace.
- Parallel file systems are distributed file systems that are specifically optimized to efficiently support concurrent file access from parallel applications. In particular, they implement synchronization mechanisms that permit the distributed application to operate on different sections of the same file or enable strided access for individual clients accessing the same file while preserving the consistency of data and metadata for multiple accessors.
- The POSIX standard defines a local file access interface in Unix environments. Two modes of access are commonly supported by the runtime library: one based on system calls and another on buffered file I/O (streams).
- NFS is one of the most frequently deployed distributed file systems in small and medium cluster environments. It permits the use of the POSIX interface and implements session semantics in which the clients most efficiently operate on disjoint files with updates propagated at the end of the session (file close).
- Lustre is a high-performance open-source parallel file system supporting multiple network types and host architectures. Due to its good performance,

20.6 **Questions and Problems**

1. What are the main storage-related challenges presented by large HPC systems? Elaborate.
2. Identify parameters the values of which may be used to classify an arbitrary HDD to one of the market segment categories mentioned in the last column of Table 20.1.
3. Your product development team has been tasked with design and implementation of an in-flight entertainment system for a large airliner. Your responsibility is to select a suitable lightweight storage device from several technologies discussed in the chapter. Justify your choice, taking into account (a) cost, (b) reliability of operation, (c) required storage capacity, and (d) performance. When considering your choices, be mindful of the target operating environment for the system.
4. A 4096-node cluster runs large-scale simulations that are checkpointed every 2 hours using distributed SSDs for intermediate I/O storage. The nodes are equipped with 64 GB of memory each and the ratio of nodes to storage devices is 16:1. Calculate:
   a. The minimum required capacity of each burst buffer to keep the checkpoint phase as short as possible.
   b. The duration of a large simulation before device failures appear given that the TBW metric of each burst buffer is 400.
5. A RAID 6 system uses eight 4-TB drives, including the minimum required number of parity drives. Calculate the effective read and write data throughput for the array. What is its effective data capacity? How many drives would be needed to assemble a RAID 10 system of equivalent capacity? How would the data throughputs change?
6. A particle detector generates data streams requiring an aggregate bandwidth of 4 TB/s in bursts of up to 1 minute long. The streams are analyzed by a 2048-node system that extracts events of interest and compresses them, reducing the data volume to 1/100th of the original size. The events of interest are then archived on a dedicated robotic tape storage using LTO-9 tapes at a sustained rate of 300 MB/s per deck. Given that experiments (each producing a single burst of data) are performed in 1-hour intervals and tape change overhead is factored into sustained storage bandwidth, answer the following:
   a. How many tape decks working in parallel are necessary to accommodate the extracted event data without forced interruptions to the experiment schedule or additional intermediate data buffers?
   b. If the capacity of tape cartridge is 18 TB, how many tapes are required to provide data storage for experiments performed over the span of 1 year?

What is the estimated shelf volume required to archive all cartridges written in 1 year if the dimensions of a single one are 102 mm × 106 mm × 22 mm?

c. Assuming data processing requires a negligible amount of memory in addition to that needed to hold the input data, how much DRAM (in powers of two) much each node be equipped with to avoid the use of intermediate data buffers?

7. Summarize the main challenges of creating efficient persistent data storage for an HPC system. How may they be solved?

8. What are the differences between system-call-based and streaming I/O interfaces in POSIX? What are their implications for file access performance?

9. Write a program that saves an array of 1000 double-precision floating-point numbers to a file using in-memory layout and an array of 1000 structures consisting of one character and one double-precision number to another file. Do the sizes of the generated files match the estimated values based on the sizes of the involved elementary data types multiplied by array size? If not, what is the reason for the discrepancy? Can the inefficiency (if any) be eliminated?

10. Consider the following code that prints array elements to a file and reads them back:

```
001 #include <stdio.h>
002
003 #define SIZE 512
004 #define FILENAME "myfile"
005
006 int main() {
007    double data[SIZE], iodata[SIZE];
008    for (int i = 0; i < SIZE; i++) data[i] = i+1/(double)(i+1);
009
010    FILE *f = fopen(FILENAME, "w");
011    for (int i = 0; i < SIZE; i++) fprintf(f, "%lf\n", data[i]);
012    fclose(f);
013
014    f = fopen(FILENAME, "r");
015    for (int i = 0; i < SIZE; i++) {
016       fscanf(f, "%lf", &iodata[i]);
017       if (data[i] != iodata[i])
018          printf("ERROR: item %d should be %lf, got %lf\n", i, data[i], iodata[i]);
019    }
020    fclose(f);
021    return 0;
022 }
```

a. Is running the code going to produce any error messages? Why? Verify your answer by compiling and executing the program.

b. How would you fix the encountered problem(s)?

c. Based on this experience, would you recommend saving floating-point data as text? Justify your answer.

11. Contrast distributed and parallel file systems. Which solutions provided by the latter improve the efficiency of concurrent accesses to shared files?

References

[1]   IBM Corp., RAMAC, The First Magnetic Hard Disk, [Online]. Available: http://www-03.ibm.com/ibm/history/ibm100/us/en/icons/ramac/.

[2]   H.M. Edwards, Galois Theory, Springer-Verlag, 1984.

[3]   IEEE and The Open Group, The Open Group Base Specifications Issue 7, IEEE Standard 1003 (2016) 1−2008. Edition, [Online]. Available: http://pubs.opengroup.org/onlinepubs/9699919799.

[4]   ISO/IEC 9899:201x C Language Standard Draft, 12 April 2011. [Online]. Available: http://www.open-std.org/jtc1/sc22/wg14/www/docs/n1570.pdf.

[5]   IETF Network Working Group, RFC 5531: RPC: Remote Procedure Call Protocol Specification Version 2, 2009 [Online]. Available: https://tools.ietf.org/html/rfc5531.

[6]   IETF Network Working Group, RFC 4506: XDR: External Data Representation Standard, 2006 [Online]. Available: https://tools.ietf.org/html/rfc4506.

[7]   R.H. Arpaci-Dusseau, A.C. Arpaci-Dusseau, The Andrew File System (AFS), in: Operating Systems: Three Easy Pieces, Arpac-Dusseaui Books, 2014.

[8]   Microsoft TechNet Library, Common Internet File System, Microsoft, [Online]. Available: https://technet.microsoft.com/en-us/library/cc939973.aspx.

[9]   IETF, RFC 7862: Network File System (NFS) Version 4 Minor Version 2 Protocol, 2016 [Online]. Available: https://datatracker.ietf.org/doc/html/rfc7862.

[10] Kerberos: The Network Authentication Protocol, Massachusetts Institute of Technology, 2016 [Online]. Available: http://web.mit.edu/kerberos/.

[11] IETF Network Working Group, RFC 2847: LIPKEY - A Low Infrastructure Public Key Mechanism Using SPKM, 2000 [Online]. Available: https://tools.ietf.org/html/rfc2847.

[12] G. Grider, The ASCI/DOD Scalable I/O History and Strategy, 2004 [Online]. Available: https://www.dtc.umn.edu/resources/grider1.pdf.

[13] OFED Overview, OpenFabrics Alliance, [Online]. Available: https://www.openfabrics.org/index.php/openfabrics-software.html.

[14] N.P. Kronenberg, H.M. Levy, W.D. Strecker, VAXcluster: a closely-coupled distributed system, ACM Transactions on Computer Systems 4 (2) (1986) 130−146.

Intermediate MPI

21

21.1 User-Defined Data Types

A simplified type management introduced in Section 14.5.2 in Chapter 14 is easy to understand and satisfies many fundamental communication patterns. However, as presented it is essentially limited to scalars or contiguous vectors derived from native types of the C language. Application developers may need to create custom user-defined data types. These can be prescribed using structures of the message-passing interface (MPI) predefined types listed in Table 14.1 of Chapter 14. Most frequently, the use of user-defined data types is motivated by the need to incorporate heterogeneous structures (e.g., C struct) in MPI programs. The MPI construct to create user-defined data types is MPI_Type_create_struct and MPI_Type_commit.

```
MPI_Type_create_struct(int number_items, int *blocklengths,
                       MPI_Aint *array_of_offsets,
                       MPI_Datatype *array_of_types,
                       MPI_Datatype *new_datatype_name)
MPI_Type_commit(MPI_Datatype *new_datatype_name)
```

High Performance Computing. https://doi.org/10.1016/B978-0-12-823035-0.00021-3

435

Creating a user-defined data type consists of providing the number of different partitions of existing MPI data type elements (*number_items*); three separate arrays of length *number_items* containing the number of elements per block, byte offsets of each block, and MPI data types of each block; and the new name for the user-defined type. This new name is then passed as an argument to MPI_Type_commit, after which it can be used in all existing MPI functions.

An example of creating a user-defined data type from a C struct and broadcasting it to all processes is provided in Code 21.1. In this example, a C struct containing some typical variable names for a simulation is populated with values on process 0. The user-defined data type for this C struct, *mpi_par*, is created and committed on lines 38−39. The values for the structure are then broadcast to all other processes in line 41.

```
01 #include <stdio.h>
02 #include <stddef.h>
03 #include "mpi.h"
04
05 typedef struct {
06    int max_iter;
07    double t0;
08    double tf;
09    double xmin;
10 } Par;
11
12 int main(int argc,char **argv) {
13
14    MPI_Init(&argc,&argv);
15    int rank;
16    int root = 0;  // define the root process
17    MPI_Comm_rank(MPI_COMM_WORLD,&rank); // identify the rank
18
19    Par par;
20    if (rank == root) {
21      par.max_iter = 10;
22      par.t0 = 0.0;
23      par.tf = 1.0;
24      par.xmin = -5.0;
25    }
26
27    int nitems = 4;
28    MPI_Datatype types[nitems];
29    MPI_Datatype mpi_par;  // give my new type a name
30    MPI_Aint offsets[nitems];  // an array for storing the element offsets
31    int blocklengths[nitems];  // an array for storing block lengths
32
33    types[0] = MPI_INT; offsets[0] = offsetof(Par,max_iter); blocklengths[0] = 1;
34    types[1] = MPI_DOUBLE; offsets[1] = offsetof(Par,t0); blocklengths[1] = 1;
35    types[2] = MPI_DOUBLE; offsets[2] = offsetof(Par,tf); blocklengths[2] = 1;
36    types[3] = MPI_DOUBLE; offsets[3] = offsetof(Par,xmin); blocklengths[3] = 1;
37
38    MPI_Type_create_struct(nitems,blocklengths,offsets,types,&mpi_par);
39    MPI_Type_commit(&mpi_par);
40
41    MPI_Bcast(&par,1,mpi_par,root,MPI_COMM_WORLD);
42
43    printf("Hello from rank %d; my max_iter value is %d\n",rank,par.max_iter);
44
45    MPI_Finalize();
46
47    return 0;
48 }
```

CODE 21.1

Example of creating and using a user-defined data type in an MPI collective.

```
> mpirun −np 4 ./code1
Hello from rank 0; my max_iter value is 10
Hello from rank 2; my max_iter value is 10
Hello from rank 1; my max_iter value is 10
Hello from rank 3; my max_iter value is 10
```

Another useful type constructor is the *indexed* type builder. Being able to send only the contiguous parts of a vector is often quite limiting. To do so may result in either many disjoint calls or propagation of unnecessary data over the network that is later discarded at its destination. Fortunately, one can build a derived type that may skip over arbitrary sequences of items located at different offsets in the original data array. The construct to achieve this is MPI_Type_indexed:

```
MPI_Type_indexed(int count, int *blocklengths, int *displacements,
                 MPI_Datatype intype, MPI_Datatype *outtype)
```

Its application is straightforward. The programmer must fill in the displacement and block-length arrays containing respectively the start index of each portion of the original vector to be used in communication calls and the length of each such contiguous block. These arrays contain the same number of elements, which is passed as the *count* parameter; the parameters are located at corresponding indices in each array applied to the same block. The blocks are defined as vectors of elements of type *intype*, which can be any predefined or user-defined MPI type. Specifically, one could use the resulting type of MPI_Type_create_struct to access arbitrary subsets of a potentially large vector of structs, a common data layout in many practical applications. The call produces the derived data type in *outtype*, which should be committed before further use in data access calls.

As a simple example, consider blocklengths[] = {1, 3} and displacements[] = {2, 5}. Passing these arrays as arguments to MPI_Type_indexed (with *count* value of 2) will create a type that ignores the first two data elements of the array (at indices 0 and 1), includes a one-element block at index 2, skips the next two elements (indices 3 and 4), and includes a three-element block starting with the element at index 5 (indices 5, 6, and 7). With this single call, a data type is constructed that not only has a "hole" in the middle but also whose first accessed element is not aligned with the start of the data buffer (Fig. 21.1).

Another example of MPI_Type_indexed may be found in Section 21.5.

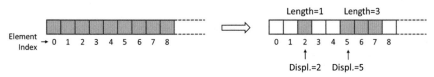

FIGURE 21.1

Example use of MPI_Type_indexed.

21.2 Enhanced Point-to-Point Communication

The standard version of the fundamental point-to-point communication interface involving the ubiquitous MPI_Send/MPI_Recv pair makes a series of implicit assumptions related to the circumstances in which these functions are invoked and their performance. In many cases, the details are left to the implementors, who often strive to make their MPI libraries portable, fast, and error- or deadlock-free. Fulfilling all of these requirements at once is not always possible, requiring judicious compromise.

This section offers additional understanding of how better performance may be extracted through additional variants of point-to-point calls and how explicitly communicating the programmer's intent to the MPI system may unlock more efficient programs. The nonblocking calls are introduced in which the requirement of strict pairing of each send to every receive may be substantially relaxed. In this mode, a nonblocking call effectively behaves as if another thread has been forked solely for the purpose of independently executing the body of either the MPI message send or receive operation. The call returns as soon as possible after internally storing information passed by the user. It also gives the user an illusion that nonblocking calls run in parallel with the main thread of the application, even though the actual implementation may not use any additional threads at all. An alternative to certain usage aspects of nonblocking calls, a combined send–receive function is presented in the following section along with an illustrative example.

Three new variants of the basic MPI_Send command will be explained that rely on specific usage of message buffers. They exploit some additional information that may be known to the user but difficult to determine by the message-passing subsystem. They include buffered send, ready send, and synchronous send. Additional buffer management functions are also presented.

Finally, the section focuses on the MPI_Status object and obtaining useful information from it.

21.2.1 Nonblocking Communication

The point-to-point communication calls introduced in Chapter 14, MPI_Send and MPI_Recv, do not return from the respective function call until the send and receive operations have completed. While this ensures that the send and receive buffers used in the MPI_Send and MPI_Recv arguments are safe to use or reuse after the function call, it also means that unless there is a simultaneously matching send for each receive, the code will deadlock, resulting in the code hanging. This common type of bug is examined in Chapter 14. One way to avoid this is using nonblocking point-to-point communication.

Nonblocking point-to-point communication returns immediately from the function call before confirming that the send or the receive has completed. These nonblocking calls are MPI_Isend and MPI_Irecv. They are used coupled with MPI_Wait, which waits until the operation is completed. When querying whether a nonblocking point-to-point communication has completed, MPI_Test is often paired with MPI_Isend and MPI_Irecv. Nonblocking point-to-point calls can simplify code development to more easily avoid such deadlocks while also potentially enabling the overlap of useful computation and checking to see if the communication has completed at the same time.

The syntax of each of these calls is the same as the blocking calls except for the addition of a request argument and the elimination of the status output in the MPI_Recv arguments.

```
int MPI_Isend(void *message, int count, MPI_Datatype datatype,
              int dest, int tag, MPI_Comm comm, MPI_Request *send_request)
int MPI_Irecv (void *message, int count, MPI_Datatype datatype,
              int source, int tag, MPI_Comm comm, MPI_Request *recv_request)
```

Because both MPI_Isend and MPI_Irecv return immediately after calling without confirming that the message-passing operations have completed, the application programmer needs a way to specify when these operations have to complete. This is done with MPI_Wait:

```
int MPI_Wait (MPI_Request *request, MPI_Status *status)
```

When MPI_Wait is called, the nonblocking request originating from MPI_Isend or MPI_Irecv is provided as an argument. The status that was previously provided directly from MPI_Recv is now supplied as an output from MPI_Wait.

Similar to MPI_Wait, MPI_Test can be paired with an MPI_Isend or MPI_Irecv call to query whether the message passing has completed while performing other work. MPI_Test shares similar syntax to MPI_Wait, adding only a flag that is set to true if the request being queried has completed.

```
int MPI_Test (MPI_Request *request, int *flag, MPI_Status *status)
```

An example of using nonblocking communication is presented in Code 21.2. In this example, the send commands are issued first, followed by the receive commands. If using blocking communication and sending a sufficiently large message, this would normally result in a deadlock, while nonblocking communication avoids this pitfall.

```
01 #include <stdlib.h>
02 #include <stdio.h>
03 #include <mpi.h>
04
05 int main(int argc,char* argv[]) {
06    int a, b;
07    int size, rank;
08    int tag = 0; // Pick a tag arbitrarily
09    MPI_Status status;
10    MPI_Request send_req, recv_req;
11
12    MPI_Init(&argc,&argv);
13    MPI_Comm_size(MPI_COMM_WORLD,&size);
```

```
14    MPI_Comm_rank(MPI_COMM_WORLD,&rank);
15
16    if (size != 2) {
17      printf("Example is designed for 2 processes\n");
18      MPI_Finalize();
19      exit(0);
20    }
21    if (rank == 0) {
22      a = 314159; // Value picked arbitrarily
23
24      MPI_Isend(&a,1,MPI_INT,1,tag,MPI_COMM_WORLD,&send_req);
25      MPI_Irecv (&b,1,MPI_INT,1,tag,MPI_COMM_WORLD,&recv_req);
26
27      MPI_Wait(&send_req, &status);
28      MPI_Wait(&recv_req, &status);
29      printf("Process %d received value %d\n",rank,b);
30    } else {
31      a = 667;
32
33      MPI_Isend(&a,1,MPI_INT,0,tag,MPI_COMM_WORLD,&send_req);
34      MPI_Irecv(&b,1,MPI_INT,0,tag,MPI_COMM_WORLD,&recv_req);
35
36      MPI_Wait(&send_req,&status);
37      MPI_Wait(&recv_req,&status);
38      printf("Process %d received value %d\n",rank,b);
39    }
40
41    MPI_Finalize();
42    return 0;
43 }
```

CODE 21.2

Example of nonblocking point-to-point communication. Process 0 sends the integer 314159 to process 1, while process 1 sends the integer 667 to process 0. The particular order of the Isend and Irecv calls in lines 24–25 and 33–34 doesn't matter because the functions are nonblocking.

```
> mpirun —np 2 ./code2
Process 0 received value 667
Process 1 received value 314159
```

21.2.2 Combined Send–Receive

Informing the MPI library that the program anticipates receiving a reply as a result of a send call is helpful in many practical situations. One of them is the *remote procedure call*, in which a *client* process sends a request to the *server* process. The latter receives a request, performs local computation using client-supplied data, and emits a response containing the computation result. Another scenario has to do with implementation of circular communication patterns, where some processes within a communicator are sending messages to their neighbors while expecting to receive messages from possibly a different set of neighbors (with neighbors selected by some logical ordering of process ranks). Arranging communication for such process groups may be difficult in the general case, especially if the total number of processes is odd.

The sendrecv call used to handle such cases has the following signature:

```
MPI_Sendrecv(void* send_buf, int send_count, MPI_Datatype send_type,
             int destination, int send_tag,
             void *recv_buf, int recv_count, MPI_Datatype recv_type,
             int source, int recv_tag, MPI_Comm communicator,
             MPI_Status *status)
```

As a simplifying and space-saving measure, MPI also provides a version of combined send and receive in which the received message is simply replacing the content of the send buffer:

```
MPI_Sendrecv_replace(void* buffer, int count, MPI_Datatype type,
                     int destination, int send_tag,
                     int source, int recv_tag,
                     MPI_Comm communicator, MPI_Status *status)
```

In the example shown in Code 21.3, every rank of the world communicator sends a message to a logical neighbor with a rank two units higher than its own and attempts to receive a message from a neighbor with a rank two units lower (the final rank is taken modulo world size, to ensure their values fall in a valid range). The first part of the MPI_Sendrecv call passing the send arguments can be found in line 13, while the arguments pertaining to the receive part are in line 14.

```
01 #include <stdio.h>
02 #include <mpi.h>
03
04 int main(int argc,char **argv)
05 {
06   int rank, size;
07   MPI_Status stat;
08   MPI_Init(&argc,&argv);
09   MPI_Comm_rank(MPI_COMM_WORLD,&rank);
10   MPI_Comm_size(MPI_COMM_WORLD,&size);
11
12   int n = 0;
13   MPI_Sendrecv(&rank,1,MPI_INT,(rank+2)%size,0,
14                &n,1,MPI_INT,(size+rank-2)%size,0,MPI_COMM_WORLD,&stat);
15   printf("Rank %d: received %d\n",rank,n);
16
17   MPI_Finalize();
18
19   return 0;
20 }
```

CODE 21.3

Example of sendrecv in which each process is sending to a neighbor separated by two units in rank and receiving from a process two ranks away in the opposite direction.

When run with five MPI processes, the program produces the following result:

```
> mpirun -np 5 ./code3
  Rank 4: received 2
  Rank 2: received 0
  Rank 0: received 3
  Rank 3: received 1
  Rank 1: received 4
```

21.2.3 Additional Buffering and Synchronization Modes

Message buffering plays an important role in communication systems. Even though it is associated with some overhead (copying data from one memory location to another is not free), it provides several benefits. First, it relaxes the requirement of coincidence of both send and receive invocation that, as mutually remote activities, would require additional communication. Second, it removes the reliance on specific capacities of hardware buffers in network interface controllers. Third, it may reduce the amount of time the sender spends inside the send call invocation, returning the control to the user thread more quickly.

As an example, consider two approaches shown in Fig. 21.2: (1) An eager send, which may be a viable option for sending short messages, need not reach out to the receiver to make sure that the corresponding receive activity has started. A holding buffer instantiated by the MPI library within every process will be most likely able to accumulate the message until the receive is posted. (2) Alternatively, sending large messages eagerly would be susceptible to varying potential failure modes. Even if the default buffer would be able to accumulate one or two such messages, it would be quickly overwhelmed if multiple ranks attempted communication at the same time. Therefore, the full handshake approach is safer in such situations.

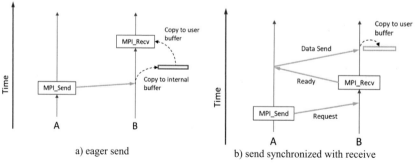

a) eager send   b) send synchronized with receive

FIGURE 21.2

A couple of several possible scenarios of message buffering for point-to-point communication.

For clarity, Fig. 21.2 doesn't show buffering that may also be performed by the sender process. This type of buffering is the motivation for the *buffered send* variant shown below:

```
MPI_Bsend(void *buffer, int count, MPI_Datatype type, int destination,
          int tag, MPI_Comm communicator)
```

The prototype of a buffered send is identical to that of the conventional MPI_Send. However, even for large messages, the buffered send is going to exit as soon as message buffering is complete. As this is purely a local operation, there is no added latency of communication with the destination process. The function is typically used when the user thread needs to resume its execution as soon as possible.

MPI provides additional buffer association and removal calls that are specifically used by the MPI_Bsend:

```
MPI_Buffer_attach(void *buffer, int size)
MPI_Buffer_detach(void *buffer_ptr, int *size_ptr)
```

The first call takes the pointer to the new buffer, possibly allocated by the programmer using one of the standard memory allocation functions, as well as its size in bytes. Only one user-specified buffer may be used at a time. After passing it under MPI control, the user should not modify its contents. The second call requires pointers to variables capable of storing an address and an integer. The successful invocation returns the address of the associated buffer and its size, which may be used to deallocate the buffer when its use is no longer necessary.

On occasion, the user may want to strictly synchronize the send call with the matching receive on a remote node, akin to the situation illustrated in Fig. 21.2(b). The MPI function with this semantics is MPI_Ssend (*synchronous mode* send):

```
MPI_Ssend(void *buffer, int count, MPI_Datatype type, int destination,
          int tag, MPI_Comm communicator)
```

Unlike MPI_Bsend, this call returns only when the matching receive has been started by the remote process.

Finally, another variant of send, the *ready send*, may result in a significant boost in performance but also requires very careful planning from its user. This call is MPI_Rsend (*ready send*):

```
MPI_Rsend(void *buffer, int count, MPI_Datatype type, int destination,
          int tag, MPI_Comm communicator)
```

It should only be called when one is certain a matching receive has been posted by the remote process; it is erroneous otherwise. In this mode the extra handshake can be completely eliminated, even for large messages, thus minimizing the overall communication latency. A natural question to ask is: how can anyone be certain of the communication status on another node? Below are a couple of examples showing how this can be guaranteed through a careful arrangement and ordering of MPI calls, possibly in connection with other message-passing operations within the application:

- On the receiving node, call a nonblocking receive followed by MPI_Barrier. On the sender node, the barrier is invoked prior to ready send, providing the necessary synchronization.
- A send—receive call is used to send a message to the future ready-send originator. The reply to that message can directly use MPI_Rsend knowing that the receive is already pending as the second half of the send-recv call.

Unlike MPI_Isend, in all blocking variants of MPI send, including the original MPI_Send and variants discussed in this section, the user data buffer may be reused immediately after the call completes. The counterpart receive-calls does not require similarly varied semantics and may be accomplished by either the standard MPI_Recv, the nonblocking receive, or even the receive portion of combined send-receive calls introduced earlier.

21.2.4 Wildcards and MPI Status

The student is already familiar with one type of the MPI wildcards, MPI_ANY_-TAG, that may be used by the receiver as a catch-all for any tag value. Certain computing models, such as client—server, may demand that one server process is permitted to receive data sent by multiple remote clients. To avoid dealing with the plethora of concurrent receive calls—each tuned to a specific sender—the MPI_ANY_SOURCE constant can be used in place of sender rank in a single call to achieve the same effect.

The point-to-point receive functions either directly fill out the contents of the status object or are retrieved through MPI_Wait or MPI_Test after completion of their nonblocking incarnations. Some processing may be avoided by passing MPI_STATUS_IGNORE in place of the pointer to status. This is beneficial in cases where the communication is organized predictably or the user does not wish to receive this information. MPI_Status directly exposes three fields that may be dereferenced using conventional C syntax for struct data members:

- MPI_SOURCE, storing the sender's rank within the communicator used for message send.
- MPI_TAG, containing the assigned tag value.
- MPI_ERROR, holding the error code of the operation.

Additionally, the count of data elements received may be retrieved via:

```
MPI_Get_count(MPI_Status *status, MPI_Datatype type, int *count)
```

Code 21.4 shows a practical use of wildcards and status information in a client–server arrangement. Multiple wildcards are among MPI_Recv arguments in line 22, while the status information is extracted and displayed in lines 25–28:

```
01 #include <stdio.h>
02 #include <mpi.h>
03
04 int main(int argc,char **argv)
05 {
06   int rank, size;
07   MPI_Status stat;
08   MPI_Init(&argc,&argv);
09   MPI_Comm_rank(MPI_COMM_WORLD,&rank);
10   MPI_Comm_size(MPI_COMM_WORLD,&size);
11
12   // check size
13   if (size < 2) {
14     printf("Error: at least two processes required\n");
15     MPI_Abort(MPI_COMM_WORLD, 1);
16   }
17
18   double sum = 0, number;
19   if (rank == 0) { // server
20     int items = 0;
21     for (int i = 1; i < size; i++) {
22       MPI_Recv(&number,1,MPI_DOUBLE,MPI_ANY_SOURCE,MPI_ANY_TAG,
23               MPI_COMM_WORLD,&stat);
24       // show request details
25       int count, client = stat.MPI_SOURCE;
26       MPI_Get_count(&stat,MPI_DOUBLE,&count);
27       printf("Server: request from %d, tag %d, contains %d double(s)\n",
28               client,stat.MPI_TAG,count);
29
30       sum += number;
31       // send back result
32       MPI_Send(&sum,1,MPI_DOUBLE,client,client,MPI_COMM_WORLD);
33       items++;
34     }
35     // print the final result
36     printf("Server: total=%f (of %d numbers)\n",sum,items);
37   }
38   else { // client
39     number = (double)rank;
40     MPI_Sendrecv_replace(&number,1,MPI_DOUBLE,0,rank,0,rank,MPI_COMM_WORLD,&stat);
41     printf("Client %d: current sum=%f\n",rank,number);
42   }
43
44   MPI_Finalize();
45   return 0;
46 }
```

CODE 21.4

Remote procedure call–like communication achieved using wildcards for message sender rank and tag.

The execution of compiled code on five nodes may produce output as follows:

```
> mpirun -np 5 ./code4
Client 2: current sum=2.000000
Client 4: current sum=6.000000
Server: request from 2, tag 2, contains 1 double(s)
Server: request from 4, tag 4, contains 1 double(s)
Server: request from 1, tag 1, contains 1 double(s)
Server: request from 3, tag 3, contains 1 double(s)
Server: total=10.000000 (of 4 numbers)
Client 1: current sum=7.000000
Client 3: current sum=10.000000
```

21.3 Custom Communicators and Topologies

Every MPI coding example presented thus far relied on the predefined MPI_-COMM_WORLD communicator encompassing all processes started by the mpirun command. Another predefined communicator handle is MPI_COMM_-SELF, which includes only the local process itself. These two choices may be sufficient for most straightforward communication patterns. In practice, however, in many sophisticated applications, especially those that perform different kinds of computations on different nodes, they would be inconveniencing the programmer, who effectively must resort to global rank remapping by hand. Fortunately, MPI provides additional support for custom communicator creation and virtual topologies.

21.3.1 Communicator Constructors

While MPI exposes powerful mechanisms for building arbitrary communicators using the concept of process *groups*, in most situations the user can accomplish practically any kind of grouping of MPI processes into subsets through just one call: MPI_Comm_split. Its prototype is surprisingly simple:

```
MPI_Comm_split(MPI_Comm in_comm, int color, int key,
               MPI_Comm *out_comm)
```

It takes the "parent", an existing communicator in_comm, and divides it into separate process groups based on the values of the color argument. The processes specifying the same color value are going to belong to the same output communicator. The key parameter influences the order of ranks in the created communicator. They are assigned in order according to key values; if there are any ties among those, a default ordering based on the ranks within the parent communicator is imposed. The resultant communicator handle is returned in out_comm. This is a collective call and therefore has to be called by every process of the parent communicator. If one or more ranks have to be excluded from grouping, their color can be set to MPI_UNDEFINED. In those cases, the local value of out_comm will be set to MPI_COMM_NULL, preventing it from participating in communication.

A short example shown in Code 21.5 demonstrates how a world communicator can be split into disjoint "odd" and "even" communicators where a parity of the original world rank determines the new communicator membership. The key is set to the constant value (zero) to indicate that the default (world communicator rank) ordering should be used.

```
01 #include <stdio.h>
02 #include <stdlib.h>
03 #include <mpi.h>
04
05 int main(int argc,char **argv)
06 {
07   int rank, size;
08   MPI_Status stat;
09   MPI_Init(&argc,&argv);
10   MPI_Comm_rank(MPI_COMM_WORLD,&rank);
11   MPI_Comm_size(MPI_COMM_WORLD,&size);
12
13   // split the communicator
14   MPI_Comm mycomm;
15   int color = rank & 1;
16   MPI_Comm_split(MPI_COMM_WORLD,color,0,&mycomm);
17
18   int new_rank, new_size;
19   if (rank & 1) {
20     MPI_Comm_rank(mycomm,&new_rank);
21     MPI_Comm_size(mycomm,&new_size);
22     printf("World rank %d -> \"odd\" rank %d (size=%d)\n",
23             rank,new_rank,new_size);
24   }
25   else {
26     MPI_Comm_rank(mycomm,&new_rank);
27     MPI_Comm_size(mycomm,&new_size);
28     printf("World rank %d -> \"even\" rank %d (size=%d)\n",
29             rank,new_rank,new_size);
30   }
31
32   MPI_Finalize();
33
34   return 0;
35 }
```

CODE 21.5

Creation of two disjoint communicators using MPI_Comm_split.

When run on an odd number of nodes, the program outputs different sizes for the resultant communicators.

```
> mpirun -np 5 ./code5
World rank 3 -> "odd" rank 1 (size=2)
World rank 4 -> "even" rank 2 (size=3)
World rank 0 -> "even" rank 0 (size=3)
World rank 1 -> "odd" rank 0 (size=2)
World rank 2 -> "even" rank 1 (size=3)
```

The created communicators may be destroyed when they are no longer needed using the call below:

```
MPI_Comm_free(MPI_Comm *communicator)
```

21.3.2 Virtual Topologies

A vast number of scientific simulations are executed on regularly spaced lattices aligned with a coordinate system. The conventional linear ordering of process ranks in a communicator is intuitive and easy to understand but requires an additional translation step for application-specific coordinate grids. To ameliorate this, a mapping to Cartesian grid topology of arbitrary dimensionality can be associated with an existing communicator. This makes the implementation of tasks such as "fetch data from a grid point one unit away along the z axis" quite straightforward.

The Cartesian topology constructor creates a new communicator that may be subsequently used in dedicated MPI calls to access the resulting topology. This communicator is created by calling MPI_Cart_create:

```
MPI_Cart_create(MPI_Comm in_comm, int num_dims, int *dimensions,
                int *periods, int reorder, MPI_Comm *out_comm)
```

The *num_dims* parameters specify the number of dimensions and correspond to the number of elements in input vectors *dimensions* and *periods*. The first of these determines the overall size of the Cartesian grid of processes by specifying the number of processes along each coordinate axis. The periodicity of the grid, i.e., whether the last coordinate is logically connected to the first one in each dimension, is controlled by the *periods* array, with values of zero disabling the linking and nonzero enabling it. This enables building of multidimensional toroidal lattices. The Boolean parameter *reorder* signals to MPI if it is permitted to reorder the ranks in the resulting communicator. When enabled (nonzero), this may potentially remap the processes for more efficient communication; otherwise the ranks in the created communicator will be the same as in the parent. If the *in_comm* includes more processes than the total count based on the contents of the *dimensions* array, the unassigned processes will receive MPI_COMM_NULL in *out_comm*.

To figure out the local process coordinates given its rank in the Cartesian communicator, the MPI_Cart_coords function may be used:

```
MPI_Cart_coords(MPI_Comm communicator, int cart_rank,
                int num_dims, int *coordinates)
```

It fills out the *coordinates* array, whose size has to be not smaller than the *num_-dims* value used to create the Cartesian communicator.

A frequent communication pattern performed on a Cartesian grid is propagation of data to the nearest neighbor(s) along a certain coordinate axis; this may be used, for example, to update the contents of ghost cells to values suitable for use in the next iteration. The preparation for this is accomplished by the MPI_Cart_shift function followed by a conventional message send and receive.

```
MPI_Cart_shift(MPI_Comm cart_comm, int direction, int displacement,
                    int *source, int *destination)
```

This function returns rank numbers within *cart_comm* that should be used as the source and destination of data transfer by the local process given the shift *direction* (index of dimension along which the shift is performed) and the *distance* (which may be negative to shift toward lower coordinates). Note that an MPI_PROC_NULL may be returned in *source* or *destination* for nodes located on the edge of an aperiodic grid.

The example in Code 21.6 puts all these bits of information together. A 3 × 2 two-dimensional toroidal grid is created in line 21. Due to fixed grid size, the count of participating processes cannot be lower than six. If the zeroth dimension corresponds to the x axis and the first dimension to the y axis, the MPI_Cart_shift in line 36 calculates the source and destination ranks necessary to move the data along the x axis toward the lower coordinates by one coordinate unit. Finally, the MPI_Sendrecv_replace call (line 39) performs the data move in one invocation.

```
01 #include <stdio.h>
02 #include <mpi.h>
03
04 int main(int argc,char **argv)
05 {
06    int rank, size;
07    MPI_Status stat;
08    MPI_Init(&argc,&argv);
09    MPI_Comm_rank(MPI_COMM_WORLD,&rank);
10    MPI_Comm_size(MPI_COMM_WORLD,&size);
11
12    // check size
13    if (size < 6) {
14       printf("Error: at least 6 processes required\n");
15       MPI_Abort(MPI_COMM_WORLD,1);
16    }
17
18    // build a periodic 2D Cartesian communicator
19    int dim[2] = {3,2}, per[2] = {1,1};
20    MPI_Comm cart;
21    MPI_Cart_create(MPI_COMM_WORLD,2,dim,per,1,&cart);
22
```

```
23   if (cart != MPI_COMM_NULL) {
24     int coords[2], cart_rank;
25     MPI_Comm_rank(cart,&cart_rank);
26     MPI_Cart_coords(cart,cart_rank,2,coords);
27     printf("World rank %d -> Cartesian rank %d, coordinates (%d,%d)\n",
28         rank,cart_rank,coords[0],coords[1]);
29
30     // set local value
31     int n = coords[1]*10+coords[0];
32     printf("Initial value at (%d,%d): %d\n",coords[0],coords[1],n);
33
34     // identify local neighbors for shift along dimension 0
35     int src, dst;
36     MPI_Cart_shift(cart,0,-1,&src,&dst);
37
38     // perform data shift
39     MPI_Sendrecv_replace(&n,1,MPI_INT,dst,9,src,9,cart,&stat);
40     printf("New value at (%d,%d): %d\n",coords[0],coords[1],n);
41   }
42   else printf("World rank %d unused\n",rank);
43
44   MPI_Finalize();
45
46   return 0;
47 }
```

CODE 21.6

Illustration of data shift across zeroth dimension on a two-dimensional torus.

When executed on seven nodes, the following output may be produced. The world rank 6 has been eliminated since the entire grid requires six processes (ranks 0 through 5).

```
> mpirun -np 7 ./code6
World rank 3 -> Cartesian rank 3, coordinates (1,1)
Initial value at (1,1): 11
New value at (1,1): 12
World rank 4 -> Cartesian rank 4, coordinates (2,0)
Initial value at (2,0): 2
New value at (2,0): 0
World rank 5 -> Cartesian rank 5, coordinates (2,1)
Initial value at (2,1): 12
New value at (2,1): 10
World rank 6 unused
World rank 0 -> Cartesian rank 0, coordinates (0,0)
Initial value at (0,0): 0
New value at (0,0): 1
World rank 1 -> Cartesian rank 1, coordinates (0,1)
Initial value at (0,1): 10
New value at (0,1): 11
World rank 2 -> Cartesian rank 2, coordinates (1,0)
Initial value at (1,0): 1
New value at (1,0): 2
```

21.4 **Collective Operation Redux**
21.4.1 **Variable Size Collectives**

This section revisits collective operations introduced in Chapter 14 to discuss their extended versions that may be useful in implementing some algorithms in fewer calls or avoiding the use of potentially less efficient point-to-point communication. The collective data exchange functions such as *scatter*, *gather*, *allgather*, and *alltoall* support several practical patterns of distributing data originating from single or multiple nodes. However, a common deficiency of these calls was that the amount of data transferred from or to individual nonroot nodes had to be the same. Here, the prototypes of those collective calls that may accept different sizes of data are listed. They retain the name of their originals but append the letter "v".

The extended version of MPI scatter is:

```
MPI_Scatterv(void *send_buffer, int *send_counts,
              int *displacements, MPI_Datatype send_type,
              void *recv_buffer, int recv_count, MPI_Datatype recv_type,
              int root, MPI_Comm communicator)
```

By comparing this signature to that of MPI_Scatter, two differences are apparent: *send_counts* is now an array, and one more argument, *displacements*, has been added. The displacement value specifies an offset, counted units of *send_type*, at which the specific section of *send_buffer* that is going to be delivered to the *i*th recipient begins (with *i* being the index in the array). The *send_counts* vector defines how many elements should be sent to that recipient. This is illustrated by the example in Code 21.7, which partitions a square matrix into upper and lower triangular portions but only scatters the upper one across the target processes. The displacements and data amounts are prepared in lines 24–27:

```
01 #include <stdio.h>
02 #include <stdlib.h>
03 #include <mpi.h>
04
05 int main(int argc,char **argv)
06 {
07   int rank, size;
08   MPI_Init(&argc,&argv);
09   MPI_Comm_rank(MPI_COMM_WORLD,&rank);
10   MPI_Comm_size(MPI_COMM_WORLD,&size);
11
12   // initialize matrix
13   double *mat = malloc(size*size*sizeof(double));
14   if (rank == 0) {
15     for (int i = 0; i < size; i++)
16       for (int j = 0; j < size; j++)
17         mat[i*size+j] = 1000.0*i+j+1;
18   }
19
20   // scatter rows of upper triangular matrix
21   double *row = calloc(size,sizeof(double));
22   int *offset = malloc(size*sizeof(int));
```

```
23    int *count = malloc(size*sizeof(int));
24    for (int i = 0; i < size; i++) {
25      offset[i] = size*i;
26      count[i] = size-i;
27    }
28
29    MPI_Scatterv(mat,count,offset,MPI_DOUBLE,row,size,MPI_DOUBLE,0,MPI_COMM_WORLD);
30
31    // print received data
32    for (int j = 0; j < size; j++)
33      printf("Rank %d, element %d: %f\n",rank,j,row[j]);
34
35    MPI_Finalize();
36
37    return 0;
38 }
```

CODE 21.7

Distribution of upper triangular matrix portion to remote nodes using MPI_Scatterv.

When run on four nodes, the program produces the output below. Only rank 0 receives a full matrix row, while the other nodes collect data amounts consecutively shortened by one element. A *calloc* allocator has been used to make sure that row storage is cleared before *scatterv* is invoked.

```
> mpirun -np 4 ./code7
Rank 0, element 0: 1.000000
Rank 0, element 1: 2.000000
Rank 0, element 2: 3.000000
Rank 0, element 3: 4.000000
Rank 1, element 0: 1001.000000
Rank 1, element 1: 1002.000000
Rank 1, element 2: 1003.000000
Rank 1, element 3: 0.000000
Rank 2, element 0: 2001.000000
Rank 2, element 1: 2002.000000
Rank 2, element 2: 0.000000
Rank 2, element 3: 0.000000
Rank 3, element 0: 3001.000000
Rank 3, element 1: 0.000000
Rank 3, element 2: 0.000000
Rank 3, element 3: 0.000000
```

The corresponding prototype for *gatherv* is:

```
MPI_Gatherv(void *send_buffer, int send_count, MPI_Datatype send_type,
            void *recv_buffer, int *recv_counts, int displacements,
            MPI_Datatype recv_type, int root, MPI_Comm communicator)
```

The parameter arrays defining the individual offsets and sizes have now been moved to the receive portion of the call, thus providing additional flexibility in choosing the storage place and space for the transferred data on the root process.

The *allgatherv* call looks identical to *gatherv*:

```
MPI_Allgatherv(void *send_buffer, int send_count, MPI_Datatype send_type,
               void *recv_buffer, int *recv_counts, int *displacements,
               MPI_Datatype recv_type, MPI_Comm communicator)
```

Analogous to *allgather*, all involved processes receive the result of a gather operation. In addition, a useful shortcut is allowed for this call by specifying a predefined constant MPI_IN_PLACE instead of *send_buffer*. This "in place" transformation causes all other send parameters to be ignored. The input data for the operation is collected from the initial contents of the receive buffers at specified offsets and quantities through *displacements* and *recv_counts*. The local regions of *recv_buffer* corresponding to these receive parameters are then overwritten by data values resulting from the execution of the call.

Finally, the most complex (and most flexible) *alltoallv* function is defined as:

```
MPI_Alltoallv(void *send_buffer, int *send_counts, int *send_displacements,
              MPI_Datatype send_type, void *recv_buffer, int *recv_counts,
              int *recv_displacements,
              MPI_Datatype recv_type, MPI_Comm comm)
```

The operation is similar to that of the conventional *alltoall* except it provides the programmer with the possibility to define data offsets and counts for both the send and receive portion of the collective operation. Replacing *send_buffer* by MPI_IN_PLACE is possible and, similarly to *allgatherv*, will result in the MPI library ignoring the send parameters.

21.4.2 User-Defined Reduction Operators

The description of *reduce* and *allreduce* calls in Chapter 14 introduced a rich set of predefined operators that support the most commonly encountered reduction arithmetic in typical applications. Certain situations, however, call for custom-defined operators primarily to minimize the number of distinct reduction operation invocations required to achieve the final desired result.

To create a custom operator, the programmer first must write a function that computes the reduction result from component pieces. Its signature is:

```
void custom_reduce(void *in_arg, void *inout_arg, int *size,
                   MPI_Datatype *type)
```

The first two arguments are arrays providing the inputs for computation, with the second of these also used for result storage. The length of these vectors is defined in a variable pointed to by the *size* argument. The data for computation is passed in vectors to permit multiple reductions per invocation, whenever possible, to improve the performance; the actual reduction is done pair-wise over corresponding elements of *in_arg* and *out_arg*. The *type* argument defines the input vector element's data type and, in some applications, can be used to select the appropriate branch of computation if overloading is used. For typical specialized implementations, the type argument doesn't need to be accessed.

This custom processing function needs to be registered with the MPI library using:

```
MPI_Op_create(MPI_User_function *fn, int commutative, MPI_Op *operator)
```

The created user reduction function is passed in the first argument to the call, followed by a Boolean flag indicating whether the reduction operation is commutative (i.e., it produces the same result if the input operands are swapped). In general, the reduction operators are required to be associative, but additional performance gains may be obtained if the overall evaluation order may be changed. The call returns a handle to the user operator registered with the MPI. This association can be removed when no longer needed via:

```
MPI_Op_free(MPI_Op *operator)
```

The example in Code 21.8 shows a custom operator that performs the weighted average of elements (lines 11–21). If the weights are equal, it computes the conventional average, and if they equal one, it also returns the count of elements as a side result. Since each vector element consists of two values, the average computed so far and the corresponding sum of weights, each of which are floating-point doubles, the appropriate type has to be created first. This is done in lines 42–44. As each process contains a vector of elements to average, local reduction has to be calculated first (lines 38–39). After all this preparatory work we can sit back and watch the final result being computed in just one reduction call in line 49.

```
01 #include <stdio.h>
02 #include <stdlib.h>
03 #include <mpi.h>
04
05 // vector element type
06 typedef struct {
07   double value, weight;
08 } mean_t;
09
10 // custom operation: weighted mean
11 void mean(void *inarg,void *ioarg,int *len,MPI_Datatype *dt) {
12   mean_t m;
13   mean_t *in = (mean_t *)inarg;
14   mean_t *io = (mean_t *)ioarg;
15   for (int i = 0; i < *len; i++) {
16     m.weight = in[i].weight+io[i].weight;
17     m.value = (in[i].value*in[i].weight+io[i].value*io[i].weight) /
18               m.weight;
19     io[i] = m;
20   }
21 }
22
23 int main(int argc,char **argv)
24 {
```

```
25   int rank, size;
26   MPI_Init(&argc,&argv);
27   MPI_Comm_rank(MPI_COMM_WORLD,&rank);
28   MPI_Comm_size(MPI_COMM_WORLD,&size);
29
30   // initialize vector
31   double *vec = malloc(size*sizeof(double));
32   for (int i = 0; i < size; i++)
33     vec[i] = (double)rank*size+i;
34
35   // compute local average
36   mean_t m, res;
37   m.value = 0; m.weight = size;
38   for (int i = 0; i < size; i++) m.value += vec[i];
39   m.value = m.value / m.weight;
40
41   // define custom type
42   MPI_Datatype mytype;
43   MPI_Type_contiguous(2,MPI_DOUBLE,&mytype);
44   MPI_Type_commit(&mytype);
45
46   // compute the overall average
47   MPI_Op mean_op;
48   MPI_Op_create(mean,1,&mean_op);
49   MPI_Reduce(&m,&res,1,mytype,mean_op,0,MPI_COMM_WORLD);
50
51   // print result
52   if (!rank)
53     printf("Average: %f (of %.0f elements)\n",res.value,res.weight);
54
55   MPI_Finalize();
56
57   return 0;
58 }
```

CODE 21.8

Creation and application of custom reduction operator computing weighted average.

Running the code produces the following output:

```
> mpirun -np 5 ./code8
Average: 12.000000 (of 25 elements)
```

21.5 Parallel Input/Output

The MPI also supports access to files. It provides a user interface that is more sophisticated than the bare-bones POSIX file access functions. The MPI-IO, a dedicated section of the MPI standard related to file input/output operations, takes advantage of the available data type machinery and parallel processing to give the powerful means to both library implementors and system users to construct algorithms achieving high performance access to data in persistent storage.

The MPI-IO files look just like conventional files; they are in essence sequences of bytes. It is worth noting that due to the requirement of concurrent access from multiple computing nodes, they should be stored on file system partitions (1) that are uniformly visible and accessible from all nodes in the system and (2) whose underlying storage can handle multiple I/O requests at a time, in terms of both aggregate bandwidth to the disks or solid-state devices and network bandwidth to the remainder of the system. Otherwise, the achieved data throughput rates may be degraded.

MPI-IO introduces several concepts that describe the way files are accessed. The first is the notion of file *view*. Each MPI process may define its own view, which describes which fragments of a file are accessible to that process. These fragments need not be contiguous or identical for each MPI process. The view starts after a user-specified offset (*displacement*) given in bytes and is expressed in units of *elementary type,* or *etype* for short. The displacement may be used to skip over a fixed file header (if such is present) or to bypass portions of the file that need not be accessed or perhaps use an incompatible etype. Fig. 21.3 shows the example of three processes defining different views of the same file. The first two skip over a header at the start of the file and set up a nonoverlapping access pattern (identified by fully shaded rectangles) using a common elementary type 1. View 3 advances the displacement to the start of the file segment that uses a different elementary type (etype 2). Another important concept of MPI-IO is *file type*, which describes the unit of file access within a view. It could be as small as a single etype. However, as shown in the example, it may also contain holes that simplify tiling of file content for easy access.

Just like in POSIX, the files first must be *opened* for access by the following routine:

```
MPI_File_open(MPI_Comm communicator, char *file_name, int access_mode,
              MPI_Info info, MPI_File *handle)
```

As the open operation is collective, it must be executed by all processes in the communicator. It is possible to open a file on just one process by passing MPI_-COMM_SELF as the communicator. The file name value should be a string containing a valid path to the target file; note that implementations are free to use additional prefixes to identify specific file systems or hosts on which files are residing. Therefore, programmers are encouraged to consult their system's documentation to obtain

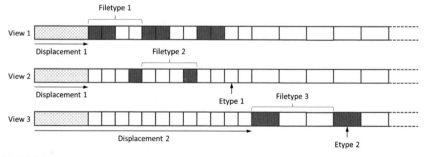

FIGURE 21.3

Example of different file views associated with the same file.

the related details. The access mode contains an OR-ed combination of flags listed below:

- MPI_MODE_RDONLY—open file only for reading.
- MPI_MODE_WRONLY—open file only for writing.
- MPI_MODE_RDWR—open file for both reading and writing.
- MPI_MODE_CREATE—create file if nonexistent.
- MPI_MODE_EXCL—fail with an error if creating a file that already exists.
- MPI_MODE_DELETE_ON_CLOSE—create a temporary file.
- MPI_MODE_UNIQUE_OPEN—notify MPI that there are no other accessors of the file.
- MPI_MODE_SEQUENTIAL—only sequential access will be performed.
- MPI_MODE_APPEND—open file for write at its end.

Certain combinations of these flags are erroneous. For example, precisely one of the first three flags should be given. The file info object may provide additional access hints. As implementations are free to ignore any and all such hints, the reader is again referred to system documentation for further explanation. File accesses still work correctly when an empty MPI_INFO_NULL value is passed instead. The call returns a file handle to be used by subsequent data access calls. After use, the file may be closed using another collective function:

```
MPI_File_close(MPI_File *file_handle)
```

The next step involves setting the file view on each process:

```
MPI_File_set_view(MPI_File *file_handle, MPI_Offset displacement,
                  MPI_Datatype etype, MPI_Datatype filetype,
                  char *data_rep, MPI_Info info)
```

The only additional argument requiring an explanation is data representation (*data_rep*). It is a string that may assume one of three values and should be identical on all processes setting the view:

- "native" should be used in homogeneous environments (e.g., running exclusively on ×86_64 CPUs) and typically avoids most of the data conversions, thus preserving the precision of data in memory. It is likely to achieve the highest performance.
- "internal" representation chooses the actual format of the file data and may be used on either heterogeneous or homogeneous platforms.
- "external32" will always perform conversion to the common canonical representation, providing the best portability across MPI environments and implementations.

MPI-IO supports many data access calls, three types of which will be discussed here. The file function prototypes for file access with *explicit offsets* are:

```
MPI_File_read_at(MPI_File file_handle, MPI_Offset offset,
                 void *buffer, int count, MPI_Datatype type,
                 MPI_Status *status)
```

```
MPI_File_write_at(MPI_File file_handle, MPI_Offset offset,
                  void *buffer, int count, MPI_Datatype type,
                  MPI_Status *status)
```

First, an explicit offset for the operation is given, counted in etypes from the start of the file view and iterating over accessible entries of the file type in that view (corresponding to the shaded boxes in Fig. 21.3). Second, yet another data type is given, which specifies the data layout in memory describing the contents of the memory region pointed to by *buffer*. This type can be different from etype as long as they are congruent, meaning that one is an integer multiple of the other and fundamental MPI types that compose each of these types occur in the same order. Finally, even though the directions of data movement are different, both calls provide status information. This is to verify the actual number of elements accessed using a function introduced earlier, MPI_Get_count.

The functions described above have collective equivalents that may enable substantial performance advantages. Even though individual processes may define their file types to be completely disjoint, their union may fully cover the accessed sections of the file. In those cases, it is frequently faster to perform a single large read and later redistribute the data across processes by performing memory-to-memory copies (in addition to message communication if necessary). The collective interface provides the necessary synchronization of access for multiple processes. The function signature is the same as for the noncollective variant:

```
MPI_File_read_at_all(MPI_File file_handle, MPI_Offset offset,
                     void *buffer, int count, MPI_Datatype type,
                     MPI_Status *status)
MPI_File_write_at_all(MPI_File file_handle, MPI_Offset offset,
                      void *buffer, int count, MPI_Datatype type,
                      MPI_Status *status)
```

Finally, file access with individual file pointers is much like in the C library. MPI maintains an internal file pointer associated with the file handle in every process. This pointer is initialized to offset 0 (again, counted in etypes) in each opened file view and advanced in agreement with the number of etype elements transferred by each successful call. Because of that, these functions no longer include the *offset* parameter:

```
MPI_File_read(MPI_File file_handle, void *buffer, int count,
              MPI_Datatype type, MPI_Status *status)
MPI_File_write(MPI_File file_handle, void *buffer, int count,
               MPI_Datatype type, MPI_Status *status)
```

One of the features of the MPI file interface is that the file can tailor in-memory types to achieve more efficient storage. It is not subjected to alignment restrictions forced by the compiler on structure members. One can skip data elements that need not be stored (for example, when they could be easily recomputed). The example in Code 21.9 uses an array of structs describing atoms in three-dimensional space. Their coordinates are double-precision floats, while the IDs and mass are integers (lines 13—16). Assume that atom IDs are to be discarded to introduce a difference between in-memory types and etypes. First, the memory data type is created in lines

32—42; this is to describe the layout of the vector of atoms in the just-initialized buffer. The final definition applies MPI_Type_create_resized with the following prototype:

```
MPI_Type_create_resized(MPI_Datatype in_type, MPI_Aint lower_bound,
                        MPI_Aint extent, MPI_Datatype *out_type)
```

to inform MPI about the true extent and lower bound of the atom struct. While for many common architectures and compilers its use here is not strictly necessary, it may avoid potential problems if the compiler adds unexpected padding following the final data member in the structure. The packed etype is defined in lines 44—47 and sets its true extent simply to the sum of sizes of all saved members (mass, x, y, and z), but without any provisions for alignment or padding; these are no longer required in a file. Finally, file types are constructed for each process separately (lines 54—57) such that each represents a contiguous chunk offset from the start of the file by the combined etype count required to store all datasets created by processes of lower rank. Line 58 installs a view for each process. As there is no file header, the initial displacement is set to 0.

```
01 #include <stdio.h>
02 #include <stdlib.h>
03 #include <mpi.h>
04
05 int main(int argc,char **argv)
06 {
07   int rank, size, N = 1000;
08   MPI_Status stat;
09   MPI_Init(&argc,&argv);
10   MPI_Comm_rank(MPI_COMM_WORLD,&rank);
11   MPI_Comm_size(MPI_COMM_WORLD,&size);
12
13   typedef struct {
14     int id, mass;
15     double x, y, z;
16   } atom;
17
18   // initialize local data
19   atom *data = malloc(N*sizeof(atom));
20   for (int i = 0; i < N; i++) {
21     data[i].id = N*rank+i;
22     data[i].mass = (i+rank)%10+1;
23     data[i].x = i+rank*1000;
24     data[i].y = i+rank*2000;
25     data[i].z = i+rank*5000;
26   }
27   if (rank == 0)
28     printf("Total size of memory data: %ld\n", size*N*sizeof(atom));
29
30   // create memory and file datatypes;
31   // assume atom IDs do not need to be saved
32   MPI_Datatype tmpt, mem_elem, etype, file_type;
33   int blen[2] = {1,3};
34   MPI_Aint adisp[2] = {0,0};
35   MPI_Datatype type[2] = {MPI_INT,MPI_DOUBLE};
36   // compute actual memory displacements
37   adisp[0] = offsetof(atom, mass);
38   adisp[1] = offsetof(atom, x);
39   // create memory struct datatype
40   MPI_Type_create_struct(2,blen,adisp,type,&tmpt);
```

```
41   MPI_Type_create_resized(tmpt,0,sizeof(atom),&mem_elem);
42   MPI_Type_commit(&mem_elem);
43   // create packed datatype for file element
44   adisp[0] = 0; adisp[1] = sizeof(int);
45   MPI_Type_create_struct(2,blen,adisp,type,&tmpt);
46   MPI_Type_create_resized(tmpt,0,sizeof(int)+3*sizeof(double),&etype);
47   MPI_Type_commit(&etype);
48
49   // open file and set the view
50   MPI_File fh;
51   MPI_File_open(MPI_COMM_WORLD,"/tmp/example.dat",
52               MPI_MODE_CREATE|MPI_MODE_WRONLY,MPI_INFO_NULL,&fh);
53   // filetype: each process gets its own contiguous chunk
54   blen[0] = N;
55   int disp = N*rank;
56   MPI_Type_indexed(1,blen,&disp,etype,&file_type);
57   MPI_Type_commit(&file_type);
58   MPI_File_set_view(fh,0,etype,file_type,"native",MPI_INFO_NULL);
59   // write local data
60   MPI_File_write_at(fh,0,data,N,mem_elem,&stat);
61
62   MPI_File_close(&fh);
63   MPI_Finalize();
64
65   return 0;
66 }
```

CODE 21.9

Parallel I/O example illustrating on-the-fly removal of holes in memory data types to achieve a compact data storage in the file system.

MPI automatically eliminated the unwanted struct member when writing each dataset to file. The savings amount to $4 \times 1000 \times 4 = 16,000$ bytes, which is the total volume occupied by 1000 integers in each of the four processes.

```
> mpirun -np 4 ./code9
Total size of memory data: 128000
> ls -l /tmp/example.dat
-rw-r--r-- 1 user20 user20 112000 Apr 25 02:08 /tmp/example.dat
```

21.6 Summary and Outcomes

- MPI offers nonblocking semantics to avoid strict reliance on call ordering and to prevent tying the program flow to completion of communication phases.
- Additional point-to-point send and combined send–receive functions give the user more control over message buffering and synchronization with the corresponding receive calls.
- MPI provides powerful means for defining custom data types capable of describing practically any data layout. They are derived from predefined MPI data types.
- MPI programmers can create and employ user-defined communicators spanning an arbitrary subset of processes and apply virtual topologies that better match data distribution used in simulations.

- Collective communications include interfaces that support buffers of different sizes and different data strides across individual participating processes.
- Creation of custom operators is a way to lower the number of collective reduction calls in a program, potentially leading to improved performance.
- File I/O is supported by the subset of MPI standard called MPI-IO. It defines additional data type concepts and custom views associated with accessed files.

21.7 Exercises

1. Rewrite the program in Exercise 1 of Chapter 14 to work with arbitrary process counts (including odd counts) using calls introduced in the current chapter. Can you think of another alternative implementation? Provide the related program(s).

2. Modify Code 21.1 of this chapter to simply send and receive back and forth on two processes the user-defined data type *mpi_par*. Add an integer to the Par struct to count how many times back and forth the data has been passed.

3. Section 21.2.3 provides two examples of side-effect synchronization that enables the use of MPI_Rsend. Can you come up with another two? Explain using relevant snippets of source code.

4. Write a program in which each process in a 4×4 grid exchanges single-layer ghost zones with their nearest neighbors using an aperiodic two-dimensional Cartesian communicator.

5. A file contains a sequence of double-precision floating-point numbers. Design an MPI-IO program in which each process with rank r in a communicator of size n retrieves numbers at index $r + n * i$ for $i = 0, 1, 2, \ldots$ and stores them in a contiguous local buffer. Use both collective and noncollective implementations that access a user-specified count of items in each I/O call and compare their performance.

Reference

[1] M.P.I. Forum, MPI: A Message Passing Interface Standard Version 4.0, 9 June 2021 [Online]. Available: https://www.mpi-forum.org/docs/mpi-4.0/mpi40-report.pdf.

Checkpointing

22

Chapter outline

22.1 Introduction

Many high performance computing (HPC) applications take a very long time to run even when using many concurrent compute resources. Some examples of such applications that have historically required very long runtimes on HPC resources include molecular dynamics simulations, fluid flow simulations, astrophysical compact object merger simulations, and mathematical optimization problems. Apart from these, an application that does not strongly scale very well may also require large runtimes because it can only effectively use a limited number of compute resources and would see no time-to-solution benefit when adding more. Applications with long execution times run a significant risk of encountering a hardware or software failure before the completion. Long execution times also frequently violate some supercomputer usage policies where a maximum wallclock time limit for a simulation is established to better accommodate the multiuser environment of a supercomputer. In either case, the consequences from having a job killed because of a time-usage policy violation or due to a hardware or software failure can be very significant and costly in terms of time lost and computing resources wasted. Checkpointing is one way to help mitigate this risk.

At designated points during the execution of an application on a supercomputer, the data necessary to allow later resumption of the application at that point in the execution can be output and saved. For example, when running machine learning training, a checkpoint may be triggered by when the loss function drops below a certain value. The dataset written is called a checkpoint, and the resumption of application execution from the checkpoint is called a restart. It is no surprise that checkpoint files can be extremely large. Apart from mitigating the cost of an execution failure during a simulation that runs for a long time, checkpoint files also provide snapshots of the application at different simulation epochs, help in debugging, aid in performance monitoring and analysis, and can help improve load-balancing decisions for better distributed-memory usage. This chapter explores two different approaches to checkpointing frequently encountered in HPC: system-level approaches and application-level approaches. It also gives a brief overview of checkpointing when training a machine learning model.

22.2 System-Level Checkpointing

System-level checkpointing performs the checkpoint and restart procedures via a full memory dump. This type of checkpointing does not require any changes to the application in order to use, and the writing of the checkpoint may be triggered either by the system or by the user. Examples of such approaches transparent to the user for HPC support include Checkpoint/Restore in Userspace (CRIU) [1] and Distributed MultiThreaded CheckPointing (DMTCP) [2]. These system-level approaches are generally fully integrated with the resource management system on a supercomputer including SLURM or PBS and provide checkpoint/restart support for multithreaded applications and message-passing interface (MPI)-based distributed memory applications. They are fully transparent to the user, requiring no changes to an application code, although they generally require a preload library step and inputs to specify the checkpoint interval, checkpoint directory, and restart directory.

The key advantage of system-level checkpoint/restart approaches over application-level approaches is that they require no changes to the application source code. Additionally, many system-level approaches also incorporate access to kernel resource information such as process IDs that can simplify restarting the application. However, because the system-level checkpointing strategy includes a full memory dump, those checkpoint files may be significantly larger than just saving the smallest amount of relevant information as would be done with an application-level approach.

As an example of interactive system-level checkpointing, the OpenMP code shown in Code 22.1 is used in conjunction with the DMTCP tool in this section.

DMTCP provides several easy-to-use commands for transparent system-level checkpointing. Installation of DMTCP is as follows:

```
1  #include <omp.h>
2  #include <unistd.h>
3  #include <stdio.h>
4  #include <stdlib.h>
5  #include <math.h>
6
7  int main (int argc, char *argv[])
8  {
9   const int size = 20;
10   int nthreads, threadid, i;
11   double array1[size], array2[size], array3[size];
12
13   // Initialize
14   for (i=0; i < size; i++) {
15    array1[i] = 1.0*i;
16    array2[i] = 2.0*i;
17   }
18
19   int chunk = 3;
20
21  #pragma omp parallel private(threadid)
22   {
23    threadid = omp_get_thread_num();
24    if (threadid == 0) {
25     nthreads = omp_get_num_threads();
26     printf("Number of threads = %d\n", nthreads);
27    }
28    printf(" My threadid %d\n",threadid);
29
30    #pragma omp for schedule(static,chunk)
31    for (i=0; i<size; i++) {
32     array3[i] = sin(array1[i] + array2[i]);
33     printf(" Thread id: %d working on index %d\n",threadid,i);
34     sleep(1);
35    }
36
37   } // join
38
39   printf(" TEST array3[199] = %g\n",array3[199]);
40
41   return 0;
42  }
```

CODE 22.1

Example OpenMP code, checkpoint_openmp.c, for demonstrating system-level checkpointing. A "sleep" statement has been added to line 34 to add a pause to the execution after each thread performs the operation of line 32.

```
git clone https://github.com/dmtcp/dmtcp.git
cd dmtcp/
mkdir build
cd build/
../configure --prefix=$HOME/dmtcp_install
make
make install
```

Once installed, several executables will appear in the installation directory. The *dmtcp_coordinator* acts as a command-line interface to DMTCP for examining the checkpoint interval, accessing status messages, and forcing a manual checkpoint outside the specified checkpoint interval from the command line. The *dmtcp_coordinator* is launched in a separate terminal and awaits command-line input instructions and outputs status messages as shown in Fig. 22.1.

To checkpoint the code illustrated in Code 22.1, it is compiled just as if it were not being checkpointed:

```
gcc -fopenmp -O3 -o checkpoint_openmp checkpoint_openmp.c -lm
```

The math library ("-lm") is added for the sin(x) function used in line 32 of Code 22.1, and the executable is named "checkpoint_openmp."

The number of OpenMP threads is also set in the normal way through the environment variable OMP_NUM_THREADS (illustrated here using bash shell syntax; for tcsh shell, use *setenv*):

```
export OMP_NUM_THREADS=16
```

The checkpoint interval can be changed using *dmtcp_command*, which sends the command to the *dmtcp_coordinator* that was already launched in Fig. 22.1:

```
andersmw@cutter:~/dmtcp-dmtcp-35386c2/bin$ ./dmtcp_coordinator
dmtcp_coordinator starting...
    Host: cutter (156.56.64.43)
    Port: 7779
    Checkpoint Interval: disabled (checkpoint manually instead)
    Exit on last client: 0
Type '?' for help.

?
COMMANDS:
    l : List connected nodes
    s : Print status message
    c : Checkpoint all nodes
    i : Print current checkpoint interval
        (To change checkpoint interval, use dmtcp_command)
    k : Kill all nodes
    q : Kill all nodes and quit
    ? : Show this message
```

FIGURE 22.1

The dmtcp_coordinator for status updates and interactions with DMTCP via the specific commands listed here including forcing a checkpoint outside the checkpoint interval by issuing the "c" command.

```
dmtcp_command --interval <checkpoint interval in seconds>
```

Because Code 22.1 executes very quickly, a checkpoint request will be manually input into the *dmtcp_coordinator* command interface. The executable is launched with checkpoint capability using the *dmtcp_launch* tool:

```
dmtcp_launch ./checkpoint_openmp
```

The executable will begin to run as normal, and if a checkpoint interval has been supplied, every specified interval of wallclock time of a checkpoint is written to the filesystem. Additionally, if the command "c" is supplied to the *dmtcp_coordinator* command interface, a checkpoint will also be written to the filesystem at that point. DMTCP checkpoint files have the naming convention of "ckpt_<executable name>_<client identity>.dmtcp" and are written in the directory where the executable was launched. A manually issued checkpoint request is illustrated in Fig. 22.2, which creates, in this example, a checkpoint file named *ckpt_checkpoint_openmp_16707112e4c8f-42000-8687a700c18a5.dmtcp*.

The checkpoint file is restarted using the *dmtcp_restart* command:

```
dmtcp_restart <checkpoint file>
```

A snippet of the standard output for Code 22.1 with and without checkpoint restart is shown in Fig. 22.3. The same OpenMP threads operate on the same array indices, and all operations are identical in the restarted case to the nonrestarted case. No changes were made to the code to enable checkpoint/restart capability, and the checkpoint files written could also be used for debugging, for execution snapshots, or as part of a strategy for fault tolerance.

Interactive system-level checkpoint/restart using DMTCP for an MPI application is similar to that for an OpenMP application with small differences. An example

```
c
[40367] NOTE at dmtcp_coordinator.cpp:1071 in startCheckpoint; REASON='starting checkpoint, suspending all nodes'
    s.numPeers = 1
[40367] NOTE at dmtcp_coordinator.cpp:1073 in startCheckpoint; REASON='Incremented computationGeneration'
    compId.computationGeneration() = 1
[40367] NOTE at dmtcp_coordinator.cpp:413 in updateMinimumState; REASON='locking all nodes'
[40367] NOTE at dmtcp_coordinator.cpp:419 in updateMinimumState; REASON='draining all nodes'
[40367] NOTE at dmtcp_coordinator.cpp:425 in updateMinimumState; REASON='checkpointing all nodes'
[40367] NOTE at dmtcp_coordinator.cpp:449 in updateMinimumState; REASON='building name service database'
[40367] NOTE at dmtcp_coordinator.cpp:465 in updateMinimumState; REASON='entertaining queries now'
[40367] NOTE at dmtcp_coordinator.cpp:470 in updateMinimumState; REASON='refilling all nodes'
[40367] NOTE at dmtcp_coordinator.cpp:510 in updateMinimumState; REASON='restarting all nodes'
```

FIGURE 22.2

A manually issued checkpoint request followed by the associated status messages from DMTCP for checkpointing Code 22.1.

MPI "pingpong" code, referred to as pingpong.c, using *MPI_Send* and *MPI_Recv* is shown in Code 22.2, which passes back and forth an integer, incrementing that integer for each iteration.

```
1  #include <stdio.h>
2  #include <stdlib.h>
3  #include <unistd.h>
4  #include "mpi.h"
5
6  int main(int argc,char **argv)
7  {
8   int rank,size;
9   MPI_Init(&argc,&argv);
10  MPI_Comm_rank(MPI_COMM_WORLD,&rank);
11  MPI_Comm_size(MPI_COMM_WORLD,&size);
12
13  if ( size != 2 ) {
14   printf(" Only runs on 2 processes \n");
15   MPI_Finalize();    // this example only works on two processes
16   exit(0);
17  }
18
19  int count;
20  if ( rank == 0 ) {
21   // initialize count on process 0
22   count = 0;
23  }
24  for (int i=0;i<10;i++) {
25   if ( rank == 0 ) {
26    MPI_Send(&count,1,MPI_INT,1,0,MPI_COMM_WORLD); // send "count" to rank 1
27    MPI_Recv(&count,1,MPI_INT,1,0,MPI_COMM_WORLD,MPI_STATUS_IGNORE); // receive it back
28    sleep(1);
29    count++;
30    printf(" Count %d\n",count);
31   } else {
32    MPI_Recv(&count,1,MPI_INT,0,0,MPI_COMM_WORLD,MPI_STATUS_IGNORE);
33    MPI_Send(&count,1,MPI_INT,0,0,MPI_COMM_WORLD);
34   }
35  }
36
37  if ( rank == 0 ) printf("\t\t\t Round trip count = %d\n",count);
38
39  MPI_Finalize();
40 }
```

CODE 22.2

Example MPI "pingpong" code for demonstrating system-level checkpoint/restart using DMTCP. A "sleep" command has been added to line 21 to slow down the execution for checkpoint demonstration purposes. This code is designed to only work on two processes and will print out the "count" integer at each message epoch.

```
andersmw@cutter:~/textbook$ dmtcp_restart ckpt_checkpoint_openmp_16707112e4c8f-42000-8687a700c18a5.dmtcp
  Thread id: 15 working on index 141
  Thread id: 14 working on index 138
  Thread id: 7 working on index 117
  Thread id: 12 working on index 132
  Thread id: 1 working on index 99
  Thread id: 2 working on index 102
  Thread id: 8 working on index 120
  Thread id: 5 working on index 111
  Thread id: 11 working on index 129
  Thread id: 13 working on index 135
  Thread id: 3 working on index 105
  Thread id: 10 working on index 126
  Thread id: 9 working on index 123
  Thread id: 6 working on index 114
  Thread id: 4 working on index 108
  Thread id: 0 working on index 96
```

```
  Thread id: 15 working on index 141
  Thread id: 14 working on index 138
  Thread id: 8 working on index 120
  Thread id: 1 working on index 99
  Thread id: 2 working on index 102
  Thread id: 4 working on index 108
  Thread id: 12 working on index 132
  Thread id: 7 working on index 117
  Thread id: 0 working on index 96
  Thread id: 13 working on index 135
  Thread id: 11 working on index 129
  Thread id: 5 working on index 111
  Thread id: 3 working on index 105
  Thread id: 9 working on index 123
  Thread id: 6 working on index 114
  Thread id: 10 working on index 126
```

FIGURE 22.3

The standard output from Code 22.1 after checkpoint restart (left) and without restart (right). The same OpenMP threads operate on the same indices, and all operations are identical in the restarted case to the nonrestarted case. As is standard in system-level checkpointing, no changes to Code 22.1 were made to enable checkpoint capability.

Just as in the OpenMP checkpoint/restart example, the code is not modified and is compiled as usual without including any extra libraries specific to checkpoint/restart:

```
mpicc -O3 -o pingpong pingpong.c
```

In this example MPICH-2 is the MPI implementation used; DMTCP supports several different implementations of MPI. After the *dmtcp_coordinator* is started in a separate window in order to issue manual checkpoint commands and monitor status messages, the pingpong executable is then launched on two processes using a combination of *dmtcp_launch* and *mpirun* as follows:

```
dmtcp_launch --rm mpirun -np 2 ./pingpong
```

After five message epochs, the command for generating the checkpoint ("c") is issued to the *dmtcp_coordinator*, as illustrated in Fig. 22.4.

Four checkpoint files result from the checkpoint command: one from each process and two associated with the MPI launcher. A restart script specific to the checkpoint files generated is also created to simplify the restart process. This script is

```
c
[22984] NOTE at dmtcp_coordinator.cpp:1071 in startCheckpoint; REASON='starting checkpoint, suspending all nodes'
    s.numPeers = 4
[22984] NOTE at dmtcp_coordinator.cpp:1073 in startCheckpoint; REASON='Incremented computationGeneration'
    compId.computationGeneration() = 1
[22984] NOTE at dmtcp_coordinator.cpp:413 in updateMinimumState; REASON='locking all nodes'
[22984] NOTE at dmtcp_coordinator.cpp:419 in updateMinimumState; REASON='draining all nodes'
[22984] NOTE at dmtcp_coordinator.cpp:425 in updateMinimumState; REASON='checkpointing all nodes'
[22984] NOTE at dmtcp_coordinator.cpp:449 in updateMinimumState; REASON='building name service database'
[22984] NOTE at dmtcp_coordinator.cpp:465 in updateMinimumState; REASON='entertaining queries now'
[22984] NOTE at dmtcp_coordinator.cpp:470 in updateMinimumState; REASON='refilling all nodes'
[22984] NOTE at dmtcp_coordinator.cpp:510 in updateMinimumState; REASON='restarting all nodes'
```

FIGURE 22.4

Status messages generated after issuing the command to checkpoint ("c") to the dmtcp_coordinator. Each process generates a checkpoint file, which is stored in the directory where the executable was launched.

```
[andersmw@cutter textbook]$ ./dmtcp_restart_script_129b065bca8bba11-56000-87bae5e9cb04.sh
 Count 6
 Count 7
 Count 8
 Count 9
 Count 10
                         Round trip count = 10
```

```
Count 1
Count 2
Count 3
Count 4
Count 5
Count 6
Count 7
Count 8
Count 9
Count 10
                Round trip count = 10
```

FIGURE 22.5

The standard output from the MPI "pingpong" from Code 22.2 after checkpoint restart (left) and without using any checkpoint/restart (right). The checkpoint restart case (left) began from checkpoint data generated after the fifth epoch and consequently the first output seen after restart is the sixth epoch.

created in the directory where the *dmtcp_coordinator* was launched and is called *dmtcp_restart_script_<client identity>.sh*. This script requires no arguments and already knows where to find the checkpoint files in the file system. Launching this shell script will restart the job, as illustrated in Fig. 22.5.

Both the OpenMP and MPI examples explored here using the DMTCP system-level checkpointing tool were performed interactively for ease of demonstration. However, on most supercomputing systems a user will not attempt to perform a checkpoint/restart interactively but will launch applications through a resource management system like PBS or SLURM. DMTCP, like the other system-level checkpointing tools mentioned here, is integrated with PBS and SLURM and provides example scripts for launching and restarting applications through a resource management system. In the case of DMTCP, using a resource management system to checkpoint an MPI or OpenMP application requires the *dmtcp_coordinator* to be launched as a daemon in the PBS or SLURM script while the other commands (*dmtcp_launch, dmtcp_restart_script*) remain the same, as was demonstrated in interactive mode. On HPC resources with the Infiniband network, the *dmtcp_launch* command also requires the flag "*–infiniband*" for checkpoint/restart support of MPI-based applications using Infiniband.

22.3 Application-Level Checkpointing

In application-level checkpointing the application developer has the responsibility to perform all checkpoint/restart operations. As opposed to system-level checkpointing, application-level checkpointing requires changes to the application code. While inconvenient, application-level checkpoint/restart tends to produce checkpoint files that are smaller than system-level checkpoint/restart where a full memory dump is performed. Checkpoint files originating from application-level checkpointing are generally smaller than checkpoint files originating from system-level checkpointing approaches simply because the application developer will only output the most pertinent information necessary for application restart. The system, in contrast, must dump the entire application memory because it can't single out what data is relevant for restart.

For distributed-memory applications based on MPI, application-level checkpoint/restart approaches often share some basic characteristics:

- Only one checkpoint file is written per MPI process.
- Only one MPI rank accesses a single checkpoint file.

- Checkpoint files do not contain data from multiple checkpoint epochs.
- Checkpoint files are generally written to the parallel file system by the compute nodes.
- Checkpoint/restart overheads can be large.

Application-level checkpoint/restart implementations generally pick designated points in the computational phase in the simulation algorithm for checkpointing to ensure computational phase consistency in the checkpoint epoch. For example, in a timestepping algorithm, a natural place to incorporate checkpoint/restart would be at the end of one timestep, thereby ensuring that all checkpoint files are at the same computational phase even if they each reached this phase at different wallclock times. This contrasts with system-level checkpointing where regardless of what phase of computation the process may be at, a checkpoint is dumped as designated by a wallclock time interval or an event such as a manual request for checkpoint given in the command line. Consequently, application-level checkpoint/restart implementations may not specify a checkpoint interval in terms of wallclock time as in system-level approaches but rather require the interval of computational phases for checkpoint/restart.

Application-level checkpoint/restart is very popular in large-scale MPI applications and toolkits because it can be tailored for the application to be as efficient and minimal as possible. However, checkpoint/restart overhead is still very high, and there are checkpoint/restart libraries written to assist in reducing this overhead for application-level checkpoint approaches. One such library is SCR: Scalable Checkpoint/Restart for MPI [3].

The Scalable Checkpoint/Restart (SCR) library assists application-level checkpoint strategies by reducing the load on a parallel file system and by partially utilizing nonparallel fast storage local to a compute node for checkpoint file storage with some redundancy in the event of a failure on the local storage. SCR provides several different checkpoint file redundancy schemes with varying levels of resilience and performance. It requires the parallel remote shell command (PDSH) [4] and the Perl module for date/time interpretation [5] and works natively with the SLURM resource manager. Installation of SCR is as follows:

```
wget https://github.com/LLNL/scr/releases/download/v3.0/scr-v3.0.tgz
tar -zxf scr-v3.0.tgz
cd scr-v3.0
mkdir build
cd build
cmake -DCMAKE_INSTALL_PREFIX=$HOME/scr_install
make install
```

The SCR library is built around an application-level checkpoint strategy like that illustrated in Code 22.3 where only one checkpoint file is written by an MPI process. When using the SCR library, the library needs to know when to start a checkpoint and when to finish a checkpoint through application processing interface (API) calls that are collective across all MPI processes. The SCR library can also determine if a checkpoint file is needed rather than having some user-defined checkpoint frequency as was done in Code 22.3. This is done by configuring SCR with system information to estimate checkpoint costs and frequency of failure and then using the API call *SCR_Need_checkpoint* to let SCR decide the frequency of checkpointing.

```
1 #include <stdio.h>
2 #include <stdlib.h>
3 #include "mpi.h"
4
5 int write_checkpoint()
6 {
7  // get our rank
8  int rank;
9  MPI_Comm_rank(MPI_COMM_WORLD, &rank);
10
11  char file[128];
12  sprintf(file,"checkpoint/%d_checkpoint.dat",rank);
13
14  FILE *fp = fopen(file,"w");
15
16  // write sample checkpoint to file
17  fprintf(fp," Hello Checkpoint World\n");
18  fclose(fp);
19
20  return 0;
21 }
22
23 int main(int argc,char **argv)
24 {
25  MPI_Init(&argc,&argv);
26
27  int max_steps = 100;
28  int step;
29  int checkpoint_every = 10;
30
31  for (step=0;step<max_steps;step++) {
32   /* perform simulation work */
33
34   if ( step%checkpoint_every == 0 ) {
35    write_checkpoint();
36   }
37  }
38
39  MPI_Finalize();
40  return 0;
41 }
```

CODE 22.3

Simple example of common application-level checkpoint strategy. Each process writes its own checkpoint data to a single checkpoint file. The frequency of writing the checkpoint is determined by the user, set here to be 10 (line 29).

The modifications to Code 22.3 needed to incorporate the SCR library are limited to adding the calls *SCR_Init*, *SCR_Finalize*, *SCR_Start_checkpoint*, *SCR_Complete_checkpoint*, and *SCR_Route_file*. Optionally, the checkpoint frequency can be determined by SCR using the call *SCR_Need_checkpoint* as already noted. *SCR_Init* and *SCR_Finalize* initialize and shut down the SCR library analogous to *MPI_Init* and *MPI_Finalize*. *SCR_Start_checkpoint* and *SCR_Complete_checkpoint* indicate that a checkpoint is about to begin to write and that a checkpoint has successfully been written, respectively. *SCR_Route_file* is used for getting the full path and file name for SCR access. Each SCR API call is collective across all MPI processes. The SCR version of Code 22.3 is provided in Code 22.4.

```
1  #include <stdio.h>
2  #include <stdlib.h>
3  #include "scr.h"
4  #include "mpi.h"
5
6  int write_checkpoint()
7  {
8    SCR_Start_checkpoint();
9
10   // get our rank
11   int rank;
12   MPI_Comm_rank(MPI_COMM_WORLD, &rank);
13
14   char file[128];
15   sprintf(file,"checkpoint/%d_checkpoint.dat",rank);
16
17   FILE *fp = fopen(file,"w");
18
19   char scrfile[SCR_MAX_FILENAME];
20   SCR_Route_file(file,scrfile);
21
22   // write sample checkpoint to file
23   fprintf(fp," Hello Checkpoint World\n");
24   fclose(fp);
25
26   int valid = 1;
27
28   SCR_Complete_checkpoint(valid);
29
30   return 0;
31 }
32
```

CODE 22.4

SCR version of Code 22.3 application-level checkpointing. Calls to the SCR API include SCR_Init (line 37), SCR_Finalize (line 53), SCR_Start_checkpoint (line 8), SCR_Complete_checkpoint (line 28), SCR_Need_checkpoint (line 48), and SCR_Route_file (line 20). The SCR_Need_checkpoint call is optional and allows SCR to control the checkpoint frequency. Relatively few changes are needed to an existing application-level checkpoint strategy to take advantage of the benefits of SCR.

```
33 int main(int argc,char **argv)
34 {
35  MPI_Init(&argc,&argv);
36
37  if ( SCR_Init() != SCR_SUCCESS ) {
38    printf(" SCR didn't initialize\n");
39    return-1;
40  }
41
42  int max_steps = 100;
43  int step;
44  for (step=0;step<max_steps;step++) {
45   /* perform simulation work */
46
47    int checkpoint_flag;
48    SCR_Need_checkpoint(&checkpoint_flag);
49    if ( checkpoint_flag ) {
50     write_checkpoint();
51    }
52  }
53  SCR_Finalize();
54  MPI_Finalize();
55  return 0;
56 }
```

CODE 22.4, cont'd

To use SCR and execute Code 22.4, SCR must be integrated with the supercomputer's resource management system. In the case of SLURM, an SCR-enabled code would launch using *scr_srun* instead of *srun*.

22.4 Machine Learning Checkpointing

Training a machine learning model can go for tens of thousands of epochs and go on for hundreds of hours. The end of each training epoch marks a natural boundary in the training phase for writing a checkpoint of the weights at that point in the training. Machine learning frameworks like PyTorch and Tensorflow leverage this boundary for executing application-level checkpointing of the weights. For example, using Tensorflow:

```
1 checkpoint_filepath = "/tmp/checkpoints"
2 model_checkpoint_callback = tensorflow.keras.callbacks.ModelCheckpoint(
3          filepath=checkpoint_filepath,
4          save_weights_only=True,
5          save_freq='epoch')
6
7 model.fit(X,Y,epochs=num_epochs,batch_size=1024, callbacks=
  [model_checkpoint_callback])
```

A callback is defined on line 2 using the ModelCheckpoint callback where the training weights are saved each epoch. This callback is then used when training the model in line 7 as a callback. Other frequent options for checkpointing frequency in machine learning are save_best_only, where the previous checkpoint will only be overwritten if a monitored quantity like accuracy improves. The training can be easily restarted by reading in the latest or best checkpoint:

```
model.load_weights(checkpoint_filepath)
```

The programming interfaces for machine learning frameworks invariably include support for application-level checkpointing.

22.5 **Summary and Outcomes**

- Applications with long execution times run a significant risk of encountering a hardware or software failure before the completion.
- Long execution times also frequently violate some supercomputer usage policies where a maximum wallclock limit for a simulation is established.
- The consequences from a hardware or software failure can be very significant and costly in terms of time lost and computing resources wasted for long running jobs.
- At designated points during the execution of an application on a supercomputer the data necessary to allow later resumption of the application at that point in the execution can be output and saved. This data is called a checkpoint.
- Checkpoint files help mitigate the risk of a hardware or software failure in a long running job.
- Checkpoint files also provide snapshots of the application at different simulation epochs, help in debugging, aid in performance monitoring and analysis, and can help improve load-balancing decisions for better distributed memory usage.
- In HPC applications, two common strategies for checkpoint/restart are employed: system-level checkpointing and application-level checkpointing.
- System-level checkpointing requires no modifications to the user code but may require loading a specific system-level library.
- System-level checkpointing strategies center on full-memory dumps and may result in very large checkpoint files.
- Application-level checkpointing requires modifications to the user code. Libraries exist to assist this process.
- Application-level checkpoint files tend to be more efficient since they only output the most relevant data needed for restart.
- Machine learning frameworks provide application-level checkpoint capability and leverage the natural boundary for checkpointing at the end of a training epoch.

22.6 Exercises

1. List the tradeoffs between system-level checkpointing and application-level checkpointing. Survey some of the many scientific computing toolkits available for download that have checkpoint/restart capability. What form of checkpointing is the most popular in these toolkits?

2. How might checkpoint files be used for debugging? Illustrate this by introducing a race condition into Code 22.1 such as a reduction operation without the appropriate reduction clause and then expose the bug by using a checkpoint file. Use system-level checkpointing.

3. For an application that runs on 100,000 cores for 9 days of wallclock time, estimate the likelihood that the application will encounter a hardware failure during the simulation. Use the reported annualized failure rate for a hypothetical collection of hard drives, processors, and power supplies.

4. What could happen if a system failure occurs while a checkpoint is being written? What are ways to mitigate this type of failure?

5. How do checkpoints/restarts in reinforcement learning frameworks differ from checkpoints in a framework like TensorFlow or PyTorch?

22.7 References

1. CRIU. Checkpoint/Restore In Userspace. [Online] https://criu.org/.
2. DMTCP: Distributed MultiThreaded CheckPointing. [Online] http://dmtcp.sourceforge.net/.
3. Lawrence Livermore National Laboratory. Scalable Checkpoint/Restart Library. [Online] http://computation.llnl.gov/projects/scalable-checkpoint-restart-for-mpi/software.
4. Parallel Remote Shell Command (PDSH). [Online] http://sourceforge.net/projects/pdsh.
5. Perl Date Manipulation. [Online] http://search.cpan.org/~sbeck/Date-Manip-6.56.

Computing in the Future: A Personal Perspective

23

Chapter outline

23.1 Introduction

Practical goal-oriented students with near-term objectives need not read further. No content of this chapter will advance the needed skills to apply state-of-the-art high performance computers to leading-edge applications, even as they evolve in areas such as machine learning. Surprisingly, application programming interfaces mature and change slowly and incrementally even as performance opportunities grow more aggressively. This chapter does not discuss more advanced programming methods expected in the near future because they are likely to be only slightly improved from those of the present as addressed in this textbook and in most cases backward compatible. In the immediate future, hardware architectures in all likelihood will be heterogeneous in form, with some variability from the vendors in offered accelerators. But details cannot be predicted to a degree of accuracy that is useful enough to take on now. The same is not true for new libraries, which can always be improved, extended, or added as the need arises.

An important near-term change clearly needed in the field but rarely discussed is in the average level of performance available from supercomputers for the domain user. An obsessive focus on the fastest computer in the world at least by one or a few benchmarks dominates formal discussions about progress with such decades-long codification as the Top 500 list as one example. This is natural and interesting and provides a degree of animated competition among systems, deployments, vendors, and even nations. Again related to the Top 500 list, instead of a uniform

High Performance Computing. https://doi.org/10.1016/B978-0-12-823035-0.00023-7

distribution of existing deployed systems on that list at any one year, there is really a highly disparate capability of available systems on the list in a pattern the authors refer to as the "three-world model". It clearly shows that although, for example, high performance computing (HPC) is now declared to be in the "post-exascale era", it is only true for one or a few such systems, but the vast majority of the listed systems are within a narrow performance regime of from a couple of petaflops to just above 10 Petaflops. The hyperperformance regime represented is at most among the top 10 machines. This gap of more than an order of magnitude is the immediate challenge. The normal user only has access to a few Petaflops, not a thousand Petaflops, even if the latter exists in principle. This textbook serves both classes of system capabilities such that if the user is effective in using the majority of machines at the Petaflops range, they can pretty much take the same skill sets to run on the very biggest systems such as Frontier or Aurora if fortunate enough to have such access. So, this chapter need not add to this challenge as the textbook already spans this gap; the inchoate HPC user is already good to go.

If doing this is the reader's goal, then proceed no further. But if you are curious or have a driving intellectual need to consider the future, want to explore the possibilities of 21st-century computing, or want to be part of its revolutionary advances in hardware invention or software innovation, then you will find this chapter a good basis for considering the reasons for change, the leading-edge principles that may motivate it, and the possible conceptual alternatives that are even now being considered by both the research and development HPC community.

This chapter does not intend to convince readers of one or another approach but rather inform readers of the diversity of strategies, some of them highly innovative, that are exhibiting promise even now and may open future career paths. Readers will benefit and even possibly enjoy the following content. It's kind of cool, actually. The authors have many years of experience and expertise in these admittedly tentative forward-looking areas, so much of the material can be internalized with some confidence. But first, the next section discusses what the problems are with current supercomputer hardware and software systems to justify various alternative approaches even now being considered. Nonetheless, the authors acknowledge that although current research can be identified with confidence, any projections of these or further predictions are only subjective and may be circumvented with as-yet-unforeseen events in enabling technologies and concepts. Enjoy.

23.2 Limitations of Modern High Performance Computing Systems and Methods

After reading about the extraordinary revolution and successes of HPC through the previous 22 chapters of this up-to-date text, as well as effectively applying the techniques presented to produce correct results on real-world supercomputing problems, it is reasonable to be suspicious of any claims of serious deficiencies with technical strategies that, with incremental but exponential improvements, have appeared to work well over so many decades with a legacy of constant advances. Nonetheless, as will be discussed, a backlog of constraining facets of common methods is accruing to devastating effect for the future of cost-effective HPC. Even with the long-awaited accomplishment of demonstrated Exaflops R_{max} performance, the rate of growth has slowed significantly, for a number of reasons. The long-term implications of these issues are to promote innovation of future system design and operation, extending the capabilities of HPC both in performance and in class of applications, at least through the remainder of this decade and perhaps beyond. To suggest what such innovations are required and how they may be addressed, the inherent and in some cases inherited fundamental problems must be laid out.

A major source of limitation looking forward is the foundational assumptions of the legacy of the von Neumann architecture. It goes without saying that even to this day, more than 7 decades later, this model of execution has sustained the field of computing and established an almost axiomatic basis for all subsequent computing systems, including supercomputers. Before subjecting this major historical invention to criticism, it is acknowledged that the von Neumann architecture was a breakthrough invention that transformed the modern world from an analog to a digital modality and was formulated in the context of the emerging technologies at the conclusion of World War II, which was just at the hairy edge of the possible. It is hard to imagine a better conceptual fit to the properties and limitations of the physical devices available at the time. But again, that was more than 7 decades ago. The technologies today and their tradeoffs are entirely different from those early years.

The von Neumann computer architecture and its derivatives of the following decades are based on the assumption that the arithmetic unit of the system is the precious resource and that the objective function is the optimization of its utilization. The arithmetic units initially delivered the functionality of basic integer arithmetic and Boolean logical bit-wise functions, with additional necessary accumulators and buffers as well as necessary electrical signal—conducting wires between components. These first arithmetic logic units (ALUs) were huge in size, exceeding more than 1 square foot just for a single bit of the functional component. Over time, applications became more sophisticated and real numbers rather than just discrete integers assumed an important role in scientific and engineering problems as the range of values extended well beyond the original hardware integer formats, initially at 16 bits. Floating-point operations were particularly costly in time and space because the first realization of real numbers was through assembler-level software, which was slow. Over years of technology and design progress, floating-point calculations became more strongly supported by hardware and firmware. Before the turn of the century, floating-point hardware was an integral element of very large-scale integration microprocessors. Architectures continued to treat the ALU and then the floating-point unit (FPU) as precious resources. But ultimately, this stopped being the case when the rest of the processor core exceeded in die area that of the total arithmetic logic. Eventually, and currently, these arithmetic functional units themselves only consume a small part of the processor core die, and much of the rest of the core design provides added means to keep the arithmetic units busy. This is poor economics.

A second overriding assumption derived from the legacy of the von Neumann model was the physical separation between processor logic and main memory that exists to this day. The original driving factor was the highly disparate enabling technologies used. Logic was most heavily composed of vacuum tubes with additional passive electronic components. Main memory was provided by capacitor banks, mercury delay lines (referred to as "tanks"), phosphorous screen Williams tubes, spinning drums with ferromagnetic coatings, magnetic cores, and other forms of secondary storage such as magnetic tapes, disks, punched cards, and paper tapes. But today, both processor core logic and main memory (dynamic random access memory) are fabricated from silicon semiconductors. It is therefore realistic to expect that low-latency and high-bandwidth structures of merged memory and logic might be far more efficient and yield higher performance than the continued separation that has come to be referred to as the "von Neumann bottleneck".

The third counterintuitive assumption of the von Neumann architecture that retains traction even to this day is that of sequential instruction fetch. This is central to all conventional parallel HPC systems and includes the underlying semantics of sequential memory consistency in which the ordering of changes to the memory state must emulate that of the idealized machine model of sequential (nonoverlapped or parallel) access. There are a number of other more subtle but no less constraining assumptions with heritage from the beginning of digital electronic computing. Innovations across decades have retained the effects of these demands while overcoming many of their performance shortcomings. But the processor cores have grown enormously in footprint on the semiconductor die and, for example, with speculative memory fetching, impose substantially more demand on the communication fabric and energy for data transfer. Over the era of Moore's law, these tradeoffs were justified because of the exponential gains in device density and performance. But with the end of Moore's law, such benefits no longer accrue, and alternative innovative strategies, quite different from those of the past, may be required.

23.3 Cloud Computing

As has been represented throughout this textbook, the assumed environment and infrastructure for the user, the provider, and the supply vendor is the data center, a large facility potentially on the order of 8000 to 40,000 square feet of raised floor space with full accommodations for power, cooling, mass storage, internet access, and high-speed system interconnect as well as access for maintenance. More routinely, such an established environment augments a world-class supercomputer with one or more modest HPC systems, usually commodity clusters with Linux and PBS or SLURM, to manage secondary workloads such as smaller jobs, software development, student (short and low-cost) practice problem sets, external input/output (I/O) infrastructure, and maybe even some administrative jobs. However, this typical framework, though traditionally pervasive in government labs and centers, financial houses, a few industry sites, and major academic institutions, may not serve all circumstances and may benefit from an alternative business model and arrangement of shared resources. Enter the "cloud".

The idea of shared computing is neither new nor unique and in fact has a long tradition, albeit in diverse modalities. From submission of punched-card decks (data and programs) in the 1960s and teletype (110 baud) mechanical terminals in the 1970s, a single system could be shared by a multitude of users in batched or time-shared mode. By the 1980s, a multitasking system would support a cohort of concurrent users through many command-line "terminals", usually via video screens and mostly connected by means of dedicated hardlines and center switch. Although shared among multiple users at any one time, it is largely a single, previously designated and fixed system being so used.

The advent of the single-user workstation, the personal computer, the local area network (LAN) (e.g., Ethernet), and the inchoate internet in combination dramatically changed the means of computing. The dedicated user desktop or desk-side system became a primary platform with shared LAN-accessible central file systems (e.g., Network File System), group printers and I/O devices, possibly a large-scale multiprocessor, and national and international internet service. While conducting most cycles locally, the first infrastructures for use of many remote systems established the methodology for universally shared systems such as the National Science Foundation–sponsored centers (e.g., National Center for Supercomputer Applications).

In the 21st century, a new business model of the cloud expanded availability and access to commercially provisioned and provided computing facilities. Potentially, large-scale remote systems are provided for large problems, and more typically streams of remote jobs are directed on single-node to medium multinode computer systems both tightly coupled and distributed for throughput processing (rather than strong scaled execution). The cloud, in its general sense, offers, at least potentially, a number of advantages in accomplishing workloads, although less so HPC applications. In the extreme, there are some who believe that the cloud will ultimately replace HPC as a commercial service.

The presumed advantages are that of operational cost and organizational resource flexibility. A cloud is not a new HPC technology but rather an alternative arrangement between service provider and user organization. In principle, the user only pays for what it uses. The user organization does not incur the high operational costs of a large-scale HPC facility, including the initial outlay for the data center, the procurement of one or more HPC systems and their infrastructure, the sustained costs of systems administrators, operational costs (including power), and system depreciation. The cloud presumably absorbs all of these, only billing for time of usage. Additionally, the cloud business model includes replacement and updating of deployed computing to deliver state-of-the-art capabilities to the user. These features appear very attractive compared with the more conventional role of your own computer. But for certain classes of workload, including that of very HPC, there are secondary issues that may still dominate and for which the cloud is ill suited.

This textbook has illustrated the properties of HPC platforms that distinguish them from far more conventional data processing systems. For serial job stream workloads, the distinction may, in fact, impose little difference. But HPC does differ in multiple critical ways for important high-speed and highly parallel mission-critical working sets. Heterogeneous HPC is sensitive to the precise accelerators required for a given job. But the cloud provider may not support the specific graphics processing unit (GPU) needed. The nodes made available at the time of request may not be relatively local for minimal latency effects but rather more loosely and non-uniformly coupled, and this may change from run to run. Cloud providers are focused on serving a much broader and presumably more profitable market than the small boutique domain of specialized HPC. Therefore, it is in their best interest to try to satisfy to the extent possible the needs of the HPC user, not configure or customize for them. Subtle as it may seem, clouds do not readily respond at full capacity and optimality to unplanned (not previously arranged) HPC demands, which may include large resources and dataset storage and communication. This is a currently existing challenge. Finally, cost advantage does not necessarily favor the cloud when compared with in-house platforms and infrastructures, as complex as they may prove. For the industry, the cloud as it relates to HPC is a work in progress but may not yield to a realistic business model. Nonetheless, the HPC cloud model is one possible option for future supercomputing.

23.4 Memory-Centric Computing

As presented in the earlier parts of this textbook, the processor core or central processing unit (an anachronism) has been the centerpiece of the computer system, even as a multiplicity of these complicated devices are used in parallel or distributed system structures. In most of these scalable organizations, main memory devices were slaved to the processor cores via system area networks. Shared-memory access semantics among processor cores is supported among limited-scale multiprocessors complete with physical caches and hardware mechanisms for cache coherence. Distributed-memory access, which delivers a framework for extensive scalability, adds an additional burden of message passing between the nodes, each with a partition of the global memory. Although there are variations on these configurations, they nonetheless impose the longest delays between main memory, the system area network, and the controlling processor core(s). These accumulated delays occur to the fundamental factors of latency, overheads, and additional waiting because of contention for shared resources. Historically, there have been significant improvements in enabling technologies over the multiple decades of which this formula has served as the mainstay HPC system design. As device speeds and densities continued to improve, incremental system architecture design advances were the most productive trajectory of progress. But with the limits of nanoscale fabrication, performance gains can no longer rely on technology alone. Another path is required.

Memory-centric architectures reverse many of the conventional approaches as they diminish in effectiveness. Innovative strategies based on concepts tightly coupling memory with processing logic have been explored through research extending back more than 3 decades, including Exacube (Kogge et al.) and Terasys (Iobst). Though promising, they did not catalyze commercial success. Memory-centric architectures have recently undertaken modern ideas benefiting from nanoscale but have dramatically altered the relationships of the devices to correct the prior constraints.

The active memory architecture (AMA) (Sterling and Brodowicz) is a recent revolutionary memory-centric architecture being investigated to circumvent the previously discussed barriers to performance progress and expanding on the new capabilities favoring today's technologies. Other memory-centric architectures are being pursued as well. For AMA, many of the legacy properties of conventional MPPs are being precluded and replaced by alternative structures. In so doing, many of the legacy assumptions of conventional processors are eliminated. The FPU and ALU are no longer treated as precious resources as they once were. Instead, those aspects most valued and for which structure is optimized are (1) latency of data access from memory to nearest arithmetic logic; (2) waiting because of contention for access to physical and logical resources. including memory and network bandwidth; (3) starvation caused by serial instruction execution and the overheads for software management of exposing and synchronizing parallel flow control; and (4) creation of a new execution model to guide future designs and operation for efficiency, scalability, and productivity.

The challenges faced by memory-centric architectures are many, and this is a transitional period of HPC when current and near-term semiconductor technologies can still offer significant performance opportunity through revolutionary supercomputer architecture. But even if successful, memory-centric-based systems may prove disruptive to the large body of existing application codes, libraries, and programming interfaces in which enormous investment has already been made throughout the prior half century. Initial use of such systems may serve as attached accelerators to otherwise conventional host systems for dynamic graph-based applications supported by runtime system software exporting high-level service calls, much as is done today with GPUs, easing the transition to new supercomputer capabilities.

23.5 Neuromorphic Computing

Brain-inspired devices, circuits, and systems are as enticing as they are currently problematic. The human brain comprises on the order of 89 billion elements called "neurons", in a volume of about 1250 cubic centimeters weighing about 1.3 kg. Yet all knowledge, behavior, senses, motor control, and higher mental abstractions are accomplished within this single organ and the associated central nervous system.

What if a computing machine could be devised that was as powerful as the brain, even constructed similar to the brain but with semiconductor and optical technologies rather than biology? Today's transistors operate more than 1 million times faster than a brain's neurons, send signals near the speed of light, and are orders of magnitude smaller. Admittedly, the brain is very power efficient, consuming about 20 W. But the attraction of creating a thinking machine drives international research. Although highly varied in detail, this research shares the common strategy of emulating in some form the underlying building block of the brain, the neuron, and then synthesizing a system that operates these in highly interconnected topologies. The goal: achieve unprecedented levels of computation performance as an emergent property of a "neural network".

Although much is known about properties of the brain and details of the underlying biological neurons, no one actually knows how a brain works, let alone how to fabricate one. Yet there is a kind of pervasive assumption that if a synthetic neuron of sufficient fidelity can be fabricated, then combining many of them into a single topology will result in a very high performance computer with all the advantages of modern technology but with the additional miracle of thought. The goal extends far beyond mere numeric computational capability to the edge of cognition and the quest for artificial intelligence.

Neuron avatars have been created in many forms and with diverse technologies. These include analog devices, digital devices, hybrids of the two, and software emulations. Other more arcane technologies are being explored such as memristors and spintronics. Some limited success has been achieved for relatively simple processing such as speech processing, image pattern recognition (e.g., face recognition), and a number of other functionalities not easily performed by conventional processor cores. Many of these engage in pattern matching of many forms.

23.6 Analog Computing

Even before the earliest digital electronic logic devices and the computers constructed from them, sophisticated analog computers were already in operation and being applied to complex computational problems. In its most simple form, a digital logic gate can only represent a "1" or a "0" but nothing in between. This has shown to be advantageous for reasons of noise immunity, formal design principles, and general purpose. But an analog computing device can in the ideal case represent an infinite number of values (not realistically). For certain operations both simple and more complex, an analog computer can perform these much faster than their digital counterparts, though with certain restrictions.

As a curious note to the history of computing, both analog and their digital equivalences in the 17th and 18th centuries had their forerunners. On the digital side, primitive calculating mechanisms such as the Pascaline used wheels, gears, and images of numerals to do simple arithmetic operations on multidigit integer operands. Almost 3 centuries of evolution of such mechanical calculators dominated the desks and counters of businesses, banks, accountants, and other applications up into the middle of the past century. Analog computing also had its early introduction in the 17th century in the form of the early slide rules, which could perform multiplication to three significant digits, among other operations. By the 20th century, this was a staple of any engineer's toolkit, students and professionals alike.

Analog computers from the 1930s to as late as the 1970s served important roles in solving complex computing problems in engineering, science, and dynamic process controls. Several generations of technologies advanced the analog computer from mechanical gears and cams to electronics, including vacuum tubes, transistors, and integrated circuits. The operational amplifier fabricated from these was able to perform summations, differentiation, integration, and multiplication or division by a constant. These complex structures derived from sets of first-order differential equations could provide modeling of dynamical linear engineering systems and scientific phenomena with speeds that outperformed digital computers well into the 1970s for those purposes. Mechanical analog computers were widely used during World War II for, among other things, fire control systems on naval vessels such as battleships and destroyers.

Analog computing has progressed very far since then, with a wide variety of new analog devices to perform specific functions that in combination form very complicated computations. As range, stability, numbers of states, and speed increase, analog computers may take on new roles in the 21st century. In neuromorphic computing, some means of fabricating synthetic neurons are based on analog devices. The future may not be closed to additional analog methodologies.

23.7 Superconducting Supercomputing

One question when considering the future of supercomputers is what current or future technologies could be used to replace the semiconductor transistor while delivering on speed and energy advances?

In materials research, a number of possibilities are at least conceptually under investigation. There are more advanced semiconductors beyond silicon complementary metal oxide semiconductor, nonlinear photonics in optical technologies, amorphous phase change devices, and biological chemistry such as DNA. One additional prospect is superconductivity, which has been demonstrated in the laboratory. Single-flux quantum (SFQ) gates of logic circuits are devised from the basic building block of the Josephson junction (JJ), which is a superconducting two-pin switch. When two JJs and an inductor are connected in a loop and a current is induced in it, a magnetic flux is created by this current. Because it is superconducting, there is no electrical resistance in this loop, so the flux is retained indefinitely. This simple SFQ gate may sustain a flux or exhibit no flux; that is, it can hold one of two states—but not just any flux state.

The quantum mechanical physics enabling this phenomenon only permits the value of the flux to exist at a very specific level, or at a level of zero. Significant properties support SFQ as a basis of future supercomputers. First is their switching speed. Components created from such SFQ devices (e.g., high-speed analog-to-digital converters) routinely exhibit switching speeds of between 25 and 60 GHz, which is more than the order of 10 times today's semiconductors. But SFQ can go much faster. In the laboratory, demonstrated switching speeds have repeatedly exceeded 700 GHz.

Second only to its speed is the energy consumption of SFQ. Because there is no resistance in supercooled niobium wires and switches, the wasted heat is minimal, and the power lost is comparably very low. Thus, the speed-to-power ratio is enormous. But this is not just for the lab; complete logic circuits have been fabricated from SFQs and shown that in principle any Boolean logic circuit and therefore any digital device should be possible.

Such superconducting supercomputing logic has existed for more than 2 decades, and one might wonder where all these terrific computers are. The devil is in the details. There was a time when the worst challenge was the need to cool SFQs down to about 4 Kelvins to make them superconduct. That may sound very cold (it is). But this is about the temperature of liquid helium, which is readily available. Further mitigation comes with the advent of experimental quantum computers, which are regularly chilled to below 40 millikelvins. With respect to this, liquid helium is like a balmy day on the beach. A third challenge is device density. Industrial-grade engineering has simply not been conducted yet to bring the feature size down to tens of nanometers to prove its viability. Finally, the most nuanced challenges are the speed of light and the resulting latencies of signal transmission. At these speeds, a signal can only cover a distance of a small fraction of 1 cm or less, which is a small part of a die size. New circuit designs will be essential to make best use of the opportunities enabled by superconducting SFQs. Its practical commercial development beyond specialty circuits has yet to be demonstrated.

23.8 Quantum Computing

No discussion of the future of HPC would be complete without the consideration of quantum computers. At least in conception, quantum computing could exhibit remarkable computational properties if practical systems could be implemented. The reason for the level of international interest from industry, governments, and academic institutions is driven by several factors, not least of which is a disproportionate degree of undue hype. But the vision, at least in theory, is legitimate, with the prospect of performing specific classes of currently unachievable applications at speeds thousands of times greater than conventional platforms. Claims of the potential of executing problems to completion that would take today's biggest supercomputers longer than the lifetime of the universe, although few, are nonetheless well founded in theory. Of course, no such aspirations can be demonstrated by current-generation preprototypes of quantum devices today. But even the hint of ultimate realization has inspired many to explore the possibilities and means of such revolutionary performance gains. Giant companies such as Google and IBM are dedicating significant resources to this quest, and relatively young companies such as D-Wave have already delivered multiple generations of early quantum-annealing computers for optimization searching.

The overloaded term "quantum" in this case relates to the fundamentals of quantum mechanics and its nonintuitive operational properties, including its "particle–wave" duality. Trying to explain quantum computing is like teaching computer science at Hogwarts. But the outline of the concept and its potential for the future of HPC can be described with some clarity. In principle, a future quantum computer is general purpose and can do the same things as a conventional computer. But if successfully developed, it may be able to do certain calculations much faster. Part of the current research over the past 3 decades has been to determine these promising problems by discovering their underlying quantum algorithms. Much of the remaining investment in industry- and government-sponsored facilities has been to address the significant engineering challenges imposing barriers and explore the wide, albeit speculative, approaches that have been proposed.

The primary element of a quantum computer is the "qubit", which sounds like a video game character but stands for "quantum bit". Like a bit in a normal computer's main memory, a qubit stores information. But here the theory for the two classes of computer diverges markedly. A classical bit, determined by Claude Shannon as the foundation of information theory, may contain a value of either of two states: ordinarily a "1" or a "0". A qubit can store a 1 or 0, too. But it can also contain multiple values by means of the unique quantum mechanical behavioral property of "superposition". In so doing, its actual value can be a multidimensional value between 0 and 1 representing all of many states at once. In essence, a qubit may store both 1 and 0 at the same time. To the reader: yes, this is hard to grasp intuitively, but it is in accord with the observed nature and theoretical models of quantum mechanics. The consequences, at least in principle, can be dramatic. For certain problems, the performance gain of a quantum computer of a sufficient number of qubits can be exponential compared with a comparably sized conventional supercomputer. One such problem is in the domain of cryptography to extract the prime factors of an encrypted key value using Shore's algorithm. For yet other problems, the performance improvement can be polynomial in scale. Hence the excitement, perhaps deservedly so.

Yet such apparent miracles do not come cheaply or quickly, and the realization of practical quantum computers may be considered still in the experimental inchoate phase. There are many challenges that impose immediate barriers to success. To pick one, "decoherence" is among the most egregious. Decoherence is related to the ability of a qubit to retain its balancing act of holding the probability of many distinct states simultaneously. Any one of many sources of quantum noise may cause one or more of a set of qubits to decohere, and in doing so the stored value will collapse into a 1 or 0. This is generally likely to occur from within milliseconds to a few seconds, which restricts the duration of any computation, no matter how powerful.

Dozens of alternative ways of creating actual working qubits are being pursued, such as requiring superconducting to be cooled to approximately 20 millikelvins; optical techniques, quantum traps, electron spin, and others. Among these are super-cooled superconductors consisting of a couple of JJs and an inductor. This has been repeatedly achieved at multiple sites with dozens or even hundreds of cooperating qubits operating. Other sources of noise are being addressed through the integration of multiple qubits in a single cohort, in which an error of any single qubit is ameliorated, producing correct approximate values. Assembly and coordinated operation has led to some success.

The array of future possibilities may encompass multiple futures, and each is likely to engage a plethora of alternative, possibly interacting, solutions. All of those discussed in this closing chapter are founded on well understood principles, but none has demonstrated commercially viable technology solutions. Over the past 3 decades (or more) Moore's law and Dennard scaling have applied to drive HPC technology. This alone drove continued improvements and exceptional performance growth. But after a human lifetime (yet only one), this performance trajectory is now coming to an end with nanoscale fabrication technology. The existing gaps, some substantial, have yet to be resolved. But with the degree of urgency now confronting emerging technologies to replace past conventional practices, the field of HPC is now turning the page to a new chapter of future of this technology.

23.9 Summary and Outcomes

- Cloud computing is a business model of otherwise conventional technologies that share the investment in substantial computing resources such that a customer only pays for the degree of actual usage. This greatly reduces or eliminates many costs and increases flexibility of resource expenditures.
- Analog computing replaces digital technology with analog devices and circuits. For some classes of problems, analog computing can achieve quite substantial performance gain. But this would require substantial improvements in circuit stability and fidelity.
- Neuromorphic computing is pursuing the goal of emulating the methods of the brain for higher order functionality while retaining low volume and high performance. Although taking diverse early forms, at least experimentally, neuromorphic computing shares the common methodology of representing the basic element of a neuron in some form.
- Superconducting supercomputing replaces conventional gates with JJs in a hyper-cooled (~ 4 Kelvins) state that enables superconductivity. The high speed enabled and extremely low power combine to make computing between 1 and 2 orders of magnitude faster than conventional semiconductor logic.
- Quantum computing replaced two-state bits typical of conventional processing with qubits that may hold multiple, even many, states simultaneously and manipulate all such states at the same time.

23.10 **Exercises**

1. What are two factors limiting conventional HPC continued exponential growth in performance?

2. How does cloud computing expand performance opportunities in the immediate future?

3. Analog computing is distinguished from digital computing. Name two ways in which this is true.

4. Neuromorphic computing is inspired by what existing phenomenon?

5. What is the basic element of neuromorphic computing?

6. Superconducting HPC benefits from what key physics property that it is dependent on?

7. What is the basic circuit element of superconducting supercomputing upon which all larger logic circuits are based?

8. Quantum computing is general purpose. What is the principal device that distinguishes it from other forms of computing, conventional or otherwise?

Index

Note: Page numbers followed by *f* indicate figures and *t* indicate tables.